MULTICULTURAL EDUCATION 95/96

Second Edition

Editor

Fred Schultz
The University of Akron

Fred Schultz, professor of education at the University of Akron, attended Indiana University to earn a B.S. in social science education in 1962, an M.S. in the history and philosophy of education in 1966, and a Ph.D. in the history and philosophy of education and American studies in 1969. His B.A. in Spanish was conferred from the University of Akron in May 1985. He is actively involved in researching the development and history of American education with a primary focus on the history of ideas and social philosophy of education. He also likes to study languages.

**SCHOOL OF EDUCATION
CURRICULUM LABORATORY
UM-DEARBORN**

Cover illustration by Mike Eagle

Annual Editions

A Library of Information from the Public Press

The Dushkin Publishing Group/
Brown & Benchmark Publishers
Sluice Dock, Guilford, Connecticut 06437

The Annual Editions Series

Annual Editions is a series of over 65 volumes designed to provide the reader with convenient, low-cost access to a wide range of current, carefully selected articles from some of the most important magazines, newspapers, and journals published today. Annual Editions are updated on an annual basis through a continuous monitoring of over 300 periodical sources. All Annual Editions have a number of features designed to make them particularly useful, including topic guides, annotated tables of contents, unit overviews, and indexes. For the teacher using Annual Editions in the classroom, an Instructor's Resource Guide with test questions is available for each volume.

Printed on Recycled Paper

VOLUMES AVAILABLE

Africa
Aging
American Foreign Policy
American Government
American History, Pre-Civil War
American History, Post-Civil War
Anthropology
Archaeology
Biology
Biopsychology
Business Ethics
Canadian Politics
Child Growth and Development
China
Comparative Politics
Computers in Education
Computers in Business
Computers in Society
Criminal Justice
Developing World
Drugs, Society, and Behavior
Dying, Death, and Bereavement
Early Childhood Education
Economics
Educating Exceptional Children
Education
Educational Psychology
Environment
Geography
Global Issues
Health
Human Development
Human Resources
Human Sexuality
India and South Asia

International Business
Japan and the Pacific Rim
Latin America
Life Management
Macroeconomics
Management
Marketing
Marriage and Family
Mass Media
Microeconomics
Middle East and the Islamic World
Money and Banking
Multicultural Education
Nutrition
Personal Growth and Behavior
Physical Anthropology
Psychology
Public Administration
Race and Ethnic Relations
Russia, the Eurasian Republics, and
    Central/Eastern Europe
Social Problems
Sociology
State and Local Government
Urban Society
Violence and Terrorism
Western Civilization,
    Pre-Reformation
Western Civilization,
    Post-Reformation
Western Europe
World History, Pre-Modern
World History, Modern
World Politics

Cataloging in Publication Data
Main entry under title: Annual editions: Multicultural education. 2/E.
    1. Intercultural education—Periodicals. I. Schultz, Fred, *comp*. II. Title: Multicultural
education.
370.19′341′05   ISBN: 1-56134-364-1

Second Edition

Printed in the United States of America

Editors/Advisory Board

To the Reader

In publishing ANNUAL EDITIONS we recognize the enormous role played by the magazines, newspapers, and journals of the *public press* in providing current, first-rate educational information in a broad spectrum of interest areas. Within the articles, the best scientists, practitioners, researchers, and commentators draw issues into new perspective as accepted theories and viewpoints are called into account by new events, recent discoveries change old facts, and fresh debate breaks out over important controversies.

Many of the articles resulting from this enormous editorial effort are appropriate for students, researchers, and professionals seeking accurate, current material to help bridge the gap between principles and theories and the real world. These articles, however, become more useful for study when those of lasting value are carefully *collected, organized, indexed,* and *reproduced* in a *low-cost format,* which provides easy and permanent access when the material is needed. That is the role played by *Annual Editions.* Under the direction of each volume's *Editor,* who is an expert in the subject area, and with the guidance of an *Advisory Board,* we seek each year to provide in each *ANNUAL EDITION* a current, well-balanced, carefully selected collection of the best of the public press for your study and enjoyment. We think you'll find this volume useful, and we hope you'll take a moment to let us know what you think.

The concept of multicultural education evolved and took shape in the United States out of the social travail that wrenched the nation in the late 1960s, through the 1970s and 1980s, and into the present decade. Canada's combined English and French national heritages, coupled with Canada's generous immigration policies following World War II, saw multicultural educational programming develop there as well. There has been considerable interest in improving intercultural relations between the very culturally diverse populations of both Canada and the United States. The linkages between diverse and coexisting ethnic, racial, socioeconomic, and religious heritages are explored in the readings in this volume. There has been enthusiastic support for the idea of a volume exclusively devoted to multicultural education, and after teaching and studying courses in multicultural education for over 20 years, it is a very great pleasure to serve as editor of *Annual Editions: Multicultural Education 95/96.*

The development of multicultural education courses in teacher education originated in the field research studies of various ethnic and racial groups and various types of communities undertaken in the 1920s through the 1970s. Anthropological and sociological ethnographic inquiry into intercultural relations continue to feed the fast-growing literature on the topic, as does research and publication on the impact of prejudice and victimization on children and adolescents in pediatric psychiatry.

The critical literature on gender and other equal opportunity issues in educational studies also increases our knowledge base regarding the multicultural mosaic that so richly adorns North American cultures. When the first courses in multicultural education were developed in the 1960s, the United States was in the midst of urban and other social crises, and there were no textbooks available. Educators who taught in this area had to draw heavily from academic literatures in anthropology, sociology, social psychology, social history, sociolinguistics, and psychiatry. Today, there are textbooks available in the area, but there is also a need for an annually published volume that offers samples from the recent journal literature in which the knowledge bases for multicultural education are developed. This volume is intended to address that need.

The National Council for the Accreditation of Teacher Education (NCATE) in the United States has in place national accreditation standards requiring that accredited teacher education programs offer course content in multicultural education. A global conception of the subject is usually recommended in which prospective teachers are encouraged to develop empathetic cultural sensitivity to the demographic changes and cultural diversity that continues to develop in the public schools as a result of dramatic demographic shifts in the population.

In this volume we first explore the national and global social contexts for the development of multicultural education. Its role in teacher education is then briefly defined in the essays in unit 2. In the next unit, the nature of multicultural education as an academic discipline is discussed by James Banks, and several issues related to this topic are explored. The readings in unit 4 look at multicultural education from the perspective associated with the enculturation and acculturation of persons in the process of developing their own unique personal identities in the context of their interactions with their own as well as others' cultural heritages and personal life experiences. The readings in unit 5 focus on curriculum and instruction in multicultural perspective. Unit 6 addresses special topics relevant to development of multicultural insight, and the essays in unit 7 explore alternative future directions and the need for a critically conscious quest for emancipatory educational futures for all persons of all cultural heritages.

This volume will be useful in courses in multicultural education at the undergraduate and graduate levels. It will add considerable substance to the sociocultural foundations of education, educational policy studies, and leadership, as well as to coursework in other areas of preservice and inservice teacher education programs. We hope you enjoy this volume, and we would like you to help us improve future editions. Please complete and return the postpaid form at the back of the book. We look forward to hearing from you.

Fred Schultz

Fred Schultz
Editor

Contents

Unit 1

The Social Contexts of Multicultural Education

Six articles discuss the importance of a multicultural curriculum in sensitizing students to an integrated world society.

The concepts in bold italics are developed in the article. For further expansion please refer to the Topic Guide and the Index.

Unit 2

Teacher Education in Multicultural Perspective

Four selections examine some of the major issues being debated on how to effectively integrate the multicultural dynamic into teacher education programs.

Unit 3

Multicultural Education as an Academic Discipline

Five selections examine the dynamics of integrating multicultural education into the discipline of education.

The concepts in bold italics are developed in the article. For further expansion please refer to the Topic Guide and the Index.

Unit 4

Identity and Personal Development: A Multicultural Focus

Four articles consider the interconnections between gender, social class, racial or ethnic heritage, and primary cultural values.

The concepts in bold italics are developed in the article. For further expansion please refer to the Topic Guide and the Index.

Unit 5

Curriculum and Instruction in Multicultural Perspective

Seven articles review how curriculum and instruction must be formulated to sensitize young people to the multicultural reality of a national civilization.

The concepts in bold italics are developed in the article. For further expansion please refer to the Topic Guide and the Index.

Unit 6

Special Topics in Multicultural Education

Seven articles explore some of the ways students succeed or fail in culturally pluralistic school settings.

The concepts in bold italics are developed in the article. For further expansion please refer to the Topic Guide and the Index.

The concepts in bold italics are developed in the article. For further expansion please refer to the Topic Guide and the Index.

Unit 7

Toward a New Day in Our Visions of Education: Multiple Visions — Universal Hope

Three selections address the concerns that must be kept in mind for the future improvement of our educational system.

Topic Guide

This topic guide suggests how the selections in this book relate to topics of traditional concern to students and professional educators, involved with the study of education. It is useful for locating articles that relate to each other for reading and research. The guide is arranged alphabetically according to topic. Articles may, of course, treat topics that do not appear in the topic guide. In turn, entries in the topic guide do not necessarily constitute a comprehensive listing of all the contents of each selection.

TOPIC AREA	TREATED IN:	TOPIC AREA	TREATED IN:
African American Youth	8. Multicultural Education Training for Special Educators Working with African American Youth 17. Can Separate Be Equal? 25. Sapphires-in-Transition: Enhancing Personal Development among Black Female Adolescents 26. Racial Issues in Education 32. *Brown* Revisited 35. Investing in Our Children	**Curriculum in Multicultural**	20. Curriculum Guidelines 21. Empowering Children to Create a Caring Culture 22. Toward Defining Programs and Services for Culturally and Linguistically Diverse Learners in Special Education 23. Issues in Testing Students 24. Forming Academic Identities 25. Sapphires-in-Transition: Enhancing Personal Development among Black Female Adolescents
Brown v. Board of Education	4. Diversity without Equality = Oppression 17. Can Separate Be Equal? 32. *Brown* Revisited	**Demographic Change and Multicultural Education**	3. Intermarried . . . with Children 5. Numbers Game 27. Dynamic Demographic Mosaic Called America
Civil Rights Movement and Multicultural Education	4. Diversity without Equality = Oppression 11. Multicultural Education 14. New Word for an Old Problem 17. Can Separate Be Equal? 32. *Brown* Revisited	**Empowerment**	21. Empowering Children to Create a Caring Culture 24. Forming Academic Identities 28. Literacy, Social Movements, and Class Consciousness: Paths from Freire and the São Paulo Experience 34. Towards a Discourse of Imagery
Critical Theory and Education	28. Literacy, Social Movements, and Class Consciousness: Paths from Freire and the São Paulo Experience 34. Towards a Discourse of Imagery	**European Schools**	6. European Schools
Cultural Diversity and Equality	2. Children of Urban Poverty 4. Diversity without Equality = Oppression 17. Can Separate Be Equal? 18. Multiculturalism and Individualism	**Future Visions of Multicultural Education**	11. Multicultural Education 15. Cultural Pluralism, Multicultural Education 34. Towards a Discourse of Imagery 35. Investing in Our Children 36. Educating Citizens for a Multicultural 21st Century
Cultural Diversity in Schools	17. Can Separate Be Equal? 20. Curriculum Guidelines 21. Empowering Children to Create a Caring Culture 22. Toward Defining Programs and Services for Culturally and Linguistically Diverse Learners in Special Education 23. Issues in Testing Students 24. Forming Academic Identities 25. Sapphires-in-Transition: Enhancing Personal Development among Black Female Adolescents 26. Racial Issues in Education 29. Understanding Indian Children 30. Hollywood and the Indian Question 31. "I Wouldn't Want to Shoot Nobody:" The Out-of-School Curriculum as Described by Urban Students 32. *Brown* Revisited	**Gender Issues in Multicultural Education**	16. Intersections of Gender, Class, Race, and Culture 25. Sapphires-in-Transition: Enhancing Personal Development among Black Female Adolescents 33. How Schools Shortchange Girls
		Identity Development in Multicultural Perspective	16. Intersections of Gender, Class, Race, and Culture 17. Can Separate Be Equal? 18. Multiculturalism and Individualism 19. Lessons of Vancouver 24. Forming Academic Identities 25. Sapphires-in-Transition: Enhancing Personal Development among Black Female Adolescents
Cultural Pluralism	4. Diversity without Equality = Oppression 11. Multicultural Education 14. New Word for Old Problem 15. Cultural Pluralism, Multicultural Education 18. Multiculturalism and Individualism	**Immigration**	1. Great Migration 14. New Word for an Old Problem 19. Lessons of Vancouver 27. Dynamic Demographic Mosaic Called America 36. Educating Citizens for a Multicultural 21st Century

TOPIC AREA	TREATED IN:	TOPIC AREA	TREATED IN:
Intermarriage between Cultures	3. Intermarried . . . with Children	**Racism**	13. White Racism 26. Racial Issues in Education
Language and Multicultural Education	18. Multiculturalism and Individualism 22. Toward Defining Programs and Services for Culturally and Linguistically Diverse Learners in Special Education 23. Issues in Testing Students 24. Forming Academic Identities	**Segregation and Desegregation**	4. Diversity without Equality = Oppression 17. Can Separate Be Equal? 32. *Brown* Revisited
Literacy and Multicultural Education	28. Literacy, Social Movements, and Class Consciousness: Paths from Freire and the São Paulo Experience	**Social Contexts of Multicultural Education**	1. Great Migration 2. Children of Urban Poverty 3. Intermarried . . . with Children 4. Diversity without Equality = Oppression 5. Numbers Game 6. European Schools
Multicultural Curriculum Guidelines	20. Curriculum Guidelines		
Multicultural Education and Community Service	35. Investing in Our Children	**Special Education and Multicultural Education**	22. Toward Defining Programs and Services for Culturally and Linguistically Diverse Learners in Special Education
Multicultural Education as an Academic Discipline	11. Multicultural Education 12. Moving Beyond Tolerance 13. White Racism 14. New Word for an Old Problem 15. Cultural Pluralism, Multicultural Education	**Teacher Education in Multicultural Perspective**	7. Building Cultural Bridges 8. Multicultural Education Training for Special Educators Working with African American Youth 9. Multicultural Teacher Education 10. Preservice Teachers' Perceptions of the Goals of Multicultural Education
Native Americans	1. Great Migration 29. Understanding Indian Children 30. Hollywood and the Indian Question	**Testing and Multicultural Education**	23. Issues in Testing Students
Population and Multicultural Education	1. Great Migration 2. Children of Urban Poverty 3. Intermarried . . . with Children 5. Numbers Game 19. Lessons of Vancouver 27. Dynamic Demographic Mosaic Called America 36. Educating Citizens for a Multicultural 21st Century	**Tolerance**	12. Moving Beyond Tolerance 13. White Racism 14. New Word for an Old Problem 36. Educating Citizens for a Multicultural 21st Century
		Urban Poverty	2. Children of Urban Poverty
Preservice Teachers and Multicultural Education	7. Building Cultural Bridges 8. Multicultural Education Training for Special Educators Working with African American Youth 9. Multicultural Teacher Education 10. Preservice Teachers' Perceptions of the Goals of Multicultural Education	**Violence and Schooling**	31. "I Wouldn't Want to Shoot Nobody:" The Out-of-School Curriculum as Described by Urban Students
		White Racism	13. White Racism

The Social Contexts of Multicultural Education

We are very rapidly becoming an ever more multi-culturally unique nation-state in the United States, and Canada is also experiencing major changes in its cultural composition due to its very generous immigration policies. Both nations face multicultural futures. From its beginnings the United States has been a multicultural nation. Some demographic projections indicate that within five years a majority of the total American elementary and secondary school student body will be composed of youth who are children of the rainbow coalition (Native American, African American, Asian American, and Hispanic youth). We always were a unique nation in terms of our cultural composition, and we are becoming even more so.

Multicultural national communities have special challenges associated with the dynamics of daily life among the diverse cultural groups that comprise them. Such societies also have unique opportunities to develop truly great culturally pluralistic national civilizations in which the aesthetic, artistic, literary, and moral standards of each cultural group can contribute to the creation of new standards of national civilization. They can learn from one another, they can benefit from their respective strengths and achievements, and they can help one another to transcend problems and injustices of the past. Furthermore, there are several major multicultural national social orders worldwide, and they can learn from and help each other even more than they have heretofore. We, therefore, ought to see the multicultural national fabric that is our social reality as a circumstance of promise and hope, one of which to be very proud.

In examining the social context of multicultural education, we need to help teachers and education students to sense the promise and the great social opportunity that our multicultural social reality presents. There are many serious challenges to the social and economic well-being of children and young adults. We are heirs to social conditions yet to be rectified. We have the task of empowering students with a constructive sense of social consciousness and a will to transcend the social barriers to safety, success, and personal happiness that confront, in one form or another, almost one-third of them. It is essential that we invest in all the children and young adults of multicultural nations in order that great social promise and hope may be brought to fulfillment in our near-term future as nations.

We can ask ourselves certain very important questions as we work with children and young adults in our schools. Are they safe? Are they hungry? Are they afraid? Are they angry? Do they have a sense of angst; are they filled with self-doubt and uncertainty as to their prospects in life? For far too many children and adolescents from all socio-economic groups, social classes, and cultural groups the answers to these questions are "yes." Far greater numbers of children from minority cultural groups answer "yes" to at least some of these questions than do children from higher socioeconomic groups.

Having done this, we, as educators and civic leaders, ought to ask ourselves a few questions. What are the purposes of schooling? Are schools limited to their acknowledged mission of intellectual development? Or, are schools also capable of serving to advance, as classical Greek and Roman education advanced for the children of their citizens, education in honor, character, courage, resourcefulness, civic responsibility, and social service, in addition to achieving their intellectual development? This latter concept of the mission of schooling is still today the brightest hope for the full achievement of our great promise as a multicultural nation-state embraced in an interdependent world community of nations.

What are the problems we face in achieving this end? We need to enable each child to advance intellectually in school as far as may be possible for that child. We need to do this at the same time that we help develop a child's sense of self-respect and pride in his or her own cultural heritage as a part of a national community. As educators we need to do what we can to help each student to develop a sense of honor, pride, and self-respect that will lead them in their adult years to want to serve, help, and heal the suffering of others. We need intellectually curious and competent graduates who are both knowledgeable of their own ethnic heritages and committed to social justice for all persons, in their own nation as well as in the community of nations.

The problems we face in achieving such an intellectual and social end are not insignificant. Developing multicultural curriculum materials for schools and integrating them throughout the course content and activities of the school day and year can help to sensitize all students to the reality of the inherent worth of all persons. Also, the safety and security needs of all school-aged children must be better served. All youth deserve the opportunity to learn about their own cultural heritages, and they deserve the right to know the culturally unique national reality of America from an objective, socially scientific perspective that is not seen through the cultural lenses of Eurocentric perspectives alone.

North American nations have qualitative issues to face in the area of intercultural relations. Problems differ because of very different national experiences and very different school systems. Around the world other nations

have to wrestle with providing adequate opportunity structures for minority populations while maintaining high intellectual standards. The articles in this unit attempt to address all of these concerns.

There are dramatic demographic changes in the characteristics of the world's population as well as in the interdependence of the world's nations in a global economy. We must reconsider how we develop human talent in our schools, for the young people are the ones who will be the most basic resource in the near term. The unit also provides important background on the history of the civil rights movement in the United States as well as on the origins of many racial and cultural stereotypes that have inhibited the efforts of educators to help young people become more accepting of cultural diversity.

Young adults have the right to learn that the struggle for freedom, and against tyranny, is not really over in the world in spite of the great advances that democratic forces have made in recent years. Young persons need to be able to accept and to value cultural diversity. This unit has sought to offer a concise discussion of the nature of

the social context in which efforts to expand multicultural education have occurred.

The unit essays are relevant to courses in cultural foundations of education, educational policy studies, multicultural education, social studies education, and curriculum theory and construction.

Looking Ahead: Challenge Questions

What should every student learn about cultural diversity and their own cultural heritage?

What facets of the history of the human struggle for civil rights should be taught to students?

What should students learn about other nations and other democratic traditions?

How can the mass media more effectively inform the public on issues related to cultural diversity?

What can educators do to help students to better understand the social contexts in which they live?

What should every student know about cultural diversity and equality of opportunity?

—F. S.

The Great Migration

JOHN ELSON

The most salient fact about American history is this: the ancestors of everyone who lives in the U.S. originally came from somewhere else. That includes even the Inuits and other Native Americans, whose forebears first crossed from Siberia to Alaska on a land bridge that now lies beneath the icy Bering Sea. From its colonial beginnings, the history of America has largely been the story of how immigrants from the Old World conquered the New. As the historian Carl Wittke noted, eight nationalities were represented on Columbus' first voyage to a continent that eventually received its name from a German mapmaker (Martin Walseemüller) working in a French college, who honored an Italian explorer (Amerigo Vespucci) sailing under the flag of Portugal.

The history of America is a prodigious tale of newcomers, replete with perils, triumphs and true grit

The tide of humanity that has washed over the American continent during the last three or four decades of the 20th century has had profound consequences, to be sure. But in relative terms, it is no match for the waves that came ashore during the 19th. Between Napoleon's defeat at Waterloo in 1815 and the assassination of Austrian Archduke Franz Ferdinand at Sarajevo in 1914, more than 30 million Europeans left their homelands—some involuntarily—to settle in the U.S. It was by far the greatest mass movement in human history. The influx continues, in ever greater variety. For people in search of better lives, America remains the ultimate lure.

AFRICA
One-fifth of the population at the time of George Washington's Inauguration in 1789 was black. In the 1990s, African Americans make up 12% of Americans but remain the country's largest ethnic minority.

Eight nationalities were represented on Columbus' first voyage to a continent that eventually received its name from a German mapmaker.

BRITISH ISLES
The English, Welsh, Scots and Scotch-Irish formed a steady influx from colonial times. More familiar with the language and customs than others, they assimilated easily and dominated America's industrial and political leadership.

America's immigration story actually starts in the darkness of prehistory. Archaeologists estimate that Paleo-Indians began their great trek from Asia around 30,000 B.C., in pursuit of shaggy, straight-horned bison (now extinct) and other edible fauna. They gradually moved south and east from Alaska as the glaciers of the Ice Age melted. By 19,000 B.C., the Indians—a short, hardy people who suffered from arthritis and poor teeth, among other infirmities—had built primitive homes in cliffs along Cross Creek, a few miles from present-day Pittsburgh, Pennsylvania. One tribal nation, the Cahokia federation, had the sophisticated skills to build a thriving trade center of 40,000 people, across the river from what is now St. Louis, Missouri, between A.D. 1000 and 1250. But by 1300, this metropolis—the largest on the continent north of Mexico—had been abandoned, a victim of overdevelopment. The Cahokians had run out of food.

When the first Europeans arrived, the Indian population of North America north of Mexico was about 1 million. According to Ronald Takaki's *A Different Mirror: A History of Multicultural America,* some Indian sages had forecast the coming of white-skinned aliens. On his deathbed, a chief of New England's Wampanoag tribe said that strange white people would come to crowd out the Indians. As a sign, a great white whale would rise out of the witch pond. The night he died, the whale rose, just as he had predicted. Similar prophecies about predatory whites can be found in the lore of Virginia's Powhatans and the Ojibwa of Minnesota.

Until recently, American history texts were resolutely Anglocentric, beginning the immigration story with the first successful English settlements—at Jamestown, Virginia, in 1607 and Plymouth Rock, Massachusetts, in 1620. The British, in fact, were latecomers. In 1565 a convicted Spanish smuggler named Pedro Menéndez de Avilés, leading a ragtag army of perhaps 1,500 that included blacksmiths and brewers as well as foot soldiers, built the first permanent European settlement on American soil at St. Augustine, Florida. (The ruins of Menéndez's first fort were discovered only last summer.) Thirty-three years later, Juan de Oñate established a colonial capital at San Gabriel in what is now New Mexico.

The Spanish, typically more interested in the pursuit of gold than in settlement, easily subjugated the Indians, enslaving those who did not die of imported diseases like smallpox. The 500,000 or so Indian inhabitants of Eastern North America at the time of the first English settlements were not so easily conquered. These resilient and warlike nations—principally the Algonquin and Iroquois in the north, the Muskoghean and Choctaw in the south—were happy to trade with the white man and adopt his weapons, but not his Christian faith or his mores. And they would fight to the death to defend their lands from encroachment.

Many of the first immigrants from the British Isles were unwilling voyagers. Long before Australia became the fatal shore for millions of convicts, North America was London's principal penal colony. Others came to the New World as indentured servants, bound into service to pay the cost of their passage for specified terms—usually three to seven years—before being set free. During the 17th century, for example, 75% of Virginia's colonists arrived as servants, some of whom had been kidnapped by unscrupulous "recruiters."

And then there were the slaves. In 1619 the Virginia settler John Rolfe made a diary note of a dark moment in American history. "About the last of August," he wrote, "came in a dutch man of warre that sold us twenty Negars." In Virginia alone, the slave population grew from about 2,000 in 1670 to 150,000 on the eve of the American Revolution. Most of the slaves sailed from West Africa, chained together in dank, fetid holds for transatlantic journeys that often lasted three months or more. The conditions were unspeakable, the mortality rate horrifying: on some ships more than half the slaves died during the passage.

Initially, blacks worked alongside whites in the tobacco fields of Virginia and the Carolinas, but by 1650 field hands were invariably men and women of color. One reason: because of what science now knows is the sickle-cell trait, blacks were often less susceptible than whites to the depredations of malaria. More important, a terrible distinction had been made, first informally but then in legislation: white servants were considered persons despite their temporary state of servitude; blacks were mere property that could be bought and sold.

I N SHARP CONTRAST TO MOTHER ENGLAND, the 13 American colonies were heterogeneous in character. By the mid-18th century, Welsh and Germans had settled in Pennsylvania and the Carolinas, which also had a substantial population of Scotch-Irish. South Carolina and the major towns of New England were home to thousands of French Huguenots. There were Swedes and Finns in Delaware, Sephardic Jews from Holland and Portugal in Rhode Island and Dutch in New York. Visiting New Amsterdam in 1643, the French Jesuit missionary Isaac Jogues was amazed to discover that in this town of 8,000 people, 18 languages were spoken. In his famous *Letters from an American Farmer*, J. Hector St. John Crèvecoeur wrote in 1782, "Here individuals of all nations are melted into a new race of men, whose labors and posterity will one day cause great changes in the world."

GERMANY
Historically, Germans were the single largest additive to the melting pot, so that by 1990, nearly one-quarter of Americans identified themselves as being at least part German.

On his deathbed, a chief of New England's Wampanoag tribe said that strange white people would come to crowd out the Indians.

EASTERN EUROPE
The terrible pogroms of czarist Russia inspired more than 2 million Jews to seek asylum in the U.S. between 1881 and 1914. In 1900 fully one-third of these newcomers were employed by the garment trades.

But did these myriad groups really melt? A unique characteristic of the U.S. immigration experience, historian Daniel Boorstin has noted, is the way in which so many ethnic communities were able to preserve their separate identities. Instead of "*E pluribus unum*" (From many, one), Boorstin suggests, the American motto should have been "*E pluribus plura*." New York offers an early case history. The Dutch lost political control of the Hudson River within 40 years of New Amsterdam's founding in 1624, but their cultural influence proved longer lasting. As late as 1890, some inhabitants of villages near Albany still spoke a form of Dutch at home.

Early immigrants found their way to the New World for a variety of reasons. The Huguenots and German Mennonites were escaping religious persecution. The Irish had been deprived of their farmlands. As Crèvecoeur observed, the primary motive for most newcomers was economic: "*Ubi panis ibi patria* [Where there is bread there is country] is a motto of all emigrants." A primitive form of advertising helped the cause. William Penn wrote pamphlets extolling the attractions of what was called "Quackerthal" in German, which were circulated widely in the Netherlands and the Rhineland. "Newlanders appeared in Old World villages as living specimens of New World prosperity, dressed in flashy clothes, wearing heavy watches, their pockets jingling with coins."

Brochures promoting the New World's glories understandably did not emphasize the difficulty of getting there. An 18th century journey from, say, Amsterdam to Philadelphia or Boston could last anywhere from five weeks to six months. The tiny ships, whose height between decks seldom exceeded 5 ft., braved pirates as well as North Atlantic storms. Conditions below decks were hardly better than on slave ships. As one passenger wrote, "Betwixt decks, there can hardlie a man fetch his breath by reason there ariseth such a funke in the night that it causeth putrifaction of the blood and breedeth disease much like the plague." Fatal outbreaks of scurvy, dysentery and smallpox were common. And yet the tide of emigration could not be halted. Between 1700 and 1776, 450,000 Europeans crossed the ocean to find a new life.

Most 18th century immigrants were peasant farmers—the poor, huddled masses of Emma Laza-

rus' famous poem. Some, though, elevated the quality of life in the colonies. The Huguenots and their descendants—Paul Revere among them—maintained a tradition of craftsmanship and provided the colonies with many of their physicians. Major Pierre Charles L'Enfant designed not only the new capital of Washington but also the badge for the Society of the Cincinnati—which was one of the earliest uses of the eagle as the symbol of America. Royalist political refugees from the French Revolution turned up as dancing masters in the salons of Philadelphia.

In the early years of the new American republic, however, immigration was modest. Apart from slaves, only about 4,000 foreigners entered

WILLIAM WILLIAMS MANUSCRIPTS—N.Y. PUBLIC LIBRARY

HUDDLED MASSES: Immigrants crowd the benches of Ellis Island's main hall

the U.S. annually between 1800 and 1810. One reason for the laggard pace was Britain's Passenger Act of 1803, which raised the cost of transatlantic tickets and served to discourage a brain drain of talented workers who might carry with them England's industrial secrets.

The U.S. government did not begin to record immigration data until 1820. A decade later, the nation's population was around 13 million, of whom only 500,000 were foreign-born. But by then the century's great tide of immigration had truly begun, primarily from Ireland, Germany and Scandinavia. Profoundly influencing this exodus were the so-called America letters—glowing accounts of life in the New World by recent voyagers that became as popular in Europe as best-selling novels. In Ole Rynning's *America Book* (1838), the U.S. is described as a classless society with high wages, low prices, good land and a nonrepressive government.

Ads by shipping firms and land-speculation companies also beckoned peasants from the Old World to the New. Midwestern states, beginning with Michigan in 1848, set up their own immigration agencies and offered special inducements to newcomers, like voting rights after only six months' residency. In the Dakotas a poetasting huckster promised women that the territories were prime land for husband hunting: "There is no goose so gray, but, soon or late,/ Will find some honest gander for a mate."

In one key respect, emigrating to America was different from moving from one country to another in Europe. The newcomers would face hostility

SWEDEN
Nearly 1.2 million Swedes emigrated to the U.S. between 1851 and 1930. In 1900 Chicago had more Swedes (145,000) than any city but Stockholm.

America's introduction to slavery: "About the last of August came in a dutch man of warre that sold us twenty Negars."
—FROM THE DIARY OF JOHN ROLFE

INDIA
The vast majority of immigrants from India and its neighbors came after 1965, when national quotas were lifted. The largest number live in California and near New York City, where many have flourished in the field of medicine.

and prejudice from native-born Americans. But in the eyes of the law, once they became citizens they were fully equal to those whose ancestors had sailed aboard the *Mayflower*. In the words of Marcus Hansen, the pioneering historian of U.S. immigration, "The immigrant was to enjoy no special privileges to encourage his coming; he was also to suffer no special restrictions." With that goal in mind, Congress in 1818 rejected requests from Irish societies in Eastern cities to set aside certain frontier lands for colonies of indigent Hibernians. America was not to become "a patchwork nation of foreign settlements."

RELATIVELY FEW EMIGRANTS FOUND THE paradise promised by the ads and the letters home. The early arrivals were, by and large, poor, ill-schooled and young (two-thirds were between 15 and 39 years old). In Europe's principal ports of exodus—Liverpool and Cork, Bremen and Rotterdam—they were beset by thieves and hucksters, cheated by ship's captains (there was no set fee for tickets to America) and, until the age of steam, often even ignorant of where they would eventually land. If they survived the journey—and as many as one-third died aboard ship or within a year of landing in the New World—fresh hazards awaited them in America. Among them were streetwise recent immigrants who would rob them of their few remaining shillings or kronen.

No European nation lost proportionately more of its sons and daughters to the U.S. than Ireland: in all, some 4,250,000 from 1820 to 1920. Native-

Sometimes the Door Slams Shut

FOR MOST OF ITS HISTORY, the U.S. has been wide open to immigrants—those from Europe, that is. Countless 19th century voyagers from the Old World pursued the uniquely egalitarian shelter of a New World so different from Europe's rigidly structured nation-states. Barriers to immigration did not square with the American ideal of opportunity for all.

Not that each newcomer was welcomed by a fledgling society entirely free from fear and bias. In 1798 Congress raised the residency requirement for citizenship from 5 to 14 years, largely to exclude political refugees from Europe who might foment revolution. Later some states imposed taxes on alien ship passengers they feared might become public charges.

Such nativist sentiments only grew after the Civil War. The once vast frontier seemed less vast, and economic recessions raised fears that cheap foreign laborers might take American jobs. There was also the openly racist argument that some newcomers, Asians especially, could not be "assimilated." In 1882 Congress passed the Chinese Exclusion Act, imposing a head tax and excluding whole categories of people—convicts and the mentally ill, for example. For the first time there were real limits on European immigration. Twelve years later, a group calling itself the Immigration Restriction League adopted the pseudo science of eugenics as the basis for its contention that breeding from "inferior stock" would fatally weaken America.

After World War I, there were fears that millions of displaced Europeans, newly influenced by Bolshevism, would infect America with alien ideology. As a result, a series of racism-tinted national-origins laws passed during the 1920s established an annual immigration quota of 150,000 that favored established groups like the Germans and Irish. Some nationalities, notably the Japanese, were excluded entirely. The national-origins system was preserved in the 1952 McCarran-Walter Act, though that notorious law did establish tiny quotas—100 or so a year—for such previously barred groups as Indians and Filipinos.

Underlying these laws was the belief that preserving America's ethnic mix as it existed in 1920 was politically and culturally desirable. After World War II, the quotas were relaxed only to allow in politically favored groups, such as the 38,000 Hungarians who fled the 1956 Soviet crackdown. Inspired by Lyndon Johnson's Civil Rights Act, Congress in 1965 at last ended the national-origins system and opened America's doors to the Third World.

The 1980 Refugee Act radically expanded the definition of those eligible for political asylum. But because it has been poorly enforced and easily abused, it helped bring on today's growing demand for new limits on aliens. Still, for the first time in its history, the U.S. has an immigration policy that, for better or worse, is truly democratic. ***—J.E.***

MEXICO
Known by more labels than any other ethnic or national group, Mexican Americans are variously called Tejano, Latino, Hispano, Chicano and Mexicano, among others, depending on where they live and from whence they came.

> **"Here individuals of all nations are melted into a new race of men, whose labors... will one day cause great changes in the world."**
> —J. HECTOR ST. JOHN CRÈVECOEUR

IRELAND
The second largest immigrant group, the Irish have deeply influenced U.S. big-city politics and the Roman Catholic Church, and now rank among the most affluent Americans.

---

born Americans sniffed at these Gaels—made desperate by the potato famine that devastated their homeland in the 1840s—as filthy, bad-tempered and given to drink. The haunting, taunting employment sign NO IRISH NEED APPLY became a bitter American cliché. And yet Irish lasses made the clothmaking factories of New England hum. Irish lads built the Erie Canal, paved the highways and laid tracks for the railroads. In the South the Irish were sometimes considered more expendable than slaves and were hired, at pitifully low wages, for the dirtiest and most dangerous jobs, like clearing snake-infested swamps.

But the Irish had a gift for mutual self-help and taking care of their own. Out of this instinct,

manifest in America's dozens of "little Dublins," emerged institutions, like New York City's notorious Tammany Hall, that would transform the quality and character of urban politics in America.

ITALY
With their strong family ties, Italian immigrants early formed their own neighborhoods, many of which still flourish. Today Italian is synonymous with good food, high fashion and design.

> **"Betwixt decks... there ariseth such a funke in the night that it... breedeth disease much like the plague."**
> —PASSENGER ON AN 18TH CENTURY TRANSATLANTIC VOYAGE

As early as 1852, the immigrant vote (principally Irish) was so important that Winfield Scott, the staunchly Protestant Whig candidate for President, ecumenically attended Sunday Mass on campaign visits to New York. Some 210,000 Irish fought during the Civil War, 170,000 of them on the Union side.

As Irish migration began to recede, a second great wave—of Germans (or perhaps more properly, German speakers)—began. As Oscar Handlin pointed out in his classic study *The Uprooted*, most 19th century European immigrants thought of themselves not as ex-citizens of a national state (which, in the case of Poland, for instance, did not even exist) but as speakers of a common tongue, or residents of a particular village or province. The Germans were lured by the vision of unlimited economic opportunity and greater freedom than Central Europe offered in the post-Napoleonic era.

If the Irish brought a new spirit to American politics, the Germans brought culture in varied forms, from singing groups to vineyards to poetry societies. Some German railway workers could recite Homer in Greek. More pioneering than the Irish, they helped develop America's hinterland, from Ohio to Texas. (In 1900, 1 out of 3 Texans was German in origin.) The town of Hermann, Missouri, still known for its wines, was typical: when laid out in 1837, streets were named for Schiller, Gutenberg, Goethe and Mozart.

"The Scandinavian immigrant to the United States," wrote historian Wittke, "has been the Viking of the Western prairie country." In the mid-19th century, American newspapers carried accounts of immigrant Swedes disembarking en masse from cargo ships and marching—often with their country's flag carried aloft—to railway depots where trains would take them upriver to Buffalo, along the Erie Canal and thence to the prairie country of the upper Mississippi valley. "What a glorious new Scandinavia might not Minnesota become!" wrote Frederika Bremer in 1853, and she was right. Today about 400 place names in Minnesota are of Scandinavian origin.

AFTER 1880, IMMIGRATION CHANGED ONCE again. Most of the newcomers were from Eastern and Southern Europe: Russian Jews, Poles, Italians and Greeks. They too left the Old World to escape poverty and, in the case of the Jews, persecution. Like their predecessors, they were mostly peasants, but they faced a different and unhappy prospect. The great era of frontier settlement was coming to an end. After being processed at Ellis Island in Upper New York Bay and other immigration centers, millions of these rural folk found themselves confined to the mean streets of urban ghettos like Manhattan's festering Lower East Side, working at menial jobs and crammed into narrow railroad flats that lacked both heat and privacy.

The nativist sentiment that foreigners are somehow inferior to the American-born may be the nation's oldest and most persistent bias. (Curiously, it was not until 1850 that the U.S. Census took note of where Americans were born.) Apart from slaves, Asians (principally the Chinese) suffered most from this prejudice. Seeking fortune and escape from the turmoil of the Opium Wars, Chinese first began arriving in California during the 1840s. Initially, they were welcomed. During the 1860s, 24,000 Chinese were working in the state's gold fields, many of them as prospectors. As the ore gave out, former miners

GREECE
The New World's farm life differed so much from their own that most Greek immigrants became city dwellers, often peddling from pushcarts or running cafés. In Florida, many dove for sponges.

CHINA
By the 1870s, Chinese immigrants made up three-quarters of San Francisco's woolen-mill workers and 90% of its cigar makers. They also manned gold-fields, though ownership of the mines was limited by law.

"The Scandinavian immigrant to the United States has been the viking of the Western prairie country."
—HISTORIAN CARL WITTKE

MIDDLE EAST
Most of the immigrants from the Arab world were Christians rather than Muslims—until recent years. Culturally diverse, many began as peddlers strung across the U.S.; others opened family businesses in dry goods and groceries.

were hired to build the Central Pacific Railroad; others dug the irrigation canals that poured fertility—and prosperity—into the Salinas and San Joaquin valleys.

The Chinese were rewarded for their labor with low wages, typically a third less than what

white workers could earn. Even so, hostility forced them from many jobs as times got tough. Excluded from the mines and farms, many set up shop as laundrymen, a trade that did not exist in their homeland. They were ineligible for citizenship under a 1790 federal law that limited that privilege to whites. In 1882 Chinese workers were barred from entering the U.S. by an act of Congress that was extended indefinitely in 1902 and was not rescinded until 1943.

After the Chinese were excluded, Japanese became the principal concern of nativists who feared America's contamination by a "Yellow Peril." The shameful nadir of this bias followed the attack on Pearl Harbor in December 1941. Under pressure from security-conscious Army officials, the Federal Government exiled more than 100,000 Japanese and Japanese Americans from their homes on the West Coast to internment camps in Arizona, Arkansas, California, Colorado, Idaho, Utah and Wyoming. Despite this humiliation, 30,000 Japanese Americans served in uniform, and the all-Nisei 442nd Regimental Combat Team and the 100th Battalion became the most decorated units in U.S. military history.

American immigration is like a book with no ending. Despite a resurgence of nativism, newcomers continue to seek entry, with the same sense of hope and yearning that fired their 19th century predecessors. Illegal Irish seek jobs, escaping an 18% unemployment rate in their homeland. Jews from the former Soviet Union want relief from an ugly surge of anti-Semitism at home. Perhaps 80% of the newcomers in recent years have come from Asia and Latin America, adding to the country's unparalleled cultural and racial diversity. (New York City alone has more than 170 distinct ethnic communities.) "Of every hue and caste am I," wrote Walt Whitman in *Song of Myself.* True enough when he composed that line in 1881. Truer still today.

Children of Urban Poverty: Approaches to a Critical American Problem

David A. Hamburg

President, Carnegie Corporation of New York

No problem in contemporary America is more serious than the plight of children and youth in our decaying cities. Almost a quarter of the nation's children grow up in poverty, all too many of them in smashed families and rotting communities. Their loss is our loss. Without major, sustained, concerted efforts to work out these problems, the entire society will pay a terrible price.

I have touched on this subject in six of my nine annual essays since becoming president of Carnegie Corporation in 1982. Now I focus squarely on the critical, festering wound of lacerated childhood, because I believe it can be healed only by collaboration between those trapped in degrading environments and the powerful sectors of society—business, government, labor, scientific and professional societies, community organizations, universities, and the media. Foundations have fostered a great deal of research and innovation showing that much can be accomplished to prevent the massive damage now being inflicted on the young of our society. This essay sketches a developmental sequence of experiences, opportunities, and interventions that can make a crucial difference.

The nation is on a path that will generate an increasing proportion of warped, empty, and destructive lives. Yet the relevant scientific and professional communities have recently illuminated other paths that can lead to better

NOTE: *The president's essay is a personal statement representing his own views. It does not necessarily reflect the foundation's policies. This essay is adapted from the author's book,* Today's Children: Creating a Future for a Generation in Crisis. *New York: Times Books, Random House, 1992.*

outcomes. There is in fact an emerging action agenda for children and youth in urban poverty.

In times past, extensive formal education was not a prerequisite for making a living or getting a good job. Low-level literacy sufficed in the agricultural era and was also adequate for high-paying work in factories of the early industrial period. Most of these jobs, however, disappeared by the end of the 1970s. Today, higher standards of literacy and numeracy are necessary to obtain jobs in the modern economy. They are also essential to the full exercise of citizenship in a complex, democratic society. The quantitative skills and scientific thinking required for the most desirable vocations will only rise further in the foreseeable future. If students from very poor and socially depreciated areas have difficulty today meeting the minimal standards of education, they will be even less likely in the next century to master the skills and knowledge essential for mainstream opportunities—unless broad ameliorative action is taken now.

Poor children are at higher risk of succumbing to death, disease, disability, or injury than are economically advantaged children. They are more likely to have parents with formidable vulnerabilities that expose them to multiple hazards. Their mothers, often very young and socially isolated, may receive only minimal support from other family members or friends and have no prenatal care. Their fathers are frequently absent. As a consequence, some children stand a strong chance of being born underweight with neonatal damage; they may grow up malnourished and have untreated childhood illnesses or uncorrected early problems of hearing and vision, accidents, and injury. They may experience higher degrees of stress and violence in their social environment on a continuing, long-term basis. Many of their very early developmental or health problems will be unrecognized at home. In school,

From the Carnegie Corporation Annual Report, *Report of the President*, 1992, pp. 3-19. Reprinted by permission of the Carnegie Corporation of New York, 437 Madison Avenue, New York, NY 10022.

they will be observed to be underdeveloped in their social skills, emotionally troubled, and linguistically and cognitively well behind their peers born into more fortunate circumstances. So, poverty is a profound and pervasive exacerbating factor in illness, disability, emotional distress, and educational failure.

FAMILIES IN CRISIS, CHILDREN IN JEOPARDY

There have been dramatic changes in the structure and function of American families in just a few decades. Some of these changes represent new opportunities and tangible benefits; others represent a serious threat to the well-being of children on a large-enough scale to pose a major problem for the entire society.

Perhaps the most striking change from the perspective of child and adolescent development is the rapidity with which mothers of young children have entered the work force. By 1990, more than half of all mothers of young children, preschool as well as of school age, held jobs outside the home. Today most American children spend part of their childhood in a single-parent family. By age sixteen, close to half of the children of married parents will see their parents divorce. For nearly half of these, it will be five years or more before their mothers remarry. Compared with other societies, the United States exhibits a kind of revolving-door pattern of marriage and family disruption, jeopardizing attachments and the normal developmental paths of childhood and adolescence.

With all the radical shifts in family life, it is not surprising that Americans are deeply troubled about their offspring. In public opinion surveys, parents report concerns about their children and the likelihood of educational failure, delinquency, suicide, adolescent pregnancy, and sexually transmitted diseases. They fear the possibility of a fatal accident or homicide striking a child down. Yet two-thirds of them report they are less willing to make sacrifices for their children than their own parents were.

The total time parents spend with their children has diminished by about one-third and perhaps even one-half in the past thirty years. Not only are mothers home much less but there is little evidence that fathers spend more time with their children to compensate. Only about 5 percent of American children see a grandparent regularly. They spend a vast amount of time during their years of most rapid growth and development gazing at the mixture of reality and fantasy presented by television, hanging out in a variety of out-of-home settings, or taking care of themselves (which often means no care at all). Adolescents increasingly are immersed in a separate "teen culture," lacking adult leadership, mentorship, and support.

It will be necessary to find ways to strengthen families that are now vulnerable and to use other institutions to provide some of the conditions for healthy child development.

LAUNCHING TWO GENERATIONS: THE POTENTIAL OF PRENATAL CARE

A few years ago, an important study from the Institute of Medicine of the National Academy of Sciences concluded that prenatal care could contribute markedly to the reduction of infant mortality and low birthweight and, more generally, to improved child health. Yet in spite of the fact that good prenatal care can cost less than $1,000 per family, as against the many thousands required for intensive care for a premature or small-for-age baby, too many expectant mothers have no access to such care or they do not know of it. It is a vivid example of missed opportunity and avoidable tragedy.

To prevent such damage, efforts need to be made to identify and reduce the risks to mother and child before pregnancy occurs. Women must be given universal and equal access to high-quality prenatal care, regardless of their economic status. The content of prenatal care must be enlarged to include a strong educational component. Long-term effort must be made to educate the public about the importance of early prenatal care and ways of getting it.

In the past decade, several synthesis reports by highly credible scientific and professional groups have documented the importance of prenatal care, not only for the growing fetus but for identifying paths toward the healthy development of the newborn and for assisting the parents. The National Institutes of Health has prepared the latest of these on behalf of the United States Public Health Service. It provides the basis for new action on prenatal care, a solid foundation for healthy child development, and a program for enlarging opportunities for young mothers, especially in poor communities. The discussion of prenatal care converges around two central questions: What should be the core *content* of prenatal care for all women? How can women be assured of equitable *access* to care?

The Public Health Service report covers three essential components of prenatal care: medical care, education, and social support. It recommends the enrichment of prenatal care by placing more emphasis on preconception and the earliest weeks of pregnancy and on healthy child development, positive family relationships, and family planning.

For women at highest risk — those who are poor, uneducated, or very young — the prospects for a positive change in life associated with the birth of a baby can provide the impetus for other life changes. Most parents want to do well for their children. That inclination can lead to job training, formal schooling, or other education likely to improve prospects for the mother and her new family. Such life enhancement may in the long run lead to improved outcomes for later children and perhaps even grandchildren.

Social Support and Guidance for Young Parents

All too often, adolescent parents who are socially isolated need a dependable person to provide support for their health and education through the months of pregnancy and the ensuing year or so. Where a helper does not exist in the family, there are family-equivalent functions that are being tried in some areas of concentrated poverty. They illustrate ways to organize social support for health and education in various community settings throughout childhood and adolescence.

Efforts are being made in the United States and in other countries to get poor young mothers into comprehensive prenatal care early and keep them in it so they may take advantage of the opportunities provided. This objective has stimulated innovations that have the potential for addressing not only adolescent pregnancy and prenatal care but other adolescent problems as well.

The Prenatal/Early Infancy Project in Rochester, New York, headed by David L. Olds, is a systematic effort to mobilize social support for pregnant adolescents. It teaches parenting skills oriented toward the growth of competence and self-esteem; it provides health care and education for mother and baby, including programs to enhance the mother's capacity to care for herself; it recruits informal support from boyfriends and family friends; it uses visiting nurses to link pregnant adolescents to agencies that can provide needed services in health, education, and the social environment.

This program builds strength partly by recruiting the informal support of reliable friends and relatives for the adolescent individual, who is typically asked, "Who can you count on for help?" Those so identified are encouraged by the intervention staff to enter into the world of the pregnant adolescent — especially to provide support for maintaining healthy behaviors: to quit smoking, keep weight within appropriate bounds for the pregnancy, and avoid drug intake.

Evaluation of this study is highly encouraging. Beyond the time of the intervention, the young women enjoy greater informal social support, improve their diets more, and smoke less than do similar women exposed to conventional arrangements. On long-term follow-up, it has been shown that the mothers in this program, though poor and unmarried, are much more successful in the work force during the first four years of their children's lives than are their control counterparts. Moreover, they have substantially fewer subsequent births in that time interval. So they are able to focus serious attention on the baby they have and on employment opportunities, instead of following the more familiar pattern, manifested in the control group, of having one baby after another with no respite. Altogether, this ingenious program offers considerable hope about what can be done with respect to poor, unmarried adolescent mothers and at-risk youth in the context of sound, supportive interventions.

HOME VISITING FOR VERY POOR YOUNG PARENTS

Home visiting programs have shown that they can have positive effects on the health and well-being of poor adolescent mothers and their families. The benefits can be long lasting, as demonstrated by the best studied early intervention programs aimed at preventing damage to disadvantaged children.

Home visitors can work with family members to solve problems of housing, food, health, child rearing, child development, and family relationships. Such visitors can help young parents with information, skills, and motivation and open the door to a variety of community resources in health, education, and social services.

Home visits can be effective in teaching parenting skills to high-risk families that are the least likely to come to clinics for prenatal or well-baby care, to participate in parent education classes, to attend parent support groups, or to find quality preschool programs for their children. So this is a multifaceted opportunity to give poor children a decent start and set them on a course out of poverty.

PREVENTING DAMAGE TO CHILDREN THROUGH EARLY HEALTH CARE

The Ounce of Prevention Fund in Chicago is vigorously tackling the hardest problems of the inner city. Its pediatric care has focused on very poor children, but its emphasis on preventing disease and encouraging healthy lifestyles reflects the best pediatric practice across the entire spectrum of families — poor and rich alike. Indeed, such well-baby care is fundamental to healthy development. In addition to providing immunizations during infancy, pediatricians monitor children's growth carefully to detect nutritional and developmental problems. They provide well-informed guidance and emotional support to help families work toward healthy lifestyles. They answer and also anticipate parents' questions about their children's growth and development, helping them prepare for predictable transitions.

Ideally, a young woman's contact with a pediatrician should begin before a baby's birth so the doctor can reinforce understanding of the risks of alcohol, tobacco, and other nonprescription drugs to the fetus and promote the benefits of breast-feeding for the infant. Establishing this medical relationship can help ease the mother from pregnancy to care of the newborn.

Since pediatricians and other physicians are usually in short supply in poor city neighborhoods, it is essential to enlist the help of pediatric nurse practitioners, home visitors, parent support group workers, and public health workers. They not only provide primary health care services, they guide parents on how to meet the essential requirements for healthy child development and utilize community services.

Community health centers, originally known as neighborhood health centers, have shown over three decades how health care, medical services, and social support can be provided effectively and at low cost in very poor communities.

At present, the nation is seeking to immunize all children against the common infections of childhood. Fewer than half of poor and minority children under age four are fully vaccinated against the preventable infections. Recent outbreaks are traceable to this failure. Linking immunization to child care and preschool education can be helpful in ways analogous to requiring immunization for school entry. A system of comprehensive primary care would be optimal for this purpose and for a wide range of disease prevention activities that logically flow from immunization.

STRENGTHENING FAMILIES

Community-based early interventions to strengthen families have been developed and tested in recent decades. They serve a variety of purposes: to augment parents' knowledge and skill in child rearing; enhance their ability to cope with the vicissitudes of child development and family relations; help families gain access to services; facilitate informal support networks among parents; and organize to counteract dangerous trends in the community. They are implemented in poor neighborhoods by agencies that employ paraprofessionals from the community who link with professionals as needed.

Child development research shows that community-based early interventions can help parents become teachers of their own children or at least make clear to them the strong value of intellectual achievement and constructive human relations. They can provide emotional encouragement, cognitive stimulation, and social support.

Other evidence indicates that child care of high quality plus parent education can facilitate an infant's and a child's cognitive and social development in high-risk urban poverty populations. Adolescent mothers can be helped to go on to higher levels of education, and the effects for younger children in the family can be beneficial. So efforts to build parental competence can be useful for two generations.

This approach is beautifully exemplified by a highly innovative program begun in San Antonio, Texas. Avance is a center-based parent support and education program serving low-income Mexican American families. It has been functioning since 1973, and anyone who has visited it can hardly fail to be impressed. It has two centers in San Antonio, one in a federal housing project, and another in a low-income residential neighborhood. Directed from the start by Gloria G. Rodriguez, a skillful, dedicated, and charismatic leader, it is staffed largely by former program participants, who are trained by core professionals. Parents can enroll their children up to three years of age; all families in the community are welcome; and there is systematic, door-to-door recruitment into the program by the staff.

The core component of Avance is a nine-month parent education program consisting of monthly two-and-a-half-hour sessions. The parents are taught that they themselves can be educators, and they are shown concretely how to facilitate their own children's development. The Avance experience has also highlighted the importance of ancillary services: transportation to the center; home visits to the new parents as a transition to participating in the activities of the center; day care; pleasurable outings; graduation ceremonies as a focus for solidarity and reward for accomplishment; employment training; family planning; education in the use of community resources; driver education. In other words, Avance tries to offer one-stop support in which many needs can be met in one place.

A community survey conducted by Avance in 1980 revealed how badly knowledge was needed in the community: parents were ignorant of their children's developmental needs or how to acquire job skills; they needed help in sustaining hope in the face of long-term adversity, building a sense of control over their lives, and overcoming social isolation. A high incidence of child abuse and neglect among young parents was detected in this survey. The staff used the survey results to focus its program more sharply, emphasizing parents' own development and providing them a basis for self-esteem and perception of opportunity, improved decision-making skills, and specific knowledge of child development. In the latter respect, the staff directly demonstrated and modeled how parents could encourage play, seek points of mutual pleasure between mother and child, and give constructive feedback.

Evidence has accumulated that the program does indeed foster parents' knowledge of child development, increase their hopefulness about the future, enhance prospects in this poor community, decrease punitive approaches to child discipline, and generally improve the mother-child relationship.

Preschool Education

The past few decades have seen an almost incredible upsurge in preschool education for three- and four-year-olds. Head Start and similar opportunities have become symbols of hope. The results have generally been encouraging.

Research shows that preschool education programs such as Head Start do prepare young children, especially those from disadvantaged backgrounds, to enter kindergarten and first grade. They provide health services, involve many parents in their child's education, and open doors to community resources.

Overall, individuals who have been in early education programs like Head Start show better achievement scores in elementary school, are less likely to be classified as needing special education, and have higher rates of high school completion and college attendance than comparable students who were not in preschool programs.

So far, so good. But Head Start alone cannot neutralize a long series of noxious events. It is a valuable part of a development-promotion sequence throughout childhood and adolescence. As in other major transitions, children need special attention to cross the threshold to elementary school successfully. Fortunately, research efforts directed at these early years have given valuable guidance.

Upgrading the Earliest Years of Elementary Education

Innovative efforts and research results show that elementary schools can play a much more constructive role for poor children than they typically do today. An outstanding example is provided by Success for All in the Baltimore city schools. Researchers at Johns Hopkins University working with public school teachers have developed an elementary school experience that can help all children. The program seeks to prevent learning problems by involving parents early and consistently as well as by using high-quality research-based classroom instruction. It utilizes intensive and immediate interventions to address learning problems before

they do lasting damage. The program includes preschool education, a full-day kindergarten, a family support team, an intensive reading effort with special tutors, individual academic plans based on frequent assessments, a program facilitator, training and support for teachers, and a school advisory committee that includes parents.

An extensive, systematic evaluation of Success for All has produced interesting results. The earlier that students start the program, the more benefit they obtain. Their academic accomplishment is higher than that of students undergoing traditional instruction. They have fewer behavior problems and better attendance records, and their parents are more likely to become seriously involved in their education. This shows what can be done in very poor communities.

Another elementary school innovation is Dr. James P. Comer's pioneering work, which turned around schools in very bad shape and sustained the gains over almost two decades. Most current education reforms de-emphasize interpersonal factors, focusing on instruction and curricula. The conventional approach assumes that all children arrive at school with adequate preparation to receive instruction and perform well. But for poor minority children from alienated, non-mainstream families, the contrast between home and school has a profound effect on their psychosocial development, impeding their academic achievement. Comer's program addresses that disparity directly. His intervention team consists of a social worker, psychologist, and special education teacher.

The work of Comer and his colleagues at Yale's Child Study Center began in two inner-city New Haven elementary schools in 1968. Their program promoted children's development and learning by building supportive bonds among students, parents, and school staff members. Key ingredients included a multifaceted governance team, a program to involve parents in the school, a mental health team, and a program of life-skills training, especially in social skills useful for opportunities in the mainstream economy.

The students in the two schools at the outset ranked lowest in achievement among the city's thirty-three elementary schools. By contrast, during the past decade they have been among the highest. Attendance rates greatly improved, and serious behavior problems have become rare. A major impact of long-term significance is clear in these and other "Comerized" schools. The program has since been implemented in additional cities, including middle schools and high schools. Their outcomes have been similar to those of the original New Haven schools. The whole effort has been of authentic inspirational value for national school reform.

EARLY ADOLESCENCE: LIFELONG OPPORTUNITIES

Adolescence is a crucially formative phase of development. It begins with puberty, a profound biological upheaval. This coincides with drastic changes in the social environment, especially the transition from elementary to junior high school or middle grade school. Convergent stressful experiences make this an especially difficult period for young people who lack a perception of opportunity and a basis for hope.

These early adolescent years, ages ten to fifteen, see the formation of behavior patterns in education and health that have lifelong significance. Many patterns are dangerous and need to be recognized: becoming alienated from school and dropping out; starting to smoke cigarettes, drink alcohol, and use other drugs; driving automobiles and motorcycles in high-risk ways; not eating an adequate diet or exercising enough; risking early pregnancy and sexually transmitted diseases; and in some ways worst of all, beginning to use dangerous weapons.

Initially, adolescents explore these new possibilities tentatively. Experimentation is typical of adolescence. Before damaging patterns are firmly established, therefore, there is a vital opportunity for intervention to prevent lifelong casualties. This opportunity is tragically missed in poor communities now.

To meet the essential requirements for healthy adolescent development, we must help adolescents acquire constructive knowledge and skills, inquiring habits of mind, dependable human relationships, a reliable basis for earning respect, a sense of belonging in a valued group, and a way of being useful to others. These basic needs can be met in poor communities by a conjunction of pivotal institutions: family, schools, community-based organizations, the health care system, and the media.

ANTIDOTES TO EDUCATIONAL FAILURE

Adolescents make choices that have fateful consequences both in the short term and for the rest of their lives. These choices affect their health and education and their fate as human beings. Schools and related institutions must help adolescents find constructive expression for their curiosity and exploratory energy, provide them with knowledge and skills to make informed, deliberate decisions, and in other ways put in place the building blocks of a hopeful and competent future. The recommendations of the Corporation-sponsored report, *Turning Points: Preparing American Youth for the 21st Century*, address this challenge in middle grade schools. The report's writers recognized that the schools cannot do what needs doing in the next century without a lot of cooperation from other institutions, and they made strong recommendations for changes in the structure, teaching, and content of middle grade education:

1) Large middle grade schools should be divided into smaller communities for learning so each student will receive sustained individual attention.

2) Middle grade schools should transmit a core of common, substantial knowledge to all students in ways that foster curiosity, problem solving, and critical thinking.

3) Middle grade schools should be organized to ensure success for all students by utilizing cooperative learning and other techniques suitable for this age group.

4) Teachers and principals, not distant administrative or political bodies, should have the major responsibility and authority to transform middle grade schools.

5) Schools should be environments for health promotion with particular emphasis on the life sciences and their applications; the education and health of young adolescents are inextricably linked.

6) Families should be allied with school staff through mutual respect and opportunities for joint effort.

7) Schools should be partners with various kinds of community organizations in educating young adolescents, including involving them in the experience of community service.

8) Teachers for the middle grades should be specifically prepared to teach young adolescents and be recognized for this accomplishment.

A developmentally appropriate life sciences curriculum teaches students essential concepts in biology, relates these concepts to problems they encounter in their daily lives, and encourages healthy behaviors through the knowledge they will gain about themselves — and what they can do to their own bodies and their own lives, both for better and for worse.

In very poor and depreciated communities, middle schools can carry out some family-equivalent functions — cultivate shared aspirations and mutual aid, pool information, strengthen coping strategies, rally around a student in time of stress, help a child learn to use community resources. They can provide powerful leverage for promoting education and health.

In the transformed middle grade school, the creation of social supports can be done in a variety of synergistic ways: by breaking up large, impersonal institutions into houses or schools-within-a-school and having a durable homeroom in which each day is started; by implementing cooperative learning, peer tutoring, community service programs, team teaching, a reliable advisory system, and systematic parental involvement; and by relating schools to community organizations. All these would contribute to sustained individual attention in a supportive group that fosters education and health.

Summer school also offers disadvantaged children valuable opportunities. Research suggests that the more intensive the summer school experience, the more substantial the student's gain. Poor children tend to lose their academic gains over the summer. Having them attend school consistently can make an important difference for them. It turns out that the most useful program for disadvantaged children is simply to read regularly. Research focusing on sixth graders at the end of elementary school found that summer reading can improve reading performance regardless of socioeconomic background.

COMMUNITY SUPPORT

Across the nation, most communities have programs that offer recreation or support or teach skills to youngsters. Youth agencies serve about 25 million young people annually and thus are second only to the public schools in the extent of their influence. They offer some advantages over the schools. They are free to experiment, they can reach children early, and they typically work in small groups with ten to fifteen young people at a time.

Youth-oriented churches offer several innovative approaches to educating the disadvantaged. Many organizations within poor communities have found ways to build dependable support for children beyond what their families provide. Thousands of community organizations across the nation have strong potential for facilitating education and healthy development.

A variety of minority organizations provide mentors from similar backgrounds for inner-city youth. Minority college students in some programs devote three of their evenings a week to tutoring and recreation and help youngsters gain experience accessing community resources and developing social skills. These activities are generally attractive to adolescents and may combine entertainment with education. There is a recurring emphasis in such efforts on forming constructive human relationships, providing models of accomplishment and success, developing skills pertinent to the mainstream economy, building self-esteem, and seizing real opportunity.

Community service can have special value for disadvantaged minority youth by moving them beyond the constraints of the inner city, helping them make a valued social contribution, developing employable skills, and building their self-esteem through solid accomplishment.

Since lack of employment opportunities looms so large in the lives of disadvantaged minority families, there needs to be a stronger link between education and job prospects. One option is to offer minority students part-time or summer jobs as a strong incentive to stay in school. Indeed, some educators propose the creation of paid work-study programs in which the student's pay is made contingent on performing satisfactorily in school. But perceiving job opportunities is just the first step; disadvantaged students also need help in acquiring essential practical skills: job searches, job training, and appropriate on-the-job behavior. On-the-job training and counseling also enhance students' prospects for adapting successfully to the world of work.

ANTIDOTES TO DRUG ABUSE

Education to prevent substance abuse has made a start in recent years but has a long way to go. It must cover *all* schools, regardless of socioeconomic status, starting in late elementary school, going on to junior high or middle school, and continuing through high school. It must reach *beyond* the schools to cover the entire community. In this respect, lessons learned from adult cardiovascular disease prevention efforts in several countries can be helpful. These efforts combine broad public education with extensive community organization for health. They deliver their message through schools and media and community organizations in ways that suit particular cultural circumstances, so that the messages will be clear, pertinent, and fully intelligible.

Researchers in several countries have carried out experimental programs for adolescent students to prevent the use of cigarettes, alcohol, and other drugs. Overall, the results show it is feasible to diminish substantially the use of gateway substances in early adolescence. Furthermore, this can be done in a way that enhances personal and social competence. Much more data will soon become available on the applicability of this approach to poor minority students. So far, the results of such research efforts indicate that there are clearly beneficial effects for disadvantaged populations, especially if education is linked with social supports for education and health.

A fundamental underpinning for adequate understanding of drug abuse can be provided by the life sciences, especially in the middle grade schools. To make good use of this vital information, students need better skills in decision making, including the capacity to draw upon information carefully, to avoid jumping to conclusions, to be deliberate in considering the meaning of the information for one's own life. Thus, the decision-making component of life-skills training is very important for this purpose. Indeed, it should be considered a special branch of the movement toward critical thinking skills that is so much a part of science education and basic education reform at the present time.

The social skills component of life-skills training also is important in teaching youngsters to be assertive without being hyperaggressive; to negotiate in human relationships; to achieve at least a substantial part of what they want without disrupting important relationships; and to resist pressure to engage in destructive behaviors. Such social skills have many uses, but they certainly are pertinent to the capacity to navigate the stormy waters of adolescence without becoming dependent on drugs. Social support networks for health and education are as crucially significant in the drug context as elsewhere — especially in the setting of the transformed middle grade school.

Lessons learned from cardiovascular disease prevention programs demonstrate how important is the role of the media. We have only scratched the surface on the constructive uses of the media as an educational system in this context and in others.

The capacity of community organizations to help with this problem is also at an early stage of development, especially in poor neighborhoods. For many young people, using or selling drugs seems an attractive path to adult status. But alternate paths must be constructed, and nowhere more so than in deeply impoverished communities. Community-based organizations can provide a sense of belonging in a valued group that promotes constructive alternatives to drugs and violence.

Altogether, in school and out, we have to find ways to help adolescents build competence, earn respect, join a group of friends capable of resisting pressure to use drugs, and delineate a vision of an attractive future. An important part of this in poorer communities has to do with economic prospects: *early* opportunities must become visible to young people before the drug pathway becomes firmly established.

ANTIDOTES TO VIOLENCE

In my lifetime, the common mode of fighting in urban poverty settings has gone from fists to knives to pistols to semiautomatic weapons. In the path we are on, it may well be fully automatic weapons before long — with a capacity for wreaking slaughter beyond reason and imagination. Surely there is a better way.

Adolescent violence is as much a public health concern as other behavior-related health problems are, and what works for the latter may be applicable to the former. Teenagers' tentative exploration of new possibilities offers an opportunity to develop alternatives to violent responses. With the goal of reducing fights, assaults, and intentional injuries among adolescents, violence prevention programs train providers in diverse community settings in a special curriculum; they then translate this curriculum into concrete services for adolescents and enlist the support of the community in preventing such violence. The four principal components of these programs are curriculum development, community-based prevention education, clinical treatment services, and a media campaign. Violence prevention efforts of such a systematic and extensive sort are very recent. Evaluation is under way. We must provide solid, hopeful alternatives to the violent behavior that so often arises from empty lives and shattered families.

High-risk youth in impoverished communities urgently need social support networks and life-skills training. These can be created in a wide range of existing settings, such as school sports, school-based health clinics, community organizations, mentoring interventions, home-visiting programs, and church-related youth activities. To be successful, they must have a dependable infrastructure and foster enduring relationships with adults as well as peers. There is potential in this approach even to provide constructive alternatives to violent groups.

As social support systems have become attenuated with the recent upsurge of family and community disruptions, the explicit teaching of social skills in schools and community organizations has become crucial. One important category of social skills is constructive assertiveness. Adolescents have to learn how to be assertive in taking advantage of opportunities—that is, how to use community resources such as health and social service agencies or job-training opportunities.

Another aspect of assertiveness is how to resist pressure or intimidation to use drugs or weapons without spoiling relationships or isolating oneself. Yet another aspect is nonviolent conflict resolution — assertiveness to achieve personal and social goals in ways that make use of the full range of nonviolent opportunities.

A variety of innovative efforts have sought ways to construct dependable one-on-one relations over an extended time between an experienced, caring adult and a shaky adolescent. The findings indicate a nationwide trend to view mentoring as a powerful way to provide adult contacts for adolescents who are otherwise largely isolated from adults. These programs help adolescents prepare for social roles that can earn respect and encourage them to persist in education. The mentor is expected to provide support, guidance, and concrete assistance as the adolescent goes through a difficult time, enters a new situation, or takes on substantial new tasks. It is useful for the mentoring program to be integrated with other resources that are available in the community.

Particularly for high-risk youth, where problems tend to cluster, the connection with education, health, and social services may be crucial.

Overall, work in this field indicates that effective mentoring can improve the social chances of poor adolescents by supporting them in their efforts to move ahead in education and in health, by encouraging new patterns of behavior that fit the emerging circumstances of adolescent development, by providing a tangible perception of opportunity and steps toward the fulfillment of that opportunity, by sharing experiences of pleasure and stimulating curiosity around those experiences, and by providing some tangible resources as well as coping skills.

CONCLUDING COMMENT

The American population is one of the most heterogeneous in the world. Somehow, we have learned to live with each other reasonably amicably and with mutual respect, even across cultural divides. A great national experiment in education and health to bring all American groups into the mainstream of opportunities would suit our nation as we turn the corner into a new century.

This field is not a morass. There are many useful, constructive interventions that could be mounted across this country. It will require national leadership, long-term vision of what we really want this country to become, and long-term follow-through. That in turn requires mobilization of public opinion. Only with broad public support can the problems of disadvantaged children be effectively solved — and in the process improve the quality of life for all. If we can do that, we will have left our nation the greatest legacy it could possibly have and made it an inspiring example for the whole world.

David C. Hamburg

President

REFERENCES

Adolescent Behavior and Health. Summary of a conference held June 26-27, 1978. Washington, DC: Institute of Medicine, October 1978.

Cicchetti, D., and Toth, S. L., eds. *Advances in Applied Developmental Psychology*. Vol. 8, *Child Abuse, Child Development, and Social Policy*. Norwood, NJ: Ablex Publishing Corporation, 1993.

Comer, J. P. "Educating Poor Minority Children." *Scientific American* 259, no. 5 (November 1988).

Falco, M. *The Making of a Drug-Free America: Programs that Work*. New York: Times Books, Random House, 1992.

Feldman, S. S., and Elliott, G. R., eds. *At the Threshold: The Developing Adolescent*. Cambridge, MA: Harvard University Press, 1990.

Goldstein, A. *Addiction: From Biology to Drug Policy*. New York: W. H. Freeman, forthcoming 1993.

Graham, P. A. *S.O.S.: Sustain Our Schools*. New York: Hill and Wang, 1992.

Hamburg, B. A. *Life Skills Training: Preventive Interventions for Young Adolescents*. A working paper of the Carnegie Council on Adolescent Development. Washington, DC: Carnegie Council on Adolescent Development, April 1990.

Hamburg, D. A., and Trudeau, M. B., eds. *Biobehavioral Aspects of Aggression*. New York: Alan L. Liss, 1981.

Hamburg, D. A.; Elliott, G. R.; and Parron, D. *Health and Behavior: Frontiers of Research in the Biobehavioral Sciences*. Washington, DC: National Academy Press, 1982.

Hamburg, D. A., and Sartorius, N., eds. *Health and Behavior: Selected Perspectives*. Cambridge, England: Cambridge University Press (published on behalf of the World Health Organization), 1989.

Hamburg, D. A. "Interventions for Education and Health in Very Poor Communities." In published papers from Symposium on the Underclass presented at the American Philosophical Society, April 24, 1992.

Hamburg, D. A. *Today's Children: Creating a Future for a Generation in Crisis*. New York: Times Books, Random House, 1992.

Hamburg, D. A. "The Urban Poverty Crisis: An Action Agenda for Children and Youth." In *Western Journal of Medicine* (in press).

Hechinger, F. M. *Fateful Choices: Healthy Youth for the 21st Century*. New York: Hill and Wang, 1992.

Larner, M.; Halpern, R.; and Harkavy, O., eds. *Fair Start for Children: Lessons Learned from Seven Demonstrated Projects*. New Haven, CT: Yale University Press, 1992.

Lerner, R. M., ed. *Early Adolescence: Perspectives on Research, Policy, and Intervention*. Hillsdale, NJ: Lawrence Erlbaum Associates, 1993.

A Matter of Time: Risk and Opportunity in the Nonschool Hours. Report of the Task Force on Youth Development and Community Programs of the Carnegie Council on Adolescent Development. Washington, DC: Carnegie Council on Adolescent Development, 1992.

Millstein, S. G.; Petersen, A. C.; and Nightingale, E. O., eds. *Promoting the Health of Adolescents: New Directions for the Twenty-First Century*. New York: Oxford University Press, 1993.

Olds, D. "The Prenatal/Early Infancy Project." In *Fourteen Ounces of Prevention: A Casebook for Practitioners*, R. H. Price et al., eds. Washington, DC: American Psychological Association, 1988.

Pentz, M. A., et al. "A Multi-Community Trial for Primary Prevention of Adolescent Drug Abuse: Effects on Drug Use Prevalence." *Journal of the American Medical Association* 261, no. 22 (1989).

Price, R. H., et al. *School and Community Support Programs that Enhance Adolescent Health and Education*. A working paper of the Carnegie Council on Adolescent Development. Washington, DC: Carnegie Council on Adolescent Development, April 1990.

Prothrow-Stith, D. *Deadly Consequences: How Violence Is Destroying Our Teenage Population and A Plan to Begin Solving the Problem*. New York: HarperCollins, 1991.

Quality Education for Minorities Project, Action Council on Minority Education. *Education that Works: An Action Plan for the Education of Minorities*. Cambridge, MA: Massachusetts Institute of Technology, 1990.

Reiss, A. J., and Roth, J. A., eds. *Understanding and Preventing Violence*. Washington, DC: National Academy Press, 1993.

Rosenheim, M., and Testa, M. F., eds. *Early Parenthood and Coming of Age in the 1990s*. New Brunswick, NJ: Rutgers University Press, 1992.

Slavin, R. E., et al. *"Whenever and Wherever We Choose..." The Replication of Success for All*. Paper presented at the annual meeting of the American Educational Research Association, Atlanta, April 1993.

Television and Its Educational Potential for Children. Report of a conference held at Carnegie Corporation of New York, September 21, 1984.

Turning Points: Preparing American Youth for the 21st Century. Report of the Task Force on Education of Young Adolescents of the Carnegie Council on Adolescent Development. Washington, DC: Carnegie Council on Adolescent Development, 1989.

U.S. Congress, Office of Technology Assessment. *Adolescent Health*. Vol. I, *Summary and Policy Options*. Vol. II, *Background and the Effectiveness of Selected Prevention and Treatment Services*. Vol. III, *Crosscutting Issues in the Delivery of Health and Related Services*. Washington, DC: U.S. Government Printing Office, 1991.

Zigler, E., and Styfco, S. J., eds. *Head Start and Beyond: A National Plan for Extended Childhood Intervention*. New Haven, CT: Yale University Press, 1993.

INTERMARRIED . . . WITH CHILDREN

For all the talk of cultural separatism, the races that make up the U.S. are now crossbreeding at unprecedented rates

Jill Smolowe

Hostile stares and epithets were the least of their problems when Edgar and Jean Cahn first dated. Twice the couple—he a white Jew, she a black Baptist—were arrested simply for walking the streets of Baltimore arm in arm. When they wed in 1957, Maryland law barred interracial marriages, so the ceremony was held in New York City. Although Jean had converted by then, the only rabbi who would agree to officiate denied them a huppah and the traditional breaking of glass. As law students at Yale in the 1960s, the couple lived in a basement because no landlord would rent them a flat.

In 1963 the Cahns moved to Washington, D.C., where they raised two sons, Reuben and Jonathan. By 1971, as co-deans of the Antioch School of Law, the high profile couple had received so many death threats that they needed bodyguards. The boys' mixed ancestry caused near riots at their public school. One principal said they "brought a dark force to the school" and called for their expulsion.

Now the generational wheel has turned. In 1990 young Reuben married Marna, a white Lutheran from rural Pine Grove, Pennsylvania. Although both a rabbi and a minister officiated, none of Marna's relatives, except her mother, attended the wedding. Her father fumed, "I can't believe you expect me to accept a black person, and a Jewish one at that!" But with the birth last year of towheaded Aaron, Marna's family softened considerably.

Intermarriage, of course, is as old as the Bible. But during the past two decades, America has produced the greatest variety of hybrid households in the history of the world. As ever increasing numbers of couples crash through racial, ethnic and religious barriers to invent a life together, Americans are being forced to rethink and redefine themselves. For all the divisive talk of cultural separatism and resurgent ethnic pride, never before has a society struggled so hard to fuse such a jumble of traditions, beliefs and values.

The huddled masses have already given way to the muddled masses. "Marriage is the main assimilator," says Karen Stephenson, an anthropologist at UCLA. "If you really want to affect change, it's through marriage and child rearing." This is not assimilation in the Eurocentric sense of the word: one nation, under white, Anglo-Saxon Protestant rule, divided, with liberty and justice for some. Rather it is an extended hyphenation. If, say, the daughter of Japanese and Filipino parents marries the son of German and Irish immigrants, together they may beget a Japanese-Filipino-German-Irish-Buddhist-Catholic-American child. "Assimilation never really happens," says Stephenson. "Over time you get a bunch of little assimilations."

The profusion of couples breaching once impregnable barriers of color, ethnicity and faith is startling. Over a period of roughly two decades, the number of interracial marriages in the U.S. has escalated from 310,000 to more than 1.1 million; 72% of those polled by TIME know married couples who are of different races. The incidence of births of mixed-race babies has multiplied 26 times as fast as that of any other group. Among Jews the number marrying out of their faith has shot up from 10 to 52% since 1960. Among Japanese Americans, 65% marry people who have no Japanese heritage; Native Americans have nudged that number to 70%. In both groups the incidence of children sired by mixed couples exceeds the number born into uni-ethnic homes.

Some critics fret that all this criss-crossing will damage society's essential "American" core. By this they usually mean a confluence of attitudes, values and assumptions that drive American's centuries-old quest for a better life. What they fail to acknowledge is that legal, educational and economic changes continuously alter the priorities within that same set of social variables. A few generations back, religion, race and custom superseded all other considerations. When Kathleen Hobson and Atul Gawande, both 27, married last year, however, they based their vision of a shared future on a different set of common values: an upper-middle-class upbringing in tight-knit families, a Stanford education and love of intellectual pursuits.

Unlike many other mixed couples, Gawande, an Indian American, and Hobson, a white Episcopalian of old Southern stock, have always enjoyed a warm reception from both sets of parents. Still, when Hobson first visited the Gawandes in October not every one of their friends was ready to celebrate. "One Indian family didn't want to come because they were concerned about their children being influenced Hobson says. Their wedding in Virginia was a harmonious blend of two cultures though Kathleen wore a white gown and her minister officiated, the ceremony included readings from both Hindu and Christian texts.

Tortured solutions to mixed-marriage ceremonies are common. Weddings, funerals, are a time when family resentments, disappointments and expectations bubble to the surface. The tugging and tussling over matters that may seem frivolous set the stage for a couple's lifelong quest to create an environment that will be welcoming to both families, yet uniquely their own.

Accommodation and compromise only begin at the altar. The qualities that attracted Dan Kalmanson, an Anglo of European extraction, to Yilva Martinez in a Miami reggae club—her Spanish accent, exotic style of dance and playfulness—had a more challenging echo in their married life. After they wed in 1988, Ignacio, Yilva's then eight-year-old son by a previous marriage, moved from Venezuela to join the couple. Dan, 33, spoke no Spanish, the boy no English. The couple decided to compel Ignacio to speak English. He caught on so fast that his Spanish soon degenerated. Says Yilva: "We have literally forced him to learn Spanish again."

For Yilva, 35, the struggle is not just to preserve her native tongue; she also wants to suffuse her home, which has grown with the addition of Kristen, 3, with the Latin ethic that values family above all else. "Here, you live to work. There, we work to live," she says. "In Venezuela we take a two-hour lunch break; we don't cram in a hamburger at MacDonald's."

Children also force mixed couples to confront hard decisions about religion. Blanche Speiser, 43, was certain that Mark, 40, would yield if she wanted to raise their two kids Christian, but she also knew that her Jewish husband would never attend church with the family or participate in holiday celebrations. After much soul searching, she opted for a Jewish upbringing. "I knew it would be O.K. as long as the children had some

belief," she says. "I didn't want a mishmash." Although Blanche remains comfortable with that decision and has grown accustomed to attending synagogue with her family, she admits that it pricks when Brad, 7, says, "Mommy, I wish you were Jewish." Other couples expose their families to both religions, then leave the choice to the kids.

When it comes to racial identity, many couples feel that a child should never have to "choose" between parents. The 1990 U.S. census form, with its "Black," "White" and "Other" boxes, particularly grated. " 'Other' is not acceptable, pure and simple," says Nancy Brown, 40. "It is psychologically damaging to force somebody to choose one identity when physiologically and biologically they are more than one." Nancy, who is white, thinks the census form should include a "Multiracial" box for her two daughters; her black husband Roosevelt, 44, argues that there should be no race box at all. Both agree that people should be able to celebrate all parts of their heritage without conflict. "It's like an equation," says Nancy, who is president of an interracial family support group. "Interracial marriage that works equals multiracial children at ease with their mixed identity, which equals more people in the world who can deal with this diversity."

The world still has much to learn about living with diversity. "What people say, what people do and what they say they do are three entirely different things," says anthropologist Stephenson. "We are walking contradictions." Kyoung-Hi Song, 27, was born in Korea but lived much of her youth abroad as her father was posted from one United Nations assignment to the next. Despite that cosmopolitan upbringing, her parents balked when

Kyoung-Hi married Robert Dickson, a WASP from Connecticut. They boycotted the 1990 wedding, and have not contacted their daughter since. The Dicksons hope that the birth of their first child, expected in April, will change that.

Intolerance need not be that blatant to inflict wounds. If Tony Jeffreys, 34, and Alice Sakuda Flores, 28, have a child, that hypothetical Japanese-Filipino-German-Irish-Buddhist-Catholic-American will become flesh and blood. In their one year of marriage, Tony says, "I've heard friends say stupid stuff about Asians right in front of Alice. It is real hypocritical because a lot of them have Mexican or black girlfriends or wives." Sometimes the more subtle the rejection, the sharper the sting. Says Candy Mills, 20, the daughter of black and Native American parents, who is married to Gabe Grosz, a white European immigrant: "I know that people are tolerating me, not accepting me."

Such pain is evidence that America has yet to harvest the full rewards of its founding principles. The land of immigrants may be giving way to a land of hyphenations, but the hyphen still divides even as it compounds. Those who intermarry have perhaps the strongest sense of what it will take to return America to an unhyphenated whole. "It's American culture that we all share," says Mills. "We should capitalize on that." Perhaps her two Native American-black-white-Hungarian-French-Catholic-Jewish-American children will lead the way.

—Reported by Greg Aunapu/ Miami, Sylvester Monroe/Los Angeles, Andrea Sachs/New York and Elizabeth Taylor/Chicago

Diversity Without Equality
=
Oppression

Meyer Weinberg

Meyer Weinberg is a professor in the Graduate School of Education, California State University, Long Beach.

Civil rights are legally enforceable claims to equal treatment. Under the United States Constitution, many such rights are enjoyed by citizen and noncitizen alike. One example is the Fourteenth Amendment, under which a state is forbidden to "deny any **person** within its jurisdiction the equal protection of the laws."

Any government can grant rights to persons or groups, or it may choose to annul such rights after a time. For many years, Americans had the legal right to own other human beings. The prospect of withdrawing this right led to the outbreak of the Civil War. The Thirteenth Amendment ended slavery.

Possessors of certain civil rights frequently are hesitant about extending such rights to others. The right to vote in America was for decades closely held by a tight little group of white, property-holding men. Large-scale movements of African-Americans and women arose to ultimately extend this right. The results of such efforts are embodied in the Fourteenth, Fifteenth, and Nineteenth Amendments (1868, 1870, 1920) and the Voting Rights Act (1965).

The Civil Rights movement of the 1950s through 1970s was a largely successful effort to solve certain enduring weaknesses of American democracy. It was conceived, organized, and led principally by African-Americans. In the North, some whites also joined in.

What were the aims of this movement?

In the area of civil rights, to be equal does not mean being the **same**. Rather, equal means to be of the **same worth**. In other words, people striving for civil rights insist that they be treated with the

same respect as anyone else. The word dignity derives from the Latin word *dignus*, worthy. Being treated with dignity is thus to have one's human worth acknowledged. During the historic Civil Rights demonstrations of the 1960s, one was often struck by the overwhelming dignity of demonstrators whose message was simply: we are as good as you and deserve the same human consideration.

The Civil Rights movement thrived in the streets where imposing numbers were obvious. They had to resort to the streets because all the other arenas of power were closed to them. The courts, legislatures, executive offices—almost all were lily-white. The viewpoints of millions of people were simply not being heard and certainly they were not being consulted. Blacks, Hispanics, and other excluded people objected in the name of democracy. This keynote strengthened their stature as it appealed to many Americans outside the movement.

How was this growing support translated into specific laws and regulations that extended democracy in the United States? Six lines of action were discernible.

1. Create fairer patterns of living. Simply talking about better living would no longer do. Actual changes in day-to-day affairs needed to materialize.

2. Establish a more just distribution of political and community power. Having others speak for you would need to be replaced by people representing themselves.

3. Enforce the actual application of new patterns. Government would not remain content with the passage of resounding measures but would require practical implementation.

4. Broaden the types of activities meriting government protection. Governmental measures will be enacted to

protect the rights of women, the disabled, of privacy, and others.

5. Minimize barriers to change. Education and information through mass media and school and colleges will deepen popular understanding.

6. Develop a politics of fairness. Insist that political parties discuss problems of creating a more just society and require that mass media repay their privileges by opening their facilities to broad ranges of opinion. Facilitate organization of congressional caucuses for a fairer society.

During the 1960s and 1970s, these lines of action penetrated many institutions, including schools and colleges.

Foremost was an effort to abolish racial discrimination based on segregation. New laws forbade the use of federal funds to discriminate against minorities. School districts were directed to desegregate when evidence in court established that the segregation was deliberately created. Segregation meant separateness, but it also almost always led to shortchanging minority children educationally.

Courts sought to make all public schools open to every child. After equal access was assured, other steps were taken: faculties were desegregated, compensatory education was made available to children who had been denied an equal education, special educational programs were opened to hitherto-excluded students, and discriminatory rules governing promotion and transfer were abolished.

. . . .

Between 1954 and 1973, the U.S. Supreme Court turned aside all appeals involving northern school segregation. The latter year, in a case involving Denver, the court extended its 1954 *Brown v. Board of*

From *Multicultural Education*, Spring 1994, pp. 13-16. © 1994 by the National Association for Multicultural Education. Reprinted by permission.

Education decision. Thereafter, a number of northern and western cities saw their segregated school systems undergo significant change. The greatest changes, North and South, occurred whenever federal courts, Congress, and the executive officer acted in the same spirit. This happened especially during the years 1968 through 1972.

Looking back at historical events, there is often a tendency to imagine that a certain inevitability was at work. Opposition to the changes is passed over, and thus the ease with which the new course occurred is exaggerated. It should not be forgotten, for example, that the central impetus for desegregation was the people whose children suffered most from segregation. Professional organizations of educators remained silent or even antagonistic. Professional journals of education, published by well-known universities, found little or no space to analyze the problems of segregation. In cities undergoing or facing desegregation battles, teacher unions most often supported school-board resistance to desegregation. Local newspapers and other mass media usually criticized desegregation advocates. Mayor Richard J. Daley of Chicago called Dr. Martin Luther King a Communist when the latter turned his attention to segregation in the North.

During the 1970s and 1980s, congressional ardor for civil rights cooled considerably. Federal agencies in charge of enforcement of civil rights statutes were pressed to ease up on school districts and other recipients of federal aid. Regulations governing procedures whereby new laws were to be implemented were watered down at congressional request. Always hanging over the heads of federal agencies concerned was a threat—frequently exercised—to cut agency budgets and thus hobble altogether a capacity to enforce the laws concerned. In state legislatures, parallel trends could be discerned.

During the 1980s, the federal courts retreated along a broad front of civil rights. The Supreme Court laid down standards for governmental action against racial discrimination that were almost impossible to document. These involved the manner in which a court needed to prove intention of officials to discriminate. By the close of the 1980s, the U.S. Department of Justice more frequently represented school officials than aggrieved minority parents in desegregation proceedings.

Major political candidates continue to avoid the subject of civil rights. In the election campaign of 1992, neither the Democrats nor the Republicans initiated any programmatic demand in the area of desegregation. Professional educators more or less follow the same pattern of inattention. You can search the texts of one school reform proposal after another and still not come up with a single demand in this area.

Inevitably, the meaning of civil rights has changed. For many years, mention of the term brought to mind Blacks and Whites. Thus, everyday controversy as well as more academic discourse assumed a black-white framework. Not only is this incorrect today; it has been so for decades.

During the first half of the present century, Mexican-American children and youth were educated under conditions of extreme segregation, especially in Texas. School boards did not hesitate to build three schools within a few blocks of each other, designating them explicitly for African-Americans, Mexican-Americans, and Whites. Schools built for the Blacks and Mexican-Americans were inferior to those for whites. Mexican-American parents and residents organized local protests, but little heed was paid them. Meanwhile, the children were subjected to various forms of discrimination inside the schools. It was a common practice to compel them to repeat early grades for their ethnicity rather than academic ability. In a number of districts, they were excluded from high schools. I.Q. exams were administered in English without an allowance for the unfamiliar language. Throughout the Southwest, school children were forbidden to speak Spanish, even while at play.

During World War II, some Mexican-Americans gained seats on local government agencies, where they could blunt at least some of the worst practices. After the war, Mexican-American veterans formed the American GI Forum which, during the next quarter-century, filed over 200 lawsuits against segregated schools. Parents protested at the unequal funding by the state of Texas of segregated elementary schools. Segregation and unequal funding were also attacked by the League of United Latin American Citizens (LULAC), the first Mexican-American national ethnic-protest organization. LULAC, founded in 1949, was a civil rights group that used legal and demonstrative tactics extensively.

. . . .

Civil rights demonstrations were conducted throughout Mexican-American communities during the late 1960s and 1970s. Many dealt with school issues related to special ethnic themes, but as many or more were aimed at introducing democratic practices into the schools.

In March 1968, for example, thousands of students in five Los Angeles high schools boycotted the schools and made a number of demands. Some called for Mexican-American administrators in predominantly Mexican-American schools, compulsory bilingual and bicultural education for Mexican-American students in such schools, and textbooks that would accurately and truthfully portray the life and history of Mexican-Americans, as well as other similar issues. In addition, however, they requested an end to homogeneous grouping, abolition of corporal punishment, and elimination of ROTC. The combination was characteristic of demands made by African-American students in contemporaneous civil rights actions.

Some five years after enactment of the Civil Rights Act of 1964, Mexican Americans began to benefit from the measure. Title VI of the law had outlawed the discriminatory use of federal funds on the grounds of national origin as well as race and color. Late in 1969, the federal Office for Civil Rights (OCR) began systematic exploration of discrimination against national origin minority group children. The next year, OCR issued a memorandum assigning school districts the affirmative obligation to provide special instruction whenever "inability to speak and understand the English language excludes national origin-minority group children from effective participation" in a district's educational program.

First applying this rule in Texas, OCR recommended errant districts offer bilingual programs. Because, however, the districts almost always regarded these measures as "extra," they sought outside funds rather than provide support from their regular budget. When federal funding for bilingual education fell far short of requests, little changed in the classrooms.

During the 1968 to 1972 period, the U.S. Commission on Civil Rights conducted the most detailed survey ever made of Mexican-American education. Its findings confirmed the essential characteristics of Mexican-American education in the United States: (1) a high degree of segregation, (2) an extremely low academic achievement, (3) a predominance of exclusionary practices by schools, and (4) a discriminatory use of public finance to the detriment of Mexican-American children. A quarter-century later, the situation continues to be marked by similar characteristics.

Asian Americans constitute another group which has pursued civil-rights methods in its century and a half of American history.

During the years 1850 to 1900, Chinese Americans were subjected to sweeping racial discrimination by federal, state, and local governments. Until 1882, Chinese were free to enter the United States as immigrants. They could not, however, become naturalized citizens as the federal Naturalization Act of 1790 reserved this right to Whites only. This law remained in force for more than a century and a half.

Only Asian-Americans born here could be citizens. In 1882, the Chinese Exclusion Act barred the further immigration of Chinese laborers and certain others. It was the first time in United States history that a specific racial-ethnic group was excluded by law. Further enactments were made by Congress to regulate or restrict Chinese-American immigrants, including a provision that they must carry an identification card; no other people were so required.

. . . .

Asian Americans sought protection of their civil rights in the courts. Historian Sucheng Chan reports that "tens of thousands of Asians sought justice through legal action." (See Asian Americans: An Interpretive History, Twayne, 1991, p. 90). According to Chan, over 90 percent of the cases dealt with the issue of immigrant exclusion. Two other subjects—naturalization and economic discrimination—covered the remaining cases. Chinese-Americans were also deprived of an equal opportunity to gain an education for most of their years here. California public schools for decades excluded Chinese students by state law. Nevertheless, Chinese continued to pay school taxes to support white attendance where their own children were turned away. Finally, Chinese-Americans were permitted to attend California schools, but not with white students. In the 1920s, a Chinese-American girl was refused admission to a white-only school in Mississippi. the U.S. Supreme Court upheld the exclusion.

Other Asian-Americans suffered similarly. During World War II, when some 120,000 Japanese Americans-—most American citizens-—were arrested and incarcerated in concentration camps, their children were given a sub-standard educa-

tion. This cataclysm was preceded by decades of discrimination in many areas of ordinary living. Both Chinese- and Japanese-Americans were not employed by large or small U.S. enterprises, even if they had earned a university degree in a field of relevant to such employment. In 1924, the latter were also excluded from further immigration.

As a result of the Spanish-American War, which ended in 1898, the American suppression of the Philippine revolt for independence, which followed immediately, a secular public school system was installed in the Philippines. The United States, however, refused to provide funds for operating it. Also withheld from the Philippines were any federal land grants to help finance the public schools. Previously, every new state had received such aid, which was indispensable in building a school system. As a result, only a weak foundation had been provided for the schools by 1946, when the Philippines became independent.

Asian Americans benefited in a major way from the civil rights movement after World War II. State laws restricting land ownership by them were stricken from the books. Asian Americans were no longer barred from naturalized-citizenship. The growth of the civil rights movement, including the Civil Rights Acts of 1964 and 1965, created a favorable atmosphere for a very major improvement in immigration law: In 1965, Congress passed a law ending discriminatory immigration quotas of Asian Americans and others. Until then, western Europeans were favored with high quotas and eastern Europeans, Asians, and Africans received low ones. Now, all countries receive the same basic quotas. Many civil rights groups fought for this change as did a number of ethnic and

immigrant organizations. Not least important, Asian Americans started to organize civil rights groups.

In the Japanese-American community, an effort was launched to bring about reparations payments to those who had been victimized during World War II. The campaign was successful. Chinese-Americans organized groups aiming to abolish discrimination in employment, particularly in public employment. Under affirmative-action requirements, Asian Americans were entitled to remedial action. The U.S. Commission on Civil Rights published reports documenting areas of American life in which discrimination against Asian Americans could still be found.

. . . .

This historical review suggests that a strong tie exists between the civil rights movement and multicultural education. Both are based on a powerful movement towards equality.

Multicultural education is teaching and learning about the equal human worth of distinctive groups of people acting in customary spheres of social life. As indicated in the opening paragraphs of this article, equal human worth is the core of civil rights concerns. So, too, is it of multicultural education. Mere plurality of cultures is not the heart of the matter. Diversity without equality is oppression. Nazi Germany contained Jews, Poles, foreign workers, and Serbs, as well as Germans. That did not make Germany a truly multicultural society. During the course of American history, multiculturalism has waxed and waned. It has never been stronger than it is today. But its future is far from assured.

The Numbers Game

Altogether, the foreign born had a higher per capita income than the native born ($15,033 vs. $14,367) in 1989, but their median family income was almost $4,000 less than that of the native born ($31,785 vs. $35,508).

% of population under 18 that is foreign-born

Los Angeles 21%
San Francisco 19%
Dade County (Miami) 18%
New York City 12%
Houston 10%
Chicago 7%
U.S. 3%

In 1976 there were 67 Spanish-speaking radio stations. Now there are 311, plus 3 Spanish–language TV networks and 350 Spanish-language newspapers.

Source: Market Segment Research, Inc.

Sources: Census Bureau, INS except where otherwise noted

Current Top 10 ancestry groups

		millions
1	German	58
2	Irish	39
3	English	33
4	African	24
5	Italian	15
6	Mexican	12
7	French	10
8	Polish	9
9	Native American	9
10	Dutch	6

32 MILLION PEOPLE IN THE U.S. (13%) SPEAK LANGUAGES OTHER THAN ENGLISH AT HOME.

JAPANESE AMERICANS marry non–Japanese Americans about 65% of the time, an out-marriage rate so high that since 1981 the number of babies born in the U.S. with one Japanese and one white parent has exceeded the number with two Japanese parents.

IN 1940, 70% OF IMMIGRANTS CAME FROM EUROPE. IN 1992, 15% CAME FROM EUROPE, 37% FROM ASIA AND 44% FROM LATIN AMERICA AND THE CARIBBEAN.

FOREIGN BORN AS A PERCENT OF TOTAL POPULATION

- 0%
- 0% > 0.5%
- 0.5% > 2%
- 2% > 5%
- 5% > 20%
- 20% > 44%

Source: Claritas/NPDC

Top 10 languages

		Number of speakers in millions
1	English only	198.6
2	Spanish	17.3
3	French	1.7
4	German	1.5
5	Italian	1.3
6	Chinese	1.2
7	Tagalog	.8
8	Polish	.7
9	Korean	.6
10	Vietnamese	.5

The unemployment rate for the foreign born was 7.8% in 1990, compared with 6.2% for the native born.

In 1990 the population was: Anglo 76%, Black 12%, Latino 9%, Asian 3%. By 2050 the breakdown is projected to be: Anglo 52%, Black 16%, Latino 22%, Asian 10%.

% who eat these ethnic foods at least once a week

Italian, other than pizza	39%
Mexican	21%
Chinese	18%
Cajun	5%
French	3%
Middle Eastern	3%
Indian	1%

Source: "Shopping for Health," Food Marketing Institute

Americans use 68% more spices today than a decade ago. The consumption of red pepper rose 105%, basil 190%.

Source: American Spice Trade Association

IN 1990 THERE WERE MORE EUROPEAN DESCENDANTS— including German, Irish, English, French, Dutch, Scots-Irish, Scottish, Swedish, Welsh and Danish, Portuguese, British and Swiss—living in California than in any other state. New York led in the number of Italians, Poles and Russians; Minnesota in Norwegians; Texas in Czechs; Pennsylvania in Slovaks; and Ohio in Hungarians.

Top 10 countries of origin for immigrants in fiscal year 1992

Mexico	22%
Vietnam	8.0%
Philippines	6.3%
Soviet Union	4.5%
Dom. Republic	4.3%
China	4.0%
India	3.8%
El Salvador	2.7%
Poland	2.6%
United Kingdom	2.1%

More than 100 languages are spoken in the school systems of New York City, Chicago, Los Angeles and Fairfax County, Va.

Source: Newcomers in American Schools, Rand

The foreign-born population in 1990 totaled a record 19.8 million (8%), surpassing previous highs of 14 million in 1930 and 1980.

Since 1901, 30% of the U.S. Nobel prize-winners have been immigrants.

88% of African-born residents had a high school education or higher in 1990, compared with 76% of Asian-born, 57% of Caribbean-born and 77% of native-born.

Seven out of 10 residents of Hialeah, Fla., are foreign-born. Other cities where more than half the population is foreign-born:
Miami, Fla. **60%**
Huntington Park, Calif. **59%**
Union City, N.J. **55%**
Monterey Park, Calif. **52%**
Miami Beach, Fla., Santa Ana, Calif. **51%** each

Top 5 non-Christian religions

		% of population
1	Jewish	1.8%
2	Muslim/Islamic*	.5%
3	Buddhist*	.4%
4	Hindu*	.2%
5	Bahai	.01%

*Adjustments for undercounts due to language problems

Top 10 Christian religions

		% of population
1	Roman Catholic	26.2%
2	Baptist	19.4%
3	Protestant (no denomination supplied)	9.8%
4	Methodist	8.0%
5	Lutheran	5.2%
6	Christian (no denomination supplied)	4.8%
7	Presbyterian	2.8%
8	Pentecostal	1.8%
9	Episcopalian/Anglican	1.7%
10	Mormon/LDS	1.4%

Source: One Nation Under God: Religion in Contemporary American Society by Barry A. Kosmin and Seymour P. Lachman. Based on a telephone survey of 113,000 randomly dialed American households

European Schools Offer Contrasts and Similarities

Nations vary in beginning ages, years of compulsory schooling, and numbers going on to higher education

Arlette Delhaxhe

Arlette Delhaxhe is chief of the Department of Studies and Analyses, United European Eurydice.

As the demand for more training grows and the required levels of qualification keep going up and up, Europe's schools have had to take in a growing number of pupils for a greater number of years.

Today, compulsory schooling generally spans nine or 10 years, and as many as 12 in Belgium and Germany. Southern Europe is slowly bringing itself up to date: Although Turkey and Italy still have only five and eight years of compulsory school attendance, respectively, Portugal and Spain are catching up with their northern neighbors: Portugal requires nine years of schooling, and Spain, which currently requires eight years, will have 10 years of compulsory schooling beginning in 1996.

With the creation of all sorts of educational centers and the recognized importance of the education of young children,

Eurydice information network was created in 1976 to support cooperation in education within the European Community. It was acknowledged in 1990 to be a major means of information about national and Community education structures, systems, and developments. According to their education structures, each member-state has delegated at least one unit to participate in the network, and the EC Commission has established the Eurydice European Unit to coordinate the network. Eurydice is funded in cooperation among the units.

it is no longer the law that determines at what age a child starts school. Children start very young even though it is still optional (except in Northern Ireland and Luxembourg): usually age 3 or 4, and sometimes as young as age 2 or 3, as in France and Belgium. Northern countries, on the other hand, where the role of the family in the small child's life is greater, put off school until much later (age 5 in Denmark and Norway, for example).

Even if they agree with the principle of early education, not all southern European countries have the capacity to cater to the young child. In the countryside, for example, preschool education is often a luxury few can afford.

All the same, it is true to say that the majority of children start school at least a year before they are obliged to by law. The striking exceptions: Only 50 percent of Greek children, 40 percent of Portuguese, and a mere 5 percent of Turks preempt their summons to school.

Countries that require their young people to stay in school the longest also turn out the most university students: On average 30 to 40 percent of their 18-to-24-year-olds go to university. Yet some of these countries are so selective that university attendance rates fall to the level of countries such as Turkey: fewer than 15 percent for England and the Swiss canton of Zurich. In the United States, by contrast, more than half the 18-to-24-year-olds are in higher education.

Systems may differ, but European elementary-school classrooms look much the same. Coeducation, an average class size of 20 to 22 pupils (except in Turkey, where it can reach 45), and one teacher

for all subjects per age-group (except in Scandinavia): All Europe's primary schools are built on more or less the same pattern.

The choice of the basic subjects to be taught varies little: reading and writing, mathematics, an introduction to the sciences, sports, and art. One difference is in the importance given to foreign languages. At first, only the Anglo-Saxon countries went for it, but it is growing steadily throughout the European Community.

As for the new technology, it has not found its way into all European schools. France and Belgium allow only a minimum of educational television programs, and Greece has just banned them completely. Northern and central European countries have included the ABC's of computers in their general educational aims (especially at secondary level) and have equipped most schools. Southern Europe, along with France and Belgium, uses the computer simply as a teaching aid.

Timetables are where the real differences show. Greece, Norway, Germany, and Italy all favor a half day, usually the morning from 8 a.m. to 1 p.m. Other countries—France, Belgium, Turkey, or Switzerland—prefer a full day with a break for lunch.

Schoolchildren in southern Europe get the longest summer holidays, between 10 and 12 weeks. The others have eight weeks or even as few as five or six, as in Switzerland, England, Germany, and Denmark.

Having to repeat a year is the bugbear of German, Swiss, and Turkish schoolchildren, while their Scandinavian and

British counterparts automatically move up from one class to the next. For pupils in France, Spain, and Portugal, the threat of repeating looms only when they are about to move from one cycle of studies to the next. Some countries, such as Belgium and Spain, have decided to limit the number of times a student can repeat a year.

Northern Europe makes no distinction between elementary and secondary school: School just flows from Day 1 until the end of compulsory schooling at 16. At the other extreme, the Benelux countries, the German-speaking countries, Switzerland, and Ireland oblige their pupils to make a choice between general, technical, or even professional education as they are entering the secondary cycle or after only one transitional year.

Other countries lie between the two poles: Everyone follows the same junior cycle of secondary school, with few optional extras. Such is France's *collège unique*, the Italian *scuola media*, the Greek *Gymnasio*, and the last stage of basic teaching in Spain and Portugal. This puts off the moment of decision until the pupils reach 15 or so.

The experience European pupils have as they work their way up in school varies considerably from country to country. The same is less true for their teachers. The profession is going through a crisis, barely mitigated by the social recognition teachers enjoy in Austria, Switzerland, or Hungary.

Except in Luxembourg and Switzerland, where teachers earn more than similarly qualified workers in the private sector, teachers' pay is never an inducement. As a general rule, university teachers are better paid than primary-school teachers even if, as in Scandinavia, the difference is small.

In spite of it all, teachers practice their profession on a full-time basis, rarely seeking to add to their earnings through other work. The exception is Greece, where lessons given outside school represent the larger part of teachers' earnings. Over the years, the teaching profession has become feminized, especially at the elementary level. In most European countries, two-thirds of all teachers are women.

ANGELA ULM – STAFF

How Much Schooling: An International Comparison

This information about the amount of time students around the world spend in school is based on a World Media questionnaire sent to the participating newspapers.

	How many hours in an average school day?		How many days are there in a school year?		How many years of compulsory education?		At what age must students make decisions affecting their education and vocational prospects?
	PRIMARY	SECONDARY	PRIMARY	SECONDARY	YEARS	AGES	
ARGENTINA	n/a	n/a	180	150	7	7-14	17-18
AUSTRIA	4-5	6-7	237	237	9	6-15	15
BELGIUM	4.5	5	182	182	12	6-18	12
BRAZIL	3.5	4	180	180	n/a	n/a	16-17
BRITAIN	6	7	190	190	11	5-16	14
DENMARK	5-7	7	200	200	9	7-16	15-17
FRANCE	6	6	180	180	10	6-16	15-16
GERMANY	5	7	200*	200*	12	6-18	10
GREECE	4-5	7	175†	175†	9	6-15	14
HUNGARY	5	6-8	170	170	10	6-16	14 or 18
MEXICO	4.5-5	4-6	188	188	9	n/a	15-16
NORWAY	5	6	190	190	9	7-16	16
PORTUGAL	5-6	6-7	172	172	9	6-15	14-15
SENEGAL	5	7	168	168	5	6-11	17
SPAIN	5	6	175	170	8	6-14	14
SWITZERLAND	5-6	6-7	195	195	9	6-16★	15-16
TURKEY	5	6-8	180	180	5	9-14	15
UNITED STATES	7	7	180	180	10	6-16	16

Source: World Media Project, 1993   *Except in areas with six-day school week   †Half-days   ★Canton Zurich

Teacher Education in Multicultural Perspective

Multicultural educational programming of some sort is now an established part of teacher education programs, but there are still major issues being debated as to how it can be integrated effectively into these programs. The National Council for the Accreditation of Teacher Education (NCATE) has established a multicultural standard for the accreditation of programs for teacher education in the United States. Many educators involved in teaching courses in multicultural education have frequently wondered why multicultural education coursework is so often a segregated area of teacher education curricula. And many who are involved in multicultural teacher education believe that all teacher educators should become knowledgeable in the area of multicultural education. Teaching preservice teachers to respect cultural diversity can reinforce their studies in learning to respect individual student's diversity in learning styles and beliefs. All persons who become teachers need to be sensitized to the reality of cultural diversity and to the need to learn about the values and beliefs of their students. The demographic changes in the population characteristics of Canada and the United States ensure that many North American teachers will have students from a wide array of differing cultural heritages.

There is still much misunderstanding as to what multicultural education is within the teacher education establishment. This will continue as long as many of its opponents consider it a political rather than an intellectual or educational concept. If all children and young adults are to receive their educational experiences in schools that nourish and recognize their respective heritages as persons, teachers must learn those intellectual and affective skills that can empower them to study and to learn about diverse cultures throughout their careers. Multicultural education course content in teacher education programs is, at one and the same time, about both cultural diversity and about individual students from differing cultural heritages.

Teachers will have to consider how a person's (especially their students') development is shaped by the powerful force of those values into which they are enculturated in their homes and neighborhoods. In a civilization rapidly becoming more culturally pluralistic, resistance to overwhelmingly Eurocentric domination of social studies and language arts curricula in the schools will continue. By the year 2000 about 5 billion of the projected 6 billion people on Earth will be persons with a non-Eurocentric conception of the world. Scholars in the social sciences, humanities, and teacher education in North America who study minority-majority relations in the schools now realize that the very terms "minority" and "majority" are changing when we speak of the demographic realities of the cultural configurations existent in most major urban and suburban educational systems. This is also true when we consider minority-majority relations in vast isolated rural or wilderness areas where those of western or northern European descent can be found to be "minorities" in the midst of concentrations of indigenous peoples. Many teachers will teach students whose values and views of the world are very different from their own, hence the relevance of teachers' learning how to study human cultures and belief systems so that they can understand the lives and heritages of their students.

Many teachers of European ethnic heritage are having difficulty understanding the importance of the fact that national cultures in North America really are becoming more culturally pluralistic. From a multicultural perspective, one of the many things course content seeks to achieve is to help all prospective teachers realize the importance of becoming learners themselves throughout their life. The knowledge base of multicultural education is further informed by the history of the struggle for civil rights in North American societies. Multicultural educational programming in teacher education programs seeks to alter how prospective teachers perceive society as a whole, not just its current minority members. We must take a broad view, not a narrow view, of multicultural education. Culturally pluralistic themes need to be apparent throughout teacher education programs and integrated into the knowledge bases of teacher education. Broadly conceived, multicultural education seeks to help members of all ethnic, cultural backgrounds to appreciate one another's shared human concerns and interrelationships; it should not be conceived as simply the study of minority cultural groups. Teachers need to be prepared in such a manner that they learn genuine respect for cultural as well as personal diversity.

Teachers should be prepared to take a global perspec-

differing cultural traditions in childrearing, entry into adulthood (rites of passage), and differing cultural styles of child-adult interaction in school settings.

The essays in this unit explore why it is important not to see multicultural education as just a political concept, but rather as an area of critical inquiry from which we can all learn alternative diverse styles of teaching appropriate to the learning styles and cultural backgrounds of students. The articles stress the importance of teachers being able to learn differing ways, share in social interaction in classroom settings, and in seeing the impact of how we perceive the ideas of race, gender, and social classes interacting in teachers' formation of their ideas about themselves as teachers, how they perceive other teachers, and how they perceive their students.

This unit's articles are relevant to courses that focus on introduction to the cultural foundations of education, educational policy studies, history and philosophy of education, and curriculum theory and construction, as well as methods courses in all areas of teacher education programs.

Looking Ahead: Challenge Questions

Why is multicultural education so frequently seen as an isolated, segregated part of teacher education programs?

What are the reasons for so much resistance to coursework in the area of multicultural education in teacher education programs?

What can we learn about teaching styles and methods from case studies of teachers from cultures other than our own?

Why can it be said that our understanding of the relevance of multicultural perspectives on teacher education emerged from the struggle for human rights in general?

What seem to be the major points of disagreement about the role of multicultural education in teacher education programs?

What attitudes need to be changed regarding multicultural education?

tive of the world and to think critically about the issues confronting them, their students, and society as a whole (seen as part of an interdependent community of nations). Multicultural education should not be politicized. It should be a way of seeing the world as enriched by cultural and personal diversity. Preservice teachers should learn from case studies that exemplify and report on the differing learning styles which develop in differing cultural contexts. Different styles of teaching can be learned from

—F. S.

BUILDING CULTURAL BRIDGES

A Bold Proposal for Teacher Education

Geneva Gay

University of Washington

One of the most compelling features of current school demographics is the growing sociocultural gap between teachers and students. Although the percentage of citizens and students who are Hispanic, Asian, Indian, African-American, poor, and limited English speaking is increasing significantly, the number of teachers from similar backgrounds is declining. This distribution has some major implications for the professional preparation of teachers and for how classroom instruction is conducted. The discussion that follows describes some of the specific demographic characteristics of students and teachers, explains some of the implications of these for teacher education, and offers some suggestions for how teacher preparation programs should be designed to respond to these demographic realities.

STUDENT AND TEACHER DEMOGRAPHICS

The percentage of students of color in U.S. schools has increased steadily since the 1960s. They now compose 30% of the total population of elementary and secondary schools. During the 1980s Hispanics and Asians/Pacific Islanders accounted for the greatest increases, by 44.7% and 116.4%, respectively (*The Condition of Education,* 1992). Although their percentages are not evenly distributed throughout the United States, the trend of increasing numbers of children of color in all school districts across the country is. Already, in at least 18 states and Washington, DC, between 30% and 96% of the public school students in grades K–12 are children of color (*Digest of Education Statistics,* 1992; *Education That Works,* 1990).

The increasing number of ethnically and culturally diverse students is attributable to two major factors—the relative youth of groups of color and their higher birthrates and increased immigration from non-White, non-Western European countries in Asia, the Caribbean, Central and South America, Africa, and the Middle East. By the beginning of the 1990s, more than one third of Hispanics (39%) and African-Americans (33%) were 18 years old or younger, compared to 25% of Anglos. Also, a greater proportion of the population of these groups fell within the prime childbearing years and produced a larger average number of children per family unit. The median ages of Hispanics, African-Americans, and Anglos were 25.5, 27.3, and 33.1 years, respectively (*The Condition of Education,* 1992; *Statistical Abstract of the United States,* 1991).

During the 1980s, the pattern of immigration to the United States shifted radically from previous generations. People coming from Western European nations declined to a mere trickle, whereas those from other parts of the world, such as Southeast Asia, Central and South America, and the Caribbean, increased (*Statistical Abstract of the United States,* 1991). The reunification of Germany, the fall of the USSR, the democratization of Eastern European nations formerly under communistic control, and political shifts in Arabic nations also are having a major impact on immigration patterns. As more people from these parts of the world arrive in the United States, even more strands of ethnic, religious, cultural, and language diversity are being added to the American mosaic. The overall impact of these demographic changes on U.S. society led Time magazine, in its April 9, 1990, cover story, to describe it as the "browning of America" (Henry, 1990).

Increasing levels of poverty are another salient characteristic of today's students. According to the latest statistics from the Bureau of the Census (*Statistical Abstract of the United States,* 1991), 38.4% of Hispanic and 44% of African-American children under the age of 18 live in poverty. Rather than stabilizing or declining in the near future, these rates are expected to continue to increase.

The statistics on ethnic identity, immigration, and poverty among public school students have major ramifications for teacher education because there are direct correlations between these social descriptors and the educational opportunities and outcomes of different groups of students. Also, they are significant because the ethnic, racial, and cultural diversity among school-teachers and administrators does not reflect similar trends.

From *Education and Urban Society,* Vol. 25, No. 3, May 1993, pp. 285-299. © 1993 by Sage Publications, Inc. Reprinted by permission of Corwin Press, Inc.

Ethnic minorities now compose less than 15% of the teaching force, and less than 12% of school administrators. About 8.0% of all K–12 public school teachers are African-Americans, 3.0% are Hispanics, 1.4% are Asians/Pacific Islanders, and 0.9% are American Indians/Native Alaskans (*Status of the American School Teacher*, 1992). Among public school principals and central office administrators there are 8.6% African-Americans; 3.2% Hispanics; 1.1% American Indians, Eskimos, and Aleuts; and 0.6% Asians/Pacific Islanders (*The Condition of Education*, 1992; De La Rosa & Maw, 1990; *The Hispanic Population in the U.S.*, 1991).

DEMOGRAPHIC IMPLICATIONS GREATER THAN NUMBERS

A closer scrutiny of the demographics summarized above suggests that the problem is greater than the numbers and that the solution is more complex than merely recruiting teachers of color. There is a growing cultural and social distance between students and teachers that is creating an alarming schism in the instructional process. In addition to racial disparities, other key factors accounting for these widening gaps are residence, generation, gender, social class, experiential background, and education levels.

Many teachers simply do not have frames of reference and points of view similar to their ethnically and culturally different students because they live in different existential worlds. Whereas a growing percentage of students are poor and live in large urban areas, increasing numbers of teachers are middle class and reside in small- to medium-size suburban communities (*Statistical Abstract of the United States*, 1991; *Status of the American School Teacher*, 1992). Furthermore, there is not much mobility in the profession, which means that the teaching population is aging, and relatively few opportunities are available for significant numbers of new and younger individuals to enter the profession. The most recent summary of U.S. teachers compiled by the National Education Association (*Status of the American School Teacher*, 1992) indicate that their mean age is 42 years. Although 60% live within the boundaries of the school district where they are employed, only 37% live in the attendance area of the school where they teach. This percentage drops to 17.3 for schools in large systems, where the greater number of ethnically diverse and poor children are enrolled. The overwhelming majority of teachers continue to be Anglo (86.8%). More than 72% are female. By comparison, the student population in public schools is increasingly children of color.

Disparities in educational levels also contribute to the growing social distance between students and teachers. More and more teachers are achieving higher levels of education, whereas students of color and poverty are becoming less educated. Teachers with 5 years of college education, and a master's degree, or its equivalent, are common occurrences throughout the country.

Another distancing phenomenon in who teaches and who is taught is that students are far more technologically adept than most teachers. Thus they are accustomed to high levels of multiple sensory stimulation and mediated information processing. These conditions are rather alien in most conventional classrooms, which tend to emphasize single sensory stimulation, similarity, passivity, and mental activities (Goodlad, 1984). These orientations and dispositions challenge the basic foundations of how teaching and learning are customarily organized and practiced. This challenge is apparent in the frustrations frequently voiced by teachers throughout the United States that they can no longer teach; they have to entertain. From the vantage point of students, many of them find it difficult to become personally invested in classroom learning because too often it lacks the "special effects" that characterize the dissemination of information they are accustomed to from constant exposure to technological media. Consequently, many of the assumptions, premises, programs, and strategies that have been used previously to teach students do not work any more. Therefore, radical changes must be made in how teacher preparation programs are conceived, designed, and implemented to meet these new challenges.

In classroom interactions, these sociocultural factors can become impenetrable obstacles to effective teaching and learning. The conduits or carriers of personal meaning in teaching and learning are examples, illustrations, vignettes, and scenarios. Understandably, teachers tend to select these from their own personal experiences and frames of reference. These examples, which are supposed to make subject matter and intellectual abstractions meaningful to culturally different students, often are irrelevant, too. The experiences, values, orientations, and perspectives of middle-class, highly educated, middle-aged Anglo teachers who live in small to mid-size suburban communities are very different from those of students who are poor, under-educated, racial and ethnic minorities, living in large urban areas. Yet establishing effective communication between students and teachers is imperative for academic success. Preparing teachers to connect meaningfully is the ultimate challenge of teacher education in an ethnically and culturally pluralistic and technologically complex world. Meeting this challenge requires reform in both the conceptual frameworks and substantive components of the preparation programs.

NEW CONCEPTUAL FRAMEWORKS NEEDED

In addition to the idea of *social distance*, there are several other behavioral science and multicultural education paradigms that offer some new and challenging directions for preparing teachers to work effectively with culturally diverse students and issues. Five are discussed here: cultural discontinuities, stress and anxiety, learned helplessness, situational competence, and cultural context teaching.

A growing body of behavioral science research and scholarship suggests that the burden of school failure does not rest on individual students and teachers but is nested in the lack of "fit" or syncretization between the cultural systems of schools and diverse groups. Spindler (1987), and other contributing authors to *Education and Cultural Process,* refer to this phenomenon variously as *cultural incompatibilities, cultural discontinuities,* and *cultural mismatches.* They and others (Gibbs, Huang, & Associates, 1989; Kochman, 1981; Shade, 1989; Trueba, Guthrie, & Au, 1981) agree that many of these mismatches occur at the level of procedures rather than substance. That is, culturally diverse students often have difficulties succeeding in school because *how* they go about learning is incompatible with school expectations and norms, not because they lack desire, motivation, aspiration, or academic potential. Opportunities to participate in the substantive components of teaching and learning frequently are a condition of the extent to which students conform to the "correct procedures and social protocols" (Holliday, 1985) of teaching. Failure to master these virtually ensures academic failure as well.

Some of the most crucial cultural discontinuities in classrooms occur in the areas of cultural values, patterns of communication and cognitive processing, task performance or work habits, self-presentation styles, and approaches to problem solving. That many of these incompatibilities happen without deliberate and conscious intent does not distract from their importance. If anything, this increases their significance as obstacles to successful teaching and learning in culturally pluralistic classrooms and as variables to be targeted for inclusion in multicultural teacher preparation programs.

Living and functioning effectively in culturally pluralistic classrooms can be highly stress provoking for both students and teachers. Trying to negotiate two or more different cultural systems can take psychoemotional priority over attending to academic tasks. *Stress and anxiety* correlate inversely with task performance. As psychoemotional stress levels increase in culturally pluralistic classrooms, teaching and learning task performance declines, thereby reducing the overall quality of academic efforts and achievement outcomes (Beeman, 1978; Gaudry & Spielberger, 1971). Teachers spend inordinate amounts of time on classroom control and maintaining the Anglocentric cultural hegemonic status quo. Culturally different students spend much of their psychoemotional and mental resources defending themselves from attacks on their psychic senses of well-being. Many find themselves in what Boykin (1986) calls a "triple quandary," having to negotiate simultaneously in three often-disparate realms of experience: the mainstream school culture, their natal ethnic cultures, and the status of being members of oppressed, powerless, and unvalued minority groups.

These conditions do not create "safe and supportive" environments for learning, one of the commonly accepted requirements for effective schooling. Instead, the result is classroom climates charged with adversarial opposition, distrust, hostility, and heightened levels of discomfort and tension. Neither students nor teachers can function at their best under these circumstances. Thus being able to identify stress-provoking factors in cross-cultural instructional interactions and knowing how to alleviate them can be a vital way to improve the overall quality of teaching in pluralistic classrooms.

An assumption held by many teachers is that children from certain ethnic groups and social classes are "universally disadvantaged or incompetent" because they do not do well on school tasks. These teachers further assume that the normative ways of doing things in school, whether they deal with social adaptation or academic issues, are the only "correct" and acceptable ones. Research conducted by cultural anthropologists, social psychologists, ethnographers, and sociolinguists (Boggs, Watson-Gegeo, & McMillen, 1985; Florio & Schultz, 1979; Greenbaum, 1985; Holliday, 1985; Kochman, 1981) indicate that ethnically and socially diverse students are very capable in their own cultural communities and social contexts. But these skills do not necessarily transfer to schools. A case in point is African-American youths who are verbally adept, creative, imaginative, and fluent among other African-Americans but appear inarticulate and unthinking in the classroom. The Kamehameha Early Education Program (KEEP) demonstrates the positive benefits of modifying the schooling process to incorporate the social competences native Hawaiian children exhibit in their homes and cultural communities (Au & Jordon, 1981; Boggs et al., 1985).

Furthermore, all individuals are not equally capable in all intellectual areas. Some are artistic; others are more scientific, mechanical, literary, or musical. Gardner (1983) reaffirms this point in his work on multiple intelligences, and Barbe and Swassing (1979) explain the merits of teaching to different students' modality strengths. But teachers frequently do not extend this principle to functioning in different cultural systems. They assume that deficiency in one area extends to all others. Thus children who are poor and from racial minority groups become "culturally deprived," "at risk," "learning disabled," and "socially maladaptive," and *all* of their educational experiences are so affected. Children with limited English proficiencies are too often assumed also to have limited intellectual potential in mathematics, science, computers, and critical thinking. These orientations need to be replaced with ones that emphasize *situational competence* and the understanding that all students are competent in some things within certain environments. The challenge is for teachers to determine what individual strengths and cultural competencies different students bring to the classroom and to design learning experiences to capitalize on them.

Irrespective of their ethnic identity, socioeconomic status, gender, or cultural background, most children begin school eager to demonstrate their abilities and excited about engaging in new learnings, experiences, and interactions. However small the rest of the world might think their achievements are, these youngsters see them as major accomplishments. They do not focus their energies on what they do not have and cannot do; they naturally take great pride in showing off what they do have and can do. They have the dispositions and perspectives on their own experiences that Giovanni (1970) praised in the poem, "Nikka Rosa," and lamented about these strengths being ignored or abused by those who do not understand them. Giovanni explains that what she remembers most about her childhood is self-pride, a strong sense of accomplishment, love, and happiness, not the constraints of poverty that others outside her social network feel define her essence.

These positive perceptions of personal competence begin to erode for many culturally different students shortly after they start their formal schooling. A persistent message is sent to them, in innumerable ways, of all the things they do not have and cannot do. The longer they stay in school, the more persuasive this message becomes. They become helpless, insecure, and incompetent. This concept of *learned helplessness* is crucial to understanding the plight of these students in schools and developing teacher attitudes and behaviors to avoid its perpetuation.

Basic principles of learning (Gagne, 1985) suggest that students are more likely to master new learnings when they build on previous learnings. These principles apply to the content to be learned, as well as to the structures, conditions, and environments under which learning occurs. Ecological psychologists have found that setting, environment, and climate are important factors in fostering desired behavior (Shade, 1989). Thus students who are accustomed to work being framed in informal social relations and group structures outside school will perform better if this tradition is continued in the classroom, rather than in formal, highly competitive, and individualistic situations.

This continuity can be achieved by doing *cultural context teaching.* That is, placing the mechanics and technical components of teaching and learning into the cultural frameworks of various ethnic, racial, and social groups. Stated somewhat differently, cultural context teaching is synchronizing various cultural styles of teaching and learning and creating culturally compatible classrooms that provide genuine invitations and opportunities for all students to engage maximally in academic pursuits without any one group being unduly advantaged or penalized (Barbe & Swassing, 1979; Shade, 1989).

Cultural context teaching is somewhat analogous to *segmented marketing* in business and industry. As the United States evolved from a factory-driven to a consumer-driven economy, corporations moved rapidly from total reliance on mass media advertising to marketing strategies designed for specifically targeted segments of the population. The shift involves identifying the values, institutions, connections, concerns, experiences, and motivations of key consumer segments; affiliating with esteemed individuals, organizations, and activities that embody these features to enter into the "circles of trust" of different consumer groups; and packaging products and services to match the life-styles of the various groups (Swenson, 1990). The merits of these strategies are readily apparent—"increased consideration translates into increased sales" (Swenson, 1990, p. 12).

Educational institutions are very susceptible to the opinions of business and industry. They have a long tradition of borrowing models from the corporate world and using economic reasoning to justify program priorities. Education, like other consumer goods and services, must be marketed effectively if it is to "sell" and succeed. Just as mass, homogeneous advertising is obsolete in the economic marketplace, so is it in the educational marketplace.

The questions now are (a) What knowledge and skills do teachers need to acquire to respond to the practical implications of *consumer-segmented teaching* and other paradigms for understanding cultural pluralism in the classroom? and (b) How should teacher preparation programs be redesigned to address these needs?

TEACHERS AS CULTURAL BROKERS

No one should be allowed to graduate from a teacher certification program or be licensed to teach without being well grounded in how the dynamic of cultural conditioning operates in teaching and learning. To achieve this goal, the preparation programs should be designed to teach teachers how to be *cultural brokers* (Gentemann & Whitehead, 1983) in pluralistic classrooms and to be competent in *cultural context teaching* (e.g., *segmented marketing of pedagogy*).

A cultural broker is one who thoroughly understands different cultural systems, is able to interpret cultural symbols from one frame of reference to another, can mediate cultural incompatibilities, and knows how to build bridges or establish linkages across cultures that facilitate the instructional process. Cultural brokers translate expressive cultural behaviors into pedagogical implications and actions. They model maneuvers within and negotiations among multiple cultural systems without compromising the integrity of any. They provide mechanisms for establishing continuity between ethnically and socially diverse cultures and mainstream school culture. Cultural brokers are *bicultural actors* who are able to straddle or syncretize different cultural systems and integrate elements of ethnic cultures into classroom procedures, programs, and practices (Gentemann & Whitehead, 1983). How they function epitomizes cultural context teaching at the levels of interpersonal interactions with students, pedagogical strategies employed in the classroom, and the infusion of multiculturalism throughout the entire instructional process.

Several skills are necessary for teachers to become cultural brokers. These can be classified as acquiring cultural knowledge, becoming change agents, and translating cultural knowledge into pedagogical strategies. They should form the substantive core of all teacher preparation programs.

ACQUIRING CULTURAL KNOWLEDGE

This component of preparing teachers to be cultural brokers should have three aspects: learning factual information about the specific characteristics of different ethnic and cultural groups, understanding the pedagogical implications of these cultural characteristics, and developing a philosophy for cultural context teaching. The students enrolled in the preparation programs should declare a cultural or ethnic group for concentrated study. They also may choose more than one group to concentrate on with the understanding that this choice will extend the time they spend in the preparation program. When they finish the program, the graduates will have a culturally diverse area of specialization (e.g., African-Americans, Mexican-Americans, children of poverty), as well as a subject matter major and endorsement.

Knowledge about cultural diversity should be acquired through two primary means: studying the accumulated research and scholarship on different ethnic and cultural groups and first-hand experiences gained from participatory observations in various cultural communities. Both of these should be in-depth experiences, guided by the methodologies, orientations, conceptual frameworks, and knowledge funds generated by behavioral scientists, ethnic studies scholars, and expressive artists (such as cultural anthropologists, social psychologists, sociolinguists, ethnomusicologists, ethnographers, cultural artists, and literary authors). College of education faculties will need to establish previously unexplored instructional partnerships with some university divisions and scholars. These partnerships in search of accurate and authentic knowledge about cultural patterns and functions are as essential as the more traditional ones between educationists and social scientists designed to increase mastery of the subject matter taught in schools.

Some dimensions of culture are more applicable than others to understanding and remediating cultural conflicts in pluralistic classrooms. These include cultural values, relational patterns, learning styles and work habits, communication styles, rewards and punishments, social etiquette and decorum, cultural ethos, self-presentation styles, and patterns of ethnic identification and affiliation. Students enrolled in teacher education programs should be expected to take relevant behavioral science courses to learn specific content about each of these cultural components for specific ethnic groups. They may take courses in ethnic literature, cultural values, folklore, family, art and aesthetics, celebrations and ceremonies, customs and traditions, and developmental psychology.

The cultural content courses should be complemented with education seminars that have three primary purposes. The first is the extrapolation of pedagogical principles and practices embedded in the cultural content. Seminars should be sequenced so that students' enrollment in the content courses and the seminars coincide with each other or follow closely thereafter. The courses could even be team taught by behavioral scientists and educationists working together. A second component of the seminars is a field-based practicum in which students spend concentrated periods of time in culturally pluralistic school sites. During these experiences, students will function as participant observers to document how the cultural characteristics they are studying are expressed in actual classroom settings and interactions. The third element of the seminars should be the development of students' philosophies for cultural context teaching. The emphasis here is on developing an understanding and appreciation of cultural pluralism in the classroom as a vital, creative, and enriching phenomenon, as well as its potential for transforming the quality of schooling for students from historically disenfranchised groups. The conceptual paradigms discussed earlier should be the foundations of this philosophy.

BECOMING CHANGE AGENTS

To be effective cultural brokers and cultural context teachers, students in teacher education programs must be taught how to be change agents. This role requires a commitment to institutional transformation and developing skills for incorporating cultural diversity into the normative operations of schools and classrooms. A four-step process should constitute this aspect of teacher education.

First, teacher education students should be taught skills of critical analysis and self-reflection. These skills will help them learn to analyze systematically the structures and procedures in schools and classrooms and their own habitual ways of behaving in instructional settings, from various cultural vantage points; to identify points of conflict between the culture of the school and different ethnic groups; and to determine which of these offer the best and the worst opportunities for negotiation and change to serve the academic needs of culturally different students better.

Second, education students should be taught how to deconstruct mainstream hegemonic assumptions, values, and beliefs embedded in the normative structures and procedures of conventional classroom teaching. This requires a thorough understanding of how cultural values shape classroom policies, procedures, and practices; points in the instructional process that are most susceptible to cultural conflict; and the ability to discern those structural components that are most significant to incorporating cultural pluralism into routine classroom procedures.

Commitments to making teaching more culturally relevant need to be grounded in principles of organizational behavior and change (e.g., Belasco, 1990; Bowditch & Buono, 1985; Meltzer & Nord, 1980; Robbins, 1991). Many teacher education students recognize the need for change and have strong affinities for making their classroom teaching more culturally sensitive. But they do not know how to anchor it in a realistic and reliable operational framework. They seem to believe that desire alone is sufficient to bring about change. In the long run, this naïveté is a serious obstacle to real change. Students must understand the organizational culture, climate, and psychology of schools; why schools are self-perpetuating institutions; obstacles to change; cooperative strategies for planned change; and techniques to initiate and sustain change.

An integral feature of success as cultural brokers is being able to relate well to students from culturally, ethnically, and racially diverse backgrounds. Therefore, a fourth part of becoming effective change agents is developing competencies in cross-cultural communications and multicultural counseling. Both of these fields of research and scholarship have rich data bases from which students can acquire conceptual skills and practical techniques. The emphases should be on sociolinguistic and paralinguistic communication components (Cazden, John, & Hymes, 1985; Greenbaum, 1985; Hall, 1981; Kochman, 1981; Smitherman, 1977; Trueba et al., 1981). In some instances, language studies and principles of bilingual education and second language learning also are appropriate. Techniques of cross-cultural counseling are important because teachers need to know how to help students deal with the stress and strain of living and functioning in culturally pluralistic settings. Some of the specific associated needs are style shifting across cultures, self-declaration for different ethnic group members, dealing with interracial and interethnic group hostilities, editing cultural nuances out of public behaviors, and coping with traumas and anxieties related to functioning in cross-cultural settings (Beeman, 1978; Schofield, 1982; Spencer, Brookins, & Allen, 1985).

TRANSLATING KNOWLEDGE INTO PRACTICE

Finally, teacher education programs should provide ample opportunities for students to engage in supervised practice doing cultural context teaching and being cultural brokers in actual classroom settings. Through a combination of classroom simulations, sample demonstrations, media protocols, case studies, and field experiences, students should develop skills in diagnosing teaching and learning styles, matching teaching styles with learning styles, creating inviting classroom climates (Purkey, 1978), using culturally sensitive assessment tools and techniques, and integrating culturally diverse content into subject matter curricula. These action strategies will need to be accompanied by corresponding changes in beliefs about what knowledge is of greatest worth for citizenship in a pluralistic world and what are the best ways it can be acquired for students from different ethnic, cultural, racial, and social backgrounds. The overriding principles should be the cultural contextuality of teaching and learning and using alternative pedagogical means to achieve common learning outcomes.

All teacher education students also should be expected to participate in a cultural brokerage internship before completing their preparation program. This internship should take place in actual classroom settings and provide opportunities to practice all of the skills involved in being a cultural broker. It is to be a complement to, not a replacement for, the traditional student teaching experience. The duration of the experience should be long enough for the students to get a sampling of the wide variety of issues and challenges involved in the institutional culture of schools. The internship should be carefully monitored and assessed by experienced classroom teachers or university professors. Successful completion should be a condition of graduating from the teacher preparation program and receiving a license to teach.

CONCLUSION

The plight of many culturally different students in U.S. public schools is chronic and critical. Because teachers play a central role in resolving it, their preparation must be a prime target of reform. This need is becoming even more imperative, given shifts in school demographics that show rapid increases in the numbers of children who are poor, limited English speakers, immigrants, and members of ethnic groups of color, as well as a decline in teachers from similar backgrounds. The resulting social distance can be an impenetrable obstacle to effective teaching and learning.

Generic teacher education programs that are supposed to prepare teachers to function well in all types of school communities are no longer viable. Instead, preparation must be population based and contextually specific. Nor can participation in multicultural learning experiences be left to choice and chance—it must be mandatory and carefully planned. The best way to translate these—ideas into practice is preparation programs that emphasize developing skills in cultural context teaching and how to be cultural brokers in pluralistic classrooms. The essence of these strategies is affirming the cultures of diverse students, establishing continuity and building bridges across different cultural systems, creating supportive classroom climates where diverse students feel welcome and valued, and replacing cultural hegemonic pedagogy with one that models cultural pluralism without hierarchy. Mastering the skills necessary for cultural brokering and cultural context teaching may require longer time in preparation. But it is time well spent, and the long-range payoffs are more than worth the relative short-term investments.

Preparing teachers to work better with culturally different students and communities demands action now. Conventional approaches to teacher education must be decentered and transformed at their most fundamental core, if teachers are to be maximally prepared to teach students of the 21st century who will be increasingly racially, culturally, ethnically, socially, and linguistically pluralistic.

REFERENCES

Au, K. H. P., & Jordan, C. (1981). Teaching reading to Hawaiian children: Finding a culturally appropriate solution. In H. T. Trueba, G. P. Guthrie, & K. H. P. Au (Eds.), *Culture and the bilingual classroom: Studies in classroom ethnography* (pp. 139–152). Rowley, MA: Newbury House.

Barbe, W. B., & Swassing, R. H. (1979). *Teaching through modality strengths: Concepts and practice.* Columbus, OH: Zaner-Bloser.

Beeman, P. N. (1978). *School stress and anxiety: Theory, research and intervention.* New York: Human Sciences Press.

Belasco, J. A. (1990). *Teaching the elephant to dance: Empowering change in your organization.* New York: Crown.

Boggs, S. T., Watson-Gegeo, K., & McMillen, G. (1985). *Speaking, relating, and learning: A study of Hawaiian children at home and at school.* Norwood, NJ: Ablex.

Bowditch, J. L., & Buono, A. T. (1985). *A primer on organizational behavior.* New York: Wiley.

Boykin, A. W. (1986). The triple quandary and the schooling of Afro-American children. In U. Neisser (Ed.), *The school achievement of minority children: New perspectives* (pp. 57–92). Hillsdale, NJ: Lawrence Erlbaum.

Cazden, C. B., John, V. P., & Hymes, D. (Eds.). (1985). *Functions of language in the classroom.* Prospects Heights, IL: Waveland.

The condition of education. (1992). Washington, DC: U.S. Department of Education, National Center for Education Statistics, Office of Educational Research and Information.

De La Rosa, D., & Maw, C. E. (1990). *Hispanic education: A statistical portrait.* Washington, DC: National Council of La Raza.

Digest of education statistics, 1991. (1992). Washington, DC: U.S. Department of Education, Office of Education Research and Improvement, Center for Educational Statistics.

Education that works: An action plan for the education of minorities. (1990). Cambridge: MIT, Quality of Education for Minorities Project.

Florio, S., & Shultz, J. (1979). Social competence at home and at school. *Theory Into Practice, 18,* 234–243.

Gagne, R. M. (1985). *The conditions of learning and theory of instruction* (4th ed.). New York: Holt, Rinehart & Winston.

Gardner, H. (1983). *Frames of mind: The theory of multiple intelligences.* New York: Basic Books.

Gaudry, E., & Spielberger, C. D. (1971). *Anxiety and educational achievement.* New York: Wiley.

Gentemann, K. M., & Whitehead, T. L. (1983). The cultural broker concept in bicultural education. *Journal of Negro Education, 54,* 118–129.

Gibbs, J. T., Huang, L. N., & Associates (1989). *Children of color: Psychological interventions with minority youth.* San Francisco: Jossey-Bass.

Giovanni, N. (1970). *Black feeling, Black talk and Black judgment.* New York: William Morrow.

Goodlad, John I. (1984). *A place called school: Prospects for the future.* New York: McGraw-Hill.

Greenbaum, P. E. (1985). Nonverbal differences in communication style between American Indian and Anglo elementary classrooms. *American Educational Research Journal, 22,* 101–115.

Hall, E. T. (1981). *The silent language.* New York: Anchor.

Henry, W. A., III. (1990, April 9). Beyond the melting pot. *Time,* pp. 28–31.

The Hispanic population in the U.S. (1991, March). (Current Population Reports, Series P-20, No. 455). Washington, DC: U.S. Department of the Census.

Holliday, B. G. (1985). Towards a model of teacher-child transactional processes affecting Black children's academic achievement. In M. B. Spencer, G. K. Brookins, & W. R. Allen (Eds.), *Beginnings: The social and affective development of Black children* (pp. 117–130). Hillsdale, NJ: Lawrence Erlbaum.

Kochman, T. (1981). *Black and White styles in conflict.* Chicago: University of Chicago Press.

Meltzer, H., & Nord, W. R. (1980). *Making organizations humane and productive: A handbook for practitioners.* New York: Wiley.

Purkey, W. W. (1978). *Inviting school success: A self-concept approach to teaching and learning.* Belmont, CA: Wadsworth.

Robbins, S. P. (1991). *Organizational change: Concepts, controversies and applications.* Englewood Cliffs, NJ: Prentice-Hall.

Schofield, J. W. (1982). *Black and White in school: Trust, tension, or tolerance.* New York: Praeger.

Shade, B. J. R. (Ed.). (1989). *Culture, style, and the educative process.* Springfield, IL: Charles C Thomas.

Smitherman, G. (1977). *Talkin' and testifyin': The language of Black America.* Boston: Houghton Mifflin.

Spencer, M. B., Brookins, G. K., & Allen, W. R. (Eds.). (1985). *Beginnings: The social and affective development of Black children.* Hillsdale, NJ: Lawrence Erlbaum.

Spindler, G. D. (Ed.). (1987). *Education and cultural process: Anthropological perspectives.* Prospect Heights, IL: Waveland.

Statistical abstract of the United States (111th ed.). (1991). Washington, DC: Department of Commerce, Bureau of the Census.

Status of the American school teacher 1990–1991. (1992). Washington, DC: National Education Association, Research Division.

Swenson, C. A. (1990). *Selling to a segmented market: The lifestyle approach.* New York: Quorum.

Trueba, H. T., Guthrie, G. P., & Au, K. H. P. (1981). *Culture and the bilingual classroom: Studies in classroom ethnography.* Rowley, MA: Newbury House.

Multicultural Education Training for Special Educators Working with African-American Youth

ABSTRACT: *Inservice training in multicultural education helps provide special education classroom teachers with the additional competencies needed to work more effectively with African-American students with disabilities. A pilot study was conducted to assess the perceptions of special education administrators in Ohio about multicultural inservice training and the nature of their exposure to multicultural education. Results indicate that special education administrators perceive that special education teachers should be involved in multicultural educational training programs with special emphasis on African-American students and their families. The results also reveal that personnel responsible for conducting such inservice programs may lack formal training. Author recommendations include the need for special educators to actively participate in high-quality, ongoing, multicultural education inservice programming conducted by personnel who have been formally prepared.*

BRIDGIE ALEXIS FORD

BRIDGIE ALEXIS FORD (CEC #0138) is an Associate Professor in the Department of Counseling and Special Education at the University of Akron, Ohio.

As we prepare to enter the 21st century, African-American youth continue to remain in a crisis situation within the public school system. They are still subjected to differential patterns of treatment (Banks, 1989; Ogbu, 1978; Payne, 1984; Smith, 1988). Recent data continue to reveal their overenrollment in classes for students with mental retardation and serious emotional disturbance and disproportionate underrepresentation in gifted/talented classes (Chinn & Selma, 1987). This phenomenon exists despite the enactment of federal legislation designed to eliminate inappropriate placement of these students within special classes and efforts by professionals advocating adequate identification of African-American gifted learners. A large percentage of these students will exit school without receiving a diploma or certificate (National Education Association, 1990). And, research indicates that these African-American youth, in particular, are at a great risk for adolescent pregnancy, problems related to drugs, involvement in the juvenile justice system, and unemployment or underemployment (Jones, 1989). We must identify and systematically adopt school practices that provide African-American youth

(with and without disabilities) with access to quality educational opportunities and experiences within the total school enterprise (Gay, 1989).

Barriers to the provision of quality educational services include ethnocentric attitudes of racial superiority; low expectations and negative attitudes toward African-American students with disabilities and their families and communities; testing, misclassification, and tracking; monocultural textbooks and curricula; narrow and limited instructional techniques; differential disciplinary and reward systems; and deficit-model (genetic or cultural factors) definitions of African-American youth's academic and socioemotional behavior (Baker, 1983; Banks, 1989; Gay, 1989; Ogbu, 1978).

Furthermore, researchers have indicated (Keisler & Stern, 1977; Payne, 1984; Ogbu, 1978; Smith, 1988) that teachers hold lower expectations for African-American students. For example, the Smith study revealed that African-American males (both upper middle class and lower class) receive lower ratings on measures of teacher expectation than do white students in general. Teachers exhibit such lowered expectations, both overtly and covertly, by being less interested in these students, being more critical of them, praising them less often, providing less and nonspecific feedback, and demonstrating less acceptance of and patience toward them.

From *Exceptional Children*, October/November 1992, pp. 107-114. © 1992 by the Council for Exceptional Children. Reprinted by permission.

These kinds of behavior are as great or greater within special education programs. Until recently, special educators planned classroom instruction and developed curricula with very little consideration of the influence of sociocultural factors or the experiential backgrounds of African-American learners. Instead, the student's disability label largely determined the choices of curriculum, instructional, and management strategies (Goldstein, Arkell, Ashcroft, Hurley, & Lilly, 1975). Many special educators have not given a high priority to the positive recognition of individual differences relating to cultural backgrounds and attitudes, worldviews, values and beliefs, interests, culturally conditioned learning styles, personality, verbal and nonverbal language patterns, and behavioral and response mechanisms (Baker, 1983; Bennett, 1988).

The literature states that without specific training, special education teachers are not prepared to create and maintain complementary learning environments to meet the needs of African-American students with disabilities (Almanza & Mosley, 1980; Fox, Kuhlman, & Sales, 1988; Gay, 1989; Smith, 1988). For current special education classroom teachers, inservice programs on how to provide educational services from a multicultural educational perspective are essential in reducing or eliminating barriers to quality educational opportunities for African-American youth (Almanza & Mosley; Fox et al.; Gay). Teacher training institutions are also beginning to incorporate a multicultural orientation in all phases of their special education preparation activities (Fox et al.; Gonzales, 1979; Reuda & Prieto, 1979).

Recently Wayson (1988) examined the beliefs of student teachers concerning their level of competence in providing educational services for students from socioculturally diverse backgrounds. The results confirmed that many student teachers are graduating without basic skills, attitudes, and knowledge in promoting equal educational opportunity and preparing students to participate effectively in a just and fair society.

A variety of definitions and goals are associated with the concept of multicultural education. In a broad sense, multicultural education refers to the practices and policies that "transform the school so that male and female students, social class, racial, and ethnic groups will experience an equal opportunity to learn in school" (Banks, 1989, p. 20; see also Rueda & Prieto, 1979).

Assisting special educators to provide services from a multicultural framework entails the following experiences:

- Engaging teachers in self-awareness activities to explore their attitudes and perceptions concerning their cultural group and beliefs—as well as the effects of their attitudes on students in terms of self-concept, academic abilities, and educational opportunities.

- Exposing teachers to accurate information about various cultural ethnic groups (e.g. historical and contemporary contributions and lifestyles, value systems, interpersonal-communication patterns, learning styles, and parental attitudes about education and disabilities).

- Helping educators explore the diversity that exists between, as well as within, cultural ethnic groups.

- Showing teachers how to apply and incorporate multicultural perspectives into the teaching-learning process to maximize the academic, cognitive, personal, and social development of learners (e.g., assessment; curriculum; and instructional management, strategies, and materials).

- Demonstrating effective interactions among teachers, students, and family members.

- Providing special education teachers with opportunities to manifest appropriate applications of cultural information to create a healthy learning climate.

Multicultural education attempts to reeducate school personnel, moving them away from an inaccurate deficit model of viewing African-American learners with disabilities—as well as those in gifted/talented programs.

The critical need for multicultural training at both inservice and preservice levels is further supported by analysis of teacher employment and student enrollment trends. Available data predict a significant decline in the number of African-American teachers within the public school (Education Commission of the States, 1989; Gay, 1989; National Clearinghouse for Professions in Special Education, 1988). By the year 2000, these teachers will drop to barely 5% of all teachers.

This projected shortage of African-American teachers will be a tremendous loss to *all* students; but for African-American students, the loss will be particularly detrimental, because African-American administrators and teachers have traditionally served as role models and mentors for African-American students. This decline will occur at a time when the enrollment of African-American students will increase substantially (National Clearinghouse for Professions in Special Education, 1988). Within the school, the special education teacher has the greatest impact on the educational process in the classroom. According to Gay, the scarcity or absence of African-American educators heightens the demand for cultural sensitivity by other school personnel and in the total school environment.

The involvement and support of administrative personnel is a prerequisite to the success of any school-sponsored inservice training (Baker, 1983). Yet there is virtually no research examining the perceptions and opinions of administrators responsible for inservice training of special educators in multicultural education. Also absent from the literature is research focusing on the specific competencies and expertise level required of those who conduct multicultural inservice training for special educators. Previous literature (Gonzales, 1979; Hurley, 1979) has raised the critical issue of trainer competency. As Hurley cautions, "Trainers can only transmit those beliefs and values which they themselves hold" (p. 19). Clearly, this is an area requiring investigation. A small-scale pilot study was undertaken in Ohio to investigate (a) the perceptions of special education administrators regarding multicultural education inservice training for special education teachers working with African-American students, and (b) their background experiences in multicultural education.

METHOD

Subjects

Subjects were special education administrators in the state of Ohio. In a small district, a person who holds responsibility for special education staff and inservice training may serve full time as the coordinator of special education or may be a part-time counselor or psychologist. Therefore, to help ensure that the appropriate personnel would receive the survey questionnaire, I addressed the mailed questionnaires to the "Director of Special Education."

Thirty administrators from various geographical locations in Ohio were selected from the potential pool of subjects for participation in the study. Using public information obtained from the Ohio State Department of Education, I identified 20 school districts in which African-American students composed at least 10% of the total enrollment. Most of these districts were located in the northern part of the state, which is described as urban (large or mid-sized) and suburban. The remaining 10 districts were selected from different geographic regions within the state.

Questionnaire Construction and Procedures

A survey questionnaire was designed to investigate the perceptions of administrators concerning multicultural education inservice training, as well as their exposure to such training. The questionnaire consisted of two parts. Part 1 focused on demographic information about the administrator and the school district. The demographics included ethnicity, sex, and years of experience as director of special education. Two questions were included under structured experiences in multicultural education: (a) Have you ever taken a college course and/or participated in a workshop/seminar focusing on multicultural education? and (b) Have you ever taught a course or conducted a workshop/seminar on multicultural education? Respondents then were asked to describe their school district by checking off the following options: (a) area (urban mid-sized, urban large, suburban, rural, and other); (b) approximate percentage of African-American students enrolled in their districts (0-9%, 10-19%, 20-29%, 30-39%, 40-49%, and 50% or greater); (c) percentage of African-American students receiving special education services (same percentage options as above); and (d) socioeconomic status of the majority of African-American students enrolled in their districts (upper, middle, low, and other).

Part 2 requested administrators to indicate their degree of agreement with 14 statements (items) on a 5-point Likert-type scale. Choices ranged from strongly disagree (1) to strongly agree (5). The 14 items tapped directors' perceptions of their districts' policies and plans regarding multicultural education, teachers' attitudes and competencies, and school practices relative to African-American families.

Two published questionnaires served as models for the 14 items: The Multicultural Education Quick Assessment Test (Ogilvie, 1983) and Evaluating the Educational Context Questionnaire (Ortiz, 1988). Some items were taken from these, some were modified versions of items from models, and others were originally written. Part 2 also contained a "Comment" section that requested administrators to describe "the single biggest school-related problem experienced by African-American exceptional learners and their parents."

To examine the validity of the questionnaire regarding this study, three special educators from Ohio with expertise in multicultural education were asked to: (a) review the format of the questionnaire, (b) analyze the statements for relevancy and clarity, (c) make comments about adding or deleting items, and (d) rewrite specific statements if necessary. (Details on the questionnaire are available from the author.)

A copy of the final questionnaire was mailed to each of the 30 directors of special education. A total of 21 questionnaires were returned, for a 70% return rate.

RESULTS

The majority of the respondents were white (14/21; 66.7%) and male (15/21; 71.4%). There

TABLE 1
Demographic Information

Item	No. (N=21)	%
Ethnicity		
African-American	5	23.8
White	14	66.7
Native American	2	9.5
Structured experience in multicultural education		
(attendance/participation in a college course and/or workshop		
or seminar)		
Yes	4	19.0
No	17	81.0
Conducted a workshop and/or taught a course on multicultural		
education		
Yes	20	95.2
No	1	4.8
Percentage of African-American students in total school		
population		
0-9%	6	28.6
10-19%	2	9.5
20-29%	1	4.8
30-39%	4	19.0
40-49%	3	14.3
50% or greater	5	23.8

were 5 African Americans (23.8%) and 2 Native Americans (9.5%). On the average, the respondents had 4-6 years of experiences as directors of special education (see Table 1 for demographic results).

The school districts of the respondents were located primarily in the northern part of Ohio (11/21), in urban areas. Six of the 21 respondents were from school districts that contained 0-9% African-American students in the total population. Each of the remaining 15 directors was located in a district that had a population of 10% or greater of African-American students. Eleven directors worked in districts with a special education enrollment of more than 10% African-American students. Most (16/21) respondents described the African-American population in their districts as being in a low socioeconomic range.

Four of the 21 directors had participated in a workshop or college course in multicultural education. Each of these 4 respondents was from a different geographic location (eastern, northern, southern, and "other"). Three were male (2 white and 1 Native American), and 1 was female (white). In addition, three had 4 or more years of experience as directors, and one had 1-3 years. Three worked in districts with an African-American student population of 10% or greater. Twenty of the 21 respondents stated that they had either conducted a workshop or taught a course relating to multicultural education.

Overall, as indicated in Table 2, most respondents agreed with the statements in Part 2 of the questionnaire. For example, more than 80% believed special education teachers should participate in multicultural inservice training programs that have special emphasis on African-American learners. The exceptions were to Items 5, 9, and 11. Although the majority of administrators believed that special educators should be involved in training that focuses primarily on African-American students, only about one-third of them reported that this district-wide type of training had been conducted or planned. Only half believed teachers adjusted instructional materials to accommodate culturally conditioned learning styles and interests of African-American learners. Two-thirds felt that educators within their district were receptive to input from African-American parents, but fewer than half believed that their district provided training to facilitate involvement specifically by parents of African-American children.

In response to the question, "What, in your opinion, is the single biggest school-related problem experienced by African-American exceptional students and parents within your district?" seven of the directors stated that their African-American student enrollment was too small to comment. The remaining comments fell into three categories: (a) the problems of African-American students and their parents were no dif-

TABLE 2
Mean Response to Multicultural Survey by Directors of Special Education (N = 21)

Item	Mean	SD
1. The school board in my district has adopted an educational policy which supports multicultural education and encourages the schools to implement this policy.	4.33	1.82
2. The schools in my district support multicultural education and have developed or are developing a plan for implementation of services within a multicultural context.	3.76	1.70
3. The families of handicapped African-American students in my district are influenced by positive cultural value systems.	3.71	1.97
4. Special education teachers in my district should participate in inservices focusing on multicultural education issues relating to exceptional African-American students.	4.09	1.17
5. Systematic and districtwide training efforts addressing educational considerations in teaching exceptional African-American students have been conducted or are being conducted in my district.	2.47	1.12
6. Handicapped African-American students in my district participate in extracurricular programs as often as non-African-American handicapped students.	3.85	1.06
7. Parents of African-American handicapped students are actively encouraged by school personnel to become involved in their children's programs.	4.00	.89
8. Collectively, parents of African-American handicapped students in my district participate in the Individualized Education Program (IEP) process as often as other parents.	3.80	1.63
9. Special education teachers in my district adjust instructional approaches, materials, and activities to accommodate culturally conditioned learning styles of African-American students.	3.23	1.09
10. Special education services in my district can be described as a "positive" experience for African-American students and their parents.	3.95	.66
11. My district provides training to facilitate involvement of African-American parents in their children's education.	3.09	1.22
12. The special education curriculum in my district incorporates contemporary culture of African Americans, not only history, customs, and holidays.	3.61	2.15
13. Special education teachers in my district are open to input from parents of African-American students in decision making and generally have positive working relationships with them.	4.00	.83
14. Special education teachers in my district have a positive attitude toward African-American students.	4.07	.49

Note: 1 = strongly disagree, 2 = disagree, 3 = uncertain, 4 = agree, 5 = strongly agree.

ferent from other students; (b) problems that resulted from family/student differences in home values and school; and (c) problems within the school. Responses in the first category were academics, lack of basic skills, or dropping out of school. The second category responses included: family exhibits a pervasive sense of powerlessness; pregnancy; lack of family structure; mobility and transferring from school to school; the differences between African-American students' life experiences in the home and community and school expectations; failure to become actively involved in the educational process and system; verbally and physically aggressive behavior leading to barriers between students and teachers; perceptions that African-American students are receiving a greater percentage of punitive consequences; children often part of developmentally disabled with related concerns; acceptance of students' disabilities and recognition of their

strengths. In the third category were responses such as racial prejudice, lack of systematic plans for educating and managing the behavior of black students, greater than normal referral of black students to special education, difficulty of adjusting mainstream curriculum and methods to meet the needs of African-American students, and cultural bias present in tests used to make placement decisions.

Two of the four respondents with multicultural expertise stated that African-American students' problems centered around "the failure to adapt teaching styles and expectations to the cultural experiences of students."

DISCUSSION

The results obtained from this small-scale pilot study indicate that most of the special education administrators perceived that special education teachers who work with African-American students should participate in multicultural education inservice training that focuses directly on issues relevant to African-American youth and their families. Twenty of the 21 directors had conducted a workshop/seminar or had taught a course in multicultural education. But only four of the special education administrators stated that they had received formal training in multicultural education. Because leadership in multicultural inservice training appears to fall to them, statewide training of administrators must be addressed. Of primary importance is exposing them to a high-quality multicultural educational training program. Such a program would include the components described previously (e.g., attitudinal self-awareness activities, accurate knowledge about cultural ethnic groups, and application of this knowledge into the classroom and parental interactions).

The current study is a small exploratory one. A larger, more detailed research project is needed to acquire a better understanding of the perceptions of people who conduct multicultural educational training for special education teachers and their competency to develop and implement this training. Such research should investigate the competencies of trainers who have received formal training in multicultural education inservice programs versus those who have not. Follow-through research is also needed on how formally prepared trainers show leadership in proposing and supporting multicultural education inservice programs.

Another area of inquiry should center on how these leaders enhance a positive relationship between special education personnel and African-American families. For special educators working in school districts with large percentages of African-American youth, such training programs should include attitudinal awareness activities, specific topics, and concrete experiences that result in an accurate understanding of these students and their families.

According to Banks (1989), despite the increase in multicultural education inservice training workshops, little if any of the information may carry over into the school and classroom environment. Therefore, factors that increase the probability of carryover into daily teaching practices warrant research. One of these essential factors may be the amount of time special educators engage in multicultural education inservice programs. In general, effective inservice programs should use formats that encourage ongoing education (conducted over a period of time), not "one-shot" programs. Because learning to teach from a multicultural education perspective is a process involving attitudinal and overt behavioral change, extended training is a necessity. Research does not provide a standard timeline for such training. However, literature pertaining to

inservice models in general suggests several options: monthly training sessions focusing on a specific topic (e.g., learning styles, positive classroom interpersonal communication patterns); several (3-4) sessions every semester (fall and spring); or 2-3 weeks of daily meetings during the summer (Berry, McClain, Spencer, & Stewart, 1977). Regardless of limitations in time, self-evaluation of attitudes concerning cultural diversity must be an integral part of any multicultural education inservice training program. *Culture: Differences? Diversity!* (Lockwood, Ford, Sparks, & Allen, 1991) is an example of a comprehensive inservice/preservice training program developed for special education personnel in the state of Ohio. The training resource includes activities that lead personnel, over time, through the sequential stages of cultural awareness (beginning with self-awareness), understanding differences, appreciating diversity, valuing diversity, and a commitment to the maintenance of diversity. A key component of this resource is its adaptability. It is designed to meet the needs of individual school districts. (Contact author for more details about this resource.)

It is imperative that we establish systematic retraining programs for special educators, from a multicultural perspective, if we are to reduce or eliminate the barriers to equal educational opportunities and experiences for African-American youth with disabilities. Three essentials of high-quality programming (both preservice and inservice) are positive perceptions and attitudes of trainers concerning multicultural training, adequate qualifications of trainers, and the provision of ongoing multicultural education training.

REFERENCES

Almanza, H., & Mosley, J. (1980). Curriculum adaptations and modifications for culturally diverse handicapped children. *Exceptional Children, 46*(8), 608-613.

Baker, G. (1983). *Planning and organizing for multicultural instruction.* Reading, MA: Addison-Wesley.

Banks, J. A. (1989). Multicultural education: Characteristics and goals. In J. A. Banks & C. A. McGee Banks (Eds.), *Multicultural education: Issues and perspectives* (pp. 2-26). Boston: Allyn & Bacon.

Bennett, C. (1988) Assessing teachers' abilities for educating multicultural students: The need for conceptual models in teacher education. In C. Heid (Ed.), *Multicultural education: Knowledge and perceptions* (pp. 23-35). Bloomington/Indianapolis: Indiana University-Center for Urban and Multicultural Education..

Berry, S. R., McClain, S. R., Spencer, N. L., & Stewart, P. M. (1977, March). *Tomorrow is today: directions for change.* Paper presented at the National Association of School Psychologists Conference, Cincinnati, OH.

Chinn, P. C., & Selma, H. (1987). Representation of minority students in special education classes. *RASE, 8*, 41-46.

Education Commission of the States. (1989, May). A

close look at the shortage of minority teachers. *Education Week,* p. 29

Fox, L. C., Kuhlman, N. A., & Sales, B. T. (1988). Crosscultural concerns: What's missing from special education training programs? *Teacher Education and Special Education, 11*(4), 155-161.

Gay, G. (1989). Ethnic minorities and educational equality. In J. A. Banks and C. A. McGee Banks (Eds.), *Multicultural education: Issues and perspectives* (pp. 167-188). Boston: Allyn & Bacon.

Goldstein, H., Arkell, C., Ashcroft, S. C., Hurley, O., & Lilly, S. (1975). Schools. In N. Hobbs (Ed.), *Issues in the classification of children* (Vol. 2, pp. 4-61). San Francisco: Jossey-Bass.

Gonzales, E. (1979). Preparation for teaching the multicultural exceptional child: Trends and concerns. Teacher Education and Special Education, 2(4), 12-17.

Hurley, O. (1979). Preparation for integration (squared). *Teacher Education and Special Education, 2*(4), 19-20.

Jones, R. (1989). *Black adolescents.* Berkeley, CA: Cobb & Henry.

Keisler, C., & Stern, E. (1977). Teacher attitudes and attitudes change: A research review. *Journal of Research and Development in Education, 229*(6), 59-67.

Lockwood, R., Ford, B. A., Sparks, S., & Allen, A. (1991). *Cultural: Differences? Diversity!* Columbus: Ohio Department of Education.

National Education Association. (1990). *Academic tracking: Report of the NEA Executive Committee/Subcommittee on academic teaching.* (ERIC Document Reproduction Service No. ED 322642.)

National Clearinghouse for Professions in Special Education. (1988). *Information on personnel supply and demand: The supply of minority teachers in the United States.* Reston, VA: The Council for Exceptional Children.

Ogbu, J. (1978). *Minority education and caste.* San Francisco: Academic Press.

Ogilvie, B. A. (1983). *The multicultural education QAT (Quick Assessment Tests).* Washington, DC: Office of the State Superintendent of Public Instruction, The Office of Multicultural and Equity Education.

Ortiz, A. (Spring, 1988). Evaluating the educational context. A questionnaire included in the *Bilingual Special Education Newsletter,* p. 4.

Payne, C. (1984). Multicultural education and racism in American schools. *Theory Into Practice, 23*(2), 124-131.

Rueda, R., & Prieto, A. G. (1979). Cultural pluralism: Implications for teacher education. *Teacher Education and Special Education, 2*(4), 4-11.

Smith, M. K. (1988). Effects of children's social class, race, and gender on teacher expectations for children's academic performance: A study in an urban setting. In C. Heid (Ed.), *Multicultural education: Knowledge and perceptions* (pp. 101-117). Bloomington/Indianapolis: Indiana University-Center for Urban and Multicultural Education..

Wayson, W. (1988). Multicultural education in the college of education: Are future teachers prepared? In C. Heid (Ed.), *Multicultural education: Knowledge and perceptions* (pp. 39-48). Bloomington/Indianapolis: Indiana University-Center for Urban and Multicultural Education..

Multicultural Teacher Education:

A Call for Conceptual Change

Carla Cooper Shaw

Carla Cooper Shaw is an Assistant Professor in the Department of Curriculum and Instruction, Northern Illinois University. She is the author of "Instructional Pluralism: A means to realizing the dream of multicultural, social reconstructionist education," in Campus and Classroom: Making Schools Multicultural, edited by C.A. Grant and M.L. Gomez (1995).

By now, multicultural educators can almost chant the statistics regarding diversity in the nation's elementary and secondary schools. The demographics of the student population are rapidly changing, while the demographics of the teaching force are not. When we speak of educating teachers for diversity, we are speaking of educating, for the most part, white, middle class females.

As a group, these prospective teachers tend to be monocultural. Of the white respondents to the 1990 AACTE/Metropolitan Life Survey of Teacher Education Students, 95% reported that the racial composition of their neighborhoods while attending high school was "more whites than minorities." Regarding leisure time, 69.1% of the white respondents reported spending all or most "of my free time with students of my own racial/ethnic background," compared to 51.2% for African Americans, 47.3% for Hispanics, and 27.8% for Asian/Pacific Islanders.

In keeping with these statistics are what might be considered monocultural attitudes. Researchers have found that teacher education students express a desire to work with youth from communities similar to their own, and that they possess color-blind perspectives on diversity, attributing variation among people primarily to individual differences.

M. E. Dilworth, in *Reading Between the Lines*, writes that, unlike their counterparts of color, white teacher education students are not "advantaged in their ability to know and communicate in more than one culture"—an ability which "shows much promise for devising educational methods and curricula that can make a difference in the academic achievement of the nation's increasingly diverse student population." Further, if the findings of Lortie's landmark 1975 study, *Schoolteacher*, still hold true, those motivated to enter teaching tend to be conservative and reluctant to challenge prevailing practice. In the words of Dilworth, teachers are a "fairly docile" lot.

▨ ▨ ▨ ▨

Stimulating Change

Our job as teacher educators is cut out for us. We need to look at ways to stimulate change in prospective teachers. Conceptual change offers such a means, and it revolves around notions familiar to teacher educators: disequilibrium, assimilation, and accommodation.

By *disequilibrium*, I mean cognitive and affective dissonance or imbalance, which is prompted by new experiences. One responds to disequilibrium by either assimilating or accommodating. *Assimilation* is the incorporation of new experiences into existing schemas, or ways of thinking, without altering these schemas. *Accommodation* means restructuring ways of thinking to fit the new experiences. True change, then, occurs with accommodation.

To catalyze change in our teacher education students, we must first look at their experiences and characteristics. As much as possible, we need to get inside their heads and hearts to determine how we can help to construct bridges between our students' cultural backgrounds and those of their students. We must ask: How can we help to construct bridges between the culture of the schooling our would-be teachers have received and the culture of schooling toward which we strive, a culture recast today in light of a pluralistic society?

These two cultures often stand in stark contrast to one another. The schooling of our future teachers likely has been highly stratified due to ability grouping. The curriculum they have ingested has featured the contributions of "dead white males." When the contributions of women and people of color have been included, they often appear as sidebars—interesting but nonessential.

The learning styles to which our students' teachers have appealed are those attributed to European American males—individually competitive, analytic, overly cognitive, abstract, tolerant of out-of-context and theoretical learning, and field independent. The culture of their schooling subscribes to an anachronistic factory model in which the "workers" are passive students, pumped full of content and procedural knowledge and rewarded for spitting it back out relatively unchanged.

The culture of schooling toward which we strive is more democratic, with equality of opportunity for learning. This equality occurs largely through a convergence of three educational practices: heterogeneous grouping; a more inclusive curriculum,

From *Multicultural Education*, Winter 1993, pp. 22-26. © 1993 by the National Association for Multicultural Education.
Reprinted by permission.

⌧ ⌧ ⌧ ⌧
Experiences for Conceptual Change

1. Considering the privileges, both societal and educational, accruing to the possession of white skin. McIntosh's article provides a provocative catalyst for discussion. Students also might brainstorm privileges related to gender and being able-bodied.
2. Exploring one's own cultural heritage.
3. Investigating the nature and functions of African American English.
4. Reading and reflecting upon potent works of literature by a diversity of such authors as Louise Erdrich, Toni Morrison, Alice Walker, Sandra Cisneros, Amy Tan, and Margaret Atwood.
5. Engaging in experiences designed to induce empathy for and identification with people of color, physically and perceptually challenged individuals, and the elderly.
6. Considering the extent to which one is willing to become a multicultural person— for example, expending effort to cultivate friends of color and withdrawing from organizations with exclusionary membership policies; testing one's commitment to developing a social reconstructionist frame of mind by actively working for social structural equality
7. Engaging in no-holds-barred discussions of such books as Bell's *Faces at the Bottom of the Well*, Hacker's *Two Nations*, Studs Terkel's *Race*, and Jonathan Kozol's *Savage Inequalities*.
8. Analyzing IQ and achievement tests for cultural bias and exploring the ramifications of using such instruments to place children in academic tracks.
9. Immersion in cultural contexts, clinical and otherwise, that are radically different from one's own.
10. Placement in and reflection upon field experiences with contrasting paradigms of instruction. Ross and Smith, for example, comment upon the effects on five of their students of placements in differing settings: "Their placements in traditional classrooms helped the student teachers bring into focus the idea that curriculum can limit children's thinking. The placements in constructivist classrooms gave them concrete examples of alternatives and a model to follow."
11. Analyzing and discussing the experiences of students from a variety of cultural backgrounds, and teachers working with diverse student populations. Case studies by Baruth and Manning, Sleeter and Grant, and Nieto provide fertile ground for discussion.
12. Preparing reports based on observations of real classrooms. These observations might focus upon teachers' gender-related behavior, such as calling on students, reinforcement, use of examples, and body language.
13. Researching the real, operational cultures of schools and comparing them to the schools' idealized mission statements.
14. Exposure in their university classes, and certainly in their teacher education classes, to instruction that builds on a diversity of learning styles and modalities — instruction that has been called "culturally responsible pedagogy" and that I have called "instructional pluralism."

The Sociopolitical Context of Multicultural Education, Sonya Nieto says: "Becoming a multicultural teacher...first means becoming a multicultural person... But becoming a multicultural person in a society that still emphasizes the model of an educated person in a monocultural framework is not easy. It means reeducating ourselves in several ways." This reeducation includes learning more about different cultural groups, confronting our own racism and prejudices, and "learning to see reality from a variety of perspectives." These latter two means of reeducation involve disequilibrium, a prerequisite stage in the progression from monoculturalism to multiculturalism, according to Wurzel (1988).

The experience of disequilibrium is uncomfortable, as those of us in multicultural teacher education are aware. After reading the first few chapters of Banks and Banks' *Multicultural Education: Issues and Perspectives*, and Sleeter and Grant's *Making Choices for Multicultural Education*, both of which seem to take pains not to alienate their readers, some of my students note that the books seem "militant" and "radical" in tone. At the same point in the semester, at least one student is sure to exclaim, "Am I supposed to feel guilty about everything just because I'm a white male?" And more than one are likely to ask, "If my poor immigrant ancestors made it, why can't Blacks and Hispanics?"

Such reactions soon give way to more thoughtful, though no less troubled, responses. Cochran-Smith and Lytle describe the responses of teachers to reading articles about cultural pluralism as "unsettling" and "disturbing." They quote the essay of a student who had read McIntosh's 1989 article "White Privilege: Unpacking the Invisible Knapsack:"

> The fact that something called "white privilege" exists in our society is easy for someone who is white to ignore, and I think it made me uncomfortable to have to face up to these truths that I otherwise never consider in my everyday experiences.

which includes as an integral part the contributions of women and people of color; and a more diverse approach to learning styles.

The teachers of this new culture do not toss out instruction that draws on the forementioned learning styles. Rather, they incorporate those learning styles ascribed to females and people of color—preference for cooperation, relational and holistic thinking, strength in the affective domain, concrete thinking, need for contextualized learning with real-world relevance, and field sensitivity. The new culture grows out of a constructivist model in which students are active, empowered participants, the beneficiaries of what Christine Sleeter and Carl Grant have described as Education That Is Multicultural and Social Reconstructionist.

To bridge the chasm between the two cultures, to begin the process of conceptual change, we must stimulate disequilibrium in our students. In *Affirming Diversity:*

⌧ ⌧ ⌧ ⌧
Questioning the Status Quo

In light of this discomfort, the question becomes: How do we find the elusive line between just enough disequilibrium and too much, when our students become defensive and resistant to accommodation and change? For to experience disequilibrium with regard to multicultural education is necessarily to question the status quo—a status quo that has told our teacher education students they are good students, good citizens, good people. A status quo which has provided our teacher education students with the privileges that allow them to hold such views of themselves. A status quo that encourages complacency.

Two related faces of the status quo are relevant here. One concerns our students' views of themselves within society. The other pertains to their views of themselves as students and teachers.

As suggested previously, teachers, as a group, tend to have conservative dispositions. According to Lortie, "continuation," or the desire to engage in school-linked pursuits as adults, serves as a powerful motivator for entry into teaching. To the extent, then, that our students wish to prolong their school experiences, they have little reason to change. After all, they have enjoyed success within the monocultural context of schooling described previously.

Further solidifying the status quo are the findings of several researchers that most teacher education students tend to deliver the kinds of instruction they received as students. Without experiencing alternative pedagogies themselves, our students are unlikely to attempt any but the most traditional and monocultural of methodologies. Buoyed by the status quo, these students may never progress beyond assimilation to accommodation. Without

intervention aimed at conceptual change, they may not realize the fallacy inherent in the statement we so often hear: "Multicultural education is just good education. Period."

■ ■ ■ ■

The Experience of Disequilibrium

Conceptual change, or real growth, occurs when teacher education students engage in powerful experiences which involve the whole person, demand mental and emotional attention, and provoke disequilibrium. The experiences described on the previous page are those that I and numerous other multicultural teacher educators require of our students. The first seven pertain to views our students hold of themselves in society, while the latter seven pertain more directly to their views of themselves as teachers and learners. Some experiences, of course, lend themselves to examination of both faces of the status quo.

In view of what we know about teacher education students' tendency to mimic the kinds of instruction they have received, such modelling is crucial. All too often, teacher educators are guilty of not practicing what we preach. We must do more than tell students the virtues of cooperative

learning; we must use it in our own classrooms. We must do more than exhort our students to engage the whole person in learning. We, as teacher educators, must climb down from our ivory towers, vary our own instruction, and smile before Christmas.

Experiences such as these engage the whole person, induce disequilibrium, and contain the potential to jolt our teacher education students out of their complacency. They force our teacher candidates to consider, and perhaps to adopt, unaccustomed perspectives. In so doing, these experiences expand, revise, and modify our students' existing schemas. In short, they provoke conceptual change.

Conceptual change is suitable for shaping individual experiences and also for organizing entire courses and programs of teacher education—because conceptual change in the individual arena is but a microcosm of change in the larger sphere of education. That is, increasing diversity in our nation's classrooms provides disequilibrium to which our schools can respond in one of two ways. They can assimilate by continuing to follow cultural deficit models and conducting business as usual—with dire consequences. Or they can accommodate diversity by restructuring schooling for educational equity.

Preservice Teachers' Perceptions of the Goals of Multicultural Education: Implications for the Empowerment of Minority Students

Johanna Nel, Ph.D.

Dr. Johanna Nel is an assistant professor in the College of Education at the University of Wyoming.

Several educators and scholars have focused attention on the "culturally different" student's lack of achievement.[1] Over the past twenty years a series of costly, but apparently ineffective, educational reforms have been introduced to turn around minority school failure. Among these were compensatory preschool programs, a variety of bilingual education programs, the institution of safeguards against discriminatory assessment procedures, and the hiring of additional aides and remedial personnel.[2]

The ineffectiveness of these programs is evident in the disproportionate numbers of minority students who are still dropping out of school[3] or are being placed in lower ability groups.[4] Factors such as negative teacher attitudes toward the potential of minority children,[5] tracking practices and persistent discriminatory assessment procedures also attest to program ineffectiveness.[6] Serious efforts are needed to stop minority school failure. Colleges of education

have an important role to play. It is their responsibility to prepare teachers who are able and willing to change the negative pattern of failure to one of empowerment.

Reasons for Minority Student Failure

Many complex interrelated factors are at work when attempting to account for minority student failure.[7] Scholars such as John U. Ogbu argue that school success and cultural assimilation go "hand in hand." According to his viewpoint, minority groups who fail are predominantly those who came to this country involuntarily and are suffering from a castelike, dominated status. Other researchers such as Trueba and Erickson argue against this position on theoretical and empirical grounds. In their views, social forces alone are not the full explanation for differential achievement within and between minority groups.[8] They emphasize the need to recognize the significance of culture in specific instructional settings, prevent stereotyping of minorities, resolve cultural conflicts in school, integrate the home and school cultures, and develop communicative skills in children.

Cummins' theoretical framework for analyzing minority students' school failure[9] and the relative lack of success of previous attempts at educational reform such as compensatory education and bilingual education appears to be in line with Trueba and Erickson's theories. Based on a series of hypotheses regarding the nature of minority students' educational difficulties, Cummins suggests that classroom interactions between teachers and minority students, relationships between schools and minority communities, and intergroup power relations within the society as a whole are crucial in determining the success or failure of minority students. The central tenet of his framework is that students from "dominated" societal groups are "empowered" or "disabled" as a direct result of their interactions with teachers. Empowering relationships depend on the extent to which teachers 1) incorporate students' language and culture into the school program; 2) encourage minority community participation as an integral component of children's education; 3) promote intrinsic motivation in minority students to use

Reprinted with permission from *Educational Horizons* quarterly journal, Spring 1993, pp. 120-125. © 1993 by Pi Lambda Theta, Inc., international honor and professional association in education, Bloomington, IN 47407-6626.

language actively to generate their own knowledge; and 4) become advocates for minority students in assessment procedures.

Multicultural Education

Multicultural education is a way to break the cycle of minority student failure. Historically, preservice teachers have been educated to work effectively with only one cultural group, dominant mainstream America.[10] Various professional organizations such as the American Association of Colleges for Teacher Education[11] and the Holmes Group[12] call for a commitment to cultural pluralism. Both of these groups ask colleges of education to integrate multicultural education into their preservice teacher education programs. They urge educational institutions to affirm cultural diversity as a valuable resource that should be preserved and extended, and to encourage multilingualism and multi-dialectism. Although many educators lack enthusiasm for cultural diversity,[13] many colleges of education seeking National Council for the Accreditation of Teacher Education (NCATE) accreditation responded to these appeals by incorporating multicultural education into their instructional programs.

The term multicultural education, however, means different things to different people. In reviewing more than 200 articles and sixty books written on the subject, Sleeter and Grant[14] were able to distinguish among five different approaches. Primary goals of these approaches range from simple recognition of distinct personalities to a social activist position. Questions asked by the investigators included: What is the target student population? What is the vision of society? What goal does a teacher have in mind when multicultural education is incorporated in the curriculum?

Recognizing that a crucial factor in the ultimate success or failure of multicultural education in our schools is the teacher, it becomes important to determine, a) what preservice teachers regard as the most desirable goal for multicultural education, and b) what colleges of education should do re-

garding the multicultural education curriculum of preservice teachers.

Cummins' guidelines for reversing the cycle of minority student failure appear to have implications for the teaching of multicultural education at teacher education institutions. The implementation of principles outlined in his theory for the empowering of minority students may be dependent on individual teachers' perceptions of the goal of multicultural education and the way they choose to approach human diversity in their classrooms. What future teachers view as the most important goal of multicultural education could determine their ultimate effectiveness in altering school-minority relationships and reversing the cycle of failure. It is necessary for preservice teachers to be clear about their own beliefs, and to develop skills needed to establish empowering instead of disabling interactions with their minority students.

Rationale for the Investigation

To assess preservice teachers' perceptions of the goal of multicultural education was the main purpose of this investigation. Research literature in teacher education clearly indicates the premier roles played by attitudes towards diversity, cultural sensitivity, and commitment to the application of cultural knowledge upon minority students' academic success.[15] Culturally insensitive teachers often are not aware of obstacles created by cultural conflicts in pluralistic classrooms.[16] The identification of future teachers' perceived goals of multicultural education provides guidelines to colleges of education regarding the instructional methodology and content of multicultural education curricula. Preservice teachers will make up their own minds regarding the appropriate goals of multicultural education, but instructors in colleges of education have a responsibility to broaden the knowledge base and experiences on which students' decisions will be based. Analysis of Sleeter and Grant's five identified approaches to multicultural education appears to indicate that the closer respondents' choices

are to goal numbers four and five, the more realistic chances become that they, as future teachers, will be instrumental in the creation of empowering school-minority relationships and minority students' academic successes.

The Study

The sample for this study was 280 white, middle-class, predominantly rural, preservice teachers who have not had a course in multicultural education. Each respondent was asked the following question related to the goals of multicultural education: "You are a teacher in a pluralistic classroom. If you could teach only one of the goals listed below, which one would you select?" The five options from which to choose reflected a rewording[17] of Sleeter and Grant's five educational approaches to race, class and gender: a) Teaching the Exceptional and the Culturally Different, b) Human Relations, c) Single-group Studies, d) Multicultural Education, and e) Multicultural Education that is Social Reconstructionist. *See Figure 1.*

Option one, which appears to reflect a multicultural approach focusing mainly on teaching the culturally different, refers to the position of those who respect distinct personalities but are not really concerned with fostering cooperation and equity between cultural groups. These respondents view society as essentially good and healthy as long as individuals learn to get along with each other. Their main goal will be to assist culturally different students in acquiring the necessary knowledge, skills, and attitudes to participate successfully in mainstream society. Not choosing alternatives from numbers two to five implies that these respondents are unaware of the need to develop empathy between different cultural groups, cause positive change in the interactions between schools and minority communities, or to change intergroup power relations within society as a whole. The "appropriateness" of the respondents' own Anglo background and culture is taken for granted. Schooling is viewed as politically neutral.

where schools become active agents in the transformation of society.

Findings

Table I summarizes the responses.

Discussion

The fact that over sixty-six percent of the respondents selected options one and two appears significant. Not selecting alternatives three, four, or five indicates that these respondents view cooperation, tolerance and assimilation of minority groups as the major goals of multicultural education in our schools. This limited view creates concern. Preference for goals one and two appears to underline Cummins' theory about how relationships have failed to change significantly between educators and minority students and between schools and minority communities. These respondents will probably support the status quo in schools regarding minority-school relationships. Chances are that they will not be inclined to incorporate minority language and culture into their classrooms, encourage minority community participation in school programs, or become advocates for minority students in assessment procedures.

Respondents who selected option one appear to believe that society is essentially good and that teachers should make an effort to help the culturally different student to fit into the existing social structure. These preservice teachers plan to build on students' individual learning styles and teach as effectively and efficiently as possible to enable students to reach appropriate academic levels. Their goal is to build bridges between the minority students and the demands of the school. Chances are that they will not be working toward altering the teacher-minority student relationship as it has existed over the past twenty-five years.

Respondents who selected option two appear to desire to promote positive interactions between individuals or groups. While this group wants to improve teacher/minority

---

If you could only teach one of the goals listed below, which one would you select?

_____ 1. Youngsters would learn that all people are individuals with distinct personalities regardless of their backgrounds.

_____ 2. Youngsters would learn that we all have to learn to live together in this world regardless of any group differences. Cooperation and tolerance are vital.

_____ 3. Youngsters would learn that every person came from some ethnic group and all groups are equally fine.

_____ 4. Youngsters would learn that the U.S. is made up of many racial, ethnic, and religious groups and each must be protected and enhanced.

_____ 5. Youngsters would learn that we all have a responsibility to change the discrimination and prejudice in our society against certain groups.

Figure 1

Option two appears to reflect what Grant and Sleeter (1988) calls, the "Human Relations" approach. It refers to a position that recognizes the need for people within the existing social system to cooperate and communicate with each other. It does not imply a recognition of equity between cultural groups, as suggested by number three, or the need to protect differences, and affect social change as suggested by option numbers four and five. As is the case with option one, this approach is in essence politically neutral. Society is viewed as basically good, all students will be the target and the goal will be to promote harmony.

Option three points to the "Single Group Studies" approach. This position focuses on the need for children and youth to recognize all cultural groups as equal. While these respondents see a value in teaching about cultures and argue for the non-neutrality of education, they are not social activists. Emphasis in this approach seems to be on ethnic diversity to the exclusion of other forms of diversity such as class, gender, religion, and exceptionality.

Option four, the "Multicultural Education" approach, refers to a position that actively seeks to protect and enhance diverse groups. It is expected that these respondents will make an effort to incorporate minority students' language and culture into the school program and to encourage minority community participation. More forms of human diversity than suggested in option three are recognized. Diversity will be celebrated and students will be taught to value cultural differences in society but no active effort will be made to confront racism as suggested by option five.

Option five reflects Sleeter and Grant's "Multicultural Education that is Social Reconstructionist" approach. This alternative indicates the position of those who apparently have a strong focus on equity and justice. These respondents are activists who believe in a common responsibility to work actively towards social structural equality and equal opportunity in the school.

These perceptions, as represented by the five items, are not mutually exclusive, but viewed as a continuum that represents a pathway toward the ultimate goal of empowering minority students. Beginning with option one, which appears to represent the status quo of the way American classroom teachers interacted with minority children over the past twenty years, goals progressively advance toward the point

53

Table 1
Goals of Multicultural Education: Perception of Preservice Teachers (N=280)

Option	N	%
1. Recognize distinct personalities. Assist the culturally different student to fit into mainstream society.	112	40.00
2. Emphasize cooperation and tolerance between different cultural groups in a society that is essentially good.	74	26.42
3. Teach children that all ethnic groups are equal.	33	11.79
4. Actively seek to protect/enhance diverse groups.	28	10.00
5. Prepare future citizens to reconstruct society to better serve the interest of minority groups.	33	11.79

student relationships their emphasis on tolerance and acceptance *within* the existing social structure prevents them from affecting changes necessary to successfully empower minority students. Preservice teachers who select this position will be inclined to support the current structure of assessment processes that are geared towards locating the "problem" within the minority student. It would not seem necessary to these respondents to incorporate minority students' language into the classroom or actively encourage minority community participation as an integral part of children's education. According to Sleeter and Grant's critique, this approach reduces social problems to people's inability to get along.

Respondents selecting option three, which emphasizes that every person comes from an ethnic group and that all groups are equal, are a step closer to the creation of empowering relationships. Approximately twelve percent of the respondents chose this goal. Although respondents would emphasize teaching about the contributions and experiences of various ethnic groups they would not necessarily address the issue of racial oppression. According to Cummins' framework for intervention, however, it is necessary to address intergroup power relations within society as a whole if we

wish to reverse the pattern of school failure among minority students.

Respondents selecting option four appear to be bridging this gap to some extent. This group, which comprises ten percent of the total number of respondents, sees a responsibility to change discrimination and prejudice in society but do not view themselves as social activists. These students would probably want to promote equal opportunity in schools, cultural pluralism and respect for those who differ. Their belief in the need to protect and enhance diversity would lead them

---

Visionary leadership is needed in the education of preservice teachers.

---

to incorporate the principles as outlined in Cummins' theoretical framework. Not seeing their role as social reconstructionists, however, would prevent them from becoming active agents in changing power relations within society as a whole.

Only twelve percent of the preservice teachers surveyed (those who selected option five) appear to

have the necessary beliefs and motivation to implement effectively Cummins' framework for intervention. These students indicate that they see themselves as social reconstructionists who would be willing to change the status quo and redefine the teacher's role regarding minority students and communities.

Conclusion

This data has implications for teacher education. The content and instructional methodology used in teaching multicultural education to preservice teachers may influence their decisions regarding the goals of multicultural education. If the major obstacle in the way of reversing minority school failure indeed is disabling relationships between teachers and students and between schools and minority communities, as suggested by Cummins' model, then colleges of education have a definite goal to direct the preparation of future teachers. Accepting that theoretical analysis can have implications for practice,[18] Cummins' guidelines could have implications for teacher education institutions. The implementation of his theories for the empowering of minority students may depend on individual teachers' perception of the goals of multicultural education and the way they choose to approach human diversity in their classrooms.

The seriousness of minority school failure cannot be understated. Currently twenty-two of the twenty-six largest school districts in the country have a minority-majority school enrollment,[19] non-white school enrollments exceed twenty-five percent in half of our states, and fifteen percent of American public school students do not speak English at home.[20] Projections are that forty-eight percent of the overall student enrollment will be minority by the year 2020.[21]

Visionary leadership is needed in the education of preservice teachers. The pattern of school failure among minority students needs to be reversed. Maintaining the status quo spells disaster for the culturally different student in the United States. Minority-school relationships, assessment procedures and Eurocentric cultural curricula, need to be altered significantly. While this goal will require a combined effort on behalf of everyone involved with education, teachers may be the crucial agents to affect the necessary change that may lead to the empowerment of minority students. Because of the pivotal role played by teachers in the classroom,[22] it is necessary to guide preservice teachers into developing **a commitment to goals of multicultural education that will be translated ultimately into significantly altered relationships between educators and minority students and between schools and minority communities.** In the final analysis, teachers' perceptions and beliefs could be the contributing factor to either the empowerment or the disabling of minority students.

1. J. Cummins, "Empowering Minority Students: A Framework for Intervention," *Harvard Educational Review*, 56 (1986) no. 1: 18–36; J. Cummins, *Empowering Minority Students* (Sacramento: California Association for Bilingual Education, 1989); G.A. DeVos, "Adaptive Strategies in U.S. Minorities," *Minority Mental Health*, eds. E.E. Jones and S.J. Korchin (New York: Preager 1982) 74–117; F. Erickson, "Transformation and School Success: The Politics and Culture of Educational Achievement," *Anthropology and Education Quarterly* 18 (1987), no. 4: 335–356; M.A. Gibson, "The School Performance of Immigrant Minorities: A Comparative View," *Anthropology and Education Quarterly* 18 (1987), no. 4: 262–275; R.P. McDermott, "The Explanation of Minority School Failure, Again," *Anthropology and Education Quarterly* 18 (1987), no. 4: 361–364; L.C. Moll and S.E. Diaz, "Change as the Goal of Educational Research," *Anthropology and Education Quarterly* 18 (1987), no. 4: 300–311; J.U. Ogbu, *Minority Education and Caste: The American System in Cross-cultural Perspective*," (New York: Academic Press, 1978); J.U. Ogbu, "Origins of Human Competence: A Cultural-Ecological Perspective," *Child Development* 52, 1981: 413–429; J.U. Ogbu, "Cultural Discontinuities and Schooling," *Anthropology and Education Quarterly* 13 (1982), no. 4: 290–307; J.U. Ogbu, "Minority Status and Schooling in Plural Societies," *Comparative Education Review* 27 (1983), no. 2: 168–190; J.U. Ogbu, "Variability in Minority Responses to Schooling: Non-immigrants vs. Immigrants," *Interpretive Ethnography of Education: At Home and Abroad*, eds. G. Spindler and L. Spindler (Hillsdale, N.J.: Erlbaum 1987a) 255–278; J.U. Ogbu, "Variability in Minority School Performance: A Problem in Search of an Explanation," *Anthropology and Education Quarterly* 18 (1987b), no. 4: 312–334; J.U.

Ogbu and M.E. Matute-Bianchi, "Understanding Sociocultural Factors: Knowledge, Identity and School Adjustment," *Beyond Language: Social and Cultural Factors in Schooling Language Minority Students*, (Sacramento: Bilingual Education Office, California State Department of Education 1986) 73–142; C.B. Paulston, *"Bilingual Education: Theories and Issues,"* (Rowley, MA: Newbury House 1980); T. Skutnabb-Kangas, *Bilingualism or Not: The Education of Minorities*, (Clevedon, England: Multilingual Matters 1984); M.M. Suarez-Orozco, "Towards a Psychosocial Understanding of Hispanic Adaptation to American Schooling," *Success or Failure: Linguistic Minority Children at Home and in School*, H.T. Trueba, ed. (New York: Harper & Row 1987) 156–168; L. Wong-Fillmore, "The Language Learner as an Individual: Implications or Research on Individual Differences for the ESL Learner," eds. M.A. Clarke and J. Handscombe, *On TESOL '82 Pacific Perspectives on Language Learning and Teaching*, Washington, DC: TESOL 1983.

2. J. Cummins, *Empowering Minority Students*.

3. A. Wheelock and G. Dorman, *Before it's Too Late*, (Boston, MA: Massachusetts Advocacy Council, 1989).

4. A.A. Ortiz and J.R. Yates, "Incidence of Exceptionality Among Hispanics: Implications for Manpower Planning," *NABE Journal* 7 (1983): 41–54.

5. R.L. Jones and F.B. Wilderson, "Mainstreaming and the Minority Child: An Overview of Issues and a Perspective," ed. R.L Jones, *Mainstreaming and the Minority Child*, (Minneapolis: Leadership Training Institute, 1976).

6. G. Clark-Johnson, "Black Children," *Teaching Exceptional Children* 20 (1988), no. 4: 46–47; D. Clark, "High Expectations," eds. P. Bates and T. Wilson, *Effective Schools: Critical Issues in the Education of Black Children*, (University of Michigan: National Alliance of Black School Educators 1989); A.A. Ortiz and J.R. Yates, "Incidence of Exceptionality among Hispanics: Implications for Manpower Planning"; D.J.Reschly, "Minority MMR Overrepresentation and Special Education Reform," *Exceptional Children* 54 (1988) no. 4: 316–323; A. Yates, "Current Status and Future Directions of Research on the American Indian Child," *American Journal of Psychiatry* 144 (1987) no. 9: 1135–1142.

7. J. Cummins, "Empowering Minority Students: A Framework for Intervention"; J. Cummins, *Empowering Minority Students*; G.A. DeVos, "Adaptive Strategies in U.S. Minorities"; F. Erickson, "Transformation and School Success: The Politics and Culture of Educational Achievement"; M.A. Gibson, "The School Performance of Immigrant Minorities: A Comparative View"; R.P. McDermott, "The Explanation of Minority School Failure, Again"; L.C. Moll and S.E. Diaz, "Change as the Goal of Educational Research"; J.U. Ogbu, *Minority Education and Caste: The American System in Cross-cultural Perspective*; J.U. Ogbu, "Origins of Human Competence: A Cultural-ecological Perspective"; J.U. Ogbu, "Cultural Discontinuities and Schooling"; J.U. Ogbu, "Minority Status and Schooling in Plural Societies"; J.U. Ogbu, "Variability in Minority Responses to Schooling: Non-immigrants vs. Immigrants"; J.U. Ogbu, "Variability in Minority School Performance: A Problem in Search of an Explanation"; J.U. Ogbu, and M.E. Matute-Bianchi, "Understanding Sociocultural Factors: Knowledge, Identity and School Adjustment"; C.B. Paulston, *Bilingual Education: Theories and Issues*; T. Skutnabb-Kangas, *Bilingualism or Not: The Education of Minorities*; M.M. Suarez-Orozco, "Towards a Psychosocial Understanding of Hispanic Adaptation to American Schooling"; L. Wong-Fillmore, "The Language Learner as an

Individual: Implications or Research on Individual, Differences for the ESL Teacher."

8. H.T. Trueba, *Success or Failure: Linguistic Minority Children at Home and in School* (New York: Harper & Row 1987).

9. J. Cummins, "Empowering Minority Students: A Framework for Intervention."

10. J. Callas and L. Clark, *Foundations of Education* (New York: MacMillan Publishing Company 1983); D. Gollnick and P. Chinn, *Multicultural Education in a Pluralistic Society* (Columbus, OH.: Charles E. Merrill 1986); A. Lindsey, "Consensus or Diversity? A Grave Dilemma in Schooling," *Journal of Teacher Education* 36 (1985), no.4; 31–36.

11. American Association of Colleges for Teacher Education, *No One Model American: A Statement on Multicultural Education*, (Washington, DC: AACTE 1989).

12. Holmes Group, *Tomorrow's Teachers*, (East Lansing: Michigan State University 1986).

13. J. O'Connor, On TV: Less Separate, More Equal, *New York Times*, April 29, 1990, 1; "Profiles: You and the System," *Teacher Magazine*, April 1990.

14. C.E. Sleeter and C.A. Grant, "Analysis of Multicultural Education in the United States," *Harvard Educational Review* 57 (1987), no. 4: 421–444.

15. C.E. Sleeter and C.A. Grant, *Making Choices for Multicultural Education: Five Approaches to Race, Color and Gender* (Columbus, OH.: Charles E. Merrill 1988); J.A. Banks, *Multiethnic Education* (Boston: Allyn and Bacon 1987); R. Campbell and R. Farrell, "The Identification of Competencies for Multicultural Teacher Education," *The Negro Educational Review* 35, 1985: 137–144; D. Cruickshank, "Profile of an Effective Teacher," *educational Horizons* 64 (1986), no. 2: 80–86; D. Gollnick and P. Chinn, *Multicultural Education in a Pluralistic Society*.

16. S. Gilbert and G. Gay, "Improving the Success of Poor Black Children," *Phi Delta Kappan* 67, (1985): 133–137; C.E. Sleeter and C.A. Grant, "Success for all Students," *Phi Delta Kappan* 68, (1986): 297–299.

17. M. Haberman and L. Post, "Cooperating Teachers' Perceptions of the Goals of Multicultural Education," *Action in Teacher Education* 12 (1990), no. 3: 31–35.

18. P. Freire, *Pedagogy of the Oppressed* (New York: Seabury 1973); H. Giroux, "Theories of Production and Resistance in the New Sociology of Education," a critical analysis, *Harvard Educational Review* 53 (1983), no. 3: 257–293; P. Lather, "Critical Theory, Curricular Transformation, and Feminist Mainstreaming," *Journal of Education* 166, (1986): 49–62.

19. Editor, "Profiles: You and the System," *Teacher Magazine*, April 1990; *Education Week*, May 14, 1986; R.R. Fernandez and W. Felez, "Race, Color, Language in the Changing Public Schools," eds. C. Maldonado and D. Moore, *Urban Ethnicity in the United States*, (1985), 123–144.

20. "Ready or Not, Here They Come," *Education Week*, May 14, 1986; A. Wheelock and G. Dorman, *Before it's Too Late*.

21. H. Hodgkinson, *All one System: Demographics of Education—Kindergarten through Graduate School* (Washington, DC: Institute for Educational Leadership 1985); H. Hodgkinson, *The Same Client: The Demographics of Education and Service Delivery Systems* (Washington, DC: The Institute of Education 1989); Holmes Group, *Tomorrow's Schools* (East Lansing, MI: The Holmes Group 1990).

22. C. McCarthy, "Multicultural Education, Minority Identities, Textbooks, and the Challenge of Curriculum Reform," *Journal of Education* 172 (1990), no. 2: 118–129.

Multicultural Education as an Academic Discipline

Multicultural education has had a fascinating developmental history as an emergent area of scholarship out of the social upheavals of the 1960s and the concern of many in the scholarly community that there is critical need for research-based knowledge of the cultural contexts of education. It was in the 1960s that the first courses in "multicultural education" developed. Much of our early knowledge base came from critically important research in anthropology and sociology (as well as psychiatric studies of the impact of prejudice and victimization on targeted racial and cultural minorities) from the 1920s through to our present time. These studies examined intercultural relations in urban, suburban, small town, and rural settings in the United States. In addition, these "field studies" used ethnographic field inquiry methods developed by anthropologists initially and later used by some sociologists and educators as well. The earliest of these studies focused on such concerns as childrearing practices, rites of passage into adulthood, perceptions of other cultural groups, and the social stratification systems of communities and neighborhoods. Studies of how victimized and involuntarily segregated racial and cultural groups responded to being targeted for discriminatory treatment documented the intercultural state of affairs in American society in the 1930s and 1940s. This body of social science knowledge became very important documentation for the plaintiffs in *Brown v. Board of Education of Topeka* in 1954, the historic U.S. Supreme Court case that declared segregation on the basis of race to be unconstitutional.

As the U.S. civil rights movement of the 1950s continued to grow in momentum throughout the 1960s, anthropological and sociological inquiry about the education of minority cultural youth continued to develop. Out of the crises of the 1960s, educators became concerned about racial and cultural justice. They saw that there was a serious need for an area of educational studies which would focus on intercultural relations in the schools from a multicultural perspective. These areas would work in harmony with cultural pluralist visions of American social life that would challenge the by-then traditional Eurocentric melting pot visions of how one became American. The problem with the Eurocentric melting pot was that it was a very exclusionary pot—not everyone was welcome to jump into it, and many cultural groups were excluded. The philosophy of a cultural pluralist democracy in which all cultural heritages would be treasured and none rejected within the broader framework of a united, multicultural democratic nation-state became attractive to those who witnessed the arbitrary and cruel effects of racial and cultural prejudice in schools as well as in other areas of life in mainstream society.

The belief that all teachers should respect the cultural heritages of their students and that all students have the right to know their cultural heritages, as well as to develop self-esteem and pride in them, began to spread among socially concerned educators. The studies that had been conducted on intercultural relations among teachers and students by the early 1970s clearly demonstrated the need for an academic discipline which would specifically focus on building knowledge bases about our multicultural social reality. In addition, the need to teach about other cultural heritages and to improve the quality and the pedagogical effectiveness of instruction in multicultural school settings was recognized.

As part of the movement for civil rights, persons from linguistic minority heritages also sought to guarantee that their children would be given the opportunity to grow up both bilingual and bicultural. By the time the U.S. Supreme Court handed down its decision in *Lau v. Nichols* in 1974, there were dozens of federal court cases pending at various stages of development concerning this matter. The causes of bilingual education and English as a second language were being argued (as well as contested).

The academic leadership of the nation's cultural minorities and many other concerned scholars have forged a competent community of scholars to set standards of academic practice for multicultural education as an academic discipline. There is spirited dialogue going on as to what these standards of practice should be as well as the academic qualifications of persons involved in multicultural education. James Banks (professor of multicultural education at the University of Washington) and others are concerned about the future survival and development of multicultural education, which must also maintain its focus on classroom practice as well as defensible theoretical constructs.

Multicultural education must develop an ongoing cadre of competent scholarly leaders to direct the further development of the field and to ensure that attempts to merely infuse multicultural content into existing teacher educa-tion course content does not dilute the content or the quality of standards of practice in the field. Banks therefore argues that merely integrating multicultural education content into existing teacher education coursework must be resisted. He calls for a "Multicultural Education (MCE) + Integration" model for the practice of multicultural education. Since multicultural education is an interdiscipline that draws its knowledge base from anthropology, sociology, social history, and even psychiatry, adequately prepared specialists are necessary if it is to maintain its academic integrity as a discipline.

The essays in this unit reflect concerns regarding academic standards and goals for multicultural education as the field continues to develop and to enter a new period in its history. The authors of these essays raise important qualitative issues, which must be addressed as multicultural education enters a time when a majority of Americans will be from minority cultural heritages and when traditional conceptions of "minority" and "majority" relations in the United States will have little real meaning.

The essays in this unit are relevant to courses in curriculum theory and construction, educational policy studies, history and philosophy of education, cultural foundations of education, and multicultural education.

Looking Ahead: Challenge Questions

What should be some minimal "standards of practice" in the field of multicultural education?

What are the qualifications necessary for persons who wish to become specialists in multicultural education?

It has been argued that all American students should learn the multicultural reality of our nation. Why do you agree or disagree with this concept? How can it be accomplished?

What does it mean to speak of multicultural education as an "interdiscipline"?

What issues are raised by total infusion models of multicultural education in teacher education programs?

What should every American student know about racism and prejudice by the time he or she graduates from high school?

How do we help people to learn to accept cultural diversity? What can teachers do to foster acceptance of cultural differences?

—F. S.

Multicultural Education as an Academic Discipline

James A. Banks

James A. Banks is Professor and Director, Center for Multicultural Education, University of Washington, Seattle. His most recent book is An Introduction to Multicultural Education *(Allyn and Bacon, 1994). He is also the Editor (with Cherry A. McGee Banks) of the* Handbook of Research on Multicultural Education *(Macmillan.)*

Multicultural education is moving down the road toward academic legitimacy and institutionalization. Signs of vitality are the establishment of required multicultural teacher education courses in a large number of colleges and universities, the proliferation of multicultural education textbooks, scholarly books and articles, the brisk sales of textbooks, the establishment of a national organization (NAME) and magazine, and the publication of the first *Handbook of Research on Multicultural Education,* which will bring together the major scholarship, research, and theory that has developed since the field evolved in the seventies.

These significant markers of the development of multicultural education, a nascent and practical field, should not prevent us from recognizing and conceptualizing ways to deal with the challenges the field faces as it enters the 21st century. We should also view the progress and challenges to the field within a historical context. To provide such a context, I will briefly discuss the historical development of anthropology and sociology. (Space does not permit a discussion of the significant ways in which academic disciplines such as anthropology and sociology and fields such as multicultural education—which are grounded in practice—differ.)

During the late nineteenth and early twentieth centuries, the social science disciplines such as anthropology and sociology were in a nascent phase and had to struggle to attain academic legitimacy and institutionalization. At that time, the physical and natural sciences reigned supreme in colleges and universities. The new social sciences tried to gain legitimacy by attempting to adapt and incorporate the aims and methods of the physical and natural sciences. In fact, a number of early pioneers in these disciplines, such as anthropologist Franz Boas and sociologist Lester Frank Ward, had received their advanced degrees and training in the natural and physical sciences.

The Legitimization of Anthropology and Sociology

The social sciences, such as anthropology and sociology, survived and eventually gained academic legitimacy. They also became institutionalized as departments in the nation's leading research universities. Several factors contributed to their success and implementation. One of the most important was the strong academic leadership provided by scholars such as Boas (US) and Bronislaw Malinowski (United Kingdom) in anthropology; and by William G. Sumner and Lester Frank Ward in sociology. The "Chicago School" sociologists at the University of Chicago also greatly enhanced the academic status of sociology in the years after Sumner and Ward published their seminal works. William I. Thomas and Robert E. Park published highly influential works at Chicago during the second decade of this century.

The academic leadership provided by scholars such as Boas, Malinowski, Thomas, and Park included the development of paradigms, concepts, and theories that grew out of empirical research in field settings conducted by themselves, their students, and by scholars they heavily influenced. The pioneering empirical and theoretical work done by these early leaders in anthropology and sociology were decisive factors in building these two disciplines. Landmark publications that contributed to the growth and legitimacy of anthropology included *The Mind of Primitive Man* by Boas (1911), and *Argonauts of the Western Pacific* by Malinowski (1922). Landmark publications in sociology included *Dynamic Sociology* by Ward (1883); *Folkways* by Sumner (1907); *The Polish Peasant in Europe and America* by Thomas and Florian Znaniecki (1918-1920); and *Introduction to the Science of Sociology* by Park and Ernest W. Burgess (1921).

From *Multicultural Education,* Winter 1993, pp. 8-11, 39. © 1993 by the National Association for Multicultural Education. Reprinted by permission.

The commitment by these early scholars in anthropology and sociology to empirical research and to theory-building were the most important factors that led to the academic legitimacy and institutionalization of these disciplines on college and university campuses and in the public imagination.

. . . .

Twenty-first Century Goals

The next several decades will be critical ones for multicultural education as a discipline and field of study and practice. During this period, its fate will be determined. Multicultural education will either attain academic legitimacy and become fully institutionalized within the next several decades, or it will fade away like progressive education and intergroup education.

I believe that multicultural education will survive and become fully institutionalized in the nation's universities, colleges, and school districts. However, its survival is by no means assured. We can act thoughtfully and decisively in ways that will greatly increase its possibilities for survival and institutionalization. Toward that end, I will offer, for discussion by the profession, what I think ought to be the key goals for multicultural education as it faces the 21st century.

. . . .

The Development of Scholarly Leaders

We need to develop scholarly leaders for the future. Within the next two decades, the torch must be passed to a new generation of scholars and researchers in multicultural education. We need to invest much more of our time, energy, and resources in the development of new scholars for the field.

I am concerned that the identification of future scholars, and adequate training and mentoring programs for them, are not receiving the attention in the field that is essential for its development. To continue on a path of institutionalization, leadership within a field must be continuing and consistent over several generations. Anthropology succeeded in part because Boas trained students such as Ruth Benedict and Margaret Mead, who continued to develop the field after Boas had completed his most significant works. Yet one of the most important reasons that the intergroup education movement perished is that its leaders, such as Hilda Taba and William Van Til, left the field and pursued other professional interests.

Another positive example of the survival of a field because of long, continuing, and consistent leadership is the way in which African American history developed from the early twentieth century to the present. Carter G. Woodson devoted his entire life to research, organizational, and professional work in African American history. He also inspired and influenced an entire generation of younger historians, who pursued work in African American history and continued that work beyond Woodson's time. These historians included Rayford Logan, Charles H. Wesley, Benjamin Quarles, and John Hope Franklin.

To survive and prosper, leaders must not only devote a lifetime to its development, but must make sure that younger scholars are trained so that leadership in the field will be continuous over many decades. (By *younger scholars* I am not referring to chronological age, but rather to new recruits to the field. Ruth Benedict did not receive her doctorate until she was 36, yet she became one of the nation's most widely read and influential anthropologists.)

Strong and consistent scholarly leadership is essential for an academic field to survive over the long haul. Several generations of scholars must be willing to devote lifetimes to a discipline for it to develop and become institutionalized and to gain academic legitimacy. Respect among practitioners tends to follow respect in the academy.

Scholarship and research, whose aim is to improve practice, must be the field's top priority during the remainder of the nineties and the first decades of the 21st century. The field's quest for academic legitimacy and institutionalization should be an overarching goal that is vigorously and continually pursued. Although it is essential that multicultural education develop its own journals and publications, it is also important for multicultural scholars, researchers, and practitioners to publish frequently in the most respected and influential journals in education. These journals have academic legitimacy, professional authority, and large and influential audiences.

It is going to take several decades for multicultural education to attain the academic legitimacy and respect that it deserves. However, this respect and legitimacy must be earned the hard way—the same way that it was earned by other new fields and disciplines, such as anthropology, sociology, and special education. That is why it is essential that multicultural education invest heavily in the development and mentoring of future scholars who have a deep commitment to and interest in the field.

Since 1980, a number of significant multicultural education articles and papers have been published in highly respected mainstream journals and books. These publications have contributed greatly to the academic legitimization of the field. Among them are Barbara A. Shade's 1982 paper on African American cognitive style in the *Review of Educational Research*; Carl A. Grant and Christine E. Sleeter's 1986 paper on race, class and gender in the *Review of Educational Research;* Sleeter and Grant's influential 1987 paper describing their multicultural education typology in the *Harvard Educational Review;* and my own review of research in the field in 1993, in Volume 19 of the *Review of Research in Education*.

. . . .

Formulating Standards for the Field

The field needs to discuss the feasibility of developing criteria for determining who can practice in multicultural education, the possibility of developing standards and guidelines for multicultural professionals, and of developing minimum standards for practice.

A serious problem exists within multicultural education because people with varied—and often sparse—professional education are calling themselves multicultural professionals and are conducting training for business, health care, and educational institutions on a wide and often profitable scale. In their training sessions, these individuals often violate key principles and practices in the field that are derived from theory, research, and wisdom of practice.

It is not uncommon for individuals with varying skills and abilities to proclaim expertise and to practice in nascent fields. In the early years of their discipline, sociologists became deeply concerned because of the wide range of people who called themselves "sociologists." Writes B. Bernard, in "Re-viewing the impact of women's students on sociology," in *The Impact of Feminist Research in the Academy,* 1987: "They [sociologists] sought...to achieve an identity uncontaminated by quacks who called themselves sociologists. The rapid growth of the study of sociology had created a great shortage of teachers." Bernard quotes Lundberg, writing in 1929:

> Second-rate and half-trained men have in consequence filled important positions. As a result of the demand for men, sociology has tended to be a sort of happy hunting ground for well-meaning sentimentalists, plausible charlatans, and other worthy persons unwilling or unable to weather the rigorous discipline of real scholarship.

Sociology solved the problem of professional certification and of who could practice in the field by establishing the criterion that trained sociologists must earn a doctorate from a recognized university. The solution for multicultural education will be more difficult because the field is both a research and practical field. In its early years, sociology also had a practical component. However, this component was essentially eliminated during the discipline's quest for legitimacy. Because of the nature of multicultural education, in which practice and the improvement of practice are an integral part of what we are, practice must remain a significant part of the field. However, dialogue ought to take place about the possibility of setting minimum standards for practice in multicultural education.

. . . .

The Infusion/Separate Course Problem

One of the most difficult issues that multicultural education now faces and will increasingly face in the future is the pressure by mainstream colleagues in teacher education programs to "infuse" the content of multicultural education courses into existing or newly created general teacher education courses. This pressure is likely to mount as the popularity of infused education courses increases, caused in part by the budget crisis that exists in higher education throughout the nation.

It is essential that we give well-reasoned and thoughtful responses to requests (often disguised demands) to infuse the content of multicultural education courses to avoid the appearance of mere self-interest. I strongly believe, however, that the infusion model of curriculum reform, if widely implemented nationally, will seriously threaten the existence of multicultural education as a discipline and retard the academic legitimacy and institutionalization of the field.

A total integration model must be resisted on *academic, pragmatic,* and *political* grounds. We should argue for the implementation of a *Multicultural Education + Integration Model* (MCE + Integration Model). The *MCE + Integration Model* will assure that students will learn the key paradigms, concepts, ideologies, and knowledge in multicultural education from committed experts in the field. At the same time, instructors of courses such as foundations, general curriculum, and the subject matter methods courses will be encouraged and allowed to integrate multicultural content into their courses. If multicultural content is poorly integrated into the general courses (or is not integrated beyond the course outline—both conditions frequently exist), students will have benefited from the one or two multicultural education courses taught by specialists.

. . . .

The Academic Justification

I should make my preference for the *MCE + Integration Model* explicit. First, the academic justification for this model. Multicultural education is a distinct interdisciplinary field with a unique set of paradigms, concepts, theories, and skills. It is not highly likely that non-specialists can adequately teach the specialized content of the field to novice teachers and practitioners. They are likely to be learning the content of the field themselves, and may not have much more expertise in multicultural education than their students.

Even if non-specialists have mastered the academic content of multicultural education, they often have not had adequate opportunities to examine their attitudes, feelings, and beliefs, important factors in teaching multicultural content. We do not expect or usually permit a non-expert in reading to teach the content of the readings methods course to novice students or to infuse it into a general methods course that the non-expert is teaching. Multicultural specialists should insist that the same standards used to select instructors and to teach content in the other academic fields are used when making curricular and instructional decisions about multicultural content and courses.

. . . .

The Pragmatic Justification

Second, the pragmatic justification. Advocates of the *Infusion-Only Model* argue that by placing a multicultural specialist on a teaching team, multicultural content can be effectively integrated into the general course. This form of course integration can cause problems for the students as well as for the multicultural specialist on the team. Multicultural concepts, paradigms, and ideologies are *oppositional* to the paradigms, concepts, and theories taught in most mainstream general methods and curriculum courses. When multicultural concepts and paradigms conflict with the other concepts and paradigms in the general course, students often become angry and confused. The lone multiculturalist on the teaching team often becomes the victim of student hostility and confusion.

Multicultural education asks students to examine some of their latent and unexamined attitudes, beliefs, feelings, and assumptions about U. S. society and culture. Students often find this process a difficult and painful one. Because of the power of context, this self-introspection and self-analysis becomes even more painful and unsettling when it is experienced within the context of an integrated course in which most of the other content and concepts reinforce the students' mainstream values, attitudes, and beliefs.

. . . .

Mainstream vs. Transformative Knowledge

Most of the knowledge in teacher education courses is *mainstream academic knowledge*. Mainstream academic knowledge consists of the concepts, principles, theories, and explanations that constitute traditional and established knowledge in the behavioral and social sciences. An important tenet within mainstream academic knowledge is that it is a set of objective truths that can be verified through rigorous and objective research and is uninformed by human interests, values, and perspectives.

In reality, mainstream academic knowledge, while appearing neutral and objective, often presents propositions, concepts, and findings that reinforce dominant group hegemony and perpetuates racism, sexism, and classism. Influential examples of such mainstream knowledge are the concept of cultural deprivation that emerged in the 1960s (in David Riessman's *The Culturally Deprived Child*, 1962); Arthur Jensen's theory of Black-White intelligence, (in the 1969 article "How much can we boost IQ and scholastic achievement?" published in the *Harvard Educational Review);* and the concepts of "at-risk" youth and the "underclass" that are popular today. These concepts are heavily value-laden, yet they masquerade as neutral and objective.

Multicultural education, as conceptualized by the major theorists in the field, is a form of transformative academic knowledge. *Transformative academic knowledge* consists of the paradigms, themes, and explanations that challenge mainstream academic knowledge and that expand the historical and literary canon. Transformative scholars, unlike mainstream scholars, assume that knowledge is not neutral but is heavily influenced by human interests; that all knowledge reflects the social, economic, and political relationships within society, and that an important purpose of transformative knowledge is to help citizens improve society.

During the late 1960s and 1970s, transformative scholars (such as Baratz & Baratz in their "Early childhood intervention: The social science base of institutional racism" in the *Harvard Educational Review*) challenged some of the dominant paradigms that were heavily influencing the education of low-income students and students of color. They challenged cultural deprivation theories and theories about how mother tongue languages adversely affected the learning of standard English.

Transformative scholars such as Code, Patricia Hill Collins and Sandra Harding interrogate the assumptions, ideological positions, and political interests of the knower. Lorraine Code, in her seminal 1991 book, *What Can She Know? Feminist Theory and the Construction of Knowledge,* raises this question: "Is the gender of the knower epistemologically significant?" After a rigorous philosophical analysis of this question, she concludes that gender does have a complex influence on the knowledge produced by the knower. Harding and Collins have reached similar conclusions about the relationship between gender and the knower.

Nearly two decades before the work of Code, Collins, and Harding, Joyce Ladner explored a similar question regarding the influence of race on knowledge in her 1973 book, *The Death of White Sociology.* Ladner and her colleagues documented the effects of race on knowing in sociology. Ladner was about two decades ahead of her time. Consequently, her message was often criticized rather than praised.

Finally, the *Infusion-Only Model* must be resisted because the power of the multicultural specialist to control the content and pedagogy of the infused course is decentered and may completely disappear. Typically, the multicultural specialist is a lone member of a teacher education teaching team and is likely to have an ideology and conception of knowledge highly inconsistent with the other members of the team. The multiculturalist on such teams can easily became marginalized as the *Other.* Thus, the power relationship within the larger society and within the wider university community are likely to be reproduced on the teaching team.

The *MCE + Infusion Model* allows the multicultural specialist to control an important course and to serve as a resource person for instructors of other courses who wish to infuse their courses with multicultural concepts, paradigms, and pedagogy in a meaningful way. Many of these instructors need and want staff development in multicultural education. An important and appropriate role for the multicultural specialist is to lead an effort to implement a staff development effort within the school or college of education. Outside consultants and resources are usually required to implement such an effort. Local multicultural specialists can facilitate but can almost never conduct training within their own department, college, or school.

The ultimate fate of multicultural education as a discipline will to a large extent be determined by the kind of vision we develop and implement within the field. I believe that its fate will be more akin to anthropology and sociology than to progressive education and intergroup education. However, we must act now to set and pursue a rigorous scholarly and research agenda, develop a cadre of strong academic leaders who will shepherd the field in the future, develop standards for practice in the field, strive to improve classroom practice, and take vigorous steps to assure that multicultural education courses and programs are consistent with a transformative tradition that promotes justice, equality, and human dignity.

Affirmation, Solidarity, and Critique:
Moving Beyond Tolerance in Multicultural Education

Sonia Nieto

Sonia Nieto is a faculty member with the Cultural Diversity and Curriculum Reform Program, School of Education, University of Massachusetts, Amherst.

Tolerance: the capacity for or the practice of recognizing and respecting the beliefs or practices of others.
  —The American Heritage Dictionary, *as quoted in* Teaching Tolerance, *Spring, 1993.*

"We want our students to develop **tolerance** of others," says a teacher when asked what multicultural education means to her. "The greatest gift we can give our students is a **tolerance** for differences," is how a principal explains it. A school's mission statement might be more explicit: "Students at the Jefferson School will develop critical habits of the mind, a capacity for creativity and risk-taking, and **tolerance** for those different from themselves." In fact, if we were to listen to pronouncements at school board meetings, or conversations in teachers' rooms, or if we perused school handbooks, we would probably discover that when mentioned at all, multicultural education is associated more often with the term tolerance than with any other.

My purpose in this article is to challenge readers, and indeed the very way that multicultural education is practiced in schools in general, to move beyond tolerance in both conceptualization and implementation. It is my belief that a movement beyond tolerance is absolutely necessary if multicultural education is to become more than a superficial "bandaid" or a "feel-good" additive to our school curricula. I will argue that tolerance is actually a low level of multicultural support, reflecting as it does an acceptance of the *status quo* with but slight accommodations to difference. I will review and expand

upon a model of multicultural education that I have developed elsewhere (See Sonia Nieto, *Affirming Diversity: The Sociopolitical Context of Multicultural Education,* Longman, 1992) in order to explore what multicultural education might actually look like in a school's policies and practices.

Levels of Multicultural Education Support

Multicultural education is not a unitary concept. On the contrary, it can be thought of as a range of options across a wide spectrum that includes such diverse strategies as bilingual/bicultural programs, ethnic studies courses, Afrocentric curricula, or simply the addition of a few "Holidays and Heroes" to the standard curriculum (See James A. Banks, *Teaching Strategies for Ethnic Studies,* Allyn & Bacon, 1991), just to name a few. Although all of these may be important parts of multicultural education, they represent incomplete conceptualizations and operationalizations of this complex educational reform movement. Unfortunately, however, multicultural education is often approached as if there were a prescribed script.

The most common understanding of multicultural education is that it consists largely of additive content rather than of structural changes in content and process. It is not unusual, then, to hear teachers say that they are "doing" multicultural education this year, or, as in one case I heard, that they could not "do it" in the Spring because they had too many other things to "do." In site of the fact that scholars and writers in multicultural education have been remarkably consistent over the years about the complexity of approaches in the field (see, especially, the analysis by Christine E. Sleeter & Carl A. Grant, "An Analysis of Multicultural Ed-

ucation in the United States," *Harvard Educational Review,* November, 1987), it has often been interpreted in either a simplistic or a monolithic way. It is because of this situation that I have attempted to develop a model that clarifies how various levels of multicultural education support may actually be apparent in schools.

Developing categories or models is always an inherently problematic venture, and I therefore present the following model with some hesitancy. Whenever we classify and categorize reality, we run the risk that it will be viewed as static and arbitrary, rather than as messy, complex, and contradictory, which we know it to be. Notwithstanding the value that theoretical models may have, they tend to represent information as if it were fixed and absolute. Yet we know too well that nothing happens exactly as portrayed in models and charts, much less social interactions among real people in settings such as schools. In spite of this, models or categories can be useful because they help make concrete situations more understandable and manageable. I therefore present the following model with both reluctance and hope: reluctance because it may improperly be viewed as set in stone, but hope because it may challenge teachers, administrators, and educators in general to rethink what it means to develop a multicultural perspective in their schools.

The levels in this model should be viewed as necessarily dynamic, with penetrable borders. They should be understood as "interactive," in the words of Peggy McIntosh (see her *Interactive Phases of Curricular Re-vision: A Feminist Perspective,* Wellesley College Center for Research on Women, 1983). Thus, although these levels represent "ideal" categories that are internally consistent and therefore set,

From *Multicultural Education,* Spring 1994, pp. 9-12, 35-38. © 1994 by the National Association for Multicultural Education. Reprinted by permission.

the model is not meant to suggest that schools are really like this. Probably no school would be a purely "monocultural" or "tolerant" school, given the stated characteristics under each of these categories. However, these categories are used in an effort to illustrate how support for diversity is manifested in schools in a variety of ways. Because multicultural education is primarily a set of beliefs and a philosophy, rather than a set program or fixed content, this model can assist us in determining how particular school policies and practices need to change in order to embrace the diversity of our students and their communities.

The four levels to be considered are: **tolerance**; **acceptance**; *respect*; and, finally, **affirmation**, **solidarity**, **and critique**. Before going on to consider how multicultural education is manifested in schools that profess these philosophical orientations, it is first helpful to explore the antithesis of multicultural education, namely, **monocultural education**, because without this analysis we have nothing with which to compare it.

In the scenarios that follow, we go into five schools that epitomize different levels of multicultural education. All are schools with growing cultural diversity in their student populations; differences include staff backgrounds, attitudes, and preparation, as well as curriculum and pedagogy. In our visits, we see how the curriculum, interactions among students, teachers, and parents, and other examples of attention to diversity are either apparent or lacking. We see how students of different backgrounds might respond to the policies and practices around them. (In another paper entitled "Creating Possibilities: Educating Latino Students in Massachusetts, in *The Education of Latino Students in Massachusetts: Policy and Research Implications*, published by the Gaston Institute for Latino Policy and Development in Boston, which I co-edited with R. Rivera, I developed scenarios of schools that would provide different levels of support specifically for Latino students.)

Monocultural Education

Monocultural education describes a situation in which school structures, policies, curricula, instructional materials, and even pedagogical strategies are primarily representative of only the dominant culture. In most United States schools, it can be defined as "the way things are."

We will begin our tour in a "monocultural school" that we'll call the George Washington Middle School. When we walk in, we see a sign that says "NO UNAUTHORIZED PERSONS ARE ALLOWED IN THE SCHOOL. ALL VISITORS MUST REPORT DIRECTLY TO THE PRINCIPAL'S OFFICE." The principal, assistant principal, and counselor are all European-American males, although the school's population is quite diverse, with large numbers of African-American, Puerto Rican, Arab-American, Central American, Korean, and Vietnamese students. As we walk down the hall, we see a number of bulletin boards. On one, the coming Christmas holiday is commemorated; on another, the P.T.O.'s bake sale is announced; and on a third, the four basic food groups are listed, with reference to only those foods generally considered to be "American."

The school is organized into 45-minutes periods of such courses as U.S. history, English, math, science, music appreciation, art, and physical education. In the U. S. history class, students learn of the proud exploits, usually through wars and conquest, of primarily European-American males. They learn virtually nothing about the contributions, perspectives, or talents of women or those outside the cultural mainstream. U.S. slavery is mentioned briefly in relation to the Civil War, but African-Americans are missing thereafter. In English class, the students have begun their immersion in the "canon," reading works almost entirely written by European and European-American males, although a smattering of women and African-American (but no Asian, Latino, or American Indian) authors are included in the newest anthology. In music appreciation class, students are exposed to what is called "classical music," that is, European classical music, but the "classical" music of societies in Asia, Africa, and Latin America is nowhere to be found. In art classes, students may learn about the art work of famous European and European-American artists, and occasionally about the "crafts" and "artifacts" of other cultures and societies mostly from the Third World.

Teachers at the George Washington Middle School are primarily European-American women who have had little formal training in multicultural approaches or perspectives. They are proud of the fact that they are "color-blind," that is, that they see no differences among their students, treating them all the same. Of course, this does not extend to tracking, which they generally perceive to be in the interest of teaching all students to the best of their abilities. Ability grouping is a standard practice at the George Washington Middle School. There are four distinct levels of ability, from "talented and gifted" to "remedial." I.Q. tests are used to determine student placement and intellectually superior students are placed in "Talented and Gifted" programs, and in advanced levels of math, science, English, and social studies. Only these top students have the option of taking a foreign language. The top levels consist of overwhelmingly European-American and Asian-American students, but the school rationalizes that this is due to either the native intelligence of these students, or to the fact that they have a great deal more intellectual stimulation and encouragement in their homes. Thus, teachers have learned to expect excellent work from their top students, but little of students in their low-level classes, who they often see as lazy and disruptive.

Students who speak a language other than English as their native language are either placed in regular classrooms where they will learn to "sink or swim" or in "NE" (non-English) classes, where they are drilled in English all day and where they will remain until they learn English sufficiently well to perform in the regular classroom. In addition, parents are urged to speak to their children only in English at home. Their native language, whether Spanish, Vietnamese, or Korean, is perceived as a handicap to their learning, and as soon as they forget it, they can get on with the real job of learning.

Although incidents of racism have occurred in the George Washington Middle School, they have been taken care of quietly and privately. For example, when racial slurs have been used, students have been admonished not to say them. When fights between children of different ethnic groups take place, the assistant principal has insisted that race or ethnicity has nothing to do with them; "kids will be kids" is the way he describes these incidents.

What exists in the George Washington Middle School is a monocultural environment with scant reference to the experiences of others from largely subordinated cultural groups. Little attention is paid to student diversity, and the school curriculum is generally presented as separate from the community in which it is located. In addition, "dangerous" topics such as racism, sexism, and homophobia are seldom discussed, and reality is represented as finished and static. In summary, the George Washington School is a depressingly familiar scenario because it reflects what goes on in most schools in American society.

Tolerance

How might a school characterized by "tolerance" be different from a monocultural school? It is important here to mention the difference between the **denotation** and the **connotation** of words. According to the dictionary definition given at the beginning of this article, tolerance is hardly a value that one could argue with. After all, what is wrong with "recognizing and respecting the beliefs or practices of others"? On the contrary, this is a quintessential part of developing a multicultural perspective. (*Teaching Tolerance*, a journal developed by the Southern Anti-Poverty Law Project, has no doubt been developed with this perspective in mind, and my critique here of tolerance is in no way meant to criticize this wonderful classroom and teacher resource.)

Nevertheless, the connotation of words is something else entirely. When we think of what **tolerance** means in practice, we have images of a grudging but somewhat distasteful acceptance. To **tolerate** differences means that they are endured, not necessarily embraced. In fact, this level of support for multicultural education stands on shaky ground because what is tolerated today can too easily be rejected tomorrow. A few examples will help illustrate this point.

Our "tolerant" school is the Brotherhood Middle School. Here, differences are understood to be the inevitable burden of a culturally pluralistic society. A level up from a "color-blind" monocultural school, the "tolerant" school accepts differences but only if they can be modified. Thus, they are accepted, but because the ultimate goal is assimilation, differences in language and culture are replaced as quickly as possible. This ideology is reflected in the physical environment, the attitudes of staff, and the curriculum to which students are exposed.

When we enter the Brotherhood School, there are large signs in English welcoming visitors, although there are no staff on hand who can communicate with the families of the growing Cambodian student population. One prominently-placed bulletin board proudly portrays the winning essays of this year's writing contest with the theme of "Why I am proud to be an American." The winners, a European-American sixth grader and a Vietnamese seventh grader, write in their essays about the many opportunities given to all people in our country, no matter what their race, ethnicity, or gender. Another bulletin board boasts the story of Rosa Parks, portrayed as a woman who was too tired to give up her seat on the bus, thus serving as a catalyst for the modern civil rights movement. (The Fall 1993 issue of *Multicultural Education* includes a powerful example of how people such as Rosa Parks have been de-contextualized to better fit in with the U.S. mainstream conception of individual rather than collective struggle, thus adding little to children's understanding of institutionalized discrimination on our society; see "The Myth of 'Rosa Parks the Tired;'" by Herbert Kohl, pages 6–10, in which Kohl reports that based on his research most stories used in American schools present Rosa Parks simply as "Rosa Parks the Tired.")

Nevertheless, a number of important structural changes are taking place at the Brotherhood School. An experiment has recently begun in which the sixth and seventh graders are in "family" groupings, and these are labeled by family names such as the Jones family, the Smith family, and the Porter family. Students remain together as a family in their major subjects (English, social studies, math, and science) and there is no ability tracking in these classes. Because their teachers have a chance to meet and plan together daily, they are more readily able to develop integrated curricula. In fact, once in a while, they even combine classes so that they can team-teach and their students remain at a task for an hour and a half rather than the usual three quarters of an hour. The students seem to like this arrangement, and have done some interesting work in their study of Washington, D.C. For instance, they used geometry to learn how the city was designed, and have written to their congressional representatives to ask how bills become laws. Parents are involved in fund-raising for an upcoming trip to the capital, where students plan to interview a number of their local legislators.

The curriculum at the Brotherhood School has begun to reflect some of the changes that a multicultural society demands. Students are encouraged to study a foreign language (except, of course, for those who already speak one; they are expected to learn English and in the process, they usually forget their native language). In addition, a number of classes have added activities on women, African Americans, and American Indians. Last year, for instance, Martin Luther King Day was celebrated by having all students watch a video of the "I Have a Dream" speech.

The majority of changes in the curriculum have occurred in the social studies and English departments, but the music teacher has also begun to add a more international flavor to her repertoire, and the art classes recently went to an exhibit of the work of Romare Bearden. This year, a "multicultural teacher" has been added to the staff. She meets with all students in the school, seeing each group once a week for one period. Thus far, she has taught students about Chinese New Year, *Kwanzaa*, *Ramadan*, and *Dia de los Reyes*. She is getting ready for the big multicultural event of the year, Black History Month. She hopes to work with other teachers to bring in guest speakers, show films about the civil rights movement, and have an art contest in which students draw what the world would be like if Dr. King's dream of equality became a reality.

Students who speak a language other than English at the Brotherhood School are placed in special E.S.L. classes, where they are taught English as quickly, but sensitively, as possible. For instance, while they are encouraged to speak to one another in English, they are allowed to use their native language, but only as a last resort. The feeling is that if they use it more often, it will become a "crutch." In any event, the E.S.L. teachers are not required to speak a language other than English; in fact, being bilingual is even considered a handicap because students might expect them to use their other language.

The principal of the Brotherhood School has made it clear that racism will not be tolerated here. Name-calling and the use of overtly racist and sexist textbooks and other materials are discouraged. Recently, some teachers attended a workshop on strategies for dealing with discrimination in the classroom. Some of those who attended expect to make some changes in how they treat students from different backgrounds.

Most teachers at the Brotherhood School have had little professional preparation to deal with the growing diversity of the student body. They like and genuinely want to help their students, but have made few changes in their curricular or instructional practices. For them, "being sensitive" to their students is what multicultural education should be about, not overhauling the curriculum. Thus, they acknowledge student differences in language, race, gender, and social class, but still cannot quite figure out why some students are more successful than others. Although they would like to think not, they wonder if genetics or poor parental attitudes about education have something to do with it. If not, what can explain these great discrepancies?

Acceptance

Acceptance is the next level of supporting diversity. It implies that differences are acknowledged and their importance is neither denied nor belittled. It is at this level that we see substantial movement toward multicultural education. A look at how some of the school's policies and practices might change is indicative of this movement.

The name of our school is the Rainbow Middle School. As we enter, we see signs in English, Spanish, and Haitian Creole, the major languages besides English spoken by students and their families. The principal of the Rainbow School is Dr. Belinda Clayton, the first African-American principal ever appointed. She has designated her school as a "multicultural building," and has promoted a number of professional development opportunities for teachers that focus on diversity. These include seminars on diverse learning styles, bias-free assessment, and bilingual education. In addition, she has hired not only Spanish- and Haitian Creole-speaking teachers for the bilingual classrooms, but has also diversified the staff in the "regular" program.

Bulletin boards outside the principal's office display the pictures of the "Students of the Month." This month's winners are Rodney Thomas, a sixth-grader who has excelled in art, Neleida Cortes, a seventh-grade student in the bilingual program, and Melissa Newton, an eighth-grader in the special education program. All three were given a special luncheon by the principal and their homeroom teachers. Another bulletin board focuses on "Festivals of Light" and features information about *Chanukah*, *Kwanzaa*, and Christmas, with examples of *Las Posadas* in Mexico and Saint Lucia's Day in Sweden.

The curriculum at the Rainbow Middle School has undergone some changes to reflect the growing diversity of the student body. English classes include more choices of African-American, Irish, Jewish, and Latino literature written in English. Some science and math teachers have begun to make reference to famous scientists and mathematicians from a variety of backgrounds. In one career-studies class, a number of parents have been invited to speak about their job and the training they had to receive in order to get those positions. All students are encouraged to study a foreign language, and choices have been expanded to include Spanish, French, German, and Mandarin Chinese.

Tracking has been eliminated in all but the very top levels at the Rainbow School. All students have the opportunity to learn algebra, although some are still counseled out of this option because their teachers believe it will be too difficult for them. The untracked classes seem to be a hit with the students, and preliminary results have shown a slight improvement among all students. Some attempts have been made to provide flexible scheduling, with one day a week devoted to entire "learning blocks" where students work on a special project. One group recently engaged in an in-depth study of the elderly in their community. They learned about services available to them, and they touched on poverty and lack of health care for many older Americans. As a result of this study, the group has added a community service component to the class; this involves going to the local Senior Center during their weekly learning block to read with the elderly residents.

Haitian and Spanish-speaking students are tested and, if found to be more proficient in their native language, are placed in transitional bilingual education programs. Because of lack of space in the school, the bilingual programs are located in the basement, near the boiler room. Here, students are taught the basic curriculum in their native language while learning English as a second language during one period of the day with an ESL specialist. Most ESL teachers are also fluent in a language other than English, helping them understand the process of acquiring a second language. The bilingual program calls for students to be "mainstreamed" (placed in what is called a "regular classroom") as quickly as possible, with a limit of three years on the outside. In the meantime, they are segregated from their peers for most of the day, but have some classes with English-speaking students, including physical education, art, and music. As they proceed through the program and become more fluent in English, they are "exited" out for some classes, beginning with math and social studies. While in the bilingual program, students' native cultures are sometimes used as the basis of the curriculum, and they learn about the history of their people. There is, for instance, a history course on the Caribbean that is offered to both groups in their native languages. Nevertheless, neither Haitian and Latino students in the bilingual program nor students of other backgrounds have access to these courses.

Incidents of racism and other forms of discrimination are beginning to be faced at the Rainbow Middle School. Principal Clayton deals with these carefully, calling in the offending students as well as their parents, and she makes certain that students understand the severe consequences for name-calling or scapegoating others. Last year, one entire day was devoted to "diversity" and regular classes were canceled while students attended workshops focusing on discrimination, the importance of being sensitive to others, and the influence on U.S. history of many different immigrants. They have also hosted a "Multicultural Fair" and published a cookbook with recipes donated by many different parents.

The Rainbow Middle School is making steady progress in accepting the great diversity of its students. They have decided that perhaps assimilation should not be the goal, and have eschewed the old idea of the "melting pot." In its place, they have the "salad bowl" metaphor, in which all students bring something special that need not be reconstituted or done away with.

Respect

Respect is the next level of multicultural education support. It implies admiration and high esteem for diversity. When differences are respected, they are used as the basis for much of what goes on in schools. Our next scenario describes what this might look like.

The Sojourner Truth Middle School is located in a mid-size town with a changing population. There is a fairly large African-American population with a growing number of students of Cape Verdean and Vietnamese background, and the school staff reflects these changes, including teachers, counselors, and special educators of diverse backgrounds. There is, for example, a Vietnamese speech pathologist, and his presence has helped to alleviate the concerns of some teachers that the special needs of the Vietnamese children were not being addressed. He has found that while some students do indeed have speech problems, others do not, but teachers' unfamiliarity with the Vietnamese language made it difficult to know this.

When we enter the Sojourner Truth Middle School, we are greeted by a parent volunteer. She gives us printed material in all the languages represented in the school, and invites us to the parents' lounge for coffee, tea, and danish. We are then encouraged to walk-around and explore the school. Bulletin boards boast of students' accomplishments in the Spanish Spelling Bee, the local *Jeopardy* Championship, and the W.E.B. DuBois Club of African-American history. It is clear from the children's pictures that there is wide participation of many students in all of these activities. The halls are abuzz with activity as students go from one class to another, and most seem eager and excited by school.

Professional development is an important principle at the Sojourner Truth Middle School. Teachers, counselors, and other staff are encouraged to take courses at the local university and to keep up with the literature in their field. To make this more feasible, the staff gets released time weekly to get together. As a consequence, the curriculum has been through tremendous changes. Teachers have formed committees to develop their curriculum. The English department decided to use its time to have reading and discussion groups with some of the newly available multicultural literature with which they were unfamiliar. As a result, they have revamped the curriculum into such overarching themes as **coming of age**, **immigration**, **change and continuity**, and **individual and collective responsibility**. They have found that it is easier to select literature to reflect themes such as these, and the literature is by its very nature multicultural. For instance, for the theme **individual and collective responsibility** they have chosen stories of varying difficulty, including *The Diary of Anne Frank, Bridge to Terabithia* (by Katherine Paterson), *Morning Girl* (by Michael Dorris), and *Let the Circle be Unbroken* (by Mildred D. Taylor), among others. The English teachers have in turn invited the history, art, and science departments to join them in developing some integrated units with these themes. Teachers from the art and music departments have agreed to work with them, and have included lessons on Vietnamese dance, Guatemalan weaving, Jewish Klezmer music, and American Indian story telling as examples of individual and collective responsibility in different communities.

Other changes are apparent in the curriculum as well, for it has become more antiracist and honest. When studying World War II, students learn about the heroic role played by the United States, and also about the Holocaust, in which not only six million Jews, but millions of others, including Gypsies, gays and lesbians, and many dissenters of diverse backgrounds, were exterminated. They also learn, for the first time, about the internment of over a hundred thousand Japanese and Japanese Americans on our own soil.

It has become "safe" to talk about such issues as the crucial role of labor in U.S. history and the part played by African Americans in freeing themselves from bondage, both subjects thought too "sensitive" to be included previously. This is one reason why the school was renamed for a woman known for her integrity and courage.

The Sojourner Truth Middle School has done away with all ability grouping. When one goes into a classroom, it is hard to believe that students of all abilities are learning together because the instruction level seems to be so high. Upon closer inspection, it becomes apparent that there are high expectations for all students. Different abilities are accommodated by having some students take more time than others, providing cooperative groups in which students change roles and responsibilities, and through ongoing dialogue among all students.

Students who speak a language other than English are given the option of being in a "maintenance bilingual program," that is, a program based on using their native language throughout their schooling, not just for three years. Changing the policy that only students who could not function in English were eligible for bilingual programs, this school has made the program available to those who speak English in addition to their native language. Parents and other community members who speak these languages are invited in to classes routinely to talk about their lives, jobs, or families, or to tell stories or share experiences. Students in the bilingual program are not, however, segregated from their peers all day, but join them for a number of academic classes.

Teachers and other staff members at this middle school have noticed that incidents of name-calling and interethnic hostility have diminished greatly since the revised curriculum was put into place. Perhaps more students see themselves in the curriculum and feel less angry about their invisibility; perhaps more teachers have developed an awareness and appreciation for their students' diversity while learning about it; perhaps the more diverse staff is the answer; or maybe it's because the community feels more welcome into the school. Whatever it is, the Sojourner Truth Middle School has developed an environment in which staff and students are both expanding their ways of looking at the world.

Affirmation, Solidarity, and Critique

Affirmation, solidarity, and critique is based on the premise that the most powerful learning results when students work and struggle with one another, even if it is sometimes difficult and challenging. It begins with the assumption that the many differences that students and their families represent are embraced and accepted as legitimate vehicles for learning, and that these are then extended. What makes this level different from the others is that conflict is not avoided, but rather accepted as an inevitable part of learning. Because multicultural education at this level is concerned with equity and social justice, and because the basic values of different groups are often diametrically opposed, conflict is bound to occur.

Affirmation, solidarity, and critique is also based on understanding that culture is not a fixed or unchangeable artifact, and is therefore subject to critique. Passively accepting the status quo of any culture is thus inconsistent with this level of multicultural education; simply substituting one myth for another contradicts its basic assumptions because no group is inherently superior or more heroic than any other. As eloquently expressed by Mary Kalantzis and Bill Cope in their 1990 work *The Experience of Multicultural Education in Australia: Six Case Studies*, "Multicultural education, to be effective, needs to be more active. It needs to consider not just the pleasure of diversity but more fundamental issues that arise as different groups negotiate community and the basic issues of material life in the same space—a process that equally might generate conflict and pain."

Multicultural education without critique may result in cultures remaining at the romantic or exotic stage. If students are to transcend their own cultural experience in order to understand the differences of others, they need to go through a process of reflection and critique of their cultures and those of others. This process of critique, however, begins with a solid core of solidarity with others who are different from themselves. When based on true respect, critique is not only necessary but in fact healthy.

The Arturo Schomburg Middle School is located in a mid-size city with a very mixed population of Puerto Ricans, Salvadoreans, American Indians, Polish Americans, Irish Americans, Chinese Americans, Philippinos, and African Americans. The school was named for a Black Puerto Rican scholar who devoted his life to exploring the role of Africans in the Americas, in the process challenging the myth he had been told as a child in Puerto Rico that Africans had "no culture."

The school's logo, visible above the front door, is a huge tapestry made by the students, and it symbolizes a different model of multicultural education from that of either the "melting pot" or the "salad bowl." According to a publication of the National Association of State Boards of Education (*The American Tapestry: Educating a Nation*), "A tapestry is a hand-woven textile. When examined from the back, it may simply appear to be a motley group of threads. But when reversed, the threads work together to depict a picture of structure and beauty" (p. 1). According to Adelaide Sanford, one of the study group members who wrote this publication, a tapestry also symbolizes, through its knots, broken threads, and seeming jumble of colors and patterns on the back, the tensions, conflicts, and dilemmas that a society needs to work out. This spirit of both collaboration and struggle is evident in the school.

When we enter the Schomburg Middle School, the first thing we notice is a banner proclaiming the school 's motto: LEARN, REFLECT, QUESTION, AND WORK TO MAKE THE WORLD A BETTER PLACE. This is the message that reverberates throughout the school. Participation is another theme that is evident, and the main hall contains numerous pictures of students in classrooms, community service settings, and extracurricular activities. Although housed in a traditional school building, the school has been transformed into a place where all children feel safe and are encouraged to learn to the highest levels of learning. While there are typical classrooms of the kind that are immediately recognizable to us, the school also houses centers that focus on specific areas of learning. There is, for instance, a studio where students can be found practicing traditional Philippino dance and music, as well as European ballet, and modern American dance, among others. Outside, there is a large garden that is planted, cared for, and harvested by the students and faculty. The vegetables are used by the cafeteria staff in preparing meals and they have noticed a marked improvement in the eating habits of the children since the menu was changed to reflect a healthier and more ethnically diverse menu.

We are welcomed into the school by staff people who invite us to explore the many different classrooms and other learning centers. Those parents who are available during the day can be found assisting in classrooms, in the Parent's Room working on art projects or computer classes, or attending workshops by other parents or teachers on topics ranging from cross-cultural child-rearing to ESL. The bulletin boards are ablaze with color and include a variety of languages, displaying student work from critical essays on what it means to be an American to art projects that celebrate the talents of many of the students. Learning is going on everywhere, whether in classrooms or in small-group collaborative projects in halls.

What might the classrooms look like in this school? For one, they are characterized by tremendous diversity. Tracking and special education, as we know them, have been eliminated at the Schomburg Middle School. Students with special needs are taught along with all others, although they are sometimes separated for small-group instruction with students not classified as having special needs. All children are considered "talented" and special classes are occasionally organized for those who excel in dance, mathematics, poetry, or science. No interested students are excluded from any of these offerings. Furthermore, all students take algebra and geometry, and special coaching sessions are available before, after, and during school hours for these and other subjects.

Classes are flexible, with an interdisciplinary curriculum and team-teaching, resulting in sessions that sometimes last as long as three hours. The physical environment in classrooms is varied: some are organized with round work tables, others have traditional desks, and still others have scant furniture to allow for more movement. Class size also varies from small groups to large, depending on the topic at hand. Needless to say, scheduling at this school is a tremendous and continuing challenge, but faculty and students are committed to this more flexible arrangement and willing to allow for the daily problems that it may cause.

There are no "foreign languages" at the Schomburg Middle school, nor is there, strictly speaking, a bilingual program. Rather, the entire school is multilingual, and all students learn at least a second language in addition to their native language. This means that students are not segregated by language, but instead work in bilingual settings where two languages are used for instruction. At present, the major languages used are English, Spanish, and Tagalog, representing the most common languages spoken by this school's community. It is not unusual to see students speaking these languages in classrooms, the hallways, or the playgrounds, even among those for whom English is a native language.

Students at the Schomburg Middle School seem engaged, engrossed, and excited about learning. They have been involved in a number of innovative long-range projects that have resulted from the interdisciplinary curriculum. For instance, working with a Chinese-American artist in residence, they wrote, directed, and produced a play focusing on the "Know-Nothing" Movement in U.S. history that resulted in, among other things, the Chinese Exclusion Act of 1882. In preparation for the play, they read a great deal and did extensive research. For example, they contacting the Library of Congress for information on primary sources and reviewed newspapers and magazines from the period to get a sense of the climate that led to Nativism. They also designed and sewed all the costumes and sets. In addition, they interviewed recent immigrants of many backgrounds, and found that they had a range of experiences from positive to negative in their new country. On the day of the play, hundreds of parents and other community members attended. Students also held a debate on the pros and cons of continued immigration, and received up-to-date information concerning immigration laws from their congressional representative.

The curriculum at the Schomburg Middle School is dramatically different from the George Washington School, the first school we visited. Teachers take very seriously their responsibility of **teaching complexity.** Thus, students have learned that there are many sides to every story, and that in order to make informed decisions, they need as much information as they can get. Whether in English, science, art, or any other class, students have been encouraged to be critical of every book, newspaper, curriculum, or piece of information by asking questions such as: **Who wrote the book? Who's missing in this story? Why?** Using questions such as these as a basis, they are learning that every story has a point of view and that every point of view is at best partial and at worst distorted. They are also learning that their own backgrounds, rich and important as they may be, have limitations that can lead to parochial perceptions. Most of all, even at this age, students are learning that every topic is fraught with difficulties and they are wrestling with issues as diverse as homelessness, solar warming, and how the gender expectations of different cultures might limit opportunities for girls. Here, nothing is taboo as a topic of discussion as long as it is approached with respect and in a climate of caring.

What this means for teachers is that they have had to become learners along with their students. They approach each subject with curiosity and an open mind, and during the school day they have time to study, meet with colleagues, and plan their curriculum accordingly. Professional development here means not only attending courses at a nearby university, but collaborating with colleagues in study groups that last anywhere from half a day to several months. These provide a forum in which teachers can carefully study relevant topics or vexing problems. Some of these study groups have focused on topics such as Reconstruction and the history of the Philippines, to educational issues such as cooperative learning and diverse cognitive styles.

Especially noteworthy at this school is that **multicultural education** is not separated from **education**; that is, all education is by its very nature multicultural. English classes use literature written by a wide variety of people from countries where English is spoken. This has resulted in these classes becoming not only multicultural, but international as well. Science classes do not focus on contributions made by members of specific ethnic groups, but have in fact been transformed to consider how science itself is conceptualized, valued, and practiced by those who have traditionally been outside the scientific mainstream. Issues such as AIDS education, healing in different cultures, and scientific racism have all been the subject of study.

One of the major differences between this school and the others we visited has to do with its governance structure. There is a Schomburg School Congress consisting of students, faculty, parents, and other community members, and it has wide decision-making powers, from selecting the principal to determining reasonable and equitable disciplinary policies and practices. Students are elected by their classmates and, although at the beginning these were little more than popularity contests, in recent months it has been clear that students are beginning to take this responsibility seriously. This is probably because they are being taken seriously by the adults in the group. For instance, when students in one class decided that they wanted to plan a class trip to a neighboring city to coincide with their study of toxic wastes and the environment, they were advised to do some preliminary planning: what would be the educational objectives of such a trip? how long would it take? how much would it cost? After some research and planning, they presented their ideas to the Congress and a fund-raising plan that included students, parents, and community agencies was started.

The Schomburg School is a learning center that is undergoing important changes every day. As teachers discover the rich talents that all students bring to school, they develop high expectation for them all. The climate that exists in this school is one of possibility, because students' experiences are used to build on their learning and expand their horizons. Students in turn are realizing that while their experiences are important and unique, they are only one experience of many. A new definition of "American" is being forged at this school, one that includes everybody. Above all, learning here is exciting, engrossing, inclusive, and evolving.

Conclusion

One might well ask how realistic these scenarios are, particularly the last one. Could a school such as this really exist? Isn't this just wishful thinking? What about the reality of bond issues rejected by voters?, of teachers woefully unprepared to deal with the diversity in their classrooms?, of universities that do little more than offer stale "Mickey Mouse" courses?, of schools with no pencils, paper, and chalk, much less computers and video cameras?, of rampant violence in streets, homes, and schools?, of drugs and crime?, of parents who are barely struggling to keep their families together and can spare precious little time to devote to volunteering at school?

These are all legitimate concerns that our society needs to face, and they remind us that schools need to be understood within their sociopolitical contexts. That is, our schools exist in a society in which social and economic stratification are facts of life, where competition is taught over caring, and where the early sorting that takes place in educational settings often lasts a lifetime. Developing schools with a multicultural perspective is not easy; if it were, they would be everywhere. But schools with a true commitment to diversity, equity, and high levels of learning are difficult to achieve precisely because the problems they face are pervasive and seemingly impossible to solve. Although the many problems raised above are certainly daunting, the schools as currently organized are simply not up to the challenge. In the final analysis, if we believe that all students deserve to learn at the very highest levels, then we need a vision of education that will help achieve this end.

The scenarios above, however, are not simply figments of my imagination. As you read through the scenarios, you probably noticed bits and pieces of your own school here and there. However, because the "monocultural school" is the one with which we are most familiar, and unfortunately even comfortable, the other scenarios might seem far-fetched or unrealistic. Although they are **ideal** in the sense that they are not true pictures of specific schools, these scenarios nevertheless describe **possibilities** because they all exist to some degree in our schools today. These are not pie-in-the-sky visions, but composites of what goes on in schools every day. As such, they provide building blocks for how we might go about transforming schools. In fact, were we to design schools based on the ideals that our society has always espoused, they would no doubt come close to the last scenario.

It is not, however, a monolithic model or one that can develop overnight. The participants in each school need to develop their own vision so that step by step, with incremental changes, schools become more multicultural, and thus more inclusive and more exciting places for learning. If we believe that young people deserve to be prepared with skills for living ethical and productive lives in an increasingly diverse and complex world, then we need to transform schools so that they not only teach what have been called "the basics," but also provide an apprenticeship in democracy and social justice. It is unfair to expect our young people to develop an awareness and respect for democracy if they have not experienced it, and it is equally unrealistic to expect them to be able to function in a pluralistic society if all we give them are skills for a monocultural future. This is our challenge in the years ahead: to conquer the fear of change and imagine how we might create exciting possibilities for all students in all schools.

White Racism

Christine Sleeter

Christine E. Sleeter is a professor of education, University of Wisconsin-Parkside, Kenosha, Wisconsin.

Fifteen years ago, I wondered whether my own prospective involvement in multicultural education as a White person, could be helpful or problematic. The issue as I saw it—and still see it—is that Whites tend to take over. We find it "normal" to set the direction and agenda for things we become involved in. Or, when we do not take over, we nevertheless get in the way and deflect attention away from primary concerns of people of color. I decided, however, that racial justice requires White involvement, although exactly how White people could help best was not very clear to me.

In this article, I will discuss what I believe can be a helpful role for Whites, as well as our tendency to deflect attention away from racism, which is the main problem undergirding the need for multicultural education. As a whole, Whites do not talk about White racism. Even those of us involved in multicultural education examine and critique how White racism works far less than we ought. We are much more likely to discuss cultural differences than racism or Whiteness. If multicultural education is sometimes criticized as skirting around racism (see P. R. Mattai, "Rethinking multicultural education: Has it lost its focus or is it being misused," *Journal of Negro Education,* 1992; C. McCarthy, *Race and curriculum,* Falmer Press, 1990), I believe this is a result of Whites' reluctance to address it rather than people of color's disregard for it.

The field of multicultural education could benefit, however, from a rich discourse about White racism, to which we Whites need to contribute. White people have a good deal of knowledge about rac-ism: all of us have been well socialized to be racists, and benefit from racism constantly. I would like to challenge Whites to articulate, examine, question, and critique what we know about racism. Doing so would strengthen not only multicultural education's anti-racist stance, but also our own personal efforts to promote racial justice.

In the following, I will illustrate White silence about racism, discuss some strategies we use to deflect attention away from White racism, then provide an example of the kind of experience we should be critiquing openly. My point is that, in order to collaborate in the work of envisioning and building a just society that includes all of us, we as Whites need to engage in multifaceted and critical analyses of how White racism structures our lives, viewpoints, vested interests, and daily actions.

Naming our silence about White racism

With precious few exceptions, White people do not talk about White racism. Instead, we talk about group differences, very often in ways that simplify and devalue others while rendering Whiteness itself as invisible, or "normal." I first noticed White silence about racism about 15 years ago, although I was not able at the time to name it as such. I recall realizing, after having shared many meals with African American friends while teaching in Seattle, that racism and race-related issues were fairly common topics of dinner-table conversation, which African Americans talked about quite openly. It struck me that I could not think of a single instance in which racism had been a topic of dinner-table conversation in White contexts. Race-related issues sometimes came up, but not **racism**. For example, I could remember short discussions about what one would do if a Black family moved next door, or about a very bigoted relative, or about policies such as desegregation or immigration. In these discussions, what was viewed as problematic was people of color themselves, changes in policies that relate to race, or outspoken bigots.

Recently, I was giving a talk about multicultural education to a group of predominantly White teachers at an inservice session. My talk centered around persistent racial, class, and gender disparities in access to various resources such as jobs and housing. My main recommendation to the teachers was that we engage directly in reciprocal dialog with people of color and poor people in our own communities, in order to decide what kind of social system and what kind of schools we actually want, then begin to work collaboratively. I argued that White professionals cannot shape the vision of a multicultural society by ourselves, although we tend to use our status as professionals to assume exactly that role; shaping a vision of multicultural education in our own communities has to be done collaboratively, and must address social inequalities. Afterward, a White teacher approached me with a very puzzled expression on her face, and commented in a rather perplexed tone of voice that she had never heard multicultural education discussed that way. At least she reacted verbally to it; most of the audience simply applauded politely, then went on to the next session. This incident struck me because, although my discussion of racism was not as direct as it might have been, I was still framing multicultural education in a way the White teachers had not even thought about and had difficulty comprehending.

At a recent women's studies conference, participants were asked to divide

From *Multicultural Education,* Spring 1994, pp. 5-8, 39. © 1994 by the National Association for Multicultural Education. Reprinted by permission.

into racially homogeneous groups to compile a list of the main concerns facing their group. I was in the European-American group, and it floundered. Participants discussed mainly family history and ethnic immigrant background. I suggested that we might address our White racism, but that theme was not taken up. The group tried to place itself on a parallel status with the other racial groups, defining our problems as comparable to theirs. Our Whiteness seemed to be invisible to us— we could discuss our religious, ethnic, and social class differences, but not our common Whiteness or the privileges we gain from White racism (see R. Dyer, "White," *Screen*, 1988).

. . . .

I suspect that our privileges and silences are invisible to us partly because numerically we constitute the majority of this nation and collectively control a large portion of the nation's resources and media, which enable us to surround ourselves with our own varied experiences and to buffer ourselves from the experiences, and the pain and rage of people of color. But even still, White people do not live in a vacuum; Toni Morrison (*Playing in the dark: Whiteness and the literary imagination*, Harvard University Press, 1992) asks how Whites have managed **not** to see the "thunderous, theatrical presence" of African people in the United States (p. 13). I believe that we cling to filters that screen out what people of color try to tell us because we fear losing material and psychological advantages that we enjoy. Further, we have not yet collectively created a compelling self-identity and sense of meaning that does not entail ravenous materialism and acquisition of power over others.

By White racism (or White supremacy), I am referring to the system of rules, procedures, and tacit beliefs that result in Whites collectively maintaining control over the wealth and power of the nation and the world. For at least 500 years, Europeans and their descendants have taken huge amounts of land, wealth, labor, and other resources from peoples of color around the world. With the exceptions of small, sporadic attempts at restitution, such as that offered belatedly to Japanese American concentration camp survivors, White Americans have never returned or repaid what we have taken. We seem to have agreed tacitly to continue to reap the benefits of the past, and not to talk about it, except largely in ways that render present race relations as legitimate. Current data illustrate the continued advantages Whites enjoy. For example, a recent United Nations report ranks White Americans as having the highest standard of living in the world; Black Americans' liv-

ing standard ranks 31st and Hispanic Americans' ranks 35th. Of the six nations with the highest living standard, five are predominantly White (R. Wright, "Living standard in U. S. diverse: U. N.," *Kenosha News*, 1993).

As we grow up, Whites become aware that we tend to have more than people of color, and we learn to accept and justify our own position. Until about 40 years ago, it was acceptable in White society to talk openly about presumed shortcomings of groups of color, and the presumed superior intelligence, culture, and morality of Whites. Not all Whites accepted racist beliefs, of course, but they were widely enough held to be openly verbalized.

With the Civil Rights movement, people of color challenged the morality of racism successfully enough that most Whites no longer found it acceptable to voice racist beliefs. So, we simply stopped talking openly about race relations. In general, Whites seem to believe that racism was gone once we eliminated Jim Crow laws, created an ostensibly colorblind legal system (Williams, 1991), and stopped openly saying negative things about groups of color. We maintain a worldview, however, that continues to uphold our racial privileges. We are willing to critique the psychological impact of slavery on Blacks, but not its impact on ourselves. In addition, we continue to obliterate from our historic consciousness information about racism; for example, I have learned to expect only about half of my White teacher education students to have ever heard of Jim Crow laws. ("What, then, was the Civil Rights movement about?" "Well—I'm not sure, I guess.") Groups of color have hoped that we would genuinely accept them as equals if we appreciated the intellectual sophistication of their cultural creations. Too often, however, our response is to experience "other" cultures as a tourist or colonialist would, and tacitly accept White supremacy.

Deflecting attention from White racism

Most readers are probably aware that racism is an important issue to multicultural education, and most White readers probably do talk about it from time to time. However, I would suggest that our talk does not delve into it in much depth. As a result, we tend to incorporate into multicultural education fairly simplistic notions about racism, giving attention mainly to ideas that fit within European ethnic immigrant experiences. For example, consider the following passage from a children's book about racism: "Racism is the mistaken belief by some people that

their group, or race, is better than others" (A. Grunsell, *Let's talk about racism*, Gloucester Press, 1991, p. 7). While I applaud the book's effort to help children understand racism, the book barely hints at the power differential between Whites and groups of color, and subsequent control Whites maintain over most resources in the U.S. and world.

. . . .

Having learned the ideology of individualism well, we tend to interpret racism as an individual belief rather than an institutionalized system supported by a collective worldview. This interpretation allows us to assume that we are not racist if we have an open mind. The ideology of individualism also takes our attention away from group relations and statuses, directing it instead toward equal opportunity to achieve upward mobility. On a global level, we still do not see it as problematic to assume that we are entitled to the highest standard of living in the world, and cheer ourselves on in international competition as if we were watching a football game.

Multicultural education should challenge racism, but often to Whites it provides a way of trying to project a positive image about groups of color without actually confronting White supremacy. We do this by tapping into our own European ethnic immigrant experience for guidance. According to the dominant, White American ideology, the United States is a nation of immigrants: our ancestors all came here to seek opportunity. Ethnic identity is a choice, something to add onto a common American identity. Ethnicity is a side-bar, no longer relevant to our relationships with social institutions, which are color-blind and ethnic-blind.

For example, my ancestry is largely German. In school I learned very little about German immigration and culture until taking German language classes in high school, but at home I learned some broad ideas that White people commonly learn about our own ancestry. I do not have records of my German immigrant ancestors, but I grew up learning that they as well as other immigrants chose to come to the United States for opportunity, but faced great hardships at first. My own name, Sleeter, is Anglicized; somewhere along the line my ancestors decided that identifying markers of German-ness worked to their disadvantage. In addition, my family no longer speaks German; rather than developing bilingual competence, my ancestors decided to shed the German language (as well as recollection of historic German bilingual education programs). My paternal grandmother was a good German cook; my family's Christmas celebrations retain some German customs. Physically I learned that I had inherited a strong German constitution; temperamentally, I inherited German industriousness. In my daily life, German ancestry is irrelevant to who I associate with, where I live, where I work, and so forth; it is relevant mainly to my personal family history and identification with ethnic festivals during the summer.

Now let me apply this view of ethnicity to a non-White group, say, Native Americans. To apply it accurately, I should be tribe-specific, such as applying it to Winnebagos or Navajos. Some Whites distinguish among specific tribes, many do not. What is relevant to learn about Native Americans? The list of items above suggests: how Indians immigrated to the New World, food, customs, physical characteristics, language, temperament, and folk arts. (Sounds like many multicultural curricula, which many of us do critique but still see flourishing.) These are not irrelevant items (although many Indians dispute the notion of Indian immigration to North America), but this list completely excludes more important issues. Most importantly, it evades the fact that Whites occupy Indian land; Whites benefit in numerous ways from that occupation, while Indian people live largely in a state of poverty. The most helpful stance Whites could take would be to return large amounts of good land, and stop controlling the internal affairs of Indian people.

Whites generally have no intention of doing that, however. We have learned to justify the oppression of Indian people today by viewing them as a very small, inconsequential minority; attributing their problems to pathology (such as drinking), and locating Indian people in our own consciousness in America's past rather than its present or future. We have learned, and teach our children, to regard Indians of yesterday as colorful and interesting, past wrongs as tragic, but ourselves today as lacking much responsibility. Many of us, in fact, try to show respect for Indian people in a manner similar to that in which Whites have always acted: We take what we like for our own personal use. For example, many Whites try to adopt versions of Indian spirituality; Indian themes are popularly used in interior decor; and the buying and selling of Indian artifacts is common, regardless of whether Indian people themselves are deriving any profit from this exchange.

. . . .

A common White understanding of ethnicity, in fact, "emerged into prominence during a period when the civil rights movement was most active and racial minorities were challenging in basic respects the fairness of the American system" (R. D. Alba, *Ethnic identity: The transformation of White America*, Yale University Press, 1990, p. 317). White society felt threatened, and attempted to reframe ethnicity and race within our own worldview and experience. "The thrust of European-American identity is to defend the individualistic view of the American system, because it portrays the system as open to those who are willing to work hard and pull themselves over barriers of poverty and discrimination" (Alba, p. 317).

We evade discussion of racism because we do not want to give up the lifestyle, privileges, and resources that we control, and that are built on those our ancestors took from others. The very locations on which our homes rest should rightfully belong to Indian nations. Some of us are from families whose wealth was generated partly by slave labor; even if our own familial ancestors did not own slaves or exploit Mexican or Asian laborers, they still did have access to jobs, education, and other opportunities from which Whites barred people of color. To open up a discussion of White racism challenges the legitimacy of White peoples' very lives. Once we are able to say that aloud, we may be able to create a new White discourse that can contribute to a vision of a just future that actually includes all of us, and an agenda for action. But I do not believe we can do that without fully confronting the related layers and processes of White racism.

White people know a great deal about how racism works because we have observed White people intimately all our lives. By examining our own experiences critically, we are uniquely positioned to contribute insights into racism. There are many dimensions of White racism that we need to examine, such as the use of language to frame racial issues in ways that obscure racism (see T. van Dijk, *Elite discourse and racism*, Sage Publications, 1993), connections between White racism and capitalism, roots of White fears and psychological insecurities, the impact of colonialism and slavery on the White psyche, shifts over time in the forms racism takes and the way it is discussed, and factors that differentiate anti-racist Whites from the rest of us. Below I give one example of the kind of analysis in which I believe we should engage.

White racial bonding

In general, Whites stick together on common definitions of issues that involve race relations, and behave accordingly. We live largely with other Whites, socialize mainly with Whites, consume White media, vote for Whites, and so forth. Although today most Whites profess colorblindness and support for equal opportunity, in fact we behave in a very race-conscious manner. What are some of the processes we use to build and maintain racial solidarity?

This question struck me several months ago, when I watched my White teacher education students respond to an issue. The teacher education program in which I teach has a strong emphasis on multicultural and urban education throughout its coursework. In addition, we have hired a fairly diverse faculty: of eight full-time members, four are White, three are Black, and one is Asian; in addition, our dean is Black. The dean had been working with a committee of faculty, students, school administrators and teachers, and the dean of another institution to create an alternative certification program for prospective teachers of color. It would include a paid internship in a classroom and fewer course credits than the regular program, which is long on course credits and has no paid internship. Word of the alternative program reached White students in the regular program, and within days a large segment of the White student population had mobilized to affirm a common definition of the program: It was racially biased and wrong. When I tried to direct the few students who talked with me about it toward sources of more information about the program and reasons for its need, I realized that they did not want information; they wanted validation that the program was unfair toward Whites. In a meeting between the students and the faculty, White students vented openly a degree of racism that caught us off guard; no White student rose to defend the program (although a few did silently support it). Although part of the students' anger was frustration over the length of the regular teacher education program, part of it was racial.

I began to ask myself, given the coursework and field experiences the students had had, why did the White students coalesce so strongly and quickly around a common condemnation of the alternative program? How did they know their peers would support thinly-veiled as well as overt expressions of racial hostility? Why did the supporters of the program decide to keep quiet?

We are all familiar with some of the more overt ways Whites socialize Whites to accept racism (such as TV stereotypes and expressions of prejudice). But following this experience, I began to pay attention to what I will call "White racial bonding" processes White people engage in everyday. By "racial bonding," I mean simply interactions that have the purpose of affirming a common stance on race-related issues, legitimatizing particular interpretations of groups of color, and drawing conspiratorial we-they boundaries. These communication patterns take forms such as inserts into conversations, race-related "asides" in conversations, strategic eye-contact, and jokes. Often they are so short and subtle that they may seem relatively harmless. I used to regard such utterances as annoying expressions of prejudice or ignorance, but that seems to underestimate their power to demarcate racial lines and communicate solidarity.

• • • • • • • • • • • • • •

Inserts into conversations may go like this. Two White people are talking casually about various things. One comments, "This community is starting to change. A lot of Mexicans have been moving in." This comment serves as an invitation to White bonding, in which the other person is being asked to agree with the implication that Mexicans create problems and do not belong here, although this has not been said directly. The other person could respond very simply, "Yeah, that's a bummer," affirming the first person's viewpoint; this could be the end of a successful exchange. Or, the other person could complain about Mexicans, the ensuing conversation taking the form of Mexican-bashing. In either case, both parties will have communicated agreement that there is a linkage between "Mexicans" and "problems," and will have defined themselves as "insiders" in a network of people who view it as acceptable to articulate a negative valuation of Mexicans. Further, they will have communicated the acceptability of supporting policies limiting Mexican access to the community. Even silence can serve as tacit acquiescence for the purpose of winning approval. P. Williams (*The alchemy of race and rights*, Harvard University Press, 1991, p. 126-8) describes in exquisite detail such an exchange in which she participated passively.

How do I know this kind of exchange serves the purpose of racial bonding? I know because if I do not give the desired response, the other person very often presses the issue much more explicitly; I also may never hear from the other person again (including relatives). For example, if I change the subject, it usually reappears but more forcefully ("Mexicans bring gang problems, you know; I'm really concerned

about the future of this community."). Sometimes I give a response I know the other person is not seeking such as, "Yes, I'm really pleased to see this community becoming more multicultural, I've been working on my Spanish." More often than not, the other person responds with a lecture on problems associated with Mexican American people, and the misguidedness of my judgment. I am usually uncomfortable when people who do not know me well ask what I teach; quite often responses such as "multicultural education" or "urban education" provoke uninvited lectures on race relations, or on their own beliefs as a White liberal (hoping for validation that we share a common viewpoint).

These kinds of interactions seem to serve the purpose of defining racial lines, and inviting individuals to either declare their solidarity or mark themselves as deviant. Depending on degree of deviance, one runs the risk of losing the other individual's approval, friendship, and company. (This usually occurs in the form of feeling "uncomfortable" around the deviant White person.) Many Whites who do not support racist beliefs, actions, or policies, but who also do not want to risk breaking bonds with other Whites, simply remain silent.

Consideration of White racial bonding has several implications. No White person is exempt from pressures from other White people to "fit in," with the price of conformity to a racial norm very often being approval and friendship. While active anti-racist Whites may not be affected by such processes, I would hypothesize that it does affect Whites who are uncertain about their own racial beliefs and loyalties. J. E. Helms (editor of *Black and white racial identity: Theory, research, and practice*, Greenwood Press, 1990), for example, posits a stage of "reintegration" in White racial identity development in which the White person, after experiencing challenges to her or his previous beliefs about race, returns to those prior, more comfortable and socially acceptable (in White circles) beliefs (see also B. D. Tatum, "Talking about race, learning about racism: The application of racial identity development theory in the classroom," *Harvard Educational Review*, 1992). We all need affective

bonds with people. Given the segregation of our society, the strongest bonds are usually with members of our own race. In order to mitigate effects of White racial bonding, potential multicultural education advocates need to develop deep personal bonds with White anti-racists and people of color.

Implications for NAME

This consideration of White racial bonding is only one example of the sorts of issues we need to unearth and examine, in order to engage in constructive change. The National Association for Multicultural Education can provide an excellent forum for such engagement, if we as Whites decide to tackle White racism.

At the 1993 NAME conference, I spent time in the materials display. What struck me was an absence of materials about racism. To be sure, there were many very useful items; like other conference participants, I took home an armload of catalogs and ordered many dollars-worth of books. But by and large, the materials framed multiculturalism as learning about "other" non-White cultures, learning about heroes and heroines of color, and learning English while retaining one's own language. The lack of critical attention to White racism in the materials reflected the silence Whites maintain about it. If we expect to see materials that help children learn to critique White supremacy, we need to engage in such critiques ourselves.

NAME has the potential for developing a strong anti-racist, anti-sexist, anti-oppression approach to multicultural education. That will not happen without White members developing a very critical and explicit examination of what we know about White racism, and how all of us can dismantle it. Some members may object that doing so will drive Whites away; they will say that many, many Whites simply will not tolerate discussion of the "r" word. I would counter, however, that the organization will attract more politically conscious educators who do wish to see multicultural education framed as anti-racism. In addition, we may develop more effective ways of engaging Whites in grappling honestly with racism.

A New Word for an Old Problem

Multicultural "School Wars" Date to the 1840s

Nathan Glazer

Nathan Glazer is a professor of education at the Graduate School of Education at Harvard University, Cambridge, Massachusetts. He is also editor of The Public Interest.

Recent proposals that schools and colleges in the United States give greater emphasis to the history and accomplishments of America's racial and ethnic minorities—become more "multicultural"— have generated an intense public debate.

None of the leading critics of a multicultural curriculum—neither Arthur Schlesinger, Jr., author of *The Disuniting of America,* nor Diane Ravitch, the educational historian and former assistant secretary of education, nor Albert Shanker, president of the American Federation of Teachers—argues against a healthy diversity that acknowledges the varied sources of the American people and our culture. Still, all see a multicultural curriculum as a threat to the way we live together in a common nation.

Specifically, the critics envisage the possibility that large sections of the American population, particularly poor racial and ethnic groups that have been subjected to discrimination, will receive an education that attributes blame for their condition to the white or European majority and thereby worsen political and social splits along racial and ethnic lines. The gravest fear is that "oppression studies," as opponents label multicultural- ism, will cultivate an active hostility among some minorities to the key institutions of state and society, making effective government, as well as the economic progress of such groups, more difficult.

To its critics, multiculturalism looks like a very new thing in American education. In many respects, it is. However, viewed in the long stretch of the history of American public schooling, we can recognize it as a new word for an old problem: how public schools are to respond to and take account of the diversity of backgrounds of their students—religious, ethnic, racial. American public education, at least that part of it in our major cities, has rarely been free of this issue. For some decades, between the decline of European immigration in the 1920s and the rise of black nationalism in the 1960s, we were free of it. Undoubtedly, this halcyon period, during which many of the chief participants in the debate were themselves educated, colors their view of the current dispute.

· · · · · · · · · · · · · ·

With the origins of urban public education in the 1840s, the first of the "great school wars," as Diane Ravitch calls them in her history of New York City public education, broke out. That first war centered on the demands of Catholic leaders for something like equal treatment for Catholic students in public schools whose principal aim was to socialize children into the Protestant moral and religious world of the mid-19th century. Catholic religious leaders objected in particular to readings from the Protestant King James Bible. Why not the Catholic Douay translation? (No one dreamed, in those distant days, that the First Amendment to the Constitution, with its prohibition of an "establishment of religion," would in time be used to ban all Bible reading in schools.) The outcome of the conflict was that Catholics decided to establish their own schools, to the degree their capacities allowed and created a separate, Catholic system of education in the major cities of the country.

In the 1880s, bitter public disputes broke out about the rights of the children of German immigrants to receive instruction in German. Teaching in German was widely established in Cincinnati, St. Louis, and elsewhere, to the discomfort of nativists and those concerned with the assimilation of immigrants. In 1889, the historian David Tyack tells us, Illinois and Wisconsin "tried to regulate immigrant private and parochial schools by requiring that most instruction be conducted in English. As in the case of Protestant rituals in the schools, the contest over instruction in language other than English became a symbolic battle between whose who wanted to impose one standard of belief and those who welcomed pluralistic forms of education."

World War I, with its encouragement of a fierce national (or was it ethnic?) chauvinism, finished off the acceptance of German as a language of instruction in public schools. Nevertheless, it was during the build-up to entry into the war that the first major arguments for multiculturalism in American education were set forth.

• • • • • • • • • • • • •

"Cultural pluralism" was the term Horace Kallen, a student and follower of John Dewey, used to describe a new kind of public education, in which a variety of cultures besides that of England would receive a significant place in American public education.

To its critics, multiculturalism looks like a very new thing in American education. In many respects, it is. However, viewed in the long stretch of the history of American public schooling...

John Dewey himself, in 1916, speaking to the National Education Association, took up the cudgels for cultural pluralism:

Such terms as Irish-American or Hebrew-American or German-American are false terms, because they seem to assume something that is already in existence in America, to which the other factors may be hitched on. The fact is, the genuine American, the typical American, is himself a hyphenated character. It does not mean that he is part American and that some foreign ingredient is in his make-up. He is not American plus Pole or German. But the American is himself Pole-German-English - French - Spanish - Italian - Greek - Irish - Scandinavian - Bohemian - Jew—and so on. The point is to see to it that the hyphen connects instead of separates. And this means at least that our public schools shall teach each factor to respect every other, and shall take pains to enlighten us all as to the great past contributions of every strain in our composite make-up.

But the wave of postwar chauvinism that led Americans to deport East Europeans to Bolshevik Russia, to ban mass immigration, and to revive the Ku Klux Klan was too strong. In 1919, Nebraska forbade the teaching of any foreign language before the eighth grade (the Nebraska courts exempted Greek, Latin, and Hebrew, all presumed safely dead). In the 1920s, Oregon tried to ban any private schools at all. (Both laws were overturned by the Supreme Court.) In the public schools, Americanization was the order of the day, and prevailed without a check through the 1940s, while the children of the last great wave of European immigration were being educated.

• • • • • • • • • • • • •

I attended the schools of New York City from 1929 to 1944 (I include the public City College of New York in that stretch), and not a whiff of cultural pluralism was to be found. Americanization was strong, unself-conscious, and self-confident. Although probably two-thirds of the students in New York's public schools were Jewish or Italian, no Jewish or Italian figure was to be found in our texts for literature, for social studies, for history. All cultures but that of the founding English and its American variant were ignored, and students were left to assume, if they thought about the matter at all, that the cultures of their homes and parental homelands were irrelevant or inferior.

And that singularly unicultural educational background is having an important effect on the current debates over multiculturalism. For many protagonists in this debate, the conflicts over educating Catholic and later, German-speaking students, as well as the arguments for multi-culturalism in the age of mass immigration, are all a kind of murky prehistory, wiped out in a flood that deposited a uniform silt over our past, leaving only fossil remains of that earlier diversity and those earlier conflicts. Advocates of multi-culturalism today often do not know that they had forebears; nor do opponents of multiculturalism today know that the education they experienced was the expression of an age singularly free of conflict over issues of cultural pluralism.

The arguments for cultural pluralism began to emerge again during World War II, and the motivating force was Hitler. If he argued that one race and one people was superior and should be dominant, then it was in the interest of the war effort to teach equality and tolerance. In the 1940s, a small movement for "intercultural education" sprouted. Its aim was to teach something about the various ethnic and racial groups that made up America, and to teach tolerance. Just how extensive it actually was in the schools is not clear, but it did not survive the 1950s and 1960s, when cultural pluralism was pushed aside by the shock of Sputnik and the issue of desegregation.

Something of a contradiction existed between desegregation, as then envisaged, and cultural pluralism. The aim of black and liberal civil rights leaders was for blacks to get the same education that whites received. If whites' education had precious little of cultural pluralism or multicultur-alism in it, why should that be changed for blacks? The black objective, through the entire course of the struggle in the courts in the 1940s and 1950s for equality, was assimilation. Blacks should not be treated differently because they were black.

But that was transmuted rapidly into the demand of many militants that blacks must get something different because they were black. By the late 1960s, a "black power" movement, black Muslims, and other manifestations of black nationalism were already challenging the assimila-tionist civil-rights leadership. Black schools were started in black communities, and some were even established under the ae-gis of liberal public school systems(as in Berkeley, California).

Soon Mexican Americans and Puerto Ricans raised their own grievances against the public school system, and political activists demanded the recognition of Spanish. Civil rights laws that guaranteed equality were interpreted by the Supreme Court to mean that equality for those speaking a foreign language could require instruction in that language; liberal states passed laws giving a limited right to instruction in one's native language, and federal laws and regulations and court decisions made that a requirement in many school systems.

Bilingualism is, of course, not the same thing as multiculturalism, but it was generally taken for granted that instruction in one's native language for those speaking Spanish also meant to some degree instruction in Puerto Rican or Mexican culture and history. Through the 1970s, bilingualism and the acknowledgement of distinctive group cultures and histories in social studies and history classes spread and established themselves in the public schools.

One might well ask why multiculturalism has become such an important issue today. It has been at least 20 years since public schools started adapting themselves to the presumed cultural distinctiveness and interests of blacks and Hispanics, by modifying textbooks, introducing new reading materials, changing examinations, and instructing non-English-speaking students in Spanish for a few years. What has put the issue on the agenda today, not only in the public schools, but in colleges and universities, public and private?

I believe the basic explanation is a build-up of frustration in the black population in recent years over the failure of civil rights reforms to deliver what was expected from them. In the colleges, affirmative action—well established as it is—has not increased markedly the number of black instructors or the number of black students who can qualify for the more selective institutions without special consideration. In the public schools, black achievement as measured by NAEP scores, SAT scores, and high school completion rates has improved somewhat, but the gaps between black and white achievement remain large. Blacks on the whole do worse than Hispanic groups despite the very large numbers of new, non-English-speaking immigrants, and far worse than the Asian groups.

One can record substantial black achievement in politics, in the armed forces, in the civil service, and in some high positions in the private economy, but alongside these successes a host of social problems afflicting a large part of the black population has, by some key measures, grown, not declined, in the past 20 years.

One might have expected that the multicultural debate would be fueled by the large new immigration of the past 20 years. But that is really not the moving force. The Asian immigrants, almost half the number, seem quite content with the education they get. Nor are Hispanic immigrants making demands on the public school system that necessitate radical change. Mexican Americans would like to see their children do better in school, to have more of them graduate. But they have no strong commitment to the idea that this objective will be enhanced by more teaching in Spanish, or more Mexican cultural and historical content.

For the critics of multiculturalism, the issue that ultimately determines its acceptability is a judgment as to the underlying purpose of the curriculum reform. Is it to promote harmony and an acceptance of our society? Or to portray our society as so fatally flawed by racism, so irredeemably unfair and unequal that it must be rejected as evil?

The critics fear that the second vision underlies the strong multicultural position. On one level, they are right. But if we look more deeply into the objectives of those who promote a strong multicultural thrust, and who in doing so present a somewhat lopsided view of our history, we will find that they promote multiculturalism not because they aim at divisiveness and separation as a good, not because they—to put it in the strongest terms possible—want to break up the union, but because they aim at a fuller inclusiveness of deprived groups.

. . . .

In the short term, their vision may well mean more conflict and divisiveness, but they see this as a stage on the way to a greater inclusiveness. They are no Quebec separatists, Croatian nationalists, Sikh or Tamil separatists. They seek inclusion and equality in a common society.

Critics of the new multiculturalism will see my judgment as far too benign. Undoubtedly one can point to some leading advocates of multiculturalism whose intentions are not benign. But I would emphasize that we deal with a spectrum of views, some mild enough to gain the endorsement of Ravitch, Schlesinger, and Shanker. In the middle there is much to argue about.

What sort of students do multicultural schools turn out? The Catholic schools of the mid-19th century, so fearful to many as a threat to national unity, produced Americans as patriotic or more patriotic than the norm. Nor did the German-language schools do badly in molding upstanding Americans, though equally upstanding Americans were doing their best to stamp out those schools. Even Amish, Hasidic, and Black Muslim schools, while I do not know whether they produced patriots, turn out, I think, citizens as good by many measures as the public schools.

Our diversity has one major binding force in the Constitution under which we live and which still, through the procedures that it first laid down and that have been further developed in our history, governs at the margin what we can and cannot do in our public schools. The Constitution guarantees that Amish children need not attend schools after the age when their parents feel they will be corrupted, and that Mormons and Black Muslims can teach their own version of the truth, which is as fantastic to many of us as the further reaches of Afrocentrism. Even the most dissident call on the Constitution for protection, yet few people are ready to tear it up as a compact with the devil. This common political bond keeps us together—nationalists and anti-nationalists, Eurocentrists and Afrocentrists—and may continue to through the storms of multiculturalism.

. . . .

America has changed. It is not God's country, anymore. We can lose wars—real ones—and we can be beaten in economic competition by the Japanese. We have become only one of a number of economically powerful, democratic countries, and not in every respect the best. And America exists in the larger reality of the non-Western world. A good deal of that world is sunk in poverty and political disorder, but some of it is teaching lessons in economic effectiveness to the West. Western hubris can never again be what it was in the late 19th and early 20th centuries.

Finally, America's population is changing in its racial and ethnic composition. Its values are changing. Its notions of the proper relation of groups and individuals to the national society are changing. As hard as it may be for veterans of the educational system of earlier decades to wrench free of their own schooling, it is even harder to see how such a system can be defended in the face of these changes.

Cultural Pluralism, Multicultural Education, and Then What?

Elaine C. Hagopian

It seems to me that multicultural education works on improving the status dimension of inequality which supports the notion of cultural pluralism but does not touch structural issues of class and power for those who are doubly negative evaluated.

Elaine C. Hagopian is a professor in the Department of Sociology, Simmons College, Boston, Massachusetts. This article is based on her address to the National Association for Multicultural Education conference on February 10, 1994, in Detroit, Michigan.

Opening Remarks

My field is not education but sociology. Nonetheless, I hope that a sociological perspective on multicultural education will be of some value to this distinguished audience. Let me quickly spell out for you what my basic points will be. They are not dissimilar from many of your own, and especially the views of the distinguished President of the National Association for Multicultural Education, Carl A. Grant. What I hope will be new is some of the content and analysis of the issues the points reflect.

First, while my focus will be on racial and ethnic groups, class and power correlates will be accented.

Second, the results of the civil rights movement took us from desegration to visions of integration, and when the latter faltered, to recognition of diversity in the form of cultural pluralism—which nonetheless implied "structural integration."

What we actually witnessed was more emphasis on cultural expression and less on structural access. Cultural pluralism as the focus of solution for the problem of inequality deflected attention from the need for structural change and access.

Third, what cultural pluralism as a policy did do, along with the negative pressures created by continuing racism/ethnism, was to encourage multicultural education as a kind of "cure-all" for the tensions of the society and to offer it as proof of our commitment to democracy.

Fourth, multicultural education at its best may create greater awareness and appreciation of all categories of people within and beyond race, ethnicity, and gender, and it may create a number of activists determined to make the wider society match the goals of multicultural education, but I do not think for the immediate future that it can effect the real changes needed to provide a truly or reasonably just society. It is part of the solution, but there are too many national and international factors which presently limit its full success.

Fifth, even so, it will have a greater impact, done right, than the previous focus on cultural pluralism alone.

Analysis

Christine Sleeter and Grant in a 1987 article in the *Harvard Educational Review* define the multicultural education approach as one that:

> ...promotes cultural pluralism and social equality by reforming the school program for all students to make it reflect diversity. These reforms include school staffing patterns that reflect the pluralistic nature of American society; unbiased curricula that incorporate the contributions of different social groups, women, and the handicapped; the affirmation of the languages of non-English-speaking minorities; and instructional materials that are appropriate and relevant for the students and which are integrated rather than supplementary.

They also identify another type that embodies the above, but adds an action dimension, *i.e.*, the notion of multicultural education actually preparing "students to challenge social structural inequality and to promote cultural diversity." Theresa Perry and James W. Fraser in their book *Freedom's Plow* have phrased this somewhat differently by saying that:

> ...if a democracy which includes all of America's people is to be fostered and prefigured in this nation's education system, then multicultural education must be at the heart, and not on the margins, of all discussions about education in this country. In this situation, multicultural education becomes not a matter of simply adding new material to the school curriculum, but of fundamentally re-visioning the relationship of schooling to a democratic society.

What these definitions have in common is their focus on equality that somehow multicultural education must create and promote. To understand what we are promoting, we need to define equality. In its absolute sense, equality means sameness of outcome. Without getting into a long discussion as to whether or not this is desirable, sameness of outcome would require a level of monitoring that a democracy would not find acceptable. Nonetheless, ever since the liberal age with its concept of citizenship and civil society emerged from the enlightenment, the idea of equality became a goal insisted upon by emancipated western society.

How then can we define it? Here I am addressing myself to racial and ethnic groups, but it could be applied to other categories as well. The following definition includes the social ingredients necessary to attain equality: a state of racial/ethnic equality exists in a polyethnic society when racial/ethnic groups enjoy nondiscriminatory status (*i.e.*, that they are valued positively at the human and cultural levels), are guaranteed those basic conditions of security and services which enable them to secure credentials to their abilities (equality of condition), and actually have unimpeded opportunity to compete for positions of power and class that have the authority to shape the conditions of life. This will still lead to inequality, but it will meet the terms of the spirit of equality, *i.e.*, that the criterion of fairness is operative.

This means that whoever falls to the bottom of class and power will do so from a relatively equal playing field; they will be statistically spread throughout the populations rather than centered in particular groups; and they will not be left without the basic securities from which their children can mount their effort to rise in the system. I will return to the concepts of status, class, and power, as well as the notions of equality of condition and opportunity, later in this analysis.

• • • • • • • • • • • • • •

The same definition of equality holds for interstate relations, but requires agreements first between states, especially North/South states, and second, within the separate states themselves. This is a much more complex process and requires no less than a reordering of the world politically, economically, and socially. This will not happen without great resistance, and it may be utopian. Even so, it offers clear direction for the future. And here, I hasten to add that multicultural education must therefore include internationalization of education to its approach.

To assess the prospects of attaining the spirit of equality as I have defined it, and to have multicultural education serve as a lead into, and support of it in our own society without neglecting the international scene, we need to examine what we mean by western liberalism, the birthmother of modern, universal citizenship rights. Advocates of the latter allege that it alone is able to achieve democracy and hence by association, equality, especially since the failure of state socialism in the former USSR.

• • • • • • • • • • • • • •

First, we need to understand what the western liberal model is. Actually, there are basically three western liberal models of equality. The first is the assimilation/universalist model which came out of the enlightenment tradition and is now enshrined in the U.N. Universal Declaration of Human Rights.

It is based on the assumption that the state constitution and laws recognize universal humanity and guarantee the same rights as such to all citizens to pursue their goals, that equal opportunity is therefore one of the rights which derives from universality and constitutionally guaranteed equal rights, and that participation in the societal structures will assimilate all citizens to a common world view and experience, thus eliminating any basis for negative differentiation. In short, people will be judged individually on their own merits because they are subject to universal criteria.

• • • • • • • • • • • • • •

The second is the protection of minority rights as individual groups in polyethnic states model which was given content and focus after World War I through the League of Nations and the Minority Protection Treaties and Declarations. It was seen as an extension of liberal concepts of rights to freedom of expression. The basic assumption in this model is the right to protection and resource support by the state of all individuals as members of specific minority ethnic nations to retain their culture, language, religious practices, and identity

without jeopardizing their status, access to power, and economic opportunity and mobility in the state of citizenship.

This model insisted on the liberal value of freedom of expression in group form and the right to one's own identity. "Forced" acculturation/assimilation (the first model) was seen as a violation of their rights. Nonetheless, they were also to be guaranteed the same opportunities as other citizens of the state. Other citizens and state officials saw this as special privileges for ethnic groups who wanted resources to continue their separate cultures, schools, and languages while not forfeiting the general privileges of citizenship.

This was supposed to be a positive form of separate but equal, *i.e.*, separate culturally and somewhat structurally as well, and yet equal in terms of citizen access to positions in the wider society. Post-World War I Europe saw these treaties as a solution to the way states with various ethnic nations were formed. The treaties never really worked and some of the ethnic problems in Europe date back to these untenable arrangements.

• • • • • • • • • • • • • •

Third, the structural integration/cultural pluralism model was developed by such thinkers as Horace Kallen. It is a variation of the rights to freedom of cultural expression whereby ethnic group members are guaranteed equal access to the common economic, political, and social structures of the polyethnic state, while at the same time being allowed and encouraged to pursue, develop, and elaborate their own ethnic cultures freely but not guaranteed fully by the resources of the state.

The problem with some of the contemporary liberal polyethnic states (the United States included) is that they often adopt unconsciously more than one of these models in full or partially and in an incoherent manner, which may further exacerbate ethnic discontent. For example, in this country we use the first model when we deal with law, *i.e.*, equal treatment before the law which in fact does not work if only because of differential resources of the defendants. More, we use the cultural pluralism model (model three) in a negative way, *i.e.*, when an Arab (especially a Muslim) commits a crime, he/she is translated communally—*i.e.*, all Arabs are bad. When Congressman Joseph Kennedy met with constituents who were speaking to Palestinian rights in the Middle East, he was quoted by a constituent in the group as saying, "they [the Arabs] killed my father."

Sirhan was translated into a "they, the Arabs." This is not so for mainstream whites.

More recently, President Bill Clinton addressed a Black Church in Memphis to condemn violence. Although not conscious of his actions, he chose a Black Church to speak about violence, implying that African Americans are the group that needs to be approached about the problem, rather than to a white population. Nonetheless, cultural pluralism is still put forward as positive, while those who are members of a non-majority culture are treated negatively. They were before the cultural pluralist model, but cultural pluralism makes them more visible and objects of criticism for their alleged "special treatment," especially when "they" behave deviantly.

The protection model (model two) was produced in this country as negative Jim Crow laws, and those laws envisioned total separation with access only to menial positions in the wider society and inferior separate institutions. Today, the protective part of this model was theoretically embodied in affirmative action laws more as catch-up than guaranteed protection (entitlement), but in fact affirmative action, while benefiting some, has been gradually circumvented. In part, bilingual education derives from this model.

On the whole, however, we have the ideology of the first model of individual equality before the law, coupled with cultural pluralism which is put forward positively, but used negatively, and the perceptions on the part of some in this society that in the second model, various racial, ethnic, and gender groups have privileges not available to others. This is why we have a mess today.

. . . .

Well, okay, we have cultural pluralism as the dominant mode of relating to diversity in this country, and we are supposed to get structural access under this policy that leads to some equality. Affirmative action and equal economic opportunity are supposed to help us achieve the latter. Multicultural education is supposed to help prepare us for this new equality, or it is even supposed to help create it. But what do we have?

Our capitalist economic order is based on inequality. The question becomes one of who gets on the bottom? Because of the limited number of top positions, whoever could be kept out of the competition allowed others greater opportunity. Whether by intent or by opportunity, women, especially of color, and various racial/ethnic groups as categories, were disproportionally found on the bottom. If the spirit of equality operated, the bottom would not be consistently inhabited in a disproportional way with particular racial/ethnic groups and women of color.

When the post-civil rights legislation aimed at achieving integration to change this situation went into effect, it was challenged by sectors of society. And in and of itself, in any case, it could not meet the demands for equity by trying to put more players into the same structure, and one in which there is a shrinking job market. Hence, the focus shifted to cultural pluralism as a policy, not simply as a recognition of right to expression, but to deflect attention from the failure of structural integration. Good money was available for arts, dance, folklore, etc. to which the committed went. This made people feel good. These programs were good for self-esteem, but very little money was available for structural change to absorb people. Even so, cultural pluralism gave appearances of respect.

. . . .

Therefore, even when members of deprived groups got into positions of "power," economic or political, they were captive leaders. Who could imagine a Colin Powell using his previous position with the joint chiefs of staff to put forward the agenda of African-Americans on such matters as their disproportional death rate in Vietnam.

Can anyone really imagine Ron Brown presenting an unambiguous picture of African-American economic and health issues. No Arab-American can ever envision George Mitchell or Donna Shalala coming out forcefully for real justice in the Middle East which is tied to viewing Arab-Americans positively in this society. Or who could imagine Connie Chung doing a speak-out on Asian Americans, especially those from Vietnam, Cambodia, and Laos.

Lani Guinier was refused the post of U.S. Civil Rights Attorney because she did not have the credentials for being a captive leader. She was considered a "trouble-maker" because she held to her values. All of us know of at least one feminist, or an African-American, or an Hispanic-American, etc. who are defined as radical or aggressive in their views who are refused jobs because "they would not be good for our students, or co-workers, or organization." Take your pick. I myself have been locked out of teaching courses on the Middle East, my area speciality, because I believe in including the point of view of the victims as well as the victimizers in the area. None of my colleagues offered support on this matter. In short, the few who climb to the top as proof of American democracy are absorbed into the existing corporate culture. They are not able to change the structure in ways that allow cultural pluralism to mesh with social and political mobility.

To further dissect the situation in detail, I must now examine the dimensions of inequality, class, status, and power, and then I will tie the parts of my analysis together.

Class Stratification. When members of particular ethnic groups in a polyethnic society (and/or the global system of nation-states) are consistently in the low-income and high unemployment category, it becomes obvious that certain social and political processes are re-enforcing the pattern and that equal access is not a reality.

Social Status. This is often defined simply as a person's or group's position in society. Defined in this way, social status elicits little affect. However, if we understand that social location is a result of how a group is perceived by others, then we will understand social status to include other meanings. The social status of a racial/ethnic group is a derivative of the degree to which the group is valued in society in human and in cultural terms.

Ordinarily, to evaluate a group negatively in human terms correlates significantly with a negative evaluation in cultural terms. African Americans, Native Americans, and various misnamed Hispanic Americans illustrate this point. On the other hand, positive evaluation, even if given grudgingly, of an ethnic group in cultural terms may neutralize overt negative human evaluation. For example, the European cultural values of education and achievement which Jewish immigrants brought with them to the United States tended to subdue, but not defeat, overt antisemitism (the human level of their status evaluation) in this country over the years. Positive cultural evaluation provided Jewish peoples with the opportunity to achieve higher ranked positions in society.

In the first case, the double negative evaluation of a racial/ethnic group not only defines its social position, but correlates significantly with class. In the second case, latent negative human evaluation has the potential for surfacing under certain conditions. However, the cultural skills and achievements of the affected group offer a constraining factor and permit the group an overall desirable social status as well as greater class mobility.

In sum, an ethnic/racial group's status position is determined by the human and cultural evaluation made by those who "count" in society, and that these evaluations are relevant to economic access and degree of class mobility, and as we shall now see, to power positions as well.

Power. There are several types of power in addition to the obvious one of political power. There is economic power supplied either by ownership of significant shares in firms or property; there is bureaucratic power stemming from managerial positions in major organizations and agencies; and there is social power stemming from the prestige and authority of professional roles.

Ordinarily, ethnic/racial groups who are doubly negative evaluated do not have easy access to positions of power. Hence the only real power route open to doubly negative stereotyped groups is to organize the group itself to develop a critical mass capable of "disrupting" society in some form. In return for ceasing and desisting, agreements with governmental and institutional officials are made calling for attempts to alter the negative images through public education, enactment of laws to gain economic access, and greater efforts to open power positions.

Those ethnic groups negatively stereotyped humanly but not culturally are able to gain positions of power by exercising their citizens' rights and meeting necessary qualifications in the "open" society. However, the more power they gain in all areas, even in the "open" society, the greater the possibility for the latent human prejudice to express itself, especially in situations where the society as a whole is undergoing difficult economic times.

While the ethnic group is able to rally through their institutions important forces and resources against attempts to dislodge them from their class and power position, the hostility toward them is expressed quite often through acts of violence, but civil society rushes to condemn such violence against groups who are culturally valued. Clearly, the type of status evaluation of ethnic/racial groups tends to correlate with class and power positions.

. . . .

The next questions we must ask are what is the solution, and what does multicultural (including international) education have to do with it? Can multicultural education produce equality? What other forces are operating that may neutralize the intent of multicultural education?

It seems to me that multicultural education works on improving the status dimension of inequality which supports the notion of cultural pluralism but does not touch structural issues of class and power for those who are doubly negative evaluated. While it does sometimes focus on class and power issues, the reality of the American social structure tends to dampen the activists as they compete in a shrinking opportunity structure.

What we need to make multicultural education work are equality of condition and opportunity mentioned in my definition of equality. We have been on the periphery in this country of establishing equality of condition, *i.e.*, the recommendation of the Social Security Commission of 1935 that a policy of guaranteed employment be put in place so as to avoid the catastrophe of the great depression; the development of a minimum wage law—though very inadequate; some unemployment coverage; low-cost housing, etc.

Yet we have not seen these add up to even minimal maintenance of excluded peoples, never mind basic security to "level" the playing field. We have to have equality of condition, *i.e.*, guaranteed work at a level of pay that is livable, clean and decent low cost housing, health care, first class education for all without bias, reasonable support for the unemployed and handicapped, etc.

Only equality of condition will make equality of opportunity meaningful and produce the spirit of equality. These met, multicultural education's focus on creating positive status (human and cultural) could work toward achieving the spirit of equality. However, the three liberal models would have to be reformulated into a single, conscious, and positive model. Actually, this would mean that the universalist model could operate in treating people individually for jobs, political office, and before the law.

The cultural pluralism model would allow positive cultural identity without interfering in universal criteria for access to the economic and power structures. And it is assumed that the protection model would not be needed if multicultural education and equality of condition and opportunity worked well together. All of this requires fundamental change in our society calling for a socially responsible capitalism and government. Such changes assure identifying and promoting our best into all walks of life from all walks of life, while assuring those who do not attain the positions of great income and power in society a real cushion of security from which their children will have an opportunity to compete.

These are yet not enough. We have to move to greater international agreements and equity. We need real peace and recognition of the rights of third world peoples not to be used as cheap labor. They must be guaranteed security as well. Profits must be put into a human context that includes not only basic security, but *de facto* will also cease the destruction of our environment beyond earth's ability to replenish the resources necessary for life.

So long as we remain in a competitive national and international economic mode which relies on political and military power to control people and resources as well as control international financial institutions, polyethnic states with the most excellent multicultural education will not be able to sustain in reality the values of equality promoted in school.

What this all means is that a NAFTA would not be enacted, and hence would not pit American labor against Mexicans and Mexican Americans in a racist/ethnist battle for jobs. It means that a World Trade Center explosion would not direct hatred to Arab Americans and other Muslim groups in America.

For even if we ever get equality of condition and opportunity, and we could work out the problem of liberal models, we must ask if multicultural education focused on creating positive human and cultural statuses can work when national and international events and policies are enacted that can immediately wipe out its effects. One need only think of the treatment of Iranian-origin peoples in the United States after the Khomeini revolution and the holding of American Embassy workers as hostages in Iran for over one year that led to hostility to Iranian-origin people in the United States.

Some 90 years ago, Emile Durkheim thought he could promote moral behavior in our modern industrial societies through education; and we still keep trying through liberal arts. Thankfully, we do turn out a core of students who keep the embers burning, but the reality is before us. I hope that multicultural education will be more successful. It is the right thing to do, but we need the rest of society and the world, or those who make decisions in those arenas to walk with us. Given the fact that most people live in polyethnic states and within a competitive global economic system, the efforts required to achieve the spirit of equality are enormous and complex, but the goal is worth our very best efforts.

Identity and Personal Development: A Multicultural Focus

The development of each person's unique conception of self (the development of one's identity as a person) is the most important developmental learning task that any of us undertake from birth to death. The preschool, elementary, and secondary school years are ones in which each of us learns critically important cognitive and affective strategies for defining ourselves, others, and the world. Multicultural education seeks to help people develop intellectual and emotional responses to other people that will be accepting and empathic. There has been much psychological and psychiatric research over the past few decades on the differences between prejudiced and tolerant (accepting) personalities. One opportunity educators

have as they work with students in school settings is to provide good examples of accepting, tolerant behavior and to help students develop positive, affirmative views of themselves and others. Gordon Allport, in his classic book, *The Nature of Prejudice,* commented in his chapter on "The Tolerant Personality" that we could be "doubly sure" that early instruction and practice in accepting diversity is very important in directing a child toward becoming a tolerant person. Thus, we take up the topic of personal identity development in this unit.

In the education of persons we need to see the interconnections among such factors as gender, social class position in society, racial or ethnic heritage, and the primary cultural values that inform the way they see the world and themselves. We need to be perceptive of and sensitive to their visions of who they are and of how things are in the world. As Tracy Robinson argues so well from a counseling perspective in her article, we need to "see our clients whole." Perceptive teachers and therapists have always been aware of this. But all teachers need to be aware of it. Teachers, as well as parents and many others, are persons with whom students at all elementary and secondary grade levels must interact. It is important for teachers to be positive examples of accepting, open-minded persons capable of empathy, compassion, and concern for the well-being of each student.

We need to help students to understand themselves, to define their strengths and their concerns, and to empower them to critically encounter their own personal social reality. This is a task each person must learn to do in childhood and adolescence so that they may empower themselves to interpret and evaluate their own experience. This task can be integrated and effectively achieved within the intellectual mission of the school. One of the ways to do this is by encouraging students to be critically interpretive and evaluative of the texts they read and to be open and active in the discussion of issues in class. Identity development is an ongoing process. Each student needs to be able to explore the boundaries of his or her intellectual strengths and weaknesses as well as to ex-

plore the social boundaries encountered in school as well as out of school.

Multicultural education is intended for and needed by all students in order that they will have a sensitivity to the many varying heritages and backgrounds through which individuals interact in our very culturally pluralistic national social system and to enable them to forge their own conception of who they are as persons. Why should only one cultural heritage be thoroughly taught while all others are essentially ignored in elementary and secondary school years in a pluralistic national social environment, the demographics of which are changing so dramatically? Cultural values are of primary importance in the process of a person's conceptualization of him- or herself. This unit's articles explore various models of human interaction and the psychosocial foundations for the formation of knowledge bases of students. The ways in which students define themselves and their possibilities as they move across or are trapped within their perceived social boundaries in school and community settings are explored. How educators can better utilize the knowledge bases of minority cultural families in assisting minority students to achieve better social integration into mainstream school settings is also examined. The importance of educators trying to establish more effective communications linkages between students' families and cultural environments is further examined. The multiple worlds and social roles students frequently have to play in and out of school are another social phenomenon in the personality development of students that receives analysis in these essays.

Students live in a hierarchy of social contexts in which their racial, cultural, gender, and social class backgrounds, as well as the degree of their personal identification with each of these factors, impact on the processes through which they make important choices leading to individual decisions regarding their own identity. Some of the research on how desegregated schools can achieve more effective degrees of intercultural socialization is also presented in this unit. How to get all cultural group members willing to learn each others' cultural heritages is

one of the challenges being studied. Helping students to learn from the cultural perspectives of other groups so that all students might better comprehend alternative, diverse definitions of their social environments is one of the tasks of multicultural education. One purpose of multicultural education programming is to teach tolerant, accepting attitudes toward others of differing cultural backgrounds. Allport and several other major psychiatrists and social psychologists of past decades have taught us that prejudice and tolerance (acceptance) are learned behaviors. We can learn to be accepting, caring, compassionate persons. Yes, schools can teach to overcome prejudice. Educators are not powerless in the face of the prejudiced views that many students bring to school from their homes.

The essays in this unit are relevant to courses in educational policy studies and leadership, cultural foundations of education, sociology or anthropology of education, history and philosophy of education, and curriculum theory and construction, among others.

Looking Ahead: Challenge Questions

What are the primary gender issues in multicultural school settings?

What should children learn about the cultural heritages and values of other children in their schools?

How do social class differences relate to misunderstandings among students from different social class positions in a community?

What can educators learn from developing close communications linkages with the families of their students?

What challenges do minority students encounter that majority students in a desegregated school do not encounter (putting aside the question as to which cultural group is the majority or minority culture)?

How does community structure affect adolescent identity development?

What can teachers do to foster positive personal identity development in their students?

—F. S.

The Intersections of Gender, Class, Race, and Culture: On Seeing Clients Whole

The author explores the multiple and dynamic intersections of gender with race, culture, and class in psychosocial identity formation to minimize the risk of homogenizing or polarizing our understanding of these characteristics.

Tracy Robinson

Tracy Robinson is an assistant professor in the Department of Counselor Education at North Carolina State University–Raleigh.

Gender, class, race, and culture are core components of each person's identity formation (Condry, 1984; Gibbs, Huang, & Associates, 1989; Good, Gilber, & Scher, 1990; Helms, 1984; Ibrahim, 1985; Katz, 1985; Lee & Richardson, 1991; Pinderhughes, 1989; Scher & Good, 1990; Sue & Sue, 1990; Ward, 1989). Erikson's (1968) concept of identity formation has been primary to psychologists' understanding of identity, which is psychosocial and refers to the continuity of the self in a developmental context and to one's relationships with others in society (Ward, 1989). Throughout the life span, identity constructs of gender, race, class, and culture shape an individual's image and ensuing reimage of self and one's place in the world.

The overall goal of this work is to promote dialogue among helping professionals concerning the pivotal role of these simultaneous intersections in affecting clients' lives, their problems, and ultimately, their empowerment. Such a conceptual framework is preferred over focusing on one aspect of identity for assessment purposes.

Concerning research, Reid and Comas-Diaz (1990) observed, "gender research typically fails to include race/ethnic concerns, . . . studies of ethnic groups often ignore gender issues" (p. 397). The interaction of gender, class, race, and culture in our society determines one's identity (Gollnick, 1991). Thus, one identity construct does not fully reveal an individual's character.

To illustrate the importance of attending to a client's multiple intersections, a case study example is used. A discussion of monoculturalism and its relationship to oblivion regarding these intersections is explored. Finally, approaches to change for training and practice are outlined.

A DEFINITION OF CONCEPTS

In this work, the term *socioeconomic class* refers to a person's (or to a group's) relative social position in a hierarchical ranking (Jaynes & Williams, 1989). Race has both biological origins and social dimensions (Pinderhughes, 1989). Although typical conceptions of race refer to non-Whites (Christian, 1989), race refers to both Whites and non-Whites. Clearly an immutable characteristic, race holds status and rank in society just as socioeconomic class, a mutable variable, does (Leggon, 1980). Gender has social categories in terms of roles and behaviors based on a biological given of sex (Renzetti & Curan, 1992). It refers to both men and women, although traditional notions of gender reference nonmales (Christian, 1989). Thus, there is an interrelationship between race, gender, and social class (Gibbs, Huang, et al., 1989). Finally, the term *culture* refers to total ways of living and refers to values, beliefs, norms, and traditions (Pinderhughes, 1989). It is enormous and central to our lives.

Indivisible Intersections

The importance of considering the multiple intersection of class, race, culture, and gender has been raised across a variety of disciplines (see Christian, 1989; Collins, 1989; Reid & Comas-Diaz, 1990; Siegel, 1990). Such attention is warranted, considering that every human being's psychosocial identities are an embodiment of each of these and other immutable and mutable constructs.

In her discussion of gender and race, Christian (1989) suggested that ignoring these primary intersections is to treat individual constructs as if they were pure and exhaustive categories. Such a treatment implies that certain constructs can be isolated and used solely for purposes of assessment. For example, many adult men have the roles of father and husband in common. Yet, as Carrigan, Connell, and Lee (1987) maintained, the term *men in general* is puzzling because of the underlying assumption that persons who share gender are monolithic. Clearly, socialization patterns in the United States often orient men to restrict emotion and to be aggressive, competitive, and dominant (Cook, 1990; Good & Mintz, 1990; Mintz & O'Neil, 1990). Nonetheless, the experiences, issues, and concerns of a college educated African-American man from a multigenerational, middle-class background are different from those of an African-American male laborer who has a high school diploma and is from a multigenerational, working-class family.

Whereas Bronstein and Quina (1988) suggested more variability within groups than among them, in the example just provided, there is a high degree of within-group difference that can be attributed to socioeconomic class. Invariably, individual differences come into play, because each man is different from his counterparts with similar characteristics (Lee & Richardson, 1991). Yet, socioeconomic class has a direct impact on income, housing, access to medical care, children's social environment, and a host of other indicators of life-style and life quality (Gibbs, Huang et al., 1989; Jaynes & Williams, 1989). Although both men are affected by racism, class and status affect one's economic, social, and to a large extent psychological power in this society. Considering that power relates to the capacity to produce desired effects and mastery over self, nature, and other people (Pinderhughes, 1989), the relationship between power and class is evident. The type of relationship, however, is uncertain.

Although low-income status may provoke feelings of powerlessness characterized by less comfort, less gratification, insecurity, and strong tendency to depression (Pinderhughes, 1989), racism or sexism often generates similar feelings of powerlessness, even among individuals who hold middle-class status. Although class is interrelated with gender, race, and power, it is simplistic to conclude that male gender, high socioeconomic status, and being a White American is directly associated with feelings of more power, which according to Pinderhughes (1989) is characterized by less tendency to depression, more pleasure, less pain, and feelings of superiority. Likewise it is a mistake to assume that female gender, low socioeconomic status, and being a person of color is automatically associated with feelings of less power. Such a perspective is psychologically disempowering to a client although high status is typically identified with persons who are White and middle class, whereas low status is ascribed to non-White persons, ethnic minorities, and lower-class families (Gibbs, Huang, et al., 1989).

Undeniably, a disproportionate share of people living in poverty are people of color (U.S. Department of Commerce, 1990); most jobs are stratified by race, ethnicity, and gender, with women of color at the bottom of the occupational hierarchy and White men at the top (Women for Racial and Economic Equality, 1991). A full 60% of adults receiving Aid to Families with Dependent Children (AFDC) have not completed high school (Women for Racial and Economic Equality, 1991). Economic and occupational powerlessness, however, do not dictate psychological and or moral powerlessness. Moreover, economic and occupational power do not prescribe psychological and moral strength. History and contemporary reality are replete with examples of people with economic power and impoverished morals.

Pinderhughes (1989) maintained that, however ironic, accepting the reality of one's powerless position can bring a sense of power. Reframing the situation to one's advantage (through the help of a skilled counselor) and choosing not to internalize negative behaviors and attitudes of oppressive persons are acts of empowerment.

Human Characteristics as Status

Ours is a heterogenous society, however, as diverse as this nation is and has been, diversity tends to be devalued (Pinderhughes, 1989; Sue, 1990). When differences are viewed hierarchically, disdain is probable. Naturally, intolerance for difference is not compatible with multiculturalism, and diversity and multiculturalism are not synonymous.

As an ideal state and an ongoing process wherein a person is appreciative of and comfortable with racial and cultural differences (Hoopes, 1979), multiculturalism is different from racial and ethnic monoculturalism. According to McIntosh (1990), monoculturalism is single-system seeing. It assumes that people come from the same cultural system "and that its outlines are those which have been recognized by people who have the most ethnic and racial power" (p. 1). Although non-Whites represent 24% of the U.S. population (U.S. Department of Commerce, 1991), White Americans are in the numerical majority and as such have significantly influenced U.S. culture accordingly. Components of White culture that are pervasive and dominant throughout society include individualism, competition, patriarchal family structure, the Protestant work ethic, and empiricism (Sue & Sue, 1990). These values parallel the society's adherence to the experiences of upper middle-class, Euro-American, able-bodied, heterosexual men as the referent point for normalcy, regardless of race, gender, culture, and class diversity (Bronstein & Quina, 1988; Christian, 1989; Miller, 1984; Reid & Comas-Diaz, 1990). Undoubtedly, intolerance of and disdain for differences reduces humanity and impedes moral development. In counseling, such attitudes are contradictory to the goal of client empowerment.

A Case in Point

Ms. Wing is an Asian-American lawyer who comes to counseling. She presents with problems of stress, fatigue, and feelings of being overwhelmed with her multiple responsibilities at work and at home. She has two children, ages 9 and 11 years. She is also troubled because she was not promoted at the law firm where she has been employed for 6 years. During the first session of counseling she reveals that younger and less experienced White men have been promoted above her on three different occasions. Subsequently, she is beginning to doubt her capability as a professional. She is also convinced that the overtures displayed by her male supervisor are characteristic of sexual harassment.

Although it is clear that the stress Ms. Wing is experiencing is related to multiple role conflicts many women experience as mothers, professionals, and wives (Good, Gilbert, & Scher, 1990), other issues are directly related to who the client is as an Asian American. An astute counselor, regardless of his or her gender, would be sensitive to the oppressive nature of sexual harassment and its role in provoking feelings of powerlessness, increased vulnerability, and anxiety. Feeling discriminated against because of one's race or ethnicity also conjures up feelings of powerlessness, rage, and frustration. Again, an effective counselor, regardless of his or her race or ethnicity, would have the ego strength to assess this.

Despite the professional qualifications of this client who may possess many YAVIS (young, attractive, verbal, intelligent, and successful) characteristics (Pinderhughes, 1989), high levels of educational attainment, hard work, and middle-class status are not sufficient to bypass feelings of powerlessness common among people with less education and less success. In a societal context that purports to be a meritocracy and a culture in which the Protestant work ethic is endorsed, these feelings, albeit distressing, may be new for some who thought (and had been taught) that their professional

status and middle-class income would shield them from such feelings. Once again, an effective counselor would be able to coexist with this existential realization although it may evoke feelings of vulnerability in the helping professional. Pedersen (1988) reminded counselors to have balance, which is to tolerate life's inconsistencies and to learn to coexist with dissonance. Security in one's identity as a racial, gendered, cultural, and class being minimizes countertransference (Bernardez, 1987).

Silence about any of the intersections in Ms. Wing's life is akin to believing they do not exist and are thus irrelevant and dismissable. According to Fine (1987), "silencing constitutes the process by which contradictory evidence, ideologies, and experiences find themselves buried, camouflaged, and discredited" (p. 13). Although Fine was referring to the classroom event, important parallels can be made to counseling. A counselor's silence about Ms. Wing's speculations of racial and sexual discrimination could be attributed to limited exposure to clients in cross-cultural contexts. When differences are seen as contradictory, naming them or talking about them is impeded. Silence could also be linked to one of the assumptions of monoculturalism, that everyone exists in the same cultural plane and thus desires what is valued in society.

Although a prevalent tenet of feminism maintains that women need to be more assertive in a society that has socialized them to be yielding and silent, it may not be in Ms. Wing's best interest to become more assertive with her colleagues or her spouse. Lack of assertiveness and self-denial are problems for many women (Lemkau & Landau, 1986), unquestionably in this culture and arguably in non-U.S. cultures. In many Asian cultures, however, women's identities are often defined by their relationships to others more than by occupational goals (Chan, 1986; True, 1990). Furthermore, in many microcultures (e.g., Asian, Latino, American Indian, and African-American families), collective responsibility, group solidarity, and family unity are strong values and strengths, not liabilities (Sue & Sue, 1990). Thus conferring with and even deferring to some family members may be culturally representative of the important role of family in a client's culture. If only a dominant cultural lens is used to interpret behavior, bias and stereotyping ensue (Pedersen, 1988). Because all clients are shaped by a constellation of forces (Lee & Richarson, 1991; Pedersen, 1990), a monocultural approach is undoubtedly myopic.

It is not psychologically healthy for Ms. Wing to internalize a sense of personal inadequacy. If institutional racism and sexism are involved, she should be encouraged, from a behavioral perspective, to carefully document incidents when harassment takes place, investigate policy manuals concerning her rights as an employee, and pursue mediational procedures when necessary. Cognitively speaking, it may be helpful for Ms. Wing to consider her options (a change in employment, starting her own business, hiring some help with household responsibilities, marriage counseling). These and other options should be generated from a place of power as opposed to one of powerlessness. An appropriate question for a counselor to ask is, "What would Ms. Wing like to see change in her immediate situation and what action is appropriate, given who she is and who she desires to be?" Finally, Ms. Wing should be assisted in understanding that when ascribed (more than achieved) statuses are viewed as "master" status traits, a status hierarchy results. Thus, persons not traditionally associated with a role may be regarded as unsuitable candidates, regardless of professional qualifications (Leggon, 1980). That the U.S. presidency has not been occupied by any person of color or by a woman is an example. This knowledge need not impede a client's aspirations but may in fact strengthen boundaries.

On Change

The 21st century will reflect changing conceptions of gender and population growth among racial and cultural groups (Hodgkinson, 1985; Scher & Good, 1990). To empower clients and attend to them as whole persons, counselors in training and practicing counselors need to be aware of their perceptions and assumptions about differences. One possible barrier to change is that some well-meaning and highly trained counselors are oblivious to unearned privileges associated with gender, race, class, and sexual orientation (Mcintosh, 1988). Privileges refer to an "invisible, weightless knapsack of special provisions, assurances, and blank checks" (McIntosh, 1988, p. 1). As White, female, heterosexual, highly educated, and middle class, Mcintosh identified over 40 privileges that she can use on a daily basis. For example, she can easily find academic instruction that gives attention to people of her same race and class. Moreover, she recognizes that it is not necessary that she or her children answer questions about why she lives with her husband (McIntosh, 1988). Students and professionals are encouraged to identify their own personal list of privileges as a means of increasing awareness. Helpers who are aware of their own identities are less likely to be uncomfortable with differences, particularly in cross-cultural contexts (Pinderhughes, 1989). Discomfort with differences may contribute to a counselor's inability to attend to aspects of the client's identity that are different from his or her own.

Responding to Pinderhughes's (1989) questions that focus on identity may abet the process of critical thinking for both professionals and students. Included are (a) What are your feelings about being male, female, White or a person of color? (b) How do you think others

who are different from you feel? (c) What are your experiences with power or powerlessness based on any of your identity constructs? Self-inquiry is important because countertransference can occur when counselors are unaware (Bernardez, 1987; Good, Gilbert, & Scher, 1990). Finally, operating from the client's strengths, which are independent of economic or occupational indexes, promotes empowerment.

CONCLUSION

The goal of this work was to expand understanding and to encourage dialogue about the important intersections of gender, class, race, and culture. Definitions of these terms were provided. A discussion of their relationships with one another and with power was provided. A case study example illustrated the influence of these dynamics on a client's problem, process, and empowerment. A pedagogy of change was outlined and included (a) recognizing the enormity of the intersections, (b) understanding one's personal identity constructs, (c) focusing on client's strengths toward empowerment. Such strengths are not dependent on occupational and economic indexes and may emanate from cultural traditions.

REFERENCES

Bernardez, T. (1987). Gender based countertransference of female therapist in the psychotherapy of women. *Women, Power and Therapy: Issues for Women, 6*, 25–40.

Bronstein, P. A., & Quina, K. (Eds.). (1988). *Teaching a psychology of people: Resources for gender and sociocultural awareness.* Washington DC: American Psychological Association.

Carrigan, T., Connell, B., & Lee, J. (1987). Toward a new sociology of masculinity. In H. Brod (Ed.), *The making of masculinities: The new men's studies* (pp. 63–100). Boston: Allen and Unwin.

Chan, C. (1986). Teaching about Asian women's activism: The poetry of Mila Aguilar. *Women's Studies Quarterly, XVI*(1/2), 23–25.

Christian, B. (1989). But who do you really belong to–Black studies or women's studies? *Women's Studies, 17*, 17–23.

Collins, P. H. (1989). The social construction of Black feminist thought. *Signs: Journal of Women in Culture and Society, 14*, 745–773.

Condry, J. C. (1984). Gender identity and social competence. *Sex Roles, 11*, 485–511.

Cook, E. (1990). Gender and psychological distress. *Journal of Counseling & Development, 68*, 371–375.

Erikson, E. H. (1968). *Identity, youth and crisis.* New York: Norton.

Fine, M. (1987). Silencing in public schools. *Language Arts, 64*, 157–174.

Gibbs, J. T., & Huang, L. N., & Associates. (1989). *Children of color.* San Francisco: Jossey-Bass.

Gollnick, D. M. (1991). *Race, class, and gender in teacher education* (Unpublished manuscript). Washington, DC: National Council for the Accreditation of Teacher Education.

Good, G. E., Gilbert, L. A., & Scher, M. (1990). Gender Aware Therapy: A synthesis of feminist therapy and knowledge about gender. *Journal of Counseling & Development, 68*, 376–380.

Good, G. E., & Mintz, L. B. (1990). Gender role conflict and depression in college men: Evidence for compounded risk. *Journal of Counseling & Development, 69*, 17–21.

Helms, J. E. (1984). Toward a theoretical explanation of the effects of race on counseling: A Black and White model. *The Counseling Psychologist, 12*, 153–165.

Hodgkinson, H. (1985). *All one system: Demographics of education, kindergarten through graduate school.* Washington, DC: Institute for Educational Leadership.

Hoopes, D. S. (1979). Intercultural communication concepts: Psychology of intercultural experience. In M. D. Psych (Ed.), *Multicultural education: A cross cultural training approach.* LaGrange Park, IL: Intercultural Network.

Ibrahim, F. A. (1985). Effective cross-cultural counseling and psychotherapy. *The Counseling Psychologist, 13,* 625638.

Jaynes. G. D., & Williams. R. M., Jr. (1989). *A common destiny: Blacks and American society.* Washington, DC: National Academy Press.

Katz, J. H. (1985). The sociopolitical nature of counseling. *The Counseling Psychologist, 13,* 615–624.

Lee, C. C., & Richardson, B. L. (1991). *Multicultural issues in counseling: New approaches to diversity.* Alexandria, VA: American Association for Counseling and Development.

Leggon, C. B. (1980). Black female professionals: Dilemmas and contradictions of status. In L. Rodgers-Rose (Ed.), *The Black woman* (pp. 189–202). Beverly Hills, CA: Sage.

Lemkau, J. P., & Landau C. (1986). The "selfless syndrome": Assessment and treatment considerations. *Psychotherapy, 23,* 227–233.

McIntosh, P. (1988). *White privilege and male privilege: A personal account of coming to see correspondences through work in women's studies* (Working Paper No. 189). Wellesley, MA: Wellesley College Center for Research on Women.

McIntosh, P. (1990). *Interactive phases of curricular and personal revision with regard to race* (Working Paper No. 219). Wellesley, MA: Wellesley College Center for Research on Women.

Miller, J. B. (1984). The effects of inequality on psychology. In P. P. Rieker & E. H. Carmen (Eds.). *The gender gap in psychotherapy: Social realities and psychological processes* (pp. 45–51). New York: Plenum.

Mintz, L. B., & O'Neil, J. M. (1990). Gender roles, sex, and the process of psychotherapy: Many questions and few answers. *Journal of Counseling & Development, 68,* 381–387.

Pedersen, P. (1988). Ten frequent assumptions of cultural bias in counseling. *Journal of Multicultural Counseling and Development, 15,* 16–24.

Pedersen, P. (1990). The constructs of complexity and balance in multicultural counseling theory and practice. *Journal of Counseling & Development, 68,* 550–554.

Pinderhughes, E. (1989). *Understanding race, ethnicity & power: The key to efficacy in clinical practice.* New York: The Free Press.

Reid, P. T., & Comas-Diaz, L. (1990). Gender and ethnicity: Perspectives on dual status. *Sex Roles, 22,* 397–408.

Renzetti, C. M., & Curan, D. J. (1992). *Women, men, and society.* Boston: Allyn and Bacon.

Scher, M., & Good, G. E. (1990). Gender and counseling in the twenty-first century: What does the future hold? *Journal of Counseling & Development, 68,* 388–391.

Siegel, R. J. (1990). Introduction: Jewish women in therapy: Seen but not heard. *Women and Therapy. 10*(4), 14.

Sue, D. W., & Sue, D. (1990). *Counseling the culturally different: Theory and practice.* New York: Wiley.

True. R. H. (1990). Psychotherapeutic issues with Asian American women. *Sex Roles, 22,* 477–486.

U.S. Department of Commerce, Bureau of the Census. (1990). Poverty in the U.S.: 1990. *Current Population Reports.* Washington, DC: Author.

U.S. Department of Commerce, Bureau of the Census. (1991). *Statistical Abstracts of the United States.* Washington, DC: Author.

Ward. J. V. (1989). Racial identity formation and transformation. In C. Gilligan. N. P. Lyons, & T. J. Hanmer (Eds.), *Making connections: The relational worlds of adolescent girls at Emma Willard school* (pp. 215–232). New York: Troy Press.

Women for Racial and Economic Equality. (1991). *191 facts about women.* New York: Author.

CAN SEPARATE BE EQUAL?

New answers to an old question about race and schools

James Traub

James Traub's book on City College of New York, City on a Hill, *is published by Addison-Wesley.*

Forty years have passed since the U.S. Supreme Court declared, in *Brown v. Board of Education of Topeka, Kansas,* that "in the field of public education the doctrine of 'separate but equal' has no place." No single decision the Court has rendered in this century has produced so profound a social upheaval. Hundreds of lawsuits later, black and white—and sometimes Hispanic—students are being bused back and forth to desegregated schools in Buffalo, Indianapolis, Louisville, St. Louis, Milwaukee, Oklahoma City, Wilmington, Las Vegas. The South, once the stronghold of Jim Crow, is now by far the most desegregated region of the country.

But *Brown* didn't merely launch a thousand buses; by rooting the equality of black Americans in the constitutional guarantee of the equal protection of the law, the decision established civil rights as a fundamental American principle. Six months after the decision, Rosa Parks sat down in the front of a bus in Montgomery, Alabama, and the then-unknown Martin Luther King Jr. led a boycott of the city's buses. It was King, ultimately, who demanded that America make good on *Brown's* promise of simple justice and who ennobled that promise with the language of biblical salvation and the mountaintop vision of racial harmony. What *Brown* ordered was the desegregation of the schools; but what it stands for is the hope of redemption from our original sin of slavery and racism.

Redemption, of course, hasn't come. In the great cities of the Northeast and Midwest, blacks, as well as Hispanics, live in growing isolation and increasing poverty. Desegregation is swiftly becoming a dead letter in places like Milwaukee, where in a generation the schools have gone from mostly white to overwhelmingly minority. The practical barriers to desegregation are in many places so high that the moral clarity promised by *Brown*—a simple choice between segregation and integration, between racism and justice—has blurred.

The new choice, it seems, is between separate but equal and separate but unequal. This has proved to be a welcome state of affairs not only for white suburban parents frightened by the prospect of desegregation but also for black parents and activists who despair of integration or never believed in it in the first place. For them, separate but equal is not the cynical evasion the *Brown* decision sought to eradicate but a rallying cry. Black scholars like Derrick Bell have long pointed out that in *Brown* the Court didn't declare segregation an evil in itself but rather found that segregation conferred an ineradicable stigma of inferiority on black children. Now Bell and many others look on this claim as condescending and even racist. The spokesmen for all-black "academies," which have been instituted or discussed in Miami, New York, Milwaukee, Detroit, and elsewhere, insist that separation is a precondition for black self-esteem, and many blacks now look upon integration as a white plot to undermine racial pride. So desegregation, having lost its momentum, has lost its chief constituency and beneficiary class as well.

This new separate-but-equal model is disturbing for those, like me, who grew up listening to Martin Luther King and who found in the redemptive language of the civil-rights movement a virtual substitute for religious belief. It isn't only a way of schooling that's being repudiated; it's a way of living: to accept the new ideology of separatism is to accept as well the growing obsession with racial and ethnic identity, and the assumption that each group has its own truths, its own values, even its own version of history. Desegregation has proved to be so agonizing and so impractical that it now seems almost perverse to resist the suggestion that, say, we lavish funds on ghetto schools and let them develop on their own. But it is a bargain we may live to regret.

The desegregation battle is being waged in a surprising number of places. Earlier this year I paid a series of visits to Hartford, Connecticut, a city that has been struggling to improve the dismal performance of its school system (in April, in what seemed a gesture of despair, the school board announced it was considering bringing in a private company,

Education Alternatives, to run the city's schools) and is currently facing perhaps the most ambitious desegregation lawsuit filed in recent years, *Sheff v. O'Neill.* Hartford has a virtually all-minority school system, surrounded by the virtually all-white systems of the suburbs, but *Sheff* is, pointedly, not about race but about isolation, and about the overwhelming poverty of the inner city. The decision in the case, filed in state rather than in federal court, is expected sometime later this year. A victory for the plaintiffs would fill Hartford's suburbs with fear and trembling, but it might also offer a new way to think about desegregation.

On a cold morning this past February, Don Carso, principal of the McDonough Elementary School in Hartford, stood outside the dilapidated red-brick pile of his school, greeting parents as they arrived with their children. Carso is a bespectacled middle-aged white man with thinning hair and a thickening waistline. It is his habit every morning to remain outside until he has saluted every last parent. McDonough is 78 percent Hispanic, 14 percent black, and almost all poor. Carso hallooed a number of fathers in sweatshirts who looked him over with sullen glares as they climbed back into their cars. "I treat them all like lawyers and doctors," Carso said, waving a cup of tepid coffee. "Most of them come around eventually."

Carso is the kind of principal pictured in the "effective schools" literature. He's omnipresent and indefatigable, he settles fights with Solomonic compromise, and he puts learning ahead of everything else. He treats McDonough like a sanctuary from the surrounding gloom. And it is—up to a point.

Construction of McDonough began in 1897; portions of the building can be mistaken for a museum exhibition of nineteenth-century urban-school design. The cafeteria, in which 800 children are expected to eat breakfast and lunch—both provided free to almost all of the children, owing to the poverty of the students—is a basement classroom furnished with a half-dozen folding tables; sunlight barely flickers in through two windows. The boys' bathroom, next door, is a dim, high chamber. Instead of sinks it has a single long trough fitted with trumpet-shaped spigots. Only a few of the toilets have doors. The school generally runs out of toilet paper before the end of the year, and Carso has had to borrow money from another school to keep his own supplied. McDonough is so overcrowded that nearly 200 children attend classes in trailers, known as "portables," set up on what used to be the playground. Another couple hundred students go to school in another building a few blocks away, the former Moylan School, which is just as old and decrepit as McDonough.

McDonough's condition, like the condition of elementary schools throughout Hartford's slums, is shameful—an example of the sort of "savage inequalities" that crusading writer Jonathan Kozol described in his book of the same name. But it only takes money to address physical neglect, and money can be a surprisingly elastic commodity. Thanks to a $205 million city bond issue, for which Carso helped drum up support, McDonough will have a new structure by 1997; Moylan, too, will be rebuilt and rechristened as a separate institution. McDonough will have an auditorium, a gym, and a cafeteria. Carso says he will make sure that his kids have just as many computers as the kids in Hartford's fancy suburbs. And he will then have a deeply troubled school in a pristine setting.

McDonough's Hispanic students, most of them Puerto Rican, tend to be recent arrivals whose parents speak little or no English. The families are nomadic, shuttling around Hartford's slums in search of an affordable apartment. Almost every morning, two or three or four kids show up at McDonough's door, standing shyly with an equally shy parent and often a friend or relative to translate; and as they arrive, other kids simply disappear. And yet, for all their mobility the children are so isolated by their families' poverty and lack of English that they might as well be living in an Appalachian hollow. After Carso finally agreed to leave the frozen tundra that was his school's front yard, we walked into the main building and ducked into a first-grade bilingual class. The kids were sitting in a circle, singing in Spanish. The teacher, Delia Bello, came over to see us while her pupils, obviously well-drilled, talked quietly to one another. Bello said that she never ceased to be amazed by how little contact the kids had with the world. "You show them some place on the map," she said, "and they say, 'It's Hartford,' Even Russia—'It's Hartford.' And it's the same with the sixth-graders. If you talk about going to the mall, they've never been to the mall. And if you talk about college, they'll say, 'What's college? I don't know anyone who's been to college.' "

By the time we got downstairs to his pocket-sized office, Carso had to make a call to Moylan. He rushed over to the phone and, still standing in front of his desk, said, "Is she okay? Has he been drinking again?" Connie's stepfather had pulled a knife on her mother and then cut the phone cord when she tried to call 911. Connie, a sixth-grader, had told the social worker at school, who suddenly realized why the girl's work had been deteriorating in recent weeks. Carso put down the phone and said, "It's not like they don't have these problems in the suburbs, too. But you can deal with it if it's isolated." He cupped his fingertips together into a globe. "In *this* world," he said, "we're very successful. But we can't control all the stuff on the outside."

"The solution isn't in the city; maybe it's in the state," Carso says. "We are saying to our neighbors, 'Take ownership of our problem' "

A few months earlier, a janitor had been chased off a snow blower and shot behind Moylan; apparently he was a gang member. Even the violence and the degraded physical setting mattered less than the children's isolation, their immersion in a dead-end world. McDonough wasn't altering the dismal trajectory these children had been handed at birth; not enough, anyway. On Connecticut's statewide reading test, 72 percent of the school's graduating sixth-graders had scored at the remedial level. In the normal course of things, they would fall farther and farther behind, just as the great majority of Hartford's public-school children would. As Carso said, "We have hundreds of little interventions going on in our school; but they're not going to produce fundamental change."

A year earlier Carso had, after much agonizing, testified for the plaintiffs in *Sheff v. O'Neill*. Carso's testimony did not make him very popular in his suburban neighborhood, where the case raises the specter of forced busing. "It wasn't even popular in my own family," he says, rolling his eyes behind thick glasses. Carso knows how deep is the hostility to mandatory desegregation; but he also believes that his kids have to be pried loose from their environment. He even thinks there's something to the idea of simply evacuating Hartford's public schools, though he also knows that inner-city parents will bridle at the insult of one-way desegregation. Carso considers separate but equal, or even separate but more than equal, a colossal mistake; for all that he believes in his school, he doesn't see how it can overcome the world beyond his fingertip globe. "The solution," he says, sitting in his tiny office during a brief moment of calm, "isn't in the city. Maybe it's in the state." Above all, Carso thinks, the solution has to lie with the wealthy suburbs that surround Hartford. "We are," he says, striking almost a pleading note, "saying to our neighbors: 'Take ownership of our problem.'"

The desegregation premise handed down from *Brown*, the premise of the stigma of inferiority, has always contained an insulting inference for many blacks. As Dr. Eddie Davis, the principal of predominantly black Weaver High School in Hartford, says, "It would be a total slap in the face to say that education can only happen in the suburban schools." Davis testified for the plaintiffs in *Sheff*, but only because, as he said, "Wherever white children [are], there are resources." Davis would be just as happy to have the resources in a segregated environment; he doesn't see isolation as a problem. And nowadays, resources do not, in fact, follow white children as they once did. Derrick Bell has argued that the great achievement of *Brown* was to make "it possible for black parents to gain an equal educational opportunity for their children wherever those children attended school."

The declining prestige of integrationism among blacks and the rise of new and sometimes virulent forms of ethnocentrism have a good deal to do with the growing acceptance of a new separate-but-equal model, but so does the hopefulness of an Eddie Davis. Davis considers himself a disciple of the "effective schools" movement, and it was the late Ronald Edmonds, a black education scholar generally considered one of the founders of the movement, who first formulated a serious pedagogic argument for the irrelevance of desegregation. Edmonds took umbrage, as he wrote in 1978, at "the conventional liberal wisdom which said that the educational salvation of black children depended on integration." A well-run school could overcome whatever disadvantages children brought with them. There was no sound reason, Edmonds concluded, to stand in the way of the many black parents who preferred "racially distinct" schools for their children.

Edmonds's precepts have been institutionalized in groups like Theodore Sizer's Coalition of Essential Schools, which takes the demographic makeup of the schools for granted and tries to infuse those schools with the values and culture that are correlated with academic success. Weaver High School, for example, works with Sizer's group, and Dr. Davis has overseen a restructuring of his ninth- and tenth-grade classes. What really matters, Davis insists, is not race or even resources but academic rigor, high expectations, strong leadership, a willingness to experiment. But when I asked Davis how much academic improvement he had seen after five years of reform, he said that there hadn't been any yet. By the time kids reached ninth grade, he admitted, it was too late. In fact, Weaver wasn't altering trajectories any more than McDonough was. The students were scoring 150 points below the state average on the SATs. Perhaps no more than 20 percent of entering ninth-graders would ultimately go on to four-year colleges.

Separate but equal may offer a salve to black pride and a comfort to white suburbanites; but there's not much proof that it works. In *The Closing Door*, Gary Orfield, a standard-bearer of white liberal integrationism, and co-author Carole Ashkinaze analyze the effects of the 1980 decision known as the Atlanta Compromise, in which that city's largely white power structure agreed to black control over the schools in exchange for an end to litigation that would have mandated desegregation throughout the metropolitan area. Here was separate but equal in laboratory form, presided over by a new black superintendent who had a national reputation as an educational reformer. Said former Atlanta mayor Andrew Young, "It was really the integration of the money to provide a quality education for all children that was black folks' goal. Racial balance was a means for achieving the goal." But despite an initial promise of success, Orfield concludes, "Huge numbers of children flunked grades and became more likely to drop out before completing high school," while "whites and middle-class blacks abandoned the city system in droves." Poor black students, in other words, were more isolated and even more deeply cut off from the opportunity to develop, than they had been before.

What happens when city schools reach funding parity with suburbs and poor kids still ride a conveyor belt to a second-class life?

Atlanta wasn't the only place where the resources, rather than the children, were desegregated. Over the last decade or so, old-style desegregation litigation has largely given way to suits seeking equal funding for poor and rich districts. Connecticut, in fact, became one of the first states to engage in tax "equalization" as a result of a 1977 case, *Horton v. Meskill*. Thirty-six states either have agreed to equalize spending or are facing litigation that would compel them to do so. As with the Atlanta Compromise, the Connecticut measure essentially allows white suburbanites to pay a modest tax in order to keep racial lines intact. Michigan's Republican governor recently supported a move by the state legislature to equalize school funding by substituting the state sales tax for the local property tax as the source of school funding, creating a separate-but-equal status quo.

But what happens when inner-city schools reach funding parity with the suburbs and the poor kids are still riding a conveyor belt to a second-class life? This is where Hartford and *Sheff v. O'Neill* comes in.

Hartford was, for many generations, a flourishing medium-sized Yankee city. It had a fine old museum, a fine old library, a riverfront, and the headquarters of several of America's largest insurance companies. Today you can spend half an hour staring at the great Trumbull tableaux of the Revolutionary War hanging in the Wadsworth Athenaeum without encountering another soul—not even a guard. You can walk down the center of a downtown avenue at 9:00 P.M. with little fear of bodily harm, at least from a car. The insurance companies are still there, but the people who work in them live in the suburbs. Like many of the old cities of the Northeast and Midwest, Hartford peaked in size soon after World War II, as first blacks from the South, then Puerto Ricans, then Caribbeans, mostly from Jamaica, flooded into the city from the orchards and the tobacco fields of the Connecticut Valley. (The local leaf is used largely to wrap cigars.) Thereafter the city lost tens of thousands of middle-class and working-class white families. Hartford's population of 140,000 is now 69 percent non-white. Hartford is, incredibly, one of the ten poorest cities in America. Connecticut's two other major cities, New Haven and Bridgeport, are among the poorest twenty. And yet Connecticut has the highest per-capita income in the United States.

It doesn't seem so very farfetched to expect the suburbs, whose wealth depends upon Hartford, to "take ownership" of some of its problems. The suggestion, in fact, has been made before. In 1965, a study team from Harvard recommended a system of "metropolitan cooperation," in which every suburban school would agree to take two students from one of Hartford's "poverty areas" into each of its classrooms. By 1974, according to the plan, the suburbs would accommodate 6,000 inner-city students, one-fifth of the city's total student population. The idea was not to desegregate the schools. At the time, Hartford's schools were almost perfectly balanced between white and non-white students. The Harvard plan, in fact, was "directed primarily to the amelioration of the effects of poverty on education," as the authors wrote. What mattered about the students in the poverty areas was not so much that they were black or Puerto Rican as that they were poor, and living in dense concentration.

The plan, though designed to be modest, wasn't modest enough; the state legislature ultimately authorized a program known as Project Concern, which never sent more than 1,300 inner-city kids to the suburbs in a year. (The number now hovers around 650.) And the opportunity for real change was quickly past. With an unexpected increase in Puerto Rican immigration, and the continuing departure of whites to the suburbs and to parochial schools, the gulf between the Hartford schools and the suburban schools—and between the city and the suburbs—widened all the more. Five years after the Harvard

report, the Hartford schools were 67 percent non-white. Hartford itself was a "poverty area."

By the late 1980s, Connecticut, despite its reputation as a pasturage of the white upper-middle class, had become a powerful symbol of the Johnson-era Kerner Commission's "two nations." The state's three largest cities were well on their way to becoming mass ghettos. The next largest cities—Waterbury and Stamford—were becoming poorer and more black. In 1988, Gerald Tirozzi, then-state commissioner of education, issued an impassioned report calling school segregation "educationally, morally and legally wrong." Tirozzi's language was unabashedly, and perhaps naively, idealistic. He called on the state to initiate a desegregation planning process based on the principle of "collective responsibility"—New England communitarianism for an expanded community. Tirozzi also had the monumental incaution to suggest that the State Board of Education "be empowered to impose a mandatory desegregation plan" should the voluntary plan fail.

The moment the report appeared, Tirozzi later testified, "all hell broke loose." One state legislator called for his resignation. As Tirozzi toured the state, pleading his case, he discovered that "the very word 'mandate' conjures up a feeling between and among citizens, parents, teachers that really is very negative." Tirozzi, in short, was all but tarred and feathered. Governor William O'Neill strongly objected to mandatory solutions, and in a follow-up report the next year, Tirozzi proposed a series of voluntary measures; even the word "desegregation" was stricken from the document. Tirozzi had run up against the hard kernel of resistance to a social policy that required a serious degree of sacrifice from non-beneficiaries. That was why desegregation has always required court orders.

By openly indicting desegregation, however, Tirozzi's report persuaded a group of lawyers from the ACLU, the NAACP Legal Defense and Education Fund, and several other groups that the time was ripe to file a long-discussed class-action lawsuit. From the beginning, *Sheff v. O'Neill* was a state rather than a federal case, for the simple reason that the Supreme Court had long since foreclosed the sort of remedy the Tirozzi report had proposed. In 1974, the Court had declared, in *Milliken v. Bradley,* that Detroit suburbs could not be compelled to pool their students with the city's without a finding of segregative intent—a finding, for example, that the suburban schools had been set up to permit whites to elude integrated city schools. This effectively meant that the Court would not disturb the single most powerful impediment to further desegregation— the demographic forces that were rapidly dividing America's metropolitan areas, including Hartford, Bridgeport, and New Haven, into poor black inner cities and middle-class white suburbs. But the Connecticut constitution, like that of many states, includes guarantees of "equal" and "adequate" education for all citizens; in fact, Connecticut is unusual in that it guarantees non-segregated as well as non-discriminatory education.

Sheff represents a new generation of litigation not only because it's been brought in state court but because it does not turn on the dynamics of race and racism. The Hartford schools are now equally divided between black and Hispanic students, and *Sheff* does not argue that either group is the victim of historic discrimination. John Brittain, a University of Connecticut Law School professor and a member of the plaintiffs' team, says, "The most signal fact about Hartford is not that it's 92 percent non-white but that it's 63 percent poor." *Sheff* is about poverty, not race; it argues that poor children need access to a non-poor educational environment, rather than that black children need access to a racially integrated environment.

The trial was held in late 1992 and early 1993; post-trial hearings continued for another year. The two sides called on so many of the leading scholars in the field that the case, in effect, recapitulated the debate over desegregation, in which scarcely anything seems to get definitively settled despite staggering research. Much of the testimony detailed the stunning disparity between city and suburb. Hartford's schools are 92.1 percent non-white; the suburban districts are 92.6 percent white. In Hartford, 65 percent of the children under the age of eighteen come from single-parent households; 41 percent of parents have not graduated from high school. In Glastonbury, a nearby suburb, the figures were 14 percent and 9 percent. And socio-economic status dictates performance: About two-fifths of Hartford students drop out before finishing high school and only 30 percent of graduates go on to attend four-year colleges. At Glastonbury High School, the dropout rate is about 1 percent, and more than half go on to a four-year college.

---

*"Even parts of their body they didn't know,"
Hernandez testified. "They didn't know their
underclothing, what it was called"*

Some of the trial testimony was so piercing that people wept in the courtroom. Gladys Hernandez, who taught at an elementary school called Barnard-Brown, spoke of the school's grimed-over plastic windows and recalled that in twenty-three years she could never get the proper writing paper for her students. Most of the children, Hernandez said, were Puerto Rican, and spoke neither Spanish nor English properly. "They called everything a 'thing,' " she testified. "Even parts of their body they didn't know. They didn't know their underclothing, what it was called. If they had a grandparent, they didn't know that they were a grandson or a granddaughter." Once a year, Hernandez said, the school permitted her to take the children on a trip, to a zoo or a farm. "The most extraordinary thing happened when they came to the river," she testified. "They all stood up in a group and applauded and cheered, and I was aware they were giving the river a standing ovation. And they were so happy to see the beauty of the river, something that most of us go back and forth [across] and never take time to look at."

The plaintiff's expert witnesses argued that desegregation made a measurable difference in academic outcomes. Dr. Robert Crain, of Columbia University Teachers College, testified that school desegregation is correlated with later involvement in integrated colleges, neighborhoods, and workplaces. Students in Project Concern, he found, were much more likely to graduate from high school, and more likely to complete

several years of college, than were students who stayed in Hartford schools. Mary Kennedy, director of the National Center for Research on Teacher Training, cited a study of federal survey data showing that poor children in schools with high concentrations of impoverished children were twice as likely to score below the national average as poor children in low-concentration schools; the effect on non-poor students was even more pronounced. Gary Orfield cited a number of studies that showed similar effects for both black and Hispanic students. A study he conducted in San Francisco found that additional spending on the schools produced no positive effect, and possibly even a negative effect, on outcomes, whereas low-income Hispanic students who transferred to middle-class white schools did better than those who stayed behind.

There's a strikingly conservative conclusion to be drawn from the irreproachably liberal Orfield's claim: It is values and culture, not resources, that determine academic outcomes, and middle-class children bring with them to school values that produce success—self-discipline, a faith in institutions and their rules, and, above all, an expectation of success itself. Poor kids, by contrast, often reach school with the cognitive problems that come from having poorly educated or disengaged or preoccupied parents as well as with the assumptions appropriate to their experience. It wasn't only that Don Carso's students hadn't been to the mall or seen a river; they lived in a world in which middle-class success was virtually unimaginable. Eddie Davis would say that the cure for these harmful and limiting values lies in the culture of the school itself. But Carso's reluctant response was that even a well-run school cannot be impervious to the baleful influences of the world outside. And the concentration-of-poverty argument implies that all students suffer in a school where a large number of them are deeply disadvantaged.

But, of course, the inner-city children who go to a middle-class school during the day go home to their world of troubles at night. If McDonough can't shelter Connie from the effects of her chaotic home life, then is it reasonable to expect a suburban school to do much better? The defense in *Sheff* argued that neither Orfield's San Francisco study nor Project Concern showed any real correlation between desegregation and achievement, and it cited one respected study that concluded that "recent research has not lent credence" to the proposition that minority children are likely to be "influenced by their middle class peers' stronger orientation toward achievement." The state also relied heavily on the work of David Armor, a scholar who has carved out a perennial place for himself in desegregation cases by arguing that virtually all variation in academic outcome is determined by socioeconomic status. "A good strategy for improving the academic performance of students is to improve their socioeconomic conditions," Armor testified, adding that schools, of course, could not do much in that department.

Armor has been denounced as a hired gun, and his research may be questionable; but it is undeniable that neither desegregation nor school reform, nor financing, nor any intervention, weighs very heavily in determining academic outcomes compared with a student's socioeconomic status. Even so pervasive an institution as school is less influential than a child's home and family environment. Acknowledging this truth, however, doesn't make school irrelevant; what it does mean is that the way you think about school must be linked to a larger design to uproot inner-city poverty. If it's true that what makes contemporary urban poverty so intractable is what Orfield calls "the self-perpetuating cycle of racial isolation," then the larger design must involve breaking that cycle. Certainly that's the way Don Carso or Gladys Hernandez would formulate the problem. And if you accept this finding—that racial isolation and academic underachievement and poverty are inseparable—you conclude that although desegregation is only a partial solution, separate but equal is no solution at all.

The Hopewell School, in Glastonbury, is an idyllic place, set on sprawling fields that abut a seventeen-acre nature center. The classrooms are rich with computer power. Oddly enough, though, the Glastonbury schools actually spend slightly less money per capita than the Hartford schools. Much of Hartford's money, it's true, goes to security and special-ed and bilingual classes, rather than to teachers and textbooks. But Peter Maluk, Hopewell's principal, was not shedding crocodile tears when he took me on a tour of the school and pointed out all the things that Clark, his "sister" school in Hartford's slums, had and he didn't—a big library, an auditorium, a cafeteria.

The shortage of space obviously wasn't proving crippling. On the statewide math exam, 1 percent of Maluk's fourth-graders had scored in the remedial range; 89 percent had registered "excellent." His students did only a little bit worse in writing and reading. But Hopewell was not a more "effective" school than McDonough. The kids in Glastonbury were simply replicating their parents' success, as the kids in Hartford were on their way to replicating their parents' failure.

Maluk fetched a sigh and said, "There's a sense of hopelessness at times about how you reach a conclusion that works"

Peter Maluk is not unconscious of his good fortune and of the misery next door, but thinking about it makes him gloomy and fearful. He is a big man, slightly ponderous, with watery eyes. "Anything that's going to be forced is going to cause a lot of agitation," he said. He mentioned Boston; everyone in Glastonbury talked about Boston, which was only 100 miles away and whose mid-Seventies agony over forced busing had not faded from memory. When he talks about Hartford, the first thing that comes to his mind is "the gangs and the drive-by shootings." And this phrase, too, was used so often in Glastonbury that it might as well have been a single word with dashes in it. Many of these people work in Hartford, but from the way they talked about it the city might as well have been the nightmarish setting of *Blade Runner*. Maluk agrees that the kids in Hartford deserve something better; in fact, he said, he often found himself thinking of a half-serious suggestion he recalled William Buckley making in the late Sixties to the effect that poor children be

taken from their parents and placed in a more salubrious setting. But coercing the inner-city parents didn't seem like a much better idea than coercing the suburbs. Maluk fetched a sigh and said, "There's a sense of hopelessness at times about how you reach a conclusion that works."

One of Hopewell's fifth-grade teachers, Clara Dudley, who had helped forge the sister-school relationship with Clark, told me the kids from the two schools had recently had to meet at neutral locations, since many of the parents of Hopewell students were simply too freaked out by the non-stop accounts of gang violence and drive-by shootings. Even the year before, Dudley said, parents had written letters saying things like, "You warrant that the bus will drive to the front door of the school, that the children will proceed directly from the bus into the school . . ." Dudley shook her head at the pusillanimity. It was true, she admitted, that a little girl had been "abducted" across the street from the school; but the bus "always parks on the school side of the street." That must have soothed a lot of parental concern.

Glastonbury has been somewhat more willing to welcome the huddled masses of Hartford than it has been to join them. The town was one of the earliest recipients of students from Project Concern. Now there are some sixty students—from elementary through high school—attending Glastonbury schools through the program. Two Project Concern students I spoke to, both high school seniors, said that they had never experienced any racial tension at school. Other students, though, had objected when the drama club mounted a production of *Peter Pan* and all the Native Americans turned out to be African Americans. The superintendent had agreed that *Peter Pan* wasn't really an appropriate play, what with all the stereotypes.

Faced with the reality that suburban parents won't send their children to the inner city, frustrated proponents of desegregation, like Gerald Tirozzi or Don Carso, often suggest, half-seriously, that Hartford's schools, or even Hartford itself, simply be evacuated; the overwhelming imperative to free children from an imprisoning environment lends an air of plausibility even to such doomsday scenarios. A less drastic solution would be an updated form of the 1965 Harvard plan, in which thousands of Hartford students would be dispersed to the suburbs while some modest combination of suburban and inner-city students would attend urban magnet schools. This kind of one-way desegregation plan—desegregation as dispersal—has become fairly common in recent years; St. Louis, for example, has just such a system.

Such solutions don't meet the test of ideological purity. Charles Willie, a scholar who helped craft Boston's desegregation plan, has denounced one-way plans, such as that in St. Louis, as evidence of "goal displacement," in which the goal of least offensive to whites replaces that of most helpful to blacks. Why should whites, the historical beneficiary of the oppression of blacks, benefit once again from unequally shared burdens? But that raises the question of what desegregation is *for*. Is desegregation about redress, about righting ancient wrongs? If so, where does that leave Hartford's Puerto Rican immigrants or, for that matter, its Jamaicans? And what about the middle-class black suburbanites in a place like Prince Georges County, in Maryland, who see no point in traversing the area to integrate a school with middle-class whites? But if desegregation is understood, alternatively, as a means to pierce the thick walls of isolation that perpetuate inner-city poverty, then a largely one-way system isn't racist at all, though the burden may not be shared equally.

In his State of the State speech in January 1993, Governor Lowell Weicker made a startling admission: "The racial and economic isolation in Connecticut's school system is indisputable. Whether this segregation came about through the chance of historical boundaries or economic forces beyond the control of the state or whether it came about through private decisions or in spite of the best educational efforts of the state, what matters is that it is here and must be dealt with." According to Gerald Tirozzi, Weicker had initially thought of admitting the state's guilt in *Sheff v. O'Neill*. In the end, he backed off, granting the justice of the complaint while excusing the state from actual culpability. Weicker proposed that the state do voluntarily what it might otherwise be compelled to do at the end of the judicial sword. He suggested that the state be divided into regions, and that each of these regions initiate a planning process that would result in the satisfaction of numerical goals for desegregation. It was an amazingly bold proposal; however, by the time the state legislature got through with it, the numerical goals were gone, as was the very word "desegregation."

I attended a few of the early meetings of the local advisory committees that form the base of Connecticut's voluntary process; they did not inspire hope. The Glastonbury committee, rather than devising means of bringing more minority students to the town's schools, or more minority families to the town itself, was engaged in an honest liberal dither over the supposed instances of racism, like *Peter Pan,* that made the schools inhospitable to the few minority students already there. The Hartford committee, rather than pondering the means of access to the suburban schools, was drawing up a mock-epic listing of the city's attractions, the lures with which it would snare suburban students—the parks, the symphony, the river, the municipal golf courses, "the video collection in the public library," the "fire safety company." By the end of the evening they were touting "the only methadone program in the region." It was a perfect proof of the futility of voluntary solutions, but they were doing precisely what the legislation had proposed. Even people in and around Hartford who fear the stiff goad of judicial decree generally expect the voluntary process to be a colossal waste of time.

Connecticut, then, is unlikely to desegregate of its own free will. The best that can be hoped is that should Judge Harry Hammer find for the plaintiffs in *Sheff,* he will craft a remedy with an eye to maximizing minority access to suburban schools, rather than sheer mathematical equality. In fact, John Brittain, the law professor who has worked for the plaintiffs, suggests a remedy in which up to one quarter of Hartford's students would be dispersed to the suburbs while the state would fund the construction of ten new magnet schools located in desirable sites in Hartford, including the Trinity College campus and a site near Aetna's downtown headquarters. Even then, said

Brittain, "racially identifiable" schools, both white and non-white, would remain. If this is too much collective responsibility to ask the suburbs to accept, then there's probably not much hope for desegregation.

One just criticism of mandatory-desegregation remedies is that they treat the symptom but not the disease; school desegregation, that is, has not produced residential desegregation. Blacks (and, to a lesser extent, Hispanics) are more intensely segregated than any American ethnic group has ever been, inhabiting a parallel, and very unequal, world of their own. Describing Atlanta, Gary Orfield wrote that housing patterns "defined separate educational, social and economic worlds in which young people and their families had profoundly different sets of opportunities." Orfield has little to say about the self-destructive character of ghetto life, but perhaps what is usually described as "the culture of poverty" is, in fact, "the culture of isolation."

It is vain to expect schooling by itself to cure the pathologies of the inner city. Ghetto families need access to a middle-class setting even more than their children need access to a middle-class school. The peculiar American model of the impoverished central city ringed by prosperous suburbs not only isolates the urban poor in an abandoned world but ensures that the suburbanite will feel no sense of common destiny with the city-dweller; and, of course, it denies the city access to the resources of the white-collar class that it nourishes. In a new book, *Cities Without Suburbs,* David Rusk argues that the isolation and "hyperconcentration" of the poor in our great and growing urban ghettos create conditions that are impervious to reform and that ensure further ghettoization. The old cities of the Northeast and Midwest, Rusk says, cannot save themselves through such forms of internal development as enterprise zones, school reform, and so on. "In baldest terms," he concludes, "sustained success requires moving poor people from bad city neighborhoods to good suburban neighborhoods and moving dollars from wealthy suburban governments to poorer city governments."

Separate but equal proposes to build on isolation as a source of strength; that claim sounds like an admission of defeat

---

Rusk's neo-integrationism will have to make its way in a hostile world. Many blacks now speak with an almost perverse longing of the good old days of legal apartheid, when the black community was, perforce, self-reliant and self-governing. It was also, of course, supremely unequal; and it tries the imagination to suppose that, with a fairer distribution of resources, inner-city Hartford and our innumerable other ghettos would rediscover their capacity for self-reliance. Separate but equal proposes to build on isolation, to accept it as a source of strength and solidarity. That claim, no matter how it is phrased, sounds like an admission of defeat.

And desegregation scarcely has a constituency at all among whites. Even liberals schooled on the struggle for civil rights have retreated in the face of black separatism; and the sort of "social engineering" epitomized by busing has fallen deeply out of fashion. In fact, the Democratic agenda on urban poverty has been borrowed in large part from neo-conservatives like Charles Murray, who insists that the only civil right that counts is access to the marketplace, and conservative educators like William Bennett, who believes that an infusing of character, of standards and self-discipline, is enough to save inner-city schools.

But what does all this talk about personal values, whether from the left or the right of the separate-but-equal spectrum, have to do with the children in Don Carso's class? It is not their fault that they arrive at McDonough already a year or two behind the children at Hopewell; and it's not McDonough's fault that they leave the school just as far behind, or worse. Even with more rigorous schooling and more computers, or more racial and ethnic solidarity, McDonough will not cure what ails these students. If equal opportunity means anything for these children and for others like them throughout urban America, it must mean access to a different environment.

In the forty years since *Brown,* desegregation has not become irrelevant. But the *idea* of desegregation has been shaken by a crisis of faith, and by a contraction of sympathies. A teacher at McDonough, surveying the farcical deliberations of Connecticut's voluntary process, says sadly, "There's not enough good will to go around." The remark has an ominous ring of truth.

MULTICULTURALISM AND INDIVIDUALISM

Michael Walzer

Two powerful centrifugal forces are at work in the United States today. One breaks loose whole groups of people from a presumptively common center; the other sends individuals flying off. Both these decentering, separatist movements have their critics, who argue that the first is driven by a narrow-minded chauvinism and the second by mere selfishness. The separated groups appear to these critics as exclusive and intolerant tribes, the separated individuals as rootless and lonely egotists. Neither of these views is entirely wrong; neither is quite right. The two movements have to be considered together, set against the background of a democratic politics that opens a lot of room for centrifugal force. Understood in context, the two seem to me, despite the laws of physics, each one the other's remedy.

The first of these forces is an increasingly strong articulation of group difference. It's the articulation that is new, obviously, since

difference itself—pluralism, even multiculturalism—has been a feature of American life from very early on. John Jay, in one of the *Federalist Papers*, describes the Americans as a people "descended from the same ancestors, speaking the same language, professing the same religion, attached to the same principles of government, very similar in manners and customs."

These lines were already inaccurate when Jay wrote them in the 1780s; they were utterly falsified in the course of the nineteenth century. Mass immigration turned the United States into a land of many different ancestors, languages, religions, manners, and customs. Principles of government are our only stable and common commitment. Democracy fixes the limits and sets the ground rules for American pluralism.

Two contrasts can help us grasp the radical character of this pluralism. Consider, first, the (relative) homogeneity of countries like France, Holland, Norway, Germany, Japan, and China, where, whatever regional differences exist, the great majority of the citizens share a single ethnic identity and celebrate a common history. And consider, second, the territorially based heterogeneity of the old multinational empires (the Soviet Union was the last of these) and of states like the former Yugoslavia, the former Ethiopia, the new Russia, Nigeria, Iraq, India, and so on, where a number of ethnic and religious minorities claim ancient homelands (even if the boundaries are always in dispute). The United States differs from both these sets of countries: it isn't homogeneous nationally or locally; it's heterogeneous everywhere—a land of dispersed diversity, which is (except for the remaining Native Americans) no one's homeland. Of course, there are local patterns of segregation, voluntary and involuntary; there are ethnic neighborhoods and places inexactly but evocatively called "ghettoes." But none of our groups, with the partial and temporary exception of the Mormons in Utah, has ever achieved anything like stable geographical predominance. There is no American Slovenia or Quebec or Kurdistan. Even in the most protected American environments, we all experience difference every day.

And yet the full-scale and fervent articulation of difference is a fairly recent phenomenon. A long history of prejudice, subordination, and fear worked against any public affirmation of minority "manners and customs" and so served to conceal the radical character of American pluralism. I want to be very clear about this history. At its extremes it was brutal, as conquered Native Americans and transported black slaves can testify; at its center, with regard to religion and ethnicity rather than race, it was relatively benign. An immigrant society welcomed new immigrants or, at least, made room for them, with a degree of reluctance and resistance considerably below the standards set elsewhere. Nonetheless, all our minorities learned to be quiet: timidity has been the mark of minority politics until very recent times.

I remember, for example, how in the 1930s and 1940s any sign of Jewish assertiveness— even the appearance of "too many" Jewish names among New Deal Democrats or CIO organizers or socialist or communist intellectuals—was greeted among Jews with a collective shudder. The communal elders said, "Sha!" Don't make noise; don't attract attention; don't push yourself forward; don't say anything provocative. They thought of themselves as

guests in this country long after they had become citizens.

Today all that is, as they say, history. The United States in the 1990s is socially, though not economically (and the contrast is especially striking after the Reagan years), a more egalitarian place than it was fifty or sixty years ago. No one is shushing us anymore; no one is intimidated or quiet. Old racial and religious identities have taken on greater prominence in our public life; gender and sexual preference have been added to the mix; and the current wave of immigration from Asia and Latin America makes for significant new differences among American citizens and potential citizens. And all this is expressed, so it seems, all the time. The voices are loud, the accents various, and the result is not harmony—as in the old image of pluralism as a symphony, each group playing its own instrument (but who wrote the music?)—but a jangling discord. It is very much like the dissidence of Protestant dissent in the early years of the Reformation: many sects, dividing and subdividing; many prophets and would-be prophets, all talking at once.

In response to this cacophony, another group of prophets, liberal and neoconservative intellectuals, academics, and journalists, wring their hands and assure us that the country is falling apart, that our fiercely articulated multiculturalism is dangerously divisive, and that we desperately need to reassert the hegemony of a single culture. Curiously, this supposedly necessary and necessarily singular culture is often described as a high culture, as if it is our shared commitment to Shakespeare, Dickens, and James Joyce that has been holding us together all these years. (But surely high culture divides us, as it always has—and probably always will in any country with a strong egalitarian and populist strain. Does anyone remember Richard Hofstadter's *Anti-Intellectualism in American Life*?) Democratic politics seems to me a more likely resource than the literary or philosophical canon. We need to think about how this resource might usefully be deployed.

But isn't it already deployed—given that multicultural conflicts take place in the democratic arena and require of their protagonists a wide range of characteristically democratic skills and performances? If one studies the history of ethnic, racial, and religious associations in the United States, one sees, I think, that these have served again and again as vehicles of individual and group integration—despite (or, perhaps, because of) the political conflicts they generated. Even if the aim of associational life is to sustain difference, that aim has to be achieved *here*, under American conditions, and the result is commonly a new and unintended kind of differentiation—of American Catholics and Jews, say, not so much from one another or from the Protestant majority as from Catholics and Jews in other countries. Minority groups adapt themselves to the local political culture. And if their primary aim is self-defense, toleration, civil rights, a place in the sun, the result of success is more clearly still an Americanization of whatever differences are being defended. That doesn't mean that differences are defended quietly—quietness is not one of our political conventions. Becoming an American means learning not to be quiet. Nor is the success that is sought by one group always compatible with the success of all (or any of) the others. The conflicts are real, and even small-scale victories are often widely threatening.

The greater difficulties, however, come from failure, especially reiterated failure. It is associational weakness, and the anxieties and resentments it breeds, that pull people apart in dangerous ways. Leonard Jeffries's African-American Studies Department at the City College of New York is hardly an example of institutional strength. The noisiest groups in our contemporary cacophony and the groups that make the most extreme demands are also the weakest. In American cities today, poor people, mostly members of minority groups, find it difficult to work together in any coherent way. Mutual assistance, cultural preservation, and self-defense are loudly affirmed but ineffectively enacted. The contemporary poor have no strongly based or well-funded institutions to focus their energies or discipline wayward members. They are socially exposed and vulnerable. This is the most depressing feature of our current situation: the large number of disorganized, powerless, and demoralized men and women, who are spoken for, and also exploited by, a growing company of racial and religious demagogues and tinhorn charismatics.

But weakness is a general feature of associational life in America today. Unions, churches, interest groups, ethnic organizations, political parties and sects, societies for self-improvement and good works, local philanthropies, neighborhood clubs and cooperatives,

religious sodalities, brotherhoods and sisterhoods: this American civil society is wonderfully multitudinous. Most of the associations, however, are precariously established, skimpily funded, and always at risk. They have less reach and holding power than they once did. I can't cite statistics; I'm not sure that anyone is collecting the right sorts of statistics; but I suspect that the number of Americans who are unorganized, inactive, and undefended is on the rise. Why is this so?

The answer has to do in part with the second of the centrifugal forces at work in contemporary American society. This country is not only a pluralism of groups but also a pluralism of individuals. It is perhaps the most individualist society in human history. Compared to the men and women of any earlier, old-world country, we are radically liberated, all of us. We are free to plot our own course, plan our own lives, choose a career, a partner (or a succession of partners), a religion (or no religion), a politics (or an antipolitics), a life-style (any style)—free to "do our own thing." Personal freedom is certainly one of the extraordinary achievements of the "new order of the ages" celebrated on the Great Seal of the United States. The defense of this freedom against puritans and bigots is one of the enduring themes of American politics, making for its most zestful moments; the celebration of this freedom, and of the individuality and creativity it makes possible, is one of the enduring themes of our literature.

Nonetheless, personal freedom is not an unalloyed delight. For many of us lack the means and the power to "do our own thing" or even to find our own things to do. Empowerment is, with rare exceptions, a familial, class, or communal, not an individual, achievement. Resources are accumulated over generations, cooperatively. And without resources, individual men and women find themselves hardpressed by economic dislocations, natural disasters, governmental failures, and personal crises. They can't count on steady or significant communal support. Often they are on the run from family, class, and community, seeking a new life in this new world. If they make good their escape, they never look back; if they need to look back, they are likely to find the people they left behind barely able to support themselves.

Consider for a moment the cultural (ethnic, racial, and religious) groups that constitute our supposedly fierce and divisive multiculturalism. All these are voluntary associations, with a core of militants, activists, and believers and a wide periphery of more passive men and women—who are, in effect, cultural free-riders, enjoying an identity that they don't pay for with money, time, or energy. When these people find themselves in trouble they look for help from similarly identified men and women. But the help is uncertain, for these identities are mostly unearned, without depth. Footloose individuals are not reliable members. There are no borders around our cultural groups and, of course, no border police. Men and women are free to participate or not as they please, to come and go, withdraw entirely, or simply fade away into the peripheral distances. This freedom, again, is one of the advantages of an individualist society; at the same time, however, it doesn't make for strong or cohesive associations. Ultimately, I'm not sure that it makes for strong or self-confident individuals.

Rates of disengagement from cultural association and identity for the sake of the private pursuit of happiness (or the desperate search for economic survival) are so high these days that all the groups worry all the time about how to hold the periphery and ensure their own future. They are constantly fund raising; recruiting; scrambling for workers, allies, and endorsements; preaching against the dangers of assimilation, intermarriage, passing, and passivity. Lacking any sort of coercive power and unsure of their own persuasiveness, they demand governmental programs (targeted entitlements, quota systems) that will help them press their own members into line. From their perspective, the real alternative to multiculturalism is not a strong and substantive Americanism, but an empty or randomly filled individualism, a great drift of human flotsam and jetsam away from every creative center.

This is, again, a one-sided perspective, but by no means entirely wrongheaded. The critical conflict in American life today is not between multiculturalism and some kind of cultural hegemony or singularity, not between pluralism and unity or the many and the one, but between the manyness of groups and of individuals, between communities and private men and women. And this is a conflict in which we have no choice except to affirm the value of both sides. The two pluralisms make America what it is or sometimes is and set the pattern for what it should be. Taken together, but only together, they are entirely consistent with a common democratic citizenship.

Consider now the increasingly dissociated individuals of contemporary American society. Surely we ought to worry about the processes, even though these are also, some of them, emancipatory processes, which produce dissociation and are its products:

- the rising divorce rate;
- the growing number of people living alone (in what the census calls "single person households");
- the decline in memberships (in unions and churches, for example);
- the long-term decline in voting rates and party loyalty (most dramatic in local elections);
- the high rates of geographic mobility (which continually undercut neighborhood cohesiveness);
- the sudden appearance of homeless men and women; and
- the rising tide of random violence.

Add to all this the apparent stabilization of high levels of unemployment and underemployment, especially among young people, which intensifies all these processes and aggravates their effects on already vulnerable minority groups. Unemployment makes family ties brittle, cuts people off from unions and interest groups, drains communal resources, leads to political alienation and withdrawal, increases the temptations of a criminal life. The old maxim about idle hands and the devil's work isn't necessarily true, but it comes true whenever idleness is a condition that no one would choose.

I am inclined to think that these processes, on balance, are more worrying than the multicultural cacophony—if only because, in a democratic society, action-in-common is better than withdrawal and solitude, tumult is better than passivity, shared purposes (even when we don't approve) are better than private listlessness. It is probably true, moreover, that many of these dissociated individuals are available for political mobilizations of a sort that democracies ought to avoid. There are writers today, of course, who claim that multiculturalism is itself the product of such mobilizations: American society in their eyes stands at the brink not only of dissolution but of "Bosnian" civil war. In fact, we have had (so far) only intimations of an openly chauvinist and racist politics. We are at a point where we can still safely bring the pluralism of groups to the rescue of the pluralism of dissociated individuals.

Individuals are stronger, more confident, more savvy, when they are participants in a common life, responsible to and for other people. No doubt, this relation doesn't hold for every common life; I am not recommending religious cults or political sects—though men and women who manage to pass through groups of that sort are often strengthened by the experience, educated for a more modest commonality. It is only in the context of associational activity that individuals learn to deliberate, argue, make decisions, and take responsibility. This is an old argument, first made on behalf of Protestant congregations and conventicles, which served, so we are told, as schools of democracy in nineteenth-century Great Britain, despite the intense and exclusive bonds they created and their frequently expressed doubts about the salvation of nonbelievers. Individuals were indeed saved by congregational membership—saved from isolation, loneliness, feelings of inferiority, habitual inaction, incompetence, a kind of moral vacancy—and turned into useful citizens. But it is equally true that Britain was saved from Protestant repression by the strong individualism of these same useful citizens: that was a large part of their usefulness.

So, we need to strengthen associational ties, even if these ties connect some of us to some others and not everyone to everyone else. There are many ways of doing this. First and foremost among them, it seems to me, are government policies that create jobs and that sponsor and support unionization on the job. For unemployment is probably the most dangerous form of dissociation, and unions are not only training grounds for democratic politics but also instruments of economic democracy. Almost as important are programs that strengthen family life, not only in its conventional but also in its unconventional versions—in any version that produces stable relationships and networks of support.

But I want to focus again on cultural associations, since these are the ones thought to be so threatening today. We need more such associations, not fewer, and more powerful and cohesive ones, too, with a wider range of responsibilities. Consider, for example, the current set of federal programs—matching grants, subsidies, and entitlements—that enable religious communities to run their own hospitals, old-age homes, schools, day care centers, and family services. Here are welfare societies within a decentralized (and still unfinished) American welfare state. Tax money is used to second charitable contributions in ways that strengthen the patterns of mutual assistance that arise spontaneously within civil society. But these patterns need to be greatly extended—since coverage at present is radically unequal—and more groups brought into the business of welfare provision: racial and ethnic as well as religious groups (and why not unions, co-ops, and corporations too?).

We need to find other programs of this kind, through which the government acts indirectly to support citizens acting directly in local communities: "charter schools" designed and run by teachers and parents; tenant self-management and co-op buyouts of public housing; experiments in workers' ownership and control of factories and companies; locally initiated building, cleanup, and crime prevention projects; and so on. Programs like these will often create or reinforce parochial communities, and they will generate conflicts for control of political space and institutional functions. But they will also increase the available space and the number of functions and, therefore, the opportunities for individual participation. And participating individuals, with a growing sense of their own effectiveness, are our best protection against the parochialism of the groups in which they participate.

Engaged men and women tend to be widely engaged—active in many different associations both locally and nationally. This is one of the most common findings of political scientists and sociologists (and one of the most surprising: where do these people find the time?). It helps to explain why engagement works, in a pluralist society, to undercut racist or chauvinist political commitments and ideologies. The same people show up for union meetings, neighborhood projects, political canvassing, church committees, and—most reliably—in the voting booth on election day. They are, most of them, articulate, opinionated, skillful, sure of themselves, and fairly steady in their commitments. Some mysterious combination of responsibility, ambition, and meddlesomeness carries them from one meeting to another. Everyone complains (I mean that all of them complain) that there are so few of them. Is this an inevitability of social life, so that an increase in the number of associations would only stretch out the competent people, more and more thinly? I suspect that demand-side economists have a better story to tell about this "human capital." Multiply the calls for competent people, and the people will appear. Multiply the opportunities for action-in-common, and activists will emerge to seize the opportunities. Some of them, no doubt, will be narrow-minded and bigoted, but the greater their number and the more diverse their activities, the less likely it is that narrow-mindedness and bigotry will prevail.

A certain sort of stridency is a feature of what we may one day come to recognize as *early* multiculturalism; it is especially evident among the newest and weakest, the least organized, groups. It is the product of a historical period when social equality outdistances economic equality. Stronger organizations, capable of collecting resources and delivering real benefits to their members, will move these groups, gradually, toward a democratically inclusive politics. The driving force will be the more active members, socialized by their activity. Remember that this has happened before, in the course of ethnic and class conflict. When groups consolidate, the center holds the periphery and turns it into a political constituency. And so union militants, say, begin on the picket line and the strike committee and move on to the school board and the city council. Religious and ethnic activists begin by defending the interests of their own community and end up in political coalitions, fighting for a place on "balanced" tickets, and talking (at least) about the common good. The cohesiveness of the group invigorates its members; the ambition and mobility of the most vigorous members liberalizes the group.

I don't mean to sound like the famous Pollyanna. These outcomes won't come about by chance; perhaps they won't come about at all. Everything is harder now—family, class, and community are less cohesive than they once were; local governments and philanthropies command fewer resources; the street world of crime and drugs is more frightening; individual men and women seem more adrift.

And there is one further difficulty that we ought to welcome. In the past, organized groups have succeeded in entering the American mainstream only by leaving other groups (and the weakest of their own members) behind. And the men and women left behind commonly accepted their fate or, at least, failed to make much noise about it. Today, as I have been arguing, the level of resignation is considerably lower, and if much of the subsequent noise is incoherent and futile, it serves nonetheless to remind the rest of us that there is a larger social agenda than our own success. Multiculturalism as an ideology is not only the product of, it is also a program for, greater social *and economic* equality.

If we want the mutual reinforcements of community and individuality to work effectively for everyone, we will have to act politically to make them effective. They require certain background or framing conditions that can only be provided by state action. Group life won't rescue individual men and women from dissociation and passivity unless there is a political strategy for mobilizing, organizing, and, if necessary, subsidizing the right sort of groups. And strong-minded individuals won't diversify their commitments and extend their ambitions unless there are opportunities open to them in the larger world: jobs, offices, and responsibilities. The centrifugal forces of culture and selfhood will correct one another only if the correction is planned. It is necessary to aim at a balance of the two—which means that we can never be consistent defenders of multiculturalism or individualism; we can never be communitarians or liberals simply, but now one, now the other, as the balance requires. It seems to me that the best name for the balance itself, the political creed that defends the framework and supports the necessary forms of state action for both groups and individuals, is social democracy. If multiculturalism today brings more trouble than hope, one reason is the weakness of social democracy (in this country: left liberalism). But that is another and a longer story.

Lessons of Vancouver

Immigration raises fundamental questions of identity and values.

Andrew Phillips

If the old Canada has a refuge and a stronghold these days, it may well be in legion halls across the land. It is there that veterans, their sons and their daughters have long gathered to sip rye and ginger and simply be together—upholding proud traditions of service and remembrance. These days, though, legion branches are anything but tranquil. Many are bitterly divided over whether to admit people wearing turbans—a seemingly obscure issue that starkly underlines the pain and confusion that results when the old Canada gives way to the new. For many legionnaires uncomfortable with the changes, the issue is straightforward. Turbans, as one Halifax legion member put it last week, should not be allowed because "tradition is tradition."

These days, though, even tradition isn't what it used to be. The new Canada wears not only legion caps and hockey sweaters, but saris and smart Hong Kong suits and—yes—turbans. In our big cities, and in many small towns as well, the highest levels of nonwhite immigration ever are raising fears and testing our commitment to the ideals of multiculturalism. Poll after poll shows Canadians increasingly hostile to immigration at a time of high unemployment: almost half of those surveyed by Gallup in December said the country should accept fewer immigrants. And the polite agreement among the old-line parties not to debate the issue seriously has vanished. Instead, the loudest voices in the new House of Commons openly question both the wisdom of accepting almost a quarter of a million newcomers a year and Ottawa's two-decade-old policy of officially encouraging them to stress their separate identities rather than their common Canadian citizenship. Last week alone, Reform and Bloc Québécois MPs condemned official multiculturalism in harsher language than Parliament has heard for many years.

Because they accept 60 per cent of all immigrants, the country's three biggest cities—Montreal, Toronto and Vancouver—are being most profoundly reshaped by the newcomers from Asia, the Middle East and Latin America. But if Canada has a laboratory in which its new ethnic chemistry is being most acutely tested, it is surely Vancouver. The city's position as a magnet for Asian immigrants means that change there has been most far-reaching. In typically Canadian fashion, established (mainly white) Vancouverites have for the most part expressed their concerns only in guarded fashion. But the changes are so profound that even many who regard themselves as liberal are bound to ask themselves: Is it all going too quickly? Is the city I knew being transformed into something alien? Will my children be well served by schools increasingly geared to serving youngsters whose greatest need is simply to learn English?

Until recently, it was virtually impossible to raise those questions publicly without being accused of intolerance, or even racism. But the new Commons is bound to witness confrontations between Reform MPs who want immigration levels cut drastically, and a rookie immigration minister determined to uphold the traditional Liberal openness towards newcomers. Ironically, though, the pointed debate on immigration that seems about to begin will take place in a House that includes more visible minorities than ever before—MPs of Chinese, Japanese, Indian, Filipino and West Indian heritage. Not to mention a record three native Canadians, who might justly regard all the other 292 MPs as immigrants."

Chris Wood

Jack Lee has a dilemma. The 42-year-old Vancouver-area developer's shiny new $60-million hotel, shopping and community centre in suburban Richmond, B.C., is almost complete—financed largely by would-be Canadians from Lee's native Taiwan who have each put $250,000 into his project, qualifying them for citizenship under Canada's investor-immigrant entry rules. The finishing touch on the gleaming glass-and-concrete project will be a fountain near the entrance where, Lee says, water will splash from the open mouth of one fish into that of another. One of the fish will be a carp, a symbol of the Orient; the other a dolphin, representing the West. To Asians, he adds, "water is for money." Lee's quandary: "Which fish should receive it? And which should spit it out?"

The question is on many minds in Canada's fastest-growing city. Even as Vancouver enjoys the economic benefits of record levels of immigration, the city of 1.6 million finds itself straining to accommodate the needs of an increasingly multicultural population. Citizens of longer standing, meanwhile, are asking other questions: as the face of the city changes, whose values will prevail, those of traditional Vancouver—or those of the newcomers? Indeed, in a city where street names like Blenheim and Balaclava evoke a staunchly British heritage, the visibly changing population prompts an even deeper question, one that resonates across the nation. As the number of Canadians of non-European origin approaches those of the two so-called founding nations of Canada, who, ultimately, are "we" anyway?

The sensitivity and significance of the issue were driven home again last week. After federal Immigration Minister Sergio Marchi announced that refugee claimants will now be allowed to work while awaiting a ruling on their status in Canada—lifting a load from overburdened welfare systems—critics immediately charged that the decision would deprive Canadians of jobs. In British Columbia, however, another news item drove home a different economic message. Fuelled by record immigration of 76,000 people (from both inside and outside Canada) in 1993, British Columbia generated nearly two out of every three new full-time jobs in the entire country last year.

Welcome as that news was to Vancouver residents, it did little to ease the stresses that have accompanied a sharp reversal in earlier patterns of immigration from abroad. In contrast to newcomers in previous decades, most of whom arrived with little money and a humble willingness to accept whatever work was offered, many of those who now come to the city, particularly the roughly one-fifth of them who arrive from Hong Kong, possess both wealth and high expectations. Both as investors and as consumers, their growing presence has profoundly visible consequences.

Nowhere is that more evident than in the south Vancouver suburb of Richmond. The elegant compound curves of Lee's mirror-sheathed President Plaza embrace both a Sheraton Hotel, due to open in April, and the country's largest Asian-food supermarket, which is already doing business. On its shelves, Old Dutch Potato Chips share space with Korean *kim chi* and

cans of grass jelly drink; a live seafood section boasts tanks of eels as well as lobster. Three floors above the shoppers, seven Buddhist nuns and monks clad in plain ochre habits are preparing to dedicate a 5,000-square-foot temple, the heart of a community centre that will offer adult education in Asian languages and crafts.

Lee's complex is just the latest addition to Richmond's increasingly Asian-influenced skyline. Immediately to the south of President Plaza sits the Aberdeen Centre: despite its Scottish name, the bustling complex of shops and restaurants is owned by investors from Hong Kong who modelled it on similar centres in that enclave of capitalism. "You feel very much at home when you go there," observes Joseph Li, a Hong Kong native who now works for Lee's President Asian Enterprises Inc. To the north of Lee's building stands the Yaohan Centre, the first Canadian link in an international chain of supermarkets and department stores owned by Japan's Wada Group. There, jewelry store owner May Leung surveyed the uniformly Asian shoppers beyond her counter one day recently and observed with unconscious irony: "We do not see many foreigners out here."

That Leung meant Canadians of European extraction would frankly appall some white Vancouverites. Many feel pushed aside by the Asian influx. "They make no effort to fit in," complains Elizabeth Campbell, who has lived in Vancouver almost all her life. She was speaking particularly of the large, boxy homes on bare lots, many of them owned by Chinese immigrants, that in the late 1980s began to displace the more modest bungalows with leafy landscaping that once defined her west end neighborhood of Kerrisdale. Locals promptly dubbed the dwellings "monster houses."

But the sentiment plainly has more general application. At Magee Secondary School in the city's west end, guidance counsellor William McNulty has witnessed the change over the past 19 years as the once overwhelmingly white, Anglo-Saxon and Protestant school body has become more than half Asian. "So far," he says of attempts to foster mutual understanding between the old group and the new, "it is a one-way street: Canadians wanting to understand the newcomers." But, McNulty adds, "Canadians do have a culture. There is a case for the Asians showing they want to understand the local culture." A straw poll of one typical office floor in downtown Vancouver, meanwhile, turned up complaints directed at the Asian newcomers from more than half the tenants. Sore points ranged from the inconsiderate rudeness of some new arrivals to the soaring price of real estate, fuelled in part by wealthy immigrants paying top dollar for the city's most desirable properties. "That's why I voted Reform [in last fall's federal election]," volunteered secretary Terri Richardson. She was attracted, she says, by that party's call for restrictions on immigration.

Some of the harshest criticism of Vancouver's increasingly Asian cast can be heard in a spacious book-lined basement office a few steps down from Water Street in the city's historic Gastown district. Red and black hand-painted letters across a window facing the street identify the office as belonging to the Procult Institute: "In service to Western cultural values." The institute's founder, former businessman Jud Cyllorn, has written and published a 490-page polemic against Canada's immigration policy called *Stop Apologizing*. "In 22 years," he argues, "we have completely changed who we are and what we believe in." According to Cyllorn, who is of Scots origin, Canada's "British culture, which is based on trust" has given way to an "Asian culture [of] individual greed." Cyllorn, whose tiny organization has little influence, insists he is not a racist. "Anything I say is not to raise hatred against anyone," he told *Maclean's,* "but only to raise disgust at our own laxity and stupidity in surrendering our country without even a whimper."

But history, and the numbers, tell a very different story, one that is both more complex and more reassuring than Cyllorn's crudely bipolar perspective. The purely European past that he evokes is a fiction. So, too, is the alarmist notion that Vancouver is on the verge of becoming a transplanted version of Asia's teeming city-states.

As a matter of record, the census of 1891 documented no fewer than 42 countries of origin among the 14,000 people living in Vancouver. Orientals even then outnumbered Caucasians from continental Europe, 840 to 560. Succeeding generations of immigrants have added dozens of additional ethnic flavors to Vancouver's multicultural mix. Until 1942, a prosperous Japanese community abutted Vancouver's traditional Chinatown; its residents were abruptly interned and their property confiscated following the bombing of Pearl Harbor (the Canadian government formally apologized in 1988 for the mistreatment).

During the two decades following the Second World War, further immigration added a vigorous Italian community to the city's east end, while the concentration of Germans along one downtown street earned it the nickname "Robsonstrasse." Greek, Indo-Pakistani, Portuguese and Filipino communities appeared during the 1960s and 1970s, and by 1990, the children of immigrants registering for school in Vancouver came from a breathtaking total of 79 countries. Now, a local joke asks what the shortest distance is between Iran and Hong Kong. Answer: Lion's Gate Bridge, which links North Vancouver, favored by the city's Iranians to downtown and old Chinatown. "Vancouver has always been a seaport," observes city councillor Jennifer Clarke. "It has always accepted waves of immigrants from anywhere, and it has always been enriched by them."

For that matter, Vancouver's Chinese are scarcely less diverse in outlook than the rest of the city's population. Many families trace their Canadian roots back more than a century to the Klondike Gold Rush or the building of the Canadian Pacific Railway—which drew thousands of Chinese immigrants to the young country as prospectors and laborers. Another wave of newcomers fled the Communist takeover of mainland China in the late 1940s and early 1950s. Still more arrived in the 1960s—many with professional qualifications. The latest group of Chinese immigrants hail mainly from Hong Kong, but many also arrive from Taiwan, Vietnam and elsewhere along the southeast Asian rim. "People like my parents," observes Sonny Wong, the 32-year-old founder of a successful marketing agency whose parents came to Canada in the early 1950s, "continue to work in Chinese-dominated businesses. All their friends are

Chinese. There is a tremendous amount of ethnocentric clustering." But of himself, Wong adds: "I was educated and socialized in Western society."

At the same time, foreign immigration to Vancouver continues to be outweighed by in-migration from elsewhere in Canada. In 1993, the 41,000 in-migrants who came to British Columbia from east of the Rockies outnumbered newcomers from other countries by nearly 20 per cent. Still, the 35,000 people who came to British Columbia from outside Canada last year, three-quarters of them from Asia and most of them settling in the lower mainland, were hardly insignificant. It is unarguable that Vancouver has already changed mightily and will change still more. According to Bruce MacDonald, the author of a historical atlas of Vancouver published in 1992, residents of British heritage made up a majority of the city's population as recently as 1961. But in the most recent census, in 1991, barely 24 per cent acknowledged British heritage. They were substantially outnumbered by the nearly 30 per cent of Vancouverites who told census takers they were of Asian origin—with fully 22 per cent saying they were ethnically Chinese.

The pronounced shift in Vancouver's ethnic centre of gravity has created new strains on civic institutions as well as striking changes in what constitutes businesses as usual in Canada's third-largest city. It is not just that white business executives are signing up for classes in Asian corporate etiquette at the downtown campus of Simon Fraser University, or that virtually any hip Vancouverite can negotiate his or her way through lunch using chop sticks. At City Hall, public notices are now routinely prepared in at least five languages in addition to English: Cantonese, Punjabi, Vietnamese, Spanish and French. "If it doesn't happen," declares Philip Owen, a former councillor who won election as mayor last November, "somebody is going to be reprimanded." And since October, 1992, the city's 911 emergency line has been equipped to respond to calls for help in an even larger number of tongues, thanks to a computer link to a continent-wide network of translators.

There is no identifying sign—in any language—outside the heavily secured, cream-colored cement building just south of False Creek where a special joint squad of Vancouver city police, RCMP and officers from other nearby municipalities are grappling with a different challenge. According to Staff Sgt. Andy Nimmo, commanding officer of the Asian Gang Squad, mixed in with the tens of thousands of law-abiding immigrants who have come to Canada from various Asian nations over the decades is a tiny but potent minority of gangsters. Their victims, overwhelmingly, have been others in their own community: Asian businessmen who became targets for extortion; shopkeepers and restaurateurs shaken down for protection money; youths studying in Canada who could easily be terrorized into handing over their allowances to thugs. Until recently, however, the mainly white police forces focused most of their efforts on serving and protecting the Caucasian majority.

That began to change in 1990 after a sweeping review of police policy. It uncovered a crippling lack of confidence among many Asians in the ability of the police to protect victims and

Bridging the gap

British Columbia's lieutenant-governor, 70-year old **David See-Chai Lam,** is one of Canada's most successful immigrants. He, his wife, Dorothy, and their three daughters left Hong Kong for Vancouver in 1967. Since then, he has made a fortune in real estate, become a leading philanthropist—and in 1988 was named the Queen's representative in the province. As lieutenant-governor, Lam has been on a mission to increase understanding between established Canadians and new arrivals. "It's quite natural for people to feel uncomfortable with different people," he says. "Both sides have to gradually get used to the changes."

Lam tells established Canadians that they should not be quite so proud of Canada's reputation as a tolerant country. "Tolerant is a slightly negative word," he says. "It's like saying, 'You smell, but I can hold my breath.' " Lam says he would like Canada to celebrate its immigrants, not just put up with them.

Lam is even tougher on the new arrivals. He has little patience for complaints about minor incidents of discrimination. "Don't talk to me about discrimination," he says bluntly. "The Chinese race is one of the most discriminatory in the world. I say to them, 'Do you think you will live to see the day when in one of the provinces in China, or in any of the countries in Asia, there will be a blond, blue-eyed governor?' " And he speaks against the common practice among elderly Chinese-Canadians of having their bodies sent back to China for burial. "I tell them to go out and buy a burial plot in Vancouver," he says. "That's when they'll be really committed to Canada."

In his quest to eliminate cultural misunderstandings, Lam worries about a new problem that he fears could create antagonism. He says that children who, following Canadian custom, go door-to-door selling things like Girl Guide cookies or collecting donations for school projects no longer knock on the doors of Chinese homes. "Chinese people think that if someone comes to their door and asks for money, they are a beggar and they send them away," he says. Lam is trying to get out the word to new immigrants so they will stop unknowingly offending the youngsters—and their parents. Still, Lam says his greatest contribution has been as a symbol of change. "British Columbia has a long, long history of discrimination," he says. "To have someone of the Chinese race now occupying its most important residence, that says a lot." To both sides.

BRENDA DALGLISH

witnesses who reported crimes—fuelled by a deep-seated fear of violent reprisals from the likes of the Dai Huen Jai, a shadowy Chinese group whose name means Big Circle Boys. "Without support from victims and witnesses," Nimmo says, "there is nothing we can do." Still, he was forced to acknowledge: "Their fear is real."

Last year, Nimmo secured funding for a counterattack. He doubled the number of Chinese officers on his 28-member squad to six and in October put into service a Cantonese-language hotline for crime tips. Those and other measures have already produced some successes. "We are hearing from more people than we used to," observes Nimmo, who points to a 35-per-cent jump in arrests during 1993. In one, the victim himself wore a hidden microphone to help Nimmo's unit snare an extortionist who had extracted as much as $500,000 from visa students in the Vancouver area.

The last four years have seen Vancouver's schools similarly transform their approach to the children of immigrant families. In place of one overworked English-as-a-second-language (ESL) teaching consultant tucked away in a third-floor room at the Vancouver school board main office, the Oak Ridge Reception and Orientation Centre now greets newcomers to the city who register their children for public school. There, a multilingual staff of 10 puts prospective students and their families through a penetrating series of assessments designed not only to grade a child's grasp of English, but also to prepare youngsters for classrooms that may be very different from the ones they have left. "Many Asian students are used to rote learning," observes the centre's director, Catherine Eddy. "And they come into a class where they are supposed to break up into groups and do problem solving." For many, she adds, "this is foreign, this is weird."

One measure of the distance that Vancouver has travelled towards smoothing relations between its old and new residents can be found in the leafy and lovingly manicured precincts of Kerrisdale and South Shaughnessy. In late 1992, the neighborhoods were at the epicentre of heated debate over the right of new purchasers to raze existing homes and replace them with much larger dwellings that frequently struck established residents as glaringly out of place. In a district where many long-standing homeowners are avid gardeners, it did not help that some builders felled full-grown trees in order to accommodate the ambitious scale of the new homes, and replaced shrubs and bushes with multiple parking spaces. "It is the barrenness that upsets me," Kerrisdale resident Campbell complains of many of the new buildings. "There were old houses here before, landscaped beautifully. Now, it looks like a movie set." At the same time, the owners of the offending homes, many—although by no means all—of them newly arrived immigrants from Hong Kong, insisted that they had met existing zoning rules and had a clear right to do as they wished with their property.

A series of emotional public hearings during early 1993 led to a compromise. In exchange for permission to build houses larger than any allowed elsewhere in Vancouver, City Hall now insists that builders of new homes take into account the style of the dwellings on either side. "The houses that are being produced now," says council member Clarke, who actively resisted the encroachment of large, boxy structures into her

South Shaughnessy neighborhood, "look just great. It seems to be working."

At the same time, even many of those who express discomfort with some aspects of immigration's impact on Vancouver concede that it is largely responsible for the city's buoyant economy. Businessman John Walker, for one, complains that the need to provide ESL instruction to nearly half of Vancouver's 55,000 public school students has helped to drive up his taxes. "But in some ways," he also acknowledges, "you cannot knock [immigration]. It keeps the economy going, especially construction." Indeed, construction workers in British Columbia are enjoying good times unparalleled anywhere else in the country.

Much of that activity is visible along the north shore of False Creek. There, a company controlled by Hong Kong billionaire Li Ka-Shing is slowly transforming the former site of Vancouver's Expo 86 into what will eventually be 204 acres of parks, high-rise condominiums, marinas and public services, including a community centre anchored by a roundhouse where the first steam locomotive to cross the country on the Canadian Pacific Railway now sits in silent and imposing retirement With eight buildings completed and construction slated to begin on five more later this year, Concord Pacific Place is the largest real estate development under way in the country.

But if the money that is fuelling the activity along False Creek comes largely from the Orient, the development's Hong Kong-born president, Terry Hui, the 30-year-old son of a junior partner in the $3-billion project, bristles at the suggestion that the dominant esthetic is anything but Canadian. "It is not our vision," Hui, who is now a Canadian citizen, told *Maclean's*. "It is Vancouver's vision. It is Vancouver's taste." To bolster that claim, Concord Pacific points to more than 200 public meetings it conducted to ensure that its plans had support from Vancouver's residents.

In less visible ways, many other Vancouver businesses plainly hope to share the prosperity that the city's Asian connection has brought to its builders. The various trade councils, business forums, networking circles, institutes and foundations aimed at fostering closer commercial ties between Canada and the Orient number well over a dozen. And the Vancouver Stock Exchange announced in December that it plans to establish an Asian Board that it hopes will attract Taiwanese and Hong Kong-owned companies with operations in booming mainland China.

Economic optimism aside, strains and frictions do remain. Although immigration and race do not show up as concerns in the letters from constituents that reach Clarke's desk, taxes do. And they are being driven up, at least in part, by the need for the new services that Nimmo and Eddy champion.

Even many people of Asian heritage admit that Hong Kong's frenetic and keenly competitive culture transplants with difficulty to Vancouver's more laid-back shores. "New immigrants are different from old immigrants," says Johnny Yan, a house builder who came to Canada from Hong Kong as a child in 1967. "A few rich people always look down on others." Adds Maggie Ip, a high-school teacher who emigrated from Hong Kong 28 years ago and who was elected to Vancouver city council last November: "In Hong Kong, they never look at the long term, because they can't plan anything beyond 1997," when the British colony will revert to the control of mainland China. Adds Ip: "That kind of mentality shows in their daily life. They want something instantly—they can't wait."

If those characteristics occasionally grate on the nerves of Vancouver's more settled residents, Ip and others argue that there are still compelling reasons for patience. For one thing, the newcomers eventually adjust to the city's slower pace. After three or four years in Canada, says Ip, "they will tell you, 'This is very peaceful, we have a nice climate, there's not too much rushing.' It is almost like two different people." (For at least a few recent arrivals from Hong Kong, however, Vancouver's slower tempo has proven *too* relaxed: there is a steady, if undocumented, trickle of individuals returning to the colony, lured back by its faster-paced economy.) British Columbia's Hong Kong-born lieutenant-governor, David Lam, meanwhile, offers another argument in favor of understanding. "We have what I consider a secret weapon with the Asian community in Canada," Lam told *Maclean's*. "Everyone of them could be the beginning of the best network linkage to Asia."

In fact, Vancouver stands little danger of becoming the "Hongcouver" of Jud Cyllorn's nightmares. New arrivals from places no more exotic than New Brunswick and Manitoba will continue to find places in a richly textured ethnic fabric. That many more will also come from across the Pacific should only reinforce Vancouver's claim to be, in developer Hui's phrase, "the gateway between North America and Asia." For most people in this Pacific city, there is far more to celebrate than to fear in its Asian connection. Indeed, when Vancouver's Chinatown erupts in fireworks and dragon dancers next week in celebration of Chinese New Year, many of the faces that crowd the sidewalks will not be Oriental. They will reflect a Canada of many colors. Jack Lee's fountain, perhaps, should rightly flow in both directions.

With JOHN HOWES and BOB IP in Vancouver and BRENDA DALGLISH in Toronto

Curriculum and Instruction in Multicultural Perspective

Curriculum and instruction include all concerns relative to subject matter content to be taught and all pedagogical theory of practice relating to methods of instruction. All pedagogical theory is informed and situated in some philosophical assumptions relating to ideas of what is worthy, what is true, and what is good to either know or do. Every school curriculum is a socially situated product of a knowledge production process in which those who design and approve a curriculum decide what could be included in a particular curriculum. Since classroom teachers are the "delivery systems" for a curriculum, along with whatever texts are used, teachers have the opportunity to interpret and add their own insights regarding the curricula they teach.

It is in the area of curriculum and instruction in the elementary and secondary schools, as well as in teacher education curricula, that a fundamental transformation must occur to sensitize all young people, including those living in isolated rural and small town communities, to the multicultural reality of our national civilization. The multicultural social heritage of our civilization must be integrated into what children and young adults learn in school. There are several different approaches to multicultural education programming in the schools. This area of study has developed steadily, in stages, since the events of the 1960s, 1970s, and 1980s forced a reassessment of our sense of social justice. There are programs in some school systems that merely include the study of major minority cultural groups living in the area of the particular school system, and this is often done through isolated, elective courses or units in required courses that students must take. This is not the approach to multicultural education that most current leaders in the field favor. Today, most people who are experienced in working with students and teachers in the development of multicultural education programming favor a more holistic, inclusive approach to the subject. This would involve the infusion of multicultural themes into the entire life of the school and all course content that can be related to human social life and the ongoing struggle for social justice on the part of traditionally conceived minority groups and women. Such an inclusive approach to multicultural education seeks to help students and teachers to develop a sense of social consciousness. The sense of social consciousness, coupled with a more global and integrated conception of our social reality, will empower them to assess more critically than most of our citizens have in the past such distinctions as the disparity between public democratic rhetoric and the reality that some social groups still have difficulty being accepted into society's mainstream.

The National Council for the Social Studies (NCSS) has developed comprehensive curriculum guidelines for the implementation of multicultural education in elementary and secondary schools. These guidelines were prepared by the NCSS Task Force on Ethnic Studies. A revised version of these guidelines was published in 1991. They reflect the developmental thinking on the part of many educators who have been involved in the implementation of multicultural programming in school systems as well as teacher education programs. One important reason to focus on multicultural education is that a democratic nation has a moral responsibility to see that minority ethnic, cultural, or religious groups are not isolated or marginalized in the social life of the nation. The educational institutions of a nation tend to be the primary places where children and young adults learn about their national history, literature, and scientific achievement. Multicultural educational content is necessary in all American schools because students, even in the most culturally isolated rural and small town settings, do learn opinions and beliefs about ethnic, cultural, and religious groups other than their own. What students learn in the informal social relations of their home communities about other social groups that are different from themselves is often factually misleading or incorrect. This is how our past sad heritage of racism and negative stereotypes of differing social groups evolved. There has been much progress in the area of civil rights in the past 40 years; but there has also been resurgent racism and intercultural misunderstanding. School is the one place children and adolescents go each day where it is possible for them to learn an objective view of the culturally pluralistic national heritage that is both their present social reality and their future one as well. All communities are linked in some way to the culturally pluralistic social reality of the nation. When students leave high school to go into military service, attend college, or attempt careers in other parts of the nation in the corporate sector, government, or the arts, they will encounter a multicultural world very different from the frequently isolated, and not adequately informed, social structure of their own local community or cultural groups.

Teachers should help their students to recognize and respect ethnic and cultural diversity and to value this cultural diversity because it does enhance and enrich the quality of our civilization. All students should be raised to cherish the concept of equality of social and academic opportunity as part of a democracy. Children and adolescents should also be taught that they each, individually, have the right to choose to what extent they wish to identify with the activities and organized efforts of their own particular ethnic or cultural groups. Participation in ethnic group activities is voluntary in a democracy. They need to be taught in their school studies that they are a part of a great, unified nation, a nation in which people of many diverse ethnic, cultural, and religious backgrounds work together to build an ever richer and more just nation-state in a world of interdependent political and economic systems. This commitment to the appreciation of cultural diversity, along with social justice for all, should permeate every part of the life of every school in the nation. Every youngster should grow up in such a way that upon high school graduation, he or she will honorably, honestly believe that Thomas Jefferson and others were right to swear "eternal hostility over all the forms of tyranny over the minds of men." Realizing how far we have come since Jefferson's time, we now know in our hearts what should be reflected in every school curriculum, that every man or women in the nation deserves an equal educational and social opportunity. For we are brothers and sisters as coexistent citizens of a great, culturally pluralistic nation. We should not see one another in an adversarial way simply because of our ethnic, cultural, or religious background.

The essays in this unit reflect all of the previously mentioned concerns and provide a wide variety of perspectives on how to broaden the multicultural effort in our schools. The authors seek to incorporate more intercultural and global content and experiences into the main body of curriculum and instruction. Educators will find that, taken together, these essays provide a very sound

basis for understanding what multicultural curriculum and instruction should be about. They are relevant to coursework in curriculum and instruction, curriculum theory and construction, educational policy studies and leadership, history and philosophy of education, and cultural foundations of education.

Looking Ahead: Challenge Questions

What are the relative similarities and distinctions between a "culture" and an "ethnic group"?

Why is it more effective to integrate multicultural curriculum content into all aspects of a school curriculum?

What are the varying ways in which multicultural education is defined? Which model of multicultural education do you prefer? Why?

What is the rationale for the existence of the multicultural educational effort in the elementary and secondary schools? Should all students be exposed to it?

How can inservice teachers be better prepared to engage in multicultural instruction and learning experiences?

—F. S.

Curriculum Guidelines for Multicultural Education

Prepared by the NCSS Task Force on Ethnic Studies Curriculum Guidelines
Adopted by NCSS Board of Directors, 1976, revised 1991

Introduction

Publishing a revision of *Curriculum Guidelines for Multicultural Education* is especially appropriate and timely because of the significant increase in the nation's population of people of color that has occurred since they were published sixteen years ago. The percentage of people of color in the nation will continue to rise throughout the early decades of the next century. Indeed, the 1990 census revealed that one out of every four people who live in the United States is a person of color and that one out of every three people will be a person of color by the turn of the century. Likewise, the ethnic and racial makeup of the nation's classrooms is changing significantly. Students of color constitute a majority in twenty-five of the nation's largest school districts and in California, our most populous state with a population of thirty million people. Students of color will make up nearly half (46 percent) of the nation's school-age youth by 2020, and about 27 percent of those students will be victims of poverty.

One important implication of these demographic trends is that education in the twenty-first century must help low-income students and students of color to develop the knowledge, attitudes, and skills necessary to participate in the work force and in society. This goal is not possible without restructuring schools, colleges, and universities, and institutionalizing new goals and ideals within them. As currently conceptualized and organized, schools today are unable to help most low-income students and students of color attain these goals.

Another important implication of the demographic imperative is that students from all social groups, i.e., class, racial, ethnic, cultural, and gender, must attain the knowledge, skills, and competencies necessary to participate in public discourse and civic action with people who differ from them in significant ways. People are socialized within families and in communities where they learn the values, perspectives, attitudes, and behaviors of their primordial culture. Community culture enables people to survive. It also, however, restricts their freedom and their ability to make critical choices and to reform their society.

Multicultural education helps students understand and affirm their community cultures and helps to free them from cultural boundaries, allowing them to create and maintain a civic community that works for the common good. Multicultural education seeks to actualize the idea of *e pluribus unum* within our nation and to create a society that recognizes and respects the cultures of its diverse people, people united within a framework of overarching democratic values. A unified and cohesive democratic society can be created only when the rights of its diverse people are reflected in its institutions, within its national culture, and within its schools, colleges, and universities. A national culture or school curriculum that does not reflect the voices, struggles, hopes, and dreams of its many peoples is neither democratic nor cohesive. Divisiveness within a nation-state occurs when important segments within its society are structurally excluded and marginalized.

The changing ethnic texture in the United States has stimulated a bitter debate over the extent to which the school, college, and university curricula should be revised to reflect ethnic, cultural, and gender diversity. This polarized debate has become forensic and has generated more heat than light.

The increase of our nation's students of color and the debate over the curriculum make this an appropriate time for the National Council for the Social Studies to reaffirm its commitment to educational programs and curricula that reflect the racial, ethnic, and cultural diversity within the United States and the world. As diversity in the world grows, it becomes increasingly important for students in the United States to acquire the knowledge, skills, and values essential for functioning in cross-racial, cross-ethnic, and cross-cultural situations. For democracy to function in a pluralistic nation-state, its citizens must be able to transcend their ethnic and cultural boundaries in order to participate in public discussion and action. An important goal of multicultural education is to help students from diverse cultures learn *how* to transcend their cultural borders and engage in dialogue and action essential for the survival of our democratic political system and way of life. No goal for education is more important as we approach the threshold of the new century.

When Margit McGuire, president of National Council for the Social Studies, invited me to revise these guidelines, I asked each original author to send me his or her revisions and suggestions. I have incorporated most of the suggestions they sent me. I must assume total responsibility for this revised edition, however, because I selected the ideas to incorporate and wrote the new text. I wish to publicly thank each member of the task force for sending me thoughtful revisions and suggestions in a timely fashion. We have remained warm friends and professional colleagues for nearly two decades.

I am grateful to Charlotte Anderson and the NCSS Equity and Social Justice Committee for preparing thoughtful and

From *Social Education*, September 1992, pp. 274-294. © 1992 by the National Council for the Social Studies. Reprinted by permission.

helpful comments on an earlier draft of this revised edition of the guidelines.

This revised edition of the guidelines differs from the original in many ways. The term *multiethnic education* was used in the title and throughout the first edition; in the revised edition, *multicultural education* is used. Today, *multicultural education* is the most frequently used term to refer to the issues and concerns discussed in this document. The term *multiethnic education* has almost faded from our lexicon, a trend the task force resisted and did not foresee when the guidelines were written in 1976.

Multicultural education is also used in this edition because it more readily communicates to the new generation of readers its focus and content. Furthermore, I have tried to broaden the document's scope to include cultural groups that may not be ethnic, although ethnic groups remain the primary focus. Many of the principles, concepts, and issues discussed in the guidelines are linked to issues related to gender, class, and region—and to the intersection of these variables—as much as they are to ethnic groups and ethnicity. Also, people who are ethnic also have a gender, a social class, and a region; the intersection of these variables is an important and growing concern of multicultural theorists.

This revised edition also focuses more on race than the original does. We rarely used the word *race* in the first edition, perhaps because of our vain hope that silence would facilitate racism's disappearance. The ugly racial incidents that have occurred in our society—specifically on college and university campuses—since the guidelines were first published have eroded our hope that racism would dry up like a raisin in the sun. Racism is cyclic, and is alive and well today. Both racism and sexism must be examined seriously in any sound multicultural curriculum.

New concepts, terms, and statistics have also been incorporated into this edition. The bibliography reflects the new research and the extent to which the field of multicultural education has matured and prospered since the guidelines were first published. I hope this revision will both promote further growth and development in the field and raise the level of dialogue about multicultural education, especially among the public and within the popular media.

These guidelines are divided into four sections: A Rationale for Ethnic Pluralism and Multicultural Education, Curriculum Guidelines for Multicultural Education, The Multicultural Education Program Evaluation Checklist, plus a section of references.

The rationale section describes the view of society on which these guidelines are predicated, describes the nature of educational institutions and learners in a culturally pluralistic society, and delineates goals for school reform.

The second section describes the ideal characteristics of educational environments that are consistent with the ethnic pluralism described in the rationale. The term *multicultural education*, as used in these guidelines, does not necessarily refer to educational institutions that have mixed racial and ethnic populations, but, rather, to the idealized educational institutions and curricula that reflect and are sensitive to the ethnic and cultural diversity within the United States and the world.

The third section encourages and helps in the assessment of specific educational environments to determine how they reflect an idealized educational institution. The guidelines describe goals that each educational institution can strive to achieve and provide specific guidelines intended to clarify the meaning of the general guideline and to facilitate the assessment of educational environments.

I would like to acknowledge the Center for Multicultural Education at the University of Washington for research assistance that enabled me to find time within a hectic schedule to revise these guidelines. I am grateful to Allen D. Glenn, dean of our College of Education, for his support of the Center and my work. I thank my family—Cherry, Angela, and Patricia—for paying a high price of family time and weekends for a professional duty that I felt was a high calling.

James A. Banks, Director
Center for Multicultural Education
University of Washington
Seattle, Washington

Part One: A Rationale for Ethnic Pluralism and Multicultural Education

Three major factors make multicultural education a necessity: (1) ethnic pluralism is a growing societal reality that influences the lives of young people; (2) in one way or another, individuals acquire knowledge or beliefs, sometimes invalid, about ethnic and cultural groups; and (3) beliefs and knowledge about ethnic and cultural groups limit the perspectives of many and make a difference, often a negative difference, in the opportunities and options available to members of ethnic and cultural groups. Because ethnicity, race, and class are important in the lives of many citizens of the United States, it is essential that all members of our society develop multicultural literacy, that is, a solidly based understanding of racial, ethnic, and cultural groups and their significance in U.S. society and throughout the world. Schools cannot afford to ignore their responsibility to contribute to the development of multicultural literacy and understanding. Only a well-conceived, sensitive, thorough, and continuous program of multicultural education can create the broadly based multicultural literacy so necessary for the future of our nation and world.

In the United States, ethnic diversity has remained visible despite the acculturation process that takes place in any society made up of many ethnic groups. Although ethnic affiliations are weak for many U.S. citizens, a large number still have some attachments to their ethnic cultures and to the symbols of their ancestral traditions. The values and behavior of many U.S. citizens are heavily influenced by their ethnicity. Ethnic identification is often increased by the discrimination experienced by many because of their racial characteristics, language, or culture. Ethnic identification is also increased when significant numbers of new immigrants from the homeland arrive in the United States. Thousands of immigrants from Asia and Latin America made the United States their home during the 1980s. About 85 percent of the documented immigrants that settled in the United States between 1981 and 1989 came from Asia (47 percent) and Latin America (38 percent) (Banks 1991a, 4).

During the 1980s and 1990s, a significant increase in the population of people of color in the United States and the expression of new forms of racism stimulated a vigorous and contentious debate among educators about the extent to which the curriculum should be revised to reflect ethnic and cultural diversity. At least three major groups that participated in this debate can be identified—the Western traditionalists, the Afrocentrists, and the multiculturalists. The Western traditionalists argue that content about Europe and Western civilization should be at the center of the curriculum in the nation's schools, colleges, and universities because of the extent to which Western ideas and values have influenced the development of U.S. culture and civilization (Howe 1991; Ravitch 1990; Schlesinger 1991). The Afrocentrists maintain that it is essential that an African perspective be incorporated into the curriculum (Asante 1991). The multiculturalists believe that concepts and events should be viewed from diverse ethnic and cultural perspectives (Banks 1991a; Sleeter and Grant 1987; Tetreault 1989). The multiculturalists also argue that the conception of Western civilization taught in schools should be reconceptualized to acknowledge the debt the West owes to Asian and African civilizations (Bernal 1991). The multiculturalists also believe that the conflict inherent in the West's commitment to democratic ideals and the racism and sexism still practiced in Western societies should be made explicit in the curriculum.

The bitter debate about the extent to which issues related to race and ethnicity should be reflected in the curriculum of the nation's schools indicates that race and ethnicity are cogent forces in contemporary U.S. society. The debate over the curriculum canon is an appropriate one for a pluralistic democratic society. It reflects the extent to which various interest groups are trying to shape the national identity and culture in the United States in ways that are consistent with their views of the nation's past, present, and future.

The concept of cultural diversity embraced in these guidelines is most consistent with the position of the multiculturalists—a position that incorporates important elements of both the Western traditionalist and the Afrocentrist approaches. The multiculturalists' position contributes best to the building of a society that incorporates diversity within a cohesive and unified nation-state. Multicultural education supports and enhances the notion of *e pluribus unum*—out of many, one. To build a successful and inclusive nation-state, the hopes, dreams, and experiences of the many groups within it must be reflected in the structure and institutions of society. This is the only viable way to create a nation-state in which all groups will feel included, loyal, and patriotic.

The guidelines presented in this document are predicated on a democratic ideology in which ethnic and cultural diversity is viewed as a positive, integral ingredient. A democratic society protects and provides opportunities for ethnic and cultural diversity at the same time having overarching values—such as equality, justice, and human dignity—that all groups accept and respect. Ethnic and cultural diversity is based on the following four premises:

1. Ethnic and cultural diversity should be recognized and respected at individual, group, and societal levels.
2. Ethnic and cultural diversity provides a basis for societal enrichment, cohesiveness, and survival.
3. Equality of opportunity should be afforded to members of all ethnic and cultural groups.
4. Ethnic and cultural identification should be optional for individuals.

Characteristics of an Ethnic Group

Because this document focuses on ethnic pluralism and its implications for school reform, it is essential that we establish a working definition of *ethnic group* that reflects social sci-

ence theory and research and facilitates school reform. No one definition of the term is accepted by all social scientists or is adequate for the purpose of this document. Consequently, the working definition used herein reflects a composite of existing definitions and the results of task force discussions.

An ethnic group is distinguished from other kinds of cultural groups in the definition for this document. An ethnic group is a specific kind of cultural group having all the following characteristics:

a. Its origins precede the creation of a nation-state or are external to the nation-state. In the case of the United States, ethnic groups have distinct pre–United States or extro–United States territorial bases, e.g., immigrant groups and Native Americans.
b. It is an involuntary group, although individual identification with the group may be optional.
c. It has an ancestral tradition and its members share a sense of peoplehood and an interdependence of fate.
d. It has distinguishing value orientations, behavioral patterns, and interests.
e. Its existence has an influence, in many cases a substantial influence, on the lives of its members.
f. Membership in the group is influenced both by how members define themselves and by how they are defined by others.

The definition of *ethnic group* stated above includes some groups that are distinguished primarily on the basis of race, such as African Americans and Japanese Americans, some that are distinguished primarily on the basis of unique sets of cultural and religious attributes, such as Jewish Americans, and some that are distinguished on the basis of national origin, such as Polish Americans. The criteria for characterization, of course, frequently overlap; Japanese Americans, for example, constitute an ethnic group characterized by national, cultural, and racial origins. The definition does not include cultural or regional groups of United States origin, such as those from the Appalachian region. This exclusion does not imply that such groups do not have unique cultural experiences that have teaching implications. Although they are not the primary focus of this document, many of the guidelines are applicable to the study of regional and other kinds of cultural groups. Factors such as region, race, gender, social class, and religion are variables that cut across ethnic groups. Students must examine these factors to gain a valid understanding of the nature of racial, ethnic, and cultural diversity in U.S. society.

Characteristics of a Cultural Group

A cultural group shares behavioral patterns, symbols, values, beliefs, and other human-constructed characteristics that distinguish it from other groups. Kroeber and Kluckhuhn (1952, 161), after surveying definitions of culture, concluded that "culture consists of patterns, explicit and implicit, of and for behavior acquired and transmitted by symbols, constituting the distinctive achievements of human groups, including their embodiments in artifacts; the essential core of culture consists of traditional…ideas and especially their attached values."

Like most social scientists today, Kroeber and Kluckhuhn emphasize the intangible, symbolic, and ideational aspects of culture. Ideas, ways of thinking, values, symbols, and other intangible aspects of human life—and not tangible objects such as tools, clothing, or foods—distinguish one cultural group from another in modernized societies. Two cultural groups might eat the same foods but have different meanings and interpretations for them. It is their values, perspectives, and ways of viewing reality that distinguish cultural groups from one another in the United States, not their clothing, foods, or other tangible aspects of group life.

Principles of Ethnic and Cultural Diversity

1. Ethnic and cultural diversity should be recognized and respected at the individual, group, and societal levels.

Ethnic and cultural diversity is a social reality all too frequently ignored by educational institutions, yet it deserves open recognition. Members of ethnic and cultural groups often have worldviews, values, traditions, and practices that differ from those of the mainstream society and from those of other ethnic groups.

Even in the midst of a marked degree of assimilation and acculturation, and in spite of efforts to ignore, belittle, or eliminate some ethnic differences, many U.S. citizens have strong feelings of ethnic identity (Alba 1990). Since the civil rights movement of the 1960s and 1970s, some ethnic groups have heightened their visibility and increased their demands for equal opportunity (Alba 1990). Ethnic and cultural diversity continues to permeate life in the United States. Its persistence and our nation's changing demographics suggest that it will characterize the future (Hodgkinson 1985).

Nearly half (46 percent) of school-age youths in the United States will be people of color by 2020 (Pallas, Natriello, and McDill 1989). People of color, women, and immigrants will make up more than 83 percent of the new additions to the U.S. work force between now and the turn of the century. White men born in the United States will make up only 15 percent of the new additions to the labor force during this period (Johnson and Packer 1987).

Simply recognizing ethnic and cultural diversity is not enough. Understanding and respect for diverse values, traditions, and behaviors are essential if we are to actualize fully our nation's democratic ideals. The call for understanding and respect is based on a belief that the existence and expression of differences can improve the quality of life for individuals, for ethnic and cultural groups, and for society as a whole.

For individuals, group identity can provide a foundation for self-definition. Ethnic and cultural group membership can provide a sense of belonging, of shared traditions, of interdependence of fate—especially for members of groups who have all too often had restricted access to institutions in the larger society. When society views ethnic and cultural differences with respect, individuals can define themselves ethnically without conflict or shame.

The psychological cost of assimilation has been and continues to be high for many U.S. citizens. It too often demands self-denial, self-hatred, and rejection of family and ethnic ties. Social demands for conformity, which have harmful human consequences, are neither democratic nor humane. Such practices deny dignity by refusing to accept individuals as persons in themselves and by limiting the realization of human potential. Such demands run counter to the democratic values of freedom of association and equality of opportunity.

A society that respects ethnic group differences aims to protect its citizens from discriminatory practices and prejudicial attitudes. Such respect supports the survival of these groups and augments their opportunities to shape their lives in ways they choose. For society as a whole, ethnic groups can serve as sources of innovation. By respecting differences,

society is provided a wider base of ideas, values, and behaviors that increase its capacity for creative change.

Coping with change is fundamental to the survival of culture. Adapting to new conditions is critical. Without constructive reaction to change, cultures may weaken and deteriorate. In the face of rapidly changing conditions, the United States, as a nation, has to be concerned with ensuring mechanisms for coping with change. One way cultures change is through the process of innovation: a person (or persons) introduces new ways of thinking or behaving which are accepted by society or challenge cultural views. By respecting the plurality of ethnic and cultural life-styles, and by permitting them to flourish, our national culture may expand the base of alternatives from which it can draw in responding to new conditions and new problems.

Conversely, to the extent that a culture is homogeneous, its capability for creative change is limited. When the range of tolerated differences in values and behaviors is minimal, rigidity inhibits innovation. Too much conformity and convergence is characteristic of mass culture. On the other hand, too little acceptance of common cultural values and practices can produce social disorganization. The balance is a delicate one in a culture that must face up to the challenge of changing conditions; a dynamic and pluralistic nation cannot be left without access to competing, unique, and creative ideas. Recognition and respect for ethnic and cultural differences enable society to enhance the potential of individuals and the integrity and contributions of ethnic and cultural groups, and so to invigorate the culture.

2. Ethnic and cultural diversity provides a basis for societal enrichment, cohesiveness, and survival.

The principles on which these guidelines are based seek not only to recognize and respect ethnic and cultural diversity but to establish across racial, ethnic, and cultural lines intercultural bonds that will contribute to the strength and vitality of society.

This position maintains the right of ethnic groups to socialize their young into their cultural patterns as long as such practices are consistent with human dignity and democratic ideals. Therefore, an individual's primary group associations—family relations, friendship groups, religious affiliations—may be heavily influenced by ethnic traditions. At the same time, members of ethnic groups have both the right and the responsibility to accept U.S. democratic values and to help shape the significant institutions of the larger society. Legal and educational institutions must have a strong commitment to affecting the conditions that will permit members of ethnic groups to become fully participating members of the larger society. Ethnic groups must feel that they have a stake in this society; to the extent that ethnic group members feel a sense of ownership in societal institutions, their cultural practices will reflect the inherent values of society as a whole. What is needed is a cohesive society, characterized by ethnic pluralism, wherein the self-identities of individuals allow them to say: "I am an African American (or a Polish American, or a Mexican American)—and I am an American."

Respect for ethnic differences should promote, not destroy, societal cohesion. Although separatism is not the desire of most members of ethnic groups, they strongly demand that their histories and cultures become integral parts of the school curriculum and the larger society (Asante 1987, 1991). To the extent that society creates an environment in which all ethnic groups can flourish, and in which such groups can contribute constructively to the shaping of public institutions, hostilities will be defused and the society will benefit from its rich base of ethnic traditions and cultures. In effect, unity thrives in an atmosphere where varieties of human potential are neither socially censored nor ignored, but valued.

3. Equality of opportunity must be afforded to all members of ethnic and cultural groups.

Recognition and respect for ethnic and cultural groups require legal enforcement of equal economic, political, and educational opportunity. Anything less relegates ethnic groups and their members to the inferior status that has too often limited the quality of their lives.

Ethnic and cultural groups themselves continue to demand equal participation in society as a whole. If society is to benefit from ethnic and cultural differences, it must provide for significant interactions within social institutions. To reach this goal, ethnic and cultural groups must have access to the full range of occupational, educational, economic, and political opportunities. Society will benefit from structural integration and the mutual involvement of all sorts of people in political, educational, and economic life.

4. Ethnic and cultural identification for individuals should be optional in a democracy.

Although the assimilationist ideology has dominated our national thought for two centuries, ethnicity has proved to be a resilient factor in U.S. life and culture. The centrality of Anglo-American tradition notwithstanding, many individuals continue to derive their primary identity from their ethnic group membership. At the same time, it must be recognized that widespread cultural assimilation and acculturation has taken place in U.S. society. Many individuals of white ethnic origin are no longer identified ethnically with their original or primordial ethnic group. Although a large number of these individuals have intermarried and much cultural exchange among white ethnic groups has taken place, a new collective ethnic identity has emerged among white Americans that most of them share. Alba (1990) calls this new ethnic identity and group *European Americans.*

The degree of individuals' ethnic attachments and affiliations vary greatly. The beliefs and behaviors of some individuals are heavily influenced by their ethnic culture or cultures; others maintain only some ethnic beliefs and behavioral characteristics; still others try to reject or lose, or are simply unaware of, their ethnic origins. There are also individuals of mixed ethnic origin who identify with more than one group or for whom ethnic identification may be difficult or impossible.

For many persons, then, ethnic criteria may be irrelevant for purposes of self-identification. Their identities stem primarily from, for example, gender, social class, occupation, political affiliation, or religion. Moreover, ethnic origins ought not to be romanticized. Many, though not all, who left their original homelands did so because opportunities were closed to them there. However good "the good old days" were, they are gone. The "old countries" too have been changing. Ethnicity should not be maintained artificially.

It is inconsistent with a democratic ideology to mandate ethnic affiliation. In an idealized democratic society, individuals are free to choose their group allegiances. Association should be voluntary—a matter of personal choice. In our society, however, members of some ethnic groups have this option

while others do not. Society should maximize the opportunity for individuals to choose their group identifications and affiliations.

Although a democratic society can and should protect the right to ethnic identification, it cannot insist upon it. To do so would violate individual freedom of choice. To confine individuals to any given form of affiliation violates the principles of liberty guaranteed by the basic documents upon which this nation was founded.

The Role of the School

The societal goals stated in this document are future oriented. In effect, they present a vision of our society that recognizes and respects ethnic and cultural diversity as compatible with national and societal unity rather than one that seeks to reduce ethnic and cultural differences. Further progress in that direction is consistent with the democratic ideals—freedom, equality, justice, and human dignity—embodied in our basic national documents. By respecting ethnic and cultural differences, we can help to close the gap between our democratic ideals and societal practices. Such practices are too often discriminatory toward members of ethnic and cultural groups.

It follows, therefore, that schools need to assume a new responsibility. Their socialization practices should incorporate the ethnic diversity that is an integral part of the democratic commitment to human dignity. At the same time, however, schools must help socialize youth in ways that will foster basic democratic ideals that serve as overarching goals for all U.S. citizens. The schools' goal should be to help attain a delicate balance of diversity and unity—one nation that respects the cultural rights and freedoms of its many peoples. As schools embark on educational programs that reflect multiculturalism, they must demonstrate a commitment to:

a. recognize and respect ethnic and cultural diversity;
b. promote societal cohesiveness based on the shared participation of ethnically and culturally diverse peoples;
c. maximize equality of opportunity for all individuals and groups; and
d. facilitate constructive societal change that enhances human dignity and democratic ideals.

The study of ethnic heritage should not consist of a narrow promotion of ethnocentrism or nationalism. Personal ethnic identity and knowledge of others' ethnic identities is essential to the sense of understanding and the feeling of personal well-being that promote intergroup and international understanding. Multicultural education should stress the process of self-identification as an essential aspect of the understanding that underlies commitment to the dignity of humankind throughout the world community.

The Nature of the Learner

Research indicates that individual learning styles vary, that all people do not learn in the same way. Of particular interest to multicultural education is research suggesting that learning styles may be related to ethnicity in some ways (Hale-Benson 1982; Shade 1989). On the basis of this research, schools can reject the notion that all students learn in precisely the same way. For too long, educational practices have reflected such universal views of learning and have expected all students to conform to them. Schools should recognize that they cannot treat all students alike or they run the risk of denying equal educational opportunity to all persons. Educators should be aware of behavior that is normative and acceptable in various ethnic and cultural groups. The practices of multicultural schools must be both responsive and adaptive to ethnic differences.

Goals for School Reform

Two major goals for school reform follow. Both are based on what has preceded: the principles of ethnic and cultural diversity, the role of the school, and cultural differences among individual learners.

1. Schools should create total school environments that are consistent with democratic ideals and cultural diversity.

Schools reflect their values not only in their curricula and materials, but in policies, hiring practices, governance procedures, and climate—sometimes referred to as the informal, or "hidden," curricula. It can be argued that students often learn as much about the society from nonformal areas of schooling as from the planned curriculum. Education for multiculturalism, therefore, requires more than a change in curricula and textbooks. It requires systemwide changes that permeate all aspects of school life.

2. Schools should define and implement curricular policies that are consistent with democratic ideals and cultural diversity.

Schools should not promote the ideologies and political goals of any specific group, including those of dominant groups, but should promote a democratic ideology. Too often, school curricula have promoted the interests of dominant groups and, therefore, have been detrimental to the interests of some ethnic groups. Promoting the interests of any group over those of others increases the possibility of ethnic and racial tension and conflict.

In recent years, a contentious debate has taken place about whose culture or cultures should be reflected and represented in the school and university curriculum. The debate has centered on which social science, philosophical, and literary works should constitute the canonical knowledge taught in the nation's schools, colleges, and universities.

The Western traditionalists are concerned that more content about women and people of color will result in insufficient attention to the Western roots of American civilization (Howe 1991; Ravitch 1990). Multiculturalists have pointed out that the voices, experiences, and perspectives of people of color and women are often left out or muted in many school and university courses about Western civilization and U.S. society (Lerner 1979; Sleeter and Grant 1987; Tetreault 1989). Other advocates have called for an Afrocentric curriculum for predominantly African-American schools (Asante 1987, 1990, 1991).

Curriculum transformation is necessary for the nation's schools, colleges, and universities to describe accurately the Western roots of American civilization and to depict the diversity that characterizes the West. The debt that Western civilization owes to Africa, Asia, and indigenous America should also be described in the curriculum (Bernal 1991; Diop 1974; Sertima 1988; Weatherford 1988).

The conception of Western civilization most often taught in schools, colleges, and universities should be broadened. Too often, the West is conceptualized in a narrow way to include primarily the heritage of Western European upper-class males. Yet the ideas and writings of women and people of color in

the United States are also Western. Zora Neale Hurston, Maxine Hong Kingston, Rudolfo A. Anaya, W. E. B. Dubois, Carlos Bulosan, and N. Scott Momaday—like Milton, Shakespeare, Virgil, and Locke—are Western writers. The West should also be described in ways that accurately describe the gap between its democratic ideals and realities. Western civilization is characterized by ideals such as democracy and freedom but also by struggle, conflict, and deferred and shattered dreams.

The curriculum in the nation's schools, colleges, and universities should reflect all of its citizens. When particular groups feel excluded or victimized by schools and other institutions, conflicts, tensions, and power struggles ensue. The pluralist dilemma related to the curriculum canon debate can only be resolved when all groups involved—the Western traditionalists, the Afrocentrists, and the multiculturalists—share power and engage in genuine dialogue and discussion. Power sharing is a requisite to genuine debate and conflict resolution. When groups and individuals feel victimized by the school and the larger society because of ethnicity, conflict and tension result, and struggles to gain rights occur.

Part Two: Curriculum Guidelines for Multicultural Education

1.0 Ethnic and cultural diversity should permeate the total school environment.

Effective teaching about U.S. ethnic and cultural groups can best take place within an educational setting that accepts, encourages, and respects the expression of ethnic and cultural diversity. To attain this kind of educational atmosphere, the total school environment—not merely courses and programs—must be reformed. Schools' informal or "hidden" curricula are as important as their formalized courses of study.

Teaching about various ethnic or cultural groups in a few specialized courses is not enough. Content about a variety of ethnic groups should be incorporated into many subject areas, preschool through 12th grade and beyond. Some dimensions of multicultural education, however, have higher priority in some subject areas than in others. We can identity several dimensions of multicultural education, including *content integration,* the *knowledge construction process*, and an *equity pedagogy* (Banks 1991b). In social studies, the humanities, and the language arts, content integration is often the first and most important concern. In physics, however, developing pedagogies that will help students of color and female students to excel academically might be of greater concern than content integration (Belenky et al. 1986). Students can examine how knowledge is constructed in each discipline.

Multicultural education clearly means different things in different disciplines and areas of study. To interpret or attempt to implement multicultural education the same way in each discipline or area of study will create frustration among teachers and build resistance to the concept. Nevertheless, teachers in each discipline can analyze their teaching procedures and styles to determine the extent to which they reflect multicultural issues and concerns. An equity pedagogy exists when teachers modify their instruction in ways that facilitate the academic achievement of students from diverse racial, cultural, gender, and social-class groups. This includes using a variety of teaching styles and approaches that are consistent with the wide range of learning styles found in various cultural, ethnic, and gender groups.

To permeate the total school environment with ethnic and

cultural diversity, students must have readily available resource materials that provide accurate information on the diverse aspects of the histories and cultures of various racial, ethnic, and cultural groups. Learning centers, libraries, and resource centers should include a variety of resources on the history, literature, music, folklore, views of life, and art of different ethnic and cultural groups.

Ethnic and cultural diversity in a school's informal programs should be reflected in assembly programs, classrooms, hallway and entrance decorations, cafeteria menus, counseling interactions, and extracurricular programs. School-sponsored dances that consistently provide only one kind of ethnic music, for example, are as contrary to the spirit and principles of multicultural education as are curricula that teach only about mainstream U.S. ideals, values, and contributions.

Participation in activities—such as cheerleading, booster clubs, honor societies, and athletic teams—should be open to all students; in fact, the participation of students from various racial, ethnic, and cultural backgrounds should be solicited. Such activities can provide invaluable opportunities not only for the development of self-esteem, but for students from different ethnic and cultural backgrounds to learn to work and play together, and to recognize that all individuals, whatever their ethnic identities, have worth and are capable of achieving.

2.0 School policies and procedures should foster positive multicultural interactions and understandings among students, teachers, and the support staff.

School governance should protect the individual's right to (1) retain esteem for his or her home environment, (2) develop a positive self-concept, (3) develop empathy and insight into and respect for the ethnicity of others, and (4) receive an equal educational opportunity.

Each institution needs rules and regulations to guide behavior so as to attain institutional goals and objectives. School rules and regulations should enhance cross-cultural harmony and understanding among students, staff, and teachers. In the past, school harmony was often sought through efforts to "treat everyone the same"; experience in multiethnic settings, however, indicates that the same treatment for everyone is unfair to many students. Instead of insisting on one ideal model of behavior that is unfair to many students, school policies should recognize and accommodate individual and ethnic group differences. This does not mean that some students should obey school rules and others should not; it means that ethnic groups' behaviors should be honored as long as they are not inconsistent with major school and societal goals. It also means that school policies may have to make allowances for ethnic traditions. For example, customs that affect Jewish students' food preferences and school attendance on certain religious days should be respected.

Equal educational opportunity should be increased by rules that protect students from procedures and practices that relegate them to low-ability or special education classes simply because of their low scores on standardized English reading and achievement tests.

It is especially important for educators to consider equity issues related to testing because many groups and individuals are pushing for the establishment of a national test or tests. Unless significant changes are made within schools and society that will enable low-income students and students of color to perform well on national tests, these students will become double victims—victims of both a poor educational system

and national tests that relegate them to inferior jobs and deny them opportunities for further education (Mercer 1989). If developed, these national tests should be constructed and used in ways that are consistent with the principles of ethnic pluralism and multicultural education described in these guidelines.

Guidance and other student services personnel should not view students stereotypically regarding their academic abilities and occupational aspirations, and students must be protected from responses based on such views. Counselors should be cautioned to counsel students on the basis of their individual potentials and interests as well as their ethnic needs and concerns. Counselors will need to be particularly aware of their own biases when counseling students whose ethnicity differs from theirs.

Schools should recognize the holidays and festivities of major importance to various ethnic groups. Provisions should be made to ensure that traditional holidays and festivities reflect multicultural modes of celebration. For example, the ways in which some American Indian tribes celebrate Thanksgiving, Orthodox Greeks celebrate Easter, and Jews celebrate Hanukkah can be appropriately included in school programs.

3.0 A school's staff should reflect the ethnic and cultural diversity within the United States.

Members of various ethnic and cultural groups must be part of a school's instructional, administrative, policymaking, and support staffs if the school is truly multiethnic and multicultural. School personnel—teachers, principals, cooks, custodians, secretaries, students, and counselors—make contributions to multicultural environments as important as do courses of study and instructional materials. Students learn important lessons about ethnic and cultural diversity by observing interactions among racial, ethnic, cultural, and gender groups in their school, observing and experiencing the verbal behavior of the professional and support staffs, and observing the extent to which the staff is ethnically and racially mixed. Therefore, school policies should be established and aggressively implemented to recruit and maintain a multiethnic school staff, sensitive to the needs of a pluralistic democratic society.

In addition, students can benefit from positive and cooperative interactions with students from various racial, ethnic, and cultural groups (Slavin 1983; Cohen 1986). When plans are made to mix students from diverse groups—whether through school desegregation, exchange programs and visits, or program assignment—extreme care must be taken to ensure that the environment in which the students interact is a positive and enhancing one (Banks 1991c). When students from different ethnic and racial groups interact within a hostile environment, their racial antipathies are likely to increase (Stephan 1985).

4.0 Schools should have systematic, comprehensive, mandatory, and continuing staff development programs.

A teacher is an important variable in a student's formal learning environment. Attention should be devoted to the training and retraining of teachers and other members of the professional and support staff to create the kind of multicultural school environment recommended in these guidelines. Sound materials and other instructional program components are ineffective in the hands of teachers who lack the skills, attitudes, perceptions, and content background essential for a positive multicultural school environment. An effective staff development program must involve administrators, librarians, counselors, and members of the support staff such as cooks, secretaries, and bus drivers. This is necessary because any well-trained and sensitive teacher must work within a supportive institutional environment to succeed. Key administrators, such as principals, must set by example the school norms for ethnic and cultural differences. The need to involve administrators, especially building principals, in comprehensive and systematic staff development programs cannot be overemphasized.

Effective professional staff development should begin at the preservice level, continue when educators are employed by schools, and focus on helping the staff members: (a) clarify and analyze their feelings, attitudes, and perceptions toward their own and other racial, ethnic, and cultural groups; (b) acquire knowledge about and understanding of the historical experiences and sociological characteristics of ethnic and cultural groups in the United States; (c) increase their instructional skills within multicultural school environments; (d) improve their intercultural communications skills; (e) improve their skill in curriculum development as it relates to ethnic and cultural diversity; and (f) improve their skill in creating, selecting, evaluating, and revising instructional materials.

Staff development for effective multicultural schools is best undertaken jointly by school districts, local colleges and universities, and local community agencies. Each bears a responsibility for training school personnel, at both the preservice and in-service levels, to function successfully within multicultural instructional settings.

Effective staff development programs must be carefully conceptualized and implemented. Short workshops, selected courses, and other short-term experiences may be essential components of such programs, but these alone cannot constitute an entire staff development program. Rather, sound staff development programs should consist of a wide variety of program components including needs assessments, curriculum development, peer teaching, and materials selection and evaluation. Lectures alone are insufficient. Ongoing changes should be made to make staff development programs more responsive to the needs of practicing professionals.

5.0 The curriculum should reflect the cultural learning styles and characteristics of the students within the school community.

Students in a school responsive to ethnic and cultural diversity cannot be treated identically and still be afforded equal educational opportunities. Some students have unique cultural and ethnic characteristics to which the school should respond deliberately and sensitively. Research indicates that the academic achievement of African-American and Hispanic students increases when cooperative teaching techniques such as the jigsaw are used (Aronson and Gonzalez 1988). Moreover, *all* students develop more positive racial and ethnic attitudes when teachers use cooperative, rather than competitive, learning activities (Aronson and Gonzalez 1988).

Research indicates that many students of color, especially those from low-income families, often have value orientations, behaviors, cognitive styles, language characteristics, and other cultural components that differ from those of the school's culture (Delpit 1988; Deyhle 1986; Fordham 1991; Fordham and Ogbu 1986; Gay 1991; Heath 1983; Hale-Benson [1982]; Shade 1989). These components often lead to

conflict between students and teachers. By comparison, most middle-class mainstream youths find the school culture consistent with their home cultures and are, therefore, much more comfortable in school. Many students, though, regardless of their racial, ethnic, or cultural identity, find the school culture alien, hostile, and self-defeating.

A school's culture and instructional programs should be restructured and made to reflect the cultures and learning styles of students from diverse ethnic and social-class groups (Banks and Banks 1989). Research indicates that the instructional strategies and learning styles most often favored in the nation's schools are inconsistent with the cognitive styles, cultural orientations, and cultural characteristics of some groups of students of color (Aronson and Gonzalez 1988; Fordham 1991). This research provides important guidelines and principles that educators can use to change schools to make them more responsive to students from diverse cultural groups. Educators should not ignore racial and ethnic differences when planning instruction; nor should they dismiss the question of racial and ethnic differences with the all-too-easy cliché, "I don't see racial differences in students and I treat them all alike." Research on cognitive styles and language and communication characteristics of ethnic groups suggests that if all students are treated alike, their distinctive needs are not being met and they are probably being denied access to equal educational opportunities (Cummins 1986; Heath 1983; Kochman 1981; Philips 1983).

Although differences among students are accepted in an effective multicultural school, teaching students to function effectively in mainstream society and in social settings different from the ones in which they were socialized, and helping them learn new cognitive styles and learning patterns, must also be major goals. The successful multicultural school helps students become aware of and able to acquire cultural and cognitive alternatives, thus enabling them to function successfully within cultural environments other than their own.

6.0 The multicultural curriculum should provide students with continuous opportunities to develop a better sense of self.

The multicultural curriculum should help students to develop a better sense of self. This development should be an ongoing process, beginning when the student first enters school and continuing throughout the student's school career. This development should include at least three areas:

1. Students should be helped to develop accurate self-identities. Students must ask questions such as who am I? and what am I? in order to come to grips with their own identities.

2. The multicultural curriculum should help students develop improved self-concepts. Beyond considering such questions as who they are and what they are, students should learn to feel positively about their identities, particularly their ethnic identities. Positive self-concepts may be expressed in several ways. The multicultural curriculum, for example, should recognize the varying talents of students and capitalize on them in the academic curriculum. All students need to feel that academic success is possible. The multicultural curriculum should also help students develop a high regard for their original languages and cultures.

3. The multicultural curriculum should help students develop greater self-understanding. Students should develop more sophisticated understandings of why they are the way they are, why their ethnic and cultural groups are the way they are,

and what ethnicity and culture mean in their daily lives. Such self-understanding will help students to handle more effectively situations in which ethnicity and culture may play a part.

Students cannot fully understand why they are the way they are and why certain things might occur in their future until they have a solid knowledge of the groups to which they belong and the effects of group membership on their lives. Multicultural education should enable students to come to grips with these individual and group relationships in general and the effects of ethnicity and culture on their lives in particular.

Looking at group membership should not undermine a student's individuality. Rather, it should add a dimension to the understanding of a student's unique individuality by learning the effects of belonging to groups. Neither are students to be assigned and locked into one group. Instead, students should be aware of the many groups to which they belong, both voluntarily and involuntarily, and recognize that at various moments one or more of these groups may be affecting their lives.

The multicultural curriculum should also help students understand and appreciate their personal backgrounds and family heritages. Family studies in the school can contribute to increased self-understanding and a personal sense of heritage, as contrasted with the generalized experiences presented in books. They can also contribute to family and personal pride. If parents and other relatives come to school to share their stories and experiences, students will become increasingly aware that ethnic groups are a meaningful part of our nation's heritage and merit study by all of us so that we can better understand the complexity of the nation's pluralistic experiences and traditions.

7.0 The curriculum should help students understand the totality of the experiences of ethnic and cultural groups in the United States.

The social problems that ethnic and cultural group members experience are often regarded as part of their cultural characteristics. Alcoholism, crime, and illiteracy, for example, are considered by many people cultural characteristics of particular racial or ethnic groups. Ethnicity is often assumed to mean something negative and divisive, and the study of ethnic groups and ethnicity often becomes the examination of problems such as prejudice, racism, discrimination, and exploitation. To concentrate exclusively on these problems when studying ethnicity creates serious distortions in perceptions of ethnic groups. Among other things, it stereotypes ethnic groups as essentially passive recipients of the dominant society's discrimination and exploitation. Although these are legitimate issues and should be included in a comprehensive, effective multicultural curriculum, they should not constitute the entire curriculum.

Although many ethnic group members face staggering sociopolitical problems, these problems do not constitute the whole of their lives. Nor are all ethnic groups affected to the same degree or in the same way by these problems. Moreover, many ethnic groups have developed and maintained viable life-styles and have made notable contributions to U.S. culture. The experiences of each ethnic group are part of a composite of human activities. Although it is true that each ethnic group has significant unifying historical experiences and cultural traits, no ethnic group has a single, homogeneous, historical-cultural pattern. Members of an ethnic group do not conform to a single cultural norm or mode of behavior, nor are ethnic cultures uniform and static.

Consequently, the many dimensions of ethnic experiences and cultures should be studied. The curriculum should help students understand the significant historical experiences and basic cultural patterns of ethnic groups, the critical contemporary issues and social problems confronting each of them, and the dynamic diversity of the experiences, cultures, and individuals within each ethnic group.

A consistently multifaceted approach to teaching benefits students in several major ways. It helps them to become aware of the commonalities within and among ethnic groups. At the same time, it helps counteract stereotyping by making students aware of the rich diversity within each ethnic group in the United States. It also helps students develop more comprehensive and realistic understandings of the broad range of ethnic group heritages and experiences.

8.0 The multicultural curriculum should help students understand that a conflict between ideals and realities always exists in human societies.

Traditionally, students in U.S. common schools have been taught a great deal about the ideals of our society. Conflicts between ideals, however, are often glossed over. Often values, such as freedom in the U.S. democracy, are treated as attainable ideals, and the realities of U.S. society have been distorted to make it appear that they have, indeed, been achieved. Courses in U.S. history and citizenship especially have been characterized by this kind of unquestioning approach to the socialization of youth. This form of citizenship education, "passing down the myths and legends of our national heritage," tends to inculcate parochial national attitudes, promote serious misconceptions about the nature of U.S. society and culture, and develop cynicism in youth who are aware of the gaps between the ideal and the real.

When ethnic studies emerged from the civil rights movement of the 1960s, there was a strong and negative reaction to the traditional approach to citizenship education. A widely expressed goal of many curriculum reformers was to "tell it like it is and was" in the classroom. In many of the reformed courses, however, U.S. history and society were taught and viewed primarily from the viewpoints of specific ethnic groups. Little attention was given to basic U.S. values, except to highlight gross discrepancies between ideals and practices of U.S. society. Emphasis was often on how ethnic groups of color had been oppressed by Anglo-Americans.

Both the unquestioning approach and the tell-it-like-it-is approach result in distortions. In a sound multicultural curriculum, emphasis should be neither on the ways in which the United States has "fulfilled its noble ideals" nor on the "sins committed by the Anglo-Americans" (or any other group of Americans). Rather, students should be encouraged to examine the democratic values that emerged in the United States, why they emerged, how they were defined in various periods, and to whom they referred in various eras. Students should also examine the extent to which these values have or have not been fulfilled, and the continuing conflict between values such as freedom and equality and between ideals in other societies.

Students should also be encouraged to examine alternative interpretations of the discrepancies between ideals and realities in the life and history of the United States. From the perspectives of some individuals and groups, there has been a continuing expansion of human rights in the United States. Others see a continuing process of weighing rights against rights as the optimum mix of values, none of which can be fully realized as ideals. Many argue that basic human rights are still limited to U.S. citizens who have certain class, racial, ethnic, gender, and cultural characteristics. Students should consider why these various interpretations arose and why there are different views regarding conflicts between the ideals and between the ideals and realities of U.S. society.

9.0 The multicultural curriculum should explore and clarify ethnic and cultural alternatives and options in the United States.

Educational questions regarding students' ethnic and cultural alternatives and options are complex and difficult. Some individuals, for a variety of complex reasons, are uncomfortable with their ethnic and cultural identities and wish to deny them. Some individuals are uncomfortable when their own ethnic groups are discussed in the classroom. Teachers need to handle these topics sensitively; they must not ignore them.

The degree of a class's resistance when studying ethnic or cultural groups is influenced by the teacher's approach to the study of diversity. Students can sense when the teacher or other students in the class are intolerant of their particular group or some of its characteristics. Students often receive such messages from nonverbal responses. The teacher can minimize students' resistance to studying their own heritage by creating a classroom atmosphere that reflects acceptance and respect for ethnic and cultural differences. Most importantly, teachers need to model their own acceptance of and respect for ethnic, racial, and cultural diversity.

Teachers should help students understand the options related to their own ethnic and cultural identity and the nature of ethnic and cultural alternatives and options within the United States. Students should be helped to understand that, ideally, all individuals should have the right to select the manner and degree of identifying or not identifying with their ethnic and cultural groups. They should learn, however, that some individuals, such as members of many white ethnic groups, have this privilege while others, such as most African Americans, have more limited options. Most persons of European ancestry can become structurally assimilated into the mainstream U.S. society. When they become highly assimilated, they can usually participate completely in most U.S. economic, social, and political institutions. On the other hand, no matter how culturally assimilated or acculturated members of some ethnic groups become, they are still perceived and stigmatized by the larger society on the basis of their physical characteristics.

Students should also be helped to understand that although individualism is strong in the United States, in reality many Americans, such as American Indians and Chinese Americans, are often judged not as individuals but on the basis of the racial or ethnic group to which they belong. While teachers may give American Indian or Chinese American students the option of examining or not examining their ethnic heritage and identity, such students need to be helped to understand how they are perceived and identified by the larger society. Educators must respect the individual rights of students, at the same time, however, they have a professional responsibility to help students learn basic facts and generalizations about the nature of race and ethnicity in the United States.

10.0 The multicultural curriculum should promote values, attitudes, and behaviors that support ethnic pluralism and cultural diversity as well as build and support the nation-state and the nation's shared national culture. E pluribus unum should be the goal of the schools and the nation.

Ethnicity and cultural identity are salient factors in the lives of many U.S. citizens. They helps individuals answer the question, Who am I? by providing a sense of peoplehood, identity, and cultural and spiritual roots. They provide a filter through which events, life-styles, norms, and values are processed and screened. They provide a means through which identity is affirmed, heritages are validated, and preferred associates are selected. Therefore, ethnicity and cultural identity serve necessary functions in many people's lives. Ethnicity and cultural identity are neither always positive and reinforcing, nor always negative and debilitating, although they have the potential for both. An effective multicultural curriculum examines all of these dimensions of ethnicity and cultural identity.

The curriculum should help students understand that diversity is an integral part of life in the United States. Ethnic and cultural diversity permeate U.S. history and society. Demographic projections indicate that the United States will become increasingly multiethnic and multicultural in the future. Consequently, schools should teach about ethnic and cultural diversity to help students acquire more accurate assessments of history and culture in the United States. Major goals of multicultural education include improving respect for human dignity, maximizing cultural options, understanding what makes people alike and different, and accepting diversity as inevitable and valuable to human life.

Students should learn that difference does not necessarily imply inferiority or superiority, and that the study of ethnic and cultural group differences need not lead to polarization. They should also learn that although conflict is unavoidable in ethnically and racially pluralistic societies, such conflict does not necessarily have to be destructive or divisive. Conflict is an intrinsic part of the human condition, especially so in a pluralistic society. Conflict is often a catalyst for social progress. Multicultural education programs that explore ethnic diversity in positive, realistic ways will present ethnic conflict in its proper perspective. They will help students understand that there is strength in diversity, and that cooperation among ethnic groups does not necessarily require identical beliefs, behaviors, and values.

The multicultural curriculum should help students understand and respect ethnic diversity and broaden their cultural options. Too many people in the United States learn only the values, behavioral patterns, and beliefs of either mainstream society or their own ethnic groups, cultural groups, or communities. Socialization is, in effect, encapsulating, providing few opportunities for most individuals to acquire more than stereotypes about ethnic and cultural groups other than their own. Therefore, many people tend to view other ethnic groups and life-styles as "abnormal" or "deviant." The multicultural curriculum can help students correct these misconceptions by teaching them that other ways of living are as valid and viable as their own.

The multicultural curriculum should also promote the basic values expressed in our major historical documents. Each ethnic group should have the right to practice its own religious, social, and cultural beliefs, albeit within the limits of due regard for the rights of others. There is, after all, a set of over-arching values that all groups within a society or nation must endorse to maintain societal cohesion. In our nation, these core values stem from our commitment to human dignity, and include justice, equality, freedom, and due process of law. Although the school should value and reflect ethnic and cultural diversity, it should not promote the practices and beliefs of any ethnic or cultural group that contradict the core democratic values of the United States. Rather, the school should foster ethnic and cultural differences that maximize opportunities for democratic living. Pluralism must take place within the context of national unity. *E pluribus unum*—out of many, one—should be our goal.

Although ethnic and cultural group membership should not restrict an individual's opportunity and ability to achieve and to participate, it is sometimes used by groups in power to the detriment of less powerful groups. Individuals who do not understand the role of ethnicity often find it a troublesome reality, one extremely difficult to handle. Multicultural curricula should help students examine the dilemmas surrounding ethnicity as a step toward realizing its full potential as an enabling force in the lives of individuals, groups, and the nation.

11.0 The multicultural curriculum should help students develop their decision-making abilities, social participation skills, and sense of political efficacy as necessary bases for effective citizenship in a pluralistic democratic nation.

The demands upon people to make reflective decisions on issues related to race, ethnicity, and culture are increasing as the nation's ethnic texture deepens. When people are unable to process the masses of conflicting information—including facts, opinions, interpretations, and theories about ethnic groups—they are often overwhelmed.

The multicultural curriculum must enable students to gain knowledge and apply it. Students need a rich foundation of sound knowledge. Facts, concepts, generalizations, and theories differ in their capability for organizing particulars and in predictive capacity; concepts and generalizations have more usefulness than mere collections of miscellaneous facts. Young people need practice in the steps of scholarly methods for arriving at knowledge—identifying problems, formulating hypotheses, locating and evaluating source materials, organizing information as evidence, analyzing, interpreting, and reworking what they find, and making conclusions. Students also need ample opportunities to learn to use knowledge in making sense out of the situations they encounter.

When curricular programs are inappropriate, teaching is inept, or expectations are low for students of some ethnic groups, and especially for those who are low-income, the emphasis in class is likely to be on discrete facts, memorization of empty generalizations, and low-level skills. Even if the names, dates, and exercises in using an index are drawn from ethnic content, such an emphasis is still discriminatory and inconsistent with the basic purpose of multicultural education. All young people need opportunities to develop powerful concepts, generalizations, and intellectual abilities when studying content related to ethnic and cultural diversity.

Students must also learn to identify values and relate them to knowledge. Young people should be taught methods for clarifying their own values relating to ethnic and cultural diversity. Such processes should include identifying value

problems (their own and others'), describing evaluative behaviors, recognizing value conflicts in themselves and in social situations, recognizing and proposing alternatives based on values, and making choices between values in light of their consequences.

Determining basic ideas, discovering and verifying facts, and valuing are interrelated aspects of decision making. Ample opportunity for practice in real-life situations is necessary; such practice frequently requires interdisciplinary as well as multicultural perspectives. Decision-making skills help people assess social situations objectively and perceptively, identify feasible courses of action and project their consequences, decide thoughtfully, and then act.

The multicultural curriculum must also help students develop effective social and civic action skills because many students from ethnic groups are overwhelmed by a sense of a lack of control of their destinies. These feelings often stem from their belief that, as in the past, they and other people of color have little influence on political policies and institutions (Ogbu 1990). The multicultural curriculum should help students develop a sense of political efficacy and become active and effective in the civic life of their communities and the nation. With a basis in strong commitments to such democratic values as justice, freedom, and equality, students can learn to exercise political and social influence responsibly to influence societal decisions related to race, ethnicity, and cultural freedom in ways consistent with human dignity.

The school, in many ways, is a microcosm of society, reflecting the changing dynamics of ethnic group situations. The school can provide many opportunities for students to practice social participation skills and to test their political efficacy as they address themselves to resolving some of the school's racial and ethnic problems. Issues such as the participation of ethnic individuals in school government, the uneven application of discriminatory disciplinary rules, and preferential treatment of certain students because of their racial, ethnic, cultural, and social-class backgrounds are examples of problems that students can help to resolve. Applying social action skills effectively, students can combine knowledge, valuing, and thought gained from multicultural perspectives and experiences to resolve problems affecting racial, ethnic, and cultural groups.

By providing students with opportunities to use decision-making abilities and social action skills in the resolution of problems affecting ethnic, racial, and cultural groups, schools can contribute to more effective education for democratic citizenship.

12.0 The multicultural curriculum should help students develop the skills necessary for effective interpersonal, interethnic, and intercultural group interactions.

Effective interpersonal interaction across ethnic group lines is often difficult to achieve. The problem is complicated by the fact that individuals bring to cross-ethnic interaction situations attitudes, values, and expectations that influence their own behavior, including their responses to the behavior of others. These expectations are sometimes formed on the basis of what their own groups deem appropriate behavior and what each individual believes he or she knows about other ethnic groups. Much knowledge about ethnic groups is stereotyped, distorted, and based on distant observations, scattered and superficial contacts, inadequate or imbalanced media treatment, and incomplete factual information. Attempts at cross-ethnic interpersonal interactions, therefore, are often stymied by ethnocentrism.

The problems created by ethnocentrism can be at least partially resolved by helping students recognize the forces operating in interpersonal interactions, and how these forces affect behavior. Students should develop skills and concepts to overcome factors that prevent successful interactions including identifying ethnic and cultural stereotypes, examining media treatment of ethnic groups, clarifying ethnic and cultural attitudes and values, developing cross-cultural communication skills, recognizing how attitudes and values are projected in verbal and nonverbal behaviors, and viewing the dynamics of interpersonal interactions from others' perspectives.

One of the goals of multicultural education should be to help individuals function easily and effectively with members of both their own and other racial, ethnic, and cultural groups. The multicultural curriculum should provide opportunities for students to explore lines of cross-cultural communication and to experiment with cross-ethnic and cross-cultural functioning. Actual experiences can be effective teaching devices, allowing students to test stereotypes and idealized behavioral constructs against real-life situations, and make the necessary adjustments in their frames of reference and behaviors. In the process, they should learn that ethnic group members, in the final analysis, are individuals, with all of the variations that characterize all individuals, and that ethnicity is only one of many variables that shape their personalities. Students will be forced to confront their values and make moral choices when their experiences in cross-ethnic and cross-cultural interactions produce information contrary to previously held notions. Thus, students should broaden their ethnic and cultural options, increase their frames of reference, develop greater appreciation for individual and ethnic differences, and deepen their own capacities as human beings.

13.0 The multicultural curriculum should be comprehensive in scope and sequence, should present holistic views of ethnic and cultural groups, and should be an integral part of the total school curriculum.

Students learn best from well-planned, comprehensive, continuous, and interrelated experiences. In an effective multicultural school, the study of ethnic and cultural content is integrated into the curriculum from preschool through 12th grade and beyond. This study should be carefully planned to encourage the development of progressively more complex concepts and generalizations. It should also involve students in the study of a variety of ethnic and cultural groups.

A comprehensive multicultural curriculum should also include a broad range of experiences within the study of any group: present culture, historical experiences, sociopolitical realities, contributions to the nation's development, problems faced in everyday living, and conditions of existence in society.

Students should be introduced to the experiences of persons from widely varying backgrounds. Although the study of ethnic and cultural success stories can help students of an ethnic group develop pride in their own group, the curriculum should include study of ethnic peoples in general, not just heroes and success stories. In addition, those outside of an ethnic group can develop greater respect for that group by learning about these heroes and successes. Moreover, in establishing heroes and labeling people as successes, teachers should move beyond the standards of the dominant society and consider the

values of each ethnic group and the worth of each individual life. An active contributor to an ethnic neighborhood may be more of a hero to the local community than a famous athlete; a good parent may be more of a "success" than a famous politician.

For optimum effectiveness, the study of ethnic and cultural group experiences must be interwoven into the total curriculum. It should not be reserved for special occasions, units, or courses, nor should it be considered supplementary to the existing curriculum. Such observances as African-American History or Brotherhood Week, Hanukkah, Cinco de Mayo, St. Patrick's Day, and Martin Luther King, Jr.'s birthday are important and necessary, but insufficient in themselves. To rely entirely on these kinds of occasions and events, or to relegate ethnic content to a marginal position in the curriculum, is to guarantee a minimal influence of ethnic studies.

The basic premises and organizational structures of schools should be reformed to reflect the nation's multicultural realities. The curriculum should be reorganized so that ethnic and cultural diversity is an integral, natural, and normal component of educational experiences for *all* students, with ethnic and cultural content accepted and used in everyday instruction, and with various ethnic and cultural perspectives introduced. Multicultural content is as appropriate and important in teaching such fundamental skills and abilities as reading, thinking, and decision making as it is in teaching about social issues raised by racism, dehumanization, racial conflict, and alternative ethnic and cultural life-styles.

14.0 The multicultural curriculum should include the continuous study of the cultures, historical experiences, social realities, and existential conditions of ethnic and cultural groups, including a variety of racial compositions.

The multicultural curriculum should involve students in the continuous study of ethnic groups of different racial compositions. A curriculum that concentrates on one ethnic or cultural group is not multicultural. Nor is a curriculum multicultural if it focuses exclusively on European ethnics or exclusively on ethnic groups of color. Every ethnic group cannot be included in the curriculum of a particular school or school district—the number is too large to be manageable. The inclusion of groups of different racial compositions, however, is a necessary characteristic of effective multicultural education.

Moreover, the multicultural curriculum should include the consistent examination of significant aspects of ethnic experiences influenced by or related to race. These include such concepts as racism, racial prejudice, racial discrimination, and exploitation based on race. The sensitive and continuous development of such concepts should help students develop an understanding of racial factors in the past and present of our nation.

15.0 Interdisciplinary and multidisciplinary approaches should be used in designing and implementing the multicultural curriculum.

No single discipline can adequately explain all components of the life-styles, cultural experiences, and social problems of ethnic groups. Knowledge from any one discipline is insufficient to help individuals make adequate decisions on the complex issues raised by racism, sexism, structural exclusion, poverty, and powerlessness. Concepts such as racism, anti-Semitism, and language discrimination have multiple dimensions. To delineate these requires the concepts and perspectives of the social sciences, history, literature, music, art, and philosophy.

Single-discipline or mono-perspective analyses of complex ethnic and cultural issues can produce skewed, distorted interpretations and evaluations. A promising way to avoid these pitfalls is to employ consistently multidisciplinary approaches in studying experiences and events related to ethnic and cultural groups. For example, ethnic protest is not simply a political, economic, artistic, or sociological activity; it is all four of these. Therefore, a curriculum that purports to be multicultural and is realistic in its treatment of ethnic protest must focus on its broader ramifications. Such study must address the scientific, political, artistic, and sociological dimensions of protest.

The accomplishments of the United States are due neither to the ingenuity and creativity of a single ethnic or cultural group, nor to accomplishments in a single area, but rather to the efforts and contributions of many ethnic groups and individuals in many areas. African American, Latino, American Indian, Asian American, and European immigrant group members have all contributed to the fields of science and industry, politics, literature, economics, and the arts. Multidisciplinary analyses will best help students to understand them.

16.0 The multicultural curriculum should use comparative approaches in the study of ethnic·and cultural groups.

The study of ethnic and cultural group experiences should not be a process of competition. It should not promote the idea that any one ethnic or cultural group has a monopoly on talent and worth, or incapacity and weakness, but, instead, the idea that each individual and each ethnic group has worth and dignity. Students should be taught that persons from all ethnic groups have common characteristics and needs, although they are affected differently by certain social situations and may use different means to respond to their needs and to achieve their objectives. Furthermore, school personnel should remember that realistic comparative approaches to the study of different ethnic and cultural group experiences are descriptive and analytical, not normative or judgmental. Teachers should also be aware of their own biases and prejudices as they help students to use comparative approaches.

Social situations and events included in the curriculum should be analyzed from the perspectives of several ethnic and cultural groups instead of using a mono-perspective analysis. This approach allows students to see the subtle ways in which the lives of different ethnic group members are similar and interrelated, to study the concept of universality as it relates to ethnic groups, and to see how all ethnic groups are active participants in all aspects of society. Studying such issues as power and politics, ethnicity, and culture from comparative, multicultural perspectives will help students to develop more realistic, accurate understandings of how these issues affect everyone, and how the effects are both alike and different.

17.0 The multicultural curriculum should help students to view and interpret events, situations, and conflict from diverse ethnic and cultural perspectives and points of view.

Historically, students have been taught to view events, situations, and our national history primarily from the perspectives of mainstream historians and social scientists sympathetic to the dominant groups within our society. The perspectives of other groups have been largely omitted in the school curriculum. The World War II Japanese-American internment and the Indian Removal Act of 1830, for example, are rarely studied from the points of view of interned Japanese Americans or the American Indians forced to leave their homes and move west.

To gain a more complete understanding of both our past and our present, students should look at events and situations from the perspectives of the mainstream and from the perspectives of marginalized groups. This approach to teaching is more likely to make our students less ethnocentric and more able to understand that almost any event or situation can be legitimately looked at from many perspectives. When using this approach in the classroom, the teacher should avoid, as much as possible, labeling any perspective "right" or "wrong." Rather, the teacher should try to help students understand how each group may view a situation differently and why. The emphasis should be on understanding and explanation and not on simplistic moralizing. For example, the perceptions many Jewish Americans have of political events in the United States have been shaped by memories of the Holocaust and anti-Semitism in the United States.

Ethnicity and cultural diversity have strongly influenced the nature of intergroup relations in U.S. society. The way that individuals perceive events and situations occurring in the United States is often influenced by their ethnic and cultural experiences, especially when the events and situations are directly related to ethnic conflict and discrimination or to issues such as affirmative action and busing for school desegregation. When students view a historical or contemporary situation from the perspectives of one ethnic or cultural group only—whether majority or minority—they can acquire, at best, an incomplete understanding.

18.0 The multicultural curriculum should conceptualize and describe the development of the United States as a multidirectional society.

A basic structural concept in the study and teaching of U.S. society is the view that the United States has developed mainly from east to west. According to this concept, the United States is the product of the spread of civilization from Western Europe across the Atlantic Ocean to the east coast of what is today the United States and then west to the Pacific. Within this approach, ethnic groups appear almost always in two forms: as obstacles to the advancement of westward-moving Anglo civilization or as problems that must be corrected or, at least, kept under control.

The underlying rationale for this frame of reference is that the study of U.S. history is for the most part an account of processes within the national boundaries of the United States. In applying this frame of reference, however, educators have been inconsistent, including as part of the study of the United States such themes as pre–United States geography, the pre–United States British colonies, the Texas revolution, and the Lone Star Republic. In short, the study of the United States has traditionally included phenomena outside the boundaries of the political United States.

Yet, while including some non–United States themes as part of the traditional study of the United States, school programs have not adequately included study of the Native American, Hispanic, and Mexican societies that developed on land that ultimately became part of the United States. Nor has sufficient attention been devoted to the northwesterly flow of cultures from Africa to the United States, the northerly flow of cultures from Mexico, Latin America, and the Caribbean, the easterly flow of cultures from Asia, and the westerly flow of latter-day immigrants from Eastern, Central, and Southern Europe.

Multicultural education, from the early years of school onward, must redress these intellectually invalid and distorting imbalances by illuminating the variety of cultural experiences that compose the total U.S. experience. Multicultural education must consistently address the development of the entire geo-cultural United States—that area which, in time, was to become the United States and the peoples encompassed by that area. Moreover, the flow of cultures into the United States must be viewed multidirectionally.

19.0 Schools should provide opportunities for students to participate in the aesthetic experiences of various ethnic and cultural groups.

The study of ethnic and cultural groups should be based on more than the social sciences. Although incorporating statistical and analytical social science methodologies and concepts into the study of ethnic and cultural groups is valuable, an overreliance on these methods lacks an important part of the multicultural experience—participation in the experiences of ethnic and cultural groups.

A number of teaching materials can be used. Students should read and hear past and contemporary writings of members of various ethnic and cultural groups. Poetry, short stories, folklore, essays, plays, and novels should be used. Ethnic autobiographies offer special insight into what it means to be ethnic in the United States.

Ethnic music, art, architecture, and dance—past and contemporary—provide other avenues for experiential participation, interpreting the emotions and feelings of ethnic groups. The arts and humanities can serve as excellent vehicles for studying group experiences by focusing on these questions: What aspects of the experience of a particular ethnic group helped create these kinds of musical and artistic expressions? What do they reveal about these groups?

Studying multiethnic literature and arts, students should become acquainted with what has been created in local ethnic communities. In addition, members of local ethnic communities can provide dramatic "living autobiographies" for students; invite them to discuss their viewpoints and experiences with students. Students should also have opportunities for developing their own artistic, musical, and literary abilities, even to make them available to the local community.

Role playing of various ethnic and cultural experiences should be interspersed throughout the curriculum to encourage understanding of what it means to belong to various ethnic groups. The immersion of students in multiethnic experiences is an effective means for developing understanding of both self and others.

20.0 The multicultural curriculum should provide opportunities for students to study ethnic group languages as legitimate communication systems and help them develop full literacy in at least two languages.

A multicultural curriculum recognizes language diversity and promotes the attitude that all languages and dialects are valid communicating systems for some groups and for some purposes. The program requires a multidisciplinary focus on language and dialect.

Concepts about language and dialect derived from disciplines such as anthropology, sociology, and political science expand students' perceptions of language and dialect as something more than correct grammar. For example, the nature and intent of language policies and laws in the United States can be compared to those in bilingual nations. Students can also be taught sociolinguistic concepts that provide a framework for understanding the verbal and nonverbal behavior of others and themselves. Critical listening, speaking, and reading habits should be nurtured with special attention to the uses of language.

Research indicates that a school's rejection of a student's home language affects the student's self-esteem, academic achievement, and social and occupational mobility. Conversely, a school's acceptance and use of a student's home language improves the student's self-esteem, academic achievement, and relationships among students in a school (U.S. Commission on Civil Rights 1975). In a multicultural curriculum, students are provided opportunities to study their own and others' dialects. They become increasingly receptive to the languages and dialects of their peers. Such an approach helps students develop concepts in their own vernaculars whenever necessary at the same time promoting appreciation of home language environments.

Literacy in U.S. English is a time-honored goal of schools and should be maintained. Another important goal of the multicultural curriculum, however, is to help all students acquire literacy in a second language. Second language literacy requires students to understand, speak, read, and write well enough to communicate effectively with native speakers of the second language. Equally important, students should study the cultures of the people who use the second language. Ultimately, effective communication in the second language requires an understanding of its people and their culture.

Some students come to school speaking two languages. These students should be provided the opportunity to develop full literacy in their native language. In turn, these students and their parents can be used as resources for helping other students acquire a second language proficiency.

Second language literacy complements other areas of the multicultural curriculum. For example, approaches for studying the culture of other people are described in several of the above guidelines. As students are learning a second language, they can learn skills in interpersonal and intercultural communications. Further, because these guidelines encourage multidisciplinary approaches, second language literacy can be achieved while other areas of the language arts and the social studies are taught.

21.0 The multicultural curriculum should make maximum use of experiential learning, especially local community resources.

An effective multicultural curriculum includes a study of ethnic and cultural groups not only nationally, but locally as well. An effective multicultural curriculum must expand beyond classroom walls. Teachers should use the local community as a "laboratory" in which students can develop and use intellectual, social, and political action skills. Planned field trips and individual or group research projects are helpful. Continuous investigation of the local community can provide insights into the dynamics of ethnic and cultural groups. It can create greater respect for what has been accomplished.

It can promote awareness of and commitment to what still needs to be done to improve the lives and opportunities of all local residents.

Every member of the local community, including students' family members, is a valuable source of knowledge. There are no class, educational, or linguistic qualifications for participating in the U.S. experience, for having a culture or society, for having family or neighborhood traditions, for perceiving the surrounding community, or for relating experiences. Teachers should invite local residents of various ethnic backgrounds to the classroom to share their experiences and views with students, relate their oral traditions, answer questions, offer new outlooks on society and history, and open doors of investigation for students. Special efforts should be made to involve senior citizens in school multicultural programs both to help them develop a higher sense of self-worth and to benefit the students and the school community.

It is important that students develop a sensitivity to ethnic differences and a conceptual framework for viewing ethnic differences before interacting with ethnic classroom guests or studying the local ethnic communities. Otherwise, these promising opportunities may reinforce, rather than reduce, ethnic stereotypes and prejudices.

In study projects, students can consider such topics as local population distribution, housing, school assignments, political representation, and ethnic community activities. Older students can take advantage of accessible public documents, such as city council and school board minutes, minutes of local organizations, and church records for insight into the community. To separate the local community from the school is to ignore the everyday world in which students live.

22.0 The assessment procedures used with students should reflect their ethnic and cultural experiences.

To make the school a truly multicultural institution, major changes must be made in the ways in which we test and ascertain student abilities. Most of the intelligence tests administered in the public schools are based upon a mainstream conformity, mono-ethnic model. Because many students socialized within other ethnic and cultural groups find the tests and other aspects of the school alien and intimidating, they perform poorly and are placed in low academic tracks, special education classes, or low-ability reading groups (Oakes 1985). Research indicates that teachers in these kinds of situations tend to have low expectations for their students and often fail to create the kinds of learning environments that promote proficiency in the skills and abilities necessary to function effectively in society (Oakes 1985).

In the final analysis, standardized intelligence testing frequently serves to deny some youths equal educational opportunities. The results of these tests are often used to justify the noneducation of students of color and low-income students and to relieve teachers and other school personnel from accountability (Deyhle 1986; Mercer 1989). Novel assessment devices that reflect the cultures of ethnic youths need to be developed and used. Moreover, teacher-generated tests and other routine classroom assessment techniques should reflect the cultures of ethnic youths. It will, however, do little good for educators to create improved assessment procedures for ethnic youths unless they also implement multicultural curricular and instructional practices.

23.0 Schools should conduct ongoing, systematic evaluations of the goals, methods, and instructional materials used in teaching about ethnic and cultural diversity.

Schools should formulate attainable goals and objectives for multicultural education. To evaluate the extent to which these goals and objectives are accomplished, school personnel must judge—with evidence—what occurs in their schools in three broad areas: (1) school policies and governance procedures; (2) everyday practices of staff and teachers; and (3) curricular programs and offerings, academic and nonacademic, preschool through 12th grade. These guidelines and the checklist that follows in part 3 will help schools' evaluation programs.

Many sources of evidence should be used. Teachers, administrators, support staff, parents, students, and others in the school community ought to participate in providing and evaluating evidence.

Evaluation should be construed as a means by which a school, its staff, and students can improve multiethnic and multicultural relations, experiences, and understandings. Evaluation should be oriented toward analyzing and improving, not castigating or applauding, multicultural programs.

(continued)

Part Three: The Multicultural Education Program Evaluation Checklist

	Rating			Guidelines
Strongly ◄——————► Hardly at all				

<table>
<tr><td></td><td></td><td></td><td></td><td>

1.0   Does ethnic and cultural diversity permeate the total school environment?
    1.1   Are ethnic content and perspectives incorporated into all aspects of the curriculum, preschool through 12th grade and beyond?
    1.2   Do instructional materials treat racial and ethnic differences and groups honestly, realistically, and sensitively?
    1.3   Do school libraries and resource centers offer a variety of materials on the histories, experiences, and cultures of many racial, ethnic, and cultural groups?
    1.4   Do school assemblies, decorations, speakers, holidays, and heroes reflect racial, ethnic, and cultural group differences?
    1.5   Are extracurricular activities multiethnic and multicultural?

2.0   Do school policies and procedures foster positive interactions among the various racial, ethnic, and cultural group members of the school?
    2.1   Do school policies accommodate the behavioral patterns, learning styles, and orientations of those ethnic and cultural group members actually in the school?
    2.2   Does the school provide a variety of instruments and techniques for teaching and counseling students of various ethnic and cultural groups?
    2.3   Do school policies recognize the holidays and festivities of various ethnic groups?
    2.4   Do school policies avoid instructional and guidance practices based on stereotyped and ethnocentric perceptions?
    2.5   Do school policies respect the dignity and worth of students as individuals *and* as members of racial, ethnic, and cultural groups?

3.0   Is the school staff (administrators, instructors, counselors, and support staff) multiethnic and multiracial?
    3.1   Has the school established and enforced policies for recruiting and maintaining a staff made up of individuals from various racial and ethnic groups?

4.0   Does the school have systematic, comprehensive, mandatory, and continuing multicultural staff development programs?
    4.1   Are teachers, librarians, counselors, administrators, and support staff included in the staff development programs?
    4.2   Do the staff development programs include a variety of experiences (such as lectures, field experiences, and curriculum projects)?
    4.3   Do the staff development programs provide opportunities to gain knowledge and understanding about various racial, ethnic, and cultural groups?
    4.4   Do the staff development programs provide opportunities for participants to explore their attitudes and feelings about their own ethnicity and others'?
    4.5   Do the staff development programs examine the verbal and nonverbal patterns of interethnic group interactions?
    4.6   Do the staff development programs provide opportunities for learning how to create and select multiethnic instructional materials and how to incorporate multicultural content into curriculum materials?

5.0   Does the curriculum reflect the ethnic learning styles of students within the school?

</td></tr>
</table>

Rating				Guidelines
Strongly ←			→ Hardly at all	
				5.1 Is the curriculum designed to help students learn how to function effectively in various cultural environments and learn more than one cognitive style?
				5.2 Do the objectives, instructional strategies, and learning materials reflect the cultures and cognitive styles of the various ethnic and cultural groups within the school?
				6.0 Does the curriculum provide continuous opportunities for students to develop a better sense of self?
				6.1 Does the curriculum help students strengthen their self-identities?
				6.2 Is the curriculum designed to help students develop greater self-understanding?
				6.3 Does the curriculum help students improve their self-concepts?
				6.4 Does the curriculum help students to better understand themselves in light of their ethnic and cultural heritages?
				7.0 Does the curriculum help students understand the wholeness of the experiences of ethnic and cultural groups?
				7.1 Does the curriculum include the study of societal problems some ethnic and cultural group members experience, such as racism, prejudice, discrimination, and exploitation?
				7.2 Does the curriculum include the study of historical experiences, cultural patterns, and social problems of various ethnic and cultural groups?
				7.3 Does the curriculum include both positive and negative aspects of ethnic and cultural group experiences?
				7.4 Does the curriculum present people of color both as active participants in society and as subjects of oppression and exploitation?
				7.5 Does the curriculum examine the diversity within each group's experience?
				7.6 Does the curriculum present group experiences as dynamic and continuously changing?
				7.7 Does the curriculum examine the total experiences of groups instead of focusing exclusively on the "heroes"?
				8.0 Does the curriculum help students identify and understand the ever-present conflict between ideals and realities in human societies?
				8.1 Does the curriculum help students identify and understand the value conflicts inherent in a multicultural society?
				8.2 Does the curriculum examine differing views of ideals and realities among ethnic and cultural groups?
				9.0 Does the curriculum explore and clarify ethnic alternatives and options within U.S. society?
				9.1 Does the teacher create a classroom atmosphere reflecting an acceptance of and respect for ethnic and cultural differences?
				9.2 Does the teacher create a classroom atmosphere allowing realistic consideration of alternatives and options for members of ethnic and cultural groups?
				10.0 Does the curriculum promote values, attitudes, and behaviors that support ethnic and cultural diversity?
				10.1 Does the curriculum help students examine differences within and among ethnic and cultural groups?
				10.2 Does the curriculum foster attitudes supportive of cultural democracy and other unifying democratic ideals and values?
				10.3 Does the curriculum reflect ethnic and cultural diversity?

Rating					Guidelines
Strongly ←——————→ Hardly at all					

10.4 Does the curriculum present diversity as a vital societal force that encompasses both potential strength and potential conflict?

11.0 Does the curriculum help students develop decision-making abilities, social participation skills, and a sense of political efficacy necessary for effective citizenship?
   11.1 Does the curriculum help students develop the ability to distinguish facts from interpretations and opinions?
   11.2 Does the curriculum help students develop skills in finding and processing information?
   11.3 Does the curriculum help students develop sound knowledge, concepts, generalizations, and theories about issues related to ethnicity and cultural identity?
   11.4 Does the curriculum help students develop sound methods of thinking about issues related to ethnic and cultural groups?
   11.5 Does the curriculum help students develop skills in clarifying and reconsidering their values and relating them to their understanding of ethnicity and cultural identity?
   11.6 Does the curriculum include opportunities to use knowledge, valuing, and thinking in decision making on issues related to race, ethnicity, and culture?
   11.7 Does the curriculum provide opportunities for students to take action on social problems affecting racial, ethnic, and cultural groups?
   11.8 Does the curriculum help students develop a sense of efficacy?

12.0 Does the curriculum help students develop skills necessary for effective interpersonal and intercultural group interactions?
   12.1 Does the curriculum help students understand ethnic and cultural reference points that influence communication?
   12.2 Does the curriculum help students participate in cross-ethnic and cross-cultural experiences and reflect upon them?

13.0 Is the multicultural curriculum comprehensive in scope and sequence, presenting holistic views of ethnic and cultural groups, and an integral part of the total school curriculum?
   13.1 Does the curriculum introduce students to the experiences of persons of widely varying backgrounds in the study of each ethnic and cultural group?
   13.2 Does the curriculum discuss the successes and contributions of group members within the context of that group's values?
   13.3 Does the curriculum include the role of ethnicity and culture in the local community as well as in the nation?
   13.4 Does content related to ethnic and cultural groups extend beyond special units, courses, occasions, and holidays?
   13.5 Are materials written by and about ethnic and cultural groups used in teaching fundamental skills?
   13.6 Does the curriculum provide for the development of progressively more complex concepts, abilities, and values?
   13.7 Is the study of ethnicity and culture incorporated into instructional plans rather than being supplementary or additive?

14.0 Does the curriculum include the continuous study of the cultures, historical experiences, social realities, and existential conditions of ethnic groups with a variety of racial compositions?
   14.1 Does the curriculum include study of several ethnic and cultural groups?

Rating				Guidelines
Strongly ←			→ Hardly at all	
				14.2 Does the curriculum include studies of both white ethnic groups and ethnic groups of color?
				14.3 Does the curriculum provide for continuity in the examination of aspects of experience affected by race?
				15.0 Are interdisciplinary and multidisciplinary approaches used in designing and implementing the curriculum?
				15.1 Are interdisciplinary and multidisciplinary perspectives used in the study of ethnic and cultural groups and related issues?
				15.2 Are approaches used authentic and comprehensive explanations of ethnic and cultural issues, events, and problems?
				16.0 Does the curriculum use comparative approaches in the study of racial, ethnic, and cultural groups?
				16.1 Does the curriculum focus on the similarities and differences among and between ethnic and cultural groups?
				16.2 Are matters examined from comparative perspectives with fairness to all?
				17.0 Does the curriculum help students view and interpret events, situations, and conflict from diverse ethnic and cultural perspectives and points of view?
				17.1 Are the perspectives of various ethnic and cultural groups represented in the instructional program?
				17.2 Are students taught why different ethnic and cultural groups often perceive the same historical event or contemporary situation differently?
				17.3 Are the perspectives of each ethnic and cultural group presented as valid ways to perceive the past and the present?
				18.0 Does the curriculum conceptualize and describe the development of the United States as a multidirectional society?
				18.1 Does the curriculum view the territorial and cultural growth of the United States as flowing from several directions?
				18.2 Does the curriculum include a parallel study of the various societies that developed in the geo-cultural United States?
				19.0 Does the school provide opportunities for students to participate in the aesthetic experiences of various ethnic and cultural groups?
				19.1 Are multiethnic literature and art used to promote empathy and understanding of people from various ethnic and cultural groups?
				19.2 Are multiethnic literature and art used to promote self-examination and self-understanding?
				19.3 Do students read and hear the poetry, short stories, novels, folklore, plays, essays, and autobiographies of a variety of ethnic and cultural groups?
				19.4 Do students examine the music, art, architecture, and dance of a variety of ethnic and cultural groups?
				19.5 Do students have available the artistic, musical, and literary expression of the local ethnic and cultural communities?
				19.6 Are opportunities provided for students to develop their own artistic, literary, and musical expression?
				20.0 Does the curriculum provide opportunities for students to develop full literacy in at least two languages?
				20.1 Are students taught to communicate (speaking, reading, and writing) in a second language?

Rating				Guidelines
Strongly ⟵ ⟶ Hardly at all				

20.2 Are students taught about the culture of the people who use the second language?

20.3 Are second language speakers provided opportunities to develop full literacy in their native language?

20.4 Are students for whom English is a second language taught in their native languages as needed?

21.0 Does the curriculum make maximum use of local community resources?

    21.1 Are students involved in the continuous study of the local community?

    21.2 Are members of the local ethnic and cultural communities continually used as classroom resources?

    21.3 Are field trips to the various local ethnic and cultural communities provided for students?

22.0 Do the assessment procedures used with students reflect their ethnic and community cultures?

    22.1 Do teachers use a variety of assessment procedures that reflect the ethnic and cultural diversity of students?

    22.2 Do teachers' day-to-day assessment techniques take into account the ethnic and cultural diversity of their students?

23.0 Does the school conduct ongoing, systematic evaluations of the goals, methods, and instructional materials used in teaching about ethnicity and culture?

    23.1 Do assessment procedures draw on many sources of evidence from many sorts of people?

    23.2 Does the evaluation program examine school policies and procedures?

    23.3 Does the evaluation program examine the everyday climate of the school?

    23.4 Does the evaluation program examine the effectiveness of curricular programs, both academic and nonacademic?

    23.5 Are the results of evaluation used to improve the school program?

Part Four: References

Alba, Richard D. *Ethnic Identity: The Transformation of White America*. New Haven, Conn.: Yale University Press, 1990.

Aronson, Elliot, and Alex Gonzalez. "Desegregation, Jigsaw, and the Mexican-American Experience." In *Eliminating Racism: Profiles in Controversy*, edited by P. A. Katz and D. A. Taylor, 301–14. New York: Plenum Press, 1988.

Asante, Molefi Kete. *The Afrocentric Idea*. Philadelphia: Temple University Press, 1987.

_____. *Kemet, Afrocentricity, and Knowledge*. Trenton, N.J.: African World Press, 1990.

_____. "The Afrocentric Idea in Education." *The Journal of Negro Education* 60, no. 2 (Spring 1991): 170–80.

Banks, James A. *Teaching Strategies for Ethnic Studies*, 5th ed. Boston: Allyn and Bacon, 1991a.

_____. "The Dimensions of Multicultural Education." *Multicultural Leader* 4, no. 1 (Winter/Spring 1991b): 3–4.

_____. "Multicultural Education: Its Effects on Students' Racial and Gender Role Attitudes." In *Handbook of Research on Social Studies Teaching and Learning*, edited by James P. Shaver, 459–69. New York: Macmillan, 1991c.

Banks, James A., and Cherry A. McGee Banks, eds. *Multicultural Education: Issues and Perspectives*. Boston: Allyn and Bacon, 1989.

Belenky, Mary F., Blythe M. Clinchy, Nancy R. Goldberger, and Jill M. Tarule. *Women's Ways of Knowing: The Development of Self, Voice and Mind*. New York: Basic Books, 1986.

Bernal, Martin. *Black Athena: The Afroasiatic Roots of Classical Civilization*. Vol. 2, *The Archaeological and Documentary Evidence*. New Brunswick, N.J.: Rutgers University Press, 1991.

Cohen, Elizabeth G. *Designing Groupwork: Strategies for the Heterogeneous Classroom*. New York: Teachers College Press, 1986.

Cummins, Jim. "Empowering Minority Students: A Framework for Intervention." *Harvard Educational Review* 56, no. 1 (February 1986): 18–36.

Delpit, Lisa D. "The Silenced Dialogue: Power and Pedagogy in Educating Other People's Children." *Harvard Educational Review* 58, no. 3 (August 1988): 280–98.

Deyhle, Donna. "Success and Failure: A Micro-Ethnographic Comparison of Navajo and Anglo Students' Perceptions of Testing." *Curriculum Inquiry* 16, no. 4 (1986): 365–89.

Diop, Cheikh Anta. *The African Origins of Civilization: Myth or Reality?* New York: Lawrence Hill and Co., 1974.

Fordham, Signithia. "Racelessness in Private Schools: Should We Deconstruct the Racial and Cultural Identity of African-American Adolescents?" *Teachers College Record* 92 (Spring 1991): 470–84.

Fordham, Signithia, and John U. Ogbu. "Black Students' School Success: Coping with the Burden of 'Acting White.'" *The Urban Review* 18, no. 3 (1986): 176–206.

Gay, Geneva. "Culturally Diverse Students and Social Studies." In *Handbook of Research on Social Studies Teaching and Learning*, edited by James P. Shaver, 144–56. New York: Macmillan, 1991.

Hale-Benson, Janice E. *Black Children: Their Roots, Culture and Learning Styles*. Baltimore: John Hopkins University Press, 1982.

Heath, Shirley Brice. *Ways with Words: Language, Life and Work in Communities and Classrooms*. New York: Cambridge University Press, 1983.

Hodgkinson, Harold L. *All One System: Demographics of Education, Kindergarten through Graduate School*. Washington, D.C.: The Institute for Educational Leadership, 1985.

Howe, Irving. "The Value of the Canon." *The New Republic* 204, no. 7 (18 February 1991): 40–47.

Johnson, William B., and Arnold E. Packer. *Workforce 2000: Work and Workers for the 21st Century*. Washington, D.C.: U.S. Government Printing Office, 1987.

Kochman, Thomas. *Black and White: Styles in Conflict*. Chicago: University of Chicago Press, 1981.

Kroeber, Alfred, and Clyde Kluckhuhn. *Culture: A Critical Review of Concepts and Definitions*. New York: Vintage, 1952.

Lerner, Gerda. *The Majority Finds Its Past: Placing Women in History*. New York: Oxford University Press, 1979.

Mercer, Jane R. "Alternate Paradigms for Assessment in a Pluralistic Society." In *Multicultural Education: Issues and Perspectives*, edited by James A. Banks and Cherry A. McGee Banks, 289–304. Boston: Allyn and Bacon, 1989.

Oakes, Jeannie. *Keeping Track: How Schools Structure Inequality*. New Haven, Conn.: Yale University Press, 1985.

Ogbu, John. "Overcoming Racial Barriers to Equal Access." In *Access to Knowledge: An Agenda for Our Nation's Schools*, edited by John I. Goodlad and Pamela Keating, 59–89. New York: The College Board, 1990.

Pallas, Aaron M., Gary Natriello, and Edward L. McDill. "The Changing Nature of the Disadvantaged Population: Current Dimensions and Future Trends." *Educational Researcher* 18, no. 5 (June/July 1989): 16–22.

Philips, Susan U. *The Invisible Culture: Communication in Classroom and Community on the Warm Springs Indian Reservation*. New York: Longman, 1983.

Ravitch, Diane. "Multiculturalism E Pluribus Plures." *The American Scholar* 54 (Spring 1990): 337–54.

Schlesinger, Arthur M., Jr. *The Disuniting of America: Reflections on a Multicultural Society*. Knoxville, Tenn.: Whittle Direct Books, 1991.

Sertima, Ivan Van, ed. *Great Black Leaders: Ancient and Modern*. New Brunswick, N.J.: Africana Studies Department, Rutgers University, 1988.

Shade, Barbara J., ed. *Culture, Style and the Educative Press*. Springfield, Ill.: Charles C. Thomas, 1989.

Slavin, Robert E. *Cooperative Learning*. New York: Longman, 1983.

Sleeter, Christine E., and Carl A. Grant. "An Analysis of Multicultural Education in the United States." *Harvard Educational Review* 57, no. 4 (1987): 421–44.

Stephan, Walter G. "Intergroup Relations." In *The Handbook of Social Psychology*, vol. 2, 3d ed., edited by Gardner Lindzey and Elliot Aronson, 599–658. New York: Random House, 1985.

Tetreault, Mary K. Thompson. "Integrating Content about Women and Gender into the Curriculum." In *Multicultural Education: Issues and Perspectives*, edited by James A. Banks and Cherry A. McGee Banks, 124–44. Boston: Allyn and Bacon, 1989.

United States Commission on Civil Rights. *A Better Chance to Learn: Bilingual-Bicultural Education*. Washington, D.C.: U.S. Government Printing Office, 1975.

Weatherford, Jack. *Indian Givers: How the Indians of the Americas Transformed the World*. New York: Fawcett Columbine, 1988.

---

*Task Force on Ethnic Studies Curriculum Guidelines

James A. Banks, Chair, University of Washington

Carlos E. Cortés, University of California, Riverside

Geneva Gay, University of Washington

Ricardo L. Garcia, University of Idaho

Anna S. Ochoa, Indiana University

Empowering Children To Create a Caring Culture in a World of Differences

Louise Derman-Sparks

Louise Derman-Sparks is Director, Anti-Bias Leadership Project, Pacific Oaks College, Pasadena, California. This article is based on her keynote address at the ACEI Study Conference in Phoenix, Arizona, April 8, 1993.

Racism, sexism, classism, heterosexism and ableism are still deeply entrenched and pervasive in society, making it very difficult for millions of children to be "Freedom's Child." What must we do as educators to ensure that all children can develop to their fullest potential—can truly become "Freedom's Child"?

Children's Development of Identity and Attitudes

Take a moment to listen to the voices of children. Members of the Anti-Bias Curriculum Task Force developed the anti-bias approach after a year spent collecting and analyzing children's thinking and trying out activities. They collected the following anecdotes:

- Steven is busy being a whale on the climbing structure in the 2-year-old yard. Susie tries to join him. "Girls can't do that!" he shouts.
- Robby, 3 years old, refuses to hold the hand of a dark-skinned classmate. At home, he insists, after bathing, that his black hair is now "white because it is clean."

- "You aren't really an Indian," 4-year-old Rebecca tells one of her child care teachers. "Where are your feathers?"
- "Malcolm can't play with us. He's a baby," Linda tells their teacher. Malcolm, another 4-year-old, uses a wheelchair.

Those voices reflect the impact of societal bias on children. Now, listen to voices of children in programs that practice anti-bias curriculum:

- Maria, 4 years old, sees a stereotypical "Indian warrior" figure in the toy store. "That toy hurts Indian people's feelings," she tells her grandmother.
- Rebecca's kindergarten teacher asks the children to draw a picture of what they would

From *Childhood Education*, Winter 1993/94, pp. 66-71. © 1993 by the Association for Childhood Education International. Reprinted by permission of the Association for Childhood Education International, 11501 Georgia Avenue, Suite 315, Wheaton, MD.

like to be when they grow up. Rebecca draws herself as a surgeon—in a pink ball gown and tiara.

- After hearing the story of Rosa Parks and the Montgomery bus boycott, 5-year-old Tiffany, whose skin is light brown, ponders whether she would have had to sit in the back of the bus. Finally, she firmly asserts, "I'm Black and, anyway, all this is stupid. I would just get off and tell them to keep their old bus."

- In the school playground, 5-year-old Casey and another white friend, Tommy, are playing. Casey calls two other boys to join them. "You can't play with them. They're Chinese eyes," Tommy says to him. Casey replies, "That's not right. All kinds of kids play together. I know. My teacher tells me civil rights stories."

Children do not come to preschool, child care centers or elementary school as "blank slates" on the topic of diversity. Facing and understanding what underlies their thoughts and feelings are key to empowering children to resist bias. The following is a brief summary of research about how children develop racial identity and attitudes:

- As early as 6 months, infants notice skin color differences. (Katz, 1993)
- By 2 years of age, children not only notice, they also ask questions about differences and similarities among people. They soon begin forming their own hypotheses to explain the diversity they are seeing and hearing. When my daughter was 3, she commented one day, "I am thinking about skin color. How do we get it?" I launched into an explanation about melanin, which was clearly above her level of understanding. Finally, I asked her, "How do you think we get skin color?" "Magic markers!" she replied. (Derman-Sparks, Tanaka Higa & Sparks, 1980)

At my family's 1991 Passover Seder (the Seder honors the ancient Jewish Exodus from slavery in Egypt), my niece announced, "I'm half Jewish." "Uh huh," I replied (one parent is Jewish). She continued, "The Jewish people went through the water and they didn't get wet. They got to the other side. The people who weren't Jewish got drowned."

"That is what the Passover story tells us, that the Egyptian soldiers drowned," I affirmed, but her expression remained quizzical. So, I decided to ask her, "What do you think happened to the people who were half Jewish?"

"They got to the other side, too," she replied, paused and then concluded, "but they got a little bit wet." Afterward, a cousin wondered, "How did you ever think of that question?" (the Passover story does not mention people being "half Jewish").

I don't know if my question was "right" in any absolute sense, but trying to follow my niece's line of thinking, I sensed that the issue was important to her. She seemed emotionally satisfied with her solution. Moreover, it was a cognitively clever one—she got to the other side safely AND she ac-

knowledged her identity as she understood it.

■ How we answer children's questions and respond to their ideas is crucial to their level of comfort when learning about diversity. Statements such as, "It's not polite to ask," "I'll tell you later" or "It doesn't matter," do not help children form positive ideas about themselves or

---

The following poem by Bill Martin, Jr. (1987) captures the essence of what I think it means to empower children to create a caring culture in a world of differences.

I like me, no doubt
about it,
I like me, can't live
without it,
I like me, let's shout
about it,
I am Freedom's Child.

You like you, no doubt
about it,
You like you, can't live
without it,
You like you, let's shout
about it,
You are Freedom's Child.

We need all the
different kinds of people
we can find,
To make freedom's dream
come true,
So as I learn to like the
differences in me,
I learn to like the
differences in you.

I like you, no doubt
about it,
You like me, can't live
without it,
We are free, let's shout
about it,
Hooray for Freedom's
Child!

Reprinted by permission of SRA/Macmillan/ McGraw-Hill School Publishing Co.

pro-diversity dispositions toward others. (Derman-Sparks & ABC Task Force, 1989)

■ Between 2 1/2 to 3 1/2 years of age, children also become aware of and begin to absorb socially prevailing negative stereotypes, feelings and ideas about people, including themselves. All children are exposed to these attitudes in one form or another, usually through a combination of sources (parents, extended family, neighbors, teachers, friends, TV, children's books, movies). (Derman-Sparks & ABC Task Force, 1989)

■ Throughout the early childhood period, children continue to construct and elaborate on their ideas about their own and others' identities and their feelings about human differences. In the primary years, children's development goes beyond the individual to include a group identity. Some researchers believe that after age 9, racial attitudes tend to stay constant unless the child experiences a life-changing event. (Aboud, 1988)

■ The research literature also points to the great damage racism, sexism and classism have on *all* children's development. Young children are harmed by a psychologically toxic environment. How they are harmed depends on how they are affected by the various "isms"— whether they receive messages of superiority or inferiority. (Clark, 1955; Dennis, 1981)

For children of color, the wounds can be overt. Often, however, they are quite subtle. Chester Pierce calls these subtle forms of racism "micro-contaminants" (Pierce, 1980). Kenyon Chan notes that these micro-contaminants "are carried by children like grains of sand, added one by one, eventually weighing children down beyond their capacity to carry the sand and to grow emotionally and intellectually to their fullest" (Chan, 1993).

Racism attacks young children's growing sense of group, as well as individual, identity. Thus, the chil-

dren are even less able to resist racism's harm. Chan cites an example: A Chinese American girl enrolled in a suburban kindergarten in Los Angeles. Her European American teacher claimed that her name was too difficult to pronounce and promptly renamed her "Mary," calling it an "American" name. This young child is forced to wonder what is wrong with her name and what is wrong with her parents for giving her such a "bad" name. And her doubts originated with the very person who is responsible for supporting and cultivating her development.

● ———

R acism attacks young children's growing sense of group, as well as individual, identity.

——— ●

Moreover, as Lily Wong-Fillmore's research documents, young children who come from homes where a language other than English is spoken pay a terrible price if they experience a too-early loss of continued development in their home language. The price includes the gradual impoverishment of communication between the child and parents (and other family members) and the potentially serious weakening of the "family's continued role in the socialization of its children" (Wong-Fillmore, 1991).

White, English-speaking children also experience psychological damage. Although this issue has been less studied, the research we do have suggests some disturbing problems:

■ First, racism teaches white children moral double standards for treating people of racial/ethnic groups other than their own. This leads to the possibility of general ethical erosion (Clark, 1955) and to a form of hypocrisy that results in primary school-age children saying words that sound like acceptance of diversity, while acting in ways that demonstrate the opposite (Miel, 1976).

■ Second, children may be constructing identity on a false sense of superiority based on skin color. White children's self-esteem will be rather vulnerable if/when they come to realize that skin color does not determine a person's value.

■ Third, racism results in white children developing fears about people different from themselves. They do not gain the life skills they need for effectively interacting with the increasing range of human diversity in society and the world.

Racial stereotyping is not the only danger. Children's absorption of gender stereotypes limits their development. As young as 3 and 4, children begin to self-limit their choices of learning experiences because of the gender norms they are already absorbing. One of the negative consequences of this process is a pattern of uneven cognitive development, or "practice deficits," related to the types of activities boys and girls choose (Serbin, 1980, p. 60). Girls tend to function below potential in math and boys in expression of their feelings.

Furthermore, research on children's development of ideas and feelings about disabilities indicates that by 2 and 3, they notice, are curious about and sometimes fear people with a disability and their equipment (Froschl, Colon, Rubin & Sprung, 1984; Sapon-Shevin, 1983). Children's fears appear to come from developmental misconceptions that they might "catch" the disability, as well as from adults' indirect and direct communication of discomfort. Moreover, the impact of stereotypes and biases about people with disabilities affects primary age children's treatment of any child who does not fit the physical "norms" of attractiveness, weight and height.

Research also suggests that young children who learn about people with disabilities through a variety of concrete activities are much more likely to see the whole person, rather than just focusing on the person's disability.

What Empowering Children To Create a Caring Culture Requires of Us

Clarity About Goals. The following goals are for *all* children. The specific issues and tasks necessary for working toward these goals will vary for children, depending on their backgrounds, ages and life experiences.

■ *Nurture each child's construction of a knowledgeable, confident self-concept and group identity.* To achieve this goal, we must create education conditions in which all children are able to like who they are without needing to feel superior to anyone else. Children must also be able to develop biculturally where that is appropriate.

■ *Promote each child's comfortable, empathic interaction with people from diverse backgrounds.* This goal requires educators to guide children's development of the cognitive awareness, emotional disposition and behavioral skills needed to respectfully and effectively learn about differences, comfortably negotiate and adapt to differences, and cognitively understand and emotionally accept the common humanity that all people share.

■ *Foster each child's critical thinking about bias.* Children need to develop the cognitive skills to identify "unfair" and "untrue" images (stereotypes), comments (teasing, name-calling) and behaviors (discrimination) directed at one's own or others' identities. They also need the emotional empathy to know that bias hurts.

■ *Cultivate each child's ability to stand up for her/himself and for others in the face of bias.* This "activism" goal requires educators to help every child learn and practice a variety of ways to act: a) when another child acts in a biased manner toward her/him, b) when a child acts in a biased manner toward another child, c) when an adult acts in a biased manner. Goal 4 builds on goal 3 as critical thinking and empathy are necessary components of acting for oneself or others in the face of bias.

These four goals interact with and build on each other. We cannot accomplish any one goal without the other three. *Their combined intent is to empower children to resist the negative impact of racism and other "isms" on their development and to grow into adults who will want and be able to work with others to eliminate all forms of oppression.* In other words, the underlying intent is not to end racism (and other "isms") in one generation by changing children's attitudes and behaviors, but rather to promote critical thinkers and activists who can work for social change and participate in creating a caring culture in a world of differences.

Preparing ourselves. Effective anti-bias education requires every teacher to look inward and commit to a lifelong journey of understanding her/his own cultural beliefs, while changing the prejudices and behaviors that interfere with the nurturing of all children. Teachers need to know:

■ how to see their own culture in relationship to society's history and current power realities

■ how to effectively adapt their teaching style and curriculum content to their children's needs

■ how to engage in cultural conflict resolution with people from cultural backgrounds other than their own

■ how to be critical thinkers about bias in their practice

- how to be activists—engaging people in dialogue about bias, intervening, working with others to create change.

Achieving these goals takes commitment and time, and is a developmental process for adults as well as for children. One must be emotionally as well as cognitively involved and ready to face periods of disequilibrium and then reconstruction and transformation.

Implementation Principles and Strategies

To create a caring culture in which children can be empowered, teachers must be "reflective practitioners" who can think critically about their own teaching practice and adapt curriculum goals and general strategies to the needs of their children.

Critical thinking. Be aware of "tourist multicultural curriculum" and find ways to eliminate tourism from your program. Tourist multicultural curriculum is the most commonly practiced approach in early childhood education and elementary school today. The majority of commercial curriculum materials currently available on the market and many published curriculum guides reflect a tourist version of multicultural education. Unfortunately, tourist multicultural curriculum is a simplistic, inadequate version of multicultural education.

In a classroom practicing a tourist approach, the daily "regular" curriculum reflects mainstream European American perspectives, rules of behavior, images, learning and teaching styles. Activities about "other" cultures often exhibit the following problems:

- *Disconnection*: Activities are added on to the curriculum as special times, rather than integrated into all aspects of the daily environment and curriculum.
- *Patronization*: "Other" cultures are treated as "quaint" or "exotic." This form of tourism does

not teach children to appreciate what all humans share in common.

- *Trivialization*: Cultural activities that are disconnected from the daily life of the people trivialize the culture. A typical example is multicultural curriculum that focuses on holidays—days that are different from "normal" days. Children do not learn about how people live their lives, how they work, who does what in the family—all of which is the essence of a culture. Other forms of trivialization include: turning cultural practices that have deep, ritual meaning into "arts and crafts" or dance activities, or asking parents to cook special foods without any further lessons about the parents' cultures.
- *Misrepresentation*: Too few images of a group oversimplifies the variety within the group. Use of images and activities based on traditional, past practices of an ethnic group rather than images of contemporary life confuse children. Misusing activities and images that reflect the culture-of-origin of a group to teach about *the life of cultures in the U.S.* conveys misconceptions about people with whom children have little or no face-to-face experience.

In sum, tourist multicultural curriculum does not give children the tools they need to comfortably, empathetically and fairly interact with diversity. Instead, it teaches simplistic generalizations about other people that lead to stereotyping, rather than to understanding of differences. Moreover, tourist curriculum, because it focuses on the unusual and special times of a culture and neglects how people live their daily lives, does not foster children's understanding and empathy for our common humanity. Moving beyond tourist multicultural curriculum is key to our profession's more effective nurturing of diversity.

Incorporate multicultural and anti-bias activities into daily curriculum planning. Diversity and anti-bias topics are integral to the entire curriculum at any education

level. One practical brainstorming technique for identifying the numerous topic possibilities is "webbing."

Step one is determining the center of the "web." This can be: 1) an issue raised by the children (e.g., a person who is visually impaired cannot work); 2) any number of traditional preschool "units" (e.g., my body, families, work); 3) High/Scope's (Weikart, 1975) "key experiences" (e.g., classification or

---

Critical thinking and activism activities should rise out of real life situations that are of interest to children.

---

seriation); 4) any of the traditional content areas of the primary curriculum (science, math, language arts, physical and health curriculum).

Step two involves brainstorming the many possible anti-bias, multicultural issues that stem from the subject at the web's center. *Step three* involves identifying specific content for a particular classroom based on contextual/developmental analysis. *Step four* involves listing possible activities that are developmentally and culturally appropriate for your particular class.

Cultural Appropriateness: Adult/Child Interactions

Effective teaching about diversity, as in all other areas, *is a continuous interaction between adults and children.* On the one hand, teachers are responsible for brainstorming, planning and initiating diversity topics, based on their analyses of children's needs and life experiences. On the other hand, careful attention to children's thinking and behavior, and to "teachable moments," leads educators to modify initial plans.

Find ways to engage children in critical thinking and the planning and carrying out of "activism" activities appropriate to their developmental levels, cultural backgrounds and interests.

Critical thinking and activism activities should rise out of real life situations that are of interest to children. The purpose of such activities is to provide opportunities for children, 4 years old and up, to build their empathy, skills and confidence and to encourage their sense of responsibility for both themselves and for others. Consequently, activities should reflect *their* ideas and issues, not the teacher's. The following two examples are appropriate activism activities.

In the first situation, the children's school did not have a "handicapped" parking space in their parking lot. After a parent was unable to attend open school night because of this lack, the teacher told the class of 4- and 5-year-olds what had happened and why. They then visited other places in their neighborhood that had "handicapped" parking and decided to make one in their school lot. After they did so, they then noticed that teachers were inappropriately parking in the "handicapped" spot (their classroom overlooked the parking lot), so they decided to make tickets. The children dictated their messages, which their teacher faithfully took down, and drew pictures to accompany their words. They then ticketed those cars that did not have "handicapped parking" plaques in their windows.

In the second example, a class of 1st- through 3rd-graders visited a homeless shelter and talked to the director to find out what people needed. They started a toy and blanket collection drive, which they promoted using posters and flyers. They visited several classrooms to talk about what they were doing. They also wrote to the Mayor and the City Council to say that homeless people needed more houses and jobs.

Parents and Family Involvement

Find ways to involve parents and other adult family members in all aspects of anti-bias education. Education and collaboration with parents is *essential*. Educators have to be creative and ingenious to make this happen. Parents can help plan, implement and evaluate environmental adaptations and curricular activities. They can serve on advisory/planning committees with staff, provide information about their lifestyles and beliefs, participate in classroom activities and serve as community liaisons. Teachers can send home regular short newsletters to share ongoing plans and classroom activities, and elicit parent advice and resources. Parent meetings on child-rearing and education issues should also incorporate relevant diversity topics.

When a family member disagrees with an aspect of the curriculum, it is essential that the teachers listen carefully and sensitively to the issues underlying the disagreement. Objections may include: 1) family's belief that learning about differences will "make the children prejudiced" ("color-blind" view), 2) parent's belief that teaching about stereotyping and such values belongs in the home, not at school, 3) family members' strong prejudices against specific groups.

Staff need to find out all they can about the cultural and other issues that influence the family's concerns, and then work with family members to find ways to meet their needs while also maintaining the goals of anti-bias education. The techniques for working with parents on anti-bias issues are generally the same as those used for other child development and education topics. The difference, however, lies in the teachers' level of comfort about addressing such topics with other adults.

Teacher Education and Professional Development

Teacher training must incorporate liberating pedagogical techniques that:

- engage students on cognitive, emotional and behavioral levels
- use storytelling to enable students to both name and identify the ways that various identity contexts and bias have affected their lives
- use experiential activities that engage learners in discovering the dynamics of cultural differences and the various "isms"
- provide new information and analysis that give deeper meaning to what is learned through storytelling and experiential activities
- create a balance between supporting and challenging students in an environment of safety, not necessarily comfort.

The most useful way to work on our own development is to join with others (staff, or staff and parents) in support groups that meet regularly over a long period of time. By collaborating, sharing resources and providing encouragement, we can work on our self-awareness issues, build and improve our practices, strengthen our courage and determination and maintain the joy and excitement of education.

In sum, children of the 21st century will not be able to function if they are psychologically bound by outdated and narrow assumptions about their neighbors. To thrive, even to survive, in this more complicated world, children need to learn how to function in many different cultural contexts, to recognize and respect different histories and perspectives, and to know how to work together to create a more just world that can take care of all its people, its living creatures, its land.

Let's remember the African American novelist Alice Walker's call to "Keep in mind always the present you are constructing. It should be the future you want" (Walker, 1989, p. 238).

References

Aboud, F. (1988). *Children and prejudice*. London: Basil Blackwell.

Chan, K. S. (1993). Sociocultural aspects of anger: Impact on minority children. In M. Furlong & D. Smith (Eds.), *Anger, hostility, and aggression in children and adolescents: Assessment, prevention, and intervention strategies in schools*. Brandon, VT: Clinical Psychology Publishing.

Clark, K. (1955). *Prejudice and your child*. Boston: Bacon.

Dennis, R. (1981). Socialization and racism: The White experience. In B. Bowser & R. Hunt (Eds.), *Impacts of racism on White Americans* (pp. 71-85). Beverly Hills, CA: Sage.

Derman-Sparks, L., Tanaka Higa, C., & Sparks, B. (1980). Children, race, and racism: How race awareness develops. *Bulletin, 11*(3 & 4), 3-9.

Derman-Sparks, L., & ABC Task Force (1989). *Anti-bias curriculum: Tools for empowering young children*. Washington, DC: National Association for the Education of Young Children.

Froschl, M., Colon, L., Rubin, E., & Sprung, B. (1984). *Including all of us: An early childhood curriculum about disability*. New York: Educational Equity Concepts.

Katz, P. (May, 1993). *Development of racial attitudes in children*. Presentation given to the University of Delaware.

Martin, B., Jr. (1987). *I am freedom's child*. Allen, TX: DLM Teaching Resources.

Miel, A. (1976). *The short-changed children of suburbia*. New York: Insitute of Human Relations Press.

Pierce, C. (1980). Social trace contaminants: Subtle indicators of racism in TV. In Withey & Abelis (Eds.), *Television and social behavior*. New Jersey: Lawrence & Erlbaum.

Sapon-Shevin, M. (1983). Teaching young children about differences. *Young Children, 38*(2), 24-32.

Serbin, L. (1980). Play activities and the development of visual-spatial skills. *Equal Play, 1*(4), 5.

Walker, A. (1989). *The temple of my familiar*. New York: Pocket Books.

Weikart, D. (1975). *Young children in action*. Ypsilanti, MI: High Scope Press.

Wong-Fillmore, L. (1991). Language and cultural issues in early education. In S. L. Kagan (Ed.), *The care and education of America's young children: Obstacles and opportunites. The 90th yearbook of the National Society for the Study of Education* (pp. 3-49). Chicago: University of Chicago Press.

Toward Defining Programs and Services for Culturally and Linguistically Diverse Learners in Special Education

Shernaz B. García
and Diana H. Malkin

Shernaz B. García *(CEC Chapter # 101), Lecturer and Associate Director, Bilingual Education Program and* **Diana H. Malkin** *(CEC Chapter # 101), recently completed a máster's degree, Department of Special Education, The University of Texas at Austin.*

Effective program design for services for students from culturally and linguistically diverse (CLD) backgrounds who also have disabilities is based on the same principles and purposes of multicultural education that create supportive learning environments in general education. In the absence of appropriate programs in regular and special education, these students are at higher risk of being misidentified as having disabilities, and their educational experiences may not take into account the reality that linguistic and cultural characteristics coexist and interact with disability-related factors. For example, a girl with a learning disability may also have limited English proficiency (LEP), be living in poverty, and come from a family of migrant farm workers. Special education programs for this student must address the interacting influence of these variables. How will bilingual education and English as a second language (ESL) in-struction be modified for this child? How do the family and larger community respond to her disability? How does the presence of an impairment influence the family's goals and expectations for their daughter? Would these differ if the child were male? How? Do her language characteristics—in the native language and in English—reflect linguistic differences, or do they, instead, result from socioeconomic factors? Failure to consider such issues may result in inadequate student progress or dropping out of school.

Special education services must be culturally and linguistically appropriate if they are to be truly inclusive. To meet the needs of CLD students with exceptionalities, special educators need knowledge and skills in four specific areas: (1) information about the language characteristics of learners with disabilities who are bilingual or have limited English proficiency that will assist in the development of a language use plan (Ortiz & García, 1990; Ortiz & Yates, 1989); (2) information about cultural factors that influence educational planning and services; (3) characteristics of instructional strategies and materials that are culturally and linguistically appropriate; and (4) characteristics of a learning environment that promotes success for all students.

Addressing Language Characteristics

Several aspects of the individualized education program (IEP) are influenced by students' language characteristics. Even when students are proficient in English, their cultural backgrounds may influence language use in academic settings. Dialectal differences, different patterns of language use and function among varied language communities, and nonverbal communication style differences among cultures can have a significant impact on student performance.

Gathering Essential Language Information

An accurate description of the language characteristics of students from language minority backgrounds, obtained from many sources, is necessary before decisions can be made regarding the language(s) of instruction as well as type(s) of language intervention to be provided in special education. For each language spoken by the student, several aspects of language proficiency and use should be considered, including information about the student's (a) language

From *Teaching Exceptional Children*, Vol. 26, No. 1, Fall 1993, pp. 52-58. © 1993 by the Council for Exceptional Children. Reprinted by permission.

dominance and proficiency; (b) acquisition of the surface structures (grammar, syntax, vocabulary, phonology, etc.), as well as functional language use (pragmatics); and, (c) receptive and expressive language skills. Language information should be current to ensure that educational planning is reponsive to language shifts that may have occurred since any previous testing. (Readers interested in a more detailed discussion of language profiling are referred to Ortiz & García, 1990.)

Developing the Language Use Plan

When educators assume that students with disabilities who have limited English proficiency will be confused by two languages, or that services for their disability-related difficulties should receive priority over services for their language needs, they are likely to remove students from language programs, or they may fail to realize the importance of coordinating services across bilingual and special education settings. However, students with LEP are entitled to bilingual and ESL instruction and should receive both to ensure that goals and strategies are pedagogically appropriate for their disability, as well as their language status. Foremost in the IEP should be a language use plan that specifies the language(s) of instruction for each goal and related objectives, the person(s) responsible for instruction in the targeted language(s), and the type of language intervention recommended (Ortiz & Yates, 1989).

In all instances except ESL instruction, ways of providing native language or bilingual instruction to these students should be explored, even if such services are not readily available. Alternatives may include the use of bilingual paraprofessionals, parent and community tutors in the native language(s), bilingual peer tutoring, collaboration with the student's bilingual/ESL teacher, and any other resources available in the district. Even when students do not qualify for bilingual education and ESL programs or have recently exited from these programs, some may

still need language support to succeed in academic tasks that demand greater English proficiency than they possess. Unless teachers understand that the English performance of students from language minority backgrounds may reflect language status rather than cognitive ability, instruction may be geared to the former rather than the latter. These students need instruction that accommodates their language level while teaching concepts that are at the appropriate cognitive level. The learning environment should support the language of instruction in a variety of contextualized, nonverbal, multisensory ways.

The Influence of Cultural Factors

In the most general sense, culture provides a world view that influences our ways of perceiving the world around us. It defines desirable attitudes, values, and behaviors, and influences how we evaluate our needs. As a result, the culture and subcultures of the school are likely to impact what and how children should be taught, as well as when and how successfully it is taught (Lynch, 1992). These culturally conditioned influences on educational programs and curriculum development are more difficult to perceive if educators do not have adequate cultural self-awareness and an understanding of other cultures. In order to truly understand how culture mediates school experiences, it is important to go beyond the "tourist" curriculum that focuses on external characteristics such as food, music, holidays, and dress (Derman-Sparks, 1989). An awareness of the internal (values, thoughts, cognitive orientations) and hidden (unspoken rules, norms) aspects of culture is also needed. For instance, it is helpful to understand the influence of culture on the size and structure of the family; standards for acceptable behavior (decorum and discipline); language and communication patterns (including rules for adult, adult-child, child-child communication); religious influences on roles, expectations and/or diet; and

traditions and history (e.g., reason for immigration, contact with homeland) (Saville-Troike, 1978).

Influences on Childrearing Practices

Enculturation is the part of the socialization process through which children acquire the language and characteristics of their culture (Gollnick & Chinn, 1986). For example, the community's values and orientation toward dependence-independence-interdependence will influence parents' goals for their son or daughter from infancy through adulthood. How the roles and status of children in the family and community are defined influences acceptance or rejection of specific behavior in a range of situations, including child-child, child-adult, family-school, and family-community interactions. In the case of students with disabilities, it is also helpful to know how parents' expectations and goals for their child have been influenced by cultural values, beliefs, and expectations for individuals with disabilities. Cultures vary in their definition of *family*; consequently, "the term...must be defined in a way that is relevant to the targeted cultural groups; otherwise, a very important resource for classroom learning and motivation may be overlooked" (Briscoe, 1991, p. 17). Failure to do this can lead to false assumptions about the role of parents in the care and education of their children and the extent to which parents or other primary caregivers should be involved in formal schooling activities, as well as the beliefs of school personnel that minority parents do not value education.

Finally, how children acquire strategies for learning and which patterns of thinking and learning are reinforced by the family have also been shown to vary across cultural contexts (Philips, 1983; Ramirez & Castaneda, 1974). When the culture of the classroom values behaviors such as independent seatwork, self-direction, and competition, or when success is defined primarily in academic terms, students whose families value interdependent behavior, or those for whom family well-being supersedes individual success, may have difficulty in school and are at risk of being mislabeled as "overly dependent," seeking "excessive" adult approval, or lacking the ability to become independent learners.

Influences on Communication Styles

Effective cross-cultural communication requires a knowledge of the cultural referents as well as individual and situational factors that influence how students use language in conversational and academic contexts. Examples include pragmatic variables such as turntaking behavior, greeting conventions, proximity, and rules of conversation—including unspoken rules (Cheng, 1987). In addition, cultural values and orientations are influential in defining the norms, rules, roles, and communication networks that govern interpersonal and intercultural communication. How students process information (their cognitive style); how they deal with conflict; and which strategies they prefer during negotiation, persuasion, or other types of communication may be influenced by the cultural context in which they are raised. Their self-concept and social identity (the influence of group membership on self-concept) are also affected by their membership in a particular cultural community (Gudykunst & Ting-Toomey, 1988). Given the "hidden" nature of many of these rules, norms, roles, and expectations, our awareness of their existence may develop only when they are violated and we attempt to identify the source of the misunderstanding.

Variations in communication styles also exist as a function of gender, socioeconomic status, and/or ethnicity (e.g., Heath, 1986; Hecht, Collier, & Ribeau, 1993), and they are present in any language, including native English-speaking communities. For example, African-American students, Appalachian children, or individuals from rural or low-income environments whose language does not reflect the language and language uses valued at school may experience some of the same difficulties as speakers of other languages if they are not accustomed to the way language is used by teachers and in textbooks and other materials. In fact, class differences may negatively influence teacher responses, even when teachers and students are members of the same ethnic community. In such instances, teachers using an inclusive approach would acknowledge and respect the language a child brings to school while focusing on building and broadening the child's repertoire of language varieties to include Standard English.

Instructional goals and strategies should be instrumental in helping students experience academic success, provide opportunities for them to try new learning situations, and increase the range of learning environments in

Table 1. Cultural and Linguistic Considerations Related to IEP Development

Selection of IEP Goals and Objectives

Considerations for IEP Development	Classroom Implications
IEP goals and objectives accommodate the student's current level of performance.	• At the student's instructional level • Instructional level based on student's cognitive level, not the language proficiency level • Focus on development of higher level cognitive skills as well as basic skills
Goals and objectives are responsive to cultural and linguistic variables.	• Accommodates goals and expectations of the family • Is sensitive to culturally based response to the disability • Includes a language use plan • Addresses language development and ESL needs

Selection of Instructional Strategies

Considerations for IEP Development	Classroom Implications
Interventions provide adequate exposure to curriculum.	• Instruction in student's dominant language • Responsiveness to learning and communication styles • Sufficient practice to achieve mastery
IEP provides for curricular/instructional accommodation of learning styles and locus of control.	• Accommodates perceptual style differences (e.g., visual vs. auditory) • Accommodates cognitive style differences (e.g., inductive vs. deductive) • Accommodates preferred style of participation (e.g., teacher- vs. student-directed, small vs. large group) • Reduces feelings of learned helplessness
Selected strategies are likely to be effective for language minority students.	• Native language and ESL instruction • Teacher as facilitator of learning (vs. transmission) • Genuine dialogue with students • Contextualized instruction • Collaborative learning • Self-regulated learning • Learning-to-learn strategies
English as a second language (ESL) strategies are used.	• Modifications to address the student's disability • Use of current ESL approaches • Focus on meaningful communication
Strategies for literacy are included.	• Holistic approaches to literacy development • Language teaching that is integrated across the curriculum • Thematic literature units • Language experience approach • Journals

which they can be successful. When parents' goals and expectations for their child are not consistent with the school's definition of success, attempts to "re-educate" the family should be avoided in favor of working collaboratively to determine mutually acceptable goals and helping parents in the decision-making process by sharing pertinent information.

Selection of Appropriate Instructional Strategies

Given the high frequency with which IEPs focus on instructional goals related to reading and language arts, this section addresses language and literacy development. However, many of the principles of effective literacy instruction are appropriate for use in other subject areas. In general, teaching/learning strategies and materials should be selected that facilitate high levels of academic content. Recent literature examining the instructional processes that foster literacy for students with disabilities (Cummins, 1984; Englert & Palincsar, 1991; García, Ortiz, & Bergman, 1990; Goldman & Rueda, 1988; Graves, 1985; Ruiz, 1989; Willig & Ortiz, 1991) emphasize the role of interactive learning environments. A critical assumption is that culture determines how literacy is defined, instructed, and evaluated. From this perspective, literacy is developed in environments that engage students and teachers in meaningful dialogue through activities that are authentic, holistic, and relevant (Cummins, 1984; Englert & Palincsar, 1991). Specifically:

1. Language and dialogue are essential to learning because they scaffold cognitive growth and mediate new learning for students.
2. Instructional goals should focus on student ownership of the literacy process to the extent that students can transform what they have learned into authentic writing activities.
3. Instruction cannot be transmitted or totally scripted by teachers, because learning occurs through student-

Table 2. Checklist for Selecting and Evaluating Materials

☐ Are the perspectives and contributions of people from diverse cultural and linguistic groups—both men and women, as well as people with disabilities—included in the curriculum?

☐ Are there activities in the curriculum that will assist students in analyzing the various forms of the mass media for ethnocentrism, sexism, "handicapism," and stereotyping?

☐ Are men and women, diverse cultural/racial groups, and people with varying abilities shown in both active and passive roles?

☐ Are men and women, diverse cultural/racial groups, and people with disabilities shown in positions of power (i.e., the materials do not rely on the mainstream culture's character to achieve goals)?

☐ Do the materials identify strengths possessed by so-called "underachieving" diverse populations? Do they diminish the attention given to deficits, to reinforce positive behaviors that are desired and valued?

☐ Are members of diverse racial/cultural groups, men and women, and people with disabilities shown engaged in a broad range of social and professional activities?

☐ Are members of a particular culture or group depicted as having a range of physical features (e.g., hair color, hair texture, variations in facial characteristics and body build)?

☐ Do the materials represent historical events from the perspectives of the various groups involved or solely from the male, middle-class, and/or Western European perspective?

☐ Are the materials free of ethnocentric or sexist language patterns that may make implications about persons or groups based solely on their culture, race, gender, or disability?

☐ Will students from different ethnic and cultural backgrounds find the materials personally meaningful to their life experiences?

☐ Are a wide variety of culturally different examples, situations, scenarios, and anecdotes used throughout the curriculum design to illustrate major intellectual concepts and principles?

☐ Are culturally diverse content, examples, and experiences comparable in kind, significance, magnitude, and function to those selected from mainstream culture?

teacher dialogue and classroom interactions that connect what students need to know to their current knowledge and experiences.
4. Teachers must view errors as a source of information regarding the emergence of new literacy skills rather than as student deficits or undesired behaviors.
5. Student difficulties should be interpreted as areas in which teachers need to provide greater mediation, rather than problems that reside in the student.

Table 1 summarizes key variables to be considered when selecting instructional strategies for students with disabilities who are also culturally and/or linguistically different and suggests approaches that are more likely to be responsive to issues of student diversity.

Creating Supportive Learning Environments

Achievement of IEP goals and objectives depends on the context in which teaching and learning occur. A supportive classroom culture is part of the larger "psychological environment" of the school, and it can increase student motivation and attitudes toward learning (Maehr, 1990). Three ways in which the learning environment can be enhanced are by careful selection and evaluation of instructional materials, incorporation of students' language and culture, and involvement of parents and community.

Selecting and Evaluating Instructional Materials

Careful selection of instructional materials that promote high interest, motivation, and relevance to their sociocultural, linguistic, and experiential backgrounds increases the likelihood that students will respond to them positively. Materials published after the early 1970s are more likely to give attention to issues of diversity (Derman-Sparks, 1989). When using older instructional materials, teachers should develop and use relevant guidelines to determine whether they can be adapted and will be useful in increasing students' awareness of issues such as stereotyping, prejudice, and discrimination or it would be better to replace them. This is not meant to imply that classical literature that reflects gender or racial bias, for example, should be totally eliminated from the curriculum. Rather, in addition to appreciating the literary value of these materials, students can develop a better understanding of the historical contexts in which oppression occurs and can learn to identify ways in which discrimination against people, including individuals with disabilities, can be reduced or eliminated. Table 2 lists guidelines to assist special educators in developing their own criteria for evaluating materials they currently have available.

Incorporating Students' Language and Culture

Bilingual education programs are designed not only to provide native language instruction and ESL development, but also to enhance cognitive and affective development and provide cultural enrichment (Baca & Cervantes, 1989). Even in schools and communities where bilingual programs are not available and in situations where educators do not speak the students' language, it is possible to communicate a positive attitude toward students' backgrounds and heritage (Cummins, 1989). The following strategies are examples of ways in which classrooms and materials can reflect the diversity of backgrounds that is present in many schools and in the larger society (Cummins, 1989; Derman-Sparks, 1989).

1. Students are encouraged to use their first language around the school in various ways, even when they are not receiving native language instruction. For example, books are provided in several languages in each classroom and in the library for use by students and parents; bulletin boards, signs, and greetings employ various languages; and students are encouraged to use their native language to provide peer tutoring support.

2. Pictures and other visual displays show people from various backgrounds and communities, including individuals with varying abilities, elderly people, and men and women in blue-collar and white-collar roles. Images accurately depict people's contemporary daily lives—at work as well as in recreational activities.

3. Units developed for reading and language arts include literature from a variety of linguistic and cultural backgrounds and reflect the diversity in U.S. society across race, religion, language, class, gender, and ability. In addition to making children aware of a range of lifestyles, values, and characteristics of diverse groups, literature can reflect their struggles, achievements, and other experiences. Reflecting on such accounts, fictional as well as biographical, may also help some students understand and deal with their own struggles and difficulties.

4. Teachers and other school personnel understand that their interactions and behaviors, even if inadvertent and unintentional, may teach their students gender, racial, and other biases. This is reflected in educators' attention to their own verbal and nonverbal behaviors; avoidance of sexist or ethnocentric language; and parallel expectations for academic performance for girls, students with varying abilities, children from low-income environments, and so on.

5. The seating arrangement and organization of the classroom reflect consideration of learning style differences and encourage students to try new ways of interacting and learning.

Involving Parents and Families

As diversity in the student population increases, alternative models of parent involvement will have to be developed (Harry, 1992). Historically, many parents from language minority groups have had to overcome barriers to their effective participation in the regular and special education process, including educators' perceptions about these parents and their communities; their values regarding educational, linguistic, and cultural differences; and socioeconomic factors. Rather than being part of the problem, parents from culturally and linguistically diverse backgrounds can be effective advocates for their children. They represent a largely untapped resource to assist educators in responding effectively to multicultural issues (Briscoe, 1991).

Implementing Multicultural Special Education

Developing Intercultural Competence

Intercultural competence is an essential ingredient in teachers' ability to implement multicultural special education. Educators who possess such competence can feel comfortable and effective in their interactions with people from a variety of cultures, and they can help students and families feel comfortable as well. Finally, these skills are necessary to accomplish IEP goals. Acquisition of these skills is a gradual process, progressing through several stages. The following elements are helpful in this process (Lynch, 1992):

1. Developing an understanding and appreciation of one's own culture. This process of self-awareness and introspection allows us to examine our own assumptions and values, particularly those that may have been taken for granted because they are so much a part of our own family and community systems.

2. Gathering information about the other target cultures and analysis of this information with respect to individual students and families who reside within the community. Through our interactions with each family, we can determine the extent to which the family and its individual members share the cultural characteristics of their ethnic group. (Ethnic identity is determined by the individual and should not be assigned by others based on their observation of external traits.)

3. Discovering the parent's (or other primary caregiver's) orientation to childrearing issues, values, and orientations, including the family's goals and aspirations for their child with special needs.

4. Applying this knowledge to the development of cross-cultural skills. This results in interventions and interactions that are successful with students from diverse cultures.

Strategies for Enhancing Intercultural Understanding

The following questions may arise as special educators explore implications of multicultural education for their own programs.

While it sounds good, how can I, as one teacher, respond to so many diverse characteristics without being overwhelmed? How long will it take? Where do I start? Focusing on the cultures included at your school and within your community can be a good start, because this allows you to identify materials and strategies that are inclusive of the students you teach on a regular basis. It is a good idea to review your needs periodically—perhaps once at the beginning of each school year—to make sure that the information is updated. Which cultures are represented among your students? Does the information include any new families recently arrived in the community? Once a profile has been developed, you can reflect on your own knowledge of these cultural groups. How much do you know about each one? Which one is the most familiar? The least? This information will be useful as you evaluate what you feel comfortable about and identify areas in which you want to learn more.

How accurate is my current knowledge? What were my sources? Think about what you already know. How did you acquire this information? How extensive is your contact with the communities this knowledge presents? Is this information based on the students' country of origin, or does it encompass the experiences of the group in the United States (e.g., Mexican vs. Mexican American)? Is it based on traditional or contemporary life-styles? Pitfalls to avoid include information that is stereotypic; sources that fail to acknowledge within-group differences based on class, gender, language, religion, ethnicity, and geographic region; and information and experiences that are limited to a "tourist curriculum" (music, food, dress, holidays, etc.), which fail to highlight aspects of culture such as historical experiences related to the group's arrival in the United States, reasons for migration, accomplishments in various fields, values and belief systems, and communication patterns.

Where can I get more information? There are many ways of learning more about cultures, including formal study, reading, workshops, travel, and audiovisual materials. In addition, activities that allow students to share their experiences and the participation of parents and other community members in the school (e.g., speaking to the class about their language, culture, or religion) will make this information a part of the ongoing routine of school activities, and it will be acquired in a natural context. The following are some strategies to consider:

• As you prepare the demographic profile of your own classroom, school, or community, ask parents whether they would be willing to speak to the students about their cultural heritage, their own accomplishments, and any barriers they have overcome. Develop a resource directory that can support other curriculum development and planning efforts as well.

• Identify community organizations and groups that can provide access to audiovisual materials and other resources for personal study as well as instructional use.

• Identify print materials, journals, and other professional publications that highlight model programs, instructional strategies and curricula, and resources for multicultural education.

What if my classes do not reflect much cultural or linguistic diversity? Even in schools where students from diverse cultural and linguistic backgrounds are represented in very small numbers, or in predominantly middle-class communities, the larger culture is made up of subcultures from different religious, gender, and geographic backgrounds. White students also represent diverse ethnic backgrounds, and even when they may perceive their identity as "American," several cultures are represented in their ethnic heritage (Boutte & McCormick, 1992). Family histories and other activities can offer opportunities for them to explore and appreciate their unique characteristics. Finally, it is important to examine the influence of gender on teacher expectations, career counseling, and referral to special education.

A related, and equally important, issue for all students, regardless of color, gender, religion, or other differences, is the development of cross-cultural competence. As the diversity in U.S. society continues to increase, students must be prepared to become members of a workforce that is much more heterogeneous. Multicultural education can help *all* students increase their appreciation of diversity; develop positive self-concepts; respect individuals' civil and human rights; understand the historical context in which prejudice, oppression, and stereotyping occur; and ultimately fulfill their own potential while resisting and challenging stereotyping and barriers to success that exist in the society (Sleeter, 1992).

Conclusion

Efforts to implement multicultural special education services are more likely to succeed when teachers' individual efforts are supported by a school- or district-wide orientation toward improving academic achievement for all students from culturally and linguistically diverse backgrounds. Ensuring that all educators possess the necessary knowledge and skills is a long-term process. Ongoing staff development efforts must supplement preservice teacher preparation programs. In addition, effective instruction in multicultural special education requires greater collaboration between special educators and general educators, including bilingual educators, ESL specialists, migrant educators, Chapter I teachers, and other individuals who serve CLD students with disabilities. The school's multicultural resources can be considerably enhanced when collaborative efforts also involve parents and the community in meaningful ways. Effective services for a multicultural student population in general and special education requires a comprehensive, multidimensional approach that is capable of accommodating the diverse needs of students. We must develop a more effective interface with the programs that have traditionally served these children.

References

Baca, L. M., & Cervantes, H. T. (Eds.) (1989). *The bilingual special education interface* (2nd ed.). Columbus, OH: Merrill.

Briscoe, D. B. (1991). Designing for diversity in school success: Capitalizing on culture. *Preventing School Failure, 36*(1), 13-18.

Boutte, G. S., & McCormick, C. B. (1992). Avoiding pseudomulticulturalism: Authentic multicultural activities. *Childhood Education, 68*(3), 140-144.

Cheng, L. L. (1987). *Assessing Asian language performance: Guidelines for evaluating limited-English-proficient students.* Rockville, MD: Aspen.

Cummins, J. (1984). *Bilingualism and special education: Issues in assessment and pedagogy.* Clevedon, Avon, England: Multilingual Matters.

Cummins, J. (1989). A theoretical framework for bilingual special education. *Exceptional Children, 56,* 111-119.

Derman-Sparks, L. (1989). *Anti-bias curriculum: Tools for empowering young children.* Washington, DC: National Association for the Education of Young Children.

Englert, C. S., & Palincsar, A. S. (1991). Reconsidering instructional research in literacy from a sociocultural perspective. *Learning Disabilities Research and Practice, 6*(4), 225-229.

García, S. B., Ortiz, A. A., & Bergman, A. H. (1990, April). *A comparison of writing skills of Hispanic students by language proficiency and handicapping condition.* Paper presented at the annual conference of the American Educational Research Association, Boston, MA.

Goldman, S., & Rueda, R. (1988). Developing writing skills in bilingual exceptional children. *Exceptional Children, 54,* 543-551.

Gollnick, D. M., & Chinn, P. C. (1986). *Multicultural education in a pluralistic society* (2nd ed.). Columbus, OH: Merrill.

Graves, D. (1985). All children can write. *Learning Disability Focus, 1*(1), 36-43.

Gudykunst, W. B., & Ting-Toomey, S. (1988). *Cultural and interpersonal communication.* Newbury Park, CA: Sage.

Harry, B. (1992). Restructuring the participation of African-American parents in special education. *Exceptional Children, 59,* 123-131.

Heath, S. B. (1986). Sociocultural contexts of language development. In *Beyond language: Social and cultural factors in schooling language minority students* (pp. 143-186). Los Angeles: Evaluation, Dissemination and Assessment Center, California State University.

Hecht, M. L., Collier, M. J., & Ribeau, S. A. (1993). *African American communication: Ethnic identify and cultural interpretation.* Newbury Park, CA: Sage

Lynch, J. (1992). *Education for citizenship in a multicultural society.* New York: Cassell.

Maehr, M. (1990, April). *The psychological environment of the school: A focus for school leadership.* Paper presented at the annual meeting of the American Educational Research Association, Boston, MA.

Ortiz, A. A., & García, S. B. (1990). Using language assessment data for language and instructional planning for exceptional bilingual students. In A. L. Carrasquillo & R. E. Baecher (Eds.), *Teaching the bilingual special education student* (pp. 25-47). Norwood, NJ: Ablex.

Ortiz, A. A., & Yates, J. R. (1989). Staffing and the development of individualized educational programs for the bilingual exceptional student. In L. M. Baca & H. T. Cervantes (Eds.), *The bilingual special education interface* (pp. 183-203). Columbus, OH: Merrill.

Philips, S. U. (1983). *The invisible culture: Communication in classroom and community on the Warm Springs Indian reservation.* New York: Longman.

Ramírez, M. III, & Castañeda, A. (1974). *Cultural democracy: Bicognitive development and education.* New York: Academic Press.

Ruiz, N. (1989). An optimal learning environment for Rosemary. *Exceptional Children, 56,* 130-144.

Saville-Troike, M. (1978). *A guide to culture in the classroom.* Rosslyn, VA: National Clearinghouse for Bilingual Education.

Sleeter, C. (1992). *Keepers of the American dream: A study of staff development and multicultural education.* Bristol, PA: Palmer.

Willig, A. C., & Ortiz, A. A. (1991). The nonbiased individualized education program: Linking assessment to instruction. In E. V. Hamayan & J. S. Damico (Eds.), *Limiting bias in the assessment of bilingual students* (pp. 281-302). Austin, TX: Pro-Ed.

Issues in Testing Students from Culturally and Linguistically Diverse Backgrounds

Richard A. Figueroa and Eugene Garcia

Richard A. Figueroa is a professor with the California Research Institute on Special Education and Cultural Diversity at the University of California, Santa Cruz, and Eugene Garcia is director of the Office of Bilingual Education and Minority Language Affairs, United States Department of Education, Washington, D.C.

The Learning Contexts of Diversity

Demographic analyses sketch macro portraits of life parameters confronting ethnic families in our country. At the micro level, however, such parameters translate to living conditions that present children with cognitive and linguistic "curricula" often unimagined and incomprehensible to the larger society in general and to test protocols in particular.

Our society has children from nurturing, intact ethnic homes. The language of the home, the media that informs and entertains, and the communication patterns in many neighborhoods involve more than English and another language. They also include code-switching, varying levels of bilingualism and genres unique to such contexts. Biculturalism is a constant, evolving experience for many families as they negotiate competing practices in socialization, child-rearing and relationships. Large communities where English is seldom spoken are commonplace and provide social and linguistic contexts that are unique in what they teach and in how they socialize. Moving between countries on an annual basis creates unique conditions for shifts in language proficiencies and cultural adaptations. Families often live in housing projects where danger preoccupies the family's waking hours. Anomie permeates the condition of many homes, exacerbated by periodic deportations and exploitation in the work

place. Some parents are broken by marginalization and isolation. In communities where ethnic groups are in the majority, powerlessness breeds loss of faith in authority and in the political process.

All of these conditions and life situations are not new in the history of the country (Figueroa, 1990). Every new group of immigrants has walked these same paths. What is unique at present is the demography of these conditions. In many areas of the country, a new majority is emerging.

Immigration Trends: Roots of Diversity

From 1981 through 1990 some 7,388,062 people immigrated to the United States, marking a 63 per cent increase in the immigrant population over the previous decade (see Table 1). Apart from the sheer magnitude in the numbers of immigrants to the U.S., what are the characteristics of this population? That is, in relative terms, from which country does this population originate? And perhaps more importantly, what are the greatest changes and emerging immigration trends?

• • • • • • • • • • • • • •

Over the past two decades. Mexico has remained the country of origin for the majority of immigrants to the U.S. An estimated 1,655,843 Mexican citizens have emigrated here since 1981. This figure outnumbers any other single nation of origin by over a million for the same time period. The Philippines have ranked second in number of U.S.-bound emigrants for some 20 years now (1971-1980: 354,987; and 1981-1990: 548,764). China (346,747), Korea (333,747), and Vietnam (280,782) fol-

lowed. In terms of the greatest numbers, this ranking of countries of origin has remained relatively stable (since 1971), with the exception of Cuba. The U.S. has seen a decline of Cuban emigrants from 264,863 in the 1970s to 144,578 in the 1980s.

Comparing the past two decades, what countries of origin exhibit the greatest **growth** rates in migrations to the U.S.? In the last ten years more then six times as many Salvadorans have fled to the U.S. from war-torn El Salvador than in the previous decade (1980's: 213,539; 1970's: 34,346). Irish immigration has increased 178 per cent to 31,969. The numbers of Iranian and Haitian immigrants have more than doubled in this same time frame. Eastern European countries, such as Hungary, Poland, and Romania averaged approximately a 100 per cent increase (18,348; 83,252; 30,857 respectively, as of 1990). The Vietnamese community continues to grow at a rate 62 per cent greater than previously.

These statistics describe a U.S. immigrant population which is comprised of vastly different peoples. It is not only rapidly growing but rapidly intensifying in diversity as well. These immigrants come with families and often live in their own, large ethnic communities. More than ever before, we are a nation of immigrants/refugees. This reality has never existed in our country quite as it does now, and as it will increasingly do so in the future.

Future Projections of Student Populations

At the student level, the most comprehensive report with regard to trend towards diversity was published in 1991 by The College Board and the Western Interstate Commission for Higher Education, *The Road to College: Educational Progress by Race and Ethnicity.* This report indicates that the U.S. non-White and Hispanic student population will increase from 10.4 million in 1985-86 to 13.7 million in 1994-95. These pupils will constitute 34 per cent of public elementary and secondary school enrollment in 1994-95, up from 29 per cent in 1985-86. White enrollment, meanwhile, will rise by just five per cent, from 25.8 million to 27 million, and their share of the student population will drop from 71 per cent to 66 per cent in 1994-95. Non-White and Hispanic student enrollment will grow from 10 million in 1976 to nearly 45 million in 2026. These students will grow from 23 per cent to 70 per cent of our nation's school enrollment during this relatively short period of time. **In 2026, we will have the exact inverse of student representation as we knew it in 1990 when White students made up 70 per cent of our enrolled K-12 student body.**

Of distinctive educational significance is the reality that in 1986, 30 to 35 per cent (3 million) of non-White and Hispanic students were identified as residing in homes in which English was not the primary language (August & Garcia, 1988). Using these figures and extrapolating from the projections displayed in Tables 1 and 2, by the year 2,000, our schools will be the home for six million limited English proficient students. By the year 2026, that number will conservatively approximate 15 million students, or somewhere in the vicinity of 25 per cent of total elementary and secondary school enrollments.

The Language Minority Student and Testing

Within this discussion of student diversity, one distinctive subpopulation should be highlighted due to its growing size, both relatively and absolutely, and its precarious situation within our educational institutions. These students come to the schooling process without the language in which that process is imbedded. Demographic data has indicated that in the next two decades some 15 per cent of U.S., K-12 student population, will be comprised of these students. Moreover, they present a special challenge to our social and educational institutions and practices (such as testing) due to their linguistic diversity. Much of the formal, pre-K-12, teaching/learning/testing enterprise requires effective communication of specific facts, concepts, ideas, and problem solving strategies. Most of these students are able to do that, but, they do so in another language and through different communication skills (August & Garcia, 1988). These often do not match those of the service provider, teacher, school, or test.

• • • • • • • • • • • •

As one searches for a comprehensive definition of the "language minority" student, a continuum of possibilities unfolds. At one end of the continuum are general definitions such as "students who come from homes in which a language other than English is spoken." At the other end of that continuum are highly operationalized definitions, "students scored in the first quartile on a standardized test of English

language proficiency." Regardless of the definition adopted, these students come in a variety of linguistic shapes and forms.

The language minority population in the U.S. continues to be linguistically very heterogeneous. There are over 100 distinct language groups identified. Even in the largest language group, some are monolingual Spanish speakers while others are to some degree bilingual. Other non-English speaking minority groups in

Table 1
Immigration to the United States by Region 1820-1990 with Special Emphasis On 1971-1980 and 1981-1990.

Region and Country of Origin	1820-1990	1971-1980	1981-1990
All Countries	**56,994,014**	**4,493,314**	**7,338,062**
Europe	**37,101,060**	**800,368**	**761,550**
Austria-Hungary	4,342,782	16,028	24,885
Austria	1,828,946	9,478	18,340
Hungary	1,667,760	6,550	6,545
Belgium	210,556	5,329	7,066
Czechhoslovakia	145,801	6,023	7,227
Denmark	370,412	4,439	5,370
France	787,587	25,069	32,353
Germany	7,083,465	74,414	91,961
Greece	703,904	92,369	38,377
Ireland	4,725,133	11,490	31,969
Italy	5,373,108	129,368	67,254
Netherlands	374,232	10,492	12,238
Norway-Sweden	2,145,954	10,472	15,182
Norway	801,224	3,941	4,164
Sweden	1,284,475	6,531	11,018
Poland	606,336	37,234	83,252
Portugal	501,261	101,710	40,431
Romania	204,841	12,393	30,857
Soviet Union	3,443,706	38,961	57,677
Spain	285,148	39,141	20,433
Switzerland	359,439	8,235	8,849
United Kingdom	5,119,150	137,374	159,173
Yugoslavia	136,271	30,540	18,762
Other Europe	181,974	9,287	8,234
Asia	**5,019,180**	**1,588,178**	**2,738,157**
China	914,376	124,326	346,747
Hong Kong	302,230	113,467	98,215
India	455,716	164,134	250,786
Iran	176,851	45,136	116,172
Israel	137,540	37,713	44,273
Japan	462,244	49,775	47,085
Korea	642,248	267,638	333,746
Philippines	1,026,653	354,987	584,764
Turkey	412,327	13,399	23,233
Vietnam	458,277	172,820	280,782
Other Asia	1,030,718	244,783	648,354
America	**13,067,548**	**1,982,735**	**3,615,255**
Canada	4,295,585	169,939	156,938
Mexico	3,888,729	640,294	1,655,843
Caribbean	2,703,177	741,126	872,051
Cuba	748,710	264,863	144,578
Dominican Republic	510,136	148,135	252,035
Haiti	234,757	56,335	138,379
Jamaica	429,500	137,577	208,148
Other Caribbean	780,074	134,216	128,911
Central America	**819,628**	**134,640**	**648,088**
El Salvador	274,667	34,436	213,539
Other Central America	544,961	100,204	254,549
South America	**1,250,303**	**295,741**	**461,847**
Argentina	131,118	29,897	27,327
Columbia	295,353	77,347	122,849
Ecuador	155,767	50,077	56,315
Other South America	668,065	138,420	255,356
Other America	110,126	995	458
Africa	**334,145**	**80,779**	**176,893**
Oceania	204,622	41,242	45,205
Not Specified	**267,459**	**12**	**1,032**

the U.S. are similarly heterogeneous. Describing the "typical" language minority student is highly problematic. However, one might agree that this student is one: (a) who is characterized by substantive participation in a non-English speaking social environment; (b) who has acquired the normal communicative abilities of that social environment; (c) who is exposed to a substantive English-speaking environment, more than likely for the first time, during the schooling process; and (d) who tests poorly on verbal, English-language tests.

Estimates of the number of language minority students have been compiled by the federal government on several occasions (O'Malley, 1981; Development Associates, 1984; Waggoner, 1991). These estimates differ because of the definition adopted for identifying these students, the particular measure utilized to obtained the estimate, and the statistical treatment utilized to generalize beyond the sample obtained. For example, O'Malley (1981) defined the language minority student population by utilizing a specific cutoff score on an English language proficiency test administered to a stratified sample of students. Development Associates (1984) estimated the population by utilizing reports from a stratified sample of local school districts. Estimates of language minority students have ranged from 1,300,000 (Development Associates, 1984) to 3,600,000 (O'Malley, 1981).

The U.S. Department of Education (1993) recently sketched a demographic and educational portrait of these students. Table 2 summarizes this information.

Notwithstanding, the statistical portrait of LEP children and their low status in the public schools, at an ideographic level the picture is just as dramatic. Children come to school with language genres, behavior patterns, motivations, attitudes, and expectations that are either unacknowledged by the schools or seen as developmental deficits that must be "remediated" or proscribed before school learning can begin. In the standoff between what the schools require and what ethnic children bring, the children usually loose. Instead of acknowledging that these pupils are learners with unique and intact systems of knowledge (Moll, Velez-Ibanez, Greenberg, & Rivera, 1990) and processes for learning, they are tracked into programs that attempt to "cure" the deficits or to diagnose cultural and linguistic differences as mental handicaps to be dealt with in special education.

• • • • • • • • • • • • •

In terms of the middle class normative frameworks that undergird tests, children from diverse learning environments have traditionally been described as developmentally deficient in language, cognition, attention, memory, perception, learning ability, IQ, and just about every major benchmark of "normal" growth and development. Virtually every "objective" test used to assess individual skills or aptitudes has been instrumental in profiling these deficits.

Ironically, from their inception, "standard" assessments, and particularly tests, have operated under a key, robust assumption. They assume equal or comparable exposure to the content of the assessments prior to the assessment. They assume a high degree of homogeneity of experiences. Regretably, when such homogeneity has not actually existed, test and test users have enforced it by labeling individuals with average scores as "normal" and those with below average scores as "deviant." This, in spite of historical admonishments about the assumption buttressing normative measures:

> ...The validity of **all** mental testing rests on the fundamental assumption that those tested have had a **common opportunity to learn** the skills, facts, principles and methods of procedure exemplified in the tests. [emphasis added] (Colvin, 1921, p. 137.)

> The assumption is made that if one samples the results of learning in matters where all individuals tested have had an **equal chance** at learning, he may arrive at an estimate of the capacity to learn. [emphasis added] (Dearborn, 1921, p. 211.)

> One's actual present capacity for doing any particular thing is obviously dependent upon his training and learning, or, in general, upon his past experience: whereas in the measurement of intelligence, the attempt is always to minimize the effects of past experience by utilizing performances, the acquisition of the capacity for which is presumably **favored equally** by the past environments of all individuals measured. [emphasis added] (Woodrow, 1921, p. 207.)

The Fragility of Tests and Testing

Tests have high status in our society. At the turn of the century, they propelled the new science of psychology into the limelight by politically enhancing nativist notions about American intelligence and by providing an efficient system for tracking army recruits into various jobs in the military during the first and second World

---

TABLE 2
"DESCRIPTIVE STUDY OF SERVICES TO LIMITED ENGLISH PROFICIENT STUDENTS" (U.S. DEPARTMENT OF EDUCATION. 1993)—SUMMARY OF DATA

1. Since 1984, there has been a 70 per cent increase in the number of LEP students (currently totalling 2.31 million);
2. Across the country, 43 per cent of all school districts serve LEP pupils;
3. 82 per cent of the LEP student population is in grades K-9, making it an exceedingly young population of school-age children;
4. Almost 75 per cent speak Spanish, 4 per cent Vietnamese, 2 per cent speak Hmong, Cantonese, Cambodian and Korean (each), and and the rest speak from 29 Native American languages;
5. 41 per cent of LEP students were born in the U.S;
6. The larger the school district, the more likely that language assessment proficiency is measured through a standardized procedure;
7. English is the predominant language assessed; only 33 per cent of the districts measure oral language proficiency in the native language; only 12 per cent measure academic achievement in the home language;
8. The larger the number of LEP pupils in a school district, the more likely that services are provided in the native language;
9. 20 per cent of the states do not require native language services for LEP pupils and almost 33 per cent of the states require some form of primary language service in academic content areas;
10. Only 22 states make special allocations for instructing LEP students;
11. ESL is the predominant instructional adaptation for LEP pupils; only 17 per cent of schools provide a significant degree of primary language instruction;
12. Instructional aides provide a large amount of the instructional and translation services;
13. Though over 363,000 teachers provice some service to LEP pupils, only 10 per cent are credentialed bilingual teachers;
14. Only 33 per cent of the teachers serving LEP pupils have ever taken a college course on culture, language acquisition or teaching English to LEP pupils; and
15. The majority of teachers serving Spanish-speaking pupils have no proficiency in Spanish

Wars (Cronbach, 1957). Tests are perceived as scientific, objective, and useful. In high stakes assessments, they tend to carry the day in decisions about jobs, educational placements, diagnosis, etc. Yet, their true source of power has always resided in their ability to predict, to predict better than human judgment.

• • • • • • • • • • • • •

However, tests are quite fragile. They rest on some key assumptions (above), and they are generally plagued by shortcomings in technical properties. The *Buros Mental Measurement Yearbooks*, for example, typically fault most available normative measure on the issues of reliability or validity. However, the primary source of discontent by test reviewers resides in tests' weak or modest predictive validities. It is generally rare to find a test that predicts to real-life situations (grades, job success, program completion rates, etc.) with anything above a .5 or .6 correlation. This essentially means that anywhere from 75 to 64 per cent of the variance of the criterion (what is predicted to) remains unexplained. By and large, the further a test score gets from similar test scores (for example, from a developmental test score, to another developmental test score, to an achievement test score, to grades, to graduation rates), the lower the predictive validities become.

We have attempted to examine this with tests commonly given to young children. Table 3 presents the predictive coefficients or evaluations of validity reported by three well known test evaluators (Sattler, 1988; Salvia & Ysseldyke, 1988; Bredekamp & Shepard, 1989). By and large, the data in Table 3 show that these tests are fragile.

It should be noted that almost all the predictive coefficients cited in Table 3 involve achievement test scores as criteria. Few studies actually ever report on grades or other more "existential" criteria. Usually when such indices are used, test scores predict in the .2 to .3 range. In other words, they account for approximately 4 to 9 per cent of grade variance. Many argue that this is due to the low reliability and subjectivity involved in such real-life "scores." Paradoxically, it is these type of "scores" that usually decide on promotions, suspensions, and other real life outcomes. For tests, however, they remain too "subjective."

Given the fragile nature of the technical data reviewed in Table 2, some of the precautions and requisites in this are worth quoting:

> There are...major dilemmas in assessing readiness...the performances of preschoolers are so variable that there is relatively little long-term prediction...while readiness tests are used exclusively to predict a person's success or failure in an instructional sequence or program. Therefore, certain technical characteristics, such as predictive criterion-referenced validity, are extremely important. Moreover, since readiness tests are routinely used to make individual placement decisions, these test must conform to the highest standards of technical excellence. (Salvia & Ysseldyke, 1988, p. 454).

Table 3
Predictive Validity and Evaluations of Validity for Some of the Most Widely Used Tests of School Readiness

Name of Test	Predictive Coefficients	Evaluations
Boehm Test of Basic Concepts	.40 (Mdn. Corr; Achievement tests)* .54 (Spelling)** .54 (Ach. Tests)** .27 (Rdng. Test)** .27-.72 (Ach. subtests)**	"correlates modestly with achievement...has inadequate reliability and norms."*p.442 "acceptable validity but only minimally adequate validity." **p.344
Form C	.52 (Mdn; Ach. Tests)**	
Form D	.50 (Mdn; Ach. Tests)**	
Boehm Preschool	.67 (vocabulary)** .57 (vocabulary)**	
Denver Developmental Screening Test		"reliability and validity are adequate...although the norms are questionable." **p.440 "has several weaknesses...should be used with caution" ** pg. 352
Metropolitan Readiness Test	.34-.65 (Ach.subtests)** .48-.83 (Ach. subtests)**	"The MRT's predictive validity particular curricula or other achievement tests is unknown and therefore...should not be used as a predictive devise." * p. 451 "...the evidence for validity is scant" * p. 453
Gessel School Readiness Test	.28-.64 (Ach.,intell)***	"The psychometric properties of the Gesell test do not meet the standards of professional test development." ***p.16
Preschool Inventory-R		"..empirical validity is generally lacking." * p. 445
Test of Basic Experience		"Evidence for predictive validity is not reported." * p. 446
Developmental Indicators for the Assessment of Language-R		"Norms are questionnable...reliability is poor... Validity is not clearly established." *p.449
Developmental Profile II		"..norms are unrepresentative, the degree of reliability unknown, and evidence for validity is scant." * p.453
Columbia Mental Maturity Scale	.31-.61 (Ach.tests)	"..appears technically adequate." *p.195
Detroit Test of Learning Aptitude-R	.51 (Mdn; ach. tests)	"data on validity is scarce." *p. 175
Extended Merrill		"No validity indeces are reported in the manual."
Palmer		** pg. 307
McCarthy Scales of Childrens' Abilities	.66 (Mdn; ach. tests)** .58 (ach. tests)**	"Evidence about validity is still limited." *p. 139
Wechsler Preschool and Primary Scale of Intelligence	.58, .30,.37,.58, .36, .36, .60, .62, .68, .43, NS, .27, .61, .41, .73 (Ach. tests)**	"evidence on validity is...very limited." *p.169 "Excellent reliability and validity..." **p. 214

* (Salvia & Ysseldyke, 1988)
** (Sattler, 1988)
*** (Bredekamp & Shepard, 1989)

• • • • • • • • • • •

Recently, even the most powerful tests (IQ) have also come under criticism for not being very useful in helping to plan educational interventions (Shinn, 1989). Also, ethnographic studies of what actually happens in the most controlled testing situations also show that the much touted objectivity of the enterprise may be more illusory than real:

Proponents of testing describe tests as objective, standardized and norm-referenced. In a standardized test, procedures, apparatus, and scoring have been fixed so that precisely the same test can be given to many different students on different occasions. The emphasis here is standardization of procedure. Technically, testing kits are uniform. We found, however, that the administration of tests in practical situations is not routine. The act of testing involves a complex social relationship...that makes the uniform and objective measure of intelligence a social activity. (Mehan, Hertweck, & Meihls, 1986, p. 94)

Mehan also found that in testing situations inappropriate feedback was given, and incorrect cues were provided. In effect, social factors played as important a part as the test directions. The distinct impression given by Mehan's descriptions of the testing sessions he videotaped is that testing is not "reliable" in that it does not follow the script provided by the test manuals.

We have confirmed the findings of many previous researchers...who have shown that treating test results as...facts obscures the constitutive process by which testers and students jointly produce answers in individual tests. (Mehan, et al., 1986, p. 100)

There is one other factor to consider. Most of the predictive correlation's cited in Table 3 come from studies where White, middle-class children are used as subjects. In the few studies where minority children are involved (Sattler, 1988), the outcomes are often in the direction of lowering the predictive correlations. In effect, for many minority populations, evidence is beginning to accumulate indicating that test fragility may well be test bias.

The Historical Context

Virtually every ethnic group in the U.S. since the early 1900s has fared badly on American tests (Brigham, 1923; Figueroa, 1990; Valdes & Figueroa, in press):

On the other hand, with regard to more purely intellectual traits, the Japanese are judged as inferior. This is shown in the ratings of general intelligence, desire to know and originality. (Darsie, 1926, p. 76)

In a comprehensive review of intelligence and achievement testing with linguistic minorities, Figueroa (1990) outlined some of the key historical issues and findings regarding the effects of culture and bilingualism on these two categories of American tests.

With respect to culture, Figueroa (1990) found that the typical way in which test researchers dealt with this variable was to operationally define it in a group. Rather than set forth a continua of factors associated with a culture, test researchers ascribed it to a group. Hence, when American Indian culture was being studied, it resided in the test scores of the American Indian group being investigated. Accordingly, Garth (1920) talked about the "mental fatigue" trait in American-Indian and Mexican-American culture. The effects of poverty, segregation, biased teacher perceptions, and the general anti-immigrant social and political sentiment of the early part of this century played no part in explaining the large differences between the test scores of "minority" populations and the dominant cultural group. Test scores had the force of science behind them and differences in group scores were seen as real differences in mental abilities and genetic potential.

Similar to culture, bilingualism was not taken seriously. However, as Figueroa (1990) demonstrates, this variable left its imprint on every study on intelligence and achievement test conducted with populations from non-English backgrounds. First, any test that required the use of English in even the most elemental task (e.g., repeating digits in English) and even with groups that already spoke English, registered the impact of the second language in a lower than expected score. Interestingly, some of the most conservative test makers and advocates came to appreciate the pervasive impact of a second language on test scores:

For purposes of comparing individuals or groups, it is apparent that tests in the vernacular [English] must be used only with individuals having equal opportunities to acquire the vernacular of the test. This requirement precludes the use of such tests in making comparative studies of individuals brought up in homes in which the vernacular of the test is not used, or in which two vernaculars are used. The last condition is frequently violated here in studies of children born in this country whose parents speak another tongue. It is important, as the effects of bilingualism are not entirely known. (Brigham, 1930, p. 165.)

Second, bilingualism never affected internal indices (reliability, concurrence) of test adequacy. But in several studies, there was evidence that bilingualism lowered predictive validity (Figueroa, 1990). Third, anomalous data showed up: for bilinguals, recalling digits backward was easier than recalling them forward; middle class bilingual test-takers often did better than middle-class English speakers; and finally, older bilinguals who had been educated in their primary language also often did better than English speakers. Fourth, though verbal tests were always hypersensitive to bilingualism, school grades were not.

• • • • • • • • • • • • •

The "solutions" that test users and test makers often tried to apply when it came to testing bilingual populations pre-1950s included the following: (a) ignore bilingualism and test in English, (b) use non-verbal tests, (c) translate the test into the native language and use the same norms, and (d) norm the test in the primary language. Some of these solutions exist to the present. However, as Figueroa (1989, 1990) has pointed out, none of them have any merit. In many ways, the caveats that were articulated in the 1920s and 1930s about the bilingual pupil and testing remain just as poignant today (Brigham, 1930, above).

It is regrettable, however, that test users and test makers have chosen to repeat the mistakes of the past when it comes to culturally and linguistically diverse students. Since the 1960s, the federal courts and Congress have had to step in and legislate testing practices. This is uniquely the case in special education.

Special Education Testing

The contemporary issue of testing and minorities first came to the attention of the courts in a non-special education case, *Hobsen v. Hansen*. In this case, Black children in the Washington, D.C. area, after being integrated at the high school level (as per *Brown v. Board of Education*), began failing in large numbers. The district superintendent initiated a testing system designed to tailor educational programs to individual abilities. An elaborate testing system was set in place to direct the students into their most appropriate program. Since neither the tests nor the test givers paid attention to the fact that pre-integration, Black pupils attended "disadvantaged" school and were exposed to "disadvantaged" curricula, in a few years the vocational tracks in the high schools were all Black and the academic tracks were all White. In the subsequent trial, the judge in *Hobsen v. Hansen* ruled that the tests were responsible for the new segregation and that these instruments could not measure the learning potential of Black students because they did not account for their cultural background.

Hobsen v. Hansen is a benchmark in the field of testing because all the language linked to prejudice, racism and segregation became associated with the adverse impact that tests often have on culturally diverse pupils. From this case, the stage was set for a legal challenge to the sort of testing that goes on in special education.

• • • • • • • • • • • •
In the early 1960s, an old phenomenon (Reynolds, 1933) began receiving attention from researchers (Mercer, 1973). Classes for the mildly handicapped (mild mental retardation, learning handicaps) were found to be over-populated by Black and Hispanic pupils (the same could have been reported about American Indian children). In *Diana v. California Board of Education*, the Ninth Circuit oversaw an out of court settlement entitling bilingual pupils to testing in English and in their primary language. The settlement also called for yearly monitoring of the effects of testing on overrepresentation rates in classes for the mildly handicapped.

In *Larry P. v. Riles*, the same Ninth District federal judge ruled, after a lengthy trial, that IQ tests were biased against Black children because they did not take into account their cultural background. He banned the use of such tests for Black children who were being considered for placement into the Educable Mentally Retarded programs.

• • • • • • • • • • • •
Since these two cases, there have been a series of similar legal challenges to testing in special education (*Lora v. Board of Education of the City of New York; Jose P. v. Ambach; PASE v. Hannon*). Most of these have been framed within the facts and issues surrounding *Diana* and *Larry P.* Most of the time the rulings have gone in the same direction as *Diana*. In the matter of *Larry P.*, some judges have ruled in a diametrically different direction and at present a legal challenge to *Larry P.* in California (*Crawford v. Honig*) is moving the state on the side of Black children and possibly towards the elimination of IQ tests, psychometric tests, the Medical Model used to "diagnose" problem learners as handicapped learners, and the very existence of separate classes for the mildly handicapped. These moves, it should be pointed out, are not without support from the research community (Skrtic, 1991).

In 1975, in P.L. 94-142, Congress included testing language that flowed directly from the court cases. In special education for young children and for the K-12 population, tests and testing have to be racially and culturally non-discriminatory and have to be provided in the primary language, if it is at all feasible to do so.

The Regulatory Context

Since the 1960s, the testing professions have published many editions of the testing *Standards* (American Psychological Association, 1954; American Educational Research Association & National Council on Measurement, 1955; American Psychological Association, American Educational Research Association, & National Council on Measurement, 1966, 1974; American Educational Research Association, American Psychological Association, National Council on Measurement, 1985), and periodic texts on issues confronting testing (Cleary, Humphreys, Kendrick, & Wesman, 1975; Wigdor & Garner, 1982; Heller, Holtzman, & Messick, 1982). Most have either asserted that cultural bias in testing cannot be found (Cleary, Humphreys, Kendrick, & Wesman, 1975) or they have reiterated the same historical cautions about bilingualism and testing without any real sense of sanctions or proscriptions. Among these, however, there are two key exceptions.

First, the National Academy of Sciences, in an indirect way, has framed some of the cultural concerns surrounding the testing of ethnic pupils in an interesting manner (Heller, Holtzman, & Messick, 1982). In its report on the overrepresentation of minority pupils in special education, the Academy endorsed one suggestion (pp. 68-72): before the very high-stakes testing for special education, there should be an assessment of the **instructional context** where the student is currently placed. In effect, the recommendation is for educators to take into account at least one of the key background variables that affects children's learning: the quality of their learning experience in the classroom.

• • • • • • • • • • • •
Specifically, the Academy set four dimensions in order to gauge the effectiveness of the classroom: (a) there should be evidence that the curriculum offered works with the pupil's cultural group, (b) there should be documented evidence that such curriculum is effectively implemented by the teacher, (c) there should be evidence that the child in question has not really learned the material taught, (d) there should be evidence of early intervention when the problems in learning first appeared. If all these conditions are met, then and only then does the assessment move on to consider the possibility that the problem resides in the pupil. This is a major departure in the history of testing. For once, there is now a directive to examine the historical caveats and assumptions on which tests rest: the homogeneity of experience. This is to be done prior to the administration of the test and prior to the interpretation of any score.

Second, all the major national organizations involved with testing, in the *Standards for Educational and Psychological Testing*, (AERA, APA, NCM, 1985) finally come to terms with the historical, complex, intervening variable of bilingualism. In a chapter on "Testing Linguistic Minorities" the *Standards*, like the National Academy of Sciences, break new ground. First, it is

acknowledged that for bilingual learners who may not have had "substantial" exposure to English, any test given in English becomes in unknown degrees a test of English language or English literacy.

Third, a bilingual individual's linguistic background must be taken into account in any type of testing. "Bilingualism" is multifactorial and includes individuals with a broad range of speaking, reading, writing, and understanding abilities in each language. Further, some "bilinguals" not only speak two languages they also codeswitch as per the social demands of communicative events. Also, for some bilingual individuals, processing information in the weaker language is a more demanding undertaking than for a monolingual.

Fourth, translating tests does not translate psychometric properties. The same vocabulary item in two languages can have different frequency (p) values, degrees of propriety and meaningfulness.

Fifth, there is a need for multifactorial language tests ("communicative competence, literacy, grammar, pronunciation, comprehension" p. 74) in English and in primary languages in order to help make educational placement decisions.

Sixth, linguistic proficiency in English is at least a dual phenomenon: that which is manifest in informal communication and that which is required in formal and academic situations.

• • • • • • • • • • • •
Seventh, language is culturally embedded, and the unique linguistic genre typically used in testing ("an adult who is probing for elaborate speech with only short phrases" p. 74) may elicit culturally appropriate ways of responding rather than test appropriate ways of answering ("short phrases or...shrugging their shoulders" p. 74) leading to "interpretations and prescriptions of treatment [that] may be invalid and potentially harmful to the individual being tested" (p. 74).

The issues raised in the chapter on "Testing Linguistic Minorities" in the *Standards* virtually preclude the use of psychometric and normative tests with linguistically and culturally diverse individuals in the U.S. Paradoxically, this paper and the *Standards* themselves barely scratch the surface on the biasing effects of culture and bilingualism. The *Standards* are currently being revised. It will be interesting to see whether the testing professions retreat from their 1985 directives or actually move towards correcting the testing abuses of the last 75 years.

Culture and Bilingualism

Testing psychology has yet to cope with culture. In studies on test bias, "culture" continues to be defined by the group that supposedly has the "culture" (Sandoval, 1979; Sandoval, Zimmerman & Woo-Sam, 1980).

• • • • • • • • • • • •

As a variable, "culture" in testing psychology is a black box. The one large attempt to operationally define it, the *System of Multicultural Pluralistic Assessment* (SOMPA) (Mercer, 1979), failed because it relied on more testing (as a way to capture its complexity) while ignoring any sources of test variance unique to African-American or Hispanic cultures. At its core, SOMPA failed because it did not know how to cope with bias in the criteria to which tests are expected to predict and because it did not dare to really measure those elements in African-American and Latino cultures which constitute the curricula, pedagogy, and contexts to which cross-cultural children in our society are exposed (Tharp, 1989; Moll *et al.*, 1990; Miller-Jones, 1989).

SOMPA did do something unique. It treated each ethnic group as a separate norming population of 700 youngsters. But it used this wonderful sampling opportunity to norm the same White, culture-bound tests on culturally different children and then expected these tests to provide something more than measures of sociological distance from the majority culture. As diagnostic tools, the SOMPA tests continued the tradition of mismeasuring children because of their differentness all the while ignoring what they had learned in their unique demographic and cultural worlds. In the end, the SOMPA tests also proved to be just as fragile and modest in helping to predict future performance (Figueroa & Sassenrarth, 1989; Figueroa, 1989).

The Courts have been just as unspecific in operationalizing "culture." But, paradoxically, they have been insistent that since neither in their development nor validation have tests taken "culture" into account, they are inappropriate and invalid for pupils from diverse cultural backgrounds.

Notwithstanding, the breakthrough re-presented by the *Standards*, bilingualism also continues to be ignored by test developers and test users. The current, favorite "solution" to the challenge of bilingualism for testing is to either have a bilingual adult translate a test extemporaneously while testing a child (a practice that is widespread and proscribed by the current *Standards*) or to produce seemingly comparable versions of the U.S. tests in another language. The Spanish versions of the *Woodcock Johnson Psychoeducational Battery* and the *Boehm Test of Basic Concepts* are primary examples of this trend.

This "solution" has a unique appeal since it appears to solve the problem. But it is naive and misguided. To begin with, a bilingual learner in the U.S. is not like a monolingual English learner nor like a monolingual Spanish speaker. As Grosjean (1989) explains, the last 20 years of educational, psychological, neurological, and information-processing research has shown that:

> A bilingual (or holistic) view of bilingualism proposes that the bilingual is an integrated whole which cannot be decomposed into two separate parts.

Table 4
Comparison of Predictive Validity Coefficients of Several Tests of Ability (Predicting to Standardized Measures of Reading and Math) for Hispanic Children from three Home-Language Groups (E=English; E/S=English/Spanish; S=Spanish) and for Anglo Children

	Reading Hispanic E	E/S	S	Anglo+	Math Hispanic E	E/S	S	Anlgo+
WISC-R								
VIQ								
(a)*	.60	.50	.45	.66	.55	.50	.42	.56
(b)			.37	.57			.42	.62
(c)			.33	.66			.43	.56
PIQ								
(a)	.52	.40	.39	.47	.54	.44	.23	.48
(b)			.34	.50			.41	.59
(c)			.26	.47			.20	.48
FSIQ								
(a)	.61	.53	.47	.65	.60	.55	.37	.58
(b)			.35	.62			.42	.52
(c)			.37	.65			.41	.58
Binet								
3 yrs.								
(c)			.34				.33	
4 yrs.								
(c)			.27				.31	
McCarthy Scales								
(c)			.37	.66			.41	.66
K-ABC Mntl Procss Compos								
(d)		.23		.56		.32		.56**
K-ABC Achieve.								
(d)		.67		.80		.49		.80**
Bohem.								
(e)	.66	NS		.67	.64	.47		.65**
Tchers. Ratings Pre K to End 1st Grade								
(f)	NS	NS		.49	NS	NS		.64
Nunber Profic.								
(f)	.31	NS		.57	.21	.60		.51

+ Values taken from Sattler (1988), unless otherwise indicated.

* Sources: (a) Figueroa, 1990; (b) Mishra, 1983; (c) Johnson & McGowan, 1984; (d) Valencia & Ranking, 1988; (e) Pilkington, Piercel & Pontorotto, 1981 (f) Gandara, Keogh & Yoshioka-Maxwell, 1980.

** Values taken from row sources.

The bilingual is NOT the sum of two complete or incomplete monolinguals, rather, he or she has a unique and specific linguistic configuration. The coexistence and constant interaction of the two languages in the bilingual has produced a different but complete linguistic entity. (Grosjean, 1989, p. 6)

Because of the *Lau v. Nichols* Supreme Court decision in 1975, bilingualism and bilingual education have received an unparalleled degree of attention and

A List of References for Issues in the Testing of Culturally and Linguistically Diverse Students

American Educational Research Association, American Psychological Association,The National Council on Measurement. (1985). *Standards for educational and psychological testing.* Washington, DC: American Psychological Association.

American Educational Research Association, The National Council on Measurement. (1955). *Technical recommendations for achievement tests.* Washington, DC: National Education Association.

American Psychological Association (1954). *Technical recommendations for psychological tests and diagnostic techniques.* New York: American Psychological Association.

American Psychological Association, American Educational Research Association, The National Council on Measurement. (1966). *Standards for educational and psychological tests and manuals.* Washington, DC: American Psychological Association.

American Psychological Association, American Educational Research Association, The National Council on Measurement. (1974). *Standards for educational and psychological tests.* Washington, DC: American Psychological Association.

August, D. & Garcia, E. (1988). *Language minority education in the U.S.: Research, policy and practice.* Chicago, IL: Charles C. Thomas.

Bredekamp, S. & Shepard, L. (1989). How best to protect children from inappropriate school expectations, practices and policies. *Young Children,* 44(3), 14-24.

Brigham, C. C. (1923). *A study of American intelligence.* Princeton: Princeton University Press.

Brigham, C. C. (1930). Intelligence tests of immigrant groups. *Psychological Review,* 37, 15-165.

California Department of Education. (1992). LEP growth in the last two decades. *Bulletin of the California State Department of Education,* 12, 3-4.

Cleary, T. A., Humphreys, L. G., Kendrick, S. A. & Wesman, A. (1975). Educational uses of tests with disadvantaged students. *American Psychologist,* 30, 15-40.

Colvin, S. S. (1921). Intelligence and its measurement: A symposium (IV). *Journal of Educational Psychology,* 12, 136-139.

Cronbach, L. J. (1957). The two disciplines of scientific psychology. *American Psychologist,* 12, 671-684.

Darsie, M. L. (1926). The mental capacity of American-born Japanese children. *Comparative Psychology Monographs,* 3(15), 1-89.

Dearborn, W. F. (1921). Intelligence and its measurement: A symposium (XII). *Journal of Educational Psychology,* 12, 210-212.

Development Associates (1984). *Final report descriptive study phase of the national longitudinal evaluation of the effectiveness of services for language minority limited English proficient students.* Arlington, VA: Author.

Diversity and Equity in Assessment Network (1993). Guidelines for Equitable Assessment. Cambridge, MA: Fair Test.

Figueroa, R. A. (1989). Psychological testing of linguistic minority students in special education.

Exceptional Children, 56(2), 145-152.

Figueroa, R. A. (1990). Assessment of linguistic minority group children. In C. R. Reynolds & R. W. Kamphaus (Eds.), *Handbook of psychological and educational assessment of children: Intelligence and achievement.* New York: Guilford Press.

Figueroa, R. A. (1991). Bilingualism and psychometrics. *Diagnostique,* 17(1), 70-85.

Figueroa, R. A. & Sassenvath, J. M. (1989). A longitudinal study of the predictive validity of the system multicultural pluralistic assessment (SOMPA). *Psychology in the Schools,* 26(1), 5-19.

Gandara, P., Keogh, B. K., & Yoshioka-Maxwell, B. (1980). Predicting academic performance of Anglo and Mexican American kindergarten children. *Psychology in the Schools,* 17(2), 174-177.

Garth, T. R. (1920). Racial differences in mental fatigue. *Journal of Applied Psychology,* 4, 235-244.

Grosjean, F. (1989). Neurolinguists, beware! The bilingual is not two monolinguals in one person. *Brain and Language,* 36, 3-15.

Hakuta, K. (1986). *Mirror of language: The debate on bilingualism.* New York: Basic Books.

Heller, K. A., Holtzman, W. H., & Messick, S. (1982). *Placing children in special education: A strategy for equity.* Washington, DC: National Academy Press.

Johnson, D. L. & McGowan, R. J. (1984). Comparison of three intelligence tests as predictors of academic achievement and classroom behaviors of Mexican American children. *Journal of Psychoeducational Assessment,* 2, 345-352.

Mehan, H., Hertweck, H. & Meihls, J. L. (1986). *Handicapping the handicapped.* Palo Alto, CA: Stanford University Press.

Meisels, S. J. (1987). Uses and abuses of developmental screening and school readiness testing. *Young Children,* 42(2), 4-6.

Mercer, J. R. (1973). *Labeling the mentally retarded.* Berkeley, CA: University of California Press.

Mercer, J. R. (1979). *The System of Multicultural Pluralistic Assessment.* New York: The Psychological Corporation.

Miller-Jones, D. (1989). Culture and testing. *American Psychologist,* 44(2), 360-366.

Mishra, S. P. (1983). Validity of WISC-R IQs and factor scores in predicting achievement for Mexican-American children. *Psychology in the Schools,* 20(4), 442-444.

Moll, L. C., Velez-Ibanez, C., Greenberg, J., & Rivera, C. (1990). *Community knowledge and classroom practice: Combining resources for literacy instruction.* Tucson: The University of Arizona, College of Education.

Neill, M. (1993). Some pre-requisites for the establishment of equitable, inclusive multicultural assessment systems. Cambridge, MA: Fair Test.

Office of Bilingual Bicultural Education. (1982). *Basic principles for the education of language minority students: An overview. 1982 Edition.* Sacramento, CA: California State Department of Education.

O'Malley, M. J. (1981). *Language minority children with limited English proficiency in the U.S.. Children's English and services study.* Rosslyn, VA: National Clearinghouse for Bilingual Education.

Pilkington, C., Piersel, W. & Ponterotto, J. (1988). Home language as a predictor of first-grade achievement for Anglo- and Mexican-American

children. *Contemporary Educational Psychology,* 13(1), 1-14.

Poplin, M. S. (1988a). The reductionist fallacy in learning disabilities: Replicating the past by reducing the present. *Journal of Learning Disabilities,* 7, 389-400.

Poplin M. S. (1988b). Holistic/Constructivist principles of the teaching/learning process: Implications for the field of learning disabilities. *Journal of Learning Disabilities,* 21, 401-423.

Resnick, L. B. & Renick, D.P. (1989). Assessing the thinking curriculum: New tools for educational reform. In B.R. Gifford & M.C. O'Connor (Eds.), *Future assessments: Changing view of aptitude, achievement, and instruction.* Boston, MA: Kluwer.

Reynolds, A. (1933). *The education of Spanish-speaking children in five southwestern states (Bulletin No. 11).* Washington, DC: U.S. Department of the Interior.

Salvia, J. & Ysseldyke, J. E. (1988). *Assessment in special and remedial education (Fourth Edition).* Dallas, TX: Houghton Mifflin.

Sandoval, J. (1979). The WISC-R and internal evidence of test bias with minority groups. *Journal of Consulting and Clinical Psychology,* 47(5), 919-926.

Sandoval, J., Zimmerman, I. L. & Woo-Sam, J. M. (1980, September). *Cultural differences on WIS-R verbal items.* Paper presented at the annual convention of the American Psychological Association, Montreal, Canada.

Sattler, J. M. (1988). *Assessment of children (Third Edition).* San Diego: Jerome M. Sattler.

Skrtic, T. M. (1991). The special education paradox: Equity as the way to excellence. *Harvard Educational Review,* 61(2), 148-206.

Skutnabb-Kangas, T. & Toukomaa, P. (1976). *Teaching migrant children's mother tongue and learning the language of the host country in the context of the sociocultural situation of the migrant family.* Helsinki, Finland: Finnish National Commission for UNESCO.

Tharp, R. G. (1989). Psychocultural variables and constants. *American Psychologist,* 44(2), 349-359.

Valdes, G. & Figueroa, R. A. (in press). *Bilingualism and psychometrics: A special case of bias.* New York: Ablex.

Valencia, R. R. & Rankin, R. J. (1988). Evidence of bias in predictive validity on the Kaufman assessment battery for children in samples of Anglo and Mexican American children. *Psychology in the Schools,* 25(3), 257-263.

Waggoner, D. (1991). *Language minority census newsletter.* Washington, DC: Waggoner Incorporated.

Wigdor, A. & Garner, W. R. (Eds.). (1982). *Ability testing: Uses, consequences and controversies.* Washington, DC: National Academy Press.

Woodrow, H. (1921). Intelligence and its measurement: A symposium (XI). *Journal of Educational Psychology,* 12, 207-210.

debate (Hakuta, 1986). The extant knowledge base about bilingualism in the U.S. and abroad is very large and continues to document the complexity of this human trait and the complexity of learners who operate in bilingual contexts. Because of the available knowledge and because of the demographic profile of our country as an emerging bilingual society, there is a growing understanding of the multivariate, developmental conditions that can affect a bilingual learner.

• • • • • • • • • • • •

Children learn two languages either simultaneously or sequentially. The latter is the more common phenomenon and includes wide differences in linguistic varieties (e.g. dialect, codeswitching); in second language (L2) acquisition rates and correlates (proficiency in L1, access to L2 peers, extroversion, motivation, formal instruction); in proficiencies (in L1 and L2); and in degrees of loss (either of L1 when it is not supported in the instructional setting or L2 when there is migration between countries).

At a more psychological level, several theoretical formulations have been proposed to account for the range of linguistic differences and the reasons for bilingual underachievement. Among the most widely known is the following: The Threshold Hypothesis—"the degree to which proficiencies in L1 and L2 are developed is positively associated with academic achievement" (Office of Bilingual, Bicultural Education, 1982, p. 7). The worst case scenario for bilingual children is when neither their primary nor their secondary languages are developed to near native capacity. Bilingualism in this situation is "subtractive," leading to underachievement (Skutnabb-Kangas & Toukomaa, 1976) and limited access to language-mediated cognitive functions (metaphor, similarities, analogy). This is most often caused by an emphasis on the acquisition of English above everything else.

• • • • • • • • • • • •

At an atomistic level, other features of bilingualism have been mapped out with considerable specificity by research on information processing. Studies not only suggest topographical differences in the left cerebral hemisphere of bilingual individuals (Figueroa, 1991), they also indicate that bilinguals may have memory storage systems with non-overlapping and overlapping areas. In the former, the implication is that in one language, say English, a particular piece of information, such as the meaning of a vocabulary item on a test, may not be accessible even though it is known in the other, primary language. Extensive research from both Europe and the U.S. also points to the disadvantage that bilingual learners face when asked to perform encoding tasks in the weaker language. Not only is the process potentially slower, it is also more amenable to blockage due to stress, task complexity or noise. For tasks such as reading, where naming speed is critical for comprehension, the bilingual learner can be put at a considerable disadvantage when artificially induced speed or timed tasks (such as in tests) are required.

It should be pointed out that this line of research has also mapped out the strategic advantages of bilingualism. For example, using two languages to process information (with tasks as simple as taking bilingual notes) produces greater learning. There is some indication that creativity is enhanced in bilingual processing. Children who are taught in effective bilingual classrooms show greater academic gains than those taught in English-only programs. There is even the possibility of enhanced cognitive functioning in bilingual individuals.

This knowledge base exists with virtually no influence on the field of assessment. However, the imprint of bilingualism is being discovered in the key *raison d'etre* of tests: predictive validity. This is new ground in the field of psychometrics and assessment in general. From their very beginnings, formal assessments have registered large ethnic and racial differences on group averages. But the argument has always been that this is not evidence of bias. The true test of bias resides in demonstrating differential rates of predictive validities. These have seldom if ever been demonstrated. Table 4 presents some of the emerging findings on the impact of linguistic backgrounds on predictive validities. As the available studies now show, the greater the use of a non-English language in the home, the lower the predictive validity of some of the most well known and respected psychometric instruments of mental ability. Table 4 shows how this applies to children's and to **young** children's measures. Interestingly, the data also indicate that non-verbal measures may be the most hypersensitive to linguistic background and the most flawed with respect to bias in predictive validity.

What is the Alternative?

The testing technology currently in existence is very fragile and has not improved its percent reduction in total error beyond 40 per cent (predictive coefficients above .6). This has been the case for over 75 years in spite of progressively more and more sophisticated statistical tools for analyzing scores. When it comes to testing young children the tests are extremely tenuous in what they can do. Add to this the complex, multifactorial challenges posed by the variables of culture and bilingualism and the "objective," "scientific," "accurate," and "useful" attributions made to testing become more myth than fact. It should be recalled that the diverse contexts in which children develop in our country is growing geometrically as the diversity of our population grows arithmetically.

• • • • • • • • • • • •

Taking all these considerations into account: (1) psychometric, norm-based assessments of school readiness and high-stakes testing for all diverse learners in schools and outside of schools should be abandoned, and (2) the Medical Model paradigm which undergirds testing should also be abandoned. The first recommendation is not new. It has been proposed since the 1970s when the court cases involving tests received a great deal of media and public attention. Recent versions of this recommendation (Diversity and Equity in Assessment Network, 1993; Neill, 1993), however, break new ground in not just calling for the removal of "multiple-choice, norm-referenced, standardized tests in the U.S." They also call for redefining the principles that govern school-based testing: appropriateness, instructional validity, and limited role in decision-making. The most critical dimension in the new debate on the tests and testing, however, is the call for authentic, performance-based assessments. This includes the recognition, sometimes underemphasized, that authentic assessments must hold the instructional setting accountable and must also assess its impact on the learner.

• • • • • • • • • • • •

What is often missing in the new demands for a sea change in assessments is the call for a change in paradigm. The psychology of "individual differences" has been such a powerful influence that entire professions view IQs as measures of intelligence, achievement test scores as measures of what children know, personality profiles as what a person is, and vocational aptitude scores as indicators of what a person can do. Scores derived from one, two, or three hours of small responses to small stimuli (test items) do not account for much of real-life functioning, nor for the situated and unpredictable nature of human behavior. The same student with the same academic task can use many different cognitive strategies depending on the day, the teacher, or the mood. Only assessments that recognize that contexts often influence or even define outcomes actually begin to work under a different paradigm, and under a more contextualist and constructivist view of human functioning and human measurement. Such assessments are by nature longitudinal and bifocal. That is, they inherently measure the individual's work and the context in which it happened.

In education, the movement towards portfolio assessment is particularly promising. Attempts, however, at using old psychometric benchmarks in order to legitimize portfolio assessments, or at attributing portfolio work-products exclusively to individual mentation (the "individual differences" model), or at developing portfolio measurement systems that do not account or build on cultural and linguistic diversity (*e.g.*, Resnick & Resnick, 1989) are not really reform efforts. A paradigm shift begins with a refutation of the Medical Model myth that what is behaviorally measured is really what is inside the individual in actuality and inmutably (like "intelligence," or "mental retardation," or "learning disabilities"). Without such a change, dynamic assessment, criterion-referenced and "authentic" assessment models will still lead to ethnic overrepresentation in special education classes because the search will still be for the broken mental process, for the disability **inside** the individual.

Portfolio assessment is uniquely intriguing since it inherently provides a portrait of the type of educational opportunity that a pupil has been given. In classrooms that are driven by a Reductionist pedagogical model (Poplin, 1988a,b), the portfolio will include worksheets, phonics drills, and spelling lists. In classrooms that are taught without regard for the use of the primary language, the portfolios of limited English-speakers will provide a portrait of many futile struggles at making meaning. In classrooms that are optimal learning environments (where constructivism, biliteracy, literature, and authentic writing projects occur) the portfolio will track development and academic achievement in-context.

Forming Academic Identities: Accommodation without Assimilation among Involuntary Minorities

Hugh Mehan, Lea Hubbard, and Irene Villanueva
University of California, San Diego

Hugh Mehan is a professor of sociology and a coordinator of teacher education at UCSD. Lea Hubbard is a graduate student in sociology at UCSD. Irene Villanueva is a supervisor of student teaching and lecturer in teacher education at UCSD.

Institutional mechanisms influence students' ideology, which in turn has a positive influence on their academic performance. Latino and African American students who have participated in an untracking program for their high school careers develop a critical consciousness about their educational and occupational futures. The Latino and African American students in this untracking program become academically successful without losing their ethnic identity. They adopt the strategy of "accommodating without assimilating," a pattern that Gibson associates with voluntary minorities but not involuntary minorities. IDEOLOGY, ACHIEVEMENT, MINORITY STUDENTS

Students from linguistic and ethnic-minority backgrounds and low-income families do poorly in school by comparison with their majority and well-to-do contemporaries. They drop out at a higher rate. They score lower on tests. Their grades are lower. (Coleman et al. 1966; Haycock and Navarro 1988; Jencks et al. 1972). And most importantly for the topic of this paper, they do not attend college as often (Carter and Wilson 1991; Center for Education Statistics 1986).

Students from linguistic and ethnic-minority backgrounds are expected to compose an increasing percentage of the U.S. population through the early years of the 21st century (Carter and Wilson 1991; Pelavin and Kane 1990). Jobs that require higher education are expected to increase in number (CSAW 1990; NCEE 1990). The current census data, however, show that students from linguistic and ethnic-minority backgrounds are not enrolling in college in sufficient numbers to qualify for the increasing number of jobs that will require baccalaureate degrees. If the enrollment of students from underrepresented backgrounds in colleges and universities does not increase and if these same students do not obtain college degrees, then the nation will not have achieved the educational and economic and social equity that it has sought. Neither will it have the skilled workforce it needs to ensure a healthy and competitive economy. Nor will it have the well-educated and thoughtful citizenry it needs for a vibrant and energetic democracy. Indeed, if the current college enrollment trends continue, then the social and economic gaps that exist between ethnic groups in the United States will widen. We have been studying an "untracking" program in San Diego that is closing one of the educational gaps between minority and majority, low-income and upper-income students: college enrollment. The San Diego untracking experiment places students from low-income ethnic and linguistic-minority backgrounds in college prep classes along with their high-achieving peers. In addition to placing high- and previously low-achieving students in the same heterogenously grouped courses, this program provides the students with a special elective class that emphasizes collaborative instruction, writing, and problem solving.

In a previous report (Mehan et al. 1992), we described the commendable college-enrollment record of the graduates of this program, compared to San Diego and national averages. As we conducted interviews of the untracked students and observed them in their classrooms and out of school, we discovered additional social consequences of this untracking effort that extend beyond its manifest educational consequences.

The African American and Latino students in the untracking program formed academically oriented peer groups and developed strategies for managing an academic identity at school and a neighborhood identity among friends at home. From these new voluntary associations, new ideologies developed. The students' belief statements displayed a healthy disrespect for the romantic tenets of achievement ideology and an affirmation of cultural identities, and they acknowledged the necessity of academic achievement for occupational success. Gibson calls this ideology, and the course of action that flows from it "accommodation without assimilation" (1988). This is a unique ideology, not usually expressed by low-income Latino and African American youth. Gibson found it operating among *voluntary minorities* (such as Sikhs, Japanese, and Chinese) but not *involuntary minorities* (such as Latinos and African Americans).

In this article, we present the contours of the accommodationist ideology that we found among the Latino and African American youth in this untracking program. Then we describe some of the cultural processes and organizational practices that seem to have nurtured its development. Before doing so, we place this discussion in the context of the debate attempting to explain the educational inequities that break out along class, ethnic, and gender lines in the United States.

EXPLAINING EDUCATIONAL INEQUALITY

Why are students from minority and working-class backgrounds not as successful in school as their middle- and upper-income contemporaries? Why is there a strong tendency for working-class children to end up in working-class jobs? One of the most persuasive explanations of the inequality in educational outcomes is *reproduction theory,* which suggests that inequality is the consequence of capitalist structures and forces that constrain the mobility of lower-class youth.

The Reproduction of Inequality by Economic and Cultural Means

Bowles and Gintis posited a correspondence between the organization of work and the organization of schooling which trained elites to accept their place at the top of the class economy and trained workers to accept their lower places at the bottom of the class economy (1976). The sons and daughters of workers, placed into ability groups or tracks that encourage docility and conformity to extremal rules and authority, learn the skills associated with manual work. By contrast, the sons and daughters of the elite are placed into tracks that encourage them to work at their own pace without supervision, to make intelligent choices among alternatives, and to internalize rather than externally follow constraining norms.

Bourdieu and Passeron provide us with a more subtle account of inequality, by proposing cultural elements that mediate the relationship between economic structures and the lives of people (1977; cf. Bourdieu 1986). Distinctive cultural knowledge is transmitted by the families of each social class. As a consequence, children of the dominant class inherit substantially different cultural knowledge, skills, manners, norms, dress, styles of interaction, and linguistic facilities than do the sons and daughters of lower-class origin. Students from the dominant class, by virtue of a certain linguistic and cultural competence

acquired through family socialization, are provided the means of appropriating success in school. Children who read good books, visit museums, attend concerts, and go to the theatre acquire an ease, a familiarity with the dominant culture which the educational system implicitly requires of its students for academic attainment. Schools and other symbolic institutions contribute to the reproduction of inequality by devising a curriculum that rewards the *cultural capital* of the dominant classes and systematically devalues that of the lower classes.

Bourdieu and Passeron's more nuanced view (1977) overcomes some of the problems in Bowles and Gintis's economic formulation (1976), but the representation of the cause of inequality contained in cultural reproduction theory, while powerful, still suffers from an overly deterministic worldview. It emphasizes structural constraints while virtually ignoring the social organization of school practices and individuals' actions (Mehan 1992). Students are treated mainly as bearers of cultural capital—a bundle of abilities, knowledge, and attitudes furnished by parents (Apple 1983; Giroux 1983; MacLeod 1987). As a result, we second the motion made by Giroux and Simon (1989) and MacLeod (1987), who call for a reflexive relationship between social agency and social constraints.

Resistant and Oppositional Behavior: Students' Contributions to Their School Failure

A series of articulate ethnographies have begun to establish a balance between structural determinants and social agency in explaining inequality. While acknowledging that structural constraints inhibit mobility and that school practices contribute to inequality, they focus on students own contributions to their difficulties. In these ethnographies, students from lower-income, ethnic- and linguistic-minority backgrounds have been represented as having a belief system that is different than the mainstream. While mainstream students are characterized as believing in the value of hard work and individual effort (oftentimes called the *achievement ideology*) low-income and minority students either directly challenge or disengage from the prevailing ideology of American society. Either they do not buy into, or they have given up on, the belief in hard work and individual effort. If they have beliefs at all, they are said to be antiestablishment. If not anti-intellectual, they are at least antiacademic because these students see little reason for their course-work and cannot envision how schooling will help them achieve their goals (LaCompte and Dworkin 1991).

Willis's 1977 study of disaffected white working-class males in a British secondary school is the hallmark study in this so-called resistance tradition. He found the "lads," a group of high-school dropouts who rejected achievement ideology, subverted teacher and administrator authority, and disrupted classes. Willis says that the lads' rejection of the school is partly the result of their deep insights into the economic condition of their social class under capitalism. But their cultural outlook limited their options; equating manual labor with success and mental labor with failure prevented them from seeing that their actions led to dead-end, lower-paying jobs. Blind to the connection between schooling and mobility, they *choose* to join their brothers and fathers on the shop floor, a choice apparently made happily and freely from coercion. Thus, what begins as a potential insight into the social relations of production is transformed into a surprisingly uncritical affirmation of class domination. This identification of manual labor with masculinity ensures the lads' acceptance of their subordinate economic fate and the successful reproduction of the class structure.

Following in Willis's path, MacLeod (1987) and Foley (1991) invited us to listen to the antiestablishment ideology of the working class. Like the lads in England, the sons of the working class in the United States have developed a critique of the capitalist system which rationalizes their lack of academic and economic success. The "Hallway Hangers" in Boston and the "vatos" in South Texas realize that, no matter how hard they work, they will still be relegated to low-paying jobs or, worse, no jobs at all. These words are translated into deeds; they withdraw from academic pursuits, act up in class, ignore assignments and homework, and cut classes. Their critique, like that of the "lads," is somewhat shortsighted, however, because their ideology leads to actions that contribute to their stagnant position in the status hierarchy.

Ogbu's research into the folk models of schooling associated with voluntary minorities and involuntary minorities sharpens the oppositional and resistant representation of minority and working-class youth (1978, 1987). Voluntary minorities (such as Japanese, Koreans, and Chinese) accept school norms, work hard, and alternate their academic identity at school with a nonacademic identity with friends, Ogbu says. African Americans and Latinos have a different folk model of schooling that encourages different patterns of behavior. These involuntary minorities tend to equate schooling with assimilation into the dominant group, a course of action that they actively resist. As a result, they do not try to achieve academically; instead, they engage in collective actions of resistance against school and societal norms.

Ogbu implies that the ideology that African Americans, Latinos, and other encapsulated minority groups have developed contributes to their relatively poor academic and economic success. Because it is collectivist and oppositional, the ideology of involuntary or encapsulated minorities has led them to adopt strategies that scorn the idea of individual achievement that is so important in American society, in favor of collective strategies that blame failure on racial discrimination and other structural forces.

Labov reported that low-income black students formed group identity based on in-group linguistic codes, Black English Vernacular (BEV), for example (1982). While these communication patterns help maintain group cohesion, they also have alienating effects. BEV use—like rap and raggae—distinctive dress, and demeanor are a source of distinction and pride (from the low-income black student's point of view) but are signs of opposition and irritation (from the white teacher's point of view). In Labov's study, the folk model within the low-income black peer culture required speech that was markedly different from the "good English" expected in school. Students who spoke "school English" and did well in school marked themselves as different and risked rejection by their peers. Because

they valued peer praise, these students opted out of academic pursuits and into oppositional pursuits, which meant they spent more time resisting authority and being confrontational and much less time and effort in their schoolwork (1982).

Fordham and Ogbu (1987) expanded Labov's argument. Because involuntary immigrant groups still experience prejudice, they have come to believe that social and economic success is only possible by adopting the cultural and linguistic patterns of the majority culture. This puts high-achieving blacks in a bind, because they must choose between maintaining their ethnic identity or striving for high achievement, which their ethnic peers regard as acting superior, or "acting white." To resolve this dilemma, many blacks reject academic life in favor of an oppositional lifestyle.

Apple and Weis contribute to this tradition by saying that U.S. working-class students see schooling as tacitly teaching middle-class norms, values, and dispositions through institutional expectations and the routines of day-to-day school life (1983). Working-class subcultures oppose the rigid rules, the respect for external rewards, the orderly work habits, and the demand for subordination.

Solomon reports a similar pattern among West Indian children in a major Canadian city (1992). These newly arrived immigrants come to school with beliefs and actions that work against their academic success. These attitudes lead them to respond to their treatment by the school in a manner that compounds their problem: they form separatist groups, they do not follow school rules, and they play sports rather than do schoolwork. Solomon, like Foley, MacLeod, Ogbu and Weis, and Willis before him, gives student subcultures some political savvy: they oppose school culture because they see limited economic opportunities ahead of them. The net result is that these newly arrived immigrant students fail, in spite of their expressed desire to succeed in school.

Weis places the history of school antagonisms between blacks and whites in the history of relationships between blacks and whites in the wider society:

> The fact that blacks constitute a castelike group in American society means that student culture will automatically take a somewhat different shape and form from that of the white working class. Student cultural forms is [sic] also affected by the nature of the historic struggle for particular groups. [1985:132]

In short, poor black and Latino students are said to have an ideology and a course of action that directly challenges conventional American wisdom about the relationship between academic performance and occupational success. When black high school students rebuke their black peers for "acting white," they are actively resisting white structure and domination (Fordham and Ogbu 1987). Likewise, when black college students go through the routine of schooling but exert little effort in their study, they are resisting an education that they see as "only second best" to that available to whites (Weis 1985). So too, when West Indians in Toronto form separatist groups, refuse to follow school rules, and play sports to the exclusion of their schoolwork, they are creating a "lived culture" that contributes to their own school difficulties (Solomon 1992). The ideology and practice of resistance contribute to the lowly position of blacks and Latinos in the occupational structure, according to "resistance" theorists, because working-class students refuse to develop the skills, the attitudes, the manners, and the speech that are necessary for the achievement of success in capitalist societies.

The agency attributed to students, then, distinguishes these ethnographic accounts from the theorizing of either Bowles and Gintis or Bourdieu and Passeron. Unlike the students in Bowles and Gintis's rendition who passively internalize mainstream values of individual achievement or the students in Bourdieu and Passeron's theory who simply carry cultural capital on their backs or in their heads, these working-class, linguistic- and ethnic-minority students make real choices in their everyday lives. While at first glance, the working-class students' rebellious behavior, their low academic achievement, and their high dropout rate seem to stem from dullness, laziness, inability to project themselves into the future, and lack of self-discipline, their actual causes are quite different. Their unwillingness to participate comes from their assessment of the costs and benefits of playing the game. It is not that schooling will not propel them up the ladder of success; it is that chances are too slim to warrant the attempt. Given this logic, the oppositional behavior of MacLeod's Hallway Hangers, Foley's vatos, Willis's lads, and the others is a form of resistance to an institution that cannot deliver on its promise of upward mobility for all students.

Adding the notion of *resistance* to the lexicon employed to understand inequality in schools, then, reveals the contributions that social actors make to their own plight. As Ogbu phrases it, this line of research shows how victims contribute to their own victimization (1991).

INSTITUTIONAL ARRANGEMENTS MEDIATING THE RELATIONS BETWEEN SOCIAL CONSTRAINTS AND EDUCATIONAL OUTCOMES

We encountered a set of institutional arrangements in which the sons and daughters of the working poor develop a much different ideology and adopt a much different course of action than has been previously described. Poor African American, Latino and European American high school students who have participated in an untracking program express a belief in their own efficacy and a belief in the power of schooling to improve their lives and the lives of others. They translate belief into action by participating actively in school. Yet they do not adopt a romantic or naive commitment to achievement ideology. They are all too aware of the barriers erected in front of them by the history of racism and discrimination. To handle the complexities of the world that they confront, they adopt strategies that many researchers have attributed to recent immigrants to the United States (Cummins 1986; Gibson 1988; Gibson and Ogbu 1991: Ogbu 1978, 1987; Suárez-Orozco 1989), but not to encapsulated minorities: they maintain their ethnic identity while actively engaging schooling.

The AVID Untracking Program

These students who accommodate to the norms of school and society without assimilating or compromising their ethnic iden-

tity participate in an "untracking" program in San Diego high schools, called AVID, an acronym that stands for Advancement Via Individual Determination. The idea of untracking low-achieving students was introduced to San Diego in 1980 at Claremont High School, a predominantly white school, by Mary Catherine Swanson, then a member of the English department, as a way to educate minority students bused to that school from predominantly ethnic-minority schools in Southeast San Diego under a court's desegregation order. Unwilling to segregate African American and Latino students into a separate, compensatory curriculum, Swanson and the Claremont faculty placed the bused students in regular "college-prep" classes.

The expressed goals of the AVID untracking program are to motivate and prepare underachieving students from underrepresented linguistic-and ethnic-minority groups to perform well in high school and to seek a college education. Since 1991, 14 other "city schools," 50 high schools in San Diego County, and 84 high schools outside the county have introduced AVID programs.

AVID coordinators select students for the untracking program. Low-income, ethnic- and linguistic-minority students in the eighth or ninth grade who have average-to-high achievement test scores but low junior high school grades are eligible for AVID. Once teachers identify these high-potential/low-performance students, their parents are advised. Those parents who agree to support their children's participation in the academic program sign contracts to have their children participate in AVID as soon as they enroll in high school.

Once selected, students take a special elective class as part of their course load. This class emphasizes writing, inquiry, and collaboration (Swanson n.d.). Writing is seen as a tool of learning. Students are taught a special form of note taking, the Cornell system, in which they are to jot detailed notes from their academic classes in a wide right-hand margin and, as homework, develop questions based on the notes, in a narrow left-hand column. The questions students develop as homework are supposed to be used the following day in the AVID class. In addition to note taking, the students are supposed to keep learning logs and practice "quick writes" to facilitate their learning (Swanson n.d.).

Inquiry refers to the instructional strategy that teachers and tutors are to employ with the students in the elective AVID class. The program provides tutors (usually students recruited from local colleges, some of whom participated in AVID while they were in high school) to assist AVID students. Tutors are trained to lead study groups in specific subjects, such as math or English, based on the students' notes and questions. Tutors are not to give answers: they are to help the AVID students clarify their thoughts based on their questions. AVID encourages the use of the inquiry method so that the AVID class does not become a glorified study hall or homework session (Swanson n.d.).

Collaboration is the instructional strategy that organizes students to work together to achieve instructional goals. Collaborative groups or study teams enable students to serve as sources of information for each other. Collaboration, AVID asserts, shifts the responsibility for learning from the teacher who directs lessons, to the students who participate in them (Swanson n.d.).

The AVID central office suggests a basic plan for the weekly instructional activities within AVID classrooms. Two school days are designated tutorial days. On these days students are to work in small groups with the assistance of a tutor. On the other two days, writing as a tool for learning is emphasized. On these days, students engage in a variety of writing activities, including essays for their English classes and essays for college applications. One day a week, usually Fridays, is a "motivational day." Guest speakers are invited to address the class, and field trips to colleges are scheduled on these days.

The Academic Consequences of Untracking

This untracking program has been successful in preparing its students for college. In 1990 and 1991, 253 students who had participated in the AVID untracking experiment for 3 years graduated from 14 high schools in the San Diego City Schools (SDCS) system. In those years an additional 288 students started the program but left after completing one year or less. We interviewed 144 of the "graduates" and 72 of the students who left the program within one year (Mehan et al. 1992).

Of the 144 students who graduated from AVID, 72 (50 percent) reported attending four-year colleges, 60 (42 percent) reported attending two-year or junior colleges, and the remaining 12 students (8 percent) said they are working or doing other things. The 50 percent four-year college enrollment rate for students who were "untracked" compares favorably with the SDCS's average of 37 percent and the national average of 39 percent. It also compares favorably with the college enrollment rate of students who started but did not complete the untracking program; 31 percent of them enrolled in four-year colleges within a year of graduating from high school.

Furthermore, the untracking experiment assists students from low-income families and the two major ethnic groups that are underrepresented in college. African Americans and Latinos from AVID enroll in college in numbers that exceed local and national averages. Of the Latino students who participated in AVID for three years, 44 percent enrolled in four-year colleges. This figure compares favorably to the SDCS's average of 25 percent and the national average of 29 percent. African American students who participated in AVID for three years also enrolled in college at rates higher than the local and national averages: 54 percent of black students in AVID enrolled in four-year colleges, compared to 35 percent from the SOS and the national average of 33 percent.

AVID students from the lowest income strata (parents' median income below $19,999) enrolled in four-year colleges in equal or higher proportion to students from higher income strata (parents' median income between $20,000 and $65,000). Furthermore, AVID students from families in which their parents do not have a college education enrolled in four-year colleges more often than students from families with parents who have a college education.

Students who completed three years of AVID enrolled in college in greater proportion than students who completed one

year or less of AVID, regardless of the family's income level: 60 percent of three-year AVID students from families who earned less than $20,000 enrolled in college, compared to 29 percent of one-year AVID students whose families were in this income bracket; 44 percent of three-year AVID students from families in the $20 to 39 thousand income range enrolled in college versus 30 percent of one-year AVID students whose families were in this range; 59 percent of three-year AVID students whose families were in the $40 to 59 thousand range and 43 percent of the one-year AVID students whose families were in this income range enrolled in college.

The Social Consequences of Untracking

Improving the college enrollment of students from underrepresented linguistic- and ethnic-minority backgrounds is the expressed purpose of the AVID untracking program. And our research shows that the program is successful in this regard.

As we conducted interviews of the AVID students and observed them in their classrooms and out of school, we discovered additional social consequences of this untracking effort that extend beyond its manifest educational consequences. The African American and Latino students in AVID developed a reflective system of beliefs, a critical consciousness if you will, about the limits and possibilities of the actions they take and the limitations and constraints they face in life.

After we describe our research methods, we present the contours of the accommodationist ideology that we found among the Latino and African American youth in this untracking program. Then we describe some of the cultural processes and organizational practices that seem to have nurtured its development.

Data and Methods

We used materials from many sources in this study: official school records, interviews of students, teachers, parents, and school officials, as well as observations in classrooms. The San Diego City Schools (SDCS) kindly supplied us with the Cumulative School Records (CSRs) of AVID students in the classes of 1990 and 1991. We used information from the CSRs to determine students' ethnicity and to calculate their academic record in high school (AVID classes taken, CTBS scores, college-prep courses taken and completed, etc.).

Of the 1,053 students enrolled in AVID in 1990 and 1991, we found 253 students in 14 high schools who had completed three years of AVID during their high school careers when they graduated. We also identified 188 students who had entered AVID in the same academic year as the "untracked" group but did not complete three years of the program. Instead, they left after one semester or one year.

In order to determine students' activities since they graduated from high school, we attempted to interview the 253 graduates of the classes of 1990 and 1991 and the 188 students who started but did not complete AVID. We were able to interview 144 of the program grads and 72 of the AVID comparison group. We asked both groups of students about their activities since they graduated from high school, that is, whether they had enrolled in four- or two-year colleges, were working, or were doing other things. In order to place students' college enrollment and work information in context, we asked students about their family background (e.g., parents' education, languages spoken in the home). We also discussed their high school and AVID experiences with them. This information helped us answer the question: *does* untracking work?

We recognized that, in order to answer the question of *how* untracking works, we needed to go beyond correlational data and examine school practices and cultural processes. To do so, we conducted case studies of four of the San Diego high schools that are participating in this untracking experiment. We chose the four schools—Churchill, Monrovia, Pimlico, and Saratoga (all pseudonyms)—based on their ethnic enrollments, their college enrollment rate, and of course, their willingness to participate in the study. From October 1991 to August 1992, we observed in AVID classrooms, and Hubbard and Villanueva interviewed AVID teachers, students, and their parents from these four schools. In some cases we also observed in the academic classes that AVID students take and interviewed the parents of AVID students.

THE DEVELOPMENT OF A REFLECTIVE ACHIEVEMENT IDEOLOGY

The involuntary-minority students in AVID have developed an interesting set of beliefs about the relationship between school and success. They do not have a naive belief in the connection between academic performance and occupational success. While they voice enthusiastic support for the power of their own agency, their statements also display a critical awareness of structures of inequality and strategies for overcoming discrimination in society.

Belief in Individual Effort, Motivation, and Opportunity

AVID teaches a version of achievement ideology, telling students they can be successful (which AVID defines as going to college) if they are motivated and study hard. The AVID coordinator at Saratoga High School stated this philosophy succinctly when greeting her incoming freshman class:

The responsibility for your success is with you. AVID is here to help. Your goal should be to go to a four-year college. There is lots of work to be done, but you will have more help, support, and love than you will ever need.

Interviews with AVID students suggest that they internalize this ideology, articulating success in a way that reflects the message that AVID teaches. The following students highlight the value of motivation in providing equal opportunity:

Before AVID I was unsure about college. I was always changing my mind. AVID teaches you that you have the same opportunity to get to college as anybody if you just stay motivated.
I am more motivated to go to college because AVID made me want to go. Before I got into AVID, I didn't think I had many opportunities. I thought I couldn't afford it and that I couldn't get good-enough grades. Mrs. Lincoln says we can get financial aid. And well, now my grades are really good.

These students assert that their opportunity to achieve success is the result of their individual effort:

I have a better opportunity than others because I am really striving for it. AVID helps me know what to do. I try hard; so I have to say I have the opportunity because of who I am. I have my own individual identity and not the identity of a group of people.

Students also echo the sentiments of the AVID program when they claim that they have the same opportunity to achieve as anyone else, regardless of their racial or ethnic background. An African American male at Saratoga maintains that he has an opportunity to succeed because "the key to success is your own body, your own self."

Experience with Prejudice and Discrimination

AVID students' believe in individual effort, motivation, and opportunity. But these students also recognize that the world out there is full of discrimination, prejudice, and racism.

Many AVID students have personally experienced prejudice. In a group discussion Lea Hubbard had with African American AVID students at Saratoga, David and Rocky, two Saratoga seniors, said that they had stopped at a traffic light and that a white man in the car next to them got out of his car and pulled a gun on them for no reason. They took off "like fast." AVID students have experienced scrutiny and harassment from the police in ways that resonate with the tales told by Anderson (1991:190–206). Here are some incidents that these students rattled off to Hubbard during that discussion which suggest that the police define their social-control work as keeping middle-income white neighborhoods "safe" from low-income blacks:

Rocky and two other friends were walking home from a school dance behind some white guys. A police patrol stopped and harassed them, but never stopped the white guys.
Kam was at home one night when cops just burst into his home without reason and left without explanation.

When Lea Hubbard said to them, "It sounds like you are getting a bum deal," the boys agreed. But they were not resigned to these conditions; they believed they could overcome them: "If you work hard, you will succeed."

Dora, a black female student at Saratoga, relayed similar experiences to Lea Hubbard in an interview:

I'm gonna tell you something—I don't care if I should—but there's a whole lot of racism. My friend and I were alternates on the flag team . . . and when they needed to replace some permanent members, they got two new white girls and not my friend and I.

Khalada, another African American female student at Saratoga, also expressed an awareness of discrimination. She said her mother told her that she had to watch out. She might be friends with whites now, but when it came to the business world later, they would let you down.

Experience with prejudice and discrimination is not confined to black and Latino students. John Sing, a junior in AVID at Saratoga, is an ethnic Chinese born in Vietnam. Although he is doing well academically (carrying a 3.3 GPA), he confided to Lea Hubbard that he is afraid of the verbal portion of the SAT because he considers it a racist test. He is also afraid that his chances of going to college will be hampered by a quota system, which limits the number of Asian students, and that "there are lots of Asians smarter than me."

Strategies for Dealing with Discrimination

AVID students are not only aware of these structures of discrimination, but they have developed strategies for dealing with them. When Hubbard asked Dora about what happened after the flag-team incident (reported above), she said:

> My mom raised heck. [But] teacher don't care. They just think they are here to teach: "You've got to get yourself through." Except for three teachers. Mrs. Lincoln is one of them. Teachers don't say you are capable. No one really cares.

Later in this interview, she reinforced her earlier statement that individual motivation overcomes racism:

> Most blacks in the community are faced with prejudice and will be held back, not me.

Tipoli, a Saratoga junior, recognized there are barriers erected in her path and in the path of African American students generally:

> I think teachers expect more out of us [blacks]. Colleges recruit blacks because of sports, but they don't get an education. That's dumb. There's lots of hurt and prejudice. People need to learn about different cultures and read about black people. They always look at us when we study about slaves as if we were slaves.

In addition to her general appeal for more culturally sensitive curricula, her more personal strategy for dealing with prejudice is to "go to college. I want to be there. It's the only way to get a job."

This opinion was reinforced by David, an African American student, who says he does not have an equal opportunity to succeed because of his race:

> There is more pressure because we are black and we are athletes. They are always looking to us to do the right thing, and if we do anything wrong, we're nobody.

Before he became involved with AVID, David said that his athletic prowess would lead him to success. Since he has been in AVID, his strategy for dealing with the prejudice he has experienced has changed; now he plans to get good grades and not rely on athletics as his ticket to success.

Several African American males reported tales of systematic discrimination at the hands of a particular counselor at Saratoga. In a group interview with Lea Hubbard, they reported that this counselor repeatedly tells African American males that they "won't make it to a big time college." One student reported asking for information about a four-year college and being told, "What for? It's just a waste of your time and mine. You won't make it anyway." The counselor then gave him only information about two-year colleges and vocational schools. Even though the students say they have protested the counselor's ill treatment of them, he is unwilling to help them. When one male student tried to add a chemistry course to his schedule, this same counselor said no and that "he didn't need that for

what he was going to do after graduation. Only college-bound kids need academics." To deal with this prejudicial situation, the AVID students have devised ways to avoid this counselor. Instead of going to him for advice, they rely on the AVID teacher to counsel them about college. They also advise each other and make it clear to new AVID students that they should avoid this counselor.

Students report incidents at Monrovia that suggest they are victims of backlash from their academic teachers. It appears as though some teachers think that AVID students are only in advanced classes because they are AVID students. This "sorting privilege" can operate against AVID students. One Monrovia student commented that her advanced-English teacher told her on her first day that "she wouldn't make it in her class." Her AVID teacher intervened on her behalf the next day, telling the English teacher that "the student would make it because she was getting extra help from AVID." The student finished the semester with a grade of B. Hubbard asked the student why she felt she was able to succeed. She said:

> I knew if I tried, I could, and I really wanted to show her I could do it. [The AVID coordinator] told me to work with the tutor. But boy was I hurt that [the advanced-English teacher] thought I couldn't do it. I know it was because I was a minority student. She didn't even know my ability.

Some African American males [among] AVID students talk about their race strategically. In doing so, they sound like the "Brothers" in MacLeod's 1987 ethnography of urban youth. The Brothers said they thought they had more opportunity to succeed than their parents because of the influence of governmental civil rights laws. Darius, a black male from Saratoga High School, is typical of many African American males in AVID in this respect. He feels he has a better opportunity because of his race. Colleges, especially those in California, are trying to meet affirmative-action goals, he says. Therefore, they recruit African American males such as himself to meet quotas. That is, in a civil rights climate, his race gives him an advantage, a fact that he can use strategically.

Discrimination can cut two ways. Darcey, one of a minority of white students in AVID, indexed what would be called reverse discrimination. He says that he does not have an equal opportunity because of his race: colleges are accepting Asians over white kids.

Accommodation without Assimilation

AVID students recognize that academic performance is necessary for occupational success, but they have not bought the naive proposition that their individual effort will automatically breed their success. The Latino and African American students in AVID (which Ogbu would call "involuntary minorities") have also developed provocative beliefs and practices about culture contact. They affirm their cultural identities while at the same time recognize the need to develop certain cultural practices, notably achieving academically, that are acceptable to the mainstream. Following Gibson (1988) we talk about this aspect of their ideology as "accommodation without assimilation."

Marta Garcia represents many Latino students in AVID who affirm their cultural identity while achieving academically.

Marta confided to Lea Hubbard that her Latino cultural background is very important to her. In fact, when she was in third grade, she pledged to become perfectly bilingual, maintaining her native Spanish while developing acceptable English and academic skills. She has fulfilled this promise to herself and entered the University of Ihao Americana, Tijuana, Mexico, in the fall of 1992.

When Lea Hubbard and Irene Villanueva interviewed Marta's Spanish-speaking parents, it was clear that Marta's identification with her Mexican heritage has been kept actively alive by her intense involvement with her parents. Spanish is the predominant language in the home; the family takes frequent trips to Mexico; religious and cultural symbols are prevalent in the home. Marta's parents respect her bicultural moves. On the one hand, they are pleased that Marta and her friends are respectful of their background. On the other hand, they encourage the academic path their children are taking. It is perhaps symbolic of the way the parents are juggling these two worlds that Marta's older brother, also an excellent student, will be attending college with Marta.

Marta has two close friends, Serena and Maria, both of whom are in AVID. These girls reinforce each other's love of their cultural heritage and desire to succeed. They often discuss college plans and share their concerns and excitement in Spanish, a sure sign of their cultural accommodation.

Another sign of Serena's accommodation is found in her interactions with her mother about college. Serena's mother is a widow who speaks very little English and works as a domestic and food-services worker at the University of San Diego. Serena interacts with her mother in Spanish at home but seldom about academic matters, apparently. Mrs. Castro told Irene Villanueva that she provided Serena with general moral support (*apoyo morao*) but felt ill-quipped to provide the detailed technical skills Serena needed in school. Mrs. Castro always supported Serena's plans to go to college, although she did not want her to leave the San Diego area in order to pursue this goal. She is pleased, therefore, that Serena will attend the University of California at San Diego. When Irene asked Mrs. Castro about Serena's financial aid, Mrs. Castro laughed in an embarrassed way because she was completely unaware of what Serena will be receiving, what her fees are, or how they will be paid. Serena has assumed all the responsibilities associated with college matriculation and, in the process, simultaneously maintained her family life with her mother and her school life with her friends.

Managing Dual Identities

The space AVID has created is productive, because it helps AVID students foster academic identities. But this same space also creates problems for AVID students, because they must deal with their friends who are academically oriented and their friends who are not academically oriented. AVID students develop a variety of strategies for balancing or managing this dilemma.

Gándara found that college-bound Latino students used "denial" as a strategy to keep up their grades while still keeping up their friendships (in press). One Latino student told her, "I didn't let on that I was studying or working hard. I mean you were cool if you didn't study."

While some AVID students submerged their academic identity entirely, most students maintained dual identities, one at school and one in the neighborhood. Because they were segregated by classes at school, it was not difficult to keep the two peer groups separate. At school, they were free to compete academically; at home in the afternoon, they would assume a different posture.

Laura is a Latina who lives in what she described as "the ghetto":

> You don't know how awful it is there. They don't give a damn about themselves. My mom doesn't have any education. My friends in the neighborhood think I am really stupid for staying in school. They tell me that, since I have enough credits to graduate, I ought to quit school and get a job. They think the most important thing is to get married and have babies.

Laura wants to be a lawyer, and she knows the only way to achieve that goal is to "put forth the effort and go to college." But she also wants to keep her friends. So she is active in AVID during school hours and continues to date boys from her neighborhood and go to the movies with her girlfriends who live on her street.

An African American male from Monrovia said in so many words that he lives two lives. Chris said he really wants to go to college and that AVID provides him a place where his academic pursuits are encouraged and where he has academically oriented peers. But he has street friends, too. While he feels they are "wasting their lives" because "they are into being bad," he still hangs out with them. Chris also spends some of his free time as a peer counselor for Saratoga's African American students. His counseling activities bridge the two different worlds that he occupies.

The story of Hazzard, an African American male who attended Pimlico High School, exemplifies a third strategy for managing dual identities. He brought his nonacademic friends with him into academic settings. Hazzard was a member of a gang when he was selected into AVID. He retained his gang friends, while simultaneously developing new acquaintances in AVID. Like other AVID students, he wanted to go to college. He was, in fact, accepted at the University of California at Berkeley, San Diego State University, and a local junior college. Instead of enrolling at the Berkeley campus, he said he chose to attend the college closer to his home so that he could stay with his friends. Indeed, he brought them to classes with him. Hazzard was doing what he needed to do to pass academically, while retaining his membership in his peer group.

These "border crossing" strategies (Delgado-Gaitan and Trueba 1991; Giroux 1992; Rose 1989) have special utility for minority students because, by the time they graduate, they will have had experience in moving between two cultures. They will have interacted with high-achieving Anglos and still be comfortable in the company of friends who would never leave the fields or the barrios or go to college (cf. Gándara, in press).

GROUP FORMATION AND THE CONSTRUCTION OF ACADEMIC IDENTITIES

The African American and Latino students who participated in the AVID untracking program for three years developed strategies for managing dual identities and developed new ideologies. Importantly, these ideologies were neither conformist nor assimilationist. Instead, their belief statements displayed a healthy disrespect for the romantic tenets of achievement ideology and affirmed their cultural identities, while acknowledging the necessity of academic achievement for occupational success.

In the next few pages, we describe the institutional arrangements and cultural processes that contributed to the formation of academic identities and the development of a reflective achievement ideology.

Isolation of Group Members

In order to transform raw recruits into fighting men, the military isolates them from other, potentially conflicting social forces. Religious orders and gangs operate in a similar manner, shielding their recruits from competing interests and groups (Goffman 1964; Jankowski 1991).

Whether intentionally or not, AVID has adopted this principle. AVID selects promising students and isolates them in special classes that meet once a day, every day of the school year. Once students are in these classes, AVID provides them social supports that assist them through the transition from low-track to academic-track status. These scaffolds include explicit instruction in a special method of note taking, test-taking strategies, and general study tips. The note-taking technique stresses compiling and abstracting main ideas and generating questions to guide students' reading. Students are expected to apply these techniques in notebooks that they keep for their academic courses.

Test-taking skills were taught in all AVID classrooms, albeit differentially emphasized. At a minimum, students were given drill and practice on vocabulary items likely to appear on the Scholastic Aptitude Test (SAT). When a more extensive approach to test preparation was taken, students were provided explicit instruction in ways to eliminate distracting answers on multiple choice questions, strategies for approximating answers, and probabilities about the success of guessing. One AVID teacher devoted two successive weeks to SAT preparation, including practice with vocabulary items, administering practice tests, reviewing wrong answers, and teaching strategies for taking tests. This teacher reviewed the kinds of analogies typically found on the SAT with her students so that they could practice the kinds of problems they would encounter on their tests. This teacher also sent her students to an expert math teacher for assistance on math test items. She reinforced this teaching by explaining that she was teaching them the same academic tricks found in the expensive Princeton Review SAT preparation class. While note-taking skills, test-taking strategies, and study tips were taught routinely, by far the most prevalent activity in the four AVID programs we studied during [the] 1991–92 school year revolved around the college-applica-

tion process. Procedures for filing applications, meeting deadlines for SAT tests, and requesting financial aid and scholarships dominated discussion. At Pimlico High, for instance, students must complete a weekly AVID assignment in which students do writing and/or reading tasks directly related to college. The junior class at Saratoga received a handout, Choosing Your College, containing a checklist of information typically found in college catalogs. Students were instructed to fill in the information for that college according to the assigned checklist. This task presumably made them more familiar with college catalogs and would help them choose a college to fit their personal needs.

By dispensing these academic tricks, AVID is giving students explicit instruction in the hidden curriculum of the school. That is, AVID teaches explicitly in school what middle-income students learn implicitly at home. In Bourdieu's terms (1986), AVID gives low-income students some of the cultural capital at school that is similar to the cultural capital that more economically advantaged parents give to their children at home.

Public Markers of Group Identity

In addition to isolating students and providing them with social supports, AVID marks their group identity in a public manner. The special class set aside for their exclusive use is one such marker. Instead of going to shop or driver's education for their elective class period, they go to the AVID room, a classroom identified by signs and banners. Students often return to the AVID room at lunchtime or after school to do homework or socialize, actions that further mark their distinctive group membership.

AVID students are given special notebooks, emblazoned with the AVID logo, to take AVID-style class notes. These notebooks signal their membership in this special group. Some schools have designed distinctive ribbons and badges that AVID students wear on their clothes. Others have adorned their graduation gowns or mortarboards with AVID ribbons. Still other AVID classes publish a newspaper that reports the accomplishments of AVID students. All of these actions further distinguish AVID students as members of a special, academically oriented group.

These markers influence teachers as well as students. Teachers report that, when they saw AVID students with notebooks, taking notes in class and turning in neat assignments on time, it indicated to them that AVID students were serious.

Formation of Voluntary Associations

Special classrooms, badges of distinction—these are physical, material markers that define the space for AVID students to develop an academically oriented identity. Within this space, AVID students develop new academically oriented friends or join academic friends who were already in AVID.

Several Saratoga students told us that they really did not know anyone in AVID when they joined, but after a few years almost all their friends were from AVID. These friendships developed because they were together in classes throughout the day and worked together in study groups. Coordinators encouraged these friendships by minimizing competition. The AVID coordinator at Monrovia High School, for example, told her students that they should think of themselves on "parallel ladders with each other. There should be no competition between students, but rather an opportunity to share notes and to help one another."

Some AVID students did join AVID to be with their friends. Cynthia, a Latina from Monrovia High School, said her friends were already in AVID, and because they were doing well, she wanted to be with them. Now all her friends are in AVID. Thomas, an African American male at Saratoga, said that he told his two good friends from elementary school that "they had to get into AVID because it would really help with their grades." He even called one of his friend's mother to convince her that AVID was good for her son. These three boys have remained good friends for their four AVID years and always study together.

AVID encourages the development of academically oriented associations among students through formally organized activities such as college visits. AVID coordinators take their students to such colleges as San Diego State University (SDSU), the University of California at San Diego (UCSD), the University of California at Los Angeles (UCLA), and the University of Southern California (USC). Of particular note, the AVID coordinator at Pimlico High takes her AVID students on a two-week trip to traditionally black colleges and universities in Washington, D.C., and Atlanta, every other year. In addition to the usual college tours and dorm sleepovers, the current generation of AVID high school students meet AVID students who enrolled in these schools in previous years.

Less formal activities also do this work of developing academically oriented associations. Students in AVID classrooms often talk among themselves and discuss matters relevant to their adolescence. Students use this period of time to bounce their values and troubles off one another, to test their principles and ideas, and to react to others. In those schools where African American and Latino students are bused in, the AVID classroom may be the only time minority students see each other during school hours. In those classes in which older and younger AVID students mix, the younger students observe older students' behavior and how teachers interact with them.

The longer students are in the program, the more ties seem to intensify. A Latina who attends Monrovia articulated these sentiments. AVID provides a different environment for her. "At home they expect me to get married. Here they expect me to go to college." Because of the pressures she receives from home, Maria attributes much of her academic success to the girlfriends she has cultivated in AVID. She studies together with her two friends and:

[we] chat a lot about college and what we want out of life. Our study group really opens up a lot of issues. Everyone is really motivated to go to college. It really helps to be around others that want to go. It makes you want it more.

We thought the highly visible markers of AVID (the notebooks required to be carried to classes, the special class periods established for them, the college visits arranged for them, the newspapers they publish) would stigmatize AVID students in the eyes of their peers. But this marking process has had the opposite effect. AVID students reported that their friends who were not in AVID were jealous. They wanted to be in AVID for the comradarie to be sure, but also because they wanted to take advantage of the resources that AVID made available to its students, such as information about scholarships, college-entrance exams, and visits to colleges.

Many Monrovia AVID students told us in interviews that their non-AVID friends were jealous and "wanted into" the program. One Latina student stated that her friends, who were mostly white, felt racially threatened by the advantages given to AVID students: "They don't like AVID because they feel racially threatened. They don't really know what it is. They are jealous and think AVID is unfair." Another Latina student, Maria, expressed a similar view:

Many are really jealous of the help that AVID gives me. One friend told me that it wasn't fair that [the AVID coordinator] helped me with my composition. [But] they forget that I don't have a mother to proofread my papers like they do. I can't get any help from my parents."

Ngoc, a Vietnamese student who attended Monrovia High School, suggested that this jealousy can take on overtones of reverse discrimination; his friends think that the only reason he got into USCD was because he was in AVID: "They think that AVID can get you in," he said. While these peer attitudes lead Maria and Ngoc to feel defensive about their participation in this untracking program, such attitudes also seem to fuel an increased commitment and loyalty. Pressure from outside the group creates a bond inside the group. Many students felt they were lucky to be "chosen" for the program and know that they were chosen because they need help academically.

CONCLUSIONS

The actions that working-class African American and Latino youths take against limitations in the capitalist system have been blamed for their poor academic performance. The sons and daughters of the poor withdraw from academic pursuits because they realize that their access to high-paying jobs is limited. Their critique is limited and ironic, however, because their unwillingness to play the academic game ensures that they will stay in lowly economic positions.

Ogbu maintains that the status that African Americans, Latinos, and other involuntary immigrant groups have in the power structure contributes to this condition. While voluntary minorities accept achievement ideology, involuntary minorities tend to equate schooling with assimilation into the dominant group, an equation they detest. As a result, they do not try to achieve academically: instead, they engage in collective actions of resistance against school and societal norms. Ogbu implies that the collectivist and oppositional ideology that blacks, Latinos, and other involuntary minority groups have developed contributes to their relatively poor academic and economic success. They fail in school because they blame failure on racial discrimination and other structural forces and do not take personal responsibility for their own actions and individual initiative, a course of action that Ogbu feels is fundamental for success in American society.

We did not find an oppositional ideology or pattern of resistance among the black and Latino students who participated in the AVID untracking program. Instead, we found that AVID kids formed an academic identity and developed a reflective and critical ideology. Strictly speaking, their ideology was neither conformist nor assimilationist. Instead, it included a critique of many tenets of achievement ideology, an affirmation of cultural identity, while acknowledging the necessity of academic achievement for occupational success.

By isolating students for significant portions of the school day, marking them as members of a special group, and providing them social supports, AVID fostered the academic identity of its students. This newly acquired academic identity posed problems for AVID students who had many nonacademic friends, however. AVID students resolved this dilemma by managing dual identities, an academic identity with academic friends at school, and a nonacademic identity with friends after school. This border-crossing strategy is useful for minority students, because it provides them experience in moving between two cultures, a high-achieving academic culture and a supportive community culture.

AVID students face discrimination and racism to be sure. But these antagonisms do not result in the acts of cultural inversion suggested by Winis, MacLeod, Foley, and Ogbu. In fact, AVID students invite us to reexamine the typology Ogbu constructs that designates separate and distinct ideologies for voluntary and involuntary immigrant groups. The blacks and Latinos who participate in AVID do not fit the typology proposed by Ogbu. While many African American students in AVID describe a system that is not sympathetic to students in general and discriminatory to blacks in particular, they speak of their own opportunity in terms of their own individual hard work. One black male from Saratoga summarizes this argument for us:

> We know that the teacher is not doing what's right. He is a real racist jerk, but if you work hard, you will succeed. If you get good grades, he can't hurt you.

The ethnic and linguistic minority students in this untracking project seem to have developed an ideology, a consciousness if you will, that is neither oppositional nor conformist. Instead, it combines a belief in achievement with a cultural affirmation, becoming more critical than conformist.

The ideology of AVID students, which is simultaneously culturally and academically affirming, puts a new twist on the traditional connection between academic achievement and economic success. Black and Latino AVID students sense the need to develop culturally appropriate linguistic styles, social behavior, and academic skills. And they develop these skills, but without erasing the cultural identity of theirs that is nurtured and displayed at home and in the neighborhood.

Furthermore, these students' ideology provides an interesting counterpoint to the ideology of resistance. Here we encounter circumstances in which members of ethnic- and linguistic-minority groups eschew oppositional ideologies in favor of the "accommodation without assimilation" belief system (Gibson 1988), which is presumably reserved for members of voluntary

immigrant groups (Cummins 1986; Gibson and Ogbu 1991; Ogbu 1978; Suárez-Orozco 1989).

In a sense, AVID students (who are successful by anyone's standards) have developed the ideology that Fine seems to think is reserved for the rejects of the educational system (1991). She found that high school dropouts had developed a much more sophisticated critique of class, gender, and ethnic politics than high school graduates, who naively accepted the connection between hard work and academic success. It is important to note that AVID produces minority students who are successful in school and who have developed a critical consciousness. This means that a critical consciousness is not reserved only for the students rejected by the system. We have uncovered at least one set of social circumstances in which a critical consciousness develops among students who are academically successful.

In closing, we want to make a final comment about the concept of resistance which resides in many parts of reproduction theory. Our study shows that the expressive and behavioral repertoire of Latino and African American students is much more extensive than is portrayed in reproduction theory. The actions of Latino and African American students in AVID were not limited to opposing or resisting structures of constraints; they took positive courses of action to achieve socially accepted goals and attempted to break down constraining barriers. The students in our study did not passively respond to structural forces; rather they shaped and defined those forces in creative ways.

Circumscribing students' actions as only negative or oppositional produces a limited portrait of their social agency. Having witnessed a wide and diverse range of students' actions, it is clear to us that we need a more subtle and inclusive conception of social agency in order to understand how the inequality between rich and poor, "majority" and "minority," is sustained generation after generation. This more comprehensive sense of agency to which we have alluded in this study attempts to capture the processes by which people give meaning to their lives through complex cultural and political processes while appreciating the power of the constraints under which they labor (cf. Giroux and Simon 1989:147).

NOTES

Acknowledgments. Portions of this article were presented by Mehan to the Ethnography and Education Forum, the University of Pennsylvania, March 1993, and by Hubbard to the Linguistic Minority Research Institute, the University of California, Santa Barbara, May 1993.

This research was funded by grants from the Linguistic Minority Research Institute of the University of California and the office of Educational Research and Improvement, U.S. Department of Education. Our thanks to the San Diego City Schools, especially John Griffith and Peter Bell, for encouraging this research. We especially appreciate the support and cooperation of Mary Catherine Swanson and the AVID coordinators, teachers, and students at the four high schools.

REFERENCES CITED

Anderson, Elijah, 1991. Streetwise: Race, Class and Change in an Urban Community. Chicago: University of Chicago Press.
Apple, Michael W., 1983. Education and Power. Boston: Routledge and Kegan Paul.

5. CURRICULUM AND INSTRUCTION IN MULTICULTURAL PERSPECTIVE

Apple, Michael W., and Lois Weis, eds., 1983. Ideology and Practice in Education: A Political and Conceptual Introduction. Philadelphia: Temple University Press.

Bourdieu, Pierre, 1986. The Forms of Capital. In Handbook of Theory and Research for the Sociology of Education. John G. Richardson, ed. Pp. 241-258. New York: Greenwood Press.

Bourdieu, Pierre, and Claude Passeron, 1977. Reproduction in Education, Society and Culture. Los Angeles: Sage.

Bowles, Samuel, and Herbert I. Gintis, 1976. Schooling in Capitalist America. New York: Basic Books.

Carter, Deborah J., and Reginald Wilson, 1991. Minorities in Higher Education: Ninth Annual Status Report. Washington, DC: American Council on Education.

Center for Education Statistics, 1986. The Condition of Education: A Statistical Report. Washington, DC: U.S. Department of Education.

Coleman, James, et al., 1966. Inequality of Educational Opportunity. Washington, DC: U.S. Government Printing Office.

CSAW (Commission on the Skills of the American Workforce), 1990. America's Choice: High Skills or Low Wages! Rochester, NY: National Center on Education and the Economy.

Cummins, Jim, 1986. Empowering Minority Students: A Framework for Intervention. Harvard Educational Review 56(1):18-36.

Delgado-Gaitan, Concha, and Henry Trueba, 1991. Crossing Cultural Borders. New York: Falmer Press.

Fine, Michelle, 1991. Framing Dropouts: Notes on the Politics of an Urban Public High School. Albany: State University of New York Press.

Foley, Doug, 1990. Learning Capitalist Culture: Deep in the Heart of Tejas. Philadelphia: University of Pennsylvania Press.

Fordham, Signithia, and John U. Ogbu, 1987. Black Students' School Success: Coping with the Burden of 'Acting White.' Urban Review 18(3):1-31.

Gándara, Patricia. In press. Choosing Higher Education: Antecedents to Successful Educational Outcomes for Low Income Mexican American Students.

Gibson, Margaret, 1988. Accommodation without Assimilation: Sikh Immigrants in an American High School. New York: Cornell University Press.

Gibson, Margaret, and John U. Ogbu, eds., 1991. Minority Status and Schooling: A Comparative Study of Immigrant and Involuntary Minorities. New York: Garland.

Giroux, Henry, 1983. Theory and Resistance in Education. London: Heinemann Education Books.

_____ 1992. Border Crossing: Cultural Workers and the Politics of Education. London: Routledge & Kegan Paul.

Giroux, Henry, and Roger Simon, 1989. Popular Culture and Critical Pedagogy. In Critical Pedagogy, The State and Cultural Struggle. Henry Giroux and Peter MacLaren, eds. Pp. 236-252. Albany: State University of New York Press.

Goffman, Erving, 1964. Asylums. New York: Doubleday.

Haycock, Kati, and Susanne Navarro, 1988. Unfinished Business. Oakland: The Achievement Council.

Jankowski, Martín Sánchez, 1991. Islands in the Street: Gangs and American Urban Society. Berkeley: University of California Press.

Jencks, Christopher, et al., 1972. Inequality: A Reassessment of the Effect of Family and Schooling in America. New York: Basic Books.

Labov, William, 1982. Competing Value Systems in the Inner City Schools. In Children in and out of School: Ethnography and Education. Perry Gilmore and Alan Glathorn, eds. Pp. 148-171. Washington, DC: Center for Applied Linguistics.

LeCompte, Margaret, and Anthony Dworkin, 1991. Giving Up on School: Student Dropouts and Teacher Burnouts. Newberry Park, CA: Corwin Press.

MacLeod, Jay, 1987. Ain't No Makin' It: Leveled Aspirations in a Low-Income Neighborhood. Boulder, CO: Westview Press.

Mehan, Hugh, 1992. Understanding Inequality in Schools: The Contribution of Interpretive Studies. The Sociology of Education 65(1):1-20.

Mehan, Hugh, et al., 1992. Untracking and College Enrollment. Research Report, 4. Santa Cruz, CA: National Center for Research on Cultural Diversity and Second Language Learning.

NCEE (National Center for Education and the Economy), 1990. America's Choice: High Skills or Low Wages? Washington, DC: NCEE.

Ogbu, John U., 1978. Minority Education and Caste: The American System in Cross-Cultural Perspective. New York: Academic Press.

_____ 1987. Variability in Minority School Performance: A Problem in Search of an Explanation. Anthropology & Education Quarterly 18(4):312-334.

_____ 1991. Immigrant and Involuntary Minorities in Comparative Perspective. In Minority Status and Schooling. M. Gibson and J. Ogbu, eds. Pp. 3-37. New York: Garland Publishing.

Pelavin, Sol H., and Michael Kane, 1990. Changing the Odds: Factors Increasing Access to College. New York: College Entrance Examination Board.

Rose, Mike, 1989. Lives on The Boundary. New York: The Free Press.

Solomon, R. Patrick, 1992. Black Resistance in School: Forging a Separatist Culture. Albany: State University of New York Press.

Suárez-Orozco, Marcello M., 1989. Central American Refugees and U.S. High Schools: A Psychosocial Study of Motivation and Achievement. Stanford: Stanford University Press.

Swanson, Mary Catherine, n.d. AVID: A College Preparatory Program for Underrepresented Students. San Diego: San Diego County Office of Education.

Weis, Lois, 1985. Between Two Worlds: Black Students in an Urban Community College. Boston: Routledge & Kegan Paul.

Willis, Paul, 1977. Learning to Labor. New York: Columbia Teachers College Press.

Sapphires-in-Transition: Enhancing Personal Development Among Black Female Adolescents

Joyce Lynom Young

Joyce Lynom Young is an associate professor in the Department of Counseling, Educational Psychology and Research, University of Memphis, P.O. Box 11832, Memphis, TN 38111.

The author describes a counselor intervention program used for facilitating the personal development of adolescents. Intervention occurred through activities that were designed for Black female adolescents in a secondary public school. Goals were met through structured developmental activities, counseling sessions, and organized network support. Results indicated the program was successful.

Various interventions for secondary school students occur through counseling program initiatives (Cole, 1991; Coy, 1991; Moles, 1991; Olson & Perrone, 1991; Young, 1991). Such initiatives enable school counselors to assume pivotal leadership roles in planning, implementing, and evaluating innovative affective education programs that address specific concerns and issues of diverse student populations.

Kowitz and Dronberger (1970) wrote of the difficulty involved in measuring change based on affective education. They indicated that assessment using observational techniques may be superior to more formal, standardized approaches. These authors added that very few recommendations have been made on converting observational data into quantitative evaluations. In discussing measurement concerns in counseling program evaluations, Bardo and Cody (1975) recommended that criterion-referenced measuring devices be designed to reflect the objectives of specific counseling programs. Ciechalski (1990)., Gerler (1990), and Campbell and Robinson (1990) wrote of action research and its applicability for use in planning and evaluating school counseling programs. *Action Research* was defined as focusing on immediate problem solving, using and applying the practical results directly to the counselor's school setting.

I describe a counselor intervention program for facilitating the personal development of Black female adolescents enrolled in a secondary public school in the southeast United States. The counselor intervention program was titled Sapphires-in-Transition (SIT). The title was selected by the Black counselor because of the Sapphire association with Black women (Spears, 1981). In addressing the shrewish connotation involving Black women and the name "Sapphire," King (1971) wrote, "Saddled with the image of a menacing matriarch and long demeaned . . . as Sapphire and Saphronia, Black women are . . . expending their energies in 'redefining their image' " (p. 70).

Such a redefinition involved making lemonade out of a lemon, for example, wearing the Sapphire title proudly as one wore the sapphire jewel (Young, 1978). Indeed, the positive symbolism of Sapphire suggested an ideal title for a program focusing on the Black female adolescent in her developmental emergence.

PROGRAM DESCRIPTION

The school setting was a predominantly lower middle-class suburban area with two female counselors, one Black and one White. There were approximately 450 Black students and 450 White students in grades 7 through 12. Intervention occurred through a counselor-designed program that involved Black female adolescent participants, their peers, parents, selected relatives, faculty, administrators, and community volunteers (Coy, 1991; Dedmond, 1991).

The Black counselor was familiar with the Black female student population and knew that many of these students exhibited inappropriate external behaviors. Such behaviors were manifested in their attire, attitudes, demeanor, and grooming; moreover, their behaviors (in combination with data that indicated poor academic performance and negligible involvement in extracurricular activities) spawned speculation that many of these adolescents were also internalizing inappropriate behaviors, including poor self-concepts (Gainor & Forrest, 1991; George, 1986; Poussaint & Atkinson, 1972).

Both Black counselor and White counselor agreed that some of the Black female students could benefit from structured developmental activities if appropriated assistance in affective education were provided to address students' concerns and needs (Brantlinger, 1992; Moles, 1991; Olson & Perrone, 1991; Pine, 1975; Young, 1991).

These counselors used daily observation as a needs assessment tool (Collison, 1982) to determine specific needs. Thereafter, the White counselor and the guidance committee (an advisory group composed of three teachers and two community representatives who were selected each year by the school principal) collaborated and provided general ancillary services to assist the Black counselor in meeting the specific needs through a program intervention approach. The approach included formulating the program mission and goals, designing program activities, and implementing and evaluating the program. The counselors' daily observations yielded information that indicated several general areas of need for many of the Black female adolescents who exhibited inappropriate external behaviors. Those areas included (a) developing positive self-concepts, (b) building self-esteem, (c) heightening consciousness of personal and career success opportunities for Black female adolescents who reflect societally appropriate behaviors, and (d) learning and practicing appropriate behaviors (Evans & Herr, 1991; Nassar, Hodges, & Ollendick, 1992; Page & Berkow, 1991). The aforementioned areas of need were used as reasons for adopting the program mission of helping participants develop positive self-concepts and build self-esteem through the adoption of appropriate behaviors for effective societal functioning. Program goals focused on participants learning and practicing the specific external behaviors of (a) modulating voices, (b) grooming properly, and (c) developing assertive demeanor. Goals were met through three program facets: group counseling sessions, structured developmental activities, and procedural network support.

Participants

A total of 69 Black female students in grades 7 through 12 (grade 7 =15 students, grade 8 =14 students, grade 9 =10 students, grade 10 =10 students, grade 11 =10 students, grade 12 =10 students) were selected to participate in the SIT program for approximately 5 weeks. Participants were referred by teachers who observed students and who used the following criteria in the selection process: (a) exhibiting inappropriate behaviors, (b) projecting negative self-concepts, and (c) showing potential to benefit from special attention. Participants were also expected to show interest in the SIT program and have written parental permission to participate.

Teachers, peers, parents, selected family members, and participants were required to read and sign contracts to verify their interest and voluntary involvement in the program. Parents were requested to attend parent workshops to learn about program goals, activities, and procedures as well as to heighten their sensitivities regarding the special concerns of Black female adolescents. Moreover, parents were sensitized to the importance of providing a supportive home environment (Crosbie-Burnett & Pulvino, 1990; Palmo, Lowry, Weldon, & Scioscia, 1984; Penick & Jepsen, 1992). They were also continually reminded of their pivotal roles in the formation of positive self-concepts, crucial prerequisites for adopting and practicing appropriate external behaviors (Fitts, 1964; Holloman, 1989).

To help attain the program goals as well as reinforce positive growth among participants, the counselors organized a network of teachers, administrators, students, peers, parents, significant family members, and community leaders (networkers). These networkers provided baseline data on the participants in the program. Networkers also provided leadership, consultation, intervention, seminars, workshops, evaluation, and general support services.

INTERVENTION

SIT Group Counseling

SIT participants were involved in a variety of activities that were designed to motivate Black female adolescents to learn appropriate internal and external behaviors. Activities began with counselor-facilitated group guidance, orientation, and group counseling, which included self-awareness and societal-awareness sessions (Cole, 1991; Drury, 1984) that were held every day for 2 consecutive weeks. These Facet 1 program sessions reflected the program mission and focused on participants developing positive self-concepts and building self-esteem by making them cognizant of their individual and collective worth as beautiful people and motivating them to consider their personal as well as societal potential as young Black women. To encourage self-awareness, participants received help in (a) identifying their assets, strengths, and talents; (b) becoming aware of the practical and aesthetic dimensions of developing as well as using their assets, strengths, and talents; and (c) learning to strengthen, reverse, or minimize their weaknesses. To promote awareness of societal perceptions and career opportunities for young Black women, participants received guidance in (a) comprehending their traditional and transitional images and roles, (b) acquiring knowledge of the achievements of historical and contemporary Black women role models to validate the individual and collective achievements and potential of young Black women, and (c) clarifying values, solving problems, making decisions, and setting goals regarding their directions for the future as productive students and citizens. Group counseling sessions continued throughout the program on a weekly basis after the initial 2 weeks of daily, intensive intervention. These sessions complemented the SIT developmental activities and provided opportunities for processing the activities.

SIT Developmental Activities

SIT participants attended Facet 2 consciousness-raising developmental activities that were conducted daily by community leaders for 3 consecutive weeks. These activities focused on helping participants learn and practice behaviors, attitudes, and skills deemed societally appropriate. Workshops, seminars, and interest sessions involved contemporary issues and relevant topics that included personal grooming (hygiene, makeup, hair care, nails, wardrobe), social skills, demeanor, poise, career and academic planning, job etiquette, voice modulation, assertive behavior, tact, college life, leadership development, citizenship, marriage, and family.

SIT Procedural Support
Throughout all SIT activities, the networkers (teachers, administrators, counselors, community leaders, parents, significant family members, and student peers) constituted a procedural support system (Dedmond, 1991; Miller & Grisdale, 1975; Stilwell, Baffington, DeMers, & Stilwell, 1984). This system of observation, positive reinforcement and informal assessment was used to augment group counseling, guidance sessions, and other developmental activities that were part of the SIT program. As a component of the Facet 3 Network Support System, observation was used as a procedural tool.

Observation Component
Each SIT participant was observed by two peers (Larrabee & Terres, 1984; Robinson, Morrow, Kigin, & Lindeman, 1991), one Black and one White, who were selected by the participants themselves. The peer evaluators, either young men or young women, observed the SIT participant whenever possible; however, observers were specifically charged to attend the Facet 2 structured activities with the participants for approximately 3 weeks. The evaluators were charged to observe the participants for specific positive and negative behavior manifestations before, during, and after the structured activities. Peer evaluators were expected to provide feedback regarding the relevance of the activities for the SIT participants. They were also charged to assess behaviors and determine any behavior changes in the participants.

In addition to the peer evaluators, each SIT participant selected one family evaluator, not necessarily a parent, to observe her behaviors away from school and to provide appropriate feedback. Parents, teachers, and administrators were involved in the program as informal observers, and they provided feedback occasionally.

Because participants were aware of the observation component in the support system, they sought, dutifully, to exhibit positive behaviors as often as possible during the activities, school day, and at home. The feedback received from evaluators served as reminders when inappropriate behaviors were noted. Moreover, such feedback activated positive reinforcement, the second component in the network support system.

Positive Reinforcement Component
Parents, peer evaluators, teachers, and family evaluators were the designated networkers who provided positive reinforcement to participants showing improvement in external behaviors. Verbal reinforcers were given for any positive behaviors observed; however, when appropriate, reinforcement could assume the form of specific awards, honors, or general recognition. Reinforcement of some type was continually provided at school and at home. Analyses of reinforcement efforts activated informal assessment, the third component in the network support system.

Informal Assessment Component
The subjective impressions or empirical evidence (Kowitz & Dronberger, 1970) gleaned from results of the observation and positive reinforcement procedures represented an informal assessment. Although the empirical evidence suggested that appropriately selected verbal reinforcement was a valuable strategy in helping young Black women practice appropriate behaviors, criterion-referenced devices were used at the end of Facet 3 of the SIT program to obtain additional data regarding goals, objectives, achievement, and program viability. Such procedures represented a formal, objective evaluation.

EVALUATION
Evaluation of the SIT program indicated that participants learned, practiced, and adopted specific external behaviors deemed societally appropriate. They all showed dramatic improvement on a daily basis in voice modulation, proper grooming, and assertive behavior. Additionally, the evaluation indicated that participants, teachers, administrators, peers, parents, and family evaluators (a) reacted favorably to the participants' behavioral changes and (b) perceived the SIT program as successful.

The program evaluation was based on data derived from several devices: the SIT Pre/Post Assessment Forms, SIT Self-Awareness Scale, SIT Self-Evaluation Scale, SIT Parent Survey, and SIT Program Evaluation Form. These self-report devises were designed and field tested at the school (before initiating the SIT program) with students and parents who would not be involved with the program.

Participants were administered the SIT Pre/Post Assessment Forms, SIT Self-Awareness Scale, SIT Self-Evaluation Scale, and SIT Program Evaluation Form. Parents were administered the SIT Pre/Post Assessment Forms, SIT Parent Survey, and SIT Program Evaluation Form. Other networkers were administered the SIT Pre/Post Assessment Forms and SIT Program Evaluation Form. All devices were administered at the school after completion of Facet 3 except for the SIT Pre/Post Assessment Forms, which were administered prior to initiating Facet 1 program sessions.

Additionally, written observations and perception reports were obtained from the networkers. Participants responded favorably (100%) regarding their perceptions of the SIT program's success. They also responded favorably (98%) to perceived personal behavioral changes. Parents responded favorably (99%) to perceived personal behavioral changes. Parents responded favorably (99%) regarding their perceptions of the SIT program's success. They also responded favorably (95%) to observing positive behavioral changes in their children. Other networkers responded favorably (100%) regarding their perceptions of the SIT program. Many noted that the program should be expanded and made available to all students enrolled at the school. They also responded favorably (98%) to observing positive behavioral changes in specific students and peers.

IMPLICATIONS
In this article I have described counselor intervention in facilitating the personal development of Black female adolescents.

Intervention occurred through a counselor-designed program. Sapphires-in-Transition, that was targeted to help Black female adolescent students in a secondary public school. Program evaluation indicated that participants learned, practiced, and adopted specific behaviors deemed societally appropriate. Moreover, participants, student peers, teachers, administrators, parents, relatives, and community volunteers all responded affirmatively regarding the positive impact and value of the program for the Black female adolescent participants.

The SIT program was designed from a project approach as opposed to a purely experimental perspective. The SIT program evaluation was outcome oriented and focused on several approaches (case study, experiment, expert opinion, self-evaluation, and satisfaction survey; Lewis, 1983). These approaches were congruent with the criterion-referenced devices, program mission, and goals.

As a program model, SIT was flexible and could easily be adapted for use with other populations. If redesigned from an experimental approach, however, this program model would have tremendous potential for yielding valuable data to use in assisting at-risk adolescents and other populations.

The SIT program provided valuable service to the Black female adolescent participants in making them aware of their individual and collective beauty and potential. Counselor intervention facilitated personal development for these adolescents by exposing them to attitudes and activities that encouraged (a) knowledge of behaviors deemed societally appropriate for effective functioning in a culture essentially controlled by neither Blacks nor women, (b) practice of such societal behaviors when appropriate, and (c) recognition, respect, acceptance, and glorification of Black standards and images of physical beauty. Such exposure was instrumental in forming positive self-concepts, building self-esteem, and reflecting positive images during a transitional period for the participants—a transitional period for them as adolescents, at ages between childhood and adulthood, and as Black women, members of an often maligned and misunderstood group (Brown, 1993; Evans & Herr, 1991; Wallace, 1979).

REFERENCES

Bardo, H. R., & Cody, J. J. (1975). Minimizing measurement concerns in guidance and evaluation. *Measurement and Evaluation in Guidance,* 8(3), 175–179.

Brantlinger, E. (1992). Unmentionable futures: Postschool planning for low-income teen-agers. *The School Counselor,* 39, 281–291.

Brown, J. F. (1993). Helping black women build high self-esteem. *American Counselor.* 2(1), 9–11.

Campbell, C. A., & Robinson, E. H. (1990). The accountability and research challenge: Training future counselors. *Elementary School Guidance & Counseling,* 25, 72–77.

Ciechalski, J. C. (1990). Action research, the Mann-Whitney U, and thou. *Elementary School Guidance & Counseling,* 25, 54–62.

Cole, C. (1991). Counselors and students' self-concept. *The School Counselor,* 38, 162.

Collison, B. B. (1982). Needs assessment for guidance program planning: A procedure. *The School Counselor,* 30, 115–121.

Coy, D. R. (1991). The role of the counselor in today's school. *The Journal for Middle Level and High School Administrators,* 75(534), 15–19.

Crosbie-Burnett, M., & Pulvino, C. J. (1990). Children in non-traditional families: A classroom guidance program. *The School Counselor,* 37, 286–293.

Dedmond, R. M. (1991). Establishing, coordinating school-community partnerships. *The Journal for Middle Level and High School Administrators,* 75(534), 28–35.

Drury, S. S. (1984). Counselor survival in the 1980's. *The School Counselor,* 31, 234–240.

Evans, K. M., & Herr, E. L. (1991). The influence of racism and sexism in the career development of African American women. *Journal of Multicultural Counseling and Development,* 19, 130–135.

Fitts, W. F. (1964). *Tennessee self-concept scale.* Nashville, TN: Counselor Recordings and Tests.

Gainor, K. A., & Forrest, L. (1991). African American women's self-concept: Implication for career decisions and career counseling. *The Career Development Quarterly,* 39, 261–271.

George, V. D. (1986). Talented adolescent women and the motive to avoid success. *Journal of Multicultural Counseling and Development,* 14, 108–115.

Gerler, E. R., Jr. (1990). Children's success in school: Collaborative research among counselors, supervisors, and counselor educators. *Elementary School Guidance & Counseling,* 25, 64–71.

Holloman, L. (1989). Self-esteem and selected clothing attitudes of black adults: Implications for counseling. *Journal of Multicultural Counseling and Development,* 17, 50–61.

King, H. H. (1971). The black woman and women's lib. *Ebony.* 26(5), 68–76.

Kowitz, G. T., & Dronberger, G. B. (1970). Accountability in affective education. *Measurement and Evaluation in Guidance,* 8(4), 200–205.

Larrabee, M. J., & Terres, C. K. (1984). Groups: The future of school counseling. *The School Counselor,* 31, 256–264.

Lewis, J. D. (1983). Guidance program evaluation: How to do it. *The School Counselor,* 31, 111–119.

Miller, J. V., & Grisdale, G. A. (1975). Guidance program evaluation: What's out there? *Measurement and Evaluation in Guidance,* 8(3), 145–154.

Moles, O. C. (1991). Guidance programs in American high schools. *The School Counselor,* 38, 163–177.

Nassar, C. M., Hodges, P., & Ollendick, T. (1992). Self-concept, eating attitudes and dietary patterns in young adolescent girls. *The School Counselor,* 39, 338–343.

Olson, M. J., & Perrone, P. A. (1991). Changing to a developmental guidance program. *The School Counselor,* 39, 41–46.

Page, R. C., & Berkow, D. N. (1991). Concepts of the self: Western and eastern perspectives. *Journal of Multicultural Counseling and Development,* 19, 83–93.

Palmo, A. J., Lowry, L. A., Weldon, D. P., & Scioscia, T. M. (1984). Family counseling. *The School Counselor,* 31, 272–284.

Penick, N., & Jepsen, D. A. (1992). Family functioning and adolescent career development. *The Career Development Quarterly,* 40, 208–222.

Pine, G. (1975). School guidance programs: Retrospect and prospect. *Measurement and Evaluation in Guidance,* 8(3), 136–144.

Poussaint, A., & Atkinson, C. (1972). Black youth and motivation. In R. L. Jones (Ed.), *Black psychology* (pp. 113–123). New York: Harper & Row.

Robinson, S. E., Morrow, S., Kigin, T., & Lindeman, M. (1991). Peer counselors in a high school setting: evaluation of training and impact on students. *The School Counselor,* 39, 35–40.

Spears, R. A. (1981). *Slang and euphemism.* Middle Village, New York: Jonathan David Publisher.

Stilwell, W. E., Baffington, P. W., DeMers, S. T., & Stilwell, D. N. (1984). Facilitating psychological education: A comprehensive checklist for implementation. *The School Counselor,* 31, 249–255.

Wallace, M. (1979). *Black macho and the myth of the superwoman.* New York: Dial Press.

Young, J. L. (1978). Sapphires-in transition. *Black Pearl,* 1(1), 28–29.

Young, J. L. (1991). Developmental programming in the affective domain: Leadership for the school counselor. *Creative Visions for Counseling Professionals* (The Official Journal of the West Tennessee Association for Counseling and Development). 1(2), 5–6.

Racial Issues in Education: Real or Imagined?

Gloria S. Boutte, Sally LaPoint, and Barbara Davis

Gloria S. Boutte, Ph.D., is assistant professor at the University of South Carolina in Columbia. Gloria has published a number of articles, has presented extensively, and is currently completing a book on multicultural issues. She works closely with school districts on racial and other related issues.

Sally LaPoint, Ed.D., is an assistant professor of elementary education at the University of South Carolina in Beaufort. Sally has written articles, presented at several conferences, and is currently writing a chapter in a book on racial issues.

Barbara Davis, Ph.D., is an assistant professor at the University of South Carolina in Columbia. Barbara has conducted a number of workshops and seminars and is currently writing a chapter in a book on racial issues.

> ### Recently, one of the authors was visiting a second grade classroom and witnessed children telling ethnic jokes.
>
> As the author sat in utter amazement and listened to these jokes, she was most alarmed by three other parents' and the teacher's laughter at the jokes! To further compound an already inflammatory situation, one of the parents praised a child for being a "good joke teller." After listening to the fourth or fifth joke, the author finally interrupted, telling the teacher that racial jokes were inappropriate in the classroom. At this point the teacher informed the children that they could not tell jokes that make fun of other people. After querying the children, the teacher discovered that the children did not understand the subtle, negative, racial messages in the jokes; in fact, they did not know what a "Polack" was! The most appalling part of this entire incident was the teacher's and parents' condonation of racial jokes. Unbeknownst to the teacher, racism was being perpetuated and fertilized in the classroom!

W hat's the worst ethnic joke you've ever heard? Prejudice. (It's no joke.) *

Although most of the children did not seem to understand the jokes they told in the second grade classroom situation described here, they were laughing and unconsciously learning negative messages about various ethnic groups (all of the jokes depicted various ethnic groups as being stupid). As the question about what is the worst ethnic joke indicates, racial jokes are *not* funny and serve no fruitful purpose. They are definitely inappropriate in the classroom setting. This article is an appeal to teachers, college students, and parents to become more cognizant of overt and covert racial slurs and defamations. In light of the racial disharmony in this country, early childhood professionals and parents, who have a tremendous influence on young children's racial attitudes, must

---

*Quote used with the permission of The Anti-Defamation League of B'nai Brith, 823 United Nations Plaza, New York, NY 10017.

From *Young Children,* November 1993, pp. 19-23. © 1993 by the National Association for the Education of Young Children. Reprinted by permission.

Incidents Involving Young Children

1. **While we were visiting a kindergarten classroom, a young girl (Robin) continuously stared at one of the authors. The staring continued throughout the large-group discussion; it was sometimes accompanied by mutual smiles between the child and the author. After large-group time Robin approached the author several times to show her work. Finally, when the time arrived for the preservice teacher we were observing to do her activity, Robin was included in the group. At this point Robin blurted out, "I didn't know that your teacher was b-b-black!"**

The nervous preservice teacher replied, "Robin, don't say that!" Robin protested, "But she's pretty." The embarrassed preservice teacher plowed through her planned activity without further discussion.

This anecdote brings up two major issues. First, as suggested by Derman-Sparks (1992), like in "The Emperor's New Clothes," many teachers think that talking about race is not polite; actually, *not* discussing it is impolite. In a multicultural classroom such discussions take place daily and in a spontaneous manner (Boutte & McCormick, 1992). As the author later told the preservice teacher, an acceptable reply to Robin's observation would have been, "Yes, Robin, my teacher is African American (or black). What other races can teachers be?"

(This question could be posed to all of the children). The activity could proceed as planned unless the children wanted to discuss the issue further.

Another issue that emerges from this example is the fact that young children do notice race and other differences (Derman-Sparks, 1992); yet, as Robin's final comment suggests, young children note race as another factual aspect of an individual (in the same way that they notice gender). Robin's intention was not to be rude but rather to make an observation. Her compliment to the author indicates that her definition of attractiveness extended beyond racial lines.

When we fail to acknowledge differences in individuals, we may send a message that differences are not appreciated or that they are negative. Additionally, when we ignore or negate racial differences, we fail to individualize and meet children's needs (Boutte & McCormick, 1992)—the needs of the child of color and the needs of the child *inquiring* about differences of color and, perhaps, culture.

2. **Each of the authors has encountered similar race-related comments from children while visiting classrooms. Prior to our visits the preservice teacher typically informs the children that her teacher will be visiting her today. Nevertheless, when we arrive the children often ask, in a puzzled manner, "That's your teacher?"**

Reactions from children that demonstrate that they did not

expect a nonwhite teacher educator imply that they have not seen people of other races in this capacity. Classroom teachers can help by making sure that pictures, literature, educational materials, and resource persons include representatives from many different cultures (Boutte & McCormick, 1992). Our observations of many classrooms have revealed that presently many children of color experience a sense of invisibility in classrooms. The particulars of African American life and culture—art, literature, political and social perspective, and music—must be presented in the mainstream culture of American schooling, not consigned to special days, weeks, or months of the year, or to special topics (Steele, 1992). As Claude Steele persuasively argues, too often children of color are asked to give up their styles of speech and appearance, value priorities, and preferences in order to be valued in school and to be accepted by the dominant racial group.

Schools must actively recruit and *retain* a diverse group of teachers, regardless of the homogeneity of the school population. Many times preservice teachers admit that they have never had an African American professor. Curiously, on the first day of classes, some raise their eyebrows (unintentionally) when we enter the classroom and begin teaching.

bring racial issues to the forefront and confront them.

As African American teacher educators at a predominantly white university who visit schools regularly and interact with potential teachers, we have the opportunity to observe firsthand numerous behaviors and ideas that are prevalent in schools. Of particular interest to us are interracial interactions and comments. We are keenly aware of these issues and are probably more likely to home in on them than are most teacher educators. In fact, many would argue that incidents such as telling ethnic jokes are insignificant and harmless and should be overlooked—and certainly not blown out of proportion. We disagree. We know firsthand the negative effect of such "playful" interactions. We can testify that the impact is great and has a cumulative effect. Jones and Derman-Sparks (1992) noted that when we fail to acknowledge or take actions to

---

Each semester, preservice teachers label children of color "the quiet one" or "the maladjusted one"

---

challenge bias, then we are helping to perpetuate oppressive beliefs and behaviors. We must understand that even if racial biases are unintentional, they are still real and hurtful for the recipients.

The incidents described above include comments that were made by children or preservice teachers. Many of the comments may seem inconsequential to individuals who are not culturally sensitive. As the subsequent commentaries illustrate, however, these

comments often send powerful messages about current perspectives on racial issues.

Many teachers think that talking about race is not polite; actually, *not* discussing it is impolite.

When teachers work with children who are culturally different from themselves, they must actively seek information that will help them understand that culture (Boutte & McCormick, 1992). This information should include differences in hair textures, diet, ways of communicating, learning styles, and so forth. Many times close observation of a child in other settings will reveal a multifaceted child who has the capability to be quiet or active depending on the circumstances. Boutte and McCormick note that each person has unique cultural idiosyncrasies, and teachers should realize that their own cultural differences seem equally as strange to others as others' seem to them. Boutte (1992) urged teachers to examine their differential expectations for and interactions with children of color. Often and unintentionally, children of color are sent negative messages that indicate low expectations. Teachers must learn to treat all children fairly. Steele (1992) suggests that the culprit of school failure among African American children is often a result of the devaluation that the children face. Furthermore, Steele argues that in many classrooms, segregation by race often occurs via ability grouping and tracking. Because these practices often do more harm than good, they should be avoided—particularly in primary grades. Unfortunately, more children fail in the teacher's lounge than in the classroom or

any other part of the school—that is, negative labels often precede children; thus, they are judged by teacher expectations rather than by their actual performance.

Steele notes that the problem of low expectations of children of color (particularly African American children) continues during college. During one of the authors' classes, a white student giving examples during an oral presentation made reference to a black student's nonverbal behavior and demeanor as "quiet," "tense," and "docile." The African American student's behavior is likely to be different outside the classroom environment; however, the "docile" behavior is categorically assigned to African American students and consistently reinforced by our "mainstream" educational system until it inevitably becomes the "self-fulfilling prophecy."

This same author has noted that African American students in her college classes hesitate to participate in class discussions, ask questions, or make comments. When prodded and encouraged by the instructor, however, these same "quiet" students comment eagerly and with much breadth. Additionally, the author has observed that African American students in other classes have typically displayed the same passive behavior. These same students from whom the instructor would have to "pry" information in class would later seek the professor, and their behavior and demeanor sharply contrasted with their passive behavior in class. Both the author and Steele suggest that the

Examples Involving Preservice Teachers

1. Over the years, a number of students have indicated that they will not discuss racial issues in their classrooms. One student said, "I'll just die if I have to say the word 'black'."

Racial issues *will* emerge in the classroom, as noted by the incident involving Robin. Teachers must realize that discussing such issues when they arise is not offensive. Teachers must also explore their reasons for feeling uncomfortable with these issues. One preservice teacher indicated that she clearly understood her discomfort with racial discussions—her father is prejudiced; yet she was willing to strive to become a multicultural teacher. Becoming multicultural is a gradual process, but the first step begins with analysis of one's beliefs. As Hendrick (1992) points out, "Everyone thinks of changing the world, but no one thinks of changing himself" (p. 275). Hendrick further notes that if we, as teachers, accept differences in others without condemning them, then we can begin to develop a wider, more tolerant view of the world. The ultimate questions that teachers must ask are, Does ignoring racial issues do more harm than good? If we ignore race, then will the issues associated with it disappear?

2. During classroom discussions of racial issues, at least one student per semester reports feeling attacked. One student, for example, emphatically articulated that she was tired of everyone picking on whites. She continued that she did not "enslave any blacks or kill any Indians."

Teachers must not view multiculturalism as an attack on any race. Society has room for all races to be included, not to the detriment of another. Telling the first Thanksgiving story from the perspectives of both Native Americans and Pilgrims does not mean that one is right and the other one is wrong. In a diverse society we must learn to appreciate different perspectives.

3. Often in the college classroom, preservice teachers express confusion about the "proper" racial terminology for a particular group. They ask, for example, "Should I say 'black' or 'African American'? 'Latino' or 'Hispanic'? 'Indian' or 'Native American'?"

Preservice teachers who pose such questions most importantly indicate a necessary awareness of possible offensiveness of certain racial terminology. Many teachers never reach this point. Preferences for a particular racial term will vary depending on who you ask. Teachers must stay abreast of the literature to find out when racial terminology becomes archaic. Additionally, teachers must be aware of changes in racial compositions in various geographic locations. If a teacher is uncertain about what term to use to refer to a particular child in her classroom, she should ask the child's parent for the preferred terminology.

4. Many teacher education students and teachers seem to, have problems understanding why fingerplays or songs with racial stereotypes are inappropriate in classrooms. Many students argue that these fingerplays are good and have been around for a long time.

Using a fingerplay just because you learned it as a child is not a very strong justification. Using that argument, many things that were done in the past could be considered appropriate that we do *not* consider appropriate today (e.g., slavery, the Holocaust). The need for teachers to grow and change is especially vital in today's society because the population of children served by public schools is changing. Currently, minorities constitute the majority of schoolchildren in 23 of 25 of the largest U.S. cities (Cangelosi, 1992). Unless teachers work in a particularly isolated school setting, their classes are likely to be characterized by cultural and ethnic diversity; therefore, fingerplays, songs, and other resources must reflect this diversity.

Another issue is the fact that young children do notice race and other differences.

lack of participation in the college classroom is attributed to years of low expectations from teachers.

Conclusion

As teachers we must realize that a child's race is an intimate part of his self-esteem. How we react to this aspect of a child has a tremendous effect on the child; hence, racial issues in the classroom must be recognized and addressed—by no means should they be ignored! In response to the question posed in the title of this article, racial issues in the classroom are *real*. As teachers we are one of the most powerful influences that young children will encounter. The way racial issues are handled will determine if racism in the classroom will be perpetuated or discouraged.

Unless educators provide encouragement and a nurturing environment in which all children and older students can learn and excel, negative misconceptions about their academic, communication, and social abilities will be perpetuated. In a diverse society, we as educators must learn to recognize subtle, negative, racial attitudes. Prejudice is no joke—it is ignorance!

References

Boutte, G.S. (1992). Frustrations of an African-American parent: A personal and professional account. *Phi Delta Kappan, 73*(10), 786–788.

Boutte, G.S., & McCormick, C.B. (1992). Avoiding pseudomulticulturalism: Authentic multicultural activities. *Childhood Education, 68*(13), 140–144.

Cangelosi, J.S. (1992). *Systematic teaching strategies.* New York: Longman.

Derman-Sparks, L. (1992, March). *Anti-bias work with parents, staff and future teachers.* Paper presented at the meeting of the Southern Association on Children Under Six 43rd Annual Conference, Tulsa, OK.

Hendrick, J. (1992). *The whole child* (5th ed.). New York: Macmillan.

Jones, E., & Derman-Sparks, L. (1992). Meeting the challenge of diversity. *Young Children, 47*(2), 12–17.

Steele, C.M. (1992). Race and the schooling of black Americans. *The Atlantic Monthly, 269*(4), 69–78.

For further reading

Clark, L., DeWolf, S., & Clark, C. (1992). Teaching teachers to avoid having culturally assaultive classrooms. *Young Children, 47*(5), 4–9.

Derman-Sparks, L., & the A.B.C. Task Force. (1989). *Anti-bias curriculum: Tools for empowering young children.* Washington, DC: NAEYC.

Gough, P.B. (1993). Dealing with diversity. *Phi Delta Kappan, 75*(1), 3.

Howard, G.R. (1993). Whites in multicultural education: Rethinking our role. *Phi Delta Kappan, 75*(1), 36–41.

Majors, R., & Billson, J.M. (1992). *Cool pose: The dilemmas of black manhood in America.* New York: Touchstone.

National Association for the Education of Young Children. (1993). Enriching classroom diversity with books for children, in-depth discussion of them, and story-extension activities. *Young Children, 48*(3), 10–12.

Phillips, C.B. (1988). Nurturing diversity for today's children and tomorrow's leaders. *Young Children, 43*(2), 42–47.

Special Topics in Multicultural Education

Each year we try to focus in this section of this volume on selected special topics that have been of particular interest to those who live or work in multicultural settings. Topics are also chosen if they have a direct bearing on issues of equality of educational opportunity of concern to many educators.

The important changes in the demographic composition of the United States are examined because of the implications of these population changes for educators. We address also the struggle to empower both youths and adults to develop their own visions of the world as they become literate persons. The stereotyping of Native American culture is addressed in two excellent articles on Native Americans and the educational system. What children and teenagers learn from their out-of-school neighborhood environments is also of interest to teachers.

The history of efforts to desegregate American schools after the historic *Brown v. Board of Education* decision of the U.S. Supreme Court in 1954 is reviewed. The many evasive moves made to avoid cultural integration of schools is also documented. The executive summary of "How Schools Shortchange Girls," published by the American Association of University Women (AAUW) is also included.

Educators who work in the area of multicultural education are more concerned with research into how students can succeed in school and transcend the impact of socioeconomic inequality and feelings of powerlessness than they are with documenting the causes of school failure. (Albeit we also have to document the causes of failure as part of the process of developing the knowledge base to prevent or minimize it.) How at-risk minority students can overcome feelings of low self-esteem and develop positive, workable strategies for working through their problems in school are matters of great importance. The students of each racial, cultural, or religious minority group have had their own special historical and sociocultural experience with mainstream school curriculum. Multicultural education seeks to help all students to locate or situate their lives in the context of their developing individual identities within a pluralistic social order.

There is a need for continuing inservice preparation and training of teachers, even of experienced teachers, in order that they can learn the many skills needed to work with the diverse populations in the schools.

The essays in this unit are relevant to courses in educational policy studies, multicultural education, and cultural foundations of education.

Looking Ahead: Challenge Questions

How will the demographic changes going on in the composition of American society impact on the public schools?

How does one "empower" one's students? How does one develop a sense of social consciousness in students?

What are some concerns of Native Americans regarding how they are portrayed in the media? What can we learn from the Native American experience?

How can educators counter the out-of-school curriculum learned by youth in urban ghettos?

Why did so much resegregation occur as the nation attempted to desegregate?

Do you think girls are treated fairly in school? Why or why not? What are the gender issues in the field of education? What needs to be done to guarantee quality of educational opportunity for girls?

—F. S.

Unit 6

The Dynamic Demographic Mosaic Called America

Implications for Education

Leobardo F. Estrada

University of California, Los Angeles

There is a simple and recognized association between demographic growth and education. An increase in children requires more classrooms, more teachers, and more resources. Less obvious is the relationship between changes in the composition of families. It is the household that relates to schools as the basis of taxpayer support, as the unit that makes up neighborhood, and also as the site that determines for the most part which school will be attended. Needless to say, the number of children in a household compounds the effects that a household will have on local schools, for it is households with children that place intense demands on the schools. Finally, the concentration of households with children in certain areas focuses these effects on particular places.

Higher education, although less constrained by space, has a different relationship to its students as individuals. Nonetheless, universities recognize that the success of their students is associated with the relationship between their students and their families.

The numerical changes are visually evident in the changing cultural landscape—significant changes in the fabric and texture of the nation. For educators, it is these demographic changes that are more crucial. In sum, numbers help us to plan for the future.

TRENDS IN POPULATION GROWTH: CHANGING DEMOGRAPHICS

The U.S. population in 1990 stood at 249 million.[1] During the decade of the 1980s, the non-Hispanic population grew by 7% compared to 53% for the Hispanic population. Differential growth rates like these are significant in considering future school-age populations.

Between 1990 and 2005, the total U.S. population is expected to increase by about 11%. The K–12 population (from age 5 to

17) in 1990 was 53.2 million, and the traditional college-age population (from 18 to 24 years old) was 19 million. It is expected that, by the year 2005, these school-age groups will increase by 4.7% and 1.3%, respectively (see Table 1).

These modest growth trends for the United States mask the underlying differential in growth for minority populations. From 1990 to 2005, the population of African-Americans is expected to grow by 21% and the population of Latinos by 33%, compared to a 7.7% growth rate for the White population. Likewise, among the K–12 population, African-American and Latino populations will exceed the growth of the White population (11% for African-Americans and 20% for Latinos, compared to 9.2% for Whites). Among traditional college-age populations, African-Americans will increase 9.3%, and Latinos will increase by 40%, compared to −2.5% for the White population. Among school-age children, minority growth will exceed that of the majority population by a factor of 3:1.

In 1990, minority populations as a whole represented one of every four U.S. residents; however, among the school-age population, minority youth represented one of every three U.S. school-age youth.

TABLE 1
Summary of Growth by Race and Ethnicity

	1990		2005	
	Number	*1980-1990 % Growth*	*Number*	*1990-2005 % Growth*
Total	248,710	9.8	274,884	10.5
White	199,686	6.0	225,048	12.7
Black	29,986	13.2	36,816	22.7
Latino[a]	22,354	53.0	30,795	37.8
Other	9,805	45.1	13,020	32.8
K-12				
White	34,476		37,118	7.6
Black	6,838		7,889	15.4
Latino	5,428		6,848	26.1
18-24				
White	17,193		21,188	23.2
Black	3,642		4,198	15.3
Latino	3,127		3,599	15.1

a. The Latino population may be of any race.

From *Education and Urban Society*, Vol. 25, No. 3, May 1993, pp. 231-245. © 1993 by Sage Publications, Inc. Reprinted by permission of Corwin Press, Inc.

TABLE 2
Fast-Growing States and the Ranking of
Population for Blacks, Latinos, and Asians

	State Rank for Group			1980-1990 % Growth
	Black	Latino	Asian	
Nevada	33	8	7	50.1
Alaska	41	21	5	36.9
Arizona	31	4	19	34.8
Florida	4	7	22	32.7
California	2	2	2	25.7
New Hampshire	43	39	32	20.5
Texas	3	3	14	19.4
Georgia	5	32	23	18.6
Utah	42	15	13	17.9
Washington	27	18	3	17.8

As will be noted in Table 2, there is a direct relationship between state population growth over the last decade and the proportion of state population represented by Latinos and Asians. Latinos and Asians, as the two fastest-growing ethnic/racial groups in the United States, fuel the growth rate of these states.

As indicated by the state data, where Hispanics, Asians, and African-Americans are concentrated in large numbers, growth invariably increased in the 1980s and is likely to continue growing in the near future. The exceptions to this pattern are New Hampshire and Utah, which grew rapidly despite the low levels of minority representation in the two states.

THE HISPANIC POPULATION OF THE UNITED STATES

Among the fastest-growing ethnic/racial groups in the United States, the Latino population numbered 22.4 million persons in 1990 (not counting the 3.5 million persons residing in Puerto Rico), which represents an increase of 53% over the 1980 figure of 14.6 million. As a result, the proportion of Latinos in the total population rose from 6% in 1980 to 9% in 1990. In 1990, 6 of every 10 Latinos said that they were of Mexican origin, making them the largest Hispanic group in the United States. Mexican-origin persons totaled 13.5 million persons, an increase of 54% over the last decade. Persons of Puerto Rican origin constitute 2.7 million persons, representing 12% of all U.S. Latinos. The slower growth of the Puerto Rican population, like that of the Cuban population, reflects a slower level of immigration but is, nevertheless, impressive compared to the growth of non-Latino groups. The category of "Other Hispanics," representing primarily Central and South American groups, grew by 67%, reflecting the high levels of immigration engendered by political and economic turmoil in their countries of origin.

With these high levels of growth, it is not surprising to find that the projections for Latinos indicate that the Latino population may reach 30 million by the year 2000, 49 million by 2020, and 80.7 million by 2050 (see Table 3).

In 1990, Latinos composed 9% of the U.S. population. These projections indicate that, by the year 2000, Latinos are likely to represent 11% of the population, rising thereafter to 15% by 2020 and possibly 21% by the year 2050. These figures are a stark reminder that Latino growth is truly impressive within a nation characterized by slow and stable growth.

THE CAUSES OF MINORITY GROWTH

Youthfulness

The causes of minority growth have been recognized for some time. The first is the youthfulness of minority populations. For example, Latinos are about 8 years younger than the non-Latino population. Youthfulness affects growth in two ways. First, a higher proportion of youthful women are likely to be in the childbearing age. Hispanic women, for example, represent 9% of the U.S. population, but they account for 12% of all births in the United States. When fertility is higher, as is the case particularly for Hispanic women, these higher proportions translate into more children for the near future. Currently, about 35% (8 million) of Latinos are below age 18, compared to 26% in the total U.S. population. By the year 2020, about 31% of Hispanics will he below the age of 18, compared to 22% of the total U.S. population.

Second, youthfulness results in a higher proportion of preteens yet to move through the childbearing ages. As these preteens move through the childbearing ages over the next 15 years, there will be more children in the far future as well. There is yet another aspect of youthfulness: A population that receives a sizable number of immigrants at the youthful working ages will "remain young" as the downward pressure on the median age balances out the upward pressure of the aging process.

Higher rates of fertility for minorities, particularly Hispanics, has the effect of restructuring the population from "below." The restructuring process is visible by the growing percentages of Hispanic, Asian, and Black public high school enrollments.

Immigration

Minority population growth, particularly among Asian and Latino populations, is fueled by continued immigration. During the last decade, the United States was the desired destination for 3.5 million immigrants from Asia, Mexico, and other Latin American nations.

The United States has historically been a recipient country for immigration. The amount of immigration has varied somewhat over time, but the largest difference in immigration has not been in magnitude but rather in the composition of immigrants.

Prior to 1960, the vast majority of immigrants were from Canada, Great Britain, and other European nations. As indicated in Table 4, since 1980, the vast majority of immigration has been from Mexico, other Latin American nations, and

TABLE 3
Projections of the Hispanic Population
of the United States (in Millions)

Year	Hispanic Population
1970	9.1
1980	14.6.
1990	22.4
1992	24.0
2000	30.0
2020	47-54
2050	74-96

TABLE 4
Origins of Foreign-Born in the United States, 1990 and 1980

		1990				1980	
Rank	Place	No. (Thousands)	%	Rank	Place	No. (Thousands)	%
	United States	19,767	100.0		United States	14,080	100.0
1	Mexico	4,298	21.7	1	Mexico	2,199	15.6
2	Philippines	913	4.6	2	Germany	849	6.0
3	Canada	745	3.8	3	Canada	843	6.0
4	Cuba	737	3.7	4	Italy	832	5.9
5	Germany	712	3.6	5	United Kingdom	669	4.8
6	United Kingdom	640	3.2	6	Cuba	608	4.3
7	Italy	581	2.9	7	Philippines	501	3.6
8	Korea	568	2.9	8	Poland	418	3.0
9	Vietnam	543	2.7	9	USSR	406	2.9
10	China	530	2.7	10	Korea	290	2.1
11	El Salvador	465	2.4	11	China	286	2.0
12	India	450	2.3	12	Vietnam	231	1.6
13	Poland	388	2.0	13	Japan	222	1.6
14	Dominican Republic	348	1.8	14	Portugal	212	1.5
15	Jamaica	334	1.7	15	Greece	211	1.5
16	USSR	334	1.7	16	India	206	1.5
17	Japan	290	1.5	17	Ireland	198	1.4
18	Colombia	286	1.4	18	Jamaica	197	1.4
19	Taiwan	244	1.2	19	Dominican Republic	169	1.2
20	Guatemala	226	1.1	20	Yugoslavia	153	1.1

Asian countries. Immigration has typically been regarded as a positive element. It is a common premise that immigration is a self-selecting process that brings risk-taking, highly motivated, and entrepreneurial individuals in search of opportunity. Many U.S. residents today are descendants of parents who were ambitious enough to move here and succeed in obtaining an economic foothold.

As indicated in Table 5, Hispanic foreign-born persons are concentrated in just a few of the states of the Union. This uneven distribution intensifies the impact of immigration on specific states and, within them, specific localities.

TABLE 5
Hispanic Foreign-Born by State, 1990

	Total Hispanic	Hispanic Foreign-Born	% Hispanic Foreign-Born
United States	21,900,089	7,699,820	35.2
California	7,557,550	3,295,826	43.6
Texas	4,294,120	1,105,591	25.8
New York	2,151,743	711,069	33.1
Florida	1,555,031	893,018	57.4
Illinois	878,682	352,302	40.1
New Jersey	720,344	268,090	37.2
Arizona	680,628	173,280	25.5
New Mexico	576,709	58,004	10.1
Colorado	419,322	46,021	11.0
Massachusetts	275,859	71,203	25.8
Pennsylvania	220,479	31,343	14.2
Washington	206,088	60,993	29.6
Connecticut	203,511	32,659	16.0
Michigan	189,915	26,690	14.0
Virginia	155,353	75,420	48.6
Ohio	131,983	16,888	12.8
Nevada	121,346	48,156	39.7
Maryland	119,984	60,802	50.7
Oregon	110,606	37,185	33.6
Georgia	101,379	43,450	42.9
Indiana	95,363	16,250	17.0
Louisiana	90,609	32,783	36.2
Kansas	90,289	20,406	22.6

The primary countries of origin of Latinos are indicated in Table 6. Mexico remains, by an overwhelming margin, the primary source of Latino immigration; yet, despite its magnitude, the base population of Mexican-origin persons born in and residing in the United States exceeds immigrants by a margin of 2:1. The other countries listed represent more recent immigration, as indicated by the high levels of "foreign-bornness" of the total population.

Finally, in the same manner that the Latino population is distributed in a concentrated manner, Latino foreign-born also arrive in the United States and distribute themselves in distinct patterns.

Immigrants are typically young, the majority being concentrated in the youthful working ages. If their numbers are large, immigration can reconstruct the population from the "middle."

TABLE 6
Hispanic Foreign-Born by Country of Origin

	Total Population	Foreign-Born	% Foreign-Born
Mexican	13,393,208	4,447,439	33.2
Cuban	1,053,197	750,609	71.3
Dominican	520,151	356,971	68.6
Central American			
Costa Rican	57,223	48,264	84.3
Guatemalan	268,779	232,977	86.7
Honduran	131,066	114,603	87.4
Nicaraguan	202,658	171,950	84.8
Salvadoran	565,081	472,885	83.7
Other Central or South American	7,010	6,339	90.4
South American			
Argentinean	100,921	97,422	96.5
Bolivian	38,073	33,637	88.4
Chilean	68,799	61,212	89.0
Colombian	378,726	303,918	80.2
Equadorian	191,198	147,867	77.3
Peruvian	175,035	152,315	87.0
Uruguayan	21,996	21,628	98.3

The United States is currently in one of its periods of nativism in which the voices calling for more restrictive immigration policies are the loudest. However, historical data confirm that, despite these cycles of anti-immigration sentiment, the United States requires immigration in order to grow and finds it economically desirable. Immigrants are highly motivated to mainstream into the economic society. This is evidenced by the 1.7 million individuals who took advantage of the amnesty provisions of the Immigration Reform and Control Act, allowing long-term residents to regularize their status. The hysteria against immigration can best be understood by recognizing the concentrated nature of immigration—one half of all Hispanic foreign-born residents reside in California, New York, and Florida (see Table 7). Not surprisingly, it is in these areas of the country that immigration issues are felt with such high levels of intensity.

Combining the restructuring process of immigration with the process of population restructuring from below attributable to the differential fertility mentioned earlier, the U.S. population is undergoing a dramatic shift in composition, with its impacts felt most in geographic areas of the United States where Asians and Hispanics are the most populous and where immigrants have settled.

Today, 1 of every 8 U.S. residents is African-American, 1 of every 11 U.S. residents is Latino, and 1 of every 34 U.S. residents is Asian or Pacific Islander. By the turn of the century, 1 of every 3 U.S. residents will be African-American, Latino, or Asian.

The primary conclusion that can be drawn from the information on population growth is that minority populations will continue to grow into the new century and beyond and that the educational demands required by this growing population will challenge educators to understand the nature of this growth.

CHILDREN AND HOUSEHOLD FORMATION

How families arrange themselves into households will condition the effects of future growth. Table 8 reminds us of the dynamic manner in which families arrange and rearrange patterns of living. Over the last two decades, the trend has been

TABLE 7
Primary State of Residence of
the Hispanic-Origin Groups, 1990

Mexican		Puerto Rican		Cuban		Salvadoran	
CA	6,070,637	NY	1,046,896	FL	675,786	CA	338,769
TX	3,899,518	NJ	304,179	NJ	87,085	TX	58,128
AZ	619,435	FL	240,673	NY	77,016	NY	47,350
IL	612,442	IL	147,201	CA	75,034	MD	19,122
NM	329,233	MA	146,015	OH	45,911	NJ	16,817
Guatemalan		Nicaraguan		Honduran		Colombian	
CA	159,177	FL	79,056	CA	30,284	NY	107,377
NY	21,995	CA	74,119	NY	26,169	FL	83,634
IL	16,017	NY	11,011	FL	23,900	NJ	52,210
FL	13,558	TX	7,911	VA	23,537	CA	41,562
TX	11,724	LA	4,935	TX	10,622	TX	16,295
Peruvian		Equadorian		Argentinean		Dominican	
CA	45,885	NY	89,838	CA	30,620	NY	357,868
NY	32,161	NJ	27,572	FL	14,226	FL	34,268
FL	24,777	CA	26,953				

TABLE 8
Changes in Family Composition 1970 and 1990 (in Percentages)

Family Households	Married Couple		Male Householder		Female Householder	
	1970	1990	1970	1990	1970	1990
White	89	83	2	4	9	13
Black	68	50	4	6	28	44
Latino	81	70	4	7	15	23

TABLE 9
Persons per Household, 1990

Group	Persons per Household
White	2.63
Owner	2.75
Renter	2.43
Black	2.87
Owner	3.14
Renter	2.68
Latino	3.44
Owner	3.56
Renter	3.36

a move toward single parenthood. This trend is found among all ethnic/racial groups.

An increase in single parenthood has influenced the decrease in average household size. Furthermore, household size is expected to decline even further with the expected increases in unmarrieds, childless couples, and lower levels of fertility for traditionally high-fertility minority populations, including Latino women.

Latinos continue to be characterized by larger than average families, in part because of higher fertility. As indicated in Table 9, the largest families are those in owner-occupied housing, a pattern similar to other ethnic/racial groups. Recent studies indicate that fertility among women from all ethnic and racial groups is decreasing and converging around the rates for White women. However, the highest fertility is found among foreign-born Latinas. With continued immigration, the fertility of Latinas will converge at a much lower rate.

Population growth occurs either from immigration, which has been shown to be high for Latinos, or from fertility, which remains higher (although at a decreasing rate) for Latinas. Thus it is not surprising that the Latino population is undergoing rapid growth. However, it is important to recognize the wide variation among those high growth rates. There exist important differences between native and foreign-born Latinos, first and subsequent generations of Latinos, and borderland and interior-residing Latinos, as well as distinct patterns that are conditioned by socioeconomic and educational attainment. For example, recent census results indicate that interethnic inter-marriage rates continue to increase among Latinos. The implications of these high rates of intermarriage are unclear for future growth rates, although a reasonable assumption is that they will moderate growth. In 1990, about one of every three Cuban and Puerto Rican marriages was an intermarriage, compared to about one of every five marriages for Central and South Americans and one of every six marriages for Mexican-origin persons.

Despite these variations, in general, where Latinos reside, household formation is high, fertility is above the average, more

6. SPECIAL TOPICS IN MULTICULTURAL EDUCATION

TABLE 10
Families by Number of Children Under 18,
1970 and 1990 (in Percentages)

Group	Number of Children Under 18			
	None	1	2	3 or more
White				
1970	45	18	18	19
1990	53	20	18	9
Black				
1970	39	18	15	29
1990	41	25	19	14
Latino				
1970	30	20	19	31
1990	37	23	21	19

Group	Number of Children Under 6		
	None	1	2 or more
White			
1990	78	15	7
Black			
1990	72	19	9
Latino			
1990	65	23	12

children are found in families (see Table 10), and the size of households is likely to be above the average as well.

REGIONAL CONCENTRATION OF GROWTH

Future growth will be concentrated in particular areas—those with concentrations of minority populations—intensifying education needs in certain places. Differential regional growth has been ongoing for over a century. In brief, the Southwest has experienced dramatic growth, whereas the Northeast and Midwest have experienced low rates of growth. Not surprisingly, it is in these high-growth regions that educational demands continue to require year-round schools to alleviate overcrowded classes, teacher shortages, school facility construction, and expansion of higher education institutions. Equally important are the educational strategies and tactics required to manage lack of growth. Retrenchment strategies, decisions regarding school closures, the redeployment of staff, and the need to redefine the mission of institutions are equally challenging when the goal is to maintain quality and be fair to all concerned.

TABLE 11
Growth of Population by Region (in Millions)

Region	1970	1980	1990	1970-1990 % Change
Northeast	49.1	49.1	50.8	3.5
New England	11.8	12.3	13.2	11.9
Middle Atlantic	37.2	36.8	37.6	1.1
Midwest	56.6	58.9	59.7	5.5
East North Central	40.3	41.7	42.0	4.2
West North Central	16.3	17.2	17.7	8.6
South	62.8	75.4	85.4	36.0
South Atlantic	30.7	37.0	43.6	42.0
East South Central	12.8	14.7	15.2	18.8
West South Central	19.3	23.7	26.7	38.3
West	34.8	43.2	52.8	51.7
Mountain	8.3	11.4	13.7	65.1
Pacific	26.5	31.8	39.1	47.6

Within the regions noted in Table 11 are numerous metropolitan areas where Latinos are concentrated. These represent the kinds of places where educational decision makers must deal with growth within the context of declining revenues.

These metropolitan areas are more than geographic areas; they represent places where Latinos are a visible presence in the community as well as in the schools (see Table 12). In many of these areas, Latinos overlap significantly with Asians, American-Indians, and African-American concentrations. These urban areas also contain high proportions of immigrants in search of an economic foothold, high numbers of non-English speakers, as well as the usual issues of all cities—community safety, lack of affordable housing, shrinking base of manufacturing jobs, growing number of homeless, deteriorating infrastructure, traffic congestion, and poverty.

SOCIOECONOMIC CONDITIONS OF LATINOS

Latinos have a low educational attainment compared to those who are non-Latino. Only about one half (53%) of Latinos 25 years and older report completing high school, compared to 82% of non-Latinos. Only 9% have graduated from college, compared to 22% of non-Latinos. Nonetheless, the decade of the 1980s was, in retrospect, a decade of educational progress for Latinos.

Low educational attainment is responsible in large part for higher levels of unemployment among Latinos. For example, in March 1992, 11.3% of Latinos were unemployed compared to 6.5% of non-Latinos. The jobs that Latinos hold are also more likely to be vulnerable to economic dislocations. Latino men are more likely to be employed in lower-paying, less stable, and

TABLE 12
Most Hispanic Metropolitan Areas, 1980-1990

Area	Number (Thousands)	1980-1990 Change (%)	% of Total Metro
Los Angeles, CA	4,779	26.4	32.9
New York, NY	2,779	3.1	15.4
Miami, FL	1,062	20.8	33.3
San Francisco, CA	970	16.5	15.5
Chicago, IL	893	1.6	11.1
Houston, TX	772	19.7	20.8
San Antonio, TX	620	21.5	47.6
Dallas-Ft. Worth, TX	519	32.6	13.4
San Diego, CA	511	34.2	20.4
El Paso, TX	412	23.3	69.6
Phoenix, AZ	345	40.6	16.3
McAllen, TX	327	35.4	85.2
Fresno, CA	237	29.7	35.5
Denver, CO	226	14.2	12.2
Philadelphia, PA	226	3.9	3.8
Washington, DC	225	20.7	5.7
Brownsville, TX	213	24.0	81.9
Boston, MA	193	5.0	4.6
Corpus Christi, TX	182	7.3	52.0
Albuquerque, NM	178	14.4	37.1
Sacramento, CA	172	34.7	11.6
Tucson, AZ	163	25.5	24.5
Austin, TX	160	45.6	20.5
Bakersfield, CA	152	34.8	28.0
Tampa, FL	139	28.2	6.7
Laredo, TX	125	34.4	93.9
Visalia, CA	121	26.9	38.8
Salinas, CA	120	22.5	33.6
Stockton, CA	113	38.4	23.4

more hazardous occupations than are non-Latinos. Most Latino men are employed in service, machine operations, precision production, and farming. Non-Latino males are more likely to be employed in managerial-professional and technical-sales occupations. Latina workers are more similar to non-Latina workers, although they are more likely to work in factories as machine operators and less likely to hold managerial-professional positions.

Given this job structure, it is not surprising to find that Latinos have lower incomes than do non-Latinos. The median family income of Latinos ($23,400) was about $14,000 less than non-Latino White families. Conversely, Latino families are more likely to he poorer than non-Latino families. About 26% of Latino families were below the poverty level in 1991 compared to 10% of non-Latino White families. Poverty disproportionately affects children. About 41% of Latino children live in poverty compared to 13% of non-Latino children.

CONCLUSIONS

For the Latino population, educational attainment represents a critical foundation for that community's struggle for self-determination. To participate fully in the U.S. economy, to engage forcefully in civic activity, requires basic skills in literacy, training in English as a second language, affordable child care, and opportunities to move into the economic mainstream.

The Latino population is numerically too large to have its needs ignored, and the educational enterprise must be responsive to the demographic context of change. Decades of neglect and wishful thinking that Latinos would not differ substantially from prior immigrant groups must come to an end. Investment in the educational enterprise demands that a large portion be devoted to the needs of Latino children and youth currently in the schools and to the needs of those who will be there over the next decades.

NOTE

1. Discussion in this and following sections is based on U.S. Bureau of the Census (1990, 1991, 1992a, 1992b, 1922c).

REFERENCES

U.S. Bureau of the Census. (1990). *The foreign born population in the United States: 1990* (CPH-L98). Washington, DC: U.S. Government Printing Office.

U.S. Bureau of the Census. (1991). *Statistical abstract of the United States: 1991* (111th ed.). Washington, DC: U.S. Government Printing Office.

U.S. Bureau of the Census. (1992a). *Current population reports: Hispanic population of the United States: March 1991* (pp. 20–455). Washington, DC: U.S. Government Printing Office.

U.S. Bureau of the Census. (1992b). *Population projections of the United States by age, sex, race, and Hispanic origin: 1992 to 2050* (pp. 25–1092). Washington, DC: U.S. Government Printing Office.

U.S. Bureau of the Census. (1992c). *Statistical abstract of the United States: 1992* (112th ed.). Washington, DC: U.S. Government Printing Office.

Literacy, Social Movements, and Class Consciousness: Paths from Freire and the São Paulo Experience

María Del Pilar O'Cadiz and Carlos Alberto Torres

María del Pilar O'Cadiz *is the After School Program coordinator for the Boyle Heights Elementary Institute, a nonprofit organization that provides educational and other services to inner-city youth in East Los Angeles. She is also a doctoral candidate in the Division of Social Sciences and Comparative Education in the Graduate School of Education at the University of California, Los Angeles.*

Carlos Alberto Torres *is a professor. He is Head of the Division of Social Sciences and Comparative Education in the Graduate School of Education at the University of California, Los Angeles. He is also Assistant Dean of Students at the GSE and the coordinator of Comparative and Topical Studies at the UCLA Latin American Center.*

During a socialist administration in São Paulo, Brazil, from 1989 to 1992, a movement for literacy training of youths and adults (MOVA) and for a curriculum reform was established in the city's elementary schools. This article describes the socialist educational projects and Freire's work in São Paulo. It provides both a theoretical discussion of the projects' Freirean premises and a narrative of the experience of a particular group of literary learners in one São Paulo favela (shantytown). The authors demonstrate a special concern for the articulation between the public sector (i.e., a government agency) and various social movements, as manifested in the MOVA literacy movement. The conclusion calls for "long life" to the creative imagination that inspires and propels such projects of education for social change. LITERACY TRAINING, PAULO FREIRE, SOCIAL MOVEMENTS

SAO PAULO, SOCIAL MOVEMENTS, AND LITERACY TRAINING: POPULAR EDUCATION IN POWER

With support from the National Academy of Education Spencer Fellowship (1990–1992), Carlos Alberto Torres studied literacy-training policy formulation in the municipality of São Paulo, Brazil, during the socialist administration of the Workers' Party, or Partido dos Trabalhadores (PT), which held the municipal government from 1989 to 1992. The PT mayor, Luiza Erundina de Sousa, appointed Paulo Freire as Secretary of Education in 1989. Freire resigned from this position in May 1991, in order to resume writing and lecturing, and continued as an *ad honorem* educational advisor to the Municipal Secretariat of Education. This collaboration is confirmed by Freire's signature—jointly with Mayor Erundina de Sousa, and the new secretary of education, Mario Sergio Cortella—to a public document addressed to the city's educators, published in the *Diário Official do Município de São Paulo* (Municipal Secretariat of Education 1992b), long after his resignation.

During his tenure as Secretary of Education, Freire implemented drastic changes in municipal education, including a comprehensive curriculum reform in the K–8 grades, new models of school management through the activation of School Councils—including teachers, principals, parents, and government officials—and the launching of the Movement of Literacy Training for Youths and Adults, or Movimento de Alfabetizaçao de Jovens e Adultos (MOVA), built on participative planning and delivery with support from nongovernment organizations or social movements (Torres 1992, 1994a, 1994b; Freire and Torres 1994).

Torres's research focused on the articulation between the public sector and social movements. Using ethnographic methods, nonparticipant observation, structured interviews, survey research, and discourse analysis in documenting the São Paulo

From *Anthropology & Education Quarterly*, Volume 25, No. 3, September 1994, pp. 208-225. © 1994 by the American Anthropological Association. Reprinted by permission. Not for sale or further reproduction.

experience, we have reached some preliminary results in our study of the Municipal Secretariat of Education's extensive educational reform efforts.[1]

Fascinating as Brazilian educational history is, the PT's electoral victory signified a unique experience in local (municipal) governance in São Paulo by a mass party. The complexities and historical ironies embodied in the PT—a party that portrays a socialist ideology—are well captured by J. Humphrey, who observes that:

> the Workers Party in Brazil is curiously out of step with both world and Brazilian political trends. It is a mass party with a commitment to socialism which has grown out of the labor movement and grass-roots activism during the 1980s. It is a party which has huge electoral success in a country where the labor movement has been weak and political parties have had little grass-roots organization. [1993:347]

This short article describes the overall educational project of the PT and the work of Paulo Freire in São Paulo, and documents how a model based on class analysis and a commitment to socialism makes use of literacy training as a means of political struggle, in new and unexpected ways. In so doing, however, the MOVA model in São Paulo is not blind to the contradictions and tensions emerging in any reformist attempt. The first section outlines the major features of the PT's educational policies. The second section describes the pedagogical philosophy of conscientization underscoring the Freirean model which inspired the PT's educational work in São Paulo and explains how this emancipatory educational paradigm and Freire's unique epistemological stance embodies the principles of popular education in Latin America. In that context, the third section offers a narrative of the experience at a micro level, focusing on the practice of a particular literacy training group in a shantytown of São Paulo. The concluding section offers an after-thought on emancipatory educational practices.

BUILDING MOVA AND CONSTRUCTING A POPULAR PUBLIC SCHOOL: THE SÃO PAULO EXPERIENCE

Truly, only the oppressed are able to conceive of a future totally distinct from their present, insofar as they arrive at a consciousness of a dominated class. The oppressors, as the dominating class, cannot conceive of the future unless it is the preservation of their present as oppressors. In this way, whereas the future of the oppressed consists in the revolutionary transformation of society, without which their liberation will not be verified, the oppressor's future consists in the simple modernization of society, which permits the continuation of its class supremacy. [Freire 1972:32]

The underlying motto of Freire's administration of the Municipal Secretariat of Education was the collective construction of an *escola pública popular* (popular public school) that guarantees the school's autonomy in the definition of its own pedagogic program. All the schools of the municipal system were given the option to either formulate their own independent project or to subscribe to the secretariat's proposed Interdisciplinary Project.[2] This choice was made at each municipal

school by a democratic consensus of school administrative personnel, teachers, and parents represented in the school councils.

On another front, given the high rate of illiteracy in Brazil (19 percent of the population over age 15), it was an imperative for the PT secretariat to include in its proposal for democratizing the city's education an explicit policy of support for the social movements that for the past three decades—beginning with the Movement for Popular Culture led by Freire in the early 1960s—have worked with the poorest sectors of the population (many of which are immigrants from the Northeast, the poorest region of Brazil and the home region for Freire and Mayor Erundina). This intent materialized immediately in the first months of Freire's administration in the development of MOVA. This historic effort to democratize literacy is unique in that the state, represented by the municipal government, lent financial resources and technical expertise to social movements already active in the area of literacy training and political conscientization of the popular sectors, rather than imposing a particular program of literacy training and/or creating a separate entity or movement parallel to already existing grassroots efforts.[4]

In October 1992 in the official organ of the municipal government, *Diário Oficial do Município de São Paulo,* Mayor Erundina, Freire, and Freire's successor, Mario Sergio Cortella (1991–1992), signed a letter addressed to "those who together with us construct a public education of quality for São Paulo." In this letter the city's educators are reminded of one of the initial statements made to them in February 1989, made by Freire, when the PT first took hold of the Municipal Secretariat of Education. Freire wrote:

> We should not call the people to school to receive instructions, postulations, recipes, threats, reprimands and punishments, but rather to participate in the collective construction of knowledge, which goes beyond the knowledge of past experience and takes into account the necessities of the people and turns that knowledge into an *instrument of struggle,* making possible the people's transformation into subjects of their own history. The popular participation in the creation of culture and of education breaks with the tradition that only the elite is competent and knows what the necessities and interests of society are. The school should also be a center for the irradiation of popular culture, at the service of the community, not to consume it but to create it. [Municipal Secretariat of Education 1992a:1, emphasis in original]

The same letter goes on to recount the achievements of the PT's project for municipal educational reform during its four-year tenure, citing the construction of 65 new schools and the renovation of 178 of the total of 691 municipal schools and the extension of preschool education of 145 thousand more children, as well as literacy training to 312 thousand adults and youths. They point to one of the major accomplishments of the administration: the passing of a new municipal legislation, *Estatuto do Magistério,* that protects teacher salaries and promotes the professional valorization of teachers. The authors of the letter point also to the fomentation of school autonomy through participative planning and administration. They affirm that it is through such a process of the construction of the autonomy of local schools that the planning of municipal education "stops being the domain only of technicians and specialists, making progressively more explicit the priorities and necessities, the difficulties and the interests of various social groups, and the limitations of the municipal government as a sphere of power, [hence making the autonomy of the schools] an excellent instrument for the construction and affirmation of citizenship." But the mayor and the former and present secretaries of education conclude by asserting that, although they are "certain that this process was not free of errors, [such mistakes] cannot be taken in isolation, for they are situated within the framework of a politics that seeks the valorization of public education" (Municipal Secretariat of Education 1992a:2). It is this same emphasis on the historical process of education as an instrument of popular struggle which was expressed by some of the leaders of the social movements that collaborated with the secretariat, in MOVA. When asked how the relationship between social movements and the state (particularly the Municipal Secretariat of Education) is carried out under the PT administration, they responded:

> Since when did we participate in something so beautiful?
> The government of Ms. Mayor Luiza Erundina is an administration oriented toward the popular masses. . . . She had already worked here in the region [the impoverished periphery of the city]. . . . This government opened up a space to our movements. [MOVA] was built upon the basis of Paulo Freire's ideas. Past experiences such as MOBRAL and Suplência [a sort of adult night school] do not reach the quality of MOVA. [MOVA] works with our reality, investigating the reality of the community. . . . MOVA is the conquering of our rights; it is not a mere "opportunity" handed down to us.
> Under the PT administration, for the first time a new experience reached the population of the city, together [the municipal government and social movements], despite the difficulties confronted, have tried to get it right.
> [From field interviews, September 1992]

When asked to speak to the future of MOVA (given the imminent possibility that the municipal government could change)[5] and to that of social movements in Brazil in general, one MOVA activist insisted: "As long as there are people, there will be a movement" (from an October 1992 interview). In all its simplicity, this statement demonstrates the inherent grassroots nature of the PT political organization and anticipated the fluid, albeit at times conflictual, relationship between the state and social movements which the PT administration in São Paulo achieved.

THE PT POLITICAL-PEDAGOGIC AGENDA AND ITS FREIREAN ROOTS

> We have worked only four years at constructing, while the Right has worked 400 years at destroying. . . . It is always the case that we never learn everything at once, but that we are constantly learning. . . . Without a doubt this administration opened up space for that learning process to occur.
> —Leader of a São Paulo grassroots movement, 1992

In accordance with the PT's grassroots tradition, instead of imposing a reform package upon the schools and the social movements that agreed to work in the MOVA coalition, the PT

secretariat insisted on the autonomy of both. However the PT does promote a specific political-pedagogical agenda that entails establishing within the schools and literacy movement a Freirean pedagogic practice within an emancipatory curriculum paradigm (Damasceno et al. 1989). To this end, the secretariat, in collaboration with university specialists, developed for the municipal schools the Interdisciplinary Project (Inter Project). Inspired by various educational approaches and theories (e.g. Cagliari 1989; Campos 1989; Campos and Freire 1991; Fazenda 1979; Ferreiro 1985, 1988; Ferreiro and Teberosky 1979; Freire and Torres 1994; Japiassú 1976; Piaget 1989; Vygotsky 1978; Weisz 1985), the Inter Project held as its basis of theory and praxis Freire's methodology of *thematic investigation*. The Freirean model calls for investigating the reality of learners in order to discover the *significant situations* of their lives that can be used as *generative themes* in the organization of knowledge within an interdisciplinary curriculum. This process is undertaken collectively (by the school community or by literacy workers and learners) and aims at the construction of a locally relevant curriculum that, at the same time, relates that local reality to a broad range of individual, community, and societal problems (e.g. interpersonal relations in the family; peer group relations in school; race, gender, and class relations in society; public transportation; electoral politics; issues of public health; crime and public safety; air and water contamination in an industrial city like São Paulo). This model also calls for a dialogical approach to teaching which favors active learning (as opposed to the passive variety) and collective discussion and debate (as opposed to lecturing) in an ongoing process that leads to raising the critical consciousness of the learners.

This educational model and its political-pedagogical principles were actively disseminated by the PT secretariat to teachers in the schools and to literacy workers participating in MOVA, through the publication of a series of pamphlets (*Cadernos de Formação*) that were used as the basis for discussion and debate in regularly scheduled seminars and teacher-training groups (Grupos de Formação). Pedagogic Coordinators in schools that voluntarily opted to join the secretariat's Inter Project were trained by secretariat personnel at the Nucleus de Ação Educativa ("Nuclei of Educational Action")—the newly formed regional administrative centers that replaced the former Delegacias de Ensino (schooling precincts that carried out more of a "policing" role). Literacy-group "supervisors," elected by their respective social movements, met regularly for training with a MOVA coordinating team of the secretariat. The supervisors, in turn, met regionally with each other to coordinate their literacy training efforts, and weekly with the literacy workers in their respective organizations to provide pedagogic orientation. The secretariat also organized, for the first time in the history of the city, two Congresses of Municipal Educators (held in 1991 and 1992) as a further means of communicating its political-pedagogic project and giving educators a forum for sharing and discussing their experiences with their peers. Overall, the model articulated by the secretariat was inspired by Freire's political philosophy of education, in the context of debates in Brazil on the role of education for social and political empowerment.

POPULAR EDUCATION, PEDAGOGY OF THE OPPRESSED, AND CONSCIENTIZATION

What has made Freire's political philosophy of education so current and universal, placing him and some of the *generative themes* suggested by his method at the center of educational debates in critical pedagogy for the last three decades? Influenced by the work of psychotherapists such as Franz Fanon and Erich Fromm, Freire argues, in his *Pedagogy of the Oppressed* (1970), that few human interpersonal relations are exempt from oppression of one kind or another; by reason of race, class, or gender, people tend to be perpetrators and/or victims of oppression. He points out that class exploitation, racism, and sexism are the most conspicuous forms of dominance and oppression, but he recognizes that there exists oppression on other grounds such as religious beliefs or political affiliation.

Freire's *Pedagogy of the Oppressed* was influenced by a myriad of philosophical currents including phenomenology, existentialism, Christian personalism, humanist marxism, and Hegelianism. Freire's new philosophical synthesis calls for dialogue and ultimately social awareness as a way to overcome domination and oppression among and between human beings. Freire's epistemological and pedagogical contributions have been very important for the constitution of different models of popular education.

The term *popular education* was first used in 19th-century Latin America to designate public schooling, that is, free compulsory education for everybody. In the early 1960s, popular education was associated with radical factions within the Latin American Left, and particularly with Freire's work in Brazil. *Pedagogy of the Oppressed* constitutes an intellectual and political manifesto of that time. Popular education starts from a political and social analysis of the living conditions of the poor and their outstanding problems (e.g., under- and unemployment, homelessness, and street children) and attempts to engage the poor in individual and collective awareness of those conditions. This strategy takes into account, in the design and operation of educational programs, the collective and individual experiences of the poor, disenfranchised, and oppressed. And it is precisely this experience that is understood as previous knowledge; that is, such knowledge is viewed as the starting point for the formulation of basic programmatic actions, both educationally and politically.

Conscientization, the neologism widely disseminated by Freire in his writings, constitutes a central aim of popular education. Conscientization goes beyond the mere acquisition of new knowledge for social awareness and becomes a political program that links, in a Gramscian fashion, cultural politics to class struggle. More contemporary though, conscientization as cultural politics has been redefined to account for nonclass forms of exclusion, including gender, race-ethnicity, minority religious affiliations, rural-urban disparities, and sexual preference.

Popular education stresses working in groups rather than individualistic approaches and emphasizes collaboration rather than competition. Despite its political aims, popular education tries to develop concrete skills or abilities including literacy or numeracy and strives to arouse pride, a sense of dignity,

personal confidence, and self-reliance among the participants. Finally, these programs are usually originated by non-governmental organizations, churches, social movements, community organizations, and political parties, but they can also be originated by governments, as in Colombia and the Dominican Republic, with projects related to integrated rural development, or as in Sandinista Nicaragua, with the collective of popular education (Arnove 1986; Torres 1990). Popular education projects may be directed toward adults as well as children. Examples in the United States can be found in the newsletter *Seeds of Fire* from the Network of North American Popular Educators, or in the recently created Popular Education Graduate Program at the Lindeman Center, Northern Illinois University, in Chicago (Torres and Fishman, in press).

Let us now look through a small window and observe what happened in the literacy-training working groups in São Paulo.

THE CONTRADICTIONS OF LITERACY TRAINING: FROM THEORY TO PRAXIS (A NARRATIVE)

The literacy group visited was made up of residents of the *favela* (shantytown) located in the southern peripheral region of São Paulo.[6] A 27-year-old male literacy monitor (adult education teacher or facilitator, working in MOVA), named Vinicius, met me at the southernmost station of the subway line. We then took a 15-minute bus ride over ill-kept roads to reach the favela. While waiting at the bus stop, after the literacy class, several buses drove past us, even though we signaled for them to stop. Vinicius explained to me that many bus drivers are afraid to pick up passengers in front of the favela in the late evening, an indication of the violence that most Brazilians associated with favela life.

After walking over open sewer channels and through narrow corridors created by the makeshift plywood, zinc, cardboard, and precariously constructed brick walls of the favela dwellings, we reached an open paved area where children were playing soccer. On that cold winter evening many wore short sleeves and sandals. As we approached them, a young girl began to announce our arrival, running around and singing out, "O professor chegou, o professor chegou (The teacher is here)!" Vinicius pointed to the small one-room structure that was the community center where the literacy classes were held three nights a week from 8 pm to 10 pm. Inside, a boy had already begun to enthusiastically arrange the desks before the arrival of the adult literacy learners. The center was constructed by the favela residents to provide a space where they could realize community organizational meetings, as well as social events like weddings and baptisms. In front of the community center stood a public telephone that residents had gained by submitting a petition to the city.

The group began to assemble in the classroom. One woman was dragged in by her niece (the girl that announced our arrival). The girl pulled on her aunt's arm and coaxed her to take a seat. The class got off to a slow start as people socialized among each other while others sat silently. Not including myself and the monitor, four men and seven women between the ages of 30 and 60 were present. (According to the monitor a few students were absent that day.) I was introduced as a North American teacher who is there to observe and learn about their literacy program. This captured the attention of the group. At this point the monitor—whose teaching style began to reveal itself as relaxed and dialogical—oriented the discussion toward a specific theme.

In an interview, Vinicius expressed his uncertainty with how to go about structuring his literacy lessons. Although he teaches history at a public high school, this was his first experience with adult literacy teaching—he had been working with this group since March 1990 (approximately five months prior to this interview). As an activist in a grassroots social movement and a sympathizer of the PT, he felt that his participation in the MOVA project was an essential part of his political activity, as an educator committed to the service of the popular sectors.[7] He was confident, however, that in its collective educational experience the class would help him to develop a methodology coherent with the learners' interests and needs. He stated that the most important aspect of his work with the literacy group was the "collective regeneration" of the students' own self-concept through the process of their reflection upon the world and themselves, their free expression of that world, and the problems of their everyday lives. Interestingly, one of the secretariat's pamphlets for the methodological orientation of literacy workers, *Reflexoes sobre o Processo Metodológico de Alfabetizaçao, Caderno de Formaçao 3,* states, in a similar fashion to Vinicius's articulation of the process of "collective regeneration," the following: "All the literacy activities should be based upon the text, on the social purpose that the literacy learners make of the language, that is, of their 'discourse' when it is they who speak and write, and from the discourse of the authors, when it is they [the literacy learners] who write" (1990:7).

The learners interviewed at this MOVA literacy group, or "nucleus," expressed satisfaction at the way their teacher was conducting the lessons. He was described as patient and respectful with them.

The two literacy classes I observed followed a cyclical structure that involves five stages. First, the monitor directs a group discussion around a theme that either he presents or emerges from the group. Next, the monitor focuses on vocabulary that emerges from the group's discussion to initiate writing activity among the students (i.e. he would write these words on the blackboard). Once a series of words that have arisen from the dialogue are written on the board, the students compose freely (according to their different levels) as the monitor circulates to provide guidance to the learners in their attempts at constructing written versions of their previous oral expressions. In the next stage, the monitor asks students to read back their compositions and writes some of their phrases on the board. In the final stage of the cycle, other students are asked to read the words or phrases on the board. From that point discussion continues with the generation of a new set of vocabulary and the initiation of a critical literacy learning process begins again. It is important to point out that during this open process of oral and written language expression there is little or no emphasis on grammatical structure or phonetic associations of letters or syllables (i.e. spelling) except for an occasional clarification made by the monitor.

The first literacy session, for example, began with the spontaneous discussion of how the favela came to be formed, as each student related their individual history coming to São Paulo, from the Northeast, and settling into the shanty town. A middle-aged woman—one of the more articulate literacy learners in the group—told of how the community had attempted to get legal permission to occupy the land:

We [the community] ran around every where with a signed paper [a petition]—we even had the documents for the land—and we went over to the city hall. . . . We live here even though we know there is an owner, but no one knows who that owner is. . . . If only everybody would act together, with a lawyer, to better [our] conditions. We would like to have a lawyer explain everything just right to us; we do not want to live this way. There is no light or water. We would like some kind of guarantee. That is what we would like.

At this point the monitor interjected with the suggestion that the group write about their own history: "How is it that you arrived here? How long ago was it? What brought you to the city?" The students then began to write words or phrases depending on their individual levels, which according to the monitor ranged from virtually completely illiterate to semiliterate. One woman had difficulty writing the name of the city of Bahia from where she comes (Palmares). She wrote it out slowly under the teachers guidance and read it back joltingly: "Pal-ma-res."

After about fifteen minutes, the monitor elicited a phrase written by one of the more advanced students, "eu trabalhava na roça (I worked in the fields)," and wrote it on the board in both cursive and print ("so that they learn to read both," he said). He read the phrase back to the class and then called on individuals to do the same. At this point another discussion evolved about who had done farmwork and the different kinds of crops with which many of them had worked. From that discussion the monitor extracted new vocabulary from the literacy learners (e.g. *milho* [corn], *café* [coffee], *mandioca* [manioc], *arroz* [rice] and wrote it on the board repeating the cycle of *discussion-writing-reading-writing-discussion*.

The final part of the evening was dedicated to deciding what the group would buy with the monies allocated to them by the secretariat. Several suggestions arose, including buying chalk, notebooks, and books and magazines to read, and setting up a bulletin board to display students' work.

In the second literacy class I attended, 15 literacy learners participated. The session's theme focused around the comparison of Brazil to the United States (as suggested by the monitor since I was there to contribute to the discussion). Ideas that emerged from the group included:

It is better there [in the United States] than it is here. I think it is a rich country.
I think that the foreigner is more intelligent than the Brazilian. In Brazil things are much more laid back. There they have more money, more intelligence. . . . They have more wealth, and so it's a problem of there being more movement over there than there is here in Brazil.

After I spoke briefly with the group about the problems we face in the United States (e.g., homelessness, racism), the monitor wrote the words *Estados Unidos* and *Brasil, país rico* (rich country) and *país pobre* (poor country) on the board. The question arose as to what constitutes a poor or rich country. The group came to the conclusion that Brazil was in reality a rich country but that its wealth and privileges are in the hands of a few. One student succinctly articulated this contradiction, relating the following axiom: "*é o pedreiro quem faz a obra e o engenheiro quem fica com a fama* (it is the worker who builds the project and the engineer who goes away with the fame)." Another added, "Yes, we build houses but don't have anywhere to live." Reflecting the discussion that ensued within the literacy group around class relations of power and domination, privilege and disadvantage, in Brazilian society, the monitor wrote on the board the words *fazenda—fazendeiro* (ranch—rancher) and *indústria—industrial* (industry—industrialist), which the students copied in their notebooks. And from there, the cyclical process of dialogue and writing continued—the reading of the world and the word (Campos and Freire 1991; Freire and Macedo 1987; Torres 1992a)—until the end of the class.

How did the students come to revise their initial intuitions about their own subordinate condition vis-à-vis the United States? This process of critical understanding was the result of the dialogue that evolved in the group under the guidance of the monitor. This dialogue challenged the common sense of the group, particularly by emphasizing the disparities between the human, cultural, and economic endowments of Brazil, and the disproportionate power of the elites in the use of those resources.

The contrast between the material conditions of Brazil and the United States was part of this common sense. For the literacy learners, the importance of mass media and the images of comfort and the "good life" portrayed around North American lifestyles—so contrasting with these Brazilians harsh conditions—helped to romanticize in their own common sense the situation in the United States. When O'Cadiz introduced the issues of racism and other disparities and social problems experienced in the United States, the participants of the dialogue began to demystify this Hollywood-like view of the world and then turned critically to look at their own contradictory reality in Brazil.

With respect to their educational history, most students in the group had at least a few years of formal schooling. The reasons most cited for not having continued their education were work and marriage:

I studied when I was very small; I think I wasn't even ten years old. I then went to work in the fields, and I thought that [school] had no importance and studied no more.
I studied in the countryside, but our school was backward; we studied and worked in the fields. Back then we were willing to learn but there was no way [to continue to study].
Father said, "What good is studying if you're not going to learn anything worthwhile; you'll only learn to write a bunch of foolishness." Then my oldest brother said, "Let's let her study, at least until she learns to write her own name."
I had 70 days of study, and that was all I studied over there in Bahia. After my boyhood, I began to work. Soon I married and

then things got harder—jut to work, to live—and so study I knew no more.

When asked what it was like to live his life as a person who is unable to read and write, the oldest student, a 64-year-old man, described the immense envy he felt when he saw someone writing: tinha a maior enveja do mundo (I had the greatest envy in the world)." A female student in her thirties spoke of how an illiterate person has to depend on others: "I think that study is a good thing because a person without an education goes around having to ask others. When we are educated, we see something and we already know it all, right?"

But the most common association was that literacy will help you get a better job and give you access to financial rewards:

I would like to study because an education is important. It can help you get a better job. As for myself, I don't have a better job because I haven't studied.
I have more motivation to learn mathematics because soon I will retire and then I will be able to take care of a small business and make a little more to help me out in life. That is what I am interested in.

From a different perspective, a 35-year-old husband and father articulated a desire for intellectual growth and a curiosity for the unknown. He muses:

We want to learn what is in the project for us to learn: to write, to do arithmetic, to read a word that we don't know, or maybe something new, that we have never seen before. . . . We want to learn about those modern things—maybe a magazine with a different name, a foreign name that we don't know of and that we want to learn about—so that we can move ahead. We are more-or-less backward. We want to leave here more aware than when we arrived.

This kind of thirst for knowledge is not an isolated incident but reflects a growing trend among illiterate populations also detected in research in other Latin American countries (Torres 1993).

In summary, the students all attached a high value to literacy. Despite the obstacles that the social and material conditions of their lives—past and present—afforded to their learning to read and write, after a long day's work, there they were, two nights a week, attempting to unfold the mysteries of the written language in an effort to understand their world better and to act upon it more effectively.

LITERACY, POLITICS, AND SOCIAL MOVEMENTS: AN AFTERTHOUGHT

O pedreiro é quem faz a obra e o engenheiro quem fica com a fama.
Tinha a maior enveja do mundo.
We want to leave here more aware than we arrived.
—Comments of members of a MOVA literacy group

The above narrative provides some small detail of the collective effort and complex process of constructing a São Paulo literacy movement of the dimensions of MOVA.[8] Yet, it also serves to give voice to some of the literacy learners involved in the movement and to reveal some of the contradictions between the theory and praxis of an emancipatory literacy training project. The intentions of the literacy monitor, who in his own words and actions expresses an affinity with the PT's political-pedagogic agenda—the collective construction of knowledge and the political formation of the popular classes—are at once complemented and contradicted by the learners' own participation in the literacy sessions and their reflections on the literacy process and its perceived benefits. In short, there is a tension between two purposes. On the one hand, they recognize the social injustices that they live and the need to gain greater awareness and to get organized to ameliorate them. On the other hand, without questioning the condition of labor markets or the structural dynamics of capitalism, they express a desire to learn to read and write for purely instrumental reasons, that is, to get a better job and make more money. While these two purposes are not in themselves wholly contradictory, they are quite different; and yet this tension is not self-reflective in the construction of learners' narratives.

Both the MOVA experience, linking the government and the social movements in Brazil, and the PT's interdisciplinary curriculum reform project in São Paulo were intimately connected to the theoretical premises and historical experience of Freirean education.[9] A basic reminder—at this point in history, a seemingly trivial one—of the Freirean principle of the indissoluble nexus between politics and education becomes a sobering lesson for political activists, teachers, and scholars. It is unavoidable that every educational activity will impact political practice, more so when the educational praxis is generated by a partnership between the state and social movements. The unity between politics and pedagogy evokes the relationship between conscientization—as a goal and actual practice—and cultural politics—as a dream, a utopia, and a new horizon for practical and purposeful transformation. The epistemological implications are many.

With his seminal work, *Pedagogy of the Oppressed,* Freire introduced an epistemological perspective in pedagogy. Knowing, for Freire, like Dewey, starts from lived experience. Problem-posing education, which is at odds with problem-solving education models, starts by discovering the theory hidden in the practice of human agency and social movements. Freire's epistemological perspective seeks, in turn, to produce new knowledge that will guide, inspire, redefine and assist in the comprehension of praxis. However, this new knowledge, this unknown theory, is not yet knowledge. It has to be discovered, invented, constructed, or recreated, in an intelligent dialogue between the logic of critical social theory and the demands of tension-ridden, complicated, contradictory practices. Certainly, as the narrative in this article indicates, the nature of the popular sectors' knowledge—a knowledge that is immanently class-, gender-, and race-oriented—makes the pedagogical work richly textured and compelling and challenging beyond and above any measure.

Thus Freire's epistemological stance has at least two major implications. On the one hand, critical pedagogy emerging from Freire's contribution is concerned with how emancipatory education can validate learners' own culture and discourse while at the same time challenging their common sense, to identify the *salutory nucleus,* the "good sense" that Gramsci, in his philo-

sophical imagination, signals as the beginning of counter-hegemony (Torres 1992b). On the other hand, Freire's recognition of the tensions between objectivity and subjectivity, between theory and practice—as autonomous and legitimate spheres of human endeavor—lead him (departing from Dewey) to recognize that these dichotomies and tensions cannot be overcome. Nor can they be captured in their entire complexity through mainstream methodologies. Long live the creative imagination!

Both the lived experience of PT's curriculum reform movement in the municipal schools of São Paulo and the large-scale literacy training effort that MOVA represents serve as an historical reference to these and many other theoretical questions and practical dilemmas of educating for liberation in a postmodern age (see McLaren 1994). Perhaps the best way to capture the essence of this experience is to say that there are no limits to the pedagogical imagination, and yet, no creative pedagogical imagination can operate freely of structural constraints. In the words of Fernando del Paso, "Si pudiéramos hacer de la imaginación la loca de la casa, la loca del castillo, y dejarla que, loca desatada, loca y con alas recorra el mundo y la historia, la verdad y la ternura, la eternidad y el sueño, el odio y la mentira, el amor y la agonía, libre, sí libre y omnipotente aunque al mismo tiempo presa, mariposa aturdida y ciega, condenada, girando siempre alrededor de una realidad inasible que la deslumbra y que la abrasa y se le escapa" (1989:644–645).[10]

NOTES

1. María del Pilar O'Cadiz, a fourth-year doctoral student, has conducted several months of fieldwork in São Paulo, Brazil, with support from the UCLA Latin American Center (August–September 1991 and August–November 1992). O'Cadiz's dissertation work is on the Freirean curriculum reform in the municipal schools, but at the same time, as a research assistant to Carlos Torres, she conducted research on literacy training in São Paulo under the PT administration, specifically interviewing over a dozen leaders of social movements active in MOVA and visiting several MOVA literacy groups. Also, O'Cadiz conducted preliminary research during June and July 1990. The field site visit to a MOVA literacy group and the interviews with literacy learners and a literacy monitor, cited in the "narrative" section of this article, were carried out during this earlier stage of her research.

2. Schools could elaborate their own independent proposal to improve the quality of their educational program and receive technical and financial support from the secretariat. By January 1992, 326 schools had their own projects, independent from the secretariat's Inter Project, underway (Municipal Secretariat of Education 1992a:10).

3. The secretariat made a "political decision" (after extensive debate among the members of Freire's initial organizing team), based on its principle of democratization, to open up the opportunity for all schools in the municipal system to participate in the project instead of carrying it out more thoroughly under more-controlled circumstances, in a few sites. The same decision was made about MOVA, in that all social movements in the city were invited to enter into the movement's coalition. In the case of the schools, Ana Maria Saúl, defended the secretariat's decision, pointing out that for the first time in the municipal school system's 50-year history an educational reform had had a profound impact on the system as a whole, reaching one-third of the schools (185 out of 691 schools) (from an October 1992 interview).

4. An example of such a top-down literacy-training program in Brazil's recent history is MOBRAL (The Brazilian Movement for Literacy Training). One of the most important experiments in adult education in Latin America during the 1970s, it served as an instrument of political legitimation for the bureaucratic-authoritarian regime that governed Brazil from 1964 to 1985 (see Torres 1990).

5. In October 1992, the PT lost the municipal elections to the Partido Democratico Social (PDS, Democratic Social Party), a conservative party led by São Paulo's current mayor, Paulo Maluf.

6. The fieldwork and interviews for this narrative were conducted by Pilar O'Cadiz in July 1990. This research consisted of two observational visits to this particular literacy nucleus in a São Paulo favela within the same week. Besides interviews with the literacy learners and the monitor of this group, O'Cadiz attended the 1st Congress for Municipal Literacy Workers, São Paulo, July 15, 1990 and visited the Municipal Secretariat of Education, interviewing the then-cabinet chief under Freire, Moacir Gadotti. Gadotti was later replaced by Mário Sérgio Cortella, who then replaced Freire as secretary in May 1991.

7. *Popular sectors* refers to lower-class sectors (peasants, workers, urban marginals and squatters, etc.).

8. The secretariat reports that 15,766 working-class students were attending 868 literacy classes within MOVA (Municipal Secretariat of Education 1992:11).

9. There are a number of works in progress regarding this significant aspect of the PT's educational activity in São Paulo, including Pilar O'Cadiz 1994 and Wong 1994. In addition, several of the educators and university specialists who participated in the formulation and implementation of the PT's educational policies in São Paulo have recently published several works reflecting on this experience (see Gadotti and Torres 1992; also see Pontuschka 1993 and articles therein by A. O. Citelli, B. H. M. Citelli, Delizoicov, Fester, Garcia, Lutti, Marques, Zanetic, Chiappini, Seabra, Mendonça, Forjaz, Pernambuco, and Moraes), including Freire himself (1991).

10. "If only we could make of imagination the crazy one of the household, the mad one of the castle, and set her free in her insane and unbound madness, insane and with wings to journey the world over and though history, truth and tenderness, eternity and dreams, hatred and lies, love and agony, free, yes free and omnipotent, yet at once imprisoned, a blind and bewildered butterfly, condemned, incessantly circling around an unattainable reality that dazzles her, scorches and escapes her" (Fernando del Paso 1989:644–645). We would like to thank Maria Christina Pons for calling our attention to this fantastic statement.

REFERENCES CITED

Arnove, Robert
1986 Education and Revolution in Nicaragua. New York: Praeger.
Cagliari, Luiz Carlos
1989 Alfabetizaçao e Linguistica. São Paulo: Scipione.
Campos, Marcio D'Olne
1989 Science Teaching Integrated in the Sociocultural Context with Some Hints from Ethno Science and Ethnoastronomy. *In* Basic Science at the Elementary Level. Patric V. Dias, ed. Pp.95–124. Frankfurt am Main: Verlag für Interkulturelle Kommunikation 2.
Campos, Marcio D'Olne, and Paulo Freire
1991 Alfabetizaçao: Leitura do mundo, leitura da palavra. Cadernos de Formaçao. São Paulo: Municipal Secretariat of Education.
Damasceno, Alberto, et al.
1989 A educaçao como ato político partidário. 2nd edition. São Paulo: Cortez.
Fazenda, Ivani Catarin Arantes
1979 Integraçao e interdisciplinaridade no ensino brasileiro. São Paulo: Loyola.
Ferreiro, Emília
1985 A Representaçao da Linguagem e o Processo de Alfabetizaçao. Cadernos de Pesquisa. Fundaçao Carlos Chagas 52(7). 1988 Alfabetizaçao em Processo. São Paulo: Cortez.
Ferreiro, Emília, and Ana Teberosky
1979 Los sistemas de escritura en el desarrollo del niño. Mexico: Siglo XXI.
Freire, Paulo
1970 Pedagogy of the Oppressed. 26th edition. Myra Bergman Ramos, trans. New York: Continuum.
1972 La misión educativa de las iglesias en America Latina. Contacto, Mexico 9(5):32.
1991 A Educaçao na Cidade. São Paulo: Cortez.

Freire, Paulo, and Donaldo Macedo
1987 Literacy: Reading the Word and the World. South Hadley, MA: Bergin & Garvey.
Freire, Paulo, and Carlos Alberto Torres
1994 Twenty Years after Pedagogy of the Oppressed. Paulo Freire in Conversation with Carlos Alberto Torres. *In* The Politics of Liberation: Paths from Freire. Peter McLaren and Colin Lankshear, eds. Pp. 100–107. London: Routledge.
Gadotti, Moacir, and Carlos Alberto Torres
1992 Estado y educaçao popular na America Latina. São Paulo: Cortez.
Humphrey, John
1993 Review of *Without Fear of Being Happy: Lula, the Workers Party, and Brazil.* Bulletin of Latin American Research 12(3):347.
Japiassú, Hilton
1976 Interdisciplinaridade e patologia do saber. Rio de Janeiro: Imago.
Paso, Fernando del
1989 Noticias del Imperio. Buenos Aires: EMECE Editores.
Piaget, Jean
1989 Linguagem e Pensamento da Criança. 5th edition. São Paulo: Martins Fontes.
Pilar O'Cadiz, Maria del
1994 The Politics of Schooling in Brazil. A Qualitative Analysis of Curriculum Reform in the Municipal Schools of São Paulo. Unpublished manuscript.
Pontuschka, Nídia Nacib, organizer
1993 Ousadia no Diálogo:Interdisciplinaridade na escola pública. São Paulo: Loyola.
McLaren, Peter
1994 Postmodernism and the Death of Politics: A Brazilian Reprieve. *In* Politics of Liberation: Paths from Freire. P. McLaren and C. Lankshear, eds. Pp. 193–215. London: Routledge.
Municipal Secretariat of Education, Government of São Paulo
1990 Reflexoes sobre o Processo Metodológico de Alfabetizaçao. Caderno de Formaçao 3. São Paulo: Municipal Secretariat of Education. 1992a Construindo a Educaçao Pública e Popular: Diretrizes e Prioridades (January).
1992b Aos que fazem conosco a Educaçao Pública de Qualidade em São Paulo. Diário Offical do Município de São Paulo 37(195):1–2.
Torres, Carlos Alberto
1990 The Politics of Nonformal Education in Latin America. New York: Praeger.
1992a From the 'Pedagogy of the Oppressed' to 'A Luta Continua': The Political Pedagogy of Paulo Freire. *In* Paulo Freire: A Critical Encounter. P. McLaren and P. Leonard, eds. Pp. 119–145. London: Routledge.
1992b The Church, Society, and Hegemony. A Critical Sociology of Religion in Latin America. Richard S. Young, trans. New York: Praeger.
1993 Cultura política de la alfabetización. Descripción y análisis de las relaciones entre educación de adultos y sectores populares urbanos en México. Revista Latinoamericana de Estudios Educativos 23(3):15–65.
1994a Intellectuals and University Life: Paulo Freire on Higher Education. *Introduction to* Paulo Freire at the National University in Mexico. A Dialogue. G. G. Niebla, A. L. Fernandez, and M. Escobar, eds. Pp. 1–25. New York: SUNY Press.
1994b Paulo Freire as Secretary of Education in the Municipality of São Paulo. Comparative Education Review 38(2):181–214.
Torres, Carlos Alberto, and Gustavo Fishman
In press Popular Education: Building from Experiences. *In* Learning through Action Technologies. Annie Brooks and Karen Watkins, eds. Jossey Bass Quarterly Sourcebooks. San Francisco: Jossey Bass.
Vygotsky, Lev S.
1978 Mind in Society: The Development of Higher Psychological Processes. Cambridge: Harvard University Press.
Weisz, Telma
1985 Repensando a Prática de Alfapetizaçao: Idéias de Emilia Ferreiro na sala de Aula. Cadernos de Pesquisa. Fundaçao Carlos Chagas (52):115–119.
Wong, Pia
1994 Constructing a Popular Public Education: Seven Case Studies of Implementation in São Paulo. Unpublished manuscript.

Understanding Indian Children, Learning from Indian Elders

J.T. Garrett, Ed.D., M.P.H.
Eastern Band of Cherokee Tribe

Dr. J.T. Garrett is the Director of the Health Care Administration and Contract Health Service for the Indian Health Service (IHS). He oversees the business office for managed care operations for 42 IHS hospitals and 123 outpatient facilities, and provides technical assistance to eight Tribally-operated hospitals, as well as 332 Tribally-operated health centers, school health clinics, health stations and Alaska village clinics.

A s an Indian Elder put it, "The (Indian) children are our future, but we (elders) are their bridge to the past, while they are the bridge to the future."

The Medicine Elder wished to remain anonymous, but he expressed concern about our Indian children learning about their unique heritage, the traditions, and their cultural way of life. As he said, "We are just a generation from losing our (Indian)

living cultural heritage. We could join the extinct ones."

The key is to learn from our elders. We can all benefit from intergenerational programs and activities that encourage involvement and sharing with our Indian Elders. As the same elder put it, children are like little sponges—he called them "spongies"—that can absorb even more than we realize thorough observation and learning.

One reason why the Indian family is changing rapidly is that family members must work outside the home and the home environment. The closeness of the family has been threatened with the "new survival," in contrast to the practice of earlier years when the family worked closely together to survive in a hostile environment. The hostile environment of today has also presented new stresses for the family, including the pervasiveness of drug and alcohol abuse and the search for independence by so many youth.

As a grandfather said, "What has

happened to the interdependence of the family, the clan, and the tribe of earlier years? We have learned too much 'independence' from the 'uneg' (white person), resulting in too much 'dependence' rather than having our life of sharing, and being 'helpers' for the greater benefit of the tribe as a whole, and giving thanks to the Great One." These are the kinds of things we learn from our Indian elders. They are lessons for all of us, regardless of race or culture.

As a young boy, my fondest memories are of the special times I had with my grandfather, Oscar Rogers. My heritage is Cherokee—beginning with the Walkingstick family on my mother's side of the family—and Irish on my father's side. My grandfather would say, "You are different, and you have a spiritual vision that will come to you when the time is right."

My mother, Ruth Rogers, guided me by encouraging me to learn and to enjoy working with nature. I remember the wonderful times learning

Reprinted from *Children Today*, Vol. 22, No. 4, 1993-1994, pp. 18-21, 40. *Children Today* is a government publication published by the Administration of Children and Families, Department of Health and Human Services, Washington, DC.

about plants and herbs, and how to use what the elders shared. Unlike the rote memorization of learning today, observation and listening to stories was the primary way that Indian people learned in earlier years.

Choice was very important in the learning process, with the focus on listening and respect, rather than on achievement. The emphasis was on preserving and strengthening the interdependence of the family, clan, and tribes, rather than on personal gain or wealth.

The lesson that I learned as a youngster was that people need people, and that we all have one purpose. I learned to give thanks each day to the Great One for all things, and that experiences were necessary to learn to spiral toward a higher level of understanding. My experience and learning is understood by all American Indians and Alaska Natives today.

As I approach the age of becoming an elder myself, I realize the need to share even more with our young people, regardless of race and culture, to help them to learn or relearn the path and ways of the Ancient Ones for survival tomorrow.

The stories shared by the Indian elders teach culturally related values for learning and encourage that we all get along with each other. The story of how the Redbird got its color is an example of value learning.

As an elder shared with me, the Raccoon and the Fox were playmates, but the Fox was always trying to "outfox" the Raccoon. One day when the Fox was showing off how fast he could run, the Raccoon ran toward the Oconaluftee River. Located in the Smokey Mountains, this river is very cold, with rapids and swift running water. The Raccoon knew that the Fox was a poor swimmer, so the Raccoon pretended that he had jumped into the water, but grabbed a yellow-root plant on the bank to keep from falling into the river. The Fox followed, but he jumped into the cold rapids of the water.

Teaching children the stories to help them learn respect for every living thing and for Mother Earth herself is critical for our children of today, and for our survival tomorrow.

The Fox fought the rapids and climbed up onto the clay bank shivering from the cold water. He was so tired that he fell asleep in the warm sunshine. The Raccoon packed his eyes with red clay that quickly hardened in the bright sunshine. As the Fox awoke, he yelled, "Help, I cannot see."

A little bird about the color of earth heard the Fox, having watched what was happening between the Fox and the Raccoon. The little bird said, "I can help you, but you must promise to always play fair with the Raccoon, who is your friend." The Fox, in panic, replied, "Yes, I promise, and I will help you, too, 'cause I know that you have always wanted to be a bright, pretty color to be recognized by the other birds!"

The little bird pecked the hard clay away from the eyes of the Fox until he could see again. The Fox was so glad that he showed the little bird where to get a special plant known in the mountains as "Red

Paint" or "Paint Brush." The little bird painted himself with the Red color, and to this day, he is recognized as the official bird of North Carolina, the Red Cardinal or the Redbird. The Fox and the Raccoon played happily for evermore.

Children are our most promising resource for the future. Their challenges will certainly be coping with the environmental stresses placed on Mother Earth, and cleaning up the harm done by human beings. Reducing the harm done to the other living beings such as plants, and animals, and easing the stresses of toxic substances on the environment, will be a real challenge for our young ones of tomorrow.

Teaching children the stories to help them learn respect for every living thing and for Mother Earth herself is critical for our children of today, and for our survival tomorrow. The story of Grandfather Rock tells us that we have the answers to all of our problems—passed along to us by the ancestors or Spirit People.

A young Indian boy was perplexed by the needs of his family's survival in the cold, long before we had fire. He sat by a large rock expressing his woe, then the large rock spoke to him. Surprised, he asked, "Who are you?" "I am Grandfather Rock," said the Rock Being. "I have a spirit and energy just like you, and we are kin by having similar Being minerals." He told the young boy stories, taught him about making fire, how to hunt, and how to use everything, including the hides, for warmth and the meat for food.

He taught him special and sacred chants and ceremonies to guide his spiritual path. The young boy would go back to his people and share what he learned. But he knew that one day the Grandfather Rock would no longer share with him. He would have to depend upon his own instinct, and be guided by the Spirit People. While this came to be, Grandfather Rock is still there overseeing the earth, standing tall in every setting of mountains.

There is even a rock called Grandfather Rock near Boone, North Carolina. Could it be the same rock that talked to the young boy in those earlier generations? Many of us still believe that we can sit on and by the large rocks on Clingman's Dome in the Smokey Mountains and still hear voices with chants.

I once asked a group of Indian elders about children and how we could provide an "understanding" of our Indianness using more traditional ways or teachings. They all seemed to be concerned about the commonly accepted way of having the child learn what is being told to them, and having to perform publicly. The emphasis on public achievement was considered by them to create an atmosphere of embarrassment. The traditional Indian way encourages the younger child to observe, then allows youth and adult guidance or mentoring. Then, with guidance, the child is encouraged to be involved in performing or demonstrating his or her understanding.

Choice was and is very important to avoid embarrassment and to assure a comfortable situation for everyone. From a traditional perspective, understanding comes from acceptance of the values in the learning situation, more than from the learning process itself. Observation, involvement, and demonstrating performance with peer and youth mentoring under adult or elder guidance, is emphasized.

Within the traditional Talking Circle, each elder seemed to think the problem was with the younger generation, except for one young person in

A message to *Children Today*—Mabel C. Cuffee, a Native American mother, speaks from her heart of her youth on Long Island Sound, with a message for all children today.

Sometimes....

Sometimes I look back at my childhood and remember certain things that have been etched in my mind like a perfectly drawn picture of the horizon, with all the perfectly wonderful colors and the fullness of the setting sun.

Seeing my mother and father driving all six of my brothers and sisters, including myself, along the Ocean dune road at dusk and showing us the wild life that comes alive at five!

The beautiful Red Fox, the Great Horned Owl, and the Marsh Hawks soaring above the salthay looking for that evening's delight.

Memories of each of them explaining to us—in our terms—the significance, the beauty and the importance, and the sheer joy of this abundance of wildlife right here where we live.

Sometimes I wonder if other people thought of this.

I can remember the expression on my mother's and father's faces as they told of stories about their encounters with wild life, and the excitement and fear they felt. I loved listening to those stories! I thought, "One day when I had children, I would tell them stories with the same excitement and enchantment."

Sometimes it's hard.

They would say, "They should leave the dunes like this so we can come and see forever. Every thing here does something for nature." There was no pollution in the water then as we know it today. You could eat clams and mussels right from the water. You can still eat the seafood right from the water....

the group. It happened to be my son, Michael, who had been listening to the elders quietly and patiently. He heard the elders placing a lot of blame on themselves for acceding to influences stemming from the non-Indian focus on achievement. He clarified the problem as focusing on what we are doing and not doing, rather than who we are. Therefore, we focus on going things, rather than on "being" things. As he talked, the others started to focus on the differences in attitudes between Indians and non-Indians. We spent the next few hours discussing what the elders value as the Indian Way.

The elders in the traditional Talking Circle discussed the importance of using the circle approach with children because the circle is a sacred teaching method. Children could relate to the circle as being similar to the family, the clan, and the tribal way, instead of focusing on the individual and achievement. The elders deemed that it was important for children to understand the value of being modest and not displaying or showing assertiveness.

Respect not related to wealth, position, or title was a resounding value to be learned by the children. Several of the elders almost became upset when talking about the lack of respect that adults, youth, and children show for elders today. In their generation, it would have been dishonorable to the family to show disrespect for any elder. Understanding and using the idea of the "talking stick" to teach group cooperation and hu-

Sometimes.

I have four children now and look back on my childhood and what was taught to me. I want my children to know that we live for the future, and that what we do today will be seen in years to come just as what we did back when I was young is seen today.

Sometimes...

The dunes have almost been destroyed by construction. There are no more foxes to see, owls or hawks to watch. I want them to understand the simple things in nature. When we take away from Mother Nature, it is only right to give her something back for her generosity to us....

Sometimes.

I would like to send a message to my children and to other children. *Respect from your heart what has been given to us from the Creator and we will live forever. Be aware of our surroundings and the creatures in that cycle, for those creatures are a part of who we are, and where we are going in the future.*
So, remember, it is good to look, feel, listen and understand with your heart rather than your mind....

Sometimes.

Mabel C. Cuffee is a Shinnecock Indian who lives on the reservation, on Long Island in New York where she grew up. She worked at the Shinnecock Oyster Hatchery for 17 years, four of them as the Director. The Oyster Hatchery was the Tribe's gift to the Long Island bay cycle, sustaining its creatures for the future.

mility was another value that would be a "helper" to the children.

The elders focused much discussion on spirituality. It seemed that all topics discussed were included in the Indian spiritual way, with the value being an emphasis on "being." This included giving thanks each day for all things, and the idea of "Giveaway"— to give to others and to teach sharing. The ideas of the Talking Stick and Giveaway can be taught in games and activities with children. One activity the elders mentioned was teaching fair play, as opposed to concentrating on competition to win.

Another activity was teaching children about nature and observing the lessons of nature. As we sat in the Circle and passed the Talking Stick, each elder shared a story or expressed an idea to be used as an activity with children. One story involved having a child go outside to find something special, understanding that nature always has something special to share. Of course, it was important to leave something—for example, a rock, tobacco, or some corn meal—in return with Mother Nature. Then the child is told to give thanks using a little chant, prayer, or song to the Four Directions, Mother Earth, and Father Sky. A simple little story had many, many

Respect

not related to wealth, position, or title was a resounding value to be learned by the children.

values that were discussed in the "coming together" of the elders.

Subsequent meetings or "coming together" Circle sessions with the Indian elders have taught me, and reminded me, of lessons—wonderful teachings about the Indian Way—that I had forgotten. I also had an opportunity to learn from a young Indian child when I shared the story with some Cherokee children.

A little girl about age four said she had found something special that Mother Nature gave her. It was a small, heart-shaped white rock. I was surprised that she wanted me to have this special gift. Of course, I asked her what she left for Mother Nature. Her quick response was, "Oh, I told her you would give her something!" Even the teacher can learn from a special understanding passed on only by children.

As a young boy, I asked Elder Medicine Man, "What is the secret of life?" The Elder meditated for a long while, then said, "It is energy and a child." I became curious about what energy was to life, and which came first. The Elder, anticipating my question, said abruptly, "Neither and both. Life is not life without energy, but energy can exist without life; it is life in another form. The difference is that a child preserves both energy and life."

Hollywood

and the

Indian Question

John Walton

John Walton holds a joint appointment as Professor in the Departments of Sociology and Anthropology at the University of California at Davis, where he is also affiliated with the Native American Studies Program. His most recent book is Western Times and Water Wars: State, Culture, and Rebellion in California *(University of California Press).*

In an emblematic scene from Michael Apted's 1992 film *Thunderheart,* fugitive Indian activist Jimmy Looks Twice explains to Ray Levoi, a sympathetic FBI agent and deracinated mixed-blood Sioux, why the Native American movement poses such a dangerous threat to White society:

"We choose the right to be who we are. We know the difference between the reality of freedom and the illusion of freedom. There is a way to live with the earth and a way not to live with the earth. We choose earth. It's about power."

In this passage, as throughout the richly informed screenplay by John Fusco, *Thunderheart* portrays Native American life on the reservation in sharply political tones. As fictional realism, the film is a fitting companion to Robert Redford's 1991 documentary *Incident at Oglala,* which

"Its about power." Thunderheart reminds us, and the Native American movement has confronted power in disputes about fundamental rights to land and sovereignty.

analyzes the uprising on the Pine Ridge Reservation of South Dakota during the mid-1970s, the killing of two FBI agents, and the subsequent show trials of AIM (American Indian Movement) members. Together the films demonstrate forcibly that if Hollywood is often guilty of exploiting ethnic conflict, it is sometimes capable of getting it right in extraordinary ways.

. . . .

The Native American occupies an ambiguous position within the status hierarchy and consciousness of white society. Indians are the poorest, sickest, least educated, and most unemployed Americans; yet they also enjoy a kind of distant and sentimentalized admiration.

Beginning with America's colonization, Indians were conceded the small virtues of "natural" beings, but their customs tied to unimproved nature stood in the path of progress as that notion was understood by the European settlers. As Roy Harvey Pearce observes in *Savagism and Civilization,* "[T]he Indian became important for the English mind, not for what he was in and of himself, but rather for what he showed civilized men they were not and must not be."

The ambiguity persists today. Native Americans suffer marked discrimination on all the standard measures of social well-being, yet lately the historically suspect notion of the Ecological Indian has become a favorable stereotype and legitimate symbol of conservation. (Native American cultures were not innocent of environmentally harmful practices such as the buffalo jump, burning of land, and soil salinization by irrigation). What's going on here? Why are Indians simultaneously rejected and romanticized? How may the new films help explain this deep-seated ambivalence about Native Americans?

Incident at Oglala is a feature-length documentary devoted to the controversial

From *Multicultural Education,* Fall 1993, pp. 12-13, 37. © 1993 by the National Association for Multicultural Education. Reprinted by permission.

Political Radical or Ecological Symbol

shootout at Pine Ridge and the protracted legal struggle that followed. As exposé, it concentrates on two trials, the first resulting in exoneration of Darrelle Butler and Bob Robideau for the murders of FBI agents Jack Coler and Ronald Williams, and the second leading to Leonard Peltier's conviction for the same crime.

The storyline follows closely Peter Matthiessen's definitive investigative work, *In the Spirit of Crazy Horse*. Two dozen Indians, including many principals in the shootout, are interviewed, along with a wide variety of white defense and prosecution lawyers, jurors, police and politicians. Appropriate attention is focused on divisions within the Oglala Sioux, between the "government Indians" who controlled the Tribal Council under Dick Wilson and his GOON (Guardians of the Oglala Nation) Squad, and the "traditionals" allied with AIM to end corruption and restore popular rule to the reservation.

Among the many persons who appear (in addition to celebrities such as William Kunstler and Leonard Peltier) are John Trudell, an AIM organizer whose wife and three children were killed in an arsonist's attack on their home, and Deborah White Plume, whose son was shot by the GOON Squad. Some of those heavies, including the odious and now deceased Dick Wilson, also appear in menacing boasts about the "tribal justice" they wield over dissidents. All sides are represented, although a judgment soon emerges in defense of the traditionals and the falsely accused AIMers—a judgment rigorously sustained in the body of the film.

On June 26, 1975, agents Coler and Williams, evidently in pursuit of a suspect, drove on to the tense reservation's Jumping Bull property where a group of approximately fifteen traditionals, including AIM warriors, women and children, was encamped. Although the precipitant is still uncertain, a gun battle broke out in which the agents were mortally wounded, heavy police reinforcements and roadblocks were brought in, and the now terrified Indians miraculously walked out unobserved through the surrounding hills. When he saw the prostrate agents, Bob Robideau thought "our lives were over."

A massive dragnet was organized and before long most of the group present on the Jumping Bull property had been arrested with the exception of Peltier who fled to Canada.

. . . .

Understandably outraged by the loss of two comrades in arms, the FBI not only swore to avenge the deaths but to fix responsibility on the presumptive cause of all the unrest, the AIM activists. Dino Butler and Bob Robideau were tried for murder in Cedar Rapids, Iowa, in a proceeding so riddled with manufactured evidence, bribed witnesses, inconsistent testimony, and prejudicial publicity that the good Iowans on the jury concluded the only guilty party before them was the FBI.

Desperate now for a fall guy, the FBI and U.S. Attorneys began cooking a new case against Peltier that would plug every evidentiary hole in the first trial, beginning with false affidavits to secure Peltier's extradition from Canadian authorities. Norman Brown, a juvenile in federal custody who witnessed the shootout, and Myrtle Poor Bear, a retarded woman, were coerced with threats to make statements implicating Peltier. New evidence suddenly appeared in the form of a gun and shell casing that supposedly linked him directly to the murder scene.

. . . .

Peltier was convicted of murder in a tightly controlled trial at Fargo, North Dakota in April 1977 and remains in federal prison today, sixteen years later, although the case against him was weaker than that against Butler and Robideau. Among many irregularities, the verdict in the first case could not be told to the second jury. The details of both trials are examined in the documentary, which is surprisingly well paced, given its meticulousness. Redford provides a softly modulated and unobtrusive narration.

As the lights come up, and before the credits roll, *Thunderheart* begins with the notice, "[T]his story was inspired by events that took place on several American Indian reservations during the 1970s." That is an understatement. *Thunderheart* intri-

cately weaves together a set of factual occurrences, real people, and honest sympathies in a political thriller that loses none of its bite because its vehicle is fiction. On the contrary, Fusco's screenplay puts fiction into the service of realism by providing the broader social context which explains the Pine Ridge uprising and the fearful tension behind the shooting.

A series of killings on the Bear Creek Indian Reservation leads the FBI in Washington to dispatch to the Badlands Special Agent Ray Levoi (played by Val Kilmer), who is expected to solve the crimes within 72 hours and at the same time legitimize the federal solution by virtue of Levoi's Native American ancestry.

Why headquarters has chosen to act now, after sixty previous murders and on behalf of the latest victim who is an ARM (Aboriginal Rights Movement) supporter, is not adequately explained. Nevertheless, Levoi teams up with the wily resident agent Frank Coutelle (Sam Shepard), who is convinced on the basis of some overly obvious clues that ARM is responsible in the person of James Looks Twice.

The factual parallels begin to multiply. Looks Twice is played effectively by the mercurial AIM activist John Trudell featured in *Incident*. Like real-life Deborah White Plume, the film's Maggie Eagle Bear (played elegantly by Indian actress Shelia Tousey) has a son who is shot by GOON Squad raiders in pickup trucks. The real killer is an Indian, coerced, like Norman Brown, into acting as an FBI informer while in prison. Regaled in black hat and leather, dark glasses, and an automatic rifle, the film's evil Tribal Council President Jack Milton matches Dick Wilson phonetically and temperamentally.

As the 72-hour deadline for producing a case against Looks Twice approaches, Coutelle claims to have found a gun of the right calibre belonging to the suspect, and a shell casing comes into play, although here in defense of the suspect, in contrast to its incriminating use in the Peltier case.

. . . .

In the end, *Thunderheart* undertakes to rewrite the mixed results of the Pine Ridge tragedy—to do justice, if only in fiction and symbol. Back in the land of his father (an alcoholic steelworker, a painful memory which he has repressed), Levoi begins to experience flashbacks and ultimately a vision of his ancestors at the Wounded Knee Massacre. It becomes obvious to Levoi that his fellow agents are cooking the evidence against ARM and Looks Twice, and using him, the "Washington Redskin," to justify their frame-up.

But Levoi is tough and smart, too. He is fortunate for the assistance he receives from beautiful, Dartmouth-educated

Maggie Eagle Bear and irreverent Indian Policeman Walter Crow Horse (played with aplomb by Graham Greene)—although one does wonder how the uncorrupted Crow Horse could keep his tribal police job with the Jack Milton/Dick Wilson regime.

. . . .

Central to the plot and the spiritual message of *Thunderheart* is tribal elder Samuel Reaches (played by veteran actor Chief Ted Thin Elk), "spiritual advisor to ARM" and Levoi's salvation. As a year-old infant, Samuel Reaches was at Wounded Knee in 1890, and he recalls the holy man Thunderheart who was killed there. In a vision, the old man sees that Thunderheart's blood runs in Levoi, that he has been sent in a time of trouble to help his people. Resistant initially, Levoi is swept along by events that validate the vision.

There is much to recommend this film. The photography moves from spectacular panoramas and aerial shots of the Badlands to sordid scenes of junked cars and tumbledown housing on the reservation. Native Americans figure importantly in the cast, ranging from several of its central

players to neatly integrated Lakota and powwow singers. A plausible subplot involves uranium prospecting and environmental degradation on the reservation as the hidden scheme that unites the resident FBI Agent and the Tribal Council President in corrupt dealings and murder.

The writing is forceful and resonates themes from the Native American Movement. As he is being arrested, Jimmy Looks Twice explains to his FBI tormentors, "It's a 500 year resistance. You can't break the connection." Fundamentally, *Thunderheart's* power as a political statement lies in its factually grounded indictment of the federal government for crimes old and new against Native Americans.

This raises again the question of the Native American's ambivalent role in our national consciousness. Why do we embrace the easy pieties of the Ecological Indian, yet ignore the mean repression of AIM's rights to free speech and assembly? Why does the benign film *Dances With Wolves* generate extensive media discussion of the question "who should get to play the hero when Kevin Costner is paying all the bills," while the equally attractive *Thunderheart* stimulates no serious dis-

cussion and, in all probability, is seen as nothing more than a rural mystery story?

. . . .

The answer is straightforward. We, as a public and a political system, do not want to confront the hard choices posed in the soliloquy of Jimmy Looks Twice—to examine "the difference between the reality of freedom and the illusion of freedom," to question the complaisant belief that AIM could organize freely by contrast to the reality of Pine Ridge. Equally important, we do not want to accede to costly and disruptive Indian demands.

"Its about power," *Thunderheart* reminds us, and the Native American movement, despite its divisions, has confronted power in disputes about fundamental rights to land and sovereignty. In the Black Hills adjacent to Pine Ridge, for example, they have rejected a large cash settlement of historic land claims in preference to the land and the principle.

In important ways, Native Americans have refused to be patronized, and in so doing they have chosen an ambivalent relationship with the dominant society. These remarkable films explain that choice.

"I WOULDN'T WANT TO SHOOT NOBODY:" THE OUT-OF-SCHOOL CURRICULUM AS DESCRIBED BY URBAN STUDENTS

Jacqueline Williams
Kay Williamson

Jacqueline Williams is an Assistant Professor in the College of Kinesiology, Teacher Education, University of Illinois, Chicago.

Kay Williamson is an Assistant Professor in the College of Kinesiology, Teacher Education, University of Illinois, Chicago.

Please note: The authors would like to thank Nikos Georgiadis and Bobby Lifka for their work on this project and for their love and support given to the children who participated in the after-school program. Also a special thank you to the 17 children who willingly shared their hopes, dreams, and struggles.

The urban child characteristically lives in a context that is epitomized by poverty, violence, drugs, gangs, and an unstable family life. Often this child is a minority who comes to know the meaning of racism and oppression at an early age (Kotlowitz, 1991). The term "at-risk," commonly attached to such children and the dangers they face, was graphically described in *Time* (1990):

> Every eight seconds of a school day, a child drops out. Every 26 seconds, a child runs away from home. Every 47 seconds, a child is abused or neglected. Every 67 seconds, a teenager has a baby. Every 7 minutes, a child is arrested for drug offense. Every 36 minutes a child is killed or injured by a gun. Every day 135,000 children bring their guns to school (Johnson, Ludtke, & Riley, 1990, p. 42).

To compound these problems, urban public education provides little hope to change the inherent societal inequity; as Fine (1991) stated: "...public secondary schools were never designed for low income students and students of color. And they have never been very successful in this work" (p. 31).

Urban schools are characteristically attended by minority children, who face problems of overcrowding, inadequate facilities, limited funding, resources and educational materials, and the daily threat of violence.

In addition, the research on urban teachers has described the dismal educational prospects teachers hold for students. The following is a brief summary of results from various research studies illustrating that inner city teachers tend to: (a) label students as followers of the rules, reluctant to make any decisions for themselves (Anyon, 1980; Rist, 1970); (b) assume minority children are unintelligent, thus do not "waste their time" working with them (Clarke, 1963); (c) do not believe students have the capacity to learn much academically (Parish, Eubanks, Aquila & Walker, 1989); and (d) perceive that a controlled and restrictive environment is what children need in order to prepare them for the "real world" (Fine, 1990). With such prevalent beliefs, teaching styles have tended to be "top down" approaches, thus giving students little opportunity for input and responsibility for their own learning. The combined effect of teacher dominance in the schools and teachers exhibiting low expectations for student performance can perpetuate the self-fulfilling prophecy (Merton, 1948; Rosenthal, 1987; Martinek, 1983).

There are many facets of the educational experience described above. One dimension is the out-of-school curriculum; a phenomenon that includes the influences of the family, community, peers, television, and other areas of involvement by the child (Schubert, 1981, 1986). As Schubert (1982) emphasized: "If school curriculum is to be effective, it must have meaning that relates to perspectives students acquire..." (p. 186). Without knowledge of the out-of-school curricula that virtually creates a student's life, schooling is guesswork" (p. 189). Fine (1991) referred to this phenomenon as the "public-private split" in which inner city schools consider only the public side and does not consider anything beyond its doors. Knowledge of the out-of-school curriculum must be better understood by educators who create curricula (Schubert, 1986) and who ought to organize the school environment to acknowledge students' personal struggles (Fine 1991).

The focus of this paper is to allow the reader an opportunity to listen to the student's own voices describe their personal world or their out-of-school curriculum, to gain a closer look at the struggles, frustrations, and joys as seen through their eyes. The changing nature of childhood in relation to family structure, school, and society is one of the challenges adults face if children are to thrive (Ayers, 1989).

The Students

The students were from two inner city neighborhoods in Chicago: the first is a low income Latin-American community and the second is an African-American community located in a public housing project. Both communities face the ubiquitous presence of violence, gangs, poverty, and oppression. The African-American public housing complex is renowned for violence and has been the subject of various national network television documentaries. The introduction to one particular story described explicitly the context in which these children live.

> Picture no-man's land with broken windows, dark abandoned buildings, no law and order. There are carefully demarcated areas controlled by rival bands of militia fighting over the rubble. Nearly every night there is sniper fire. It sounds like Beirut, but in fact it's America (Kroft, 1989, West 57).

The students who shared their out-of-school lives with us were involved in an after-school recreation program in each community designed to keep them in a safe, non-threatening environment for a few

hours in the afternoon once or twice a week. The after-school programs were designed and implemented by faculty and preservice students from the University of Illinois at Chicago. A close rapport was established with the students over a period of time ranging from 1 to 3 years. Of the 31 children in both programs, 17 volunteered to be interviewed, but due to the limited amount of space we will only share four vignettes. The interviews took approximately 45 minutes to complete and were audio taped and transcribed verbatim.

The students described their stories about family life, free time, responsibilities, hopes, fears, and future plans. What follows are the out-of-school lives told through the eyes of the students as they candidly shared their experiences and dreams.

The Students' Voices

Vignette 1: Marie

Marie is a Latin-American bilingual seventh grader who lives with both parents, two sisters, and one brother. Her parents moved from Mexico the year before her birth.

> My father's laid off work, and so he goes with my cousins to help with plumbing or anything he can in the houses. My mother has meetings on Mondays and Wednesdays at school at 5:30 to 9:00. She's in the school council for my sister's school. She has to go to some meetings 'cause nobody wants to go and she says its better for herself to go so she can understand it. My mother is studying [for a] high school [degree].

> When my mother's not home, I take care of my little brother and sisters. I have to make them do their homework and when I finish my homework I have to clean the dishes or pick up, or do anything — keep the house clean. Sometimes my mother expects me to pick up the front. . . the garbage or anything that is out there.

> In my free time I just kind of don't do anything, 'cause I just stay home, do my homework, take a bath, and watch television programs, that's all.

> My family is so far over in Mexico, [if I had three wishes] I wish we would all be here and we would have enough money to go to Mexico every single year. The second wish is that my parents are always saying they need this or they need that so I wish I could help them in whatever I could. And thirdly, I [would] give the rest of the money to other people that really need it,

which will make more homes for the homeless, or more programs for the drug [users] or the gangs.

I fear that sometimes when I'm walking out by myself, someone will get me and do the things they do to other girls, 'cause you hear all the time that there is rape or violation, there is someone kidnapped or they kill them accidently. I also fear that one time one of the ones that I like will die. Like my grandmother, she is old already. I wouldn't like her to die.

Vignette 2: Juan

Juan is also a Latin-American bilingual eighth grader, the oldest of two brothers. He lives with both parents. His mother stays at home and at the time of the interview his father was laid off from a local candy factory.

My free time on weekends we sometimes go the mall with my parents. We just hang around Jose's house playing Nintendo or we go out to the plaza. After school we play basketball. Right there in the alley is a hoop. At home I either watch television or stay in my room hearing the radio or do my chores and my homework. At home I'm responsible to clean my room and make my bed, wash dishes sometimes, pass the vacuum on the rug.

My wishes are that my mother and father would not die and that we stay together, that we never have problems with the house and that we're always comfortable. I hope that I finish high school and go to college, and have a good job when I get out.

I'm afraid if we don't have money to pay for things, then I will stop going to school and have to get a job. And I want to finish school [but] if my parents are having trouble, if they're still alive and they need more money, I'm going to have to get a job instead of going to school.

There are gangs in schools and they threaten other people and that's why [students] get scared too, and that interferes with their work in the classroom. I just feel sorry for [the people in gangs] 'cause they don't have better things to do than be out screaming and getting shot. By the time they're 20 they get shot. I know this guy, his name was Joe and I told him, "How come you don't get out of the gang?" And then he goes, "I'll get out." A couple of weeks we heard he got shot in the throat and he got shot in the appendix. He was dead. He was 17.

Vignette 3: Latisha

Latisha is African-American and 13 years old. Parts of her housing project area are more notorious than others. She lives in a more "quiet" division.

[My mother] works at the hospital, serving food. [She's worked there] for 11 years, but she's been moved to different departments. I don't know what [my dad does] because he don't live with me. My mother's boyfriend [lives with us]. He's like my step father.

[In my spare time] I just like be at home look at TV, or clean up or do my homework, or [play] basketball, [or talk on the] phone. [My three wishes would be]: to have a younger brother and sister, a car of my own, and not get killed before I'm 20 years old.

I be afraid of guns and rats. My mother she has [a gun], her boyfriend has one for protection. I have shot one before and it's like a scary feeling. My uncle taught me. He took us in the country and he had targets we had to like shoot at. He showed us how to load and cock it and pull the trigger. [When I pulled the trigger] at first I feel happy because I learned how to shoot a gun, but afterward I didn't like it too much because I don't want to accidentally shoot nobody. I wouldn't want to shoot nobody. But it's good that I know how to shoot one just in case something happened and I have to use it.

Where I live its a quiet neighborhood. If [the gangs] don't bother me or threaten me, or do anything to my family, I'm OK. If somebody say, hi to me I'll say hi to them as long as they don't threaten me...I got two cousins who are in gangs. One is in jail because he killed somebody. My other cousin, he stayed cool. He ain't around. He don't be over there with the gang bangers. He mostly over on the west side with his grandfather, so I don't hardly see him...I got friends [in gangs]. Some of them seven, eight [years old] that's too young to be in a gang...They be gang banging because they have no one to turn to...If a girl join a gang its worser than if a boy join a gang because to be a girl you should have more sense. A boy they want to be hanging on to their friends. Their friends say gangs are cool, so they join.

The school I go to now is more funner than the school I just came from. We switch classes and we have 40 minutes for lunch. The Board of Education say that we can't wear gym shoes no more. They say it distracts other people from learning, its because of the shoe strings and gang colors.

My teachers are good except two. My music and art teacher she's old and it seems like she shouldn't be there teaching. It seem like she should be retired and be at home, or traveling or something like that. And my history teacher, yuk! He's a stubborn old goat. He's stubborn with everybody.

[When I finish school] I want to be a doctor. At first I wanted to be a lawyer, but after I went to the hospital I said now I want to help people, and cure people, [so I decided] to be a doctor.

Vignette 4: Dwayne

Dwayne is African-America, 13 years old, and lives with his mother, father, and brothers.

My mother use to work, [but now] she goes to school at night...so she can get her a good job. [My dad] works at [a company] where they like make clothes. He's a carpenter. [I] have two brothers, one older and one younger.

I have to do my chores before I do anything: wash dishes or clean the living room. We all have a different turn in doing that, if I have dishes, my brother has to vacuum the room.

I like to go to the movies, or be with my tutor, or go to the gym and play basketball. [If I could wish for three things they would be]: to become a professional basketball player, that my family live safely through their life, and for my little brother to get his diploma and go to college so he can do whatever he wants. And have the best for him. Well, for all of us really, but I was saying him 'cause he's the youngest.

[The gangs] tried to get me and my [older] brother. We just refused. But then they threatened us, they say they beat us up some. We kept telling our mother and father and they say: leave my sons alone. So now they don't bother us. They try to ease talk you a bit, but we're too smart to fall for it. Like now me and my brother can go wherever we want without nobody bothering us.

[In school they should] make sure they have more supervision of gangs. They bring weapons and things in school. Like last year they brung a lot of guns. When it was cold they wore long coats and hid guns up in their coats. This boy that live on the end that I live on, he's going to this school. We were sitting by the library steps, so then this boy came out of his building and just started shooting at people. The only reason we didn't get shot was because this car was coming past and the car got shot up. Then when we tried to get up in the building everybody else they [were] trying to see what's going on. We had to push them out of the way.

Reflections

Our time working and playing with these children was characterized by struggles, frustrations, and joys. We struggled with outbreaks of violence, name calling, and disputes, while the question "do we really make a difference?" echoed in our heads. Our frustrations revolved around the insidious social inequities that these children and their families experienced. However, despite their disadvantaged out-of-school curriculum, we witnessed during our time together the child underneath the burden of adult responsibilities.

Many students spoke of the fear that they may have to drop out of school in order to support their family. Other children live with such daily violence that they have no real future plans but to live through their childhood. The benefit of studying the out-of-school curriculum is that we can "profit from knowing others more fully" (Schubert, 1981, p. 196). Listening to the voices of the four students provides some understanding of the out-of-school curriculum which is rife with violence and for many, fear — to be faced every day of their young lives.

Knowledge of these students' experiences is particularly important for teacher educators, inservice, and preservice teachers who are typically from white, middle class backgrounds (Haberman, 1987; Watkins, 1989). There is certainly a void of experience for teachers who have never been involved or immersed in multicultural educational settings. Yet, predominantly white educators are supposed to design meaningful curricula for diverse groups of students.

There has been debate to what extent teacher education programs can actually teach cultural awareness (Burnstein & Cabello, 1989; Haberman, 1991). Two key factors to promoting cultural sensitivity include: (a) providing content courses on cultural diversity and field experiences over the four to five year teacher education program (Burnstein & Cabello, 1989); and (b) having faculty who can help future teachers identify "teaching behaviors which support or inhibit the realization of multiculturalism in the classroom" (Haberman, 1991, p. 30).

As teacher educators at the University of Illinois, we have attempted to provide experiences where students confront their own values and biases through readings, films, discussion, and teaching in the inner city (Williamson & Hellison, in press). However, for us to produce meaningful experiences for our students, faculty have also felt it important to work with children in the urban setting.

Although our institution is situated in downtown Chicago, within a three mile radius one will observe opulence, poverty, diversity, drug deals, and gang graffiti, we have had to take steps to "urbanize" ourselves. Our faculty is similar to other teacher education faculty who according to Haberman (1987) are primarily from a suburban/rural orientation. Therefore, before we can begin to think about preparing our preservice teachers to work and successfully teach in the city schools, we believe teacher education faculty need to broaden their own perspectives and experiences of the urban environment.

Personally and professionally our lives as teacher educators have been enhanced by becoming immersed in the urban school setting. Our "immersion" has taken place on a number of levels: (a) observing teachers; (b) working with preservice teachers in field experiences; and (c) either teaching independently or team teaching with preservice teachers and graduate students in public schools and in after-school programs (Georgiadis, 1990; Hellison, 1990a, 1990b; Lifka, 1990). We all kept journals of our experiences when in the schools. Reflections related to pedagogical strategies, subject content, and moral aspects of teaching — for example: How did boys and girls interact? What did we notice about the racial/ethnic make-up of the class and student group dynamics? And was the environment fair and just for all children to participate? Our journals provided a forum to discuss our successes and struggles in our teaching.

At times, the children have also kept journals about their experiences in our classes, which have been insightful (Williamson & Georgiadis, in press). However, the interviews with the children added another dimension to our work. We had the one on one opportunity to listen to the stories of their lives. This made us reflect upon our own childhood experiences; and as white middle class individuals our hopes and dreams seemed foreign and remote in comparison. After completing the interviews, we feel it will be a useful endeavor for our prospective teachers to also interview children whom they worked with during a field experience. The interview pro-

cess provides the opportunity to discuss the child's background, every day existence, hopes, fears, dreams, and school experiences. These insights seem particularly important for an educator to reflect on the different influences that affect a child's life.

As mentioned earlier, inner city students are often treated in an autocratic manner and perceived by many teachers to have little educational hope. As Fine explained:

> For these students, the opportunity to a public education is hollow. It asks them to abandon family and community responsibilities; to sacrifice language, identity, and pride; to ignore the pain and suffering they witness around them and the culture and pleasure they take comfort in; and to deny fundamentally all that sits between their dreams and their circumstances, between the ideologies they so want to believe and the contradictions they so need to confront (Fine, 1991, p. 182).

Through more personal interaction with inner city children, teachers may begin to understand that despite their appalling living conditions, children can succeed — with help (Beck, 1992).

In order to overcome stereotypical views of inner city students, teacher educators, and preservice and inservice teachers need to have the opportunity to: (a) reflect upon and confront their own social biases (Williamson & Williams, 1990), and (b) understand that utilizing a variety of teaching methods provides the opportunity for all children to learn and care (Farrell, Peguero, Lindsey, & White, 1988; Fine, 1990; Kohn, 1991). With a better understanding of the plight of inner city poor and developing a sensitivity to students' culture and experiences, perhaps teachers will be more aware of student needs and out-of-school influences (Abi-Nader, 1991). As Schubert (1991) stated:

> The right to benefit from the experience of another and the right to share our experience for another's good may be an ultimate ethical end of studying the out-of-school curriculum (p. 196).

Within a research context, the child's voice has been missing (Smith, 1991). Educational research has moved out of the ivory tower to professors at least acknowledging that they do not need to operate in a vacuum when conducting research. This is apparent with the movement toward realizing that it is more meaningful for teachers to conduct their own research (Cochran-Smith & Lytle, 1990; Connelly & Clandinin, 1990). Perhaps we still need to go further down the unfortunate hierarchy of power and listen to what is important to students so that we can create and implement meaningful curricula. As Schubert stated (1981): "Those who have been considered recipients of research, i.e., teachers, administrators, and especially students, must be seen as players of key roles in the knowledge creation process" (p. 195).

References

Abi-Nader, J. (1991). Creating a vision for the future. *Phi Delta Kappan, 72*(7), 546-554.

Anyon, J. (1980). Social class and the hidden curriculum of work. *Journal of Education, 162*(1), 67-92.

Ayers, W. (1989). Childhood at risk. *Educational Leadership, 46*(2), 70-72.

Beck, J. (1992, May 21). Inner city children succeed — with help. *The Columbus Dispatch/FORUM*, p. 9A.

Burnstein, N.D., & Cabello, B. (1989). Preparing teachers to work with culturally diverse students: A teacher education model. *Journal of Teacher Education, 40*(5), 9-16.

Clandinin, D.J., & Connelly, F.M. (1988). Studying teachers' knowledge of classrooms: Collaborative research, ethics and the negotiation of narrative. *Journal of Educational Thought, 22*(2A), 269-282.

Clarke, K.B. (1963). Educational stimulation of racially disadvantaged children. In A.H. Passow (Ed.), *Education in depressed areas.* New York: Teachers College Press.

Cochran-Smith, M., & Lytle, S.L. (1990). Research on teaching and teacher research: The issues that divide. *Educational Researcher, 19*(2), 2-11.

Connelly, M., & Clandinin, D. (1990). Stories of experience and narrative inquiry. *Educational Researcher, 19*(5), 2-14.

Farrell, E., Peguero, G., Lindsey, R., & White, R. (1988). Giving voice to high school students: Pressure and boredom, Ya know what I'm saying? *American Educational Research Journal, 25*(4), 489-502.

Fine, M. (1991). *Framing dropouts.* Albany, NY: SUNY Press.

Fine, M. (1990). Silencing and nurturing voice in an improbable context: Urban adolescents in public school. In H.A. Giroux & P. McLaren (Eds.), *Critical pedagogy, the state and cultural struggle* (pp. 152-171). Albany: State University of New York Press.

Georgiadis, N. (1990). Does basketball have to be all W's and L's? An alternative program at a residential boy's home. *Journal of Physical Education, Recreation, and Dance, 61*(6), 42-44.

Haberman, M. (1987). *Recruiting and selecting teachers for urban schools.* Urban Diversity Series 95. Reston, VA: Association of Teacher Educators.

Haberman, M. (1991). Can cultural awareness be taught in teacher education programs? *Teaching Education, 4*(1), 25-31.

Hellison, D. (1990a). Teaching physical education to at-risk youth in Chicago: A model. *Journal of Physical Education, Recreation, and Dance, 61*(6), 38-39.

Hellison, D. (1990b). Making a difference-reflections on teaching urban at-risk youth. *Journal of Physical Education, Recreation and Dance, 61*(6), 44-45.

Johnson, J., Ludtke, M., & Riley, M. (1990). Shameful bequests to the next generation. *Time, 136*(15), 40-46.

Kohn, A. (1991). Teaching children to care. *Phi Delta Kappan, 72*(7), 496-506.

Kotlowitz, A. (1991). *There are no children here.* New York, NY: Doubleday.

Kroft, S. (1989, August 12). Chicago gangland: Children at war. CBS News - West 57th, Show #183.

Lifka, B. (1990). Hiding beneath the stairwell - A dropout prevention program for Hispanic youth. *Journal of Physical Education, Recreation and Dance, 61*(6), 40-41.

Martinek, T. (1983). Creating Golem and Galetea effects during physical education instruction: A social psychological perspective. In T.J. Templin & J.K. Olsen (Eds.), *Teaching in physical education.* Champaign, IL: Human Kinetics.

Merton, R.K. (1948). The self-fulfilling prophecy. *Antioch Review, 8*, 193-210.

Parish, R., Eubanks, E., Aquila, F.D., & Walker, S. (1989). Knock at any school. *Phi Delta Kappan, 70*(5), 386-394.

Rist, R.C. (1970). Student social class and teacher expectations: The self-fulfilling prophecy of ghetto education. *Harvard Educational Review, 40*(3), 411-451.

Rosenthal, R. (1987). Pygmalion Effects: Existence, magnitude, and social importance. *Educational Researcher, 16*(9), 37-41.

Schubert, W.H. (1986). *Curriculum, perspective, paradigm and possibility.* New York, NY: MacMillan Publishing Company.

Schubert, W.H. (1982). Teacher education as theory development. *Educational Considerations, 9*(2), 8-13.

Schubert, W.H. (1981). Knowledge about out-of-school curriculum. *The Educational Forum, 45*(2), 185-198.

Smith, S.J. (1991). Where is the child in physical education research? *Quest, 43*(1), 37-54.

Watkins, B.T. (1989). Colleges urged to train future schoolteachers to deal with the expected influx of immigrants. *The Chronicle of Higher Education, 36*(15), A14.

Williamson, K.M., & Georgiadis, N. (in press). Teaching in an after school program in inner city Chicago. *Journal of Physical Education, Recreation, and Dance.*

Williamson, K.M., & Hellison, D. (in press). Preservice teacher education for the inner city: Ideas and applications. *The Clearing House.*

Williamson, K.M., & Williams, J.A. (1990). Promoting equity awareness in the preparation of undergraduate physical education students. *Teaching Education, 3*(1), 117-123.

Brown Revisited

The school desegregation battle passed relatively quickly, Mr. White points out — but the scars of the efforts to forestall desegregation are far more lasting and can still be seen today.

Forrest R. White

Forrest R. White is director of budget for the Norfolk (Va.) Public Schools.

ALTHOUGH THE conventional view of *Oliver Brown, et al. v. Board of Education of Topeka, Shawnee County, Kansas, et al.*, decided by the United States Supreme Court 40 years ago last May,[1] is that the ruling came as a bolt from the blue, only the extent of the decree actually came as a surprise to most of those who were charged with the planning and leadership of southern cities. There is now compelling evidence to suggest that the 1954 *Brown* decision and its enforcement decree a year later were merely the keystone events in a decade-long effort to replace the South's elaborate system of legal (de jure) segregation with the type of de facto segregation found in northern, western, and midwestern cities as a result of well-defined racial barriers between neighborhoods.

That there would be some sort of decision from the Court overruling at least a portion of the South's elaborate system of segregated education was a foregone conclusion among many southern leaders; clearly, the "separate but equal" facilities maintained by communities, particularly those in rural areas, were so far from equivalent that only the most callous Court could disregard the distinction. Moreover, the nation was already desegregating its facilities for the military, for interstate transportation, for public accommodation, and for recreation—either through administrative action or through legal intervention—and it was hard to imagine that a country that had so recently committed itself to fighting oppressors overseas would allow its own public schools to remain bastions of racial subjugation at home.

It now appears that the individuals charged with the leadership and management of southern cities had ample time, opportunity, and motivation to prepare for the legally mandated demise of segregated schools and facilities in their communities; that they started making plans in anticipation of such a ruling long before the *Brown* case was ever decided; and that their preparations grew increasingly intense as the prospect of court-ordered integration became more and more real. Furthermore, it seems that these leaders took deliberate steps to use all the powers at their disposal — both direct (those related to the control of school construction, educational administration, and student attendance) and indirect (those that fall under the headings of redevelopment, city planning, the enforcement of codes, and urban renewal) — to forestall court-ordered school desegregation in the South. The impact of their preemptive actions has been almost as profound as the *Brown* decision itself and can still be seen today in carefully contrived boundaries of school zones and neighborhoods, mis-sized and misplaced school buildings, demolished housing, redeveloped properties, and inappropriate use of municipal land.

Thus, although the decade of the 1950s was a time in which a carefully planned and executed legal assault on school desegregation finally bore fruit, it was also the era in which the impact of the High Court's ruling was largely minimized and even negated in many communities by an equally well-planned and quietly orchestrated underground resistance. Unfortunately, the traditional histories of this decade have focused almost entirely on the shouting match that was going on in the streets and in the legislative corridors and have largely ignored the far more consequential planning sessions that were taking place in the back rooms of city halls across the South.

A Shifting Population

Even without the school desegregation controversy, the 1950s would have been a challenging enough time for school boards and municipal leaders in the urban South. The mass migration of blacks from the rural South had originally been directed toward the northern cities, but after World War II it shifted destinations to include the major southern urban centers. Most of the older cities of the South did not have a central ghetto or black district, as did their northern counterparts; instead, almost every white middle-class

The traditional histories have largely ignored the back-room planning sessions across the South.

neighborhood had a small concentration of blacks living nearby, from which it drew its domestic workers.[2] Since both the housing and the schools were strictly segregated, in accordance with state laws, the burden of maintaining separate-race schools was borne almost exclusively by black children, who had to be bused across town to achieve racially separate schools. This was exactly the situation outlawed in the *Brown* case — Linda Brown was being bused past the white schools in Topeka, Kansas[3] — and it was the circumstance most directly under attack from the National Association for the Advancement of Colored People (NAACP).[4]

The changing pattern of black migration was not, however, the only force defining the need for municipal planning and redevelopment activities. The military build-up that had taken place during World War II continued through the Korean conflict and on into the Cold War era, placing enormous pressures on Sunbelt cities to plan for the influx of people and industries. Veterans returning from the war and their "baby boom" offspring began to create their own demands for more housing, schools, shopping centers, and public services. In short, the 1950s saw shifts in population, housing, and land use, especially in the urban South, and it was here that the tools of redevelopment, land use planning, school planning, and urban renewal really came of age.[5]

Legal Precedents

Attempting to overturn centuries of discrimination, prejudice, tradition, and both statutory and unwritten codes of behavior was also a lengthy process. In the 1930s the NAACP — under the leadership of Charles Houston, dean of the Law School at Howard University, and Thurgood Marshall, his young protégé who was later to serve as a Supreme Court justice — launched a withering legal attack on the peculiar logic that provided the basis for maintaining segregated schools. Although the NAACP's assault was at first aimed at discrimination in graduate education, the intent was clearly to amass an irrefutable body of precedent that would lead to a decision striking down once and for all the notion that separate schools could be equal in American society.

In the major first victory, *Gaines* v. *Missouri* (1938), the Supreme Court struck down the argument that a government could avoid the responsibility of operating a school for blacks (in this case, a law school) when it preserved one exclusively for whites.[6] Even though Missouri helped to send its black law students to schools in other states, the logic of the NAACP was convincing to the nine lawyers who served as justices on the Court: they understood that there were certain powerful advantages associated with attending a law school in the state in which one intended to practice. In *Sweatt* v. *Painter* (1950), the Court decided that the makeshift law school provided for blacks by the state of Texas to avoid the *Gaines* precedent could not provide equal educational experience for blacks.[7] Again the lawyers on the Court were sympathetic to the argument that a law school that lacked an adequate law library, a distinguished faculty, and many of the other trappings of a high-quality legal education was clearly inferior and therefore unequal. In *McLaurin* v. *Oklahoma* (1950), the Court found that separate treatment of blacks, even when they were allowed to attend the same school as whites, was also unconstitutional discrimination. The plaintiff in this case had been forced to sit in the hall outside of his classes, had been given only limited access to the library, and had been subjected to other degrading treatment designed to limit his contact with the white students.[8]

Knowledgeable southerners knew that the U.S. Supreme Court would follow these precedents if it were faced with similar circumstances in public education (i.e., the absence of any facility for blacks, separate facilities for blacks that could be shown to be inadequate or inferior, or instances of separate and degrading treatment of black students). Four of the five cases accepted by the Court in its 1952 session had to do with precisely those issues.

In addition to the case that is the focus of this article, *Brown* v. *Board of Education*, the Court was presented with three other appeals that were based on the *Sweatt*, *Gaines*, and *McLaurin* precedents. In *Davis, et al.* v. *County School Board of Prince Edward County*, the Court was faced with a county that did not provide a senior high school for black pupils. Since those black students who wished to attend high school were bused to another county, the NAACP contended that, in line with the *Gaines* and *Sweatt* decisions, such an arrangement was separate and unequal treatment in terms of the physical plant provided, the curriculum, and the extensive transportation required.[9]

In *Briggs* v. *Elliot*, the NAACP argued that the physical facilities for blacks in Clarendon County, South Carolina, were inferior to those provided for whites. The case was designed to follow the *Sweatt* precedent: the schools for blacks in the county were older hand-me-downs from the white community, and many lacked playgrounds, ball fields, cafeterias, libraries, auditoriums, and other facilities that were present in the newer schools serving whites. In addition, this case featured a whole new realm of social/psychological research that pointed to the low self-esteem of the black children who attended these inferior schools.

To support the NAACP's contention in *Gebhart* v. *Belton*, university researchers in Delaware amassed a large body of literature to show that black schools in that state were inferior to white ones in terms of pupil/teacher ratios, teacher training, extracurricular activities, school supplies, library books, and other measures of curricular and instructional support. The plaintiffs hoped to play on the *Sweatt* decision and promote a finding that separate instructional programs, even in otherwise similar physical facilities, could be shown to be inferior and thus contrary to the equal protection provisions of the U.S. Constitution.[10]

The fact that the cases were first heard in the fall of 1952, re-argued during the 1953 session of the Court, and finally decided on 17 May 1954 gave the South plenty of time to prepare for the eventuality of an adverse ruling. Once *Brown* was decided, the Court held a second hearing on enforcement in April 1955,[11] and it was not until 31 May 1955, almost three years after the initial cases had been accepted for review, that the Supreme Court issued its implementing decree requiring desegregation "with all deliberate speed." Even then, in mandating that school districts make a "prompt and reasonable start towards full compliance," the Court recognized that a "transition period" would be necessary before such compliance could be achieved. Nevertheless, the justices indicated that courts could "consider problems related to administration, . . . the physical condition of the school plant, the school transportation system, personnel, . . . and attendance areas [in order] to achieve a system of determining admission to public schools on a nonracial basis."[12]

From De Jure to De Facto Segregation

Although most southern leaders expected to lose the *Davis* (no equal facilities), *Briggs* (unequal facilities), and *Gebhart* (unequal instructional programs) cases, in which the quantifiable differences between schools serving blacks and those serving whites could be remedied in ways that stopped short of desegregation, the outcome of *Brown* proved to be the most troublesome, since what was at issue could be remediated only by school integration. Even if the South were to build literally hundreds of new and largely unneeded schools, it still might have to integrate some buildings in order to comply with the *Brown* dictate that similarly situated students not receive separate treatment just to maintain racial separation. The *Brown* precedent, because it focused on the long crosstown bus ride, cut to the core of what many urban southern leaders, both black and white, felt was most unjust about the separate but equal system of education that had evolved in most of their cities.

The most immediate effect of the *Brown* decision was to strike down the laws requiring segregated schools — i.e., de jure segregation — in 17 states (Texas, Oklahoma, Missouri, Arkansas, Louisiana, Mississippi, Alabama, South Carolina, Georgia, Florida, North Carolina, Tennessee, Kentucky, Virginia, West Virginia, Maryland, and Delaware) and the laws permitting segregated schools in four other states (Kansas, Arizona, New Mexico, and Wyoming).[13] Clearly, the decision would have considerable impact on the local schools of thousands of communities across the Deep South and in such border states of the Confederacy as Maryland and Kentucky. A more hidden, but just as important, repercussion of the decision would be its impact on community planning, politics, and redevelopment, which up to this time had been just as completely tied

to the legal strictures of segregation as had the southern schools.

The Supreme Court left intact the kind of separate-race schools that were more typically found in the cities of the North, West, and Midwest — regions of de facto segregation. This type of segregation, defended as a "natural" outgrowth of an individual's choice of neighborhoods, was considered legitimate. Thus substantially equal schools that served separate-race neighborhoods were still permitted by the Court; only the particular circumstance presented by Linda Brown — a black living closer to a white school than to a black one — was initially found unconstitutional. At least one major study of integration in 24 northern, western, and midwestern cities found that even in the areas of the country that had already desegregated, most schools could clearly be designated as single-race institutions.[14]

Thus, as community leaders all across the South raced to discern the implications of the *Brown* decision, they found that some forms of segregation were still permitted. By carefully following the practices of northern, western, and midwestern cities, most communities in the border states could comply with the dictates of the Court with only minimal integration, and most of their schools could continue as essentially single-race schools except in the few areas of each city that were racially mixed or in transition or where two racially distinct neighborhoods would have to be served by the same school. Even then, the cities outside the South that had already desegregated had evolved an elaborate system of gerrymandered school districts, liberal transfer policies, "schools of choice," staggered enrollment procedures, in-school segregation by tracking, and other quasi-legal devices to avoid larger-scale integration or to ensure that whites would not have to attend predominantly black schools.[15] Community leaders in the South realized that some of these same techniques could potentially be applied to other facilities besides schools. They were strongly motivated to attempt to impose these lawful patterns of de facto segregation on schools and to work them into a wide range of local decisions regarding planning, redevelopment, and use of community facilities.

This careful distinction between continued segregation by place of residence and outright defiance of court-ordered integration was one of the chief reasons that reactions to the *Brown* decree were

fairly mild in most of the border states, which had relatively small black populations that were for the most part concentrated in large, central, and overcrowded downtown sections of cities and were only occasionally found in small, scattered settlements in other parts of the cities. The distinction meant that the model of de facto segregation of schools and neighborhoods found elsewhere in the country could be adopted without undue hardship, except in those few cities of the Deep South that had very large concentrations of black population, a history of racial strife, or vast class distinctions between their white and their black populations that would render even minimal integration unacceptable to large segments of the white community.[16] Although integrated facilities of any kind were opposed by the vast majority of white southerners, the prospect of large-scale race mixing in the public schools had southern leaders more concerned than any other aspect of desegregation. Indeed, several years before the Court actually rendered its call for desegregation, southern newspapers openly speculated about the magnitude of the reaction that would follow an adverse ruling:

> A decision of the Supreme Court that would provide for the admission of Negro students to public schools in areas where they would constitute a large proportion or a majority of the students might be the worst thing, rather than the best, that could happen in race relations where people of both races were not ready for such changes. The law is a living instrumentality, and if society must live under it, [then] the law must also live with society.[17]

While a number of communities in the border states, especially the larger cities, began almost immediately to take steps to comply with the dictates of the Court, the eight states of the Deep South in which blacks constituted 22% or more of the population (Florida, Georgia, South Carolina, North Carolina, Alabama, Mississippi, Louisiana, and Virginia) did not integrate at all until they were pushed to the limit by the courts.[18] In those states racial separation was more firmly entrenched — especially in those regions with the largest proportion of blacks in the population, a figure that could run as high as 70% to 80% in some rural areas. In these communities, desegregation meant not just the transfer of large numbers of blacks to previously all-white schools (a situation that was rare even in the areas of the country that had already desegregated) but also the assignment of whites to black schools — a practice that was almost unheard of anywhere else in the world.[19] This requirement was largely responsible for the violent reaction to the Court's decree.[20]

Although blacks and whites lived and worked in closer proximity to one another in the South than in other parts of the country, the history of the region presaged a more intense reaction to a desegregation ruling than was likely elsewhere. Because of the sad history of slavery, the interactions between races had evolved from a master/slave relationship — a situation that did not pertain in northern and midwestern cities, where blacks were but one more immigrant group. The area's strong states' rights philosophy, adopted as much for racial considerations as for any other cause, meant that the authority of the Court was sure to be challenged. Southern leaders had every right to fear that a ruling requiring desegregation might cause deep disruptions in their way of life, their political stability, and their economic rejuvenation.

Most of the contemporary studies of this era focused either on the communities in the border states that complied with the desegregation ruling (Baltimore; St. Louis; Topeka; Washington, D.C.; Chattanooga and Clinton, Tennessee; Louisville; and Wilmington)[21] or on the legislative maneuvering of the states in the Deep South that resisted. When actions in the resistant communities were studied, the focus was on the events that occurred after the first blacks were finally assigned by the courts to previously all-white schools. Unfortunately, neither of these approaches took into account more than a decade of planning and action by school boards, city councils, planning commissions, housing authorities, and other municipal officials who joined in a quiet but concerted attempt to forestall the impact of the *Brown* decision.

It is not surprising that local officials responded to the threat of court-ordered desegregation in the same manner as their counterparts in state capitals and the Congress and used every means at their disposal to frustrate, delay, or defuse the impact of desegregation on the schools and other public facilities in their communities. The lawyers of the NAACP legal defense team began filing court challenges against segregated schools, parks, beaches, and transportation facilities all across

the nation shortly after *Brown*,[22] and the local electorate was making the same kinds of demands as the statewide constituencies. Certainly, local officials were as adept as other elected officials at using whatever powers they possessed to frustrate and circumvent the dictates of the courts.

Since most southern leaders were aware of both the long-standing legal attack on segregated schools and the various precedents involved in this battle,[23] they immediately launched a wholesale effort to build new schools, parks, and playgrounds for blacks and thus to correct any obvious deficiencies in both funding and facilities. Several southern states were quick to adopt this approach while the *Brown* cases were still pending, hoping "to preserve segregation on a voluntary basis through [building] equal school facilities."[24] In most cases, these efforts were backed by new taxing authority, new (sales) taxes, popular referendums, and other measures that indicated strong white support for building new schools and upgrading the dilapidated school facilities used by blacks. The states obviously were keeping an eye on the NAACP victories in higher education, because their attention was on more than just the physical facilities of the schools. New playgrounds, cafeterias, auditoriums, libraries, and other amenities were added to existing school buildings, and funding for teacher salaries, textbooks, supplies, and training was increased to ensure that segregation would continue even if such "separate" facilities were required to be truly "equal" — the expected decree from the Court.[25] In many areas of the South there was such a rush to equalize facilities that a number of communities soon found that they were spending more to educate black students than white ones.[26]

Although local school boards and political leaders all across the South were initially resigned to desegregation and convinced that they could "handle" it without doing irreparable harm to public education,[27] they soon found that the state legislatures were erecting legal barriers to ensure that local schools, parks, playgrounds, and other public facilities would stay segregated. Those areas that attempted to comply with the Court's decree at the outset (i.e., Washington, St. Louis, Baltimore, and Wilmington) began to experience an unexpected level of racial turmoil that gave moderates in the Deep South cause for concern.[28] Hostili-

ty — first to the *Brown* decision and later to the Supreme Court — began to grow as southerners realized that their own communities would be granted little or no transition time. The NAACP kept up its legal pressures, and soon both the intent and the authority of the judiciary to enforce its integration orders were becoming clear as the federal courts ordered such segregated institutions as state parks, city recreation facilities, and public bus systems to desegregate.[29]

A number of communities began to adopt a "wait and see" attitude, delaying new projects until they could better discern the impact of the courts' decisions. By 1956 Mississippi was reporting that only a third of its counties had actually complied with the plan to "equalize" black schools;[30] Arkansas experienced similar delays in its own districts immediately after the *Brown* decision;[31] and Virginia newspapers indicated that "there was no longer any great pressure on local officials . . . to continue the special and costly attention to Negro school building programs."[32] When communities once again began to build schools in the period following *Brown*, the dictates of that ruling were critical in determining the location and size of new buildings. Communities abandoned sites under consideration if they were found to be too close to racial dividing lines and turned instead to new locations that could continue to carry a single-race designation.

Although initially many southern leaders assumed that blacks in their communities would be content with equal facilities, they realized that they were mistaken when they saw local blacks aligned with the NAACP efforts to desegregate schools, parks, playgrounds, and beaches through the courts. At first southerners tended to blame this shift in blacks' attitudes on "outsiders" and even to see it as a "communist plot" — a reaction that had also surfaced in several northern and midwestern cities in which the white community opposed school desegregation.[33] Just as in the cities of the border states that had already desegregated, race relations in a number of communities in the Deep South began to deteriorate as whites became aware that the blacks wanted to desegregate all schools and public facilities.[34] This growing feeling of animosity between the races found other outlets in the politics and civic life of most communities, so that the coming crisis over school desegregation affected almost every aspect of racial dialogue. Moreover, those few local school boards that did persist in their efforts to keep harmony between the races soon found themselves isolated by both the black community and the white one.[35]

Interposition

In November 1955 James Kilpatrick, editor of the *Richmond News Leader*, began to promote the doctrine of "interposition" — a long-lost constitutional interpretation that compels states to "interpose" their own authority in order to protect their citizens from unjust actions of the federal government — as the answer to continuing segregation. The idea was an immediate hit and soon dominated the rhetoric of southern politicians, even in the border states that had already begun to desegregate. Within 18 months after Kilpatrick began to promote interposition as a valid legal doctrine, all eight of the states of the Deep South had passed formal interposition resolutions and a number of laws designed to use the police powers of their states to enforce segregation of their schools, parks, and playgrounds.[36] Since it was the potential integration of the schools that caused the most public panic, the interposition argument was pushed to its greatest extreme in defense of segregated education. Even so, the states were not without creativity in their attempt to preserve segregation in other facilities, even going so far as to turn their state parks over to private contractors as a ruse to continue racial discrimination.[37]

In addition to the anti-NAACP laws that were enacted in most of the states of the Deep South, eight states passed pupil placement laws designed to block transfers between white schools and black ones, six states authorized the closing of public schools under the threat of integration, four states provided financial aid to students who attended private schools to escape court-ordered desegregation, and most weakened their laws on compulsory attendance, teacher salaries, pupil transportation, the term of teacher contracts, and the like.[38] Each of these laws was an attempt to delay desegregation by forcing the courts to peel away a layer of state government that had been interposed between the local schools and the courts. The doctrine of interposition was at the heart of the Southern Manifesto as well. Signed by 100 southern senators and congressmen, the manifesto proclaimed that integration was "contrary to established law" and professed that government offi-

cials had a duty to resist integration "with every legal means" at their disposal.[39]

Although most of the rhetoric of interposition was emanating from state political leaders, most of the active efforts to block the federal courts were undertaken by local school officials because they possessed the most direct powers to manage public schools, assign pupils, manipulate attendance zones, build new buildings, and otherwise control the racial composition of classrooms. Soon, however, local governments found that some of the same tactics that could be used to block the desegregation of schools had wide applications in preserving segregated neighborhoods as well. Suddenly the race was on to rezone, rebuild, and redevelop the cities in an all-out effort to create well-defined color barriers between neighborhoods, to isolate black populations, to demolish mixed-race areas, to relocate integrated schools, and otherwise to create an even more segregated society than had existed before *Brown*.

Foremost among the local powers of interposition were the ability actually to assign individual students to schools and the authority to control the size and shape of school attendance zones. At least seven states relied on the creative use of pupil assignment as a way to deter integration.[40] Several factors other than the race of the students could be used to support the creation of school attendance zones: the distance from home to school, the maximum utilization of school space, transportation considerations, topographical barriers, and the conformity of institutions (which was meant to prevent frequent transfers).[41]

Northern and midwestern cities intent on limiting integration already relied heavily on their authority to draw boundary lines that reflected the racial characteristics of the neighborhoods rather than the locations of the schools,[42] and it did not take long for southern school officials to become just as adept at blocking desegregation with this technique. When faced with court-ordered desegregation, the city of Charlottesville, Virginia, for instance, divided itself into six elementary school zones; the lines of one of the "black" zones were so carefully drawn that the area included almost all the black students who had applied to go to previously all-white schools.[43]

Southern leaders also found that the federal courts would grant them broad leeway to exercise their "administrative

discretion" in matters of construction and zoning — even if administrative discretion had the same effect, because of prevailing housing patterns, as designating a building as a "white" or "black" facility. Several practices related to determining the location and size of new buildings and limiting attendance zones had been used for decades in northern cities to limit integration.[44] The careful location of schools and other public buildings for the purpose of minimizing integration was not only accepted by the courts but also strongly urged by newspaper editor Kilpatrick, who was fast becoming the chief spokesman for southern defiance. "A great part of the problem, especially in the cities, could be handled by the relocation of school buildings and the gerrymandering of enrollment lines," he counseled. The Richmond school board, under the leadership of Lewis Powell, Jr., who was later to sit on the U.S. Supreme Court, responded to Kilpatrick's advice by building several new schools in black neighborhoods.[45] Norfolk created one new school by pushing six mobile classrooms off the back of a truck a few weeks after the federal district court released the addresses of the plaintiffs in its own school desegregation suit.[46] The undisputed administrative authority of the local boards extended even to the assignment of a general racial designation to a facility. Norfolk and Newport News, Virginia, both turned formerly all-white elementary schools over to their black school systems in order to deter an impending desegregation ruling from the courts.[47] Norfolk even built six minischools, with five rooms each, to ensure the single-race composition of their attendance zones.[48]

Thus in the period immediately following the *Brown* decision, almost every school board and governmental agency in the South was focusing on the proximity of black students to white schools.[49] The realization was growing that school boards, city councils, and other public agencies were not powerless before the courts. Legal scholars were careful to point out that "the Constitution . . . does not require integration. It merely forbids discrimination. It does not forbid such discrimination as occurs as a result of voluntary action [such as choice of residence, neighborhood, or city]."[50]

City councils, although generally more reluctant than their school boards to take overt actions to block the federal courts, were just as motivated to use every legal means at their disposal to delay or deter

Kentucky National Guardsmen with M-47 tank help restrain a crowd on the grounds of the Sturgis High School after nine blacks entered the building to begin classes. White students near the entrance are being urged by the crowd to leave the school.

the threat of school desegregation, even going so far as to appropriate school funds on a month-to-month basis so as to intimidate black leaders and keep their school boards in check.[51] Although most of the cities' powers were related to urban renewal — redevelopment, planning, zoning, enforcement of codes, and economic development — and not to schools, southern cities were quick to learn that they possessed a potent arsenal of tools that could be used to block integration.

Closing a threatened school was a community's most obvious defense when faced with a court order to desegregate, and school-closing powers lay at the heart of Virginia's "Massive Resistance" statutes — the governor was required to close any integrated public school — and at the heart of its more unofficial system of providing public support for segregated (white) private schools. Schools in Norfolk, Arlington, and Charlottesville were closed by the state for most of the 1958-59 school year, locking out 10,000 white students in Norfolk alone. Prince Edward County, however, provided the best example of Virginia's Massive Resistance plan: public schools there were closed for several years while a white pri-

vate academy flourished with state-supported tuition grants.

Even though closing schools was thought to be the ultimate weapon in the fight against school desegregation, closing whole neighborhoods was even more destructive, and it was the application of municipal powers related to urban renewal that had the most lasting effect on the South. Robert Weaver, who was then director of the federal Housing and Home Finance Agency, has written that, "in a few southern cities . . . urban renewal too often seemed to be an instrument for wiping out racially integrated living."[52] This was certainly the case in Norfolk, where a frantic second stage of redevelopment tore down the homes of almost 20,000 people — nearly one-tenth of the population — in little more than a year. Unlike earlier redevelopment efforts, this one did not focus on substandard multi-family structures in central city slums, although Norfolk still had plenty of those. Instead, most of the houses that were destroyed were safe, decent, and even modern homes of middle-class families living on the edge of downtown. Their sudden demolition had little to do with the quality of housing; rather, demolition was

driven by the fact that the houses were located in the mixed-race neighborhoods where all the plaintiffs in the city's school desegregation suit lived.[53]

Just as effective as tearing down all the houses in a neighborhood was the selective renewal of mixed-race areas or the resizing of neighborhoods with the careful placement of public land. Some cities — notably Mobile, Alabama — relied on their interstate highways to divide neighborhoods and school attendance zones into racially distinct areas.[54] Others, when faced with a situation in which black students lived closer to white schools than to black ones, used their powers to acquire additional land for parks, playgrounds, state colleges, industrial parks, or other public purposes, thereby placing topographical barriers between neighborhoods and thus preserving the racial character of their schools. St. Louis and Baltimore appear to have employed a combination of natural geographic barriers and selective redevelopment to keep blacks confined to racially distinct school attendance zones.[55]

Just as school boards could manipulate attendance zones, cities could change their own size through merger and annexation and thus alter the pattern of school attendance. When Newport News was faced with court-ordered desegregation in 1958, for instance, the city merged with Warwick County, and the resultant ripple effect on school attendance zones allowed it to delay integration successfully for another year.[56] Richmond also used this strategy effectively, and at least one study has indicated that this city's efforts to annex surrounding counties was motivated largely by racial considerations.[57]

Thus the local governments — even more than the states — had at their disposal a large arsenal of powers that could be "interposed" between the courts and the schools to create segregated neighborhoods, enforce well-defined color barriers, isolate black populations, relocate integrated schools, and otherwise forestall court-ordered school desegregation. This was certainly the charge by plaintiffs in a number of school desegregation suits — a claim in part supported by demographic researchers and other social scientists, but they have chosen to blame school boards rather than redevelopment authorities, planning commissions, or city councils.[58] Most educational researchers have chosen to focus on the political implications of decisions that were made by school boards only when they actually faced a court order to desegregate. Thus they lend credence to the theory that, in most communities, the school boards were the villains.

The truth is that school boards were merely being dragged along in the planning, redevelopment, and housing activities of other local officials; that is, the placement of schools and the drawing of new attendance zones in many cities were only the last acts in a far more elaborate plot to replace de jure segregation with de facto segregation. In fact, southern cities appear to have used their powers of urban renewal to forestall school desegregation more often in the 1950s than in the 1960s, the decade for which more extensive documentation exists. Not only was the motivation perhaps stronger in the 1950s, but also community groups and the courts were less inclined to scrutinize actions that bore the imprint of racial planning — partly because up to that point all planning in the South, and in most of the rest of the nation as well, was designed to support the "separate but equal" and "neighborhoods of choice" concepts that were legally permissible for several years after Brown.[59]

IN LIGHT OF the enormous controversy surrounding school desegregation, it is not hard to see how the same tools that could be used to promote new growth could just as easily be enlisted in the effort to prevent certain land uses, especially those related to integrated school districts. The building boom that was already going on in most southern communities provided ample opportunity to apply the powers of urban renewal to the preservation of segregated schools. In addition, in the older cities of the South, there was a feeling of urgency prompted by situations in which blacks lived in closer proximity to white schools than to their own. It was when these two factors — opportunity and urgency — were present to a large degree that redevelopment projects, the building of new schools and highways, and other public initiatives were undertaken, partly to achieve racially segregated school districts — that is, to move with all deliberate speed from de jure to de facto segregation.

Thurgood Marshall and the lawyers at Howard University who plotted the demise of school segregation laws for the NAACP knew that it would take years to overthrow the legal structure that both established separate-race schools and kept them unequal. They knew as well that it would take decades to overcome centuries of prejudice and the peculiar social and political conventions that supported segregated schools. They did not know, however, that they were up against forces in the South that were even then working just as hard to undermine and counteract their efforts. And they never contemplated that these same forces would be willing to wreak long-term havoc on their own communities — to close schools, demolish neighborhoods, artificially divide cities, and manipulate the size and location of school buildings — just to preserve an outdated social doctrine.

The school desegregation battle passed relatively quickly, leaving only a few brief, but indelible memories — federal troops in Little Rock, padlocked schools in Norfolk, George Wallace blocking the doors to Ole Miss — before de jure segregation faded forever from the national scene. Unfortunately, the scars of the effort to forestall desegregation through interposition are far more lasting and can still be seen today in mis-sized and misplaced schools, needlessly demolished homes and neighborhoods, poorly and hastily contrived urban renewal efforts,

and highways created partly to divide residential zones.

1. *Oliver Brown, et al.* v. *Board of Education of Topeka, Shawnee County, Kansas, et al.*, reprinted in *Race Relations Law Reporter*, February 1956, p. 8.

2. Karl E. Taueber and Alma F. Taueber, *Negroes in Cities: Residential Segregation and Neighborhood Change* (Chicago: Aldine Publishing, 1965), pp. 23-122.

3. "And Who Was Brown? Well . . . ," *Southern School News*, September 1958, p. 1.

4. Walter G. Stephan, "A Brief Historical Overview of School Desegregation," in Walter G. Stephan and Joe R. Feagin, eds., *School Desegregation: Past, Present, and Future* (New York: Plenum Press, 1980), p. 13.

5. Carl Abbott, *The New Urban America: Growth and Politics in Sunbelt Cities* (Chapel Hill: University of North Carolina Press, 1981).

6. Robert A. Leflar, "Law of the Land: The Courts and the Schools," in Don Shoemaker, ed.. *"With All Deliberate Speed"* (New York: Harper & Brothers, 1957), p. 1.

7. *Brown* v. *Board of Education*, p. 8.

8. Leflar, p. 2.

9. Milton Finklestein, Jawn A. Sandifer, and Elfreda Wright, *Minorities: U.S.A.* (New York: Globe Books, 1971).

10. Leflar, p. 3; *Brown* v. *Board*, pp. 5-7; and Stephan, pp. 11-17.

11. Leflar, pp. 3-4.

12. *Brown* v. *Board of Education*, p. 11.

13. "Reaction to Supreme Court Decision Calm, Resigned," *Southern School News*, 3 September 1954, pp. 1-2.

14. Robin M. Williams and Margaret W. Ryan, eds., *Schools in Transition: Community Experiences in Desegregation* (Chapel Hill: University of North Carolina Press, 1954).

15. Ibid., pp. 45, 57, 102, 240, 242, and 443.

16. Ibid., pp. 40, 80-110.

17. "Segregation's Summing Up — Living and Evolving Law," *Norfolk Virginian-Pilot*, 13 December 1952, p. 5.

18. "Background: 8 States Still Holdouts," *Southern School News*, September 1956, pp. 1-2; "Segregation Still Holding in Deep South; North Carolina Cities Exception," *Southern School News*, September 1957, p. 1; and W. D. Workman, Jr., "The Deep South," in Shoemaker, p. 89.

19. Williams and Ryan, op cit.

20. Workman, p. 89.

21. Robert L. Crain et al., *The Politics of School Desegregation: Comparative Case Studies of Community Structure and Policy-Making* (Chicago: Aldine Press, 1968); "Chattanooga Story — What Happened?," *Southern School News*, June 1956, pp. 6-7; "Reaction to Supreme . . ."; Jeffrey A. Raffel, *The Politics of School Desegregation: The Metropolitan Remedy in Delaware* (Philadelphia: Temple University Press, 1980); and Ray Rist, *Desegregated Schools: Appraisals of the American Experience* (New York: Academic Press, 1979).

22. Lino A. Gragila, "From Prohibiting Segregation to Requiring Integration," in Stephan and Feagin, pp. 69-96.

23. Sam Ervin, Jr., "The Case for Segregation," *Look*, 3 April 1956, pp. 32-33.

24. "Mississippi: Only ¹/₃ of Counties Complied

with Equalization Plan," *Southern School News*, July 1956, pp. 1, 12.

25. Forrest R. White, *Pride and Prejudice: School Desegregation and Urban Renewal in Norfolk, 1950-1959* (Westport, Conn.: Praeger, 1991).

26. Workman, p. 93.

27. "Reaction to Supreme. . . ."

28. "D.C.: Trouble of Anacostia High Reflects Climate of Change," *Southern School News*, 4 November 1954, p. 4.

29. "Virginia Court Strikes Down Enforced Segregation in State Park," *Southern School News*, 7 April 1955, p. 14.

30. "Mississippi. . . ."

31. "Arkansas: School Building Plans Delayed Pending Court's Decision," *Southern School News*, 1 December 1954, p. 4.

32. "Segregation Decision Curbs School Construction," *Norfolk Ledger-Dispatch*, 13 October 1954, p. 6.

33. "Blacks Push for 'Equal Facilities' Instead of Integration," *Southern School News*, 6 January 1955, p. 12; James W. Ely, Jr., *The Crisis of Conservative Virginia: The Byrd Organization and the Politics of Massive Resistance* (Knoxville: University of Tennessee Press, 1976), p. 31; and Williams and Ryan, p. 237.

34. "Leaders Blame Racial Communications Problems on Pressure to Integrate," *Southern School News*, January 1955, p. 7.

35. "Chattanooga Story. . . ."

36. Workman, p. 97.

37. "Virginia Court. . . ."

38. Patrick E. McCauley, "Be It Enacted," in Shoemaker, p. 132.

39. Stephan, p. 12.

40. " 'Background' Power to Assign Pupils Is Studied in 7 States," *Southern School News*, February 1957, p. 1.

41. "Report of the Subcommittee on Zoning," New York Board of Education, 14 December 1956, reprinted in *Race Relations Law Reporter*, October 1956, p. 847.

42. Williams and Ryan, p. 57.

43. "Virginia: Charlottesville Divides Itself into 6 School Zones," *Southern School News*, September 1958, p. 6.

44. *Shannon Marguerite Henry* v. *Walter Godsell, et al.,* U.S. District Court, Michigan, 12 August 1958, No. 14,769, reprinted in *Race Relations Law Reporter*, October 1958, pp. 914-16.

45. Ely, pp. 36, 134.

46. White, pp. 235, 264.

47. "Virginia: Newport News Board Turns School Over to Negroes Rather Than Integrate," *Southern School News*, October 1955, p. 6.

48. White, pp. 235, 265.

49. "3 North Carolina Cities Assign 12 Negroes to Previously White Schools," *Southern School News*, August 1957, p. 3.

50. "Trends: Judge John J. Parker in *Briggs* v. *Elliot*," *Southern School News*, August 1956, p. 1.

51. "Virginia: Norfolk Board Votes 'Approval in Principle' of Integration," *Southern School News*, 6 July 1955, p. 10.

52. Robert C. Weaver, "The Urban Complex," in Jewel Bellush and Murray Hausknecht, eds., *Urban Renewal: People, Politics, and Planning* (Garden City, N.Y.: Doubleday, 1967), p. 94.

53. White, op. cit.

54. Charles V. Willie and Susan L. Greenblatt, *Community Politics and Educational Change: Ten School Systems Under Court Order* (New York: Longman, 1981), p. 189.

55. Crain et al., pp. 15, 72-73.

56. "Virginia: Students in Closed Schools: Where Are They Now?," *Southern School News*, January 1959, p. 9.

57. Willie and Greenblatt, pp. 231-32.

58. Gary Orfield, "Ghettoization and Its Alternatives," in Paul E. Peterson, ed., *The New Urban Reality* (Washington, D.C.: Brookings Institution, 1985), pp. 161-96; and Karl Taueber, "Residence and Race: 1619 to 2019," in Winston A. Van Horne, ed., *Race: Twentieth Century Dilemmas — Twenty-First Century Prognoses* (Milwaukee: University of Wisconsin, 1989), pp. 229-51.

59. *Heywood, et al.* v. *Public Housing Administration*, 135 F. Supp. 217, reprinted in *Race Relations Law Reporter*, April 1956, p. 347.

The AAUW Report: How Schools Shortchange Girls
— Overview —

— Why a Report on Girls? —

The invisibility of girls in the current education debate suggests that girls and boys have identical educational experiences in school. Nothing could be further from the truth. Whether one looks at achievement scores, curriculum design, or teacher-student interaction, it is clear that sex and gender make a difference in the nation's public elementary and secondary schools.

The educational system is not meeting girls' needs. Girls and boys enter school roughly equal in measured ability. Twelve years later, girls have fallen behind their male classmates in key areas such as higher-level mathematics and measures of self-esteem. Yet gender equity is still not a part of the national debate on educational reform.

Research shows that policies developed to foster the equitable treatment of students and the creation of gender-equitable educational environments can make a difference. They can make a difference, that is, if they are strongly worded and vigorously enforced.

V. Lee, H. Marks and T. Knowles, "Sexism in Single-Sex and Coeducational Secondary School Classrooms," paper presented at the American Sociological Association annual meeting, Cincinnati, OH, August 1991; S. Bailey and R. Smith, *Policies for the Future,* Council of Chief State School Officers, Washington, DC, 1982.

Neither the *National Education Goals* issued by the National Governors Association in 1990 nor *America 2000,* the 1991 plan of the President and the U.S. Department of Education to "move every community in America toward these goals" makes any mention of providing girls equitable opportunities in the nation's public schools. Girls continue to be left out of the debate—despite the fact that for more than two decades researchers have identified gender bias as a major problem at all levels of schooling.

Schools must prepare both girls and boys for full and active roles in the family, the community, and the work force. Whether we look at the issues from an economic, political, or social perspective, girls are one-half of our future. We must move them from the sidelines to the center of the education-reform debate.

A critical step in correcting educational inequities is identifying them publicly. The *AAUW Report: How Schools Shortchange Girls* provides a comprehensive assessment of the status of girls in public education today. It exposes myths about girls and learning, and it supports the work of the many teachers who have struggled to define and combat gender bias in their schools. The report challenges us all—policymakers, educators, administrators, parents, and citizens—to rethink old assumptions and act now to stop schools from shortchanging girls.

Our public education system is plagued by numerous failings that affect boys as negatively as girls. But in many respects girls are put at a disadvantage simply because they are girls. *The AAUW Report* documents this in hundreds of cited studies.

When our schools become more gender-fair, education will improve for all our students—boys as well as girls—because excellence in education cannot be achieved without equity in education. By studying what happens to girls in school, we can gain valuable insights about what has to change in order for each student, every girl and every boy, to do as well as she or he can.

What Do We Teach Our Students?

• The contributions and experiences of girls and women are still marginalized or ignored in many of the textbooks used in our nation's schools.
• Schools, for the most part, provide inadequate education on sexuality and healthy development despite national concern about teen pregnancy, the AIDS crisis, and the increase of sexually transmitted diseases among adolescents.

• Incest, rape, and other physical violence severely compromise the lives of girls and women all across the country. These realities are rarely, if ever, discussed in schools.

Curriculum delivers the central messages of education. It can strengthen or decrease student motivation for engagement, effort, growth, and development through the images it gives to students about themselves and the world. When the curriculum does not reflect the diversity of students' lives and cultures, it delivers an incomplete message.

Studies have shown that multicultural readings produced markedly more favorable attitudes toward nondominant groups than did the traditional reading lists, that academic achievement for all students was linked to use of nonsexist and multicultural materials, and that sex-role stereotyping was reduced in students whose curriculum portrayed males and females in non-stereotypical roles. Yet during the 1980s, federal support for reform regarding sex and race equity dropped, and a 1989 study showed that of the ten books most frequently assigned in public high school English courses only one was written by a woman and none by members of minority groups.

The "evaded" curriculum is a term coined in this report to refer to matters central to the lives of students that are touched on only briefly, if at all, in most schools. The United States has the highest rate of teenage childbearing in the Western industrialized world. Syphilis rates are now equal for girls and boys, and more teenage girls than boys contract gonorrhea. Although in the adult population AIDS is nine times more prevalent in men than in women, the same is not true for young people. In a District of Columbia study, the rate of HIV infection for girls was almost three times that for boys. Despite all of this, adequate sex and health education is the exception rather than the rule.

Adolescence is a difficult period for all young people, but it is particularly difficult for girls, who are far more likely to develop eating disorders and experience depression. Adolescent girls attempt suicide four to five times as often as boys (although boys, who choose more lethal methods, are more likely to be successful in their attempts).

Despite medical studies indicating that roughly equal proportions of girls and boys suffer from learning disabilities, more than twice as many boys are identified by school personnel as in need of special-education services for learning-disabled students.
U.S. Department of Education, Office for Civil Rights, 1988.

Perhaps the most evaded of all topics in schools is the issue of gender and power. As girls mature they confront a culture that both idealizes and exploits the sexuality of young women while assigning them roles that are clearly less valued than male roles. If we do not begin to discuss more openly the ways in which

ascribed power—whether on the basis of race, sex, class, sexual orientation, or religion—affects individual lives, we cannot truly prepare our students for responsible citizenship.

These issues are discussed in detail and the research fully annotated in Part 4/Chapters 1 and 3 of The AAUW Report.

How Do Race/Ethnicity and Socioeconomic Status Affect Achievement in School?

• Girls from low-income families face particularly severe obstacles. Socioeconomic status, more than any other variable, affects access to school resources and educational outcomes.
• Test scores of low-socioeconomic-status girls are somewhat better than for boys from the same background in the lower grades, but by high school these differences disappear. Among high-socioeconomic-status students, boys generally outperform girls regardless of race/ethnicity.
• Girls and boys with the same Math SAT scores do not do equally well in college—girls do better.

In most cases tests reflect rather than cause inequities in American education. The fact that groups score differently on a test does not necessarily mean that the test is biased. If, however, the score differences are related to the validity of the test—for example, if girls and boys know about the same amount of math but boys' test scores are consistently and significantly higher—then the test is biased.

A number of aspects of a test—beyond that which is being tested—can affect the score. For example, girls tend to score better than boys on essay tests, boys better than girls on multiple-choice items. Even today many girls and boys come to a testing situation with different interests and experiences. Thus a reading-comprehension passage that focuses on baseball scores will tend to favor boys, while a question testing the same skills that focuses on child care will tend to favor girls.

These issues are discussed in detail and the research fully annotated in Part 3 of The AAUW Report.

Why Do Girls Drop Out and What Are the Consequences?

• Pregnancy is not the only reason girls drop out of school. In fact, less than half the girls who leave school give pregnancy as the reason.
• Dropout rates for Hispanic girls vary considerably by national origin: Puerto Rican and Cuban American girls are more likely to drop out than are boys from the same cultures or other Hispanic girls.
• Childhood poverty is almost inescapable in single-parent families headed by women without a high school diploma: 77 percent for whites and 87 percent for African Americans.

In a recent study, 37 percent of the female drop-outs compared to only 5 percent of the male drop-outs cited "family-related problems" as the reason they left high school. Traditional gender roles place greater family responsibilities on adolescent girls than on their brothers. Girls are often expected to "help out" with caretaking responsibilities; boys rarely encounter this expectation.

There has been little change in sex-segregated enrollment patterns in vocational education: girls are enrolled primarily in office and business-training programs, boys in programs leading to higher-paying jobs in the trades.

U.S. Department of Education, 1989.

However, girls as well as boys also drop out of school simply because they do not consider school pleasant or worthwhile. Asked what a worthwhile school experience would be, a group of teenage girls responded, "School would be fun. Our teachers would be excited and lively, not bored. They would act caring and take time to understand how students feel. . . . Boys would treat us with respect. If they run by and grab your tits, they would get into trouble."*

Women and children are the most impoverished members of our society. Inadequate education not only limits opportunities for women but jeopardizes their children's—and the nation's—future.

These issues are discussed in detail and the research fully annotated in Part 2/Chapters 4 and 6 of The AAUW Report.

The research reviewed in this report challenges traditional assumptions about the egalitarian nature of American schools. Young women in the United States today are still not participating equally in our educational system. Research documents that girls do not receive equitable amounts of teacher attention, that they are less apt than boys to see themselves reflected in the materials they study, and that they often are not expected or encouraged to pursue higher level mathematics and science courses. The implications are clear; the system must change.

We now have a window of opportunity that must not be missed. Efforts to improve public education are under way around the nation. We must move girls from the sidelines to the center of educational planning. The nation can no longer afford to ignore the potential of girls and young women. Whether one looks at the issues from an economic, political, or social perspective, girls are one-half of our future.

Significant improvements in the educational opportunities available to girls have occurred in the past two decades. However, twenty years after the passage of Title IX, the achievement of sex- and gender-equitable education remains an elusive dream. The time to turn dreams to reality is now. The

current education-reform movement cannot succeed if it continues to ignore half of its constituents. The issues are urgent; our actions must be swift and effective.

— The Recommendations —

Strengthened Reinforcement of Title IX Is Essential.

1. Require school districts to assess and report on a regular basis to the Office for Civil Rights in the U.S. Department of Education on their own Title IX compliance measures.
2. Fund the Office for Civil Rights at a level that permits increased compliance reviews and full and prompt investigation of Title IX complaints.
3. In assessing the status of Title IX compliance, school districts must include a review of the treatment of pregnant teens and teen parents. Evidence indicates that these students are still the victims of discriminatory treatment in many schools.

Teachers, Administrators and Counselors Must Be Prepared and Encouraged to Bring Gender Equity and Awareness to Every Aspect of Schooling.

4. State certification standards for teachers and administrators should require course work on gender issues, including new research on women, bias in classroom-interaction patterns, and the ways in which schools can develop and implement gender-fair multicultural curricula.
5. If a national teacher examination is developed, it should include items on methods for achieving gender equity in the classroom and in curricula.
6. Teachers, administrators, and counselors should be evaluated on the degree to which they promote and encourage gender-equitable and multicultural education.
7. Support and released time must be provided by school districts for teacher-initiated research on curricula and classroom variables that affect student learning. Gender equity should be a focus of this research and a criterion for awarding funds.
8. School-improvement efforts must include a focus on the ongoing professional development of teachers and administrators, including those working in specialized areas such as bilingual, compensatory, special, and vocational education.
9. Teacher-training courses must not perpetuate assumptions about the superiority of traits and activities traditionally ascribed to males in our society. Assertive and affiliative skills as well as verbal and mathematical skills must be fostered in both girls and boys.
10. Teachers must help girls develop positive views of themselves and their futures, as well as an understanding of the obstacles women must overcome in a society where their options and opportunities are still limited by gender stereotypes and assumptions.

---

*As quoted in *In Their Own Voices: Young Women Talk About Dropping Out,* Project on Equal Education Rights (New York, National Organization for Women Legal Defense and Education Fund, 1988), p. 12.

6. SPECIAL TOPICS IN MULTICULTURAL EDUCATION

The Formal School Curriculum Must Include the Experiences of Women and Men From All Walks of Life. Girls and Boys Must See Women and Girls Reflected and Valued in the Materials They Study.

11. Federal and state funding must be used to support research, development, and follow-up study of gender-fair multicultural curricular models.

12. The Women's Educational Equity Act Program (WEEAP) in the U.S. Department of Education must receive increased funding in order to continue the development of curricular materials and models, and to assist school districts in Title IX compliance.

13. School curricula should deal directly with issues of power, gender politics, and violence against women. Better-informed girls are better equipped to make decisions about their futures. Girls and young women who have a strong sense of themselves are better able to confront violence and abuse in their lives.

14. Educational organizations must support, via conferences, meetings, budget deliberations, and policy decisions, the development of gender-fair multicultural curricula in all areas of instruction.

15. Curricula for young children must not perpetuate gender stereotypes and should reflect sensitivity to different learning styles.

Girls Must Be Educated and Encouraged to Understand That Mathematics and the Sciences Are Important and Relevant to Their Lives. Girls Must Be Actively Supported in Pursuing Education and Employment in These Areas.

16. Existing equity guidelines should be effectively implemented in all programs supported by local, state, and federal governments. Specific attention must be directed toward including women on planning committees and focusing on girls and women in the goals, instructional strategies, teacher training, and research components of these programs.

17. The federal government must fund and encourage research on the effect on girls and boys of new curricula in the sciences and mathematics. Research is needed particularly in science areas where boys appear to be improving their performance while girls are not.

18. Educational institutions, professional organizations, and the business community must work together to dispel myths about math and science as "inappropriate" fields for women.

19. Local schools and communities must encourage and support girls studying science and mathematics by showcasing women role models in scientific and technological fields, disseminating career information, and offering "hands-on" experiences and work groups in science and math classes.

20. Local schools should seek strong links with youth-serving organizations that have developed successful out-of-school programs for girls in mathematics and science and with those girls' schools that have developed effective programs in these areas.

Continued Attention to Gender Equity in Vocational Education Programs Must Be a High Priority at Every Level of Educational Governance and Administration.

21. Linkages must be developed with the private sector to help ensure that girls with training in nontraditional areas find appropriate employment.

22. The use of a discretionary process for awarding vocational-education funds should be encouraged to prompt innovative efforts.

23. All states should be required to make support services (such as child care and transportation) available to both vocational and prevocational students.

24. There must be continuing research on the effectiveness of vocational education for girls and the extent to which the 1990 Vocational Education Amendments benefit girls.

Testing and Assessment Must Serve as Stepping Stones Not Stop Signs. New Tests and Testing Techniques Must Accurately Reflect the Abilities of Both Girls and Boys.

25. Test scores should not be the only factor considered in admissions or the awarding of scholarships.

26. General aptitude and achievement tests should balance sex differences in item types and contexts. Tests should favor neither females nor males.

27. Tests that relate to "real life situations" should reflect the experiences of both girls and boys.

Girls and Women Must Play a Central Role in Educational Reform. The Experiences, Strengths, and Needs of Girls From Every Race and Social Class Must Be Considered in Order to Provide Excellence and Equity for All Our Nation's Students.

28. National, state, and local governing bodies should ensure that women of diverse backgrounds are equitably represented on committees and commissions on educational reform.

29. Receipt of government funding for in-service and professional development programs should be conditioned upon evidence of efforts to increase the number of women in positions in which they are underrepresented. All levels of government have a role to play in increasing the numbers of women, especially women of color, in education-management and policy positions.

30. The U.S. Department of Education's Office of Educational Research and Improvement (OERI) should establish an advisory panel of gender-equity experts to work with OERI to develop a research and dissemination agenda to foster gender-equitable education in the nation's classrooms.

31. Federal and state agencies must collect, analyze, and report data broken down by race/ethnicity, sex, and some measure of socioeconomic status, such as parental income or education. National standards for use by all school districts should be developed so that data are comparable across district and state lines.

32. National standards for computing dropout rates should be developed for use by all school districts.

33. Professional organizations should ensure that women serve on education-focused committees. Organizations should utilize the expertise of their female membership when developing educational initiatives.

34. Local schools must call on the expertise of teachers, a majority of whom are women, in their restructuring efforts.

35. Women teachers must be encouraged and supported to seek administrative positions and elected office, where they can bring the insights gained in the classroom to the formulation of education policies.

A Critical Goal of Education Reform Must Be to Enable Students to Deal Effectively with the Realities of Their Lives, Particularly in Areas Such as Sexuality and Health.

36. Strong policies against sexual harassment must be developed. All school personnel must take responsibility for enforcing these policies.

37. Federal and state funding should be used to promote partnerships between schools and community groups, including social service agencies, youth-serving organizations, medical facilities, and local businesses. The needs of students, partic-ularly as highlighted by pregnant teens and teen mothers, require a multi-institutional response.

38. Comprehensive school-based health- and sex-education programs must begin in the early grades and continue sequentially through twelfth grade. These courses must address the topics of reproduction and reproductive health, sexual abuse, drug and alcohol use, and general mental and physical health issues. There must be a special focus on the prevention of AIDS.

39. State and local school board policies should enable and encourage young mothers to complete school, without compromising the quality of education these students receive.

40. Child care for the children of teen mothers must be an integral part of all programs designed to encourage young women to pursue or complete educational programs.

Toward a New Day in Our Visions of Education: Multiple Visions — Universal Hope

We look forward to the future of multicultural education with a fair degree of optimism, yet we are aware that there are serious challenges before us. The winds of demophobia are blowing across the land again; concern regarding immigration is at a fairly high level. Yet this concern was also present in all earlier decades in American history when rates of immigration were running at high levels. We all agree that there is much work to be done to accomplish the goals of multicultural education. We are going to become less and less like Western Europe and more and more a very unique national wonder such as Earth has not seen before. The next 30 to 40 years will bring that vision into reality.

We need a vision for the future of our schools that includes a belief in the worth and dignity of all persons. We need to clarify our vision for the future of education in such a way that it has a holistic character, which takes into account that ever more culturally pluralistic social reality that we are becoming. As part of this effort to construct a vision for our social future in which we embrace that great multicultural reality that we are, we need to consider the French revolutionary concept of fraternity, the female gender referent to which is sorority. Fraternity and sorority refer to brotherhood and sisterhood. We need to bond together as multicultural peoples, as brothers and sisters who care for and are committed to the well-being of each other. We need a new birth of fraternity and sorority in our national life that will enable us to truly care about what happens to one another. We need very much to communicate that sense of caring to the young people who attend our schools, for they truly are our social future. The teaching profession needs a good dose of fraternity and sorority as well. Teachers need to work together in solving problems and supporting their respective professional efforts on behalf of students.

The future of teaching and learning from a multicultural perspective should include more emphasis on cooperative learning strategies that encourage students to develop a sense of community and fraternity and sorority, which will transcend competition with one another and create a sense of trust and caring among them. We need to stop making students compete with one another, and encourage them to work together. The future should see more emphasis on competition with self and caring community with others. Along with this emphasis on building a sense of community among our students, teachers need to work as a community of concerned brothers and sisters who care about each others' professional responsibilities and autonomy as classroom decision makers. There needs to be more sharing of experience, knowledge bases, and expertise among teachers. We need to learn to team together and teach together more than we have in the past, and we need to have the professional autonomy (independence of professional judgment) to be able to do so at our own discretion and not because someone told us to.

There needs to be more democratization of the day-to-day governance structures of schools so that competent teachers can enjoy the same levels of personal professional autonomy that their colleagues in teacher education enjoy. A multicultural vision of the future of education will embrace the concept that the strengths and talents of all students need an optimum, best possible development. The problems and weaknesses of all students need resolution and assistance. We will have a commitment to the optimum educational development of each student. We need to see young people as a treasured human resource whose needs for safety, health, and cognitive and affective development are to be met by our best efforts as educators. A multicultural vision of our educational future will include an acceptance by educators of an expanded conception of their responsibility to their students to include a commitment to each student's optimum development as a person; we will see our clients whole. We will be more than concerned about their intellectual development, although this is our primary role; we will see schooling as having a therapeutic mission as well as an intellectual one. Diverse cultural backgrounds and learning styles will be accepted and nurtured as brothers and sisters in a shared national community of educational interests.

The future will also see less dependence on standardized, system-wide, behavioral objectives and more emphasis on permitting teachers at the local school level to develop models for assessing whether or not their students are achieving their educational goals. There will be more informal teacher-customized approaches to evaluation of student learning and less reliance on rigid statewide standardized learning objectives. Individual school faculties will be permitted to modify their schools' learning objectives for their students, and students will receive more individualized assessment and feedback on their progress in school.

Finally, a multicultural vision of the future of education will include a strong commitment to develop a powerful, critical sense of social consciousness and social responsibility between teachers and students. Students will be encouraged and assisted to define and to reconstruct as necessary their personal worlds with the intent that we empower them to empower themselves to see the world as it is, and to make it better if they can. In "Towards a Discourse of Imagery: Critical Curriculum Theorizing," it is noted that the educational settings of society are important terrain in the struggle to reconstruct public life along more egalitarian, just social policy lines. A multicultural vision of our educational future will encourage teachers to adopt a pedagogy of liberation that champions the development of critical social awareness among students and which empowers them to evaluate critically all that they may experience. Education will have a liberatory intent; the goal will not just be to teach children to reason critically. It will be to teach children to reason critically in the light of a clear vision of social justice worthy of all of their rights as citizens to achieve its fulfillment in our public life. The struggle to see a multicultural vision for our schools adopted by the teaching profession has always been closely aligned with the broader struggle for civil liberties and human dignity.

Looking Ahead: Challenge Questions

What would be implied, what would be possible, if the governance structure of schools was democratized to permit more teacher autonomy in how they assess their students?

What can teachers do to help students develop a sense of social consciousness and social responsibility?

Why would it help teachers and students to develop a "language of possibility" as part of the development of their critical reasoning skills?

What do "transformative intellectuals" or "teacher prophets" actually do in their elementary and secondary classrooms?

How can teachers help students to develop their talents

and to develop a vision of hope for themselves? What can teachers do to accomplish such goals?

How can we help students to develop a sense of public service?

What do you think are the most important challenges confronting multicultural educators as we enter the new century?

—F. S.

Towards a Discourse of Imagery: Critical Curriculum Theorizing

Jesse Goodman

Jesse Goodman is associate professor, School of Education, Indiana University, Bloomington, Indiana 47405.

Recently, Pinar reviewed the enormous change in thinking that has taken place during the last 20 years in the field of curriculum studies.[1] What began in the early 1970s as critiques of the positivistic ideology and practices dominating the curriculum field has emerged into a widely diverse area of study that draws upon (just to name a few) historical, political, economic, social, psychological, feminist, phenomenological, hermeneutic, linguistic, literary and, most recently, post-structuralist frames of reference as a basis of curriculum theorizing. Referred to as, among others, "reconceptualist," "critical theory," "critical pedagogy," or "feminist pedagogy," this re-oriented scholarship is now highly visible in traditional academic journals such as *Curriculum Inquiry, Journal of Curriculum Studies,* and *Journal of Curriculum and Supervision* and it is the primary focus of the *Journal of Curriculum Theorizing.* In addition, it overwhelms the proposals submitted to the Division B (Curriculum Studies) of the American Educational Research Association, and supports the existence of several Special Interest Groups within that organization (e.g., "Critical Issues in Curriculum;" "Critical Examination of Race, Ethnicity, Class and Gender in Education;" and "Lesbian and Gay Studies"). It also serves as a focal point for the annual "Curriculum Theory and Classroom Practices" conferences held in Dayton, Ohio. As Pinar stated, "So what started as an opposition to the mainstream field [of curriculum studies] and its tradition [positivism] has become the field, complicated, with several centers of theoretical formation."[2]

Although critical discourse on education has, for the past 20 years, proliferated within academic circles, it has received practically no attention in public schools or society at large. During the last decade, conservatives have set the agenda and tone for public debate regarding education in our society. The primary reason for the impotence of critical educational discourse in schools and society is that it, to a large extent, challenges those who dominate the cultural, political, and economic sectors of our society to relinquish much of their privilege and power. Obviously, certain reform proposals and reports (such as *A Nation at Risk,* Hirsch's *Cultural Literacy,* and Bloom's *The Closing of the American Mind*[3]) sustain the dominant interests in our society and, hence, they are more widely accepted by the public than reports that substantively challenge these interests. However, this lack of attention does not mean that critical educators are powerless or totally blameless for the apparent absence of critical voices beyond the symbolic walls of academia.

Language has great potency. As Foucault has shown in several of his works, systems of language and ideas serve as the foundation for systems of power.[4] Language can simultaneously reflect, illuminate, mystify, and create social reality. Through language, people's thinking can be galvanized in new directions or reestablished in accordance with previously held beliefs. Unfortunately, the rich and potentially emancipatory language that has emerged recently within the curriculum field has done little to galvanize people outside of a small circle of scholars. As Giroux and McLaren note:

> The success of the conservative educational agenda also points to a fundamental failure among progressive and radical educators to generate a public discourse on schooling. . . . One major problem facing the recent outpouring of critical discourse on schooling is that over the years it has become largely academicized. . . . In effect, critical and radical writings on schooling have become ghettoized within the ivory tower, reflecting a failure to take seriously the fact that education as a terrain of struggle is central to the reconstruction of public life and, as such, must be understood in vernacular as well as scholarly terms.[5]

In order to address the above mentioned problem, this article examines the recent history of discourse within the field of curriculum studies. Building upon the strengths

 From *The Educational Forum,* Vol. 56, No. 3, Spring 1992, pp. 269-289. © 1992 by Kappa Delta Pi, an international honor society in education. Reprinted by permission.

and weaknesses of this discourse, the discussion attempts to sketch out a vision of scholarship designed to help academics who are interested in generating curriculum theories that move beyond the confines of academia.

THE DISCOURSE OF CRITICISM

Starting in the early 70s, a few scholars in the curriculum field critically questioned the role of schooling in our society. This work quickly grew into what has come to be called a language or discourse of criticism within education. Apple articulated its purpose as follows:

> First, it aims at illuminating the tendencies for unwarranted and often unconscious domination, alienation, and repression within certain existing cultural, political, educational, and economic institutions. Second, through exploring the negative effects and contradictions of much that unquestionably goes on in these institutions, it seeks to "promote conscious emancipatory activity." That is, it examines what is supposed to be happening in say, schools if one takes the language and slogans of many school people seriously; and it then shows how these things actually work in a manner that is destructive of ethical rationality and personal political and institutional power.[6]

Given this goal, the language of criticism has provided educators with numerous insights. For example, it has uncovered the myth that schools in our society serve as the "great equalizer," which allows children from all social and economic backgrounds to compete fairly in our market place economy. The early work of Bowles and Gintis and, later, the work of Oakes illustrate the way in which schools actually limit the cultural, social, and economic mobility of children; thus reproducing the existing inequalities found in our broader society.[7] It also has exposed the way in which conventional schools in society transmit a "hidden curriculum," which undermines most of our children's sense of self esteem, efficacy, and compassion, and which also profoundly narrows whose "voices" (e.g., men over women, whites over people of color, industrialists over laborers, militarists over peace activists) and what epistemological and social values are expressed in classrooms. In addition, this discourse of criticism has carefully examined the theoretical frameworks that have been used as heuristic devices to understand schooling and society. For example, there has been active and at times acrimonious debate concerning the value of, to name a few, correspondent, theological, neo-Marxist, feminist, and post-structuralist theories, and their usefulness to the scholarly investigation of education.

Although this discourse of criticism has provided educators with a significant and substantive departure from the mechanistic and administrative language that has dominated traditional curricular discussions in our society, it has a couple of major weaknesses. One problem is centered on the linguistic complexity that runs rampant through this scholarship, or the writers' propensity to create sociological jargon. Now, it is true that, as the early critical theorists in the Frankfurt School pointed out, unique linguistic structures and terminology are at times required to move us beyond the everyday language that binds us to everyday conceptions of social reality and action. For example, terms such as "hegemony," "reproduction," and "cultural capital" have been extremely useful in conceptualizing the relationship between schools and the broader society within which children are educated. It is reasonable that some sociological analyses may take two or in some cases even three readings before one fully grasps the entire meaning of a given author, especially if he or she is addressing subtle and complex phenomena.

Therefore, it is not being suggested that educational scholars must always express themselves in everyday language. However, when the linguistic structure and terminology of this scholarship prevent the vast majority of like-minded scholars (let alone classroom teachers) from having little more than the slightest notion of what is being said after several readings, then it becomes at best a form of pretentious, self-indulgent expression in which the author simply writes for his or her individualistic pleasure and professional aggrandizement (even though its stated purpose is the "emancipation" of teachers and their students) and at worst a form of psychic oppression. Take for instance the following paragraph written by Wexler and his colleagues in which they call for a new educational movement that questions the dualistic thinking found in traditional rationality and legitimates contradiction, ambiguity, and paradox as central features of this new educational thinking.

> The free play of the signifier in the polysomic movement of language shatters the linguistic conventions of a hierarchical, paternal order. A careful but fearless approach to polysomy points towards that ambiguity which the intransitive sign suppresses. Paradox that plays with expressive excess and contradictory conversation are themselves signs of a new educational practice. Paradox and contradiction are the forms of a pedagogic relation that encourage multiple interpretation. Collective identity formation through writing, the communicative production of ambiguity and the pluralizing effect of contradiction animate education as a social relation.[8]

Even if one accepts the value of what is being said, it is hard to imagine many elementary, secondary, or university instructors (even those with radical sympathies) feeling a sense of enlightenment from the above passage or others like it. Rather, they are usually faced with the dilemma of either discounting its relevance to their own work or coming to the conclusion that they must not be intelligent enough to decipher its meaning. In either case, the experience is less than emancipatory.

Christian cogently examines this problem in her analysis of literary criticism and its relationship to Afro-American literature. Her insights apply equally well to educational scholarship, and are worth quoting at length.

I feel that the new emphasis on literary critical theory is as hegemonic as the world which it attacks. I see the language it creates as one which mystifies rather than clarifies our condition, making it possible for a few people who know that particular language to control the critical scene. . . . As a student of literature, I am appalled by the sheer ugliness of the language, its lack of clarity, its unnecessarily complicated sentence constructions, its lack of pleasurableness, its alienating quality. It is the kind of writing for which composition teachers would give a resounding F. . . . In their attempt to change the orientation of Western scholarship, they, as usual, concentrated on themselves and were not in the slightest interested in the worlds they had ignored or controlled. Again I was supposed to know *them*, while they were not at all interested in knowing *me*. Instead they sought to "deconstruct" the tradition to which they belonged, even as they used the same forms, style, language of that tradition, forms which necessarily embody its values.[9] [Christian's italics]

She goes on to point out that there are very real political, social, and intellectual dangers in not situating the theorizing of scholars within a practical context.

My fear is that when Theory is not rooted in practice, it becomes prescriptive, exclusive, elitist. . . . An example of this prescriptiveness is the approach the Black Arts Movement took towards language. For it, blackness resided in the use of black talk which they defined as hip urban language. So that when Nikki Giovanni reviewed Paule Marshall's *Chosen Place, Timeless People*, she criticized the novel on the grounds that it was not black, for the language was too elegant, too white. Blacks, she said, did not speak that way. Having come from the West Indies where we do, some of the time, speak that way, I was amazed by the narrowness of her vision. The emphasis on *one way* [her emphasis] to be black resulted in the works of Southern writers being seen as non-black since the black talk of Georgia does not sound like the black talk of Philadelphia.[10]

Whether it is found in sociological, literary, or educational discourse, the intellectual elitism that is embedded in much of the language of criticism significantly undermines its own liberatory intentions.

Secondly, the discourse of criticism often unfortunately reflects the academic tradition of building individual careers at the expense of one's colleagues. One way to be "successful" in academia is to "stand out" from the crowd and be a "leader in the field." Perhaps the most effective and quickest way to achieve this recognition is to emphasize the faulty thinking of one's colleagues (who share their general ideological commitments) rather than in addressing issues regarding the schooling of young people. These educators and sociologists are more interested and spend more energy in developing their special "brand" of educational criticism at the expense of fellow critical scholars than establishing meaningful dialogue in which people can collaboratively learn from one another.

Obviously, it is necessary to illuminate the way ideas of one's colleagues need to be expanded and reexamined in light of other assumptions, or refined in light of different information. For example, the criticisms of the "correspondence theory" as used in Bowles's and Gintis's early

work, or the criticisms of Marx's theory of economic determinism and ideology from which the concept of "hegemony" emerged, have led to a more fully developed understanding of the relationship between schools and society.[11] In addition, one can recognize the need to emphasize the points at which similar ideological schools of thought become distinct from one another. This distinction is necessary not only for the sake of clarity and insight, but also for political reasons. For example, as feminist and antiracist critiques have emerged within the discourse of criticism, it is useful to draw clear lines of distinction between these languages and the more general radical language of critical theory vis-à-vis the Frankfurt School. Drawing these distinctions protects these new languages from being dominated by more traditional languages of criticism that happen to reflect the voices of mostly white males whose analysis is rooted in the dynamics of class struggle.

However, within the discourse of criticism there exists a particular strand that seems focused primarily on gaining an "intellectual advantage" over others, which at times has been ill tempered and mean spirited. That is, it seeks to silence or arrest the work of particular individuals by questioning their basic motives and integrity, rather than advance a mutually supportive development of ideas. As Giroux states:

Instead of developing a political project and ethics that . . . connect schools and other institutions to forms of ongoing struggle, these newly emerging strains of critical educational theory appear to be suffocating in ideological narcissism, tied more closely to the self-serving tenets of vanguardism and despair than to anything else.[12]

This intellectual sectarianism potentially diverts attention away from those who are interested in building a supportive community of critical educators.

Finding ways to offer critical commentary of our colleagues' work is more complex than one might initially think. For example, references made to several individuals in this article (e.g., Wexler, Giroux, Purpel) could be viewed as another example of a "mean-spirited" attack, in which case this author is guilty of the very criticism previously discussed. While there seems to be no easy solution to this problem, one thing is certain. Our inability to speak to scholars and practitioners with similar values in ways that nurture our collective interests ends up isolating us from each other and adds to the power of those who already have it. The challenge before us is, as Apple suggests, to "stand on each other's shoulders" rather than nip at each other's ankles.[13]

Finally, this discourse of criticism has tended to weaken the resolve of many critical practitioners by emphasizing the way in which schools serve the dominant interests within society at the expense of marginalized groups such as children, women, the poor, people of color, people with disabilities, and homosexuals. Because the discourse emphasizes the way in which the interests of the most powerful members in society dominate over the lives of marginalized individuals and groups of people within various institutions such as schools, it has covertly undermined practitioners' sense of potential agency and power. At first, this critical discourse was helpful in that it brought to conscious awareness the relationship between schooling and the broader sociohistorical context within which education takes place. However, its failure to take note of the way in which teachers, students, and other interested individuals manage to oppose various forces of social, political, and educational domination has eventually helped the power structure within schools and society by demoralizing and weakening many educators' resolve to develop a language and social strategy to counter these dominant influences. The discourse of criticism thus degenerated into a "discourse of despair" by promoting the view that people with a critical consciousness are basically unable to exert a meaningful impact within society. That is, the language of criticism accentuated the way schools act as agencies for social reproduction by portraying young people and their teachers as uniformly passive in their response to a curriculum and organizational structure that serves those who dominate our market economy and culture.

Although the perpetuation of power relationships in schools and society that emerged as a by-product of the discourse of criticism was unintentional, we as scholars must seriously reflect upon our primary goals for engaging in scholarship. While the discourse of criticism has, due to its emphasis on providing a macro analysis, provided important insights into the dynamics of educational and social power, it has failed to offer a meaningful, alternative vision to the organizational structure and curriculum of conventional schooling. Focusing on the critique of schooling and society while ignoring alternative visions and realities has resulted in "a series of self-alienating options in which our [scholars'] . . . presence is [limited to] bystanders, historians or critics . . . with only marginal or rhetorical connections to the confused and frustrating politics of our own time and place."[14] Unawares, a language of criticism that is not rooted in visions of actual practice can easily become irrelevant or even dogmatic in certain circumstances.

THE DISCOURSE OF POSSIBILITY

In response, Giroux and a number of his colleagues (e.g., McLaren, Simon, and Aronowitz) have called upon critical educators to move beyond the discourse of criticism and have initiated the development of "a language of possibility."[15] Rather than just criticize schools, society, and each other, the language of possibility calls upon critical scholars to create a discourse that is accessible to most well-educated individuals and which provides a *vision* of hope and promise grounded in principles of empowerment, equality, and democracy. These principles are seen as promoting "the enhancement of human possibility" and transformation of "human capacities and social forms" which "requires an education rooted in a view of human freedom as the understanding of necessity and the transformation of necessity."[16] As McLaren states, a language of possibility will then "enable students [and teachers] to do more than simply adapt to the social order but rather to . . . transform the social order in the interests of social justice, equality, and the development of a socialist democracy."[17] Further, it would provide a basis for working "towards founding a redemptive and radically utopian social imagination grounded in hope."[18]

Two primary visions have emerged from this language of possibility. The first is a picture of schools as "democratic public spheres." This concept emerges from Giroux's understanding of English clubs, journals, coffeehouses, and periodicals that were used in the 17th and 18th centuries to question the autocracy of that society. He states:

> The classic public sphere . . . defines social criticism as part of a larger discourse concerned with cultural politics and public morality and in doing so invokes the Enlightenment principles of rational argument and free exchange of ideas to challenge notions of authority rooted in superstition, tradition, and absolutist decrees. The classic public sphere established a legacy in which writing, the study of literature, and social criticism had a broadly civilized function.[19]

A vision of schools as democratic public spheres is offered as an alternative to viewing schools as merely institutions that prepare young people for their place in a competitive market economy.

> Instead of defining schools as extensions of the work-place or as front-line institutions in the battle of international markets and foreign competition, schools as democratic public spheres are constructed around forms of critical inquiry that dignify meaningful dialogue and human agency. Students learn the discourse of public association and social responsibility. Such a discourse seeks to recapture the idea of critical democracy as a social government that supports individual freedom and social justice. Moreover, viewing schools as democratic public spheres provides a rationale for defending them along with progressive forms of pedagogy and teacher work as essential institutions and practices in the performance of an important public service. Schools are now defended in a political language as institutions that provide the ideological and material conditions necessary to educate a citizenry in the dynamics of critical literacy and civic courage, and these constitute the basis for functioning as active citizens in a democratic society.[20]

In "democratic public spheres," Giroux hopes to provide us with an alternative to the dominant vision of schools as "training centers" for a technocratic work force.

He also presents a vision of teachers as "transformative intellectuals" to replace the dominate notion of teachers as educational "technicians," "managers," or "professionals." As "transformative intellectuals," teachers can potentially play a significant role in creating schools as "democratic public spheres."

> Teachers need to develop a discourse and set of assumptions that allow them to function more specifically as

transformative intellectuals. As intellectuals, they will combine reflection and action in the interest of empowering students with the skills and knowledge needed to address injustices and to be critical actors committed to developing a world free of oppression and exploitation. Such intellectuals are not merely concerned with promoting individual achievement or advancing students along career ladders, they are concerned with empowering students so that the students can read the world critically and change it when necessary.[21]

He goes on to state:

Viewing teachers as intellectuals also provides a strong theoretical critique of technocratic and instrumental ideologies underlying an educational theory that separates the conceptualization, planning, and design of curricula from the processes of implementation and execution. It is important to stress that teachers must take active responsibility for raising serious questions about what they teach, how they are to teach, and what the larger goals are for which they are striving. This means that they must take a responsible role in shaping the purposes and conditions of schooling. . . . If we believe that the role of teaching cannot be reduced to merely training in the practical skills, but involves instead, the education of a class of intellectuals vital to the development of a free society, then the category of intellectual becomes a way of linking the purpose of teacher education, public schooling, and in-service training to the very principles necessary for developing a democratic order and society.[22]

Building upon Giroux and his colleagues' vision, Purpel proposes that teachers be "seen as educational prophets."[23] These individuals have a deep devotion to sacred, humane values such as peace, justice, love, compassion, and equality. These prophet/teachers consistently look upon these values as the core upon which to examine their everyday practices. This vision represents a rich alternative to the dominate view of teachers in our society as educational managers whose main purpose is to merely "get children through" standardized curriculum within preestablished time limits.

This language of possibility has provided visualizations of alternative educational realities that are noteworthy and have been absent within the discourse of criticism. However, these visualizations have too often remained at an overly abstract level of discourse. For instance, one might suggest that Giroux's emphasis on teachers' use of their intellect (as opposed to their wisdom, intuition, and ethos of caring) reflects a narrow, masculinist perception of the human characteristics needed to change schools or society. Others might assume that "transformative intellectuals" are little more than social activists who recruit children to engage in civil actions reflective of leftist perspectives on various issues. One might question the degree in which social activism is or should be equated with the education of children. Without providing vivid images of "transformative intellectuals" at work in educational settings, it is difficult to understand the potential impact this vision has for schools and society.

Similarly, the previously mentioned work by Purpel lays out a vision of morality and spirituality as a guide for the education of children. In doing so, he provides several insights that illuminate the way in which popular terms such as "excellence" have been used to reestablish and further entrench the type of education that benefits those within society who already possess the most power and privilege. His book is filled with calls for an education that will fight human misery, hunger, poverty, war, and help build a society based upon values of love, compassion, joy, equality, and community. However, he stopped short of illuminating what this education might actually look like within a real or even imaginary school. In his own defense, he states, "It is surely not for me to provide the last word on what the broad educational framework ought to be, never mind the absurdity of an expectation that I or anyone else could also provide a detailed blueprint of implementation and practice."[24] While a "blueprint" may in fact be inappropriate, it seems irresponsible to expect others to tackle the difficult task of implementation, if he is not willing to confront it himself. By ignoring issues of implementation he leaves the reader with vague visions and "coded" generalizations of education with which few individuals would disagree, regardless of their ideological orientations. For example, similar to Giroux's call for teachers to become "transformative intellectuals," Purpel's summons for the development of a "critical intelligence" among teachers and students could be viewed as little more than idle theorizing if there is no substantive image of what this type of intelligence could possibly look like in a given classroom.

Purpel and Giroux are not alone in their unwillingness to provide substantive images of critical educational practices, and this failure is not a trivial oversight. As Gore suggests, the substance of both the discourse of criticism and that of possibility has left many educators "paralyzed."[25] How does one translate the previously stated goals and aspirations into actions within schools? Is it even possible to "transform the social order" through schooling, and if not, does that mean teachers are failures or the "system" is too overpowering? What do "transformative intellectuals" or "teacher/prophets" actually do in their elementary and secondary classrooms? What is the content of their curriculum and in what way do they practice their craft of teaching? What steps can or should be taken by these individuals in order to reach the educational ambitions that are so eloquently articulated? The inadequacy of providing a discourse that can be digested by the educational community is not simply academic. To the contrary, it has very real and potentially negative political and educational consequences.

While the language of possibility and, in particular, expressions such as "democratic public spheres," "transformative intellectuals," or "educational prophets" offer potentially powerful alternatives to traditional and conservative perceptions of schooling, one must not confuse the words for the values and visions that initially called them forth. One way in which dominant influences within society and the field of education maintain their hegemony is to usurp the meaning of new words and phrases that gain a certain degree of popularity and threaten the status quo. Take, for instance, the term "empowerment" that is increasingly being used in reference to teachers, students, and educational programs. Initially this notion was generated as a reaction against educational practices that reduce students and teachers to passive consumers and managers of normative knowledge and skills needed to fulfill the labor needs of society as presently constituted. However, due to the failure of critical scholars to create a discourse of "empowerment" grounded in rich images of teachers and students, conservative and mainstream educators have been able to use this term to justify their own agenda.

Empowerment now often refers to providing special training programs or skill curricula that give students and teachers more "power" to take advantage of the opportunities offered by our corporate economy. Conservative forces have been able to usurp this term for their own ends by providing concrete illustrations of practice. As Maeroff's research suggests, teachers work in closer consort with and serve the interests of corporations as one way to become more empowered.[26] Since it is easier to act within the discourse provided by conservative educators who are more than willing to describe in detail what should be taught and how people should act, their impact on current educational practices is not surprising. By removing the political and cultural context from which "empowerment" emerged, conservative and traditional educators have essentially crippled it as an effective expression for critical change. Visions of schooling that have surfaced from the language of possibility are not immune to such cultural and linguistic power maneuvers. For this reason, if for no others, critical educators must illustrate practices that illuminate their lofty goals for readers.

THE DISCOURSE OF IMAGERY

Like many educators, the author plays many different occupational roles in the course of his work. At different times, I teach graduate seminars in curriculum studies, direct dissertations, and teach undergraduate courses for preservice teachers. In addition, I consult with school practitioners who are interested in developing emancipatory approaches to education and, finally, conduct my own research. In each of these roles, I have felt that, as one of many educators interested in liberatory ideals, we need to build upon the language of possibility by developing a critical educational discourse of imagery, a theoretical language that is informed by and rooted in images of real (or hypothesized) people involved in tangible actions that take place in believable settings. This then requires the development of a language that is *visual* as well as verbal.

There are several aspects of this language that need to be more fully discussed. A critical educational language

of imagery implies the importance of historical and cultural context. This discourse of imagery would attempt to situate theoretical discourse within a given social phenomenon. As Clandinin and Connelly note, a language of imagery can be seen as,

> [k]nowledge embodied in a person and connected with the individual's past, present and. . . . [Image] reaches into the past gathering up experiential threads meaningfully connected to the present. And it reaches into the future and creates new meaningfully connected threads as situations are experienced. . . . Image carries intentionality.[27]

A critical language of imagery prevents educational discourse from becoming lost in self-indulgent generalizations, coded language systems, and sacrosanct idealism. It guards against discourse that is so removed from social reality as to lose its potential for contributing ideas to those for whose benefit it is supposedly written. Critical scholars need to take the time and make the effort to directly and explicitly address the question of *how* (either hypothetically, based upon observations, or as a result of reflecting upon one's own practices) individuals or groups of people can potentially act within educational settings to advance their ideals.

This willingness to *portray* the meaning of critical discourse, rather than just to "talk about" it, provides teachers and others interested in critical pedagogy an opportunity to learn through vicarious experience. The human ability to visualize the actions that occur in one setting and apply this visualization to another setting contains a potentially powerful method through which critical pedagogy can be expanded. Unfortunately, the vast majority of critical discourse has often seemed to be more interested in the glamour of abstract theorizing than examining opportunities to tap into the vicarious learning of others.

Currently only a few examples exist that exemplify the way in which this language of imagery can be established. Obviously, one avenue is to situate one's theoretical discourse within hypothetical settings. Drawing out educational theorizing into "make-believe" classrooms or schools will challenge the theorist to work through his or her ideas more fully in ways that make sense (or fail to make sense) given a current set of circumstances. These hypothetical situations can be drawn from a variety of experiences. For example, Sarason's portrayal of the "model" teacher and principal, based upon his years as a researcher and consultant, provide a good example of the way in which abstractions can come to life through the use of hypothetical constructions.[28]

This type of theoretical "working through" can also be accomplished through the use of ethnographic data collection and analysis. Weiler's research on feminist high school teachers is a viable illustration of this type of scholarship.[29] Her work contains a comprehensive analysis of the way in which issues of gender, race, class, and interpersonal power dynamics intersect between schools and society at the theoretical level with a rich portrayal of how these forces get played out in particular classrooms. Lesko's and McLaren's studies of student life within, respectively, a Catholic high school and junior high school, Goodman's research of a democratic elementary school, and Kuzmic's work in a similar high school provide additional representations of the way in which critical theorizing can be situated within the lives of teachers and students.[30]

In addition to ethnographic data, a number of educators are currently exploring the uses of autobiographical analysis. Lewis's and Simon's account of their experiences being a student and teacher in a graduate curriculum studies course, Krall's examination of her work as a departmental chairperson in a large university, Lather's account of her teaching an undergraduate women's studies course, Berlak's account of teaching an undergraduate sociology class, and Miller's account of her collaborative inquiry with five classroom teachers are representative of this type of scholarship.[31]

Whether drawing upon hypothetical, ethnographic, or autobiographical data, these discourses have several commonalities. First, they are all attempts at critical educational theorizing rooted within a cultural and historical context. This work presents various analyses of complex and substantive issues such as the relationship between schools and society and the dynamics of power based upon race, class, and gender. However, unlike the discourse of criticism, the reader is provided with images of people engaged in efforts that illuminate the manifestations, conflicts, and dilemmas of the theorizing. At the same time, these images do not trap the scholar and reader in theoretical minutia that can have no value outside a highly specific time and cultural setting. Rather, particularistic phenomena are explored in light of larger contexts "in which it is possible to make visible those mediations, interrelations, and interdependencies that give shape and power to larger political and social systems."[32]

It must be noted that there is some danger in creating a critical discourse of imagery. First, it is important that this discourse of imagery not be seen as a mindless backlash against the linguistic complexity found in the discourses of criticism. The discourse of imagery should not be presented as a morally superior form of scholarship over that of criticism. Giroux expands upon this point as follows:

> The call to writing in a language that is touted as clear and accessible has become the political and ideological equivalent of a moral and political vision that increasingly collapses under the weight of its own anti-intellectualism. Theory is now dissolved into practice under the vote-catching call for the importance of focusing on the concrete as the all-embracing sphere of educational strategy and relevance. To argue against these concerns is not meant as a clever exercise intent on merely reversing the relevance of the categories so that theory is prioritized over practice, or abstract language over the language of imagery. Nor am I

merely suggesting that critical educators mount an equally reductionist argument against the use of clear language or the importance of practice. At issue here is the need to both question and reject the reductionism and exclusions that characterize the binary oppositions that inform the overly pragmatic sentiments.[33]

In suggesting the need to develop a discourse of imagery, it is not being proposed that it replace abstract theorizing as the new pinnacle of scholarly work. Rather, what is sought is the creation of a scholarship that is inclusive of both verbal and visual expressions in the efforts of scholars to make what is said meaningful.

It is crucial that this call for a discourse of imagery not be viewed as "the answer" for all individuals interested in curriculum theorizing. In calling for a discourse of imagery, it is not being suggested that curriculum theorizing must reflect a narrow and particularistic style. There is a clear danger that a language of imagery could conceivably be used to justify a form of anti-intellectualism that is already far too pervasive in the United States. Perhaps it would be more helpful to recognize that some forms of theorizing are valuable for certain audiences, types of questions being explored, and value systems upon which they are based. While a discourse of imagery may be helpful to myself and others with similar concerns, it may be inappropriate for individuals with different interests or agendas. Scholars engaged in abstract discourses do not *always* need to situate their discussions in a context-specific setting in order to share insights with each other. At the same time, practitioners in schools do not *always* need to have visual illustrations of ideas drawn out for them in order to be useful in their own deliberations about schooling. Suggesting, as this article does, that curriculum theorizing needs to situate itself within visual narratives can easily be used to justify a form of essentialism that is counterproductive to the free exchange of ideas. While I believe that curriculum theorizing would benefit from the development of a discourse of imagery, it should not exhaust the ways in which curriculum theory can be generated.

Finally, in calling for more detailed illustrations of people working in classrooms and schools as a basis for analytical and theoretical discourse, it is not being suggested that curriculum theorists provide cookbook descriptions of how it should be done. As previously mentioned, the dominant language within education today is one of management and control, and school-based personnel are familiar with responding to research or other types of scholarly literature with a "show-me-how-to-do-it" attitude. That is, when an "expert" provides details of how schools can be run, how classrooms can be structured, what types of instruction can be used, or what curriculum can be taught, there is the assumption that those who read such work should merely turn around and implement these practices. However, to present critical practice in these terms negates the dialectical relationship between theory and action, and it reduces the reader to a passive consumer of ideas. The call to develop an educational language of critical imagery is made with an understanding that the purpose of such scholarship is not to ask others to mimic what is presented, but to learn from the images provided and apply what is vicariously experienced to one's own particular situation and limitations.

I have suggested in this article that efforts be made to move beyond the discourses of criticism and possibility by creating a "language of critical imagery" within the field of curriculum studies. The development of this new language is necessary if critical educators wish to expand their influence beyond the small confines of academic circles. As Ellsworth suggests, the vast majority of critical curriculum theorizing has been "more appropriate (yet hardly more helpful) for philosophical debates about the highly problematic concepts of freedom, justice, democracy, and 'universal' values than for thinking through and planning classroom practices to support a political agenda."[34] Simon raises a similar concern when he states, "The move from visionary rhetoric to classroom reality, from curriculum critique to pedagogical possibility, is rarely straightforward. But we know that to forsake such a journey is to continually postpone a serious exploration of 'what must be done.' "[35] This exploration will be served best when critical educators learn to speak visually as well as verbally. When we learn how to illuminate and give voice to the actions of teachers in classrooms who are struggling to develop a critical pedagogy then we will begin to broaden our potential audience as well as our own understanding. Wexler and his colleagues are correct when they assert that the type of critical education advocated by critical scholars cannot "be theorized in the academy and successfully handed down to the classroom, with more than token effect."[36]

Although this particular article has focused on the development of a language of imagery within the field of curriculum studies, it is worth emphasizing that the development of this language alone is not enough of a response to the need for connecting scholarly analysis to the practices of those administrators, teachers, and students who work in our schools. The establishment of this language should be seen as part of a broader political effort. Rather than just writing for scholarly publications, educators interested in emancipatory pedagogy need to make their voices heard in other arenas of discourse. For example, our voices should be heard in committee hearings when state legislators are considering education reform bills. We need to begin to write columns and articles for local newspapers and practitioner-oriented magazines. In addition, it would be helpful for critical educators to locate at least one teacher or administrator (or perhaps an entire staff) in a local school district and establish a peer-mentoring relationship with the person(s). In this way, critical educators will have someone "in the field" with whom they can mutually explore pedagogical ideas and practices. The school-based individual could read and respond to what the scholar has written, and the latter could serve as a consultant to, resource guide for, and occasional co-worker with his or her peer teacher or administrator. This peer mentoring may provide critical scholars and those who work in our schools with much needed mutual support. It is the type of support that critical educators have often called for but failed to provide. While it is understood that all of these practices will not alter the basic power structure and interests that dominate our schools today, the road to genuine reform must begin somewhere and the first steps are always small.

Similar to Purpel's commentary, perhaps it is appropriate to conclude this article by putting its content into a temporal perspective.[37] The last decade has been demoralizing to many educators who, only a few years prior to the escalation of the Vietnam War, were filled with hope that our society had made a strong commitment to the values of community, caring, social justice, and political participation for all of our citizens. It seemed that although much work lay ahead in order to fulfill our democratic ideal, the direction in which we were moving was clearly marked. Since then, changes in the executive and particularly the judicial branches of our government have made it difficult to maintain the optimistic vision of a society in which the well-being of children and adults would take precedence over industrial and military interests. However, we must remember that as a species, we are relatively newcomers to this planet. Human history is filled with periods of both promise and despair. As Giroux has so often pointed out, we must not succumb to recent turns of events as if societal situations are permanently cast in stone. To the contrary, now, perhaps more than ever, is a time to situate our work within a politics of hope. Although critical and progressive elements within our society have been on the defensive during this last decade, they have not disappeared. As one of the members of the 1950s' black-listed folk music group, The Weavers, stated at a reunion concert a couple of years after President Reagan took office, "Don't despair, we've been through times like this before, and we'll persevere." The spirit within human beings from which concepts such as compassion, social equity, intellectual freedom, and caring emerged has not atrophied. Now is a time to reassert our dreams of how schooling can help young people develop their intellectual and creative talents, moral character, and civic courage that will be needed to face the difficult tasks of defining and creating the "good life" for the many species of plants and animals that share this small planet, as it temporally moves into the next century.

REFERENCES

The author would like to express his appreciation to Leslie Bloom for her thoughtful critique of an earlier version of this manuscript.

7. TOWARD A NEW DAY IN OUR VISIONS OF EDUCATION

1. William Pinar, "The Reconceptualization of Curriculum Studies, 1987: A Personal Retrospective," *Journal of Curriculum and Supervision* 3 (No. 2, 1988): 157–167.

2. Ibid., p. 167.

3. National Commission on Excellence in Education, *A Nation at Risk: The Imperative for Educational Reform* (Washington, D.C.: U.S. Government Printing Office, 1983); E. D. Hirsch, *Cultural Literacy: What Every American Needs to Know* (Boston: Houghton Mifflin, 1987); Allan Bloom, *The Closing of the American Mind: How Higher Education Has Failed Democracy and Impoverished the Souls of Today's Students* (New York: Simon & Schuster, 1987).

4. E.g., Michel Foucault, *The History of Sexuality*, Vol. 1, *An Introduction* (London: Tavistock Press, 1979); *Discipline and Punish: Birth of the Prison* (London: Allen Lane Press, 1977).

5. Henry Giroux and Peter McLaren, "Introduction: Schooling, Cultural Politics, and the Struggle for Democracy," in *Critical Pedagogy, the State, and Cultural Struggle*, eds. Henry Giroux and Peter McLaren (Albany, New York: State University of New York Press, 1989), pp. xi–xxxv. Quoted from p. xiii.

6. Michael Apple, as quoted in Karen Mazza, "Reconceptual Inquiry as an Alternative Mode of Curriculum Theory and Practice: A Critical Study," *Journal of Curriculum Theorizing* 4 (No. 2, 1982): 5–88. Quoted from p. 43.

7. Samuel Bowles and Herbert Gintis, *Schooling in Capitalist America* (New York: Basic Books, 1976); Jeannie Oakes, *Keeping Track: How Schools Structure Inequality* (New Haven, Connecticut: Yale University Press, 1985).

8. Philip Wexler, Rebecca Martusewicz, and June Kern, "Popular Educational Politics," in *Critical Pedagogy and Cultural Power*, ed. D. Livingstone (South Hadley, Massachusetts: Bergin & Garvey, 1987): 227–243. Quoted from p. 242.

9. Barbara Christian, "The Race for Theory," *Cultural Critique* 6 (No. 1, 1987): 51–63. Quoted from pp. 55 & 56.

10. Ibid., p. 58.

11. Bowles & Gintis, *Schooling in Capitalist America*; Michael Apple, *Ideology and Curriculum* (London: Routledge & Kegan Paul, 1979); Henry Giroux, *Theory and Resistance in Education* (South Hadley, Massachusetts: Bergin & Garvey, 1983); Antonio Gramsci, *Selections from Prison Notebooks* (New York: International Publishers, 1971); Raymond Williams, *Problems in Materialism and Culture* (London: New Left Books, 1980).

12. Henry Giroux, *Teachers as Intellectuals: Toward a Critical Pedagogy of Learning* (South Hadley, Massachusetts: Bergin & Garvey, 1988), p. 206.

13. Apple, *Ideology and Curriculum*.

14. Williams, *Problems in Materialism and Culture*, p. 238.

15. Giroux, *Teachers as Intellectuals*.

16. Roger Simon, "Empowerment as a Pedagogy of Possibility," *Language Arts* 64 (No. 4, 1987): 370–382. Quoted from pp. 372, 373, 375.

17. Peter McLaren, "Language, Social Structure, and the Production of Subjectivity," *Critical Pedagogy Networker* 1 (Nos. 2–3, 1988): 1–10. Quoted from p. 3.

18. Ibid., p. 9.

19. Giroux, *Teachers as Intellectuals*, p. 207.

20. Ibid., p. xxxii.

21. Ibid., p. xxxiv.

22. Ibid., p. 126.

23. David Purpel, *The Moral and Spiritual Crisis in Education: A Curriculum for Justice and Compassion in Education* (South Hadley, Massachusetts: Bergin & Garvey, 1989).

24. Ibid., p. 156.

25. Jennifer Gore, "Agency, Structure and the Rhetoric of Teacher Empowerment." (Paper presented at the annual meeting of the American Educational Research Association, San Francisco, March 1989).

26. Gene Maeroff, *The Empowerment of Teachers: Overcoming the Crisis of Confidence* (New York: Teachers College Press, 1988).

27. Jean Clandinin and Michael Connelly, "Teachers' Personal Practical Knowledge: Image and Narrative Unity" (Toronto: The Ontario Institute for Studies in Education, 1984; working paper), p. 5.

28. Seymour Sarason, *The Culture of the School and the Problem of Change* (Boston: Allyn and Bacon, 1971).

29. Kathleen Weiler, *Women Teaching for Change* (South Hadley, Massachusetts: Bergin & Garvey, 1988).

30. Nancy Lesko, *Symbolizing Society: Stories, Rites and Structure in a Catholic High School* (New York: Falmer Press, 1988); Peter McLaren, *Schooling as Ritual Performance: Towards a Political Economy of Educational Symbols and Gestures* (London: Routledge & Kegan Paul, 1986); Jesse Goodman, *Elementary Schooling for Critical Democracy* (Albany, New York: State University of New York Press, in press); Jeff Kuzmic, "Harmony High School: The Paradoxes of Creating an Empowering Educational Environment." (Paper presented at the annual conference on Curriculum Theory and Classroom Practice, Dayton, Ohio, October 1988).

31. Magda Lewis and Roger Simon, "A Discourse Not Intended for Her: Learning and Teaching within Patriarchy," *Harvard Educational Review* 56 (November 1986): 457–472; Florence Krall, "Behind the Chairperson's Door: Reconceptualizing Woman's Work," in *Contemporary Curriculum Discourses*, ed. William Pinar (Scottsdale, Arizona: Gorsuch, Scarisbrick Press, 1988), pp. 495–513; Patti Lather, "Staying Dumb: Student Resistance to Liberatory Curriculum." (Paper presented at the annual meeting of the American Educational Research Association, Boston, April 1990); Ann Berlak, "Teaching for Outrage and Empathy in the Liberal Arts." (Paper presented at the annual meeting of the American Educational Research Association, New Orleans, April 1988); Janet Miller, *Creating Spaces and Finding Voices: Teachers Collaborating for Empowerment* (Albany, New York: State University of New York Press, 1990).

32. Henry Giroux, "Postmodernism and the Discourse of Educational Criticism," *Journal of Education* 170 (No. 3, 1988): 5–30. Quoted from p. 16.

33. Henry Giroux, "Schooling as a Form of Cultural Politics: Toward a Pedagogy of and for Difference," in *Critical Pedagogy, the State, and Cultural Struggle*, eds. Henry Giroux and Peter McLaren (Albany, New York: State University of New York Press, 1989): 125–151. Quoted from p. 132.

34. Elizabeth Ellsworth, "Why Doesn't this Feel Empowering? Working Through the Repressive Myths of Critical Pedagogy." (Paper presented at the annual conference on Curriculum Theory and Classroom Practice, Dayton, Ohio, October 1988), p. 2.

35. Rodger Simon, "For a Pedagogy of Possibility," *Critical Pedagogy Networker* 1 (No. 1, 1988): 1–4. Quoted from p. 3.

36. Wexler, Martusewicz, and Kern, "Popular Educational Politics," pp. 228–229.

37. Purpel, *The Moral and Spiritual Crisis in Education*.

Investing in Our

A Struggle for America's Conscience and Future

"Too many young people of all races and classes are growing up unable to handle life, without hope or steady compasses to navigate a world that is reinventing itself technologically and politically at a kaleidoscopic pace."

Marian Wright Edelman

Ms. Edelman is president of the Children's Defense Fund, Washington, D.C.

THE 1990S' STRUGGLE is about the U.S.'s conscience and future. Many of the battles will not be as dramatic as Gettysburg or Vietnam or Desert Storm, but they are going to shape this nation's place in the 21st century. Every American in this last decade of the last century of this millennium must struggle to redefine success in the U.S., asking not "How much can I get?," but "How much can I do without and share?"; not "How can I find myself?," but "How can I lose myself in service to others?"; not just how I can take care of me and mine, but how I can help as one American to strengthen family and community values and help this great nation regain her moral and economic bearings at home and abroad.

When I was growing up, service was as essential as eating and sleeping and going to church and school. Caring black adults were buffers against the segregated outside world which told me that, as a black girl, I wasn't worth anything and was not important. However, I didn't believe it because my parents, teachers, and preachers said it wasn't so. The childhood message I internalized, despite the outside segregation and poverty all around, was that, as God's child, no man or woman could look down on me, and I could look down on no man or woman.

I couldn't play in segregated playgrounds or sit at drugstore lunch counters, so my father, a Baptist minister, built a playground and canteen behind our church. Whenever he saw a need, he tried to respond. There were no black homes for the aged in South Carolina at that time, so my parents began one across the street, and our entire family had to help out. I didn't like it a whole lot of the time, but that is how I learned that it was my responsibility to take care of elderly family members and neighbors, and that everyone was my neighbor.

I went everywhere with my parents and the members of my church and community who were my watchful extended family. The entire black community took responsibility for protecting its children. They reported on me when I did wrong, applauded me when I did well, and were very clear as adults about what doing well meant. It meant being helpful to others, achieving in school, and reading. We all finally figured out that the only time our father wouldn't give us a chore was when we were reading, so we all read a lot.

Children were taught, by example, that nothing was too lowly to do and that the work of our heads and hands were both valuable. As a child, I went with an older brother—I was eight or nine or 10 and remember the debate between my parents as to whether I was too young to go help clean the bedsores of a poor, sick woman—but I went and learned just how much the smallest helping hands can mean to a lonely person in need.

Our families, churches, and community made kids feel useful and important. While life often was hard and resources scarce, we always knew who we were and that the measure of our worth was inside our heads and hearts, not outside in material possessions or personal ambition. We were taught that the world had a lot of problems; that black people had an *extra* lot of problems, but that we could struggle and change them; that extra intellectual and material gifts brought with them the privilege and responsibility of sharing with others less fortunate; and that service is the rent each of us pays for living—the very purpose of life and not something you do in your spare time or after you have reached your personal goals.

I am grateful for these childhood legacies of a living faith reflected in daily service, the discipline of hard work, and stick-to-itiveness—a capacity to struggle in the face of adversity. Giving up, despite how bad the world was outside, simply was not a part of my childhood lexicon. You got up every morning and did what you had to do, and you got up every time you fell down and tried as many times as you had to until you got it right. I was 14 the night my father died. He had holes in his shoes, but he had two children who graduated from college, one in college, another in divinity school, and a vision that he was able to convey to me even as he was dying in an ambulance—that I, a young black girl, could be and do anything, that race and gender are shadows, and that character, self-discipline, determination, attitude, and service are the substance of life.

What kind of vision are we conveying to our children today as parents, political and business leaders, and professionals? Our children are growing up in an ethically polluted nation where instant sex without responsibility, instant gratification without effort, instant solutions without sacrifice, getting rather than giving, and hoarding rather than sharing are the too frequent signals of our mass media, popular culture, and political life.

The standard of success for far too many Americans has become personal greed, rather than common good. The standard for striving and achievement has become getting, rather than making an extra effort or service to others. Truth-telling and moral example have become devalued commodities. Nowhere is the paralysis of public or private conscience more evident than in the neglect and abandonment of millions of our shrinking pool of youngsters, whose futures will determine our nation's ability to compete economically and lead morally as much as any child of privilege and as much as any other issue.

We need to understand that investing in our children is not investing in a special interest group or helping out somebody else—it is absolutely essential to every American's well-being and future. Only two out of every 10 new labor force entrants in this decade will be white males born in the U.S. As an aging population with a shrinking pool of kids, we don't have a child to waste—we need every one of them. We either can decide to invest in them up front and give them a sense of nurturing and caring adults that are part of a community and a society that guarantees them a future, or we can continue to fear them, build more and more prisons, and worry about them shooting at us. We don't have a choice about investing in our children, only when we are going to invest and whether it's going to be positive or negative investment.

Every 16 seconds of every school day, as we talk about a competitive workforce in the future, one of our children drops out of school. Every 26 seconds of every day, an American child runs away from home. These are not just poor or black children—they are all of our children. This is not something affecting just a few families—these are national problems. Every 47

seconds, a youngster is abused. Every 67 seconds, a teenager has a baby. We produce the equivalent of the city of Seattle each year with children having children. Every seven minutes, a child is arrested for a drug offense. Every 30 minutes, one of our children is charged with drunken driving. Every 53 minutes, in the richest land on Earth, an American child dies because of poverty.

It is disgraceful that children are the poorest Americans and that, in the last year alone, 840,000 youngsters fell into poverty and that there has been a 26% increase since 1979 in poverty among children. The majority of poor youngsters in America are not black and not in inner cities. They are in rural and suburban areas and in working and two-parent families. A lot of folk who were middle class last year around the country are now in poverty and on food stamps. It can happen to any of us.

We are in a sad state when the American Dream for many middle-class young people has become a choice between a house and a child. They are worrying about how their offspring are going to make it through college, pay off their higher education loans, and get off the ground and form families. We have to begin investing in all of our kids and all of our families. I believe we have lost our sense of what is important as a people. Too many children of all races and classes are growing up unable to handle life, without hope or steady compasses to navigate a world that is reinventing itself technologically and politically at a kaleidoscopic pace. Too many are growing up terribly uncertain and fearful about the future.

Despite the global realities the nation faces and a lot of the economic and moral uncertainty of the present, there are some enduring values we have lost sight of. I agree with poet Archibald MacLeish that there is only one thing more powerful than learning from experience and that is *not* learning from experience. It is the responsibility of every adult—parent, teacher, preacher, professional, and political leader—to make sure that youngsters hear what adults have learned from the lessons of life. Author James Baldwin wrote some years back that children really don't ever do what we tell them to do, but they almost always do what we do.

Americans have to move away from the idea of being entitled to something because they are men, or wealthy, or white, or black. It is time to come together to work quietly and systematically toward building a more just America and ensuring that no child is left behind. We should resist quick-fix, simplistic answers and easy gains that disappear as fast as they come. I am sick of people talking big and making great promises, then not following up and getting it done. Too often, we get bogged down

in our ego needs and lose sight of deeper community and national needs.

Family values vs. hypocricy

As a nation, we mouth family values we do not practice. Seventy countries provide medical care and financial assistance to all pregnant women and to children—the U.S. is not one of them. Seventeen industrialized nations have paid maternity/paternity leave programs—the U.S. is not one of them. In 1992, Pres. George Bush vetoed an unpaid leave bill that would have allowed parents to stay at home when a child is sick or disabled. We need to stop the hypocrisy of talking about families when all our practices are the opposite. It is time for parents to have a real choice about whether to remain at home or work outside the home without worrying about the safety of their children.

Many families have had to put a second parent into the workforce in order to make ends meet. Even when both parents work, a vast number are not able to meet their basic housing and health care needs.

The new generation of young people must share and stress family rituals and values and be moral examples for their children, just as this generation must try even harder to be. If people cut corners, their children will too. If they are not honest, their children will not be either. If adults spend all of their money and tithe no portion of it for colleges, synagogues or churches, and civic causes, their children won't either. If they tolerate political leaders who don't tell the truth or do what they say, their children will lose faith as too many are doing in the political process.

If we snicker at racial and gender jokes, another generation will pass on the poison that our generation still has not had the will to snuff out. Each of us must counter the proliferating voices of racial, ethnic, and religious division that separates us as Americans. It's important for us to face up to, rather than ignore, our growing racial problems, which are America's historic and future Achilles' heel. Whites didn't create black or brown people; men didn't create women; Christians didn't create Jews—so what gives anybody the right to feel entitled to diminish another?

We need to ask ourselves as Americans—how many potential Martin Luther King, Jrs. or Colin Powells, Sally Rides or Barbara McClintocks our nation is going to waste before it wakes up and recognizes that its ability to compete in the new century is as inextricably intertwined with poor and non-white children as with its white and privileged ones, with girls as well as its boys? As Rabbi Abraham Heschel put it, "We may not all be equally guilty for the problems that we face, but we are all equally responsible" for building a decent and just

America and seeing that no child is left behind.

People who are unwilling or unable to share and make complicated and sometimes hard choices may be incapable or taking courageous action to rebuild our families and community and nation. Nevertheless, I have great hopes about America and believe we can rebuild community and begin to put our children first as a nation. It is going to require that each of us figure out what we're going to be willing to sacrifice and share.

Many whites favor racial justice as long as things remain the same. Many voters hate Congress, but love their own Congressman as long as he or she takes care of their special interests. Many husbands are happier to share their wives' added income than share the housework and child care. Many Americans deny the growing gap between the rich and the poor, and they are sympathetic and concerned about escalating child suffering as long as somebody else's program is cut.

Americans have to grow up beyond this national adolescence. Everybody wants to spend, but nobody wants to pay. Everybody wants to lower the deficit, but also to get everything that they can. We have to ask ourselves how we're going to come together as a people to begin to make sure that the necessities of the many are taken care of and that every child gets what he or she needs to achieve a healthy start in life. If we're not too poor to bail out the savings and loan institutions, if we're not too poor to build all those B-2 bombers, we're not too poor to rescue our suffering children and to ensure that all youngsters get what they need.

In a time of economic uncertainty and fear about the future, of rising crime, rising costs, and rising joblessness, we must never give in to the urge to give up, no matter how hard it gets. There's an old proverb that says, "When you get to your wits end, remember that God lives there." Harriet Beecher Stowe once said that, when you get into a "tight place and everything goes against you, till it seems as though you could not hang on for a minute longer, never give up then, for that is just the place and the time when the tide will turn."

We can not continue as a nation to make a distinction between our children and other people's kids. Every youngster is entitled to an equal share of the American Dream. Every poor child, every black child, every white child—every child living everywhere—should have an equal shot. We need every one of them to be productive and educated and healthy.

Let me end this article with a prayer, written by a schoolteacher in South Carolina.

She urges us to pray and accept responsibility for children who sneak popsicles before supper, erase holes in math workbooks, and never can find their shoes, but let's also pray and accept responsibility for children who can't bound down the street in a new pair of sneakers, who don't have any rooms to clean up, whose pictures aren't on anybody's dresser, and whose monsters are real. Let each of us commit to praying and accepting responsibility for children who spend all their allowance before Tuesday, throw tantrums in the grocery store, pick at their food, shove dirty clothes under the bed, never rinse out the tub, squirm in church or temple, and scream in the phone, but let's also pray and accept responsibility for those children whose nightmares come in the daytime, who will eat anything, who have never seen a dentist, who aren't spoiled by anybody, who go to bed hungry and cry themselves to sleep all over this rich nation. Let's commit to praying and accepting responsibility for children who want to be carried and for those who must be carried. Let's commit to protecting those children whom we never give up on, but also those children who don't get a second chance. Let each of us commit to praying and voting and speaking and fighting for those children whom we smother, but also for those who will grab the hand of anybody kind enough to offer it.

EDUCATING CITIZENS FOR A MULTICULTURAL 21ST CENTURY

Lily Wong Fillmore

—Lily Wong Fillmore is professor of language and literacy, University of California, Berkeley. This article is adapted from her opening session address at the Third Annual Conference of the National Association for Multicultural Education, February 11, 1993.

American society is, and has always been, a diverse, multicultural society. But there is something new. Over the past two decades, with the influx of the new immigrants—people largely from Asia and Latin America, but also the Caribbean, Africa, the Middle East, and the Indian Sub-Continent—we have become visibly diverse. We have become noticeably a more colorful and variegated people than ever before.

But this same multiculturalism and diversity that some of us celebrate represents problems to others. These forces constitute, in the eyes of some people, frightening, unwanted changes in our society. The American ideal for most citizens is a monocultural society, a society with one language, one culture, one purpose, one people. When you and I talk about the advantages of a multicultural society, when we argue about the need to accommodate the many different perspectives, histories, and experiences that are represented in our society, say in our celebrations, or in our schools, we are denounced as promoters of new heresies.

The rumblings in America these days are symptomatic of another bout of crippling xenophobia coming on. This society has never found it easy to incorporate newcomers who don't blend into the crowd easily. Despite the fact that this has always been a diverse multicultural society, Americans have never accepted that reality. We have, until recently, been able to suppress it, deny it, and even erase it—at least we have tried. We have done it by forcing people, by both subtle and not-so-subtle means, to conform to our ideal of a monocultural society. People either give up their differences or they don't get access to the society.

School is the place where this process begins and where much of it takes place. It is where children learn and come to believe that what they have been taught by their parents has no place or value in the society they live in. In what follows, I will comment on what happens, and what should be happening, in schools.

For most of us, school was the place where we—or our parents or grandparents—first came into contact with the larger society. It was where we learned English, after retiring our own languages; it was where we learned what it meant to be an American in contrast to whatever else we were when we first entered school. It was where we gained a common culture and set aside our own, the culture of our parents and our primary communities. All of that was necessary, we were told, if we wanted to be members of the larger society, if we wanted jobs, if we wanted to be Americans.

And so many of us took on American culture, the one that is about baseball, cowboys, fast cars and John Wayne, and we suppressed and set aside the other stuff—our languages, our history, our stories, ourselves—and eventually forgot about them.

This process continues. Despite our best efforts to diversify the curriculum, to accommodate the cultures and experiences of our newest Americans in the schools, it continues.

We see kids entering our schools, bringing with them a great diversity of experience, language, and cultures. Their names are novel, colorful, and delightful to the ear. In just a couple of years, these kids will be speaking English—not well, but it will be their preferred language. In dress, hair-style, and in their manner, they will become more and more American. And their names—Thuy becomes Tiffany, Guillermo is Bill, you know, like the president? and Chui-wing is no more—she's Jennifer now, please. And at home, their parents are bewildered. Their children—what has happened to their children? They have become strangers—they can hardly understand the family language anymore. When they speak to their parents at all, it is in English, a language the parents don't understand. And their tones are terse, impatient, scornful even. The parents don't understand, they just don't understand. "What has happened to our children" they ask. "What has happened to our family?"

But as we know, culture is not easily changed. The kids adopt new ways of talking, dressing, and thinking—but they nonetheless retain a lot of their parents' early teachings in the deep structure of their thought. They retain a sense of the rightness of the patterns of behavior and beliefs that their parents have inculcated in them in the early years, even if they no longer practice or are guided by them. And these patterns continue to exert an influence on their thinking well after children appear to have "adjusted," as we say, to their new circumstances.

The conflict between what is and what ought to be has to be confronted by each individual who undergoes this process, and it is harder for some than for others. All of this goes into the shaping of our national psyche. Whether we like to acknowledge it or not, we are an immigrant society, and unresolved conflicts between what we are and what we might have been do affect how we look at ourselves and at others.

Here I raise issues about American society that must be confronted head-on if we are to succeed as a multicultural society. We are undeniably a multicultural society, but we are far from the kind of multicultural society we could be. There are far too many divisions among us, and there is the backlash, exemplified in the attitudes so freely expressed these days by members of the public, who view our diversity as a violation of the American ideal.

Ethnic, cultural, linguistic, religious, social, and racial differences have remained, even after most of us have bought into the idea of a common culture, a common language, and a common purpose. Our society is riddled with divisions and polarities: majority versus minority, haves versus have-nots, whites versus blacks, Asians against non-Asians, Latinos versus Anglos, native-born versus foreign-borns, as in ABCs versus FOBs (in the parlance of young Chinese Americans, "ABC" refers to American-born Chinese, "FOB" to Chinese immigrants, those who are "fresh off the boat"), gays versus straights, men versus women.

Language, ethnicity, race, and cultural and social differences have never been so apparent as they are now. There is ample evidence that such differences can affect every aspect of life. As citizens, we have to ask why matters like children's school performance can be predicted by skin color, parental income, ethnic group, or home language.

There is a lot of racial tension in our diverse communities these days—in fact, it is often directly proportionate to the amount of diversity that is present in a community. The interracial violence in Los Angeles in the spring of 1992 following the first Rodney King trial should not have surprised anyone, and Los Angeles is not an isolated case. We have seen eruptions of violence—acts of intolerance by one group against another—by people who ought to get along a great deal better than they do in a multicultural society.

After a while, a person begins to wonder: Is a multicultural society really possible—a society in which diverse people live together harmoniously and at peace with one another? And if such a society is possible, how do you achieve it? How do we create the connections that will make a difference, as was pledged in the theme of the 1993 National Association for Multicultural Education Conference?

I will ague that connections have got to be forged on many fronts, but the most important of these must be made in the classroom. We have to help children—the next generation—acquire the means and desire to build such a society. We focus on the children, but that means that we have to include their educators—teachers and parents—the adults who must be involved in the transformation of our progeny into citizens of a diverse, multicultural world.

But how do we do it when the adults we have to begin with are people who have been socialized in ways that have created the problems we face in the first place? The separatism, the racism that has kept most people from seeing the possibility or advantages of a truly multicultural world, has been the human legacy for much of our history on earth until now. That heritage has profoundly shaped the reality we have lived with in the twentieth century.

Until recently, it was possible for us to believe that we could live in worlds separated by borders and boundaries—crossing them only to vanquish, conquer, or subjugate others. That is how our own society was formed, after all. Almost always, each group sees itself, not as equal to all others, but superior to any other. Ethnocentrism, racial-centrism, is nothing new. It is written in our histories, imprinted on our brains. We are humans—you are less than that. Thus, we can set ourselves off as special, and it is easy to demonize all others.

· · · · · · · · · · · ·

When we talk about the advantages of a multicultural society, it is easy to romanticize the idea of diversity and see only the colorful, interesting, positive aspects of other groups that are different from our own, and to glorify them. But in fact, most people come from societies with long, long histories of enmity and wars with neighbors—the outsiders, the demon others in their worlds.

We humans are just only discovering that we have to live together, and it is only after living side by side, learning that we can't afford not to get along together—that it is all too easy to end up destroying one another. Those of us who work in multicultural education—who recognize that we have to build connections between the constituent groups in this society—are pretty much ahead of the game in this regard. But not everyone is. Most of all, the kids in our schools—our future citizens and leaders—their teachers, and their parents, have got to be helped to take part in this work. And that is why we have to begin with the children, and their teachers and parents.

I will argue that multicultural education must begin in kindergarten and be continuously reinforced throughout the school years. What children must learn are some fundamental attitudes and values concerning life in a multicultural, multilingual society. They must be taught, early in life, that they live in a world where people come from many different places and backgrounds, but they are more alike than they are different. They need to recognize that differences in looks, likes, beliefs, and behavior are neither good nor bad—they are just differences. They have to learn that differences are what make people interesting, and while it might be a whole lot easier to be with people who are exactly the same as we are, it can be a whole lot more interesting to be with people who are different. Most of all, they need to discover that in order to succeed socially in a multicultural world, they have to accept and respect differences in others, rather than reject and abhor them. In short, they must be educated to think and live as citizens of a multicultural world.

These might not seem like such big things, but they are core concepts, and ought to be at the heart of any curriculum for children who live in a diverse society. They are also the hardest things to teach—and that is why we have to work together to figure out how to do it right. One might think that the kids in our classrooms do not need to be taught about diversity—they, after all, are nothing if not diverse. In reality, they have no greater reason to appreciate or to know how to live with diversity than other children in the society.

How are such concepts to be taught in school? How does one incorporate them into a curriculum, and how can we impart them to children? Can children handle such notions?

In many respects, the curricular changes I have been talking about involve the inculcation of basic, fundamental ideas that make us who we are, rather than the teaching of information and skills that enable us to perform jobs or understand ideas. Some of these fundamental ideas are learned in school, ordinarily, but the really basic set is learned at home—well before children begin school, through the socialization process that takes place as family members interact with children.

· · · · · · · · · · · ·

It is at home that children acquire an outlook on life, a set of attitudes about themselves, about others, the environment, about their place in the world. Children acquire, along with their primary languages, a set of beliefs, expectations, and practices from family members—the significant others in their lives. By the time children come to school at age five or six, they are already well-socialized members of a particular family and cultural group.

As educators, we know how differently children can behave and respond to the experience of school, depending on the group and family they come from. The most critical results of this preschool curriculum in the home are invisible, not as obvious as the results of language socialization. The most powerful aspect of the cultural package that children receive in the socialization process is the belief in the naturalness and normality of the attitudes and practices that have been inculcated in them early in life.

· · · · · · · · · · · ·

What they are used to, what they have been taught is right and appropriate, what they have learned is the way to treat people, about handling conflict, or hurt, or injustice, what they regard as good or bad, beautiful or not, desirable or undesirable— all are aspects of children's culture. How do we look at these aspects of culture that children bring to school? We acknowledge the need to recognize and to respect cultural differences that children bring to school. But we are often confused about how to reconcile what we know we must achieve instructionally in school, with the beliefs, values, and understandings children have learned in the home.

Let us be clear about what educational role the family must play at home and what role the society must play at school. The family socializes its children in ways that allow the child to fit into the family and the primary group. It inculcates in the child the values and practices that will enable the child to behave and participate appropriately and effectively in the everyday activities of the family and community—whatever they happen to be. The family also prepares the child for the experience of school, teaching it ways of learning from experience and for attacking complicated problems like those they will encounter in formal instruction.

To a large degree, this process follows the traditional patterns of the cultural group of which the family is a part, but it is affected by the family's recent experiences and history, too.

Many of the families in our communities now have gone through hell before immigrating to the United States, and many of them have been deeply shaped by the problems they encountered after immigrating to the United States. Consider the experiences that have affected the lives of the South Asian and Central American refugee and immigrant families. Think about the experiences that are even now shaping the outlook of families living in inner-city ghettos where there is danger everywhere. The messages their children are being taught no doubt reflect those experiences.

And so children go to school with the teachings of the home and family, where the set of behaviors, values, and practices acquired at home are expanded to the larger world of the school and society.

Inevitably, school expands the child's world. School, especially during the early years, is advanced socialization, a process that continues throughout the school years. Ordinarily, what happens in school is a continuation of the process that begins in the home. But what happens when the socialization that takes place in school, that is, the necessary preparation for life as a member of the larger society, is in conflict with the teachings of the home?

The kinds of things I am proposing as necessary additions to the school curriculum for a multicultural society will cause many clashes with the practices, beliefs, and attitudes that are taught in many homes. In fact, that is precisely why such curricular changes are needed, and why the changes have to be for all children. There are many families, for example, who do not believe that all people are equal, or that differences in appearance, speech, belief, and practice are just differences. There are people who, by their behavior, show their children that the way to deal with things they do not understand or like is to strike out in violence.

This obviously does not make the educator's job easy. As educators, we do have to think about where our students are coming from, and what they have been taught at home. And yet, we also have a responsibility to the society we and the children we are educating live in. In order for them to live together harmoniously, peacefully, and safely, they are going to have to get along together. And no matter what their parents and families think about others, they too will have to learn to live together and be responsible for the society they live in—that is, if there is going to be society worth living in at all.

. . . .

There is no choice, really. If we are going to have a future, we are going to have to inculcate in our children the rules that form a credo that will work for the multicultural Twenty-first Century. Can we do it alone? I don't think so. We have got to form partnerships with parents and people in our communities in the most real way. We need to work on a two-pronged plan— to be carried out at home and at school— that will insure that parents and teachers alike are involved in the important task of preparing our children for the future. The curricular changes I am proposing call for the teaching of a set of beliefs, practices, and attitudes that do not necessarily come naturally to the adults who have got to be involved.

. . . .

All of us, teachers and parents and citizens alike, must engage in a process of learning. What ought to be happening at parent and teacher meetings is planning and learning. We ought to be learning about one another's cultures. We should be reading the poetry and history and literature of the various groups that make up this country, to get a perspective on the many groups that have contributed to the many-faceted culture that is America.

Many if not most of the parents in the schools I visit are not literate in English. This is hardly a problem. Many of the important works that have come from our multicultural society have been translated into many languages. Nor is the fact that some parents are not literate even in their own languages a problem. So what? People who can read can read to them in their language—that is the advantage of having bilingual teachers and citizens in our schools and communities. And what if the parents of the kids are not educated enough to deal with such materials? They can be educated—like everyone else.

The next step is to plan a series of activities that parents, teachers, and kids might engage in that would allow everyone to gain the kind of understanding needed to transform our ways of thinking, valuing, and behaving. The things to be learned are learned through example, and by active engagement, not by indirect means.

I think one does it by working together on projects that benefit everyone—and I do not mean activities where people who are in the dominant group do something to help the "poor, unfortunate, down-trodden members of the society." Rather, I think about people from all segments of the society engaged in projects like cleaning up the city's streets, developing neighborhood parks, or raising funds for projects that will benefit everyone in the community, like a new fire truck, or an after-school program for the children of working parents. When people work together as a community, they become a community, and eventually they learn enough about their neighbors to regard them not only as neighbors, but as friends.

There are so many existing divisions to bridge—how do we pull together in the face of so much racism and cross-group friction as we have now? And that is the special part that multicultural educators can play. We begin by inviting our colleagues, the parents we work with, the public, to join us in considering what kind of a society we are going to have in the future and what we have to do to prepare all children to take part in that future. And we do it by example: as educators, we show our kids and their families what we want them to be by our behavior. That, after all, is how it is done in socialization.

• • • • • • • • • • • •

As parents we know that it is through our behavior that we teach our kids what it means to be a person. If we treat our children with respect, they learn to be respectful. If we are tolerant and accepting of our kids and of others, they become tolerant and accepting people. If we are fair with them, they learn the meaning of fairness. If such simple principles were followed by most of us, there would be fewer angry people in the world.

I end this discussion on how we ought to educate children for a multicultural society with a story that Vice President Albert Gore, Jr. tells in his best-selling *Earth in Balance*. The story is about a woman in Mahatma Gandhi's village who was worried about her young son's love of sweets. She thought it was not good for her child's health to eat so many sweets. She asked the revered teacher to speak to the boy about it, to suggest to him that he should give up sweets. Gandhi thought about the woman's request for a moment, and then told her to bring her son to him in two weeks time, and he would talk with him.

Two weeks later, the woman takes her son to see Gandhi, and Gandhi does as he had promised. The boy agrees to do as he has been advised, and the mother is happy. But she is puzzled. Why did Gandhi wait two weeks before talking to her son? Gandhi tells her: he could hardly ask the boy to give up sweets until he himself had done so, and he knew it would take him at least two weeks to learn to do without them.

Educating children for the kind of world we want to leave to them has to begin somewhere, and the only place where we can be certain about it is in ourselves. It is a beginning.

Credits/ Acknowledgments

Cover design by Charles Vitelli

1. The Social Contexts of Multicultural Education
Facing overview—United Nations photo by Y. Nagata

2. Teacher Education in Multicultural Perspective
Facing overview—Photo by Steve Takatsuno.

3. Multicultural Education as an Academic Discipline
Facing overview—United Nations photo by Shelley Rotner.

4. Identity and Personal Development
Facing overview—United Nations photo by John Isaac.

5. Curriculum and Instruction in Multicultural Perspective
Facing overview—Photo by J. Wilson—Woodfin Camp.

6. Special Topics in Multicultural Education
Facing overview—United Nations photo by John Isaac. 195-197—Illustrations by Richard Swartz.

7. Toward a New Day in Our Visions of Education
Facing overview—United Nations photo by Y. Nagata.

ANNUAL EDITIONS ARTICLE REVIEW FORM

■ NAME: _____ DATE: _____

■ TITLE AND NUMBER OF ARTICLE: _____

■ BRIEFLY STATE THE MAIN IDEA OF THIS ARTICLE: _____

_____

_____

_____

_____

■ LIST THREE IMPORTANT FACTS THAT THE AUTHOR USES TO SUPPORT THE MAIN IDEA:

_____

_____

_____

_____

_____

_____

■ WHAT INFORMATION OR IDEAS DISCUSSED IN THIS ARTICLE ARE ALSO DISCUSSED IN YOUR TEXTBOOK OR OTHER READING YOU HAVE DONE? LIST THE TEXTBOOK CHAPTERS AND PAGE NUMBERS:

_____

_____

_____

_____

_____

_____

■ LIST ANY EXAMPLES OF BIAS OR FAULTY REASONING THAT YOU FOUND IN THE ARTICLE:

_____

_____

_____

_____

■ LIST ANY NEW TERMS/CONCEPTS THAT WERE DISCUSSED IN THE ARTICLE AND WRITE A SHORT DEFINITION:

_____

_____

_____

_____

_____

ANNUAL EDITIONS: MULTICULTURAL EDUCATION 95/96
Article Rating Form

Here is an opportunity for you to have direct input into the next revision of this volume. We would like you to rate each of the 36 articles listed below, using the following scale:

1. **Excellent: should definitely be retained**
2. **Above average: should probably be retained**
3. **Below average: should probably be deleted**
4. **Poor: should definitely be deleted**

Your ratings will play a vital part in the next revision. So please mail this prepaid form to us just as soon as you complete it.
Thanks for your help!

Rating	Article	Rating	Article
	1. The Great Migration		20. Curriculum Guidelines for Multicultural Education
	2. Children of Urban Poverty: Approaches to a Critical American Problem		21. Empowering Children to Create a Caring Culture in a World of Differences
	3. Intermarried . . . with Children		22. Toward Defining Programs and Services for Culturally and Linguistically Diverse Learners in Special Education
	4. Diversity without Equality = Oppression		
	5. The Numbers Game		23. Issues in Testing Students from Culturally and Linguistically Diverse Backgrounds
	6. European Schools Offer Contrasts and Similarities		
	7. Building Cultural Bridges: A Bold Proposal for Teacher Education		24. Forming Academic Identities: Accommodation without Assimilation among Involuntary Minorities
	8. Multicultural Education Training for Special Educators Working with African American Youth		25. Sapphires-in-Transition: Enhancing Personal Development among Black Female Adolescents
	9. Multicultural Teacher Education: A Call for Conceptual Change		26. Racial Issues in Education: Real or Imagined?
	10. Preservice Teachers' Perceptions of the Goals of Multicultural Education: Implications for the Empowerment of Minority Students		27. The Dynamic Demographic Mosaic Called America
			28. Literacy, Social Movements, and Class Consciousness: Paths from Freire and the São Paulo Experience
	11. Multicultural Education as an Academic Discipline		
	12. Affirmation, Solidarity, and Critique: Moving beyond Tolerance in Multicultural Education		29. Understanding Indian Children, Learning from Indian Elders
			30. Hollywood and the Indian Question
	13. White Racism		31. "I Wouldn't Want to Shoot Nobody": The Out-of-School Curriculum as Described by Urban Students
	14. A New Word for an Old Problem: Multicultural "School Wars" Date to the 1840s		
			32. Brown Revisited
	15. Cultural Pluralism, Multicultural Education, and Then What?		33. The AAUW Report: How Schools Shortchange Girls
	16. The Intersections of Gender, Class, Race, and Culture: On Seeing Clients Whole		34. Towards a Discourse of Imagery: Critical Curriculum Theorizing
	17. Can Separate Be Equal?		35. Investing in Our Children: A Struggle for America's Conscience and Future
	18. Multiculturalism and Individualism		
	19. Lessons of Vancouver: Immigration Raises Fundamental Questions of Identity and Values		36. Educating Citizens for a Multicultural 21st Century

(Continued on next page)

ABOUT YOU

Name_____ Date_____

Are you a teacher? ☐   Or student? ☐

Your School Name _____

Department _____

Address _____

City_____ State _____ Zip _____

School Telephone #_____

YOUR COMMENTS ARE IMPORTANT TO US!

Please fill in the following information:

For which course did you use this book? _____

Did you use a text with this Annual Edition?   ☐ yes   ☐ no

The title of the text? _____

What are your general reactions to the Annual Editions concept?

Have you read any particular articles recently that you think should be included in the next edition?

Are there any articles you feel should be replaced in the next edition? Why?

Are there other areas that you feel would utilize an Annual Edition?

May we contact you for editorial input?

May we quote you from above?

ANNUAL EDITIONS: MULTICULTURAL EDUCATION 95/96

BUSINESS REPLY MAIL

First Class   Permit No. 84   Guilford, CT

Postage will be paid by addressee

 **The Dushkin Publishing Group/
Brown & Benchmark Publishers**
DPG **Sluice Dock
Guilford, Connecticut 06437**

Ill....ll...l.l..l.ll.l...ll.l.l.l..l.l.l...l.l.l